Babylonian Jews and Sasanian Imperialism in Late Antiquity

From the image offered by the Babylonian Talmud, Jewish elites were deeply embedded within the Sasanian Empire (224–651 CE). The Talmud is replete with stories and discussions that feature Sasanian kings, Zoroastrian magi, fire temples, imperial administrators, Sasanian laws, Persian customs, and more quotidian details of Jewish life under Sasanian rule. Yet, in the scholarly literature on the Babylonian Talmud and the Jews of Babylonia, the Sasanian Empire has served as a backdrop to a decidedly parochial Jewish story, having little if any direct impact on Babylonian Jewish life and especially the rabbis. *Babylonian Jews and Sasanian Imperialism in Late Antiquity* advances a radically different understanding of Babylonian Jewish history and Sasanian rule. Building upon recent scholarship, Simcha Gross portrays a more immanent model of Sasanian rule, within and against which Jews invariably positioned and defined themselves. Babylonian Jews realized their traditions, teachings, and social standing within the political, social, religious, and cultural conditions generated by Sasanian rule.

SIMCHA GROSS is an Assistant Professor of Ancient Rabbinics in the Department of Near Eastern Languages and Civilizations at the University of Pennsylvania. Coauthor of *The History of the "Slave of Christ": From Jewish Child to Christian Martyr* and coeditor of *Jews and Syriac Christians*, he was an Andrew W. Mellon Foundation Fellow for Assistant Professors at the Institute for Advanced Study, Princeton; and a recipient of an Alexander von Humboldt Foundation fellowship for experienced researchers.

Babylonian Jews and Sasanian Imperialism in Late Antiquity

SIMCHA GROSS
University of Pennsylvania

CAMBRIDGE
UNIVERSITY PRESS

CAMBRIDGE
UNIVERSITY PRESS

Shaftesbury Road, Cambridge CB2 8EA, United Kingdom

One Liberty Plaza, 20th Floor, New York, NY 10006, USA

477 Williamstown Road, Port Melbourne, VIC 3207, Australia

314–321, 3rd Floor, Plot 3, Splendor Forum, Jasola District Centre, New Delhi – 110025, India

103 Penang Road, #05–06/07, Visioncrest Commercial, Singapore 238467

Cambridge University Press is part of Cambridge University Press & Assessment, a department of the University of Cambridge.

We share the University's mission to contribute to society through the pursuit of education, learning and research at the highest international levels of excellence.

www.cambridge.org
Information on this title: www.cambridge.org/9781009280501

DOI: 10.1017/9781009280549

First published 2024
First paperback edition 2025

A catalogue record for this publication is available from the British Library

Library of Congress Cataloging-in-Publication data
NAMES: Gross, Simcha, author.
TITLE: Babylonian Jews and Sasanian imperialism in late antiquity / Simcha Gross, University of Pennsylvania.
DESCRIPTION: Cambridge, United Kingdom : Cambridge University Press, [2024] | Includes index.
IDENTIFIERS: LCCN 2023014408 (print) | LCCN 2023014409 (ebook) | ISBN 9781009280525 (hardback) | ISBN 9781009280501 (paperback) | ISBN 9781009280549 (epub)
SUBJECTS: LCSH: Jews–Iraq–Babylonia–History. | Talmud–Iranian influences. | Sassanids–Intellectual life. | Iran–Ethnic relations. | Iran–History–To 640.
CLASSIFICATION: LCC DS135.B2 G75 2024 (print) | LCC DS135.B2 (ebook) | DDC 305.892/409355–dc23/eng/20230403
LC record available at https://lccn.loc.gov/2023014408
LC ebook record available at https://lccn.loc.gov/2023014409

ISBN 978-1-009-28052-5 Hardback
ISBN 978-1-009-28050-1 Paperback

Contents

Acknowledgments *page* vii

Introduction: Toward a New History of Jews and the Sasanian Empire 1

1 Jewish Society under Sasanian Rule: From Isolation to Integration 33

2 Competing for Power: Jewish Elites and Sasanian Culture 86

3 Beyond 'Tolerance': The Logics of Sasanian Violence against Jews 132

4 Forgetting Persecution: Memory and Anti-martyrdom in the Babylonian Talmud 166

5 Rabbis and Fire Temples: Navigating a Zoroastrian Empire 197

6 Kings and Religion in the Talmud and in the Imagination of Sasanian Communities 239

Conclusion: The Sasanian Empire from the Perspective of the Jews 272

Bibliography 285

General Index 335

Source Index 341

Acknowledgments

Academic life can be isolating and lonely, and all the more so in an era of quarantine. I have been incredibly fortunate that my prevailing experience has been the opposite; throughout the research and writing of this book, I have been surrounded by beloved family, dear friends, and cherished colleagues engaged in a shared intellectual pursuit, who have enriched this book and my life in immeasurable ways.

I am eternally grateful to my mentors, teachers, and peers at Yale University, where this project initially gestated. Christine Hayes' sharp insight, boundless generosity, and tireless encouragement continue to astonish me, and my appreciation for her knows no bounds. I learned a great deal from Steven Fraade's judicious approach; conversations with Eliyahu Stern remain clarifying and a delight. Renee Reed ensured that each day at Yale was filled with joy. While at Yale I had the privilege to work with Seth Schwartz; I sought to embrace his exhortation that knowledge is produced through experimentation, and his eye-opening work has served as a touchstone throughout. Aaron Butts first initiated me into the study of Syriac Christianity and has become a lifelong friend and collaborator. His breadth, depth, and good sense inform this and my other work. Throughout my studies at Yale, and before that at Yeshiva University, I received foundational training from esteemed guides including Yaakov Elman, of blessed memory, Moshe Bernstein, Mahnaz Moazami, Jeffrey Rubenstein, Richard Kalmin, Oded Irshai, Robert Brody, and Oktor Skjaervo.

Daily conversation partners and collaborators informed this project from start to finish: Avigail-Manekin-Bamberger, Krista Dalton, Yitz Landes, Yakir Paz, Annette Yoshiko Reed, Khodadad Rezakhani, and

Shai Secunda. Each read the manuscript at different stages and improved it with their incisive and invaluable perspectives. My days are enlivened by the various sounds that signal an incoming message from each of them. Adored thought partners include Domenico Agostini, Miguel Ángel Andrés-Toledo, Adam Becker, Yehuda Bernstein, Raʿanan Boustan, Rivka Elitzur-Leiman, Liane Feldman, Amit Gvaryahu, Jae Han, Marc Herman, Yedida Koren, Eve Krakowski, Mark Letteney, Shaul Magid, Yakov Mayer, Scott McDonough, Sergey Minov, Jake Nabel, Jonathan Yoni Pomeranz, Daniel Picus, Salam Rassi, James Adam Redfield, Dan Sheffield, Michael Shenkar, Jacqueline Vayntrub, Yuhan Sohrab-Dinshaw Vevaina, Erin Galgay Walsh, and James Walters.

The book first materialized over the course of my time in the Department of History at the University of California, Irvine, and was completed in the Department of Near Eastern Languages and Civilizations at the University of Pennsylvania, and my colleagues at both institutions have left their indelible imprint on the work. At Irvine, Touraj Daryaee, Matthew Canepa, and Matthias Lehmann served as critical interlocuters and supported me at each stage.

At the University of Pennsylvania, I am surrounded by dear colleagues whose friendship, sound advice, and expertise have progressed this project towards the finish line: I am forever grateful to my colleagues in NELC, including Dan Ben Amos, of blessed memory, Paul Cobb, Huda Fakhreddine, Talya Fishman, Nili Gold, Emily Hammer, Joe Lowry, Fatemeh Shams, Heather Sharkey, Richard Zettler, among others. I am similarly indebted to colleagues across the university, especially Oscar Aguirre-Mandujano, Anne Berg, Kim Bowes, Peter Struck, Reyhan Durmaz, Steve Weitzman, Donovan Schafer, Joshua Teplitsky, Beth Wenger, and Ben Nathans. Cam Grey, Natalie Dorhmann, and Arthur Kiron read the manuscript from start to finish, and always kept my eye on the larger questions and bigger picture. Linda Greene's know-how, compassion, and good humor make the department a welcoming professional home.

The book benefited greatly from a Wolf Humanities Center Book Manuscript Development Workshop, and I owe thanks to all of the participants, and especially to Clifford Ando for serving as a dazzling respondent, and for his advice and support since then. The manuscript further benefited from the Lucius N. Littauer Foundation Faculty Research Fund from the Jewish Studies program at the University of Pennsylvania, which enabled me to enlist the keen editorial eyes of Abigail Beech, Paul Moore, and Katherin Papadopoulos. I was fortunate to serve as a fellow at the Katz Center for Advanced Jewish Studies at the

University of Pennsylvania in a critical stage of the project, and I benefited from its ready supply of ever-changing but always present colleagues who are founts of inspiration and learning; among them was Hayim Lapin, who read and commented on an earlier draft of the manuscript. The book reached its final form during a blissful year at the Institute for Advanced Study, Princeton, for which I am grateful to the faculty of the School of Historical Studies, and to Sabine Schmidtke in particular.

I am immensely grateful to Beatrice Rehl and the team at Cambridge University Press for procuring wonderfully constructive reviews, and for ushering the book along expeditiously. The arguments of the book were honed by invitations from Oxford University, Princeton University, Yale University, the University of Chicago, New York University, Dartmouth College, and the Hebrew University of Jerusalem. Sections of Chapters 2 and 4 are, respectively, heavily adapted versions of articles previously published as "A Persian Anti-Martyr Act: The Death of Rabbah Bar Naḥmani," in *The Aggada of the Babylonian Talmud and its Cultural World*, ed. Jeffrey Rubenstein and Geoffrey Herman (Providence, RI: Brown University Press, 2018), 211–242, and "Rethinking Babylonian Rabbinic Acculturation in the Sasanian Empire," *Journal of Ancient Judaism* 9 (2019): 280–310.

As a historian, it requires little to contextualize myself; I would not have pursued an academic career if not for my parents, Yaacov and Ronit Gross, who transmitted to their children their relentless love of learning and productive disagreement, a mandate to approach each matter with an open mind and a healthy dose of irreverence, and the assurance of their untiring love and constant support. My siblings and their children continue to sharpen my ability to construct an argument, keep me in my place, and remind me of what matters. Liora Tamir is a constant source of inspiration and joy, of hopes and dreams, and an always-eager thought partner. This book's chief achievement is that it brought us together.

Introduction

Toward a New History of Jews and the Sasanian Empire

In an obscure debate about inheritance, which hinges on a terse genealogical verse in Genesis, a rabbi in the Babylonian Talmud proposes an interpretation that he boasts is entirely original.[1]

Rabbah said: "I will tell you something that not even King Shapur said!"
And who is he [i.e., who is "King Shapur"]? Shmuel.

The nature of this boast is puzzling: What does the king of the Sasanian Empire, in this case Shapur I (r. 240–270 CE), have to do with rabbinic biblical interpretation? An anonymous interpolation explains that "King Shapur" in Rabbah's boast is simply a nickname for Shmuel, an earlier prominent rabbi. According to the interpolation, Rabbah is therefore making a run-of-the-mill brag about besting his eminent rabbinic colleague, Shmuel. Even so, the fact that Shmuel's high rank is conveyed through analogy to the Sasanian king is noteworthy. Such a comparison assumes that the rabbinic movement is a kind of microcosm of the Sasanian Empire, headed by prominent rabbis and kings respectively.[2]

And yet, as modern scholarship on the editing of the Talmud would suggest, the anonymous explanatory gloss in this passage was likely added decades, if not centuries, after Rabbah's boast was recorded, and

[1] b. Pesaḥ 54a = b. B. Bat. 115b. The same discussion is immediately repeated, but featuring later rabbis, a typical product of the centuries-long oral transmission of the Talmud; see Yaakov Elman, "Orality and the Redaction of the Babylonian Talmud," *Oral Tradition* 14 (1999): 52–99. This repetition appears to have led to garbled versions of the discussion in MS Munich 95 and MS Vatican 125.

[2] See Chapter 6 for further detail, and the Conclusion for an analysis of a related talmudic pericope.

may not capture its original intention. Rabbah's boast may not have compared him favorably to an earlier rabbi whose sobriquet was King Shapur, but to King Shapur himself.[3] To make such a boast, Rabbah presupposes that King Shapur can serve as a benchmark for legal and interpretive creativity, such that claiming to be cleverer than him, however hyperbolically, is praiseworthy. Ideas about the king as a wise legal authority were indeed promoted by the Sasanian Empire itself, a claim Rabbah appears to have embraced and internalized.[4] However we understand the relationship of the anonymous interpolation to Rabbah's statement, the Sasanian Empire, its leading figures, and even its projections, penetrated the narrowly focused discursive universe of the rabbis.

Between the third and seventh centuries of the Common Era, numerous Jews lived in the Sasanian Empire, ruled by an Iranian and Zoroastrian dynasty whose territory extended from Syria to Central Asia.[5] Among these Jews was a network of figures known as rabbis, who, by the end of this period, produced the Babylonian Talmud, our chief literary source by and about Jews living under Sasanian rule. Across lengthy legal discussions, colorful stories, and even seemingly trivial rabbinic boasts, the Talmud is replete with references to kings, Zoroastrian priests, fire temples, imperial administrators, imperial laws, Iranian customs, Middle Persian words, and more quotidian details of life under Sasanian rule. Even a passing reading of the Babylonian Talmud makes clear the extent to which Babylonian Jews were deeply rooted in the Sasanian Empire and its realities.

Yet in historical accounts of Jews under Sasanian rule to date, the Sasanian Empire has chiefly served as a distant backdrop to a decidedly

[3] Similarly Shai Secunda, *The Iranian Talmud: Reading the Bavli in Its Sasanian Context* (Philadelphia, PA: 2013), 104–105.

[4] See Chapters 1 and 6.

[5] Although ancient sources note how populous Jews were in these areas prior to the Sasanian period – according to Josephus' hyperbolic description (*Antiquities of the Jews* 11.133), "countless myriads whose number cannot be ascertained" – estimates of the population size of the Jews of Babylonia are entirely conjectural. For sources, see: Geoffrey Herman, *A Prince without a Kingdom: The Exilarch in the Sasanian Era* (Tübingen: 2012), 2n9; and Simcha Gross, "Babylonian Jewish Communities," in *The Routledge Companion to Jews in Late Antiquity*, ed. Catherine Hezser (Abington, Oxon: 2024), 414–434. On some Jewish settlements in Iran, see Parvaneh Pourshariati, "New Vistas on the History of Iranian Jewry in Late Antiquity, Part I: Patterns of Jewish Settlement in Iran," in *The Jews of Iran*, ed. Houman Sarshar (London: 2014), 1–32. On Jewish deportees during the Sasanian period, see Geo Widengren, "The Status of the Jews in the Sassanian Empire," *Iranica Antiqua* 1 (1961): 134–137; and Aram Topchyan, "Jews in Ancient Armenia (1st Century BC–5th Century AD)," *Le Muséon* 120 (2007): 435–476.

Jewish story.[6] The relative inattention to the Sasanian imperial context has not simply been a matter of neglect; it derives from three theses concerning Sasanian rule and its Jewish subjects that have served as the cornerstones for nearly all historical accounts to date.

First, scholars characterized Sasanian rule as detached and feudalistic, only intervening directly in the lives of its diverse inhabitants in extreme circumstances.[7] The empire instead preferred to organize its heterogenous populations, including the Jews, into semi-autonomous religious communities, led by official intermediaries. In the case of the Jews, the intermediary was the so-called Exilarch, the head of a dynastic Jewish family that claimed to descend from King David.

Second, owing to imperial sponsorship, these semi-autonomous religious communities were centralized, self-governing, and structured around their own stratified internal hierarchy. In the case of the Jews, the Exilarch again stood atop the social ladder, while the rabbis served as the formal judicial branch of the Jewish community. Rabbinic authority in Babylonia therefore "depended not upon popular acquiescence, though it was considerable, but upon the coercive capabilities of their courts," as Jacob Neusner put it.[8] By dint of their enforcement capabilities, Babylonian Jewish society was believed to be more strictly and uniformly "rabbinized" than contemporary Jewish communities elsewhere, especially in Roman Palestine. As a corporate religious community, Jewish experience under and attitudes toward the empire were considered to be roughly unified in nature, the parts thereof attesting to the whole.

Third, because of their segregation into semi-autonomous communities, Jews were isolated and insulated from their non-Jewish neighbors and Iranian influence, and they were not exposed to various facets of Sasanian rule. We should therefore anticipate few signs of Iranian acculturation among Jews, except for those elites, like the Exilarch, who were required to participate in the culture of the court, and particular rabbis who chose to engage, however sparingly, with the intellectual elites of other communities. Jews similarly had little impetus to consider proper attitudes toward a remote imperial presence or devise political strategies for how best to navigate life under Sasanian rule.

6 For a concise summary of this view, see: Isaiah Gafni, "The Political, Social, and Economic History of Babylonian Jewry, 224–638 CE," in *The Cambridge History of Judaism: The Late Roman Roman-Rabbinic Period*, ed. Steven Katz (Cambridge: 2006), 792–820.

7 For this position, see Chapter 1.

8 Jacob Neusner, "Rabbis and Community in Third Century Babylonia," in *Religions in Antiquity: Essays in Memory of Erwin Ramsdell Goodenough*, ed. Jacob Neusner (Leiden: 1970), 449.

Together, these three theses fueled romantic accounts of the Jewish embrace of Sasanian rule as an opportunity to live in relative social, cultural, and intellectual isolation from their larger non-Jewish environment. The consensus view is encapsulated by Jacob Neusner when he notes that "the Iranians primarily contributed not doctrine or other sorts of 'influence,' but the opportunity for Jewry to work out its own affairs in its own way."[9] Isaiah Gafni similarly averred that "the Jewish community of Babylonia seemed to thrive, thanks to a policy of noninterference with their internal structures and lifestyle."[10] As a result, it was "precisely in this land of ancient roots, albeit imagined ones, that the Jewish community would evince the greatest degree of cultural autonomy."[11] The Sasanian Empire provided the general conditions for Jews to live in the insular, self-segregated environment to which, these scholars believed, Jews naturally gravitated.[12] Without external interference, Babylonian Jewish society remained highly stable for nearly a millennium.[13] These

[9] Jacob Neusner, "Jews in Iran: Jewish Settlement in the Western Satrapies of Iran," in *The Seleucid, Parthian and Sasanian Periods*, vol. 3, bk. 2, *The Cambridge History of Iran*, ed. E. Yarshater (Cambridge: 1983), 923. See similarly Neusner, "How Much Iranian in Jewish Babylonia," *Journal of the American Oriental Society* 95 (1975): 184–190; and the more nuanced view in Neusner, *Israel's Politics in Sasanian Iran: Jewish Self-Government in Talmudic Times* (Lanham, MD: 1986), xi.

[10] Gafni, "Political, Social, and Economic History," 794.

[11] Isaiah Gafni, "Babylonian Rabbinic Culture," in *Cultures of the Jews: A New History*, ed. David Biale (New York: 2002), 224.

[12] See also: Robert Brody, "Judaism in the Sasanian Empire: A Case Study in Religious Coexistence," in *Irano-Judaica* II, ed. Shaul Shaked and Amnon Netzer (Jerusalem: 1990), 52–62; Brody, "Irano-Talmudica: The New Parallelomania?" *Jewish Quarterly Review* 106 (2016): 209–232, and further discussion in Chapter 1 below. The notion that Jews gravitated to insularity was common in Jewish historiography of much of the twentieth century. For critical historiography, see: Seth Schwartz, "Big Men or Chiefs: Against an Institutional History of the Palestinian Patriarchate," in *Jewish Religious Leadership: Image and Reality*, ed. Jack Wertheimer (New York: 2004), 1:155–173, esp. 158–159. In Yaakov Elman's work, the peaceable conditions allowed most Jews to be insular while also enabling *some* rabbis to engage Zoroastrian elites in religious exchange: see Elman, "The Other in the Mirror: Questions of Identity, Conversion, and Exogamy in the Fifth-Century Iranian Empire. Part Two," *Bulletin of the Asia Institute* 20 (2010), 30; and Elman and Oktor Skjaervo, "Concepts of Pollution in Late Sasanian Iran: Does Pollution Need Stairs, and Does It Fill Space?" *Aram* 26 (2013), 21.

[13] Michael Morony, "Religious Communities in Late Sasanian and Early Muslim Iraq," *Journal of the Economic and Social History of the Orient* 17 (1974): 113–135; Arietta Papaconstantinou, "Confrontation, Interaction, and the Formation of the Early Islamic Oikoumene," *Revue des études byzantines* 63 (2005): 173–174; Y. Zvi Stampfer, "Jews in Baghdad during the Abbasid Period," in *Baghdād: From Its Beginnings to the 14th Century*, ed. Jens Scheiner and Isabel Toral (Leiden: 2022), 731–764. See the extreme example of Richard Frye, *Golden Age of Persia: The Arabs in the East* (New York: 1975),

three pillars of semi-autonomy, centralized self-regulating hierarchy, and insularity, continue to undergird historical research of Jews under Sasanian rule, and serve in classical works of Sasanian history as the lynchpins for the idea of Sasanian imperial laissez faire and its organization of its subject groups into semi-autonomous religious communities.[14]

This book advances a radically different, staunchly revisionist, account of Jewish life under Sasanian rule, and consequently of Sasanian rule itself. Building upon recent studies that have begun to profoundly alter our understanding of the Sasanian Empire, this book presents a more immanent and integrationist model of Sasanian rule, which Jews could not avoid, and within and against which they positioned and defined themselves. Rather than centralized, hierarchal, or neatly divided into rigid classes, this book demonstrates how Sasanian Jewish society was highly diverse, dynamic, and in constant flux, where status was determined not by guaranteed positions in a hierarchy, but by success in competition for recognition on a crowded playing field of social actors. Jews were not insulated from their surroundings, but instead interacted with neighboring communities and the empire regularly, drawing from and internalizing Sasanian and Iranian culture in the formation of their identities and in their jockeying for power and prestige. In short, Sasanian rule shaped the social and cultural worlds of Babylonian Jews, and Jews, in turn, formulated and negotiated their traditions and identities in this distinct imperial context.

By reconfiguring our understanding of Babylonian Jewish society, we must approach our surviving Jewish material and literary evidence, especially the Babylonian Talmud, as works situated within, informed by, and responsive to the realities of Sasanian rule. Rather than a passive source providing straightforward descriptions of Jewish life, the book argues that talmudic stories and discussions are often the very sites where Jews articulated and shaped attitudes towards their imperial surroundings. The Babylonian rabbis, and Jews in general, offer remarkable evidence for how communities thought about the Sasanian Empire and defined their place within it; how those deeply invested in a certain idea of Jewish

109–110: "The ghettos of minorities which probably existed in the Sasanian empire continued into Islam." More nuanced developmental accounts include Marina Rustow, "Jews and the Islamic World: Transitions from Rabbinic to Medieval Contexts," in *The Bloomsbury Companion to Jewish Studies*, ed. Dean Phillip Bell (London: 2013), 90–120; and Philip Wood, *The Imam of the Christians: The World of Dionysius of Tel-Mahre, c. 750–850* (Princeton: 2021), 41–55.

[14] See discussion in Chapter 1.

tradition reconciled its practice in a world saturated with Sasanian and Zoroastrian institutions and imagery; and how in their efforts to gain authority and recognition, the rabbis and other Jews defined themselves by and against notions of social distinction prevalent in the Sasanian Empire. Jews sought to realize their traditions and identities and to situate themselves within the political, social, religious, and cultural conditions generated by Sasanian rule.

EMPIRE AND INHABITANTS

Emerging as a local dynasty in Fars, in the south-west region of modern Iran, the Sasanians burst onto the world stage in the early third century CE, establishing an empire that rivaled the Romans to the west, to say nothing of those empires to its east.[15] Although the empire's borders expanded and contracted over the course of its more than four centuries of rule, they consistently extended from Syria in the west, the Caucasus and Caspian regions to its north, and far into Central Asia. Yet Mesopotamia, where the rabbis and likely most of the empire's Jews lived, held an elevated position in the Sasanian expanse. Known in Persian sources by the sobriquet "the heart of Iran," this agriculturally rich and economically lucrative floodplain served as the empire's breadbasket and was a critical source of imperial revenue.[16] Mesopotamia's strategic and economic importance meant that a Sasanian imperial

[15] Overviews of Sasanian history include Klaus Schippmann, *Grundzüge der Geschichte des sasanidischen Reiches* (Darmstadt: 1990); Josef Wiesehöfer, *Ancient Persia: From 550 BC to 650 AD* (London: 1996); and Touraj Daryaee, *Sasanian Persia: The Rise and Fall of an Empire* (London: 2009).

[16] For the administrative geography of the Sasanian Empire, and the place of Mesopotamia in its western quadrant, see Philippe Gignoux, "Les quatre régions administratives de l'Iran sasanide et la symboliques des nombres trois et quatre," *Annali dell'Istituto Orientale di Napoli* 44 (1984): 555–572; and Christopher Brunner, "Geographical and Administrative Divisions: Settlement and Economy," in *The Seleucid, Parthian and Sasanian Periods*, vol. 3, bk. 2, *The Cambridge History of Iran*, ed. E. Yarshater (Cambridge: 1983), 747–777. For more on the ecology, urbanization, and productivity of Mesopotamia, see: Robert McC. Adams, *Land behind Baghdad; A History of Settlement on the Diyala Plains* (Chicago: 1965), esp. 69–83; Robert McC. Adams, *Heartland of Cities: Surveys of Ancient Settlement and Land Use on the Central Floodplain of the Euphrates* (Chicago: 1981), 183; Peter Verkinderen, *Waterways of Iraq and Iran in the Early Islamic Period: Changing Rivers and Landscapes of the Mesopotamian Plain* (London/New York: 2015); St. John Simpson, "The Land behind Ctesiphon: The Archaeology of Babylonia during the Period of the Babylonian Talmud," in *The Archaeology and Material Culture of the Babylonian Talmud*, ed. Markham J. Geller (Leiden: 2015), 6; James Howard-Johnston, "State and Society in Late

presence was ubiquitous there. As it had for the Parthians, Seleucia-Ctesiphon in central Iraq served as the center of imperial power and prestige, hosting embassies and emissaries from the Roman Empire and beyond.[17]

The lands ruled by the Sasanians presented them with many opportunities for enrichment and power, but also a distinct set of challenges deriving from the heterogenous populations who lived within them.[18] Mesopotamia, in particular, was home to a diverse range of religious and ethnic communities, including Jews who had resided there continuously since the early sixth century BCE.[19] Jews and Christians lived cheek by jowl in major Mesopotamian cities, alongside Manichaeans, a variety of so-called pagans, and others.[20] Zoroastrian Iranians lived in

Antique Iran," in *Sasanian Era*, vol. 3, *The Idea of Iran*, ed. Vesta Sarkhosh Curtis and Sarah Stewart (London: 2008), 118–120.

17 Matthew Canepa, *The Two Eyes of the Earth: Art and Ritual Kingship between Rome and Sasanian Iran* (Berkeley: 2009). Recently, Michael Shenkar, "The Coronation of the Early Sasanians, Ctesiphon, and the Great Diadem of Paikuli," *Journal of Persianate Studies* 11 (2018), 113–139, has challenged the applicability of the term "capital" for Seleucia-Ctesiphon, although not its fundamental significance as a site of Sasanian imperial administrative power and presence.

18 Richard Payne, "Iranian Cosmopolitanism: World Religions at the Sasanian Court," in *Cosmopolitanism and Empire: University Rulers, Local Elites, and Cultural Integration in the Ancient Near East and Mediterranean*, ed. Myles Lavan, Richard Payne, and John Weisweiler (Oxford: 2016), 209–230.

19 On the Jews of Mesopotamia in the Achaemenid period, see Laurie E. Pearce and Cornelia Wunsch, *Documents of Judean Exiles and West Semites in Babylonia in the Collection of David Sofer* (Ithaca, NY: 2014); and Tero Alstola, *Judeans in Babylonia: A Study of Deportees in the Sixth and Fifth Centuries BCE* (Leiden: 2020). For the Parthian period, see: Jacob Neusner, *The Parthian Period*, vol. 1, *A History of the Jews in Babylonia* (Atlanta, GA: 1965); Isaiah Gafni, *The Jews of Talmudic Babylonia: A Social and Cultural History* [in Hebrew] (Jerusalem: 1990), 26–35; David M. Goodblatt, "Josephus on Parthian Babylonia (Antiquities XVIII, 310–379)," *Journal of the American Oriental Society* 107 (1987): 605–622; David M. Goodblatt, "The Jews in the Parthian Empire: What We Don't Know," in *Judaea-Palaestina, Babylon and Rome*, ed. Yuval Shaḥar and Benjamin Isaac (Leiden: 2012), 263–278; Geoffrey Herman, "The Jews of Parthian Babylonia," in *The Parthian Empire and Its Religions*, ed. Peter Wick and Markus Zehnder (Gutenberg: 2012), 141–150; and Simcha Gross, "Hopeful Rebels and Anxious Romans: Jewish Interconnectivity in the Great Revolt and Beyond," *Historia: Zeitschrift für Alte Geschichte* 72 (2023): 1–35.

20 Erica Hunter, "Aramaic-Speaking Communities of Sasanid Mesopotamia," *Aram* 7 (1995): 319–335; and Michael Morony, *Iraq after the Muslim Conquest* (Piscataway, NJ: 2005), 169–430. Albert de Jong, "The Cologne Mani Codex and the Life of Zarathustra," in *Jews, Christians, and Zoroastrians: Religious Dynamics in a Sasanian Context*, ed. Geoffrey Herman (Piscataway, NJ: 2014), 133–136, questions the relative prominence of Aramaic speakers, given the possibility of differing epigraphic habits among Aramaic and Iranian populations in Mesopotamia. For Manichaeans, see

Mesopotamia as well, drawn by social ties, economic opportunity, and the promise of administrative positions.[21] Mesopotamia's wealth and its crucial strategic and diplomatic station at the border of empires ensured that the empire always maintained a keen interest in the goings-on of the area's inhabitants. Governing and maintaining control over their diverse subjects was therefore crucial to the success of the empire.

Recent studies have begun to challenge generalizations about the feudalistic and distant character of Sasanian rule.[22] The economic, infrastructural, and military accomplishments of the Sasanians, they contend, could not have been achieved without a centralized government capable of sustaining them.[23] Excavations from regions as diverse as Iraq, Azerbaijan, and Central Asia reveal the Sasanians' ability to amass the necessary resources and labor to direct massive infrastructural and defensive projects, perhaps best exemplified by the intricate and powerful canal

Samuel N. C. Lieu, *Manichaeism in Mesopotamia and the Roman Near East* (Leiden: 1994); and on Mani's language, see Riccardo Contini, "Hypothèses sur l'araméen manichéen," *Annali di Ca' Foscari* 34 (1995): 65–107. For Mandaeans, see most recently, Kevin van Bladel, *From Sasanian Mandaeans to Ṣābians of the Marshes* (Leiden: 2017).

21 On the presence of Iranians in Mesopotamia, see Shaul Shaked, "Religion in the Late Sasanian period: Eran, Aneran, and other Religious Designations," in *The Idea of Iran*, ed. Vesta S. Curtis and Sarah R.A. Stewart, vol. 1 of *The Sasanian Era* (London: 2008), 109, 109n30; and Michael Morony, "The Effects of the Muslim Conquest on the Persian Population of Iraq," *Iran* 14 (1976): 41–42.

22 In general, see: R. N. Frye, "Feudalism in Sasanian and Early Islamic Iran," *Jerusalem Studies in Arabic and Islam* 9 (1987): 13–18; Mohsen Zakeri, *Sāsānid Soldiers in early Muslim Society* (Wiesbaden: 1995), 13–22 and *passim*; Albert de Jong, "Sub Species Maiestatis: Reflections on Sasanian Court Rituals," in *Zoroastrian Ritual in Context*, ed. Michael Stausberg (Leiden: 2003), 354n29; Richard Payne, "Review of *Commutatio et Contention*," *Journal of Late Antiquity* 6 (2013): 187–190. Indeed, the applicability of "feudalism" to medieval Europe has also been challenged: see Elizabeth Brown, "The Tyranny of a Construct: Feudalism and Historians of Medieval Europe," *American Historical Review* 79 (1974): 1063–1088; and Susan Reynolds, *Fiefs and Vassals: The Medieval Evidence Reinterpreted* (Oxford: 1994). Changes in scholarly understanding of Sasanian rule have been occasioned, in part, by the growing effort to integrate Sasanian history into the study of Late Antiquity, on which see: Joel Walker, "The Limits of Late Antiquity: Philosophy between Rome and Iran," *Ancient World* 33 (2002): 45–69; Touraj Daryaee, "The Limits of Sasanian History: Between Iranian, Islamic, and Late Antique Studies," *Iranian Studies* 49 (2016): 193–203; Teresa Bernheimer and Adam Silverstein, eds., *Late Antiquity: Eastern Perspectives* (Exeter: 2012); and Parvaneh Pourshariati, "Further Engaging the Paradigm of Late Antiquity," *Journal of Persianate Studies* 6 (2013): 1–14.

23 James Howard-Johnston, "The Two Great Powers in Late Antiquity: A Comparison," in *The Byzantine and Early Islamic Near East, III: States, Resources and Armies*, ed. Averil Cameron (Princeton, NJ: 1995), 157–226.

network that was so central to the lives of the Jews of Babylonia.[24] Inscriptions, seals, coins, and literary evidence attest to a complex administrative hierarchy and bureaucracy at all levels of society.[25]

The growing acceptance of a more direct model of Sasanian rule has drawn increased attention to the way the Sasanian Empire, like other ancient empires, sought to legitimate itself to its diverse populations and was sustained as much by persuasion as power.[26] The Sasanians communicated with their inhabitants through sophisticated artistic, performative, and ideational programs.[27] King and administrators alike cultivated relationships with elites, communities, and other subjects. Sasanian officials even took keen interest in the images subjects produced and the stories they told of life under Sasanian rule. This is evidenced, for

[24] E. W. Sauer, et al., *Persia's Imperial Power in Late Antiquity. The Great Wall of Gorgan and Frontier Landscapes of Sasanian Iran* (Oxford: 2013); St. John Simpson, "Merv, an Archaeological Case-Study from the Northeastern Frontier of the Sasanian Empire," *Journal of Ancient History* 2 (2014): 1–28; Richard Payne, "The Archaeology of Sasanian Politics," *Journal of Ancient History* 2 (2014): 80–92; Nikolaus Schindel, "The 3rd Century 'Marw Shah' Bronze Coins Reconsidered," in *Commutatio et Contentio. Studies in the Late Roman, Sasanian and Early Islamic Middle East*, ed. Henning Börm and Josef Wiesehöfer (Düsseldorf: 2010), 23–36.

[25] Rika Gyselen, *La géographie administrative de l'empire sassanide* (Paris: 1989); Rika Gyselen, "Primary Sources and Historiography on the Sasanian Empire," *Studia Iranica* 38 (2009): 163–190; on the Sasanians' substitution of client kingdoms for direct rule, see Touraj Daryaee, "Palmyra and the Sasanians," in *Palmyra and the East*, ed. Kenneth Lapatin and Rubina Raja (Turnhout, 2022), 39–44; a process that played out longer in regions like Armenia, on which see Nina G. Garsoïan, "The Arshakuni Dynasty," in *The Armenian People from Ancient to Modern Times*, vol. 1, *The Armenia People from Ancient to Modern Times*, ed. R. G. Hovannisian (New York: 1997), 75–81. These studies participate in a broader trend questioning older models of empires as disjointed and noninterventionist, e.g. Susan Sherwin-White and Amelie Kehrt, *From Samarkhand to Sardis: A New Approach to the Seleucid Empire* (London: 1993); John Ma, *Antiochus III and the Cities of Western Asia Minor* (Oxford: 2000); and Paul Kosmin, *Land of the Elephant Kings: Space, Territory, and Ideology in the Seleucid Empire* (Cambridge, MA: 2014).

[26] For the theoretical interventions driving the consideration of how subjects acquiesce and submit to being ruled, see Ania Loomba, *Colonialism/Postcolonialism* (London: 1998), 28–34. For their application to the study of Roman imperialism, see Clifford Ando, *Imperial Ideology and Provincial Loyalty in the Roman Empire* (Berkeley: 2000); Greg Woolf, *Tales of the Barbarians: Ethnography and Empire in the Roman West. Blackwell Bristol Lectures on Greece, Rome and the Classical Tradition* (Chichester, MA: 2011); for Achaemenid imperialism, see Lori Khatchadourian, *Imperial Matter: Ancient Persia and the Archaeology of Empires* (Oakland, CA: 2016).

[27] Touraj Daryaee, "The Changing 'Image of the World': Geography and Imperial Propaganda in Ancient Persia," *Electrum* 6 (2002): 99–109; Canepa, *Two Eyes of the Earth*; Howard-Johnston, "Two Great Powers"; and Howard-Johnston, "State and Society."

instance, in the synagogue discovered in Dura Europos, which included six Middle Persian graffiti left by Iranian scribes and officials that recorded their favorable impressions of the paintings.[28] These are concentrated on the panel depicting the story of Mordecai's appearance before the Achaemenid king Ahasuerus, suggesting its resonance with contemporary Iranian officials, who saw it as evoking Jewish-Iranian cooperation in the present. The king choreographed encounters with communal elites and encouraged the production and dissemination of affirming descriptions of the king and of the empire. For instance, Yazdgird I (r. 399–420) sponsored the East Syriac ecclesiastical hierarchy, which publicly acknowledged his support of the church, and in time introduced a blessing on his behalf into the church liturgy.[29] Likewise, the king sought to repress and remove representations that undermined, belittled, or challenged the legitimacy or character of the empire.[30] Sasanian rule was attentive to the images communities produced, and sought where possible to shape them to their own advantage.

Yet even as scholars have argued for the more direct and immanent nature of Sasanian rule, they continue to perpetuate the three pillars of semi-autonomy, centralized self-regulating hierarchy, and insularity that largely silo the various subject groups from each other and from the empire.[31] The empire's communicative programs are therefore often treated as narrowly targeting elites, rather than intended to reach broader populations under its rule. Through a study of Jews in comparison with other subject communities, this book not only challenges the three pillars on which previous scholarship rests, but also demonstrates how Sasanian rule and its self-representation extended across rank, class, community, and religion to impact the social and cultural life of its inhabitants.

The Sasanian Empire was more than the nominal power within which different communities interacted and conversed. It was an inescapable, direct, and dominating presence that exerted pressures, circumscribed action, created cultural conditions, and encouraged behaviors, norms, and mores, using a variety of strategies, ranging from coaxing to violence,

[28] Touraj Daryaee, "To Learn and to Remember from Others: Persians Visiting the Dura-Europos Synagogue," *Scripta Judaica Cracoviensia* 8 (2010): 29–37. For a discussion on the identity of these Persian officials, see Steven Fine, "Jewish Identity at the Limus: The Earliest Reception of the Dura Europos Synagogue Paintings," *Cultural Identity in the Ancient Mediterranean*, ed. Erich Gruen (Los Angeles: 2011), 305–313.

[29] See Chapter 1, and Simcha Gross, "Being Roman in the Sasanian Empire: Revisiting the Great Persecution under Shapur II," *Studies in Late Antiquity* 5 (2021): 390–397.

[30] See Chapter 6. [31] See Chapter 1.

carrot and stick. For their part, the empire's inhabitants responded to imperial domination through alternating, but not mutually exclusive, modes of accommodation, compliance, and resistance, even as they were invariably shaped by imperial rule.[32] At the heart of this book is therefore the perennial dialectic between structure and agency, in which Babylonian Jews were embedded in and shaped by a context in which they were also agents, and in which the very options available to them were delineated to an extent by the structures that governed them.

The impact of life in the Sasanian Empire on its communities is observable, for instance, in the ways in which royal and elite practices were imitated and contested in both Jewish and Christian texts. For instance, Joel Walker has examined Christian articulations of identity and tradition in the context of Sasanian rule through a rich study of the Syriac *History of Mar Qardagh*, a hagiographical account about a highborn Sasanian Zoroastrian general who converts to Christianity.[33] This text simultaneously portrays a contest between Christian and Sasanian norms, even as it imitates and mimics the latter. Elite Christian ideas were shaped in other ways by imperial cosmology and elite Sasanian practices, as Richard Payne, in particular, has shown.[34] Sites sacred to Zoroastrians were sacralized into a Christian topography marked by the stories of saints and especially martyrs, forging a landscape brimming with memories of cooperation and competition with imperial authorities. Christian elites and saints expressed their status through the idiom of Sasanian elite culture, and

[32] For theoretical underpinnings, see: Doris Bachmann-Medick, *Cultural Turns: New Orientations in the Study of Culture* (Berlin: 2016), 131–173; J. Go, *Postcolonial Thought and Social Theory* (Oxford: 2016); K. A. Wagner, "Resistance, Rebellion, and the Subaltern," in *The Oxford World History of Empire*, vol. 1, *The Imperial Experience*, ed. P. F. Bang, C. A. Bayly, and W. Scheidel (New York: 2021), 416–436; helpful synthetic overview provided by Loomba, *Colonialism/Postcolonialism*, 231–245, which engages, among others, the classic studies of Gayatri Spivak, "Can the Subaltern Speak?" in *Marxism and the Interpretation of Culture*, ed. C. Nelson and L. Grossberg (Urbana, IL: 1988), 271–313; and Homi Bhabha, *The Location of Culture* (London: 1994). See also James C. Scott, *Domination and the Arts of Resistance: Hidden Transcripts* (New Haven, CT: 1990).

[33] Joel Thomas Walker, *The Legend of Mar Qardagh: Narrative and Christian Heroism in Late Antique Iraq* (Berkeley: 2006). For a different example, see Sergey Minov, "Dynamics of Christian Acculturation in The Sasanian Empire: Some Iranian Motifs in the Cave of Treasures," in *Jews, Christians and Zoroastrians: Religious Dynamics in a Sasanian Context* (Piscataway, NJ: 2015), 149–202; and Sergey Minov, *Memory and Identity in the Syriac Cave of Treasures: Rewriting the Bible in Sasanian Iran* (Leiden: 2020).

[34] Richard Payne, *State of Mixture: Christians, Zoroastrians, and Iranian Political Culture in Late Antiquity* (Oakland, CA: 2015).

adopted Zoroastrian practices, especially as they pertained to marriage and sacred feasts, while bishops inveighed against them, erecting boundaries to mark Christian practice as distinct from Zoroastrian. In a similar vein, Geoffrey Herman has shown that whether discussing biblical kings like David or the posture of an enslaved person that a worshipper should assume when praying to God, the rabbis ascribe to both the trappings and habits of the Sasanian court appropriate for their rank and status.[35] Sasanian rule formed the ubiquitous background within and against which communities expressed and fashioned themselves.

These studies, however, are the proverbial exceptions that prove the rule: To date, little attention has been devoted to how Jews and Syriac Christians were embedded in, interacted with, and responded to Sasanian imperial ideological, political, and social realities. This is due to several factors, among them the three pillars discussed above, and a tendency in the academic study of religious communities to treat them and their (reified) traditions as self-contained and internally evolving systems, a problem amplified by paradigms of the semi-autonomy of Sasanian religious communities. Approaching religious communities in this way assumes there exists a single, unadulterated, authentic religious tradition, and consequently reduces signs of participation in broader social and cultural worlds to "assimilation," and the absence thereof to resistance, as the only two options available to them.[36]

An additional reason for this enormous lacuna is Sasanian studies' near exclusive interest in the royal courts and high elites, an understandable reaction to the nature of surviving literary and archaeological evidence that often speaks more easily to the concerns of the upper crust than those of other social strata.[37] But this selective focus is also the product of conceptions of a feudalistic Sasanian imperial presence impacting mainly

[35] Geoffrey Herman, "One Day David Went Out for the Hunt of the Falconers: Persian Themes in the Babylonian Talmud," in *Shoshanat Yaakov: Jewish and Iranian Studies in Honor of Yaakov Elman*, ed. Shai Secunda and Steven Fine (Leiden: 2012), 111–136; Herman, "'Like a Slave before His Master': A Persian Gesture of Deference in Sasanian Jewish and Christian Sources," *Aram* 26 (2014): 101–108.

[36] Simcha Gross, "Rethinking Babylonian Jewish Acculturation in the Sasanian Empire," *Journal of Ancient Judaism* 9 (2019): 280–310.

[37] For helpful overviews, see Maria Macuch, "Pahlavi Literature," in *The Literature of Pre-Islamic Iran*, ed. Ronald E. Emmerick and Maria Macuch (New York: 2009), 116–196; and Matthew Canepa, "Sasanian Rock Reliefs," in *The Oxford Handbook of Ancient Iran*, ed. D.T. Potts (Oxford: 2013), 856–877. For growing scholarly interest in non-elites, see: Jack Tannous, *The Making of the Medieval Middle East: Religion, Society, and Simple Believers* (Princeton: 2018).

those Jews and Christians with direct access to the court itself. When studied in conjunction with Syriac Christians and other similarly situated groups, Jewish sources and society allow us to observe the complex negotiations of subjects with manifestations of Sasanian imperial power and ideology and Iranian culture that reached far beyond the drama and intrigue of the royal court.[38]

REPRESENTATIONS OF EMPIRE

Sasanian rulers endeavored to legitimate themselves and their institutions by shaping the thought worlds and habits of their heterogenous inhabitants.[39] Individuals and groups, in turn, had to define their own positions within the empire, and to modify, or stubbornly maintain, those practices that might draw them into conflict with it. The stories people told were one of the vehicles by which they fashioned attitudes towards empire, offered paradigms of proper conduct, and defined the terms that would allow them to flourish under Sasanian rule in a manner they determined was consistent with their traditions, histories, and identities. The salient question of these sources therefore is not only the relative historicity of their representations of the Sasanian Empire and their protagonists' encounters with it, but the nature and purpose of these literary constructions in their time and place.[40]

[38] In this, I am guided by studies like those of Seth Schwartz, *Imperialism and Jewish Society: 200 BCE to 640 CE* (Princeton, NJ: 2001), Hayim Lapin, *Rabbis as Romans: The Rabbinic Movement in Palestine, 100–400 CE* (Oxford: 2012), and Katell Berthelot, *Jews and Their Roman Rivals: Pagan Rome's Challenge to Israel* (Princeton, NJ: 2021), which consider Jews from the perspective of Roman imperialism and provincialism. See also: Ishay Rosen-Zvi, "Is the Mishnah a Roman Composition?" in *The Faces of Torah. Studies in the Texts and Contexts of Ancient Judaism in Honor of Steven Fraade*, ed. Christine Hayes, Tzvi Novick, and Michal Bar-Asher Segal (Göttingen: 2017), 487–508. Similar critiques of elite-centered paradigms of Romanization are levied by David Mattingly, "Being Roman: Expressing Identity in a Provincial Setting," *Journal of Roman Archaeology* 17 (2004): 6.

[39] The "imperialism" in the book's title refers to the system(s) of political domination that the Sasanians exerted over subjects, especially in Mesopotamia. On various definitions of the term and its applicability in different contexts, see Berthelot, *Jews and Their Roman Rivals*, 17–19, and for its application to the study of late antique Jews under Roman rule, see Alexei Sivertsev, *Judaism and Imperial Ideology in Late Antiquity* (Cambridge: 2011).

[40] See the discussion of the "linguistic turn" in Elizabeth Clark, *History, Theory, Text: Historians and the Linguistic Turn* (Cambridge, MA: 2004). For an application to a Syriac context, see Aaron Michael Butts and Simcha Gross, *The History of the "Slave of Christ": From Jewish Child to Christian Martyr* (Piscataway, NJ: 2016).

Scholars of Christianity under Sasanian rule have demonstrated the benefit of this approach.[41] They have shown how Syriac texts, from hagiography to martyrology to ecclesiastical history, performed cultural work, setting the terms of Christian integration in the Sasanian Empire. These sources define and idealize the desired relationship with the Sasanian Empire, offering saintly figures like church officials, holy men, and martyrs as models of proper comportment in and towards the empire.

The Talmud presents similar evidence with which to investigate the dynamics between Jews and the Sasanian Empire. Previous scholarly accounts have to various degrees treated the representations of Sasanian kings, Zoroastrian magi, administrators, and imperial violence in the Talmud as somewhat straightforward reflections, whether direct or indirect, of historical reality itself. As I argue in Chapters 4–6, a reappraisal of these narratives reveals that they are precisely the sites in which Jews articulated and shaped attitudes toward their imperial circumstances as they perceived them. The rabbis – a select group of Jews steeped in the contemplation, instruction, and practice of Jewish law and lore – were in an ongoing process of defining the parameters of Jewish negotiation with Sasanian rule.[42] These images addressed questions as wide-ranging as which aspects of Zoroastrianism constituted "idolatry," how and when Jews should accommodate or resist expressions of imperially sponsored Zoroastrianism, how Jews should interpret imperial violence, and in what ways Jews should support, subvert, or seek to avoid the Empire.

In considering the Sasanian Empire, the Talmud directly engages imperial rhetoric and projections. Imperial claims to power and the promotion of imperial identities in their subjects were not automatically accepted hook, line, and sinker by rabbis, Jews, or Sasanian subjects; they were altered, reshaped, rearticulated, and contested. Subjects "responded to those principles they were predisposed to accept," and challenged, modified, and rejected those with which they felt they clashed.[43]

41 Payne, *State of Mixture*; Adam Becker, "Martyrdom, Religious Difference, and 'Fear' as a Category of Piety in the Sasanian Empire: The Case of the Martyrdom of Gregory and the Martyrdom of Yazdpaneh," *Journal of Late Antiquity* 2 (2009): 300–336; and Kyle Smith, *Constantine and the Captive Christians of Persia: Martyrdom and Religious Identity in Late Antiquity* (Oakland, CA: 2016), 103.

42 On the instructive quality of rabbinic literature, see, for instance, Steven Fraade, *From Tradition to Commentary: Torah and Its Interpretation in the Midrash Sifre to Deuteronomy* (Albany: 1991).

43 Ando, *Imperial Ideology and Provincial Loyalty*, 5. See also: Natalie Dohrmann, "Law and Imperial Idioms: Rabbinic Legalism in a Roman World," in *Jews, Christians, and the Roman Empire: The Poetics of Power in Late Antiquity*, ed. Natalie Dohrmann and

This book therefore seeks to appreciate anew the agency of subjects under the Sasanian Empire to shape their own experiences and attitudes towards their surroundings, even as they were shaped and constrained by the prevailing realities and discourses of the time. Questions of Jewish engagement with their imperial context appeared less germane when Jews were thought to dwell in autonomous isolation. But as integrated subjects, such questions are critical. Babylonian Jews, like all Sasanian subjects, produced accounts that defined their place within imperial, administrative, cultural, and religious systems not of their own making, transforming their own traditions in the process.

INTEGRATING BABYLONIAN JEWS

Recent strides in the comparative study of Jews and neighboring Sasanian groups challenge any simple notion of a siloed Jewish community. Parallels between the Babylonian Talmud and Zoroastrian priestly literature confirm that Jews were exposed to Zoroastrian ideas, beliefs, and practices.[44] While Zoroastrianism has received pride of place in the works of Shaul Shaked, Yaakov Elman, and Shai Secunda, among others, there has been an increasing interest in signs of rabbinic contact with other communities.[45] Syriac Christians have become a particularly productive

Annette Yoshiko Reed (Philadelphia, PA: 2014), 73; Lapin, *Rabbis as Romans*, 4; and Ra'anan S. Boustan, "The Spoils of Jerusalem at Rome and Constantinople: Jewish Counter-Geography in a Christianizing Empire," in *Antiquity after Antiquity: Jewish and Christian Pasts in the Greco-Roman World*, ed. G. Gardner and K.I. Osterloh (Tübingen: 2008), 333.

44 For a general history of the field, see: Eli Ahdut, "Jewish-Zoroastrian Polemics in the Babylonian Talmud," in *Irano-Judaica* IV, ed. Shaul Shaked and Amnon Netzer (1999), 17–40; Secunda, *Iranian Talmud*; Secunda, "Babylonian Judaism and Zoroastrianism," in *The Routledge Companion to Jews in Late Antiquity*, ed. Catherine Hezser (Abington, Oxon: 2024), 435–446.; Jason Mokhtarian, *Rabbis, Sorcerers, Kings, and Priests: The Culture of the Talmud in Ancient Iran* (Oakland, CA: 2015); and words of caution in Simcha Gross, "Irano-Talmudica and Beyond: Next Steps in the Contextualization of the Babylonian Talmud," *Jewish Quarterly Review* 106 (2016): 248–255.

45 For Armenian, see Geoffrey Herman, "The Story of Rav Kahana (BT Baba Qamma 117a–b) in Light of Armeno-Persian Sources," in *Irano-Judaica* VI, ed. Shaul Shaked and Amnon Netzer (2008), 53–86. For Manichaean, see Geoffrey Herman, "The Talmud in Its Babylonian Context: Rava and Bar-Sheshakh; Mani and Mihrshah," in *Between Babylonia and the Land of Israel: Studies in Honor of Isaiah M. Gafni*, ed. Geoffrey Herman, Meir ben Shahar, and Aharon Oppenheimer (Jerusalem: 2017), 79–96; and Jae Han, "Mani's Metivta: Manichaean Pedagogy in Its Late Antique Mesopotamian Context," *Harvard Theological Review* 114 (2021): 346–370. For Hellenistic materials, see: Daniel Boyarin, *Socrates and the Fat Rabbis* (Chicago: 2009); and Adam Becker,

point of comparison, both for signs of contact and polemic between Jews and Christians and as conduits in the transfer of knowledge from west to east, from which the rabbis appear to have benefited.[46] These studies are primarily interested in local textual questions of religious contact, influence, and borrowing, rather than the broader political, social, and cultural impact of Sasanian rule or Jewish engagement with it. But in aggregate, these studies offer a more complex portrait of the rabbis by establishing that they were not as isolated as previously believed.

In parallel to these developments, the ongoing publication of what are known as the Aramaic incantation bowls continues to reveal moments of complex social, religious, and cultural contact between Jews and others. Inscribed on ceramic bowls between approximately the fifth and seventh centuries of the Common Era, the incantations were composed in three Aramaic dialects: Syriac, Mandaic , and, most numerously, Jewish Babylonian Aramaic. While the choice of language likely reflects the identity of the particular scribe,[47] the incantations themselves reflect the transfer of formulae, figures, and imagery between scribes of different confessional groups.[48] The names of the

"Positing a 'Cultural Relationship' between Plato and the Babylonian Talmud: Daniel Boyarin's *Socrates and the Fat Rabbis* (2009)," *Jewish Quarterly Review* 101 (2011): 255–269.

[46] See the early remarks of Adam Becker, "The Comparative Study of 'Scholasticism' in Late Antique Mesopotamia: Rabbis and East Syrians," *AJS Review* 34 (2010): 91–113; Adam Becker, "Polishing the Mirror: Some Thoughts on Syriac Sources and Early Judaism," in *Envisioning Judaism: Studies in Honor Peter Schäfer on the Occasion of his Seventieth Birthday*, ed. Ra'anan Boustan, Klaus Herrmann, Reimund Leicht, Annette Y. Reed, and Giuseppe Veltri, with the collaboration of Alex Ramos (Tübingen: 2013), 2:897–916; and Michal Bar-Asher Siegal, *Early Christian Monastic Literature and the Babylonian Talmud* (Cambridge: 2016). As conduits of transfer, see Richard L. Kalmin, *Jewish Babylonia between Persia and Roman Palestine* (New York: 2006); and Richard L. Kalmin, *Migrating Tales: The Talmud's Narratives and Their Historical Context* (Oakland, CA: 2014). A review of the literature is found in Jeffrey Rubenstein and Geoffrey Herman, "Introduction," in *The Aggada of the Bavli and Its Cultural World*, ed. Jeffrey Rubenstein and Geoffrey Herman (Providence, RI: 2018), xi–xxxv; and Aaron Michael Butts and Simcha Gross, "Introduction," in *Jews and Syriac Christians: Intersections across the First Millennium*, ed. Aaron Michael Butts and Simcha Gross (Tübingen: 2020), 1–26.

[47] Tapani Harviainen, "Pagan Incantations in Aramaic Magic Bowls," in *Studia Aramaica: New Sources and New Approaches*, ed. M. Geller, J. C. Greenfield, and M. P. Weitzman (Oxford: 1995), 53–60.

[48] See, for instance, H. Juusola, "Who Wrote the Syriac Incantation Bowls," *Studia Orientalia* 85 (1999): 75–92; and H. Juusola, "Manichaean Incantations Bowls in Syriac," *Jerusalem Studies in Arabic and Islam* 24 (2000): 58–92. On the identity of the Jewish scribes, see Avigail Manekin-Bamberger, "Who Were the Jewish 'Magicians'

clients who commissioned the bowls often contain non-Jewish theophoric elements and may either belong to Jews, reflecting a degree of Jewish acculturation in their onomastic choices, or to non-Jews, suggesting that members of one community would commission bowls from the ritual experts of other groups.[49] That individuals could patronize scribes of different religions is confirmed by evidence of several clients who commissioned bowls in multiple languages. For instance, among the incantation bowls discovered at Nippur were four bowls – two in Jewish Babylonian Aramaic and two in Syriac – produced for the same client, Dādbeh bar Asmandūch, who has a Persian theophoric name (see Figures 1 and 2). One of the Syriac bowls produced for Dādbeh invokes Rabbi Joshua son of Peraḥia, who appears in rabbinic literature and is commonly invoked on Jewish Babylonian Aramaic incantation bowls.[50] The case of Dādbeh reflects how individuals, Jewish or otherwise, had direct contact with scribes of multiple religious backgrounds, and that scribes freely shared confessionally specific formulae with each other.

behind the Aramaic Incantation Bowls?" *Journal of Jewish Studies* 71 (2020): 235–254. Most remarkably, Syriac bowls invoke the rabbinic figure Rabbi Joshua son of Peraḥia, who appears frequently in the Jewish Babylonian Aramaic bowls and rabbinic literature, while a Jewish Babylonian Aramaic bowl concludes with an invocation of the Trinity. See Dan Levene, "'... and by the name of Jesus ...' An Unpublished Magic Bowl in Jewish Aramaic," *Jewish Studies Quarterly* 6 (1999): 283–308; Shaul Shaked, "Jesus in the Magic Bowls. Apropos Dan Levene's '... and by the name of Jesus ...,' *Jewish Studies Quarterly* 6 (1999): 309–319; and Sergey Minov, "Christians, Jews, and Magic in the Sasanian Realm: Between Confrontation and Cooperation," *Entangled Religions* 13.3 (2022).

49 Dan Levene, *A Corpus of Magic Bowls: Incantation Texts in Jewish Aramaic from Late Antiquity* (London: 2003), 23; Michael G. Morony, "Religion and the Aramaic Incantation Bowls," *Religion Compass* 1 (2007): 414–429; Shaul Shaked, "Popular Religion in Sasanian Babylonia," *Jerusalem Studies in Arabic and Islam* 21 (1997): 103–117; and Idem, "Jews, Christians and Pagans in the Aramaic Incantation Bowls of the Sasanian Period," in *Religions and Cultures: First International Conference of Mediterraneum*, eds. A. Destro and M. Pesce (Binghamton, NY: 2001), 61–89. For the diverse Jewish communities represented by the bowls, see: Simcha Gross and Avigail Manekin-Bamberger, "Babylonian Jewish Society: The Evidence of the Incantation Bowls," *Jewish Quarterly Review* 112 (2022): 1–30. More generally, see G. Lacerenza, "Jewish Magicians and Christian Clients in Late Antiquity," in *What Athens Has to Do with Jerusalem: Essays on Classical, Jewish, and Early Christian Art and Archaeology in Honor of Gideon Foerster*, ed. Leonard Rutgers (Leuven: 2002), 393–419.

50 James Montgomery, *Aramaic Incantation Texts from Nippur* (Philadelphia, PA: 1913), 174–175 (#12), 188–189 (#16), 223 (#31), 230 (#33).

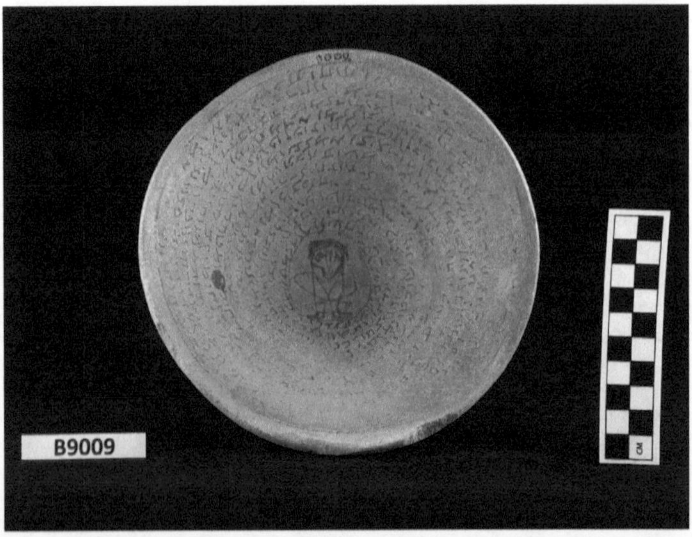

FIGURES 1 AND 2. Two incantation bowls from Nippur in the Penn Museum collection, one in Syriac and one in Jewish Babylonian Aramaic, and both written for the same client – Dādbeh bar Asmandūch – possessing a Zoroastrian theophoric name. [Penn Museum B9008 and B9009]

Other evidence similarly belies any notion of Jewish self-seclusion. The two excavated cities in Mesopotamia for which we have the strongest evidence of Jewish life – Dura Europos, north of major rabbinic centers, and Nippur, to the south – both reveal Jews living alongside other groups in dense urban environments.[51] The few descriptions of daily life in the incantation bowls similarly suggest frequent interactions between religious groups. One Jewish Babylonian Aramaic bowl requests economic success from customers who include "men and women, Jews and gentiles."[52] Contact between Jews and Christians was apparently so regular that it grew concerning to some Church elites, such that one synod revealingly lambasted Christians who, "after they receive the holy mysteries and leave the church on the days of the Eucharist, rush to the shops of Jews to drink wine."[53]

The Talmud itself depicts a social reality in which Babylonian Jews and non-Jews shared cityscapes, businesses, and courtyards, and forged personal and professional ties.[54] Rabbis, even those outside of the capital city of Seleucia-Ctesiphon, lived in densely populated Sasanian urban spaces predominately inhabited by non-Jews. Although literary evidence suggests that some Jews may have lived in concentrated Jewish neighborhoods, there is no reason to believe that even these were entirely isolated or secluded.[55] Urban patterns of Jewish life in Babylonia, together with comparative evidence and the incantation bowls, hardly evince a particular proclivity towards insularity.[56] They reveal instead a diverse religious

[51] For Dura, see Lucinda Dirven, "Religious Competition and the Decoration of Sanctuaries: The Case of Dura-Europos," *Eastern Christian Art* 1 (2004): 1–19.

[52] Dan Levene and Siam Bhayro, "'Bring to the Gates ... upon a Good Smell and upon Good Fragrances': An Aramaic Incantation Bowl for Success in Business," *Archiv für Orientforschung* 51 (2005/2006): 242–246.

[53] J.B. Chabot, *Synodicon Orientale, ou recueil de synodes nestoriens* (Paris: 1902), 225, 489; and discussion in Gross, "Babylonian Jewish Communities."

[54] For stories about interactions between Jews and non-Jews, see Gafni, "Babylonian Rabbinic Culture," 240–241. For rabbinic laws concerning commercial endeavors with non-Jews, see Christine Hayes, *Between the Babylonian and Palestinian Talmuds: Accounting for Halakhic Difference in Selected Sugyot from Tractate Avodah Zarah* (New York: 1997), 168–170.

[55] See Gross, "Babylonian Jewish Communities."

[56] On the social world revealed in the bowls, see Michael Morony, "Magic and Society in late Sasanian Iraq," in *Prayer, Magic and the Stars in the Ancient and Late Antique World*, ed. S. Noegel, J. Walker, and B. Wheeler (University Park, PA: 2005), 83–107. On the difference between the rhetoric of insularity and reality, see Albert de Jong, "Zoroastrian Religious Polemics in Their Contexts: Interconfessional Relations in the Sasanian Empire," in *Religious Polemics in Context. Papers Presented to the Second International*

and cultural landscape within which the rabbis and other Jews flourished, and invite us to consider how different individuals and groups defined themselves in relation to those around them, how they erected and conceived of borders between communities, and how permeable those borders always remained. The integrated model of the Sasanian Empire calls for a reappraisal of the fundamental assumptions about Babylonian Jewish history and demands greater appreciation for the way Jews were impacted by and participated in their local and imperial contexts, in which they were firmly entrenched.

SOURCES AND METHODS FOR THE STUDY OF BABYLONIAN JEWISH HISTORY

The primary source for Jewish life under Sasanian rule is the Babylonian Talmud. The Talmud is an enormous anthology covering an astonishing range of subjects and genres. In its sheer scope, coverage, and diversity of materials, the Talmud is unparalleled by any other literary work from the Sasanian Empire.

The Talmud's richness as a text is perhaps only equaled by the many methodological quandaries it presents to the historian. Overall, the material in the Talmud is narrowly focused on the opinions, discussions, and stories of a distinct subgroup of Babylonian Jews, whose importance it tends to inflate. The tendency of rabbinic literature to portray rabbis as prominent, even peerless, religious and judicial leaders of the Jewish community, once almost universally accepted as historically accurate, is now recognized as a reflection of the tendentious concerns and aspirations of its compilers.[57] Generalizing the effects of the Sasanian Empire on

Conference of the Leiden Institute for the Study of Religions (LISOR) Held at Leiden, 27–28 April 2000, ed. Arie van der Kooij and Theo L. Hettema (Assen: 2004), 48–63.

57 For the more critical assessment of the place of the rabbis in Palestinian Jewish society, see: Lee Levine, *The Rabbinic Class of Roman Palestine in Late Antiquity* (Jerusalem: 1990); Shaye J. D. Cohen, "The Place of the Rabbi in Jewish Society of the Second Century," in *Galilee in Late Antiquity*, ed. Lee Levine (New York: 1992), 157–173; Schwartz, *Imperialism and Jewish Society*; and Seth Schwartz, "The Political Geography of Rabbinic Texts," in *The Cambridge Companion to the Talmud and Rabbinic Literature*, ed. C. Fonrobert and M. Jaffee (Cambridge: 2007), 75–96. For some moderate pushback, see in particular Stuart Miller, *Sages and Commoners in Late Antique 'Ereẓ Israel: A Philological Inquiry into Local Traditions in Talmud Yerushalmi* (Tübingen: 2006); and the forum in *Jewish Identities in Antiquity*, ed. Lee Levine and Daniel Schwartz (Tübingen: 2009), 163–210, with the reply in Seth Schwartz, "Was there a 'Common Judaism' after the Destruction?" in *Envisioning Judaism: Studies in Honor of Peter Schäfer on the Occasion of his Seventieth Birthday*, ed. Ra'anan S. Boustan, Klaus

Babylonian Jews, let alone Jews throughout the Sasanian Empire, based on the rabbis is therefore problematic, especially once we consider how different Palestinian Jewish society appears when judged from the vantage point of rabbinic literature versus other available sources.[58] Moreover, given the anthological nature of the Talmud and the dispersed nature of the rabbinic movement at the time, it is difficult to formulate a single "rabbinic" view on almost any subject.[59] Indeed, many of the talmudic passages that address the questions animating this book include competing rabbinic opinions. This forecloses any attempt to generalize a single monolithic rabbinic, let alone Jewish, attitude or approach related to Sasanian rule. The book's primary focus on Babylonian Jews is an admission of the fact that the Talmud is mainly interested in and reflects the concerns of a narrow subset of Jews in a limited geographic region, and not necessarily of Jews across the Sasanian expanse.[60]

In addition to these questions of representativeness, the historicity of the Talmud's stories and anecdotes can hardly be taken at face value. The Talmud provides no absolute dates and rarely discusses known historical events. Even the teachings ascribed to particular sages are often pseudepigraphic or ahistorical, undermining older attempts to piece together the biographies of individual sages from an aggregate of talmudic stories.[61]

Herrmann, Reimund Leicht, Annette Y. Reed, and Giuseppe Veltri, with the collaboration of Alex Ramos (Tübingen: 2013), 1.3–22.

58 The bibliography is vast. For an overview, see Lee Levine, *Visual Judaism in Late Antiquity: Historical Contexts of Jewish Art* (New Haven, CT: 2013).

59 For the place of rabbis in Babylonian Jewish society, see: Gross and Manekin-Bamberger, "Babylonian Jewish Society"; Gross, "Babylonian Jewish Communities"; Gross, "Where Did Rav and Shmuel Preside? Lingering Institutional Assumptions in the Study of the Late Antique Babylonian Rabbis," *Jewish History* 36 (2022): 1–28 and Gross, "Prolegomena to a Study of Babylonian Rabbinization in Late Antiquity."

60 For the selective focus of the Talmud even within Babylonia, see Yakir Paz, "'Meishan is Dead': On the Historical Contexts of the Bavli's Representations of the Jews in Southern Babylonia," in *Babylonian Aggada in Its Historical Context*, ed. Geoffrey Herman and Jeffrey Rubenstein (Providence, RI: 2018), 47–102. The book does not discuss the brief period of Sasanian rule over the Jews in most of Syria, Palestine, and Egypt in the first quarter of the seventh century, on which see, for instance, Averil Cameron, "The Jews in Seventh-Century Palestine," *Scripta Classica Israelica* 13 (1994): 75–93; and Elliot Horowitz, "'The Vengeance of the Jews Was Stronger than Their Avarice': Modern Historians and the Persian Conquest of Jerusalem in 614," *Jewish Social Studies* 4 (1998): 1–39.

61 The pioneering works on these questions are Jacob Neusner, *Development of a Legend: Studies on the Traditions concerning Yohanan ben Zakkai* (Leiden: 1970); Jacob Neusner, *Eliezer ben Hyrcanus. The Tradition and the Man* (Leiden: 1973); William Scott Green, "What's in a Name? The Problematic of Rabbinic 'Biography,'" in

Talmudic stories do not offer transparent descriptions of reality, but are first and foremost literary products. They may possess various degrees of verisimilitude, but in no case is this self-evident.[62]

The problems with the Talmud's historicity are exacerbated by the growing scholarly recognition that the text before us is the product of a lengthy and substantial process of redaction and recitation which post-dates many of the figures or events that appear within it.[63] The redactors were responsible for much of the Talmud as we know it; they compiled earlier opinions into what appear to be linear legal discussions and connected one textual unit to the next. They produced the anonymous Aramaic discursive tissue that holds talmudic legal discussions and stories together, regularly interpolating explanations, questions, answers, and other material throughout. Scholars now believe that everything from individual legal opinions attributed to particular rabbis to lengthy rabbinic stories attributed to no one are at times reformulations, if not outright creations, of later editorial hands, though they are not marked as such.[64] Scholars have devised sophisticated methods to differentiate

Approaches to Ancient Judaism: Theory and Practice, ed. William Scott Green (Missoula, MT: 1978), 77–96.

[62] For the general issues, see Hillel I. Newman, "Closing the Circle: Yonah Fraenkel, the Talmudic Story, and Rabbinic History," in *How Should Rabbinic Literature be Read in the Modern World?* ed. Matthew Kraus (Piscataway, NJ, 2006), 105–113; Isaiah Gafni, "Rethinking Talmudic History: The Challenge of Literary and Redaction Criticism," *Jewish History* 25 (2011): 355–375.

[63] For helpful English language summaries, see: David M. Goodblatt, "The Babylonian Talmud," in *The Study of Ancient Judaism: The Palestinian and Babylonian Talmuds*, ed. Jacob Neusner (New York: 1981), 120–199; David M. Goodblatt, "A Generation of Talmudic Studies," in *The Talmud in Its Iranian Context*, ed. Carol Bakhos and M. Rahim Shayegan (Tübingen: 2010), 1–20; Hayes, *Between the Babylonian and Palestinian Talmuds*; and Richard Kalmin, "The Formation and Character of the Babylonian Talmud," in *The Cambridge History of Judaism*, vol. 4, *The Late-Roman Period*, ed. S. T. Katz (Cambridge: 2006), 840–876.

[64] On historicity, see Shamma Friedman, "Literary Development and Historicity in the Aggadic Narrative of the Babylonian Talmud: A Study Based upon BM 83b–86a," in *Community and Culture: Essays in Jewish Studies in Honor of the 90th Anniversary of Gratz College, 1895–1985*, ed. Nahum W. Waldman (Philadelphia, PA: 1987), 67–80; Shamma Friedman, "Historical Narrative in the Babylonian Talmud," in *Saul Lieberman Memorial Volume*, ed. Shamma Friedman (New York: 1993), 119–164; Adiel Schremer, "Stammaitic Historiography," in *Creation and Composition: The Contribution of the Bavli Redactors (Stammaim) to the Aggada*, ed. Jeffrey L. Rubenstein (Tübingen: 2005), 219–235; Jeffrey Rubenstein, *Talmudic Stories: Narrative Art, Composition, and Culture* (Baltimore, MD: 1999); Jeffrey Rubenstein, *The Culture of the Babylonian Talmud* (Baltimore, MD: 2003); David Weiss Halivni, *The Formation of the Babylonian Talmud*, trans. Jeffrey Rubenstein (New York: 2013); and Moulie Vidas, *Tradition and Formation of the Talmud* (Princeton, NJ: 2014).

earlier from later textual strata, as well as prearranged material from editorial interventions, performing a kind of textual archaeology. But talmudic sources from any textual layer are themselves literary, didactic, and tendentious. Traditional efforts to isolate historical kernel from literary husk are complicated by these sundry methodological issues.[65] Simply put: Talmudic texts cannot be treated uncritically as straightforward transcripts or reliable historical representations.

The evidentiary issues outlined above may circumscribe the type of information that can be gleaned from the Talmud and foreclose certain kinds of historical projects, such as detailed biographies of particular sages, narrative histories, or arguments of diachronic developments in Jewish society in relation to the Sasanian Empire. But recognition of these impediments does not license the abandonment of the Talmud as a crucial historical source. We must distinguish between the use of rabbinic literature to reconstruct particular events, in which its tendentiousness and artifice undermine its historical value, and the broad patterns and contours of Babylonian Jewish life presupposed in talmudic legal discussions, sayings, and stories, which are often quite revealing. The plausibility of the patterns evidenced in rabbinic literature can then be tested and corroborated through contextualization and comparison with the full array of evidence available for Sasanian rule. This approach, I argue, allows us to attempt to thread the needle and positively construct something about Babylonian Jewish life, while maintaining sensitivity to the literary, rhetorical, and at times highly tendentious character of rabbinic sources.[66]

In addition to reconstructing aspects of the social history of Babylonian Jews, the questions this study seeks to answer, especially questions pertaining to Jewish acculturation and Jewish negotiation with various aspects of Sasanian rule, are precisely attuned to the nature of the Talmud. Rabbinic sources, even when fictional, express the interests and attitudes of their authors. The Talmud may not offer transparent descriptions of historical reality, but it does reflect how rabbis imagined and contemplated their world. The artifice and *Tendenz* of rabbinic sources are themselves the objects of study, emerging at a given moment and intending to convey ideas that were legible within and intended for

65 See overview in Amram Tropper, *Rewriting Ancient Jewish History: The History of the Jews in Roman Times and the New Historical Method* (London: 2016), 31–50.

66 By focusing mainly on texts that directly address the Sasanian Empire and issues of status, I hope to avoid concerns about the overzealous contextualization of matters of rabbinic discourse and law that may be the result of internal development. For these concerns, see Hayes, *Between the Babylonian and Palestinian Talmuds*.

particular historical moments, within particular social realities, and in response to competing discourses. The methodology employed here can serve as a model for situating rabbinic discourse within its Sasanian context.[67]

Unfortunately, there are few other sources produced by Sasanian Jews that can serve to complement, supplement, corroborate, or contradict the evidence provided by the Babylonian Talmud. Medieval rabbinic sources and their descriptions of the Sasanian Jewish past have often constituted the mainstay of scholarly accounts.[68] As in many fields, and especially in the study of early Islam, a more cautious approach to these sources is necessary – one that recognizes their biases, especially their tendency to retroject continuity, rabbinic ascendancy, Jewish insularity, and a centrally organized rabbinic community.[69] Like the Talmud, medieval sources should not be rejected out of hand, nor reproduced blindly. Rather, they should be employed judiciously, their relative merits weighed with sensitivity to the presence of later agendas, and measured alongside available corroborating evidence, an approach adopted throughout this book.

Material evidence produced by Jews in the Sasanian Empire is limited to a few dozen personal stamp seals and the considerable and ever-

[67] For methodological reflections, see Michael Satlow, "Beyond Influence: Toward a New Historiographic Paradigm," in *Jewish Literatures and Cultures: Context and Intertext*, ed. Yaron Eliav and Anita Norwich (Providence, RI: 2008), 37–53.

[68] In a similar vein, one Parthian-era story about the Jews of Mesopotamia has shaped scholarly narratives. On this, see Chapter 1.

[69] On the issues attending recourse to medieval sources in the study of Sasanian history, see: Philippe Gignoux, "Problèmes de distinction et de priorité des sources," in *Prolegomena to the Sources on the History of Pre-Islamic Central Asia*, ed. Janos Harmatta (Budapest: 1979), 137–141; and Philippe Gignoux, "Pour une nouvelle histoire de l'Iran sasanide," in *Middle Iranian Studies: Proceedings of the International Symposium Organized by the Katholieke Universiteit Leuven from the 17th to the 20th of May 1982*, ed. W. Skalmowski and A. Van Tongerloo (Leuven: 1984), 253–262; and Gyselen, "Primary Sources and Historiography on the Sasanian Empire." On the study of Islamic history, see: Patricia Crone and Michael Cook, *Hagarism: The Making of the Islamic World* (New York: 1977); John Wansbrough, *Quranic Studies: Sources and Methods of Scriptural Interpretation* (Oxford: 1977); and John Wansbrough, *The Sectarian Milieu: Content and Composition of Islamic Salvation History* (Oxford: 1978). On similar problems in the study of the rabbinic past, see: David M. Goodblatt, *Rabbinic Instruction in Sasanian Babylonia* (Leiden: 1975); Simcha Gross, "When the Jews Greeted Ali: Sherira Gaon's Epistle in Light of Arabic and Syriac Historiography," *Jewish Studies Quarterly* 24 (2017): 122–144; and Lapin, *Rabbis as Romans*, 151–167.

growing collection of a few thousand Aramaic incantation bowls.[70] I make use of this material when relevant. Their evidentiary value, however, is severely circumscribed by their nature and purpose, in addition to issues of uncertain provenance. Nevertheless, as I will discuss in Chapter 5, when the images on Jewish seals are contextualized within Sasanian visual culture, they reveal how different Jews positioned themselves in relation to other neighboring groups.

The Aramaic incantation bowls provide far more extensive literary evidence and offer key insight into the imaginative worlds of scribes and clients. Given that incantations were primarily intended to ward off malevolent forces and protect their clients, they offer valuable evidence for a social history of the home, family structures, gender, medicine, and more. At the very least, they afford a glimpse of a world not entirely constrained by the principal interests of rabbinic literature.[71] They are, however, less conducive for understanding the relationship of Babylonian Jews and their imperial context.

Nevertheless, the bowls too speak to broader social-historical issues. As discussed above, the bowls reflect a social environment in which Jews, Christians, and others participated in various forms of contact and engagement. The bowls also speak to the place of the rabbis within Jewish society. The rabbis were not isolated from the marketplace of the incantation bowls; indeed, rabbis appear as clients in the bowls, and some incantations show deep familiarity with rabbinic texts and attribute great power to particular rabbinic figures and formulae.[72] They suggest that different bowl scribes and clients possessed different relations with the rabbis and rabbinic values, challenging the belief that rabbis were the exclusive, or even dominant, figures in a centralized Jewish hierarchy, and

[70] In general, see: Joseph Naveh and Shaul Shaked, *Amulets and Magic Bowls* (Jerusalem: 1985); Joseph Naveh and Shaul Shaked, *Magic Spells and Formulae* (Jerusalem: 1993); Levene, *A Corpus of Magic Bowls*; Shaul Shaked, J. N. Ford, and Siam Bhayro, *Aramaic Bowl Spells: Jewish Babylonian Aramaic Bowls* (Leiden: 2013).

[71] Geoffrey Herman, "In Search of Non-Rabbinic Judaism in Sasanian Babylonia," in *Diversity and Rabbinization: Jewish Texts and Societies between 400 and 1,000 CE*, ed. G. McDowell, R. Naiweld, J. Schlanger, and D. Stökl Ben Ezra (Cambridge: 2021), 121–138; and Geoffrey Herman, "Jewish Identity in Babylonia in the Period of the Incantation Bowls," in *A Question of Identity: Social, Political, and Historical Aspects of Identity Dynamics in Jewish and Other Contexts*, ed. D. Rivlin Katz, N. Hacham, G. Herman, and L. Sagiv (Berlin: 2019), 131–152.

[72] See Gross and Manekin-Bamberger, "Babylonian Jewish Society."

inviting more dynamic models of Babylonian Jewish society (see Chapter 1 and 2).

In addition to Jewish literary and material remains, non-Jewish sources from the period do occasionally mention Jews. However, these sources often reproduce stereotypes and carry biases that suggest that they are the literary constructions of their authors.[73] For instance, although Syriac texts frequently feature Jews, they often employ a standard repertoire of anti-Jewish tropes that is typical of the construction of an imaginary Jew rather than the reliable description of real Jews.[74] Zoroastrian texts that mention Jews postdate the Sasanian period and primarily reflect theological polemics; they too often provide little evidence immediately relevant to the questions animating this study.[75]

Thus, neither the Talmud nor our other available Jewish and non-Jewish sources enable the production of a coherent narrative account of Babylonian Jewish history. Despite these shortcomings, our available

[73] Butts and Gross, "Introduction," 11–18.

[74] In general, see the classic works of: Miriam Taylor, *Anti-Judaism and Early Christian Identity: A Critique of the Scholarly Consensus* (Leiden: 1995); Judith Lieu, *Image and Reality: The Jews in the World of the Christians in the Second Century* (Edinburgh: 1996); and Judith Lieu, "Accusations of Jewish Persecution in Early Christian Sources, with Particular Reference to Justin Martyr and the *Martyrdom of Polycarp*," in *Tolerance and Intolerance in Early Judaism and Christianity*, ed. G. Stanton and G. Stroumsa (Cambridge: 1998), 239–295. For this intervention in Syriac Christian literature, see: Adam Becker, "Anti-Judaism and Care of the Poor in Aphrahat's Demonstration 20," *Journal of Early Christian Studies* 10 (2002): 305–327; Adam Becker, "L'antijudaïsme syriaque: entre polemique et critique interne," in *Les controverses religieuses en syriaque*, ed. Flavia Ruani (Paris: 2016), 181–208 (an English version is published in Butts and Gross, *Jews and Syriac Christians*, 47–66); Christine Shepardson, *Anti-Judaism and Christian Orthodoxy: Ephrem's Hymns in Fourth-Century Syria* (Washington, DC: 2008); Naomi Koltun-Fromm, *Hermeneutics of Holiness: Ancient Jewish and Christian Notions of Sexuality and Religious Community* (Oxford: 2010); Butts and Gross, *The History of the "Slave of Christ"*; and Butts and Gross, "Introduction." For Mandaic, see Dan D. Y. Shapira, "Manichaeans (Marmanaiia), Zoroastrians (Iazuqaiia), Jews, Christians and Other Heretics: A Study in the Redaction of Mandaic Texts," *Le Muséon* 117 (2004): 243–280.

[75] Shaul Shaked, "Zoroastrian Polemics against Jews in the Sasanian and Early Islamic period," in *Irano-Judaica* II, ed. Shaul Shaked and Amnon Netzer (Jerusalem: 1990), 85–104; Albert de Jong, "Zoroastrian Self-Definition in Contact with Other Faiths," in *Irano-Judaica V*, ed. Shaul Shaked and Amnon Netzer (Jerusalem: 2003), 16–26; Albert de Jong, "Zoroastrian Religious Polemics and Their Contexts," 48–63; Samuel Thrope, "Contradictions and Vile Utterances: The Zoroastrian Critique of Judaism in the Škand Gumānīg Wizār," (PhD diss., University of California, Berkeley: 2012); and Jason Mokhtarian, "Zoroastrian Polemics against Jews in the *Doubt Dispelling Exposition*," *Mizan* 3 (2018): 53–81. For Jewish polemics against Zoroastrians, see Ahdut, "Jewish-Zoroastrian Polemics," 17–40.

evidence for Babylonian Jews offers a unique perspective on how a segment of the Jewish community, deeply invested in the study and implementation of Jewish tradition, sought to reconcile its various commitments with the demands of life in the Sasanian Empire; how Jewish elites competed within and against Sasanian imperial culture and structures to define themselves and conceptualize their place in Jewish society; and how literary representations were composed and selected to communicate foundational ideas about Jews and their place within the empire.

JEWS AND CHRISTIANS

If Jewish sources are limited, and sources about Jews by other groups are tarnished by the polemical concerns of their authors, a key method to learning about Jews is precisely by approaching them as one group of imperial subjects among many. Jews and their neighbors were subjected to the same constraints – whether administrative or discursive – that the Empire exerted on its inhabitants and would, by necessity, employ similar strategies in response to them. Triangulating between the texts and experiences of different subjects and the evidence from the Sasanian Empire can therefore help situate all within the same historical context.[76] This is not to suggest that these groups shared identical experiences or employed the same strategies. On the contrary, because of their unique traditions, histories, and positionalities, different groups embraced or contested discrete aspects of Sasanian rule and administration. They therefore developed distinct attitudes and courses of action towards the empire and were often treated differently as a result. Subject groups acted in tandem, but not necessarily in concert. A comparative approach that heeds both similarities and differences yields a textured portrait that simultaneously illuminates particular groups and the experience of subjects as a whole.

Though various Sasanian groups are discussed throughout the book, the most sustained comparison is with Syriac Christians. Over the course of Late Antiquity, Christians spread across Sasanian territories.[77] Christians and Jews occupied the same cities, towns, and neighborhoods, spoke related dialects of Aramaic, and had similarly strong ties with their

[76] Aspects of this approach can be found in Herman, *Prince without a Kingdom*.

[77] Joel Walker, "From Nisibis to Xi'an: The Church of the East in Late Antique Eurasia," in *The Oxford Handbook of Late Antiquity*, ed. Scott. F. Johnson (Oxford: 2012), 994–1052.

coreligionists under Roman rule. Christians produced a voluminous body of texts concerning life under Sasanian rule in a diverse array of genres, including martyr acts, church synod records, historiographical and hagiographical works, and more, some of which intersect with rabbinic genres, and some of which are distinctly Christian. The Jewish and Christian evidence can therefore be variously combined and juxtaposed to answer questions about each community, Sasanian subjects more abstractly, and Sasanian rule itself.[78]

This comparison is especially promising given the increased scholarly interest in Syriac Christians living under Sasanian rule.[79] Newer work has jettisoned deeply entrenched scholarly assumptions about the limited impact that the Sasanian Empire exerted on its inhabitants. Thus, previous scholarship viewed Jews as the beneficiaries of Sasanian "tolerance," Christians were viewed as the victims of consistent Sasanian "intolerance" (see Chapter 3). But recent studies have focused instead on the well-attested rise of Christians to positions of significant stature and nobility within the imperial bureaucracy, assuming roles as ambassadors, state officials, and delegates on behalf of the empire.[80] This alone gainsays any simplistic notion of a consistent Sasanian "intolerance" towards Christians.[81] The different experiences of Jews and Christians under

78 On the benefits of triangulation between these sources and communities, see: Becker, "Polishing the Mirror"; Gross, "Irano-Talmudica and Beyond"; and Butts and Gross, "Introduction," in *Jews and Syriac Christians*, 1–26.

79 On this burgeoning field, see: C. Jullien and F. Jullien, *Apôtres des confins: processus missionaires chrétiens dans l'Empire Iranien* (Bures-sur-Yvette: 2002); Scott John McDonough, "Power by Negotiation: Institutional Reform in the Fifth Century Sasanian Empire" (PhD diss., University of California, Los Angeles, 2005); Muriel Debié, "L'Empire perse et ses marges" in *Histoire générale du christianisme des origins au XVe siècle*, ed. J.- R. Armogathe, P. Montaubin, and M.- Y. Perrin (Paris: 2010), 611–646; Walker, *Legend of Mar Qardagh*; and Payne, *State of Mixture.*

80 In general, see Payne, *State of Mixture*. The prominent place of Christians is explicitly acknowledged, for instance, in the *Martyrdom of George*: Paul Bedjan, ed., *Histoire de Mar-Jabalaha, de trois autres patriarches, d'un pretre et de deux laiques, Nestoriens* (Paris: 1895), 347–348.

81 Nina Garsoïan, "Le rôle de la hiérarchie chrétienne dans les rapports diplomatiques entre Byzance et les Sassanides," *REArm* n.s. 10 (1973–1974): 119–138; Louis Sako, *Le rôle de la Hiérarchie Syriaque-Orientale dans les rapports diplomatiques entre la Perse et Byzance aux Ve–VIIe siècles* (Paris: 1986); Scott J. McDonough, "Bishops or Bureaucrats? Christian Clergy and the State in the Middle Sasanian Period," in *Current Research in Sasanian Archaeology, Art and History*, ed. Derek Kennet and Paul Luft (Oxford: 2008), 87–92; Rika Gyselen, "Les temoignages sigillographiques sur la presence chretienne dans l'empire Sassanide," in *Chrétiens en terre d'Iran: Implantation et Acculturation*, ed. R. Gyselen (Paris: 2006), 17–78; and Gross, "Being Roman in the Sasanian Empire."

Sasanian rule are a sign of the complicated and contingent ways the Sasanian Empire and subjects interacted. The works emerging from these religious groups likewise attest to strategies of negotiation that are at times strikingly comparable and at times significantly at odds, but in both cases is instructive for understanding these groups and the possibilities available to Sasanian subjects as a whole.

Although non-Zoroastrian subjects shared similar imperial backgrounds, their relationship with and experience under the Sasanian Empire was often profoundly different. A key theme throughout this book is that the different experiences of Jews and Christians under Sasanian rule resulted not from a predetermined Sasanian acceptance of Jews and intolerance toward Christians, but from the unique challenges each group posed to the Sasanians based on their social-political positions, their traditions, and the different strategies each group tended to employ in its interactions with Sasanian rule. When studied in tandem, the histories of Jews and Christians provide a valuable comparative perspective for contemplating the dynamics of subjects and empire in Iran in Late Antiquity. Together, these groups constitute essential evidence for the diverse ways in which the Sasanian Empire organized and shaped its subjects, and the ways subjects shaped their perception and experience of Sasanian rule.

CHAPTER OUTLINE

The book begins by reexamining the cornerstone of previous accounts of Babylonian Jewish society: the notion of Jewish semi-autonomy and centralization under Sasanian rule. Through a consideration of Jewish, Christian, and Sasanian sources, Chapter 1 rebuts the widespread belief that the Sasanians organized religious communities into centralized and self-governing hierarchies, headed by a recognized official representative. The consensus view arose from a problematic tendency to assume that the state monopolized all forms of power and authority, thereby inflating any suggestion of social influence into an expression of imperially authorized power. Instead, as in other imperial contexts, Sasanian legal culture simultaneously provided a primary court system for its many subjects and also created the space for alternative means of social enforcement, with which it typically did not interfere. In lieu of an approach that reads any exercise of power as an expression of official authorization and organization, Chapter 1 stresses the dynamism created by alternative means of legal and social recourse, in which local and communal legal experts competed with imperial courts, and in which individuals participated in a robust marketplace of potential means of legal resolution.

This more dynamic model of Babylonian Jewish society is embraced in Chapter 2, which situates the most prominent Jewish elites from the perspective of rabbinic literature, the Exilarch and the rabbis, within a decentralized model of Babylonian Jewish society. Rather than the beneficiaries of official imperial sponsorship, these groups necessarily competed for influence and social capital in an environment in which positions were earned, not guaranteed. They therefore sought to legitimate themselves through appeals to different discourses and symbols that were prevalent in the Sasanian Empire, while adapting them to fit their Jewish identities and traditions. Exilarch and rabbis made overlapping and competing appeals to Sasanian and Iranian culture that are diagnostic of the ways different Jewish identities were expressed within a Sasanian environment.

The notion of Jewish semi-autonomy, centralization, and insularity have been tethered to the idea that the Sasanian Empire was particularly and consistently "tolerant" towards its Jewish subjects, which created the peaceable conditions that allowed Jews to flourish culturally and intellectually. The treatment of Jews is then juxtaposed with the fate of Christians, toward whom the Sasanians were allegedly "intolerant." This assessment is based largely on the relative dearth of stories of imperial violence against Jews in the Babylonian Talmud, versus the abundance of Christian sources that describe violence against Sasanian Christians. Chapter 3 argues that the very categories of "tolerance" and "intolerance" occlude the ideological and pragmatic bases for imperial actions, and particularly imperial violence. This chapter instead offers a schematic account of the logics of Sasanian imperial violence, and probes whether and why they may have impacted Jews and Christians differently. It shows that the Sasanians did not adopt predetermined attitudes towards groups, expressing partiality for some and animus toward others. Instead, imperial violence was responsive to behaviors it sought to encourage or curb, and it exposes the imperial priorities and policies of which particular groups ran afoul. Jews may well have been subject to fewer incidents of violence than their Christian neighbors, but this was due to their traditions, social position, and the efforts they made to mitigate occasions for conflict with the Sasanian Empire.

If Jews were subjected to the same logics of violence as their neighbors, the relative absence of accounts of Sasanian violence against Jews in the Talmud requires explanation, especially considering the proliferation of such stories among Syriac Christians. Chapter 4 contends that the absence of such stories in the Babylonian Talmud is not a reflection of the dearth of Sasanian violence targeting Jews. It emerges instead from a deliberate effort in the Talmud to discourage direct conflict with the Sasanian Empire by offering stories that deny the existence of Sasanian violence or valorize accommodation to imperial domination over resistance. These stories at times appear to directly parody both earlier Palestinian accounts of rabbinic martyrs as well as the genre of Syriac Christian martyr acts in order to offer a starkly different model for Jewish life under Sasanian rule. Rather than a corpus focused on the narrow legal and interpretive interests of the rabbis on behalf of an insular and secure Jewish society, the Babylonian Talmud reveals rabbinic interest in the production of stories that promoted alternatives to direct confrontation with the Empire and sought to shape their audience's conception of Sasanian rule. Given the responsiveness of the Sasanian Empire to the behavior of its subjects, as outlined in Chapter 3, and the power of narratives to stir groups to particular kinds of action, we cannot discount the possibility that the promotion of different stories by Christians and Jews could, in fact, have had some effect on the frequency with which they were subjected to imperial violence.

The rabbis actively sought to mitigate conflict with the Sasanian Empire through other means; for instance, by minimizing potential points of friction between Jewish law and the realities of life in the Sasanian Empire. Chapter 5 examines how Babylonian Jews negotiated imperial Zoroastrianism, the state-sponsored religion. In several discussions and stories, the rabbis appear to redefine some of the most severe rabbinic prohibitions pertaining to idolatry to avoid any overt hostility towards Zoroastrian fire temples. The rabbis' approach contrasts starkly with several Syriac Christian martyr acts that treat hostility to fire temples as a *sine qua non* of Christian piety, despite recognizing their symbolic function in imperial discourse. The rabbis' accommodating approach animates other legal discussions that similarly adopt more permissive legal positions to accommodate their Sasanian context. Changes in principal domains of rabbinic law show the lengths to which rabbis went to facilitate economic and social integration in the Sasanian Empire.

Finally, Chapter 6 explores the intersection of talmudic representations of some of the leading figures of the Sasanian Empire – kings and Zoroastrian magi – with the representations offered by other subject groups and with imperial self-projection. Where the Talmud portrays kings with remarkably intimate relations with Babylonian rabbis, it portrays the magi as the sole force of religious violence against Jews. These stories served as the basis for scholarly understandings of a fundamental division between religion and state at the heart of Sasanian rule, which was a determinative feature of Jewish life therein. Kings were religiously unaligned, cynically deploying religion when it suited them, while the magi and other religious officials sought to accrue power and impose religion on the king and the empire as a whole. This dichotomy was embraced by scholars of other religious groups, who thought that it similarly explained the contrasting representations of kings and magi in their sources, even as scholars rejected the relevance of Zoroastrian sources that depicted a fundamental union between king and magi. Arguing against a dichotomous view of Sasanian royal and religious elites, this chapter seeks to understand how Sasanian imperial ideology and self-representation enabled – and perhaps intended to produce – the incongruous and competing pictures of the Sasanian kings found in the works of its varying subject groups, especially Jews, Christians, Manichaeans, and Zoroastrians. The Babylonian Talmud here reflects the way subjects internalized and responded to imperial ideology and rhetoric, which is only visible through a process of robust triangulation.

Together, the book offers an integrated model of Jewish life under Sasanian rule. Jews and other groups were informed by Iranian social norms and mores, even in intracommunal battles for recognition and prestige. Faced with the inescapable presence of imperial law, administrators, institutions, ideology, and projections, the Babylonian Talmud reveals how some subjects conceptualized and navigated Sasanian rule in ways that were similar to and strikingly different from their neighbors. Jews provide a unique vantage point from which to examine processes of acculturation, the variety of approaches adopted by non-Iranians to negotiate Sasanian rule, and the Sasanian Empire's management of its heterogenous populations.

1

Jewish Society under Sasanian Rule

From Isolation to Integration

An early medieval Middle Persian Zoroastrian source known as *The Provincial Capitals of Ērānšahr* describes the provinces and major cities of the Sasanian Empire and supplies several of them with short foundation myths. In describing the establishment of the cities of Susa and Šuštar in Khuzistan, *The Provincial Capitals* reports that they "were built by Šīšīnduxt, the wife of Yazdgird, the son of Šābuhr, since she was the daughter of the Exilarch (*rēš-galūdag*), the king of the Jews (*jahūdagān šāh*), and was also the mother of Wahrām Gōr."[1]

According to this source, a Jewish woman named Šīšīnduxt, the daughter of the Exilarch, married the Sasanian king Yazdgird I (r. 399–420), birthed the next Sasanian king Wahrām Gōr (r. 420–438), and was commanding enough in her own right to establish two major Iranian cities, Susa and Šuštar. *The Provincial Capitals* further details how Šīšīnduxt leveraged her position of prominence to benefit the Jews, as Yazdgird I transported Jews to Isfahan "by the request of Šīšīnduxt who was his wife."

Šīšīnduxt's father is identified as the Exilarch, or "head of the diaspora," the patriarch of a dynastic Babylonian Jewish family that, according to rabbinic sources, claimed genealogical descent from King David. Here, the Exilarch is identified as no less than the "king of the

[1] For text and translation, see Jivanji Jamshedji Modi, *Aiyādgār-I-Zarirān, Shatrōihā-I-Airān and Afdiya va Sahigiya-I-Sistān, Translated with Notes* (Bombay: 1899), 105; Josef Markwart, *A Catalogue of The Provincial Capitals of Ērānshahr, Pahlavi Text, Version and Commentary*, ed. G. Messina (Rome: 1931), 19; and Touraj Daryaee, *Šahrestānīhā ī Ērānšahr: A Middle Persian Text on Late Antique Geography, Epic and History* (Costa Mesa, CA: 2002), sec. 47.

Jews," who had achieved the height of prominence in the Empire. Marrying one's daughter to the king was no small feat, an honor reserved for the most aristocratic of noble families, and the Sasanian Empire was rarely willing to grant the title of "king" – even over a particular community – to anyone without some direct connection to the royal family. Judging from this source alone, one would no doubt conclude that the Exilarch was the imperially recognized leader of the Jews, and extrapolate from it about the Exilarch's responsibilities and the nature of Jewish society.

Yet there is good reason to be skeptical of this account's historicity.[2] Šīšīnduxt's existence is not corroborated by any other source, whether Jewish or not. Other elements of the story are clearly fictitious, such as the claim that the Jews settled in the region of Isfahan through Šīšīnduxt's intervention. Similarly, the name Šīšīnduxt means literally "the daughter of Susa," which suggests that Šīšīnduxt was not a real name, but rather an epithet selected to associate her with the establishment of Susa. Indeed, Šīšīnduxt's connection to Susa bears a striking similarity to that of the biblical queen Esther, who also lived in Susa and wedded an Iranian king. The Šīšīnduxt story is thus in some fashion a later adaptation of that biblical tale, in an Iranian Jewish context where Esther's example carried special cultural weight.

The story of Šīšīnduxt is most likely a fiction, the product of medieval exilarchal propaganda, as I have argued elsewhere.[3] In the early medieval period, the power and prestige of the Exilarchate was a major source of contention, with some Jews seeking to undermine and belittle it, and others, none more ardently than the Exilarch and his coterie, defending and bolstering his position, especially through appeals to the past.[4] It was at this precarious moment, from roughly the ninth to eleventh centuries CE, when the memory of the Sasanian past was imbued with particular cultural cachet across the Near East, that several dynasties, leaders, and aspiring elites began to trace their lineages back to Sasanian rulers, in a period sometimes called the Iranian Intermezzo.[5]

[2] For a full treatment of the story, see Simcha Gross, "The Curious Case of the Jewish Sasanian Queen Šīšīnduxt: Exilarchal Propaganda and Zoroastrians in Tenth- to Eleventh-Century Baghdad," *Journal of the American Oriental Society* 141 (2021): 365–380.

[3] See e.g., Gross, "Reassessing Exilarchal Authority between Sasanian and Early Islamic Rule," *Journal of Jewish Studies* 73 (2022): 263–287.

[4] Arnold Franklin, *This Noble House: Jewish Descendants of King David in the Middle Ages* (Philadelphia, PA: 2013); see also Gross, "When the Jews Greeted Ali," 122–144.

[5] Coined by Vladimir Minorsky, *Studies in Caucasian History* (London: 1953).

One of the dynasties claiming genealogical descent from the Sasanians were the Buyids, the rulers of Iraq beginning in the tenth century. They traced their lineage to none other than Wahrām Gōr, the son of Šīšīnduxt according to *The Provincial Capitals*. The story of Šīšīnduxt therefore appears to reflect a move by the medieval Exilarchate to retroject its ancestors back onto the Buyid's own Sasanian lineage, as if to say that it was the Exilarch's ancestor who birthed the Buyid's forefather. This claim appears to have resonated outside of Jewish circles, such that it made its way into a medieval Zoroastrian work, *The Provincial Capitals*, which realized the originally Aramaic term meaning "Exilarch," or head of the diaspora, into Middle Persian (*rēš-galūdag*). The Exilarch's claim was, however, also tailored to a Jewish audience, cleverly connecting himself to the Sasanians through his daughter, thereby leaving untarnished his own claim of Davidic descent, which would continue to be transmitted to, and through, his sons.

While some scholars have accepted the historicity of Šīšīnduxt and others have questioned some or all of its details, the lofty image of the Sasanian-era Exilarch and his place within Babylonian Jewish society has received widespread acceptance.[6] Whether or not the Exilarch did in fact marry his daughter to the Sasanian king, according to scholars the story was right to grant him the title of "king of the Jews." The three central tenets of previous accounts of Babylonian Jewish society – that it was semi-autonomous, ordered into a centralized and self-regulating hierarchy, and siloed from its neighbors – ultimately derive from this understanding of the Exilarch.

Accordingly, the Exilarch allegedly served as the official intermediary who brokered relations between Jews and the Empire. The Exilarch is therefore frequently described as the head of an "office," "institution," or even "government"; the leading figure in a centralized, top-down, social system.[7] The Exilarch supervised an internal Jewish bureaucracy, with

[6] For previous treatments of the story, see Gross, "The Curious Case of the Jewish Sasanian Queen Šīšīnduxt," 367–368.

[7] For instance, the preeminent nineteenth-century Jewish historian Heinrich Graetz, *Geschichte der Juden von den ältesten Zeiten bis auf die Gegenwart*, vol. 4 (Berlin: 1853), trans. Bella Lowy in *History of the Jews*, vol. 2 (London: 1891), 508ff; Felix Lazarus, *Die Häupter der Vertriebenen: Beiträge zu einer Geschichte der Exilsführsten in Babylonien unter den Arsakiden und Sassaniden* (Frankfurt: 1890); Arthur Christensen, *L'Iran sous les Sassanides* (Copenhagen: 1944), 38; Neusner, *History of the Jews*, 5.244–245; Neusner, "Rabbi and Magus in Third-Century Sasanian Babylonia," *History of Religions* 6 (1966): 170; Moshe Beer; *The Exilarchate in Babylonia in the Mishnaic and Talmudic Period* (Tel Aviv: 1970), 33–43; Moshe Beer, *The Babylonian Amoraim: Aspects of Economic Life* (Ramat Gan: 1982), 9–10; Gafni, "Political, Social,

the rabbis and other Jewish officials functioning at his behest as judges and administrators, who occasionally jostled with him for power and recognition.[8] As part of this supposedly imperially backed corporate Jewish community, the rabbis were widely recognized authority figures, shaping Babylonian Jewish practice and maintaining communal order through their courts. Under these conditions, Babylonian Jews had little reason to regularly interact with state administrators or other communities, or to be exposed to broader cultural and social pressures. They remained socially and culturally insular and segregated.[9]

Babylonian Jewish semi-autonomy was believed to be an instantiation of a consistent Sasanian policy to organize its subjects into self-governing centralized corporate communities, especially religious communities, regularly compared to the Ottoman *millet* system.[10] This was one facet of the Sasanian Empire's feudalistic predilection to delegate authority.[11]

and Economic History," 801–804; and Gafni, *Jews of Talmudic Babylonia*, 98ff. On "office," see Herman, *Prince without a Kingdom*, 179–180, and esp. 259. For "government," see Morony, *Iraq after the Muslim Conquest*, 316–319; and Wiesehöfer, *Ancient Persia*, 215–216.

8 For a review of these views, see Herman, *Prince without a Kingdom*, 2–11.

9 See the discussion in Introduction.

10 More stridently stated in F. Altheim and R. Stiehl, *ein asiatischer Staat, Feudalismus unter den Sasaniden und ihren Nachbarn* (Wiesbaden, 1954), but also found in R. N. Frye, *The History of Ancient Iran* (Munich: 1984), 318–319; R. N. Frye, "The Political History of Iran under the Sasanians," in *The Seleucid, Parthian, and Sasanian Periods*, ed. E. Yarshater, vol. 3, bk. 1, *The Cambridge History of Iran* (Cambridge: 1983), 132; Neusner, *History of the Jews*, 5.134, 244–245; Daryaee, *Sasanian Persia*, 20; Touraj Daryaee, "Ethnic and Territorial Boundaries in Late Antique and Early Medieval Persia (Third to Tenth Century)," in *Borders, Barriers, and Ethnogenesis: Frontiers in Late Antiquity and the Middle Ages*, ed. F. Curta (Turnhout: 2005), 127; Victoria Erhart, "The Development of Syriac Christian Canon Law in the Sasanian Empire," in *Law, Society, and Authority in Late Antiquity*, ed. R. W. Mathisen (Oxford: 2011), 128–129; Payne, *State of Mixture*, 15, 122, 184. Like feudalism, the characterization of the Ottoman *millet* system has been challenged and refined in many ways. For more on this, see Benjamin Braude, "Foundation Myths of the Millet System," in *The Central Lands*, ed. R. Braude and B. Lewis, vol. 1, *The Christians and Jews in the Ottoman Empire* (New York: 1982), 69–88; and Nir Shafir, "Vernacular Legalism in the Ottoman Empire: Law, and Popular Politics in the Debate over the "Religion of Abraham (millet-i Ibrāhīm)," *Islamic Law and Society* 28 (2020): 41n26.

11 Christensen, *L'Iran sous les Sassanides*, 18–25; Arthur Christensen, "Sassanid Persia," in *The Imperial Crisis and Recovery, A.D. 193–324*, ed. S. A. Cook, F. E. Adcock, M. P. Charlesworth, and N. H. Baynes, vol. 12, *The Cambridge Ancient History* (Cambridge: 1939), 114; Geo Widengren, "Recherches sur le feodalisme iranien," *Orientalia Suecana* 5 (1956): 170–176; Geo Widengren, *Der Feudalismus im alten Iran: Männerbund, Gefolgswesen, Feudalismus in der iranischen Gesellschaft im Hinblick auf die indogermanischen Verhältnisse* (Köln: 1969); Zeev Rubin, "Persia and the Sasanian Monarchy (224–651)," in *The Cambridge History of the Byzantine Empire c. 500–1492*, ed.

These paradigms were reciprocally reinforcing: Foundational works in Sasanian studies, such as Arthur Christensen's *L'Iran sous les Sassanides*, argued that Jews epitomized the Empire's propensity to grant its communities "a certain degree of autonomy."[12] The Exilarch, Catholicos, and Zoroastrian "priest of priests" (*mowbedān mowbed*) were parallel figures mediating between particular communities and the empire, who headed their own centralized and self-governing communities and generated religious societies that nearly uniformly adhered to a "normative" system of practices and beliefs.[13] A consequence of this policy was the erection of strong institutional boundaries between communities, which were thereby encouraged to live in isolation from other groups.[14]

Over the past few decades, pioneering revisionist approaches have challenged strikingly similar narratives of Jewish autonomy in other regions and periods.[15] They have drawn attention to the fact that earlier

Jonathan Shepard (Cambridge: 2008), 130–155; Zeev Rubin, "The Reforms of Khusro Anushirwan," in *States, Resources and Armies*, ed. Averil Cameron, vol. 3, *The Byzantine and Early Islamic Near East* (Princeton, NJ: 1995), 228n5; and Parvaneh Pourshariati, *The Decline and Fall of the Sasanian Empire: The Sasanian-Parthian Confederacy and the Arab Conquest of Iran* (London: 2008). More generally, see: Wiesehöfer, *Ancient Persia*, 171–191; Schippmann, *Grundzüge*, 80–86; Gignoux, "L'organisation administrative sasanide le cas du marzbān," *Jerusalem Studies in Arabic and Islam* 4 (1984): 1–29.

12 Christensen, *L'Iran sous les Sassanides*, 38. See similarly Frye, *The History of Ancient Iran*, 319, and Wiesehöfer, *Ancient Persia*, 143, 215–216.

13 Uriel Simonsohn, *A Common Justice: The Legal Allegiances of Christians and Jews Under Early Islam* (Philadelphia, PA: 2011), 51; Herman, *Prince without a Kingdom*, 200–202 and passim; and Herman, "Exilarch and Catholicos: A Paradigm for the Commonalities of the Jewish and Christian Experience under the Sasanians," in *Jews and Syriac Christians: Intersections across the First Millennium*, ed. Aaron Michael Butts and Simcha Gross (Tubingen: 2020). Challenging the notion of uniformity among Sasanian Zoroastrians, see Shaul Shaked, *Dualism in Transformation: Varieties of Religion in Sasanian Iran* (London: 1994), with response by Mary Boyce, "On the Orthodoxy of Sasanian Zoroastrianism," *Bulletin of the School of Oriental and African Studies, University of London* 59 (1996): 11–28.

14 Morony, *Iraq after the Muslim Conquest*, 316–320, 332–342, 364–372.

15 On the Patriarch in Palestine, see: Seth Schwartz, "D. Goodblatt, *The Monarchic Principle*," *Journal of Jewish Studies* 47 (1996): 167–169; Seth Schwartz, "Big Men or Chiefs: Against an Institutional History of the Palestinian Patriarchate," in *Jewish Religious Leadership: Image and Reality*, vol. 1, ed. Jack Wertheimer (New York: 2004), 155–173; Catherine Hezser, *The Social Structure of the Rabbinic Movement in Roman Palestine* (Tübingen: 1997), 8–9; and Sacha Stern, "Rabbi and the Origins of the Patriarchate," *Journal of Jewish Studies* 54 (2003): 193–215. The position of the Exilarch in the early medieval period is rather opaque; see: Robert Brody, *The Geonim of Babylonia and the Shaping of Medieval Jewish Culture* (New Haven, CT: 1998), 71–75; and Robert Brody, *Sa'adyah Gaon* (Oxford: 2013), 11–12. On Jewish semi-autonomy in the medieval period, see: Mark Cohen, *Jewish Self-Government in*

scholarship interpreted the past through a historiographical conviction that autonomy was a prerequisite for Jewish cultural efflorescence. But time and again, where earlier scholars saw rigid hierarchies, Jewish intermediaries, and self-contained social structures, Jewish society was, in fact, highly decentralized, dynamic, and deeply integrated into the prevailing legal, social, and cultural systems. Sources once thought dispositive of Jewish semi-autonomy have been dismissed, and minimalist and revisionist trends have revolutionized the study of Jews from Late Antique Palestine to early Islamic Egypt. And yet, regarding the Exilarch, and Sasanian Jewish society more generally, these paradigms persist.[16]

This chapter challenges the pillars of previous accounts and offers an integrationist portrait of Babylonian Jewish society under Sasanian rule.[17] It is driven by the recognition that despite a modern tendency to assume that power and authority are centrally distributed and monopolized by governments, ancient societies tolerated and created space for conflict resolution outside of the strict confines of the state apparatus. Elite Jewish figures who exercised various forms of power among Jews derived their position not from the empire but from the recognition of their coreligionists, which they had to earn and maintain.

In particular, the chapter shows that the Exilarch did not serve as the official Jewish communal intermediary, and that there was no self-governing Jewish bureaucracy in which rabbinic and other Jewish courts functioned as the exclusive, or even primary, means of conflict resolution available to Jews. Jewish sources, together with Syriac Christian and Sasanian evidence, reveal just the opposite: that all subjects had direct recourse to imperial courts and administration, even as the empire tolerated local

Medieval Egypt: The Origins of the Office of the Head of the Jews, ca. 1065–1126 (Princeton: 1981); Marina Rustow, *Heresy and the Politics of Community: The Jews of the Fatimid Caliphate* (Ithaca, NY: 2008), 67–69; Simonsohn, *Common Justice*, 6–10, 47; and Lev Weitz, *Between Christ and Caliph: Law, Marriage, and Christian Community in Early Islam* (Philadelphia, PA: 2018), 6.

16 Like the story of Šīšīnduxt, other both pre- and post-Sasanian stories were assimilated by scholars into the narrative of the prominent position of the Exilarch. See: Josephus, *Antiquities of the Jews*, 18.310–79, with discussion in Geoffrey Herman, "Iranian Epic Motifs in Josephus' Antiquities (XVIII, 314–370)," *Journal of Jewish Studies* 57 (2006): 245–268; and Adolf Neubauer, *Medieval Jewish Chronicles and Chronological Notes*, vol. 2 (Oxford: 1887), 76; with discussion in Herman, "The Mysterious Mar Zutra," *Segula* 27 (2015): 40–47.

17 On the need to reevaluate the Exilarch, see Schwartz, "The Political Geography of Rabbinic Texts," 89–93. Geoffrey Herman's monograph *Prince without a Kingdom* offers critical correctives to previous scholarship, but it perpetuates older paradigms of semi-autonomy and the Exilarch as formal imperial intermediary.

forms of conflict resolution. In this context, aspiring communal elites could serve as arbitrators, provided they could convince their coreligionists to submit their cases to them rather than to imperial courts or even other religious arbitrators. This marketplace of legal options drove Jewish elites to jockey among themselves and pit themselves and their expertise against the empire, in part by juxtaposing the legitimacy of Jewish versus Iranian forms of jurisprudence.

EXILARCH AS ROYAL INTERMEDIARY?

The notion of Jewish semi-autonomy is first and foremost predicated on the idea that the Exilarch served as the official intermediary between the Jews and the empire. Despite this claim's importance, it is difficult to find reliable references to encounters between Exilarchs and Sasanian kings. Scholars have mainly drawn on medieval rabbinic chronographies, which, when commenting on talmudic stories featuring encounters between kings and particular rabbis, identify those rabbis *as* Exilarchs, although any such identification is absent from the stories themselves. It has been convincingly demonstrated that these medieval accounts do not preserve reliable traditions that accurately identify these rabbis as Exilarchs. Rather, the identification is circularly predicated on the assumption of the Exilarch's role as intermediary, such that any Jew who appeared before the king *must* have been an Exilarch.[18] The following source exemplifies this dynamic between talmudic story and medieval reception:[19]

> Rav Ashi said: Huna bar Nathan told me, "I appeared before King Yazdgird, and my belt (*hemyana*) was lifted up, and he lowered it for me. He said to me: 'a kingdom of priests and a holy nation (Exod. 19.6)[20] is written about you.' When I came before Amemar, he said to me, 'And kings shall be your nursing maids (Isa. 49.23) has been fulfilled through you.'

The story itself does not identify Huna as an Exilarch, nor does it portray him functioning as an intermediary on behalf of the Jews. Yet, in his highly influential *Epistle*, composed in 987 CE in response to a question from

[18] Moshe Beer, "Exilarchs of the Talmudic Epoch Mentioned in R. Sherira's Responsum," *Proceedings of the American Academy for Jewish Research* 35 (1967): 43–74; Neusner, *History of the Jews*, 5.49–50; and most robustly Herman, *Prince without a Kingdom*, 321–329. Herman, 38 discusses other terms in rabbinic literature that scholars, following medieval rabbis, assumed referred to the Exilarch.

[19] b. Zeb. 19a, according to MS Vatican 118–119.

[20] For ancient Jewish interpretations of this verse, see Herman, *Prince without a Kingdom*, 323–325.

rabbinic leaders of the North African city of Qayrawan, Sherira Gaon, the head of the rabbinic academy of Pumbedita in Iraq, identifies Huna as the Exilarch.[21] Many scholars followed his lead.[22] Rabbinic literature, by contrast, never identifies Huna in this way. Indeed, he is labeled and functions as a rabbi, offering instruction and teaching even the great Rav Ashi.[23] Sherira appears to have identified Huna as an Exilarch based on his presuppositions about the Exilarch's role as an intermediary, rather than an authentic early tradition about Huna or the history of the Exilarchate.[24]

The main sources to unquestionably depict encounters between an Exilarch and a Sasanian king are similarly of medieval origin. These include the story of Šīšīnduxt in the *Provincial Capitals* with which the chapter began, and a related set of medieval Jewish sources according to which the Caliph 'Umar ibn al-Khaṭṭāb (r. 634–644 CE) gave one of the two captured daughters of the Sasanian king Khusro II (or, in some accounts, Yazdgird III) to the Exilarch Bustanai to wed, taking the other

[21] On the Epistle, see Robert Brody, "Epistle of Sherira Gaon," in *Rabbinic Texts and the History of Late-Roman Palestine*, ed. Martin Goodman and Philip Alexander (Oxford: 2010), 253–264.

[22] Gafni, *The Jews of Talmudic Babylonia*, 98; Beer, *Exilarchate*, 45–47, 191–195, 200–206; Neusner, *History of the Jews*, 5.12–13; Barak Cohen, "The Distinction between Sage and Exilarch in Sassanian Babylonia: The Case of (Rav) Huna bar Natan," *Jewish History* 36 (2022): 1–24 (who distinguishes between two talmudic figures of the same name, which he then unjustifiably uses to support Sherira's identification). See, however, Herman, *Prince without a Kingdom*, 321–329.

[23] On b. Giṭ. 59a as a reflection of the later redactors, and the problematic story in b. M. Qaṭ. 28a, see Herman, *Prince without a Kingdom*, 326–329.

[24] A similar case holds for another story in which three rabbis appear at the gates of the king, one named Mar Zutra (b. Ket. 61a–b), where Sherira Gaon lists Mar Zutra as an exilarch in both his *Epistle* and a related responsum, whereas another medieval rabbinic chronography, *Seder Tannaim VeAmoraim*, which shares a common source with Sherira's epistle, does not. See Beer, "Exilarchs of the Talmudic Epoch," 49–55; and Gafni, *The Jews of Talmudic Babylonia*, 98–99. Cf. Neusner, *History of the Jews*, 5.48–49; Avinoam Cohen, "More on the Question of the Amora Mar Zutra as Exilarch: A Study of Geonic Chronicles," *Sidra* 26 (2011): 19–60; and Herman, *Prince without a Kingdom*, 330–332. On the common source, see Robert Brody, "On the Sources for the Chronology of the Talmudic Period," *Tarbiẓ* 70 (2000–2001): 75–107. Other attempts to insert the Exilarch into stories in the Talmud that do not explicitly mention him are equally problematic, e.g., Beer, *Exilarchate*, 58–60; and Herman, "Midgets and Mules, Elephants, and Exilarchs: On the Metamorphosis of a Polemical Amoraic Story," in *Rabbinic Traditions between Palestine and Babylonia*, ed. Tal Ilan and R. Nikolsky (Leiden: 2014), 117–132. Both assume that a story in b. Giṭ. 14a–b, which makes no mention of the Exilarch, refers to the henchman of the Exilarch because they have Persian names and dress and are described as "close to the kingdom." This ignores several sources that characterize other figures similarly, but who are associated neither with the Patriarch nor the Exilarch (such as Jesus in b. Sanh. 43a, and Avtolmus ben Reuven in b. B. Qam. 83a and b. Soṭ. 49b).

daughter for himself.[25] Like the story of Šīšīnduxt, the tale of Bustanai is fictitious; indeed, it is an adaptation of a story about the Caliph and the two Sasanian princesses found in Islamic sources from which the Exilarch was originally absent.[26] Again, the story reflects the contest for power and prestige in the medieval period through appeals to the past, but it has little value for our understanding of the Sasanian-era Exilarch.

A final medieval account is found in *al-Maḥāsin wal-aḍdād* (*Good Qualities and [their] Opposites*), erroneously attributed to al-Jāḥiẓ (d. 869). While describing the various stages and rituals of the festival of *Nowrōz* at the Sasanian court, the text reports that:[27] "It happened that when *Nowrōz* fell on a Saturday, the king ordered to give four thousand dirham to the Exilarch."[28]

This passage is consistent with other descriptions of the highly choreographed proceedings at the royal court on Zoroastrian festivals, and indeed, it is clearly related to the description of the *Nowrōz* festivities at the court of the king in another text known as the *Kitāb al-Tāj*, or *Book of the Crown*.[29] These sources describe how an array of elite figures

[25] An earlier discussion of the Bustanai story can be found in Chaim Tykocinski, "Bustanai rosh ha-gola," *Devir* 1 (1923): 145–179. See also Moshe Gil, "The Babylonian Encounter and the Exilarchic House in Light of Cairo Geniza Documents and Parallel Arab Sources," in *Judaeo-Arabic Studies: Proceedings of the Founding Conference of the Society for Judaeo-Arabic Studies*, ed. Norman Golb (Amsterdam: 1997), 135–173; Moshe Gil, *Jews in Islamic Countries in the Middle Ages*, trans. David Strassler (Leiden: 2004), 77–81. The relevant texts, with Hebrew translation, can be found in Abraham Grossman, *Rashut ha-Golah bi-Tequfat ha-Ge'onim* (Jerusalem: 1984), 22–44. These scholars attempted to preserve the basic historicity of the story.

[26] Geoffrey Herman, "Back to Bustanay: The History of a Legend," in *Irano-Judaica* VII, ed. Geoffrey Herman and Julia Rbanovich (Jerusalem: 2018), 311–339; Gross, "The Curious Case," 365–380.

[27] Text in G. van Vloten, *Le Livre des beautés et des antithèses, attribuè á Abou Othman Amr ibn Bahr Al-Djahiz de Basra* (Leiden: 1898), 362. For an overview of Ps. Al-Jāḥiẓ's account, in the context of Sasanian court rituals, see de Jong, "Sub Specie Maiestatis," 345–366. Intriguingly, this story does not appear in the parallel text of *Kitāb al-Tāj*, and breaks the flow of the larger passage in *al-Maḥāsin wal-aḍdād*, which may suggest that it derives from a different source.

[28] Ignaz Goldziher, "Renseignements de source musulmane sur la dignité de resch-galuta," *Revue des études Juives* 8 (1884): 122; R. Ehrlich, "The Celebrations and Gifts of the Persian New Year (Now Ruz) According to the Arabic Sources," in *Dr. Modi Memorial Volume: Papers on Indo-Iranian and Other Subjects Written by Several Scholars in Honour of Sham-ul-Ulama Dr. Jivanji Jamshedji Modi*, ed. The Dr. Modi Memorial Volume Editorial Board (Bombay: 1930), 95–101, esp. 99.

[29] Charles Pellat, *Le Livre de la Couronne* (Paris: 1954), 165–169. For medieval sources on the Sasanian court, see Henning Börm, "König und Gefolgschaft im Sasanidenreich: Zum Verhältnis zwischen Monarch und imperialer Elite im spätantiken Persien," in *Die*

would appear before the king bearing gifts, and how the king would reciprocate in kind. *Nowrōz* was thus an occasion of ritualized gift exchange, where bonds of loyalty between king, nobility, and elites were reinforced and celebrated. According to the above passage, when *Nowrōz* and the Sabbath coincided, the Exilarch would receive an additional gift from the Sasanian king.[30]

We do not know if all aspects of this source accurately describe Sasanian-era realities.[31] Even granting some historical value, it need not suggest that the Exilarch was an official appointee of the Sasanian Empire or representative of the Jews as a corporate body. Instead, it only suggests that the Exilarch interacted with the Sasanian king as one elite among many.[32] If true, the story demonstrates that the Exilarch was a – perhaps the most – noteworthy Jewish elite, but hardly an official representative on behalf of the Jewish community. Ample evidence makes clear that a variety of figures regularly appeared before the Sasanian king, including elites of different ranks, Christian bishops, school masters, and others seeking the king's ruling or dispensations.[33] The festival described in Pseudo-al-Jāḥiẓ was precisely one of the formal events intended to convene a wide range of elites and reaffirm their commitment, and subordination, to the Sasanian king. The Exilarch's appearance would indicate his prominent elite status, but not his role as an intercessor on behalf of Jews.

If medieval sources do not corroborate the Sasanian-era Exilarch's intermediary role, a series of interrelated anecdotes in both the Palestinian and Babylonian Talmuds place the Exilarch alongside major officials in the Sasanian Empire. One such tradition appears in both the Palestinian and

Interaktion von Herrschern und Eliten in imperialen Ordnungen des Mittelalters, ed. Wolfram Drews (Berlin: 2018), 38.

30 The text continues and says: "And there was no reason known for this, except that their tradition was such; it had become like the *jizya*." The gloss comparing the king's gift to the Exilarch and the *jizya* is unclear. This led Goldziher, "Renseignements," 121–125, and Moshe Gil, *Jews in Islamic Countries*, 90, to instead understand the passage as a reference to the Exilarch paying four thousand dirham to the Sasanian king, which, however, does not fit the grammar.

31 Gafni, *The Jews of Talmudic Babylonia*, 157, says this encounter took place during the reign of Khusro I.

32 Noteworthily, the Catholicos does not appear in any of these texts as one of the elites. For more on the Catholicos, see below.

33 Indeed, the king's court was mobile, and thus accessible to elites from around the empire. See Florence Jullien, "Parcours à travers l'Histoire d'Īšō'sabran, martyr sous Khosrau II," in *Contributions à l'histoire et la géographie historique de l'Empire Sassanide*, ed. Rika Gyselen (Bures-sur-Yvette: 2004), 179–80. For Christian school masters, see Adam H. Becker, *Sources for the History of the School of Nisibis* (Liverpool: 2008), 155.

Babylonian Talmuds with slight variations.[34] In it, Rabbi Ḥanina offers a heuristic device to remember the two dominant shades of leprosy, each of which is further subdivided into two, by paralleling them to a hierarchal list of Sasanian figures:

Rabbi Ḥanina said "A rabbinic parable: To what shall we compare this..."
Rav Adda bar Ahava said "Such as the king, and the *alqapaṭa*, and the general, and the Exilarch."
But is this one above the other?
Rather, the king and the general, and the *alqapaṭa* and the Exilarch.

In these passages, the Exilarch appears last in a list of leading figures in the empire that includes king, general, and *arqapaṭa/alqapaṭa*, known in Middle Persian as *hargbed*.[35] While this source has served in the past to support the scholarly contention that the Exilarch was part of the imperial apparatus, it fails when subjected to critical scrutiny.[36] First and foremost, the list is intended as a heuristic device, not a precise account of the relative position of particular figures in the empire. Indeed, the list is simply one in a series of suggested heuristics which includes "two kings and two governors," "Shapur and Caesar," and "a [new white] woolen garment, and a worn-out woolen garment; and a [new white] linen garment, and a worn-out linen garment." Lacking any further details, it is unclear what the Exilarch's inclusion here means: do the rabbis really believe he is fourth in imperial rank, an impossibility given his absence from any imperial inscriptions that list, in often excruciating detail, administrative titles and elite figures? Alternatively, perhaps the Exilarch's appearance at the end of the list does not mean he was fourth in the pyramid, but simply the lowest of the four in status and position. Indeed, elsewhere the rabbis use the term *hargbed* less to refer to a particular role than to evoke the

34 B. Shebu. 6b, cf. y. Shebu. 1.2 (32d).

35 While the king and general are self-evident, the *hargbed* went from a relatively unimportant position to a highly significant role by the late third century – as evidenced by its absence from earlier Sasanian administrative lists and its prominence in the list in King Narseh's inscription in Paikuli – though we lack any clear definition of its attendant roles and responsibilities. On the *hargbed*, see: Herman, "Persia in Light of the Babylonian Talmud: Echoes of Contemporary Society and Politics: *hargbed* and *bidaxš*," in *The Talmud in Its Iranian Context*, ed. C. Bakhos and R. Shayegan (Tubingen: 2010), 61–84; Chabot, *Synodicon Orientale*, 21, 260–261; Maria Macuch, "The Case against Mar Aba, the Catholicos, in the Light of Sasanian Law," *ARAM* 26 (2014): 48n5; and Daryaee, "Palmyra and the Sasanians," 41.

36 As noted by Gafni, "Political, Social, and Economic History," 803; and Herman, *Prince without a Kingdom*, 86–92.

notion of a member of the upper crust.[37] The Exilarch's placement at the end of the list would suggest not that he is literally fourth in the empire in terms of rank, nor that he occupies a formal position in the empire, but simply that he is an elite, lower than the other three figures.

Sasanian administrative positions are put to similar heuristic use by an admittedly later author, the twelfth-century Iranian scholar al-Shahrastānī, in a section describing the teachings of the enigmatic Mazdak, whose movement is said to have wreaked havoc in the Sasanian Empire in the late fifth century. According to al-Shahrastānī, Mazdak taught that "his object of veneration … has at his disposal four powers: Discrimination, Intelligence, Preservation and Joy, as there are under the control of a king four persons: *mōbeḍān mōbēḍ*, the chief *hērbeḍ*, the *iṣbahbaḍ* and the *rāmiškar*."[38] Here too we find a heuristic list of four officials in the Sasanian Empire, this time the high priest, another kind of high priest, a general, and an entertainer or musician. This list hardly represents the four leading figures in the empire, nor does it constitute a single type of social hierarchy, and the final member of the list is not a leading figure at all. Instead, the list reflects the heuristic purposes of its author, who selected figures as counterparts to particular attributes. The same is likely true of the lists featuring the Exilarch.[39] These sources have understandably excited earlier scholars, but they are a flimsy basis upon which to build the case for the Exilarch's role as an officially recognized intermediary.[40]

37 b. Zeb. 96b. A legal discussion in b. B. Bat. 172b refers to the Sasanian king and the Exilarch together as examples of the very wealthy.

38 See Mansour Shaki, "The Cosmogonical and Cosmological Teachings of Mazdak," *Acta Iranica* 24 (1985): 527–543 (esp. 528 and 533–534).

39 A related text (y. Ber. 2.4; [5a]) appears in a series of playful anecdotes concerning the difficulties rabbis faced concentrating during prayer, including one rabbi who counts birds and another stones. In this context, Rabbi Ḥiyya notes that once, when trying to concentrate in prayer, he asked himself "who enters first before the king, the *arqabaṭa* or the Exilarch?" Herman, *Prince without a Kingdom*, 90–92 compellingly argues that this source is derivative of the heuristic device discussed above, and that the attribution to Rabbi Ḥiyya is pseudepigraphic.

40 The title Exilarch, or "Head of the Diaspora," may be an additional reason that scholars have attributed an intercessory and official role to the Exilarch, but such appellations are not uncommon. The elite figure Yazdin is called "Head of the Believers" in the *History of Isho'sabran*: J. B. Chabot, "Histoire de Jésus-Sabran, écrite par Jésus-Yab d'Adiabène," in *Archives des missions scientifiques et littéraires* 7 (1897): 520. Moreover, he is analogized in the Chronicle of Khuzistan to Joseph before Pharaoh: Nasir al-Ka'bi, *A Short Chronicle on the End of the Sasanian Empire and Early Islam* (Piscataway, NJ: 2016), 44. Figures who do not assume ecclesiastical positions are referred to as "Head of the Christians" (ܪܫܐ ܕܟܪܣܛܝܢܐ) in the *Martyrdom of Pethion*: Paul Bedjan,

In short, we lack any passages unproblematically dating to the Sasanian period that describe the appearance of the Exilarch before the king or present him as an imperial intermediary. Later Jewish and non-Jewish sources, including medieval chronographies, the story of the Exilarch's daughter Šīšīnduxt, and the story of Bustanai, largely reflect the (desired) cultural and political position of the medieval-era Exilarch retrojected onto the Sasanian past. If these passages do not offer clear evidence of the position of the Exilarch, we must turn to the functions and responsibilities attributed to the Exilarch in the Talmud to deduce his place within Jewish society. These can be divided into three areas: taxes, markets, and law.

TAXES

A common assertion is that the Exilarch was responsible for tax collection on behalf of Jews.[41] Yet we lack any evidence to support this claim.[42] The Talmud describes imperial tax collectors and royal policies pertaining to taxes without any indication that the Exilarch was involved in the process.[43] Several sources in the Babylonian Talmud portray a few Jews functioning, often begrudgingly, as low-level tax collectors working under the aegis of a more prominent – apparently non-Jewish – figure.[44] Even here, the Exilarch is absent.

The other major scholarly argument furnished to support the claim that the Exilarch was responsible for tax collection draws an analogy to the fourth-century East Syriac bishop, Simeon bar Ṣabbaʿe. Simeon is a prominent figure in the memory of East Syriac Christians and considered

ed., *Acta Martyrum et Sanctorum* (Leipzig: 1890–1897), 2.610. I note here that the one contemporary non-Jewish reference to Babylonian Jewish elites does not mention the Exilarch. See Theophylact, *History*, 5.7, 4–9 in Michael and Mary Whitby, *The History of Theophylact Simocatta* (New York: 1986), 141–142.

41 For a review of the literature, see David Goodblatt, "The Poll Tax in Sasanian Babylonia: The Talmudic Evidence," *Journal of the Economic and Social History of the Orient* 22 (1979): 270, 293; and Herman, *Prince without a Kingdom*, 176n72–73. See also y. Soṭ. 5.5 (20b), often understood to refer to taxes, with Herman, *Prince without a Kingdom*, 237–238.

42 See discussion in Goodblatt, "Poll Tax," 250; Herman, *Prince without a Kingdom*, 176–179; and contra Beer, *Exilarchate*, 118–123.

43 See the fascinating reference in b. Taʿan. 20a to the effect that Jews are not appointed to certain positions in the Sasanian Empire.

44 b. Sanh. 25b; B. Bat. 167a, 8a; Bek. 31a. See Moshe Beer, "Were the Babylonian Amoraim Exempt from Taxes and Customs?" [in Hebrew], *Tarbiẓ* 33 (1964): 249–250, and discussion in Chapter 2.

the arch-martyr of what became known as the Great Persecution under Shapur II.[45] As commonly understood, the accounts of his death attribute his martyrdom to his refusal to collect taxes on behalf of the Sasanian Empire.[46] The implication of this report is that, as a function of his position as head of the East Syriac ecclesiastical hierarchy, he was expected to collect taxes from Christians on behalf of the empire. If part of the Catholicos' remit as communal intermediary was to collect taxes, the Exilarch was thought by analogy to perform a similar function for Jews.

Some skepticism has, however, rightly been expressed about this analogy.[47] The imperial order to Simeon came at a time of increased tension between the Empire and its Christian subjects. It is difficult, therefore, to extrapolate broadly beyond it. A lack of corroborating evidence for other Catholicoi collecting taxes further problematizes the extent to which Simeon's story is representative.

Yet these cautionary notes do not go far enough. The royal order to Simeon to collect taxes from Christians is in fact a later hagiographical embellishment.[48] There are two main Syriac versions of Simeon's story: The *Martyrdom of Simeon bar Ṣabbaʿe* and the *History of Simeon bar Ṣabbaʿe*, and there is a derivative Greek account in Sozomen's *Ecclesiastical History*, composed in Constantinople in the 440s. Simeon is ordered to collect taxes in the *History* but not in the *Martyrdom*, nor in Sozomen's retelling. The significance of this disparity is illuminated by understanding the interrelationship of these sources.

In 1967, Gernot Wiessner influentially argued for the existence of a common source (ABx), of which the *Martyrdom* (A) and *History* (B) were different recensions, and from which Sozomen also drew.[49] He thus

45 For further detail, see Chapters 3 and 4.

46 For recent discussions, see: Karin Mosig-Walburg, "Die Christenverfolgung Shāpūrs II. vor dem Hintergrund des persisch–römischen Krieges," in *Inkulturation des Christentums im Sasanidenreich*, ed. A. Mustafa and J. Tubach (Wiesbaden: 2007), 171–186; Kyle Smith, *The Martyrdom and History of Blessed Simon bar Ṣabbaʿe* (Piscataway, NJ: 2014), xvii–l; Smith, *Constantine and the Captive Christians of Persia*; and Payne, *State of Mixture*, 40–44.

47 Goodblatt, "*Poll Tax*," 249–250; Herman, *Prince without a Kingdom*, 177–178.

48 For more, see Gross, "Being Roman in the Sasanian Empire," 380–382.

49 Gernot Wiessner, *Untersuchungen zur syrischen Literaturegeschichte I: Zur Märtyrerüberlieferung aus der Christenverfolgung Schapurs II* (Göttingen: 1967). Wiessner's views were popularized in English through Sebastian Brock, "Review of G. Wiessner's Zur Märtyrerüberlieferung," *Journal of Theological Studies* 19 (1968): 300–309.

contended that shared elements in the three accounts derived from the earlier common source. Following Wiessner's schema, if the king ordered Simeon to collect taxes in the *History*, and if there was a similar narrative in the *Martyrdom*, this shared story was presumed to emerge from the common source, the earliest record of Simeon's martyrdom.

Recently, Kyle Smith has convincingly challenged Wiessner's reconstruction.[50] He has argued, instead, that the *Martyrdom* was composed first, and that both the *History* and Sozomen's account were directly dependent on it. The later *History* presents a hagiographical revision of the *Martyrdom*, or a closely related source, that seeks to diminish the appearance of Christian disobedience and offer a more moderate version of Simeon's opposition to the king. For instance, whereas the *Martyrdom* speaks of Christians refusing to pay any taxes, in the *History*, Simeon refuses the draconian imperial order that Christians pay an onerous *double* tax.[51]

What continues to go unnoticed is the fact that the story in the earlier *Martyrdom* and the derivative story in Sozomen do not contain any order from the king directing Simeon himself, in his ecclesiastical capacity, to collect taxes. Instead, these texts, and Simeon as a character in them, criticize the avaricious imperial tax collectors, whose behavior causes Simeon to argue that Christians should not pay any taxes at all. In the *History* – a later adaptation offering a more moderate image of Christian opposition to Sasanian rule – the Christians as a group neither refuse to pay taxes, nor does Simeon refuse to obey the king as a matter of principle. Rather, Simeon challenges the premise that Christians should pay a double tax, and specifically that *he* should be responsible for and complicit in the double tax's collection.[52] The reason we lack

[50] Kyle Smith, "Constantine and Judah the Maccabee: History and Memory in the Acts of the Persian Martyrs," *Journal of the Canadian Society for Syriac Studies* 12 (2012): 16–33; Smith, *Constantine and the Captive Christians of Persia*, 110–111; and, especially, Smith, *The Martyrdom and History*, xvii–l.

[51] The tax is embellished further in the *Chronicle of Seert*: Addai Scher, ed., *Histoire nestorienne (Chronique de Séert)* (Paris: 1908), 1.90 (hereafter, *Chronique de Séert*). For excessive taxation against Christians in Armenia, see Robert Thomson, *History of Vardan and the Armenian War by Elishe* (Cambridge: 1982), 77.

[52] It is likely not coincidental that the same word for "edict," from Middle Persian *frawardag* ("letter"; "edict"), is used in the *History of Simeon* (Bedjan, *Acta martyrum et sanctorum*, 1.136) for the edict of the king compelling a double tax, and in the Synod of 410 for the edict gathering the bishops to the royal court. See Claudia Ciancaglini, *Iranian Loanwords in Syriac* (Wiesbaden: 2008), 238. This also suggests the *History of Simeon* is responding to a post-410 reality; on which see more below.

corroborating evidence of other bishops or Catholicoi serving as tax collectors is because this detail is an apologetic embellishment of a later account: It does not reflect the actual duties conferred by the state upon the Catholicos in any period. The case of Simeon shows how preexisting assumptions about the Sasanian Empire's supposed delegation of authority to particular religious communities skews our understanding of the textual evidence.

No evidence, therefore, supports the involvement of the Exilarch – or for that matter of the Catholicos – in tax collection. Tax collection was the remit of imperial appointees of various kinds. These appointees may occasionally have been Jews and Christians, but they owed their positions to their direct participation in the state apparatus, rather than a Jewish or Christian autonomous hierarchy.[53]

MARKETS

In a few pericopes in rabbinic literature, the Exilarch is depicted as exercising some control over agricultural markets.[54] In one story in the Palestinian Talmud, the Exilarch appoints a rabbi to oversee weights and prices in the market, using the Greek *agoranomos*, or market overseer, as his title.[55] While this source has often been taken at face value, Geoffrey Herman notes that there are reasons to doubt its facticity. The source follows a discussion that exegetically derives from the Bible an obligation for Jews to appoint an *agoranomos*.[56] The *agoranomos* in these sources is therefore not a government appointee, but rather a position within the rabbinically imagined Jewish community. The story of the Exilarch is introduced to problematize the precise nature of the *agoranomos*' responsibilities, with Exilarch and rabbi offering different understandings. Strangely, however, while the Babylonian Talmud's version of this story, which appears to be derivative of the earlier Palestinian source, states that the house of the Exilarch appoints *agoranomoi*, the Exilarch and his

[53] On Jewish tax collectors, see Chapter 2, p. 129. [54] b. B. Bat. 22a.

[55] y. B. Bat. 5.5 (15a–b). Here the Exilarch is referred to as the *resh galuta*, while in b. B. Bat. 89a his household is referred to as *be nesiya*. The figures in the story are the Babylonian rabbis Shmuel and Qarna. See Beer, *Exilarchate*, 123–126; and Herman, *Prince without a Kingdom*, 162–172. Louis Jacobs, "The Economic Conditions of the Jews in Babylon in Talmudic Times Compared with Palestine," *Journal of Semitic Studies* 2 (1957): 355, suggests that the existence of the *agoranomos* is a holdover from Hellenistic rule in Babylonia.

[56] Sifre Deuteronomy, *Ki Teṣei*, 394 (ed. Louis Finkelstein, *Sifre Deuteronomy* [New York: 1939], 313); Sifra *Qedoshim* 8 (ed. Isaac Weiss, *Sifra de-bei rav* [Vienna: 1862], 91).

household are absent from the ensuing account, again suggesting that the Exilarch did not, in reality, appoint any such figure.[57]

In general, the *agoranomos* was a Greek, and then Roman, overseer, and often one of low rank and local appointment, responsible for ensuring good order in the market.[58] There is less evidence of a widespread position akin to the *agoranomos* in Babylonia. In Shapur I's trilingual inscription at *Kaʿba-ye Zardošt* from the second half of the third century, the fifty-seventh figure on a list of officials in Middle Persian is the *wāzārbed*; a market head (the word "bazaar" derives from *wāzār*). This is translated in the Greek version of the inscription as *agoranomos*. Yet in the context of an inscription listing the top positions of the Empire, the *wāzārbed* does not sound like a position equivalent to the *agoranomos*, but instead was likely a distinct office that was best approximated in Greek by the word *agoranomos*.[59] All of this suggests, as Herman argues, that these stories "originated in Palestine" and depict "Babylonia in accordance with the reality of Palestine."[60]

In another story, the Exilarch is depicted as possessing the ability to "seize the market" in the capital city of Meḥoza, removing marketplace competition by allowing a particular merchant to complete selling their wares before others may sell theirs. According to the story, Rav Dimi from Nehardea arrives at Meḥoza with a boat filled with figs. The Exilarch instructs Rava to examine the rabbi and see whether he is in fact a "rabbinic scholar" and therefore worthy of market seizure.[61] Rava delegates this task to his junior, Rav Adda bar Ahava, who effectively insults Rav Dimi, both by his crass questions (if an elephant swallowed an Egyptian basket and expelled it through its anus, what is its status?), and subsequently by demeaning Rav Dimi himself. As Barry Wimpfheimer has shown, this story is a literary creation, comprised of a variety of sources throughout the Talmud, with the purpose of serving as a counterweight to an earlier legal discussion.[62] More to the point, the story hardly conveys

57 b. B. Bat. 89a.

58 See especially Daniel Sperber, "On the Office of the Agoranomos in Roman Palestine," *Zeitschrift der Deutschen Morgenländischen Gesellschaft* 127 (1977): 227–243.

59 There is also one case in b. B. Qam. 98a, where an Arab merchant is described as an *agoranomos* and provides rabbis with information about currency appreciation.

60 Herman, *Prince without a Kingdom*, 172.

61 The precise meaning of "rabbinic scholar" is unclear and demands further study. See Goodblatt, *Rabbinic Instruction*, 286–288 and passim.

62 Barry S. Wimpfheimer, *Narrating the Law: A Poetics of Talmudic Legal Stories. Divinations, Rereading Late Ancient Religion* (Philadelphia, PA: 2011), 122–46. See also the discussion of Marc Hirshman, *The Stabilization of Rabbinic Culture 100 C.E.–350*

the "centralized authoritative structure of the Babylonian Jewish community" as some have argued.[63] Indeed, other rabbis are similarly said to have exercised the ability to freeze the market and to intervene in market affairs.[64] For instance, according to a rabbinic discussion, local merchants sell their wares before itinerant merchants.[65] This does not appear to have been a set law, as the locals of one town asked Ravina to intercede when itinerant basket-sellers came to sell their wares, and rather than rule decisively in one direction, Ravina offers a compromise intended to appease both parties. In an adjacent story, Rava allows two rabbis to break the rules of priority so that they may return to their studies more quickly. This suggests that the ability to seize and manipulate the market stemmed not from imperial *diktat* but from communal influence, or simply lived in the literary imagination of the rabbis altogether.[66]

Indeed, the story of Rav Dimi can be read instead as a subtle critique of the way the Exilarch and his henchman doled out social privileges and deployed power and status; not in a formal capacity, but one imposed by social pressure. The story concludes with Rav Dimi disgraced and his figs spoiled and unpurchased. When Rav Dimi reports his misfortunes to Rav Joseph, the latter curses those who harmed Rav Dimi. As a result, Rav Adda bar Ahava, who ultimately did the bidding of the Exilarch by submitting Rav Dimi to questioning, dies. We find a similar condemnation of ecclesiastical use and abuse of power and privilege outside of the centralized power of the state in Aphrahat's *Demonstration* 14.[67] Composed just prior to the middle of the fourth century, Aphrahat denounces the bishop of Seleucia-Ctesiphon for exploiting his flock for the sake of his own self-exaltation and aggrandizement, and for doling out favors, titles, and honors to his corrupt cronies.[68] The bishop needlessly foments social strife, when instead he should pursue concord. According to the story of Rav Dimi, in his seizure of the markets, the

C.E.: *Texts on Education and Their Late Antique Context* (Oxford: 2009), 83–95; and Herman, *Prince without a Kingdom*, 173–176.

63 Gafni, "Political, Social, and Economic History," 803.

64 Rav Hama in b. B. Meṣ. 65a. See Herman, *Prince without a Kingdom*, 175.

65 b. B. Bat. 22a.

66 For exilarchal enforcers, see e.g., b. Giṭ. 67b (abusing Rav Amram). The rabbis depict themselves intervening in disputes involving the market. See b. B. Bat. 21b–22a.

67 Herman, *Prince without a Kingdom*, 176.

68 J. Parisot, *Aphraatis Sapientis Persae Demonstrationes I–XXI*, Patrologia Syriaca 1.1 (Paris: 1894), 577–582, 587–592, 635–650.

Exilarch similarly fosters discord in Babylonian Jewish society, pitting rabbi against rabbi and Jew against Jew in a competition for honor and privileges.

The Exilarch did not collect taxes, nor did he appoint Jews to formal governmental oversight of the markets. He may have had some power to seize the markets, but this did not derive from some official imperial position. Instead, this power was likely a product of the Exilarch's prestige and social capital and could therefore be deployed by others with some degree of social capital, including particular rabbis.

LEGAL JURISDICTION

The Exilarch is commonly thought to have overseen a system of official Jewish courts which regulated Babylonian Jewish society.[69] Few sources, however, can be mustered to support this view.[70]

According to one source, judges were present at the gate of the Exilarch:[71]

> R. Naḥman said to R. Huna, "Does the law follow our opinion or yours?"
> He replied, "The law follows your view, since you are closer to the Exilarch's court/gate (*baba*), where judges are prevalent (*škhiḥe*)."

Rav Huna argues that Rav Naḥman's legal view carried more weight by virtue of his closer proximity to the Exilarch's court or gate where judges were, depending on the translation, present, available, or prevalent.[72] Rav Naḥman is elsewhere identified as the son-in-law of the Exilarch, and his

[69] Neusner, *History of the Jews*, 2.64–72; Neusner, *A History of the Jews*, 5.244–259; Neusner, *School, Court, Public Administration: Judaism and Its Institutions in Talmudic Babylonia* (Atlanta, GA: 1987), esp. 130–131; Gafni, "Political, Social, and Economic History," 802; Simonsohn, *Common Justice*, 50–52; Herman, *Prince without a Kingdom*, 194–209.

[70] Herman, *Prince without a Kingdom*, 195n112, shows the extent to which scholars must stretch to ground exilarchal judicial authority. See also Herman, 309–319, which examines how the rabbi and judge Mar 'Uqba appears to be treated as an Exilarch only in later layers of the Talmud and is only explicitly identified as such in medieval chronographies (cf. Neusner, *History of the Jews*, 2.106–107).

[71] b. B. Bat. 65a. See discussion in David M. Goodblatt, *The Monarchic Principle: Studies in Jewish Self-Government in Antiquity* (Tübingen: 1994), 287; and Beer, *Exilarchate*, 77–78.

[72] MS Vatican 115b reads דשכיחי להו דייני.

assumed access presumably stems from his close familial relationship with the Exilarch.[73]

This brief story has been taken to suggest that the Exilarch superintended a network of courts. Yet the source makes no mention of a general court system; it refers only to a group of judges who, for whatever reason, frequent the court of the Exilarch. It is also unclear whether the word *baba* refers to the "court" of the Exilarch, which judges frequented perhaps as guests, or more specifically to the gate of his estate, which may have served as a meeting place to resolve communal affairs.[74] There is a long history in the Near East of judges adjudicating at the entrance to a city or noteworthy landmark, a phenomenon found in the Bible and also the Talmud.[75] In either case, there is no indication that the judges in question answer to the Exilarch.

The same Rav Naḥman appears in one of the other stories cited as evidence of the Exilarch's system of courts. A rabbi is encouraged to accept a summons sent by Rav Naḥman to display "the honor due to the Exilarchate."[76] In the ensuing story, there is no court, but simply Rav Naḥman in his home hearing a dispute between two litigants. Moreover, the rabbi appears before Rav Naḥman not because he has authority; indeed, he originally considers ignoring the summons. Ultimately, he agrees to appear before Rav Naḥman after a rabbi encourages him to express "honor due to the Exilarchate," but no more. This suggests that attending Rav Naḥman's summons was not mandatory, nor did it carry coercive power. In another story, Rav Naḥman issues a ruling on behalf of the Exilarch, and his ruling document is torn up in protest by another

[73] For Rav Naḥman as son-in-law of the Exilarch, see b. Ḥul. 124a. For Rav Naḥman in the court or residence of the Exilarch, see Herman, *Prince without a Kingdom*, 149 and esp. n80 there.

[74] See similarly b. B. Bat. 58a, and Becker, *Sources*, 155n510. Another story (b. Shab. 126b) describes a rabbi teaching at the entrance or "opening" of the Exilarch, although the word there is different (*pitḥa*). A story in b. Sanh. 7b, which reworks y. Bik. 3:3 (65d), pertains to the Patriarch and Palestine, not the Exilarch, contra the intimation in Herman, *Prince without a Kingdom*, 192n112.

[75] Natalie N. May, "Gates and Their Functions in Mesopotamia and Ancient Israel," in *The Fabric of Cities: Aspects of Urbanism, Urban Topography and Society in Mesopotamia, Greece and Rome*, ed. Natalie N. May and Ulrike Steinert (Leiden: 2014), 77–123; Lee Levine, *The Ancient Synagogue: The First Thousand Years* (New Haven, CT: 2005), 28–42; and b. Ned. 66b. For the formalization of the Exilarch's "gate" as a place of judgment in the medieval period, see Gil, *Jews in Islamic Countries*, 87.

[76] b. Qid. 70a. See Gross, "Rethinking Babylonian Jewish Acculturation"; and Chapter 2 for further analysis of this source.

rabbi.[77] The Exilarch asks Rav Naḥman for an explanation, and two versions of his response are offered: The latter either replied that Rav Yehuda must have had a good reason, or that Rav Yehuda's action can be dismissed because Rav Naḥman is a greater judge. Neither answer assumes the Exilarch carries any special legal authority.

There are astonishingly few additional sources that even tangentially associate the Exilarch with adjudication.[78] In one case, the Exilarch suspects that a Jew killed a man, and he instructs a rabbi to investigate the matter, and if it is confirmed, the rabbi should "dim his (i.e., the murderer's) eyes," a form of extra-judicial punishment also employed elsewhere by rabbis.[79] The Exilarch is not involved in the subsequent story. This suggests that the Exilarch may have been interested in maintaining social order but did not have a court system of his own ready to deploy. He also lacked the authority to impose punishment, or at least capital punishment, and so encouraged the rabbi to use discrete and clandestine measures, presumably to avoid the watchful eye of the actual imperial authorities.[80] In another story, the Exilarch is asked to rule in a case, but his judgment is rejected by the litigant, who instead approaches a rabbi to receive a different ruling altogether.[81] This hardly suggests formal legal authority.

As with taxes, the assumption of exilarchal legal authority was misleadingly read back into earlier sources. A particularly instructive example is an admittedly complicated, albeit brief, talmudic passage that has been instrumental to the notion of exilarchal legal authority. This short legal discussion seeks to clarify an enigmatic mishnah in tractate ʿEruvin. The tractate is dedicated to the laws for establishing a boundary marker, or *ʿeruv*, that permits people to carry objects in a city's public

77 b. B. Meṣ. 66a.

78 I have discussed the most prominent source, b. Sanh. 5a, elsewhere, and have shown that it reflects post-Amoraic developments in rabbinic imaginations about the authority of the Exilarch. See Gross, "Reassessing Exilarchal Authority," and 266n7 there for how medieval commentators and scholars have read b. Sanh. 5a into other passages, such as b. Ket. 94b, where Rav Naḥman rejects the opinion of Rav Sheshet for two reasons, one of which is that "I am judge and the master (i.e., Rav Sheshet) is not." Medieval and modern commentators have considered this again to refer to formal exilarchal appointment, but given that it is coupled with a second argument invalidating Rav Sheshet's opinion, it appears to constitute a simple boast, similar to those made by Rav Naḥman elsewhere. See also Gross, "Reassessing Exilarchal Authority," 269n18.

79 b. Sanh. 27a–b; compare with b. Ber. 58a.

80 Beer, *Exilarchate*, 62–64, claims that this proves the Exilarch had authority *even* over capital cases, arguing against Lazarus who had contended that the Exilarch was authorized to rule in civil but not capital cases.

81 b. B. Qam. 58b. To be discussed below.

spaces on Shabbat, a typically forbidden activity. In general, the theory behind the law is that one may carry in enclosed private property, and the *'eruv* is a legal fiction that turns public spaces into nominally private spaces. The mishnah discusses the unusual case of a city that was once privately owned, presumably occupied by tenants, but that has since become publicly owned and is now divided among each of its residents. The mishnah presupposes that different rules typically apply to the application of *'eruv* in privately versus publicly owned cities; in the former case, since it is privately owned already, a single *'eruv* suffices.[82] In publicly owned cities, by contrast, it must be made clear that it is only the *'eruv* that allows people to carry, lest they mistakenly infer that carrying is always permitted in public. Therefore, in publicly owned cities, a designated space was left outside of the *'eruv* to serve as a reminder that it is the *'eruv* that permits carrying on Shabbat in the rest of the city. In the ambiguous case of a privately owned city that becomes public, the mishnah rules, without explanation, that a single *'eruv* still suffices, as when it was privately owned, and no additional space must remain outside of the *'eruv* to serve as a reminder.

The Talmud seeks to identify an example of a private city that becomes public, and the reason it should be exempt from the typical requirements of a publicly owned city:[83]

What is a city of an individual [i.e., private] that became a city of the masses [i.e., public]?

R. Yehuda replied, "For example, the *disqarta* of the Exilarch."
Said R. Naḥman to him, "What is your reason [for singling out the *disqarta* of the Exilarch]? If it be suggested: Because many people meet at [the residence/office of] the *harmana* (or *kahramana*) they would remind each other – but are not all Israel assembled together on a Sabbath morning also?"
Rather said R. Naḥman, "For instance, the *disqarta* of Nitzwoi."

Previously understood as reflecting the Exilarch's imperial authority (*harmana*), careful analysis of this complex source uncovers crucial flaws with this interpretation. Rav Yehuda offers an example of a city that was privately owned and became public: the "*disqarta* of the Exilarch." *Disqarta* derives from the Middle Iranian term for an elite estate, realized as *dastgird* in Middle Persian.[84] These were large landholdings that often included both

[82] m. 'Erub. 5.6. [83] b. 'Erub. 59a.

[84] Michael Sokoloff, *A Dictionary of Jewish Babylonian Aramaic of the Talmudic and Geonic Periods* (Baltimore, MD: 2002), 344–345 (hereafter, *DJBA*). Linguistic analyses include Wojciech Skolmowski, "On Middle Iranian *dstkrt(y)*," in *Medioiranica: Proceedings of the International Colloquium Organized by the Katholieke Universiteit*

agricultural fields and living quarters.[85] These estates, as described by both Sasanian law and elsewhere in the Babylonian Talmud, required large staffs, including slaves, for upkeep and maintenance.[86] The legal discussion in the Talmud here therefore seems to refer to what was previously a privately owned estate of the Exilarch that has since become publicly owned. The process of a *disqarta* transforming from private estate to public city was, in fact, fairly common; a number of Sasanian cities in Late Antiquity were named *dastgird*, a vestige of their previous status as private estates.[87] In a similar vein, *disqarta*s also became homes to monasteries and schools, again sometimes bestowed by a single wealthy benefactor, showing how they could transition between various

Leuven, ed. Wojciech Skalmowski and Alois Van Tongerloo (Leuven: 1993), 157–162; Ciancaglini, *Iranian Loanwords in Syriac*, 153–154; and Antonio Panaino, "Between Semantics and Pragmatics: Origins and Developments in the Meaning of *dastgerd*. A New Approach to the Problem," *Sasanian Studies* 1 (2022): 215–242.

85 Dastgirds are also mentioned in b. Meg. 16a (see Chapter 2); ʿErub. 59a; and Giṭ. 40a. See P. Gignoux, "Les inscriptions en moyen-perse de Bandiān," *Studia Iranica* 27 (1998): 251–258; Gignoux, "Dastgerd," in *Dārā(b)–Ebn al-Aṯīr*, vol. 7, *Encyclopædia Iranica*, ed. Ehsan Yarshater (Costa Mesa, CA: 1994), 105–106; Jean de Menasce, "Inscriptions pehlevies en écriture cursive," *Journal asiatique* 244 (1956): 424; Herman, *Prince without a Kingdom*, 137–138; and Richard Payne, "Territorializing Iran in Late Antiquity: Autocracy, Aristocracy, and the Infrastructure of Empire," in *Ancient States and Infrastructural Power*, ed. Clifford Ando and Seth Richardson (Philadelphia, PA: 2017), 189–190. For Khusro II's opulent *dastgird*, see Frye, *History of Ancient Iran*, 337; and Hugh Kennedy, "From Shahristan to Medina," *Studia Islamica* 102 (2006): 13. Identified with Khosrow-shad-Kavadh, attested in a number of seals, this city was an estate of the king, and it featured a palace, was built on waterways, and grew in size over the course of the Sasanian period.

86 *Book of a Thousand Judgments* 18 in Maria Macuch, *Rechtskasuistik Und Gerichtspraxis Zu Beginn Des Siebenten Jahrhunderts in Iran: Die Rechtssammlung Des Farroḫmard i Wahrāmān* (Wiesbaden: 1993), 153, 158–159; and Anahit Perikhanian, *Mādayān ī Hazār ī Dādestān: Book of a Thousand Judgments, a Sasanian Law-Book* (Costa Mesa, CA: 1997), 62–63; *MHD* 39 in Macuch, *Rechtskasuistik*, 279, 284–285; and Perikhanian, *Book of a Thousand Judgments*, 106–107, where it is *MHD* 38; and *MHD* A36, in Perikhanian, *Book of a Thousand Judgments*, 314–315; and b. Giṭ. 40a.

87 *Dastgirds* appear as a toponym in b. Shab. 93a; Soṭ. 6b; and Giṭ. 28b. Similarly, a Rav Huna is said to be from *Disqarta* in b. B. Meṣ. 47a: see references in Aharon Oppenheimer, *Babylonia Judaica in the Talmudic Period* (Wiesbaden: 1983), 115–117; and *The Provincial Capitals of Ērānšahr*, sec. 20 (Touraj Daryaee, *Šahrestānīhā ī Ērānšahr: A Middle Persian Text on Late Antique Geography, Epic and History* [Costa Mesa, CA: 2002], 19). In the Synod of Dadisho in 422, one Sharbil appears to live in the *dastgird* of the king. See Nina Viktorovna Pigulevskaja, *Les villes de l'État iranien aux époques parthe et sassanide: contribution à l'histoire sociale de la basse Antiquité* (Paris: 1963), 151–153; and Smith, *Constantine and the Captive Christians of Persia*, 186.

states of private and public ownership.[88] In seeking to understand the Mishnah's ruling concerning "a private city that became public," Rav Yehuda therefore provides a local Babylonian example of such a phenomenon: The *disqarta* of the Exilarch, which was once privately owned by the Exilarch, and later publicly owned.

Based on the principle that a specific example would only be furnished due to some novelty it introduces to the discussion, the later Rav Naḥman seeks to understand whether there is something particularly instructive about the *disqarta* of the Exilarch. He wonders if perhaps Rav Yehuda selected it because of the additional novelty that people regularly meet there at the residence or office of the so-called *harmana*, a Persian loanword broadly meaning "authority," in this case, "authority figure." When gathered at the *harmana*, people would remind each other of the city's shift from private to public ownership, thereby obviating the need for a space outside the *ʿeruv* to serve as a formal reminder. He rejects this explanation, however, because Jews also regularly meet weekly on Shabbat wherever they are, and therefore the fact that people gather at the *harmana* is not a novelty. Instead, Rav Naḥman proposes that a better example is the *disqarta* of Nitzwoi, although he elaborates no further. The implication is that the *disqarta* of Nitzwoi also transitioned from private to public ownership, like many other *disqarta*s, and that even though no *harmana* resides there, the Mishnah's law still applies to it.[89] The lesson is that any city that transitions from private to public ownership can count on regular encounters, like those that occur on Shabbat, to remind residents of its status as a formerly private city.

The significance of this passage in scholarly accounts of the Exilarch derived from two fundamental misunderstandings. First, scholars simply failed to recognize that the *disqarta* of the Exilarch referred to in the text was *once* owned by him, but no longer. They therefore assumed that the *harmana* who dwelled in the *disqarta* must refer to the Exilarch himself, and to his imperial appointment and/or judicial authority.[90] The very premise of the Talmudic discussion, however, is that the *disqarta* was no

[88] Philip Wood, *Chronicle of Seert: Christian Historical Imagination in Late Antique Iraq* (Oxford: 2013), 77. See Adam Becker, *Fear of God and the Beginning of Wisdom: The School of Nisbis and Christian Scholastic Culture in Late Antique Mesopotamia* (Philadelphia, PA: 2006), 80–81.

[89] This is almost certainly a personal or family name, not an office, contra Herman, *Prince without a Kingdom*, 137n19.

[90] Herman, *Prince without a Kingdom*, 137–138.

longer privately owned by the Exilarch, and the *harmana* located there was therefore *not* the Exilarch at all.

A second error was that scholars preferred the reading *harmana*, and assumed this referred to the Exilarch, who therefore enjoyed some degree of "authority." The word *harmana*, however, is in fact a clear scribal error.[91] Most manuscripts instead have the related but less common word *kahramana*, realized in Middle Persian as *kārframān*.[92] The term can refer to a general deputy or appointed official, someone with oversight capacity or delegated authority of some kind, or to a servant.[93] The term has the former meaning elsewhere in the Babylonian Talmud, where it refers to the appointment of a lessee with authority over one's property.[94]

However, there is also a more technical use of the term in several cases in the so-called Sasanian law book, the *Book of a Thousand Judgments* (*Mādayān ī Hazār Dādestān*, hereafter *MHD*), a collection of earlier case law typically dated to the early seventh century. Here it refers to the authority conferred upon certain Sasanian judicial officials to validate documents with their seals.[95] These "seals for the exercise of authority" (*muhr ī pad kār-framān dāštan*), or just "official seals," were used by regional officials of different ranks to sign depositions, whether in criminal or civil cases. Papyri dating from the period of the Sasanian occupation of Egypt in the early seventh century feature a figure named Saralaneozan (Middle Persian, *Shahrālānyōzān*) who is identified as the *kārframān-i dar*, the *kārframān* of the court.[96] Among his other functions, he too appears to be responsible for sealing judicial documents, but also for collecting taxes and approving goods and persons for travel

[91] This should already have been clear from the fact that elsewhere in the Babylonian Talmud, the word typically appears as the "*harmana* of the king," when referring to imperial edicts and/or authorization. Yet here "of the king" is conspicuously absent.

[92] Oxford Heb. b. 10/9–12+, Oxford Heb. d. 21/6–9, CUL: T-S F 1(1).85; Vatican 109 (where the q is erased). As noted by Sokoloff, *DJBA*, 989; and Herman, *Prince without a Kingdom*, 137.

[93] For the former, see *MHD* 48, 7–10 (Macuch, *Rechtskasuistik*, 308, 324, 356–357; and Perikhanian, *Book of a Thousand Judgments*, 128–129). For the latter, see Frantz Grenet, *La geste d'Ardashir fils de Pâbag. Kārnāmag ī Ardaxšēr ī Pābagān* (Paris: 2003), 92–93 and passim. For the borrowing of the Persian word into Arabic, see Mushegh Asatrian, "Iranian Elements in Arabic: The State of Research," *Iran & the Caucasus* 10 (2006): 96n8.

[94] b. B. Bat. 46b.

[95] See Maria Macuch, "The Use of Seals in Sasanian Jurisprudence," in *Sceaux d'Orient et leur mploy*, ed. Rika Gyselen (Bures-sur-Yvette: 1997), 80–82.

[96] Dieter Weber, "Eine spätsassanidische Rechtsurkunde aus Ägypten," *Tyche* 17 (2002): 185–192.

through Sasanian territory.[97] The word *kārframān* therefore has a range of possible meanings, but all pertain to officials in a position of authority who validate legal documents and oversee other crucial administrative functions.

We may now fully understand the brief talmudic discussion. What was formerly the private *dastgird* of the Exilarch is now a public site occupied by, among other people, the *kārframān*, an imperial official. Jews would frequent the *dastgird* not to see the previous owner, the Exilarch, but to appear before the *kārframān* and perhaps avail themselves of one of his prerogatives, such as sealing relevant judicial documents. The Talmud elsewhere makes mention of Sasanian criminal deposition documents by their Middle Persian name (*pursišn-nāmag*), correctly noting that the legal case is closed once it is sealed, and in another place recognizes the need for official seals to validate documents in civil cases under Sasanian law.[98] This shows that Jews had first hand familiarity with the Sasanian legal system, presumably through access to it and to figures like the *kārframān*, a topic we will return to below. Far from pointing to the imperial authority of the Exilarch or his judicial and administrative jurisdiction, this talmudic source shows that Jews had regular and direct recourse to Sasanian administrative figures, like the *kārframān*.

In all, there is very little to support the contention that the Exilarch was responsible for overseeing the administration of judgment among Jews, a negative conclusion to be added to the absence of evidence of the Exilarch serving as formal intermediary, the Exilarch's noninvolvement in tax collection, and at best narrow deployment of social pressure in the case of markets.[99] To be clear, the Exilarch is undoubtedly viewed as a prominent Jewish figure, and by dint of his elevated social and cultural position, Jews may well have occasionally deferred to him in particular domains, such as seizure of the markets. The Exilarch may have

[97] See Patrick Sanger, "The Administration of Sasanian Egypt: New Masters and Byzantine Continuity," *Greek, Roman, and Byzantine Studies* 51 (2011): 653–665. See also Jairus Banaji, "On the Identity of Shahrālānyōzān in the Greek and Middle Persian Papyri from Egypt," in *Documents and the History of the Early Islamic World*, ed. Alexander Schubert and Petra Sijpesteijn (Leiden: 2014), 27–42.

[98] b. Giṭ. 28b and ʿErub. 62a. See below.

[99] Even Herman's more moderate position (*Prince without a Kingdom*, 195–196) in which he recognizes that "it would seem unlikely that the Jewish judicial system as a whole was subordinate to the Exilarchate," but insists that the Exilarch did possess "considerable judicial power," goes too far.

occasionally had some involvement in resolving conflicts among Jews, but this was not because they filled any formal position vis-à-vis the Empire.

BABYLONIAN RABBINIC JUDGES

If the Exilarch was considered the superintendent of a Babylonian Jewish court system, the rabbis were its official judges. The spiritual and judicial authority of rabbinic courts in both Palestine and Babylonia was once taken for granted. According to this view, the rabbis of both centers were perceived to be leaders of the Jewish community, officiating over law courts and exacting and meting out punishment.[100] Jews were governed first and foremost by Jewish law, or Halakha, as understood and promulgated by the rabbis. The history of ancient Jewish society became, in many ways, a history of rabbinic rule. And yet, while this paradigm has long since fallen out of favor for late antique Palestine, it persists in the study of Babylonia.

Over the course of the last half century, the hegemony of the rabbis in Palestine has been thoroughly challenged. Revisionist approaches that highlight what Shaye Cohen described as the "great tension between rabbinic ideology and social reality" have concluded that the rabbis were not widely recognized sources of spiritual or legal authority across Palestinian and, by extension, Mediterranean Jewish society during the first centuries of the Common Era. Indeed, the rabbis themselves were not institutionalized in any serious fashion, a fact that belies notions of a unified rabbinic movement, to say nothing of a centralized Jewish society.[101] Rabbinic influence, instead, grew gradually over many centuries.[102] Romantic notions of the elevated position of the rabbis across ancient Jewish populations and regions have grown untenable.

Palestinian rabbinic court cases recorded in rabbinic literature are no longer regarded as evidence of the formal position of the rabbis in society. Instead, rabbis functioned as arbitrators, and "depended on the consensus

[100] For a critical history of the field, see Schwartz, "Political Geography of Rabbinic Texts."

[101] Levine, *Rabbinic Class*; Hezser, *Social Structure of the Rabbinic Movement.*

[102] On the question of rabbinization, see Seth Schwartz, "Rabbinization in the Sixth Century," in vol. 3, *The Talmud Yerushalmi and Greco-Roman Culture*, ed. Peter Schäfer (Tübingen: 2002), 55–69; Lapin, *Rabbis as Romans*, 126–150; and the essays in *Diversity and Rabbinization: Jewish Texts and Societies between 400 and 1000 C.E.*, ed. Gavin McDowell, Ron Naiweld, and Daniel Stökl Ben Ezra (Cambridge: 2021).

of the ruled."[103] As a result, the rabbis used various means of social pressure to enforce their rulings; they "could threaten, plead, or cajole, but could not subpoena or impose a sentence."[104] In some Palestinian rabbinic stories, for instance, rabbis brandish excommunication to compel compliance.[105]

Even as scholars grew skeptical about the extent to which rabbis in Palestine enjoyed widespread recognition and authority, Babylonian Jewish society was thought to fall more fully under the sway of the rabbis by dint of their formal position in the centralized Jewish social hierarchy, whether deriving from or independent of the Exilarch.[106] Pioneering revisionists like E. R. Goodenough and Jacob Neusner, who challenged the hegemony of the rabbis in Palestine, insisted that in Babylonia the rabbis were authoritative, and that Jewish society therefore lived in broad conformity with their instructions. Goodenough, for instance, questioned the place of the rabbis in Palestinian Jewish society based on synagogue mosaics, which employed motifs that he argued would have been objectionable to the rabbis and evinced theologies distinct from those of the rabbis.[107] He made a similar argument about the magnificent frescoes in the Dura Europos synagogue, the only synagogue from late antique Mesopotamia to survive. Nevertheless, he believed that this community was an aberration from an otherwise rabbinized Jewish Babylonia.[108] Jacob Neusner contended that Goodenough had overstated the authority of the rabbis over other synagogues in Mesopotamia. He nevertheless held that the rabbis "exerted full and unchallenged authority" in matters of trade, real estate, civil law, marriage, and divorce, not to mention that they were revered, at least by some, as wonder workers.[109] As Neusner

[103] Schwartz, *Imperialism and Jewish Society*, 121. For courts of arbitration, see Lapin, *Rabbis as Romans*, 98–125.

[104] Schwartz, *Imperialism and Jewish Society*, 120. In a law from 392, Theodosian explicitly grants Jewish leaders the right to excommunicate without governmental interference: Amnon Linder, *The Jews in Roman Legislation* (Detroit, MI: 1987), 186–190.

[105] Schwartz, *Imperialism and Jewish Society*, 120n57; Shaye Cohen, "The Rabbi in Second-Century Jewish Society," in *The Roman Period*, vol. 3, *The Cambridge History of Judaism*, ed. William Horbury, W. D. Davies, and John Sturdy (Cambridge: 1999), 971.

[106] See Beer, *Exilarchate*, 91–93; Gafni, *The Jews of Talmudic Babylonia*, 233–234; and Jonathan Pomeranz, *Ordinary Jews in the Babylonian Talmud: Rabbinic Representations and Historical Interpretation* (PhD diss., Yale University, 2016), 150–154.

[107] Erwin R. Goodenough, *Jewish Symbols in the Greco-Roman Period* (Princeton: 1988).

[108] See discussion in Neusner, "Rabbis and Community," 441.

[109] Neusner, "Rabbis and Community," 443.

phrased it, the authority of the rabbis therefore "depended not upon popular acquiescence, though it was considerable, but upon the coercive capabilities of their courts."[110] Assuming imperial sponsorship precluded any serious need to address when and how the Babylonian rabbis attracted followers and spread their influence. Their authority and influence were guaranteed by their "coercive abilities" via the state, and therefore existed at least from the Sasanian Empire's rise in the early third century onwards. Others countered that Neusner *underestimated* the extent of rabbinic authority, arguing that the Jews of Babylonia on the whole followed rabbinic precepts, beginning in the Parthian period onwards.[111]

The rabbis were so self-assured in Babylonia, according to Richard Kalmin, that in contrast with the rabbis of Palestine, they remained aloof from and disdainful toward non-rabbinic Jews, and needless to say, non-Jews as well. They were also highly decentralized.[112] But rather than inferring from this that the rabbis were a loose collection of figures without any clear center of power or institutionalization, Kalmin concludes that "Babylonian rabbis in their own localities, part of a city, or an entire city and its environs, presided over their own 'fiefdoms.'"[113] This situation contrasted with Palestine, where, according to Gafni, lay leaders played a far greater role than in the rabbinically run Babylonian society.[114] Babylonian Jewish society was governed by the rabbis and rabbinic law.[115]

Even as this narrative of rabbinic hegemony persists, several studies have offered important correctives. In a watershed work, David Goodblatt demonstrated that the larger institutionalized rabbinic academies known from the medieval period and assumed to have originated among the earliest Babylonian rabbis, emerged in the post-talmudic

110 Neusner, *A History of the Jews*, 5.449.

111 Isaiah Gafni, "Court Cases in the Babylonian Talmud: Literary Forms and Historical Implications," *Proceedings of the American Academy of Jewish Research* 49 (1982): 23–40; Gafni, *The Jews of Talmudic Babylonia*, 26.

112 Richard L. Kalmin, *The Sage in Jewish Society of Late Antiquity* (New York: 1999), 175–214. For a critical discussion of the notion of Babylonian rabbinic insularity, see Gross, "Prolegomena to a Study of Babylonian Rabbinization in Late Antiquity."

113 Kalmin, *Sage in Jewish Society*, 11. For a critical discussion, see Gross, "Where Did Rav and Shmuel Preside."

114 Gafni, *Jews of Talmudic Babylonia*, 98–109.

115 See the credulous account in Richard Hidary, *Dispute for the Sake of Heaven: Legal Pluralism in the Talmud* (Providence, RI: 2010), 155–161, relied on by Mokhtarian, *Rabbis, Sorcerers, Kings, and Priests*, 106–108.

era.[116] The rabbis in the Talmud, by contrast, were neither centralized nor institutionalized. They were organized in small study circles, a few students congregating around a particular master in cities across Babylonia.[117] Centralized and major academies arose after the last named rabbis in the Talmud in the early sixth century, as Goodblatt and Jeffrey Rubenstein have demonstrated, even as editorial interpolations in the Talmud retrojected the later institutionalized movement onto the rabbinic past.[118] Yet these changes have been taken to narrowly reflect pedagogical and institutional developments, rather than serve as an index of the state of the rabbinic movement in Babylonia at the time.

The more marginal position of the rabbis in Babylonia is clear from the many sources that contradict the general self-presentation of the rabbis as widely respected authority figures. Although the rabbis tended not to readily describe episodes in which they were challenged, several rabbinic sources indicate that there were those in Babylonian who belittled the rabbis or did not recognize them, even in their own locales.[119] Despite the general image of a compliant Jewish society that is found throughout rabbinic literature, the rabbis sometimes do acknowledge that they were disobeyed.[120]

The insecurity of Babylonian rabbis appears to have impacted the readiness with which they deployed excommunication against those who merely disrespected them, unlike what we find among Palestinian rabbis.[121] This was not out of a "desire to protect ... the honor of the Jewish self-governmental authorities in Babylonia," as some have argued,

116 Goodblatt, *Rabbinic Instruction.*

117 Including less prominent cities. See Barak Cohen, "Local Academies in Talmudic Babylonia," *Zion* 70 (2005): 447–471.

118 Goodblatt, *Rabbinic Instruction*; Jeffrey Rubenstein, *The Culture of the Babylonian Talmud* (Baltimore, MD: 2003).

119 Yaakov Elman, "Middle Persian Culture and Babylonian Sages: Accommodation and Resistance in the Shaping of Rabbinic Legal Tradition," in *The Cambridge Companion to the Talmud and Rabbinic Literature*, ed. Charlotte Elisheva Fonrobert and Martin S. Jaffe (Cambridge: 2007), 176–178. See also b. Qid. 70a and Sanh. 99b. The latter is particularly interesting, as it suggests rabbis might be viewed as marginal and serving no purpose in broader society.

120 b. Shab. 110a; Meg. 5b; Yom. 19a; M. Qaṭ. 17a–b. Though he elsewhere assumed that rabbinic courts possessed enforcement power, even Neusner, "Rabbis and Community," 444–445, acknowledged that the rabbis depended on the willingness of Jews to obey them.

121 Bar Belinitzky and Yakir Paz, "Bound and Banned: Aphrahaṭ and Excommunication in the Sasanian Empire," in *Jews and Syriac Christians: Intersections across the First Millennium*, ed. Aaron M. Butts and Simcha Gross (Tübingen: 2020), 85–87.

but more plausibly reflects recourse to social pressure out of a lack of formal power or official means of enforcement.[122] Even stories that boast about the position of the rabbis in Jewish society often reflect a rather minor following.[123] There is little to suggest any kind of formal hierarchy or the existence of a structured court system, and the ad hoc nature of rabbinic courts is apparent.[124] There was no central governing body to determine rules, regulations, even basic laws, nor to disseminate them to the public at large.

A reappraisal of the sources typically used to support the normativity and formal authority of rabbinic courts in the Sasanian Empire shows that the notion of semi-autonomy was read into rather than derived from them. Two related stories, often cited as evidence of rabbinic judicial power, may in fact thematize precisely their lack of formal right to rule. In both cases, the rabbis sentence the guilty party to flogging. In response, it is reported to the empire that a rabbi "passes judgment (*dina*) without the authority of the king (*harmana d-malka*)."[125] As mentioned above, the term for authority here, *harmana*, is a Persian loanword used throughout the Talmud to refer to royal authority and edicts. These two rabbinic stories have typically been understood as referring to the limits of rabbinic judgment; the Sasanians allowed Jewish courts to rule in civil cases, but they lacked the "authority of the king (*harmana d-malka*)" to deliver corporal punishment.[126]

The continuations of both stories are, however, crucial. In one story, the rabbi flogged a man for fornicating with a non-Jew. When confronted by the government, he dissembles, both by mischaracterizing the offense of the guilty party and by offering praise of God that is misunderstood to be praise of the Sasanian king himself. As a result of the rabbi's "solicitousness for the government," the king hands him a staff (described by a Middle Persian loanword) and tells him: "You may judge cases."[127] This story appears to reflect a miraculous reversal of fortune: A rabbi with no

[122] Gideon Libson, "Determining Factors in Ḥerem and Nidui (Ban and Excommunication) during the Tannaitic and Amoraic Periods" [in Hebrew], *Annual of the Institute for Research in Jewish Law* 2 (1975): 292–342, esp. 335.

[123] b. Shab. 59b. See Pomeranz, *Ordinary Jews*, 132.

[124] E.g., b. Ket. 105a–b.

[125] b. Ber. 58a and Ta'an. 24b. A literary analysis of the former is provided by Jonah Fraenkel, "The Story of Rabbi Sheila" [in Hebrew], *Tarbiẓ* 40 (1970): 33–40. The related story in b. B. Bat. 58a is discussed below.

[126] See discussion in Mokhtarian, *Rabbis, Sorcerers, Kings, and Priests* 114–116; Neusner, *History of the Jews*, 2.32–2.34, understood it to refer to the increased supervision of Jewish law under the Sasanians, without challenging the notion of Jewish self-rule.

[127] On the loanword, see Sokoloff, *DJBA*, 991–992.

formal imperial authority to judge successfully tricks the king, not only evading punishment for arrogating authority, but now recognized as a judge by the empire. Notice also that the rabbi's newfound right to judge is here imagined as granted directly by the king and not as a feature of the rabbi's position in any Jewish hierarchy. In the other story, the flogging leads to the death of the guilty party, and the rabbi is defended by the king's mother Ifra Hormiz, who warns the king "do not have any dispute with the Jews." This is a signal perhaps that Jewish conflict resolution was outside of the immediate purview or interests of the state, but hardly evidence for an independent Jewish court system.[128] These stories do not indicate that, excepting cases of flogging, rabbis had power to rule. They instead show that corporal punishment was severe enough an arrogation of authority to rise to the attention of the Empire, which otherwise rarely interfered in local conflict resolution.[129] We will return to the Sasanian evidence for this below.

A more likely scenario is that, as in Palestine, Babylonian rabbis functioned as arbitrators. This explains the rabbinic discussion that advises Jewish judges to exempt themselves from liability by receiving the consent of both parties.[130] As in Palestine, Babylonian rabbis lacked the coercive powers of the empire or an internal Jewish hierarchy, resorting instead to mechanisms of social enforcement like the ban, or excommunication.[131] The ban was also used in the Babylonian Talmud to coerce Jews to appear before rabbinic courts and to obey their verdicts.

128 Indeed, the term for "dispute" here is Persian, and is particularly resonant as it is used in Persian texts to refer to both performative disputations before the king (Secunda, *Iranian Talmud*, 62) and legal disputes (Philippe Gignoux, "Une archive post-sassanide du Tabaristān (I)," in *Objets et documents inscrits en pārsīg*, ed. R. Gyselen. Res Orientales 21 [Bures-sur-Yvette, 2012], 34).

129 The idea that Sasanians particularly interfere in cases of corporal and capital punishment is the thematic core of a story in b. B. Qam. 117a, on which see Daniel Sperber, "The Unfortunate Adventures of Rav Kahana: A Passage of Saboraic Polemic from Sasanian Persia," in *Irano-Judaica* I, ed. Shaul Shaked (Jerusalem: 1982), 83–100. For a Palestinian story that conveys a similar theme, see y. Meg. 3.2 (74a); and Lapin, *Rabbis as Romans*, 118. Compare also Rabbula's *Admonitions* (Arthur Vööbus, *Syriac and Arabic Documents regarding Legislation Relative to Syrian Asceticism* [Stockholm: 1960], 45), where he warns not to flog (ܢܓܕ), but that instead it is indeed better to send the guilty party to "the judges of the world."

130 b. Sanh. 5a, with Gross, "Reassessing Exilarchal Authority."

131 Libson, "Determining Factors in Ḥerem and Nidui," 292–342; Belinitzky and Paz, "Bound and Banned," 84–85 (ample sources are cited here); Jason S. Mokhtarian, "Excommunication in Jewish Babylonia: Comparing Bavli Mo'ed Qatan 14b–17b and the Aramaic Bowl Spells in a Sasanian Context," *Harvard Theological Review* 108 (2015): 552–578. See the story in b. Qid. 39b that thematizes the liberality with which

Rabbis additionally deployed bans to prevent litigants from appearing before non-Jewish courts. We will see below that Syriac Christian sources deploy the ban similarly. This shared use of the ban reflects, according to Belinitzky and Paz, "a social reality in which leaders of minorities, who did not have the full enforcement apparatus of the Empire at their disposal, used the ban as one of their few means for consolidating their authority and upholding their honour."[132]

The Talmud includes diverse cases that were purportedly judged by individual rabbis. Thematically, they cover an impressive array of legal fields, spanning from ritual to civil law, with few cases of criminal law.[133] Granting, for the sake of argument, that most of these stories reflect the types of cases that might be judged by rabbis, it has been a standard assumption that they also indicate a centralized court system and official right to judge. However, while the rabbis may have been an attractive legal venue for some Jews, their capacity to rule derived from their popularity rather than from formal authority. More critically, as Lapin has noted in the case of Palestinian rabbinic case law, we cannot "assume that the cases, taken together, correspond in any simple way [to] the actual activity of Rabbis as judges."[134] With regard to Babylonia, many of the cases reported in the Talmud reflect the concerns of rabbis and their close adherents and were likely preserved or invented because they address a particularly uncertain area of rabbinic law. Outside of a highly romantic vision of a society entirely under the thrall of the rabbis, it is difficult to maintain that these laws constituted a central aspect of a standardized system of law.[135] Further work on these cases may offer insight into those areas of law that at least some Jews brought to the rabbis, but they are not dispositive of an official position occupied by the rabbis, and certainly not of Babylonian Jewish self-governance.

There is, therefore, little to support the notion of Babylonian Jewish semi-autonomy. The Exilarch did not enjoy any intercessory function or unique oversight of Jewish dispute resolution. Similarly, rabbinic courts

some rabbis deployed the ban. For physically binding a suspect until they confessed, see b. Nid. 25b and b. B. Bat. 167a.

132 Belinitzky and Paz, "Bound and Banned," 88.

133 Neusner, *History of Jews in Babylonia*, 3.272–338 (Neusner did not clearly distinguish between formal case law and rabbinic opinions, compromising the usefulness of his tabulations and percentages); Gafni, "Court Cases in the Babylonian Talmud"; Eliezer Segal, *Case Citation in the Babylonian Talmud: The Evidence of Tractate Neziqin* (Atlanta, GA: 1990).

134 Lapin, *Rabbis as Romans*, 104.

135 Similarly, Lapin, *Rabbis as Romans*, 106–107.

functioned outside of the direct purview of the empire. These results challenge our understanding not only of Babylonian Jewish society, but also of key paradigms concerning Sasanian imperial policy toward its religious communities. They demand an alternative model of Sasanian rule and legal culture that make sense of elite figures like the Exilarch and networks of non-imperial legal experts like the rabbis, outside of notions of semi-autonomy. For a fuller picture, we must compare the evidence of Jewish society with the other non-Zoroastrian Sasanian community for whom we have abundant sources, Christians.

CHRISTIAN INTERMEDIARIES AND LAW IN THE SASANIAN EMPIRE

Christians, too, were often thought to enjoy a form of semi-autonomy, consistent with Sasanian organization of its Jewish and other subject communities, a picture that is beginning to crumble.

Prior to the fifth century, we lack robust records of the undoubtedly many Christians who lived under Sasanian rule.[136] There is no evidence from this early period of a centralized hierarchy, single leader, or recognized representative. Our first consistent collection of evidence suggests that the increasing Christianization of the Roman Empire over the course of the fourth century fostered a growing anxiety among Sasanian officials toward their Christian subjects. Christians could be perceived as potential fifth columns for Rome, which triggered eruptions of imperial violence against them.[137] This period became known in Christian sources as the "Great Persecution," commemorated in the martyr acts relating the death of the bishop Simeon bar Ṣabbaʿe.[138]

However, in the year 410, the relationship between the Sasanian Empire and its Christian subjects underwent a profound transformation. The Roman Christian emissary Marutha of Maypherqaṭ, on behalf of other bishops in the Roman Near East, enjoined Yazdgird I to convene

[136] On Christians arriving in the Sasanian Empire, see Walker, "From Nisibis to Xian."

[137] Sebastian P. Brock, "Christians in the Sasanian Empire: A Case of Divided Loyalties," in *Religious and National Identity: Papers Read at the Nineteenth Summer Meeting and the Twentieth Winter Meeting of the Ecclesiastical History Society*, ed. Stuart Mews (Oxford: 1982), 1–19. For a review, see Gross, "Being Roman in the Sasanian Empire," 390–397.

[138] For the martyr acts concerning Simeon, see Smith, *Martyrdom and History*; and for the spinoffs, see Simcha Gross and Yakir Paz, *The Great Persecution: Martyrs at the Court of Shapur II* (Piscataway, NJ: forthcoming).

the bishops of his empire in the capital of Seleucia-Ctesiphon in order to establish a formal ecclesiastical hierarchy.[139] Marutha's own interest was to have Christians in the east ratify the canons of the Council of Nicaea and consolidate the bishops of the east into an ecclesiastical hierarchy parallel to that in the west. The Sasanian king appears to have viewed this as an opportunity to foster close ties of loyalty and dependency with a distrusted population.[140] That imperial patronage of Christians was an alternative to violence against them is explicit in the synod itself and in the epistles it attributes to the king.[141]

By patronizing the church hierarchy and its regular meetings under his aegis, the Sasanian king encouraged the identification of Christianity with the Sasanian Empire.[142] Upon arrival at the Synod of 410, the bishops, having gathered in the major church by order of the king, collectively thanked God and beseeched him to "add days unto the days of the victorious and illustrious king, Yazdgird the King of King."[143] These ties were to be reinforced biannually, as Canon 6 makes clear, with the synods convening in Seleucia-Ctesiphon, and only when the king was present. Like the Synod of 410, later synods would extoll the Sasanian kings for their patronage. In time, Sasanian kings would be added to the litanies to be recited during the liturgy.[144]

The Synod of 410 elevated the Catholicos as the leading figure of the East Syriac hierarchy backed by the Sasanian king. The Catholicos was to be the bishop of Seleucia-Ctesiphon, so that he remained in close proximity to the king.[145] The king ensured the position of the Catholicos and warned that "no one may be divided against them, and should anyone

[139] See Chabot, *Synodicon Orientale*, 17–23; and Ralph Marcus, "The Armenian Life of Marutha of Maipherkat," *The Harvard Theological Review* 25 (1932): 47–71.

[140] See similarly McDonough, "Bishops or Bureaucrats," 89. Royal support for Christians extended beyond the church hierarchy in the form of donations to churches, martyria, and more. See Chapter 6.

[141] Gross, "Being Roman in the Sasanian Empire," 390–397.

[142] On the notion of Yazdgird as a new Constantine, see Nina Garsoïan, "Armenia in the Fourth Century: An Attempt to Redefine the Concepts 'Armenia' and 'Loyalty,'" *Revue des Etudes Armeniennes* 8 (1971): 350–351; Scott McDonough, "A Second Constantine? The Sasanian King Yazdgard in Christian History and Historiography," *Journal of Late Antiquity* 1 (2008): 127–141.

[143] Chabot, *Synodicon Orientale*, 18.

[144] Chabot, *Synodicon Orientale*, 121; and see Brock, "Christians in the Sasanian Empire," 11.

[145] Indeed, according to John of Ephesus (*Ecclesiastical History*, 6.20), the Catholicos was regularly at the court of the king. See R. Payne Smith, trans., *The Third Part of the Ecclesiastical History of John Bishop of Ephesus* (Oxford: 1860), 418.

rise up against them and resist their will, they shall inform us, and we shall inform the King of Kings. He shall have himself to blame for the evil which will come heavily upon him, whoever he may be." The Catholicos' position was enforced not only by the anathema of the bishops, but, as the seventeenth canon makes clear, by the King of Kings himself. The Catholicos' power, which was contested by competing bishops several times over the course of Sasanian history, rested on the king's support, making him more pliable to the king's will. The king was often actively involved in the selection and approval of Catholicoi, and the Church experienced acephalous periods as a result of royal disapproval of the Catholicos selected by the bishops.[146] Subsequent synods were no less dependent on the king's support, who again legitimated the canons they produced.[147]

The Catholicos therefore clearly enjoyed an elevated position as part of a centralized Church hierarchy supported by the state. Yet the Catholicos was not recognized as part of a general Sasanian policy of semi-autonomy for its subject communities; otherwise, he would have been recognized long before the early fifth century, when many Christians were already living under Sasanian rule. His position instead emerged out of Sasanian anxieties over potential Christian disloyalty. The group-specific circumstances that generated the East Syriac ecclesiastical hierarchy are also clear from the fact that it was overtly modeled on its western counterpart.[148] It was, after all, western bishops who sent Yazdgird the letter, and who sought to bring the eastern churches into conformity with western Christian canons and creed. The Catholicos' elevated position parallels the elevated position of the Christian patriarch in the west. Sasanian support for the establishment of the church hierarchy was not part of a comprehensive imperial policy, but was a response to particular concerns triggered by the empire's Christian subjects.[149]

[146] See Nasir al-Kaʿbi, *A Short Chronicle on the End of the Sasanian Empire and Early Islam* (Piscataway, NJ: 2016), 16.

[147] For instance, in 497 CE a synod was convened by the order of King Jamasp, and a letter read out to the bishops in attendance reforming marriage practices such that all Christians – bishops and priests included – must eschew celibacy and take wives. Chabot, *Synodicon Orientale*, 62–68.

[148] Stephen Gerö, "The See of Peter in Babylon: Western Influences on the Ecclesiology of Early Persian Christianity," in *East of Byzantium: Syria and Armenia in the Formative Period*, ed. Nina G. Garsoïan, Thomas F. Mathews, and Robert W. Thomson (Dumbarton Oaks: 1982), 45–51.

[149] Questions about the precise nature of the Zoroastrian hierarchy and its relationship to the state are also unclear. See Rubin, "Persia and the Sasanian Monarchy," 140–144;

Even in this elevated position, however, there is little to support the notion of the Catholicos' role in Christian self-governance, or that the ecclesiastical figures were officially tasked with governing the empire's Christians. Like the Exilarch and rabbis, civil legislation was not among the official functions of the East Syriac ecclesiastical hierarchy.[150] Over the course of the Sasanian period, the Church sought to regulate a select few areas of law, especially marriage and inheritance.[151] Although scholars have had a tendency to inflate even this narrow engagement into a full-fledged officially recognized legal system, there is little to commend the notions that ecclesiastical legislation extended beyond these legal domains or that the Sasanian Empire authorized their enforcement.[152] Indeed, to the contrary; the church's interest in marriage emerged decades after the establishment of a church hierarchy in the east, out of a particular concern that members of its community, according to the Synod of 484, "imitate the Magians in impure marriage ... and violate the law of the Church of Christ."[153] In the mid-sixth century, the Catholicos Mar Aba embarked on an extensive campaign to proscribe and mark as un-Christian the close-kin marriages that were permitted and even encouraged by Sasanian and Zoroastrian law, one of the causes of imperial prosecution against him.[154] Even the church's interest in regulating these narrow areas of law should not be mistaken for a reality in which they had the power to enforce their prescriptions.

Christian sources themselves reflect the local and contested nature of Christian forays into civil law, as Richard Payne has recently shown.

Schippmann, *Grundzüge*, 92–102; and Philippe Gignoux, "Church-State Relations in the Sasanian Period," in *Monarchies and Socio-Religious Traditions in the Ancient Near East*, ed. H. I. H. Prince T. Mikasa (Weisbaden: 1984), 72–80.

150 Compare Christian litigation under Roman rule until after Constantine's reign, for instance in Caroline Humfress, *Orthodoxy and the Courts in Late Antiquity* (Oxford: 2007), 153–165.

151 For a helpful overview, see Nima Jamali, *A Study of the Interactions among Zoroastrian, Jewish and Roman Legal Systems during the 7th and 8th Centuries CE Based on a Critical Edition of Īšō'-boḵt's Corpus Juris with Commentary and an English Translation* (PhD diss., University of Toronto, 2021), 14–60; and Amir Harrak, *The Law Code of Išō'yahb I, Patriarch of the Church of the East* (Piscataway, NJ: 2022).

152 For former views, see Michael Morony, "Religious Communities in Late Sasanian and Early Muslim Iraq," *Journal of the Economic and Social History of the Orient* 17 (1974): 113–135.

153 Chabot, *Synodicon Orientale*, 623–624.

154 Payne, *State of Mixture*, 108–117; Manfred Hutter, "Mār Abā and the Impact of Zoroastrianism on Christianity in the 6th Century," in *Religious Themes and Texts of Pre-Islamic Iran and Central Asia*, ed. Carlo Cereti, Mauro Maggi, and Elio Provasi (Wiesbaden: 2003), 167–173; and Lev Weitz, *Between Christ and Caliph*, 145–171.

A particular telling example is the *History of Mar Aba*, a text which describes the accusations against Mar Aba by a high-ranking Zoroastrian *mowbed*, or priest:[155]

> He [Mar Aba] summoned away from the house of judgment many Christians who had judicial disputes with one another [resolved by] a document of acquittal [*bōxtnāmag*] with the seal of the *mowbedān mowbed*, and he broke the document of acquittal. He judges all the judicial disputes we should judge, and we suffer much violence from him.[156]

According to the *mowbed*, Mar Aba both contradicted the verdicts of the Zoroastrian high priest and improperly drew Christians away from judicial disputes under the *mowbed*'s authority.[157] Indeed, the *History of Mar Aba* earlier describes how "From four in the afternoon until the evening, [Mar Aba was occupied with] judging cases and resolving conflicts between the faithful and one another, and between pagans and the faithful."[158] In response to these attacks, Mar Aba does not argue that Christians have legal autonomy, or that they enjoy broad rights over intracommunal litigation. Instead, he downplays his involvement in the judicial process and limits the nature of his authority: "I am not commanded by the divine scriptures to restrain or strike anyone or to confiscate anything of his, but rather we pray and beseech God concerning those who err to return to true knowledge."[159] The *History of Mar Aba* makes clear that Mar Aba's forays into dispute resolution functioned outside of the formal channels of Sasanian law.[160]

Certainly, there is evidence of Christian courts. But these should be understood, as Payne notes, as "just one element of a society with

155 Payne, *State of Mixture*, 104–108.

156 *History of Mar Aba* in Bedjan, *Histoire de Mar-Jabalaha*, 234, and Florence Jullien, *Histoire de Mār Abba, catholicos de l'Orient; Martyres de Mār Grigor, général en chef du roi Khusro Ier et, de Mār Yazd-panāh, juge et Gouverneur*, vol. 1 (Louvain: 2015), 18.

157 On the term *bōxtnāmag*, see Shaul Shaked, "Some Legal and Administrative Terms of the Sasanian Period," in vol. 2, *Monumentum H. S. Nyberg* (Leiden: 1975), 216–217; and Maria Macuch, "Jewish Jurisdiction within the Framework of the Sasanian Legal System," in *Encounters by the Rivers of Babylon: Scholarly Conversations between Jews, Iranians and Babylonians in Antiquity*, ed. Uri Gabbay and Shai Secunda (Tübingen: 2014), 158.

158 *History of Mar Aba* (Bedjan, *Histoire de Mar-Jabalaha*, 226; Jullien, *Histoire de Mār Abba*, vol. 1, 13–14).

159 *History of Mar Aba* (Bedjan, *Histoire de Mar-Jabalaha*, 232; Jullien, *Histoire de Mār Abba*, vol. 1, 17).

160 On Mar Aba, see Manfried Hutter, "Mār Abā and the Impact of Zoroastrianism," 167–173; and Macuch, "The Case against Mār Abā," 47–58.

multiple sources of judicial authority," participating "in a broader legal culture rather than creating autonomous, rival courts."[161] These courts were not elements in a centralized system but were predominately local courts of voluntary arbitration. Thus, Sabrisho is praised for bringing "upright laws and just verdicts" to Lashom, thereby rendering it "a city of holiness and faith."[162] Similarly, the canons of the School of Nisibis seek to regulate disputes between its members, but in a revealing way. They rule that "a brother who has a contention with his companion or against someone else, shall not go to the court of the outsiders of his will without permission of the brothers and the steward."[163] Even here, the canons simply seek consensus before appealing to outsiders to resolve disputes they consider internal to the community. Two Christian synods similarly caution "a cleric or a monk who has a charge against a lay person" from turning "voluntarily and under no coercion ... to the tribunals of the outsiders (*barrāyē*)."[164]

This type of local Christian legislation appears to be evidenced already in Aphrahat's decidedly polemical *Demonstration* 14, dated to 344 CE.[165] The *Demonstration* rails against the elite church officials in Seleucia-Ctesiphon, and especially the bishop, for seeking their own elevation through corrupt means, such as the improper exercise of social enforcement. They "pervert justice," "declare innocent the guilty, and condemn the innocent," and appear to have been particularly eager to receive bribes. They impose bans and excommunicate without justification, just "as if to say, 'I am powerful!'"[166] They are interested in the

[161] Payne, *State of Mixture*, 107. [162] Bedjan, *Histoire de Mar Jabalaha*, 300.

[163] Arthur Vööbus, *Statutes of the School of Nisibis* (Stockholm: 1961), 80 (no. 12), 83–84 (no. 20) may allude to the court of the school itself.

[164] Chabot, *Synodicon Orientale*, 623; compare with Chabot, 117, 376. For discussion, see Uriel Simonsohn, "Seeking Justice among the 'Outsiders': Christian Recourse to Non-Ecclesiastical Judicial Systems under Early Islam," *Church History and Religious Culture* 89 (2009): 191–216, esp. 202.

[165] On the question of the authorship and dating of this *Demonstration*, see discussion in Alberto Camplani, "L'Esposizione XIV di Afraate: una retorica antiautoritaria nel contesto dell'evoluzione istituzionale della Chiesa siriaca," in *Storia e pensiero religioso nel Vicino Oriente: L'età bagratide – Maimonide – Afraate*, ed. C. Baffioni, R. Bianchi Finazzi, A. Passoni Dell'Acqua, and E. Vergani (Milan, Rome: 2014), 191–235. On questions pertaining to the authorship of the *Demonstrations* as a whole, see James Walters, "Reconsidering the Compositional Unity of Aphrahat's Demonstrations," in *Syriac Christian Culture: Beginnings to Renaissance*, ed. Aaron Michael Butts and Robin Darling Young (Washington, DC: 2020), 50–64.

[166] *Demonstration* 14.3, 7 in Parisot, *Aphraatis Sapientis Persae*, 577–582, 587–588. See Belinitzky and Paz, "Bound and Banned," 67–88.

pursuit of self-enrichment and social advancement. There is no indication that these figures serve at the behest of the empire. Intriguingly, later in the *Demonstration*, Aphrahat analogizes the relationship between God and his "stewards" the priests, to that of a king and his "prison wardens, prosecutors, and executioners," who have the right to place people in "chains, prisons, and fetters," and who use this power to excommunicate "anyone who offends them."[167] Like the rabbis, Christian judges enforced their rulings through social pressures and excommunication, not through the mechanism of an independent judicial system.

It is mainly in the post-Sasanian period that civil law is perceived by some Christian figures to fall more fully under the purview of the church.[168] This is first articulated in the Synod of 676, where it is ruled that "judgment for Christians ... should be [performed] in the church before the presence of those designated by the Bishop with the consensus of the community, by priests and the faithful, and ... they should not go outside the church to receive judgment, neither before pagans nor the unfaithful."[169] By the eighth century, a number of Christian codes of civil law appear.[170] The East Syriac cleric Isho'bokht composed the *Maktbānutā d-'al Dinē* ("A Treatise concerning Judgments"), a comprehensive overview of Christian civil law, and a shorter treatise on inheritance law is ascribed to Simeon of Rev-Ardashir.[171] Yet these do not reflect the consolidation of centuries of Christian civil law; instead, they are

[167] Aphrahat, *Demonstration* 14.44, with Adam Lehto, *The Demonstrations of Aphrahat, the Persian Sage* (Piscataway, NJ: 2010), 353–354.

[168] Payne, *State of Mixture*, 107. For an overview of East Syriac law, Hubert Kaufhold, "Sources of Canon Law in the Eastern Churches," in *The History of Byzantine and Eastern Canon Law to 1500*, ed. W. Hartmann and K. Pennington (Washington, DC: 2012), 295–313.

[169] Chabot, *Synodicon Orientale*, 219–220. Compare with Amir Harrak, *The Law Code of Simeon, Bishop of Rev-Ardashir* (Piscataway, NJ: 2020), 42–43 for the prohibition of taking a fellow Christian to a non-Christian court.

[170] Around the sixth century, the *Syro-Roman Lawbook* was translated into Syriac. For edition and German translation, see Walter Selb and Hubert Kaufhold, *Das syrisch-römische Rechtsbuch*, 3 vols. (Vienna: 2002). For an English translation, see Arthur Vööbus, *The Syro-Roman Lawbook: the Syriac Text of the Recently Discovered Manuscripts Accompanied by a Facsimile Edition and Furnished with an Introduction and Translation* (Stockholm: 1982). For the earliest dated Syriac version, see Sebastian Brock and Lucas van Rompay, *Catalogue of the Syriac Manuscripts and Fragments in the Library of Deir al-Surian, Wadi al-Natrun (Egypt)* (Leuven: 2014), 377–379.

[171] For the former, see Sachau, *Syrische Rechtsbücher* (Berlin: 1914), 3.2–201; and Jamali, *A Study of the Interactions*. It was originally composed in Middle Persian but survives only in Syriac translation replete with Persian loanwords. For the latter, see Sachau, *Syrische Rechtsbücher*, 3.207–253, and Harrak, *The Law Code of Simeon*.

replete with Iranian laws and legal technical terms, and in fact offer some of our best evidence for Sasanian law.[172] These works are ambitious attempts by post-Islamic Christians to expand the scope of church authority and legislation with little preceding Christian material to draw from, in part by coopting the legal rules that were once solely the remit of Sasanian officials.[173]

SASANIAN LEGAL CULTURE

If neither Jewish nor Christian sources support the existence of a Sasanian policy to grant religious communities semi-autonomy, Sasanian sources themselves reflect a well-defined imperial system of law that was intended to apply to all its inhabitants, though not equally, even as it made space for local forms of conflict resolution.[174]

Judging from the main source of Sasanian law, the *Book of a Thousand Judgments* (*MHD*), Sasanian law was broadly applicable to all of its subjects.[175] As such, the law enforced by the empire was not exclusively predicated on Zoroastrianism. *MHD* makes "no reference to any theological, dogmatic, ritual, or moral questions whatsoever," as Macuch notes.[176] The cases in the *MHD* address matters of family, property, procedural, and criminal law, but the work as a whole "does not discuss a single case relating to religious matters."[177] This is not to say the laws were entirely independent of Zoroastrian concerns; family law in *MHD*, in particular, is heavily informed by Zoroastrian notions of

[172] For more on these works, see Simonsohn, *Common Justice*, 99–112; Maria Macuch, "Ein mittelpersischer terminus technicus im syrischen Rechtsbuch des Īšōʿbōḫt und im sasanidischen Rechtsbuch," in *Studia Semitica necnon Iranica Rudolpho Macuch septuagenario ab amicis et discipulis dedicata*, ed. Maria Macuch, Christa Müller, and Bert Fragner (Wiesbaden: 1989), 149–160; Harrak, *The Law Code of Simeon*; and Jamali, *A Study of the Interactions.*

[173] Weitz, *Between Christ and Caliph*, 33–34.

[174] For synthetic overview of legal hierarchy and procedure, see Maria Macuch, *Das Sasanidische Rechtsbuch "Mātakdān i Hazār Dātistān,"* vol. 2 (Wiesbaden: 1981), 13–20; Mathieu Tillier, *L'invention du cadi: La justice des musulmans, des juifs et des chrétiens aux premiers siècles de l'Islam* (Paris: 2017), 385–400.

[175] On *MHD*, see Macuch, "Pahlavi Literature," 188.

[176] Maria Macuch, "Jewish Jurisdiction within the Framework of the Sasanian Legal System," in *Encounters by the Rivers of Babylon: Scholarly Conversations between Jews, Iranians and Babylonians in Antiquity*, ed. Uri Gabbay and Shai Secunda (Tübingen: 2014), 151.

[177] Macuch, "Jewish Jurisdiction," 151.

kinship.[178] But participation in the judicial system was not limited to Zoroastrians.

Nevertheless, Sasanian law recognized and reinforced a fundamental distinction between Iranians and "adherents of the good tradition" (*ērān* and *weh-dēnān*, respectively) on the one hand, and non-Iranians and "adherents of the bad tradition" (*an-ērān* and *ag-dēnān*, respectively) on the other; distinctions we will return to throughout the book.[179] These latter terms of otherness are not clearly defined, and at different points in Middle Persian literature refer to apostate Zoroastrians, non-Iranians, and non-Zoroastrians, or all of these simultaneously. Whatever these terms meant in any instance, this fundamental distinction informed Sasanian law.

In *MHD*, non-Iranians and "adherents of the bad tradition" were circumscribed in legal matters that impinged on Iranian identity.[180] For instance, a slave belonging to a Christian who became "an adherent of the good tradition" was automatically manumitted, although he owed financial remuneration to his former master.[181] Similarly, it was forbidden to

[178] Macuch, "Zoroastrian Principles and the Structure of Kinship in Sasanian Iran," in *Religious Themes and Texts of Pre-Islamic Iran and Central Asia*, ed. C. Cereti, Mauro Maggi, and Elio Provasi (Wiesbaden: 2003), 231–246.

[179] Shaked, "Religion in the Late Sasanian Period"; Maria Macuch, "Legal Constructions of Identity in the Sasanian Period," in *Iranian Identity in the Course of History*, ed. Carlo Cereti (Rome: 2010), 61; de Jong, "Zoroastrian Religious Polemics," 61; de Jong, "Zoroastrian Self-Definition," 21; and Jason Sion Mokhtarian, "The Boundaries of an Infidel in Zoroastrianism: A Middle Persian Term of Otherness for Jews, Christians, and Muslims," *Iranian Studies* 48 (2015): 99–115. For particularly acute cases of terminological blurring, see *Dādestān ī Dēnīg* 40.1–40.2 in Mohmoud Jaafari-Dehaghi, ed. and trans., *Dādestān ī Dēnīg: Part I, Transcription, Translation and Commentary* (Paris: 1998); F. M. Kotwal and P. G. Kreyenbroek, *The Hērbedestān and Nērangestān*, vol. 1 (Paris: 1992), 64–65. The categories are distinguished but serve the similar function of marking alterity in *Dēnkard* 3.140.1–140.6, on which see Philippe Gignoux, *Man and Cosmos in Ancient Iran* (Rome: 2001), 98. On the problematic translation of the word *dēn*, see Prods Oktor Skjaervø, "The Zoroastrian Oral Tradition as Reflected in the Texts," in *The Transmission of the Avesta*, ed. Alberto Cantera (Wiesbaden: 2012), 3–48 (esp. 20–25); and Yuhan S.-D. Vevaina, "'Enumerating the Dēn': Textual Taxonomies, Cosmological Deixis, and Numerological Speculations in Zoroastrianism," *History of Religions* 50 (2010): 111–143.

[180] Macuch, "Jewish Jurisdiction," 148–149. Mokhtarian, *Rabbis, Sorcerers, Kings, and Priests*, 99–106; and Mokhtarian, "Boundaries of an Infidel." For a case of an *an-ēr* who is a *weh-dēn*, see Rivāyat of Adurfarnbag 139 in Shai Secunda, *The Talmud's Red Fence: Menstrual Impurity and Religious Difference in Babylonian Judaism and Its Sasanian Context* (Oxford: 2020), 150.

[181] Perikhanian, *Book of a Thousand Judgments*, 28–29; Macuch, *Rechtskasuistic*, 22–25. Similar legislation is found in Kotwal and Kreyenbroek, *Hērbedestān and Nērangestān*, 60–61. For similar legislation in the Byzantine Empire related to Jewish slaves who

sell a slave to an "adherent of the bad tradition" (*ag-dēnān*), and in case of violation, both buyer and seller were branded.[182] Most interestingly, according to *MHD*, "adherents of the bad tradition" could not serve as substitute successors (*stūr*) to a deceased "adherent of the good tradition," an institution whose function was to produce a male heir to the sonless deceased.[183] Appointing an "adherent of the bad tradition" as substitute successor would imperil the Iranian identity of the family unit, and the legacy of the deceased believer. Further, *MHD* rules that a son who was an "adherent of the bad tradition" was exempt from the debts of his father, a financial benefit that nevertheless indicated that the son had severed his connection with his family. The law, however, hastens to add that "all other decisions concerning them (i.e., 'adherents of the bad tradition') are the same as those regarding adherents of the good tradition (*weh-dēnān*)."[184] Other references in *MHD* to adherents of the bad tradition similarly affirm their equal status under the law, an affirmation that paradoxically signals their alterity.[185] The division between these opposing groups was maintained and reinforced through specific laws intended to demarcate and reify the boundaries between them.[186] Additional Iranian sources note that non-Iranians could litigate against Iranians in court and detail a number of cases wherein Iranians must obey

converted to Christianity, see Linder, *The Jews in Roman Imperial Legislation*, nos. 11, 44, 59, 61, and discussion on 82–85. This is the only law in *MHD* to explicitly mention Christians; for other Zoroastrian texts on Christians, see Mokhtarian, "Boundaries of an Infidel," 102–103 and n14 there. On conversion of, apparently, Christians to Zoroastrianism, and the restrictions and protections placed on their wives, see Macuch, "The Hērbedestān as a Legal Source: A Section on the Inheritance of a Convert to Zoroastrianism," *Bulletin of the Asia Institute* 19 (2005): 92–93. On the value of converts in Zoroastrian literature, see Kotwal and Kreyenbroek, *Hērbedestān and Nērangestān*, 63–65; and Mokhtarian, "Boundaries of an Infidel," 105–107.

182 Perikhanian, *Book of a Thousand Judgments*, 28–29.

183 Macuch, "Legal Constructions of Identity," 202–203; Perikhanian, *Book of a Thousand Judgments*, 154–155; Simonsohn, *Common Justice*, 48; and Richard Payne, "East Syrian Bishops, Elite Households, and Iranian Law after the Muslim Conquest," *Iranian Studies* 48 (2015): 5–32.

184 Macuch, *Rechtskasuistik*, 409 (transliteration), 415 (translation), 425–426 (commentary).

185 It is worth noting that there may well be attitudinal and practical differences between how Sasanian versus Zoroastrian sources view non-Iranians/adherents of the bad tradition. On issues of intercourse and intermarriage, see de Jong, "Zoroastrian Religious Polemics," 54–56. For an example of the reduced legal status of non-Iranians in a Zoroastrian source, see Kotwal and Kreyenbroek, *Hērbedestān and Nērangestān*, 64–65. Similarly, according to the *Dēnkard* 8.20.29, non-Iranians are not admissible as witnesses. See Macuch, "Legal Constructions of Identity," 199–200.

186 Macuch, "Legal Constructions of Identity"; Mokhtarian, "Boundaries of an Infidel."

contracts with non-Iranians even to the detriment of fellow Iranians.[187] Sasanian law was therefore conceptualized as applying broadly to all subjects, yet simultaneously intended to protect and enshrine the distinctiveness of Iranians.

No Sasanian or Zoroastrian source ever acknowledges separate spheres of legal autonomy for particular communities, religious or other.[188] These sources do, however, reflect the availability within Sasanian law of different means of legal resolution. These included forms of arbitration with the consent of the litigants. Thus, the ninth-century encyclopedic Zoroastrian compilation known as the *Dēnkard* lists different means of dispute resolution, which included typical judicial disputes before a state-sanctioned judge, but also disputes in the presence of one's "own judge," a dispute held before three "good/righteous/Zoroastrian men," and a dispute before witnesses, who presumably would serve as arbitrators.[189] Some cases in *MHD* are similarly predicated on forms of arbitration.[190] Both Iranians and non-Iranians therefore had multiple legal venues open to them, from the formal courts of the empire to more local forms of arbitration. By making space for arbitration, the empire created the necessary conditions for various kinds of social collectivities to practice their laws "to a certain degree as long as they did not interfere with the law of the Sasanian state and offend the norms set in Zoroastrian society."[191]

Far from being unusual, the possibility of legal resolution on the local level outside the strict confines of the state prevailed throughout the ancient world, where arbiters and local forms of communal dispute resolution thrived alongside formal imperial courts.[192] Sasanian law similarly applied to its various inhabitants, and at no point formally

[187] Macuch, "Legal Constructions of Identity," 200–203.

[188] Shaked, "Religion in the Late Sasanian period," 104n7, incorrectly describes a text as encouraging kings to include leaders of various religions as part of his court. The text appears to refer to non-conforming Zoroastrians.

[189] *Dēnkard* 8.16.6, with Macuch, "Jewish Jurisdiction," 155–157. References to the *Dēnkard* follows the outline in E. W. West, *Sacred Books of the East: Pahlavi Texts*, Part IV (Oxford: 1892). For an attempted reconstruction of procedures of Sasanian imperial courts, see Janos Jany, "Sasanian Law," *e-Sasanika* 9 (2011): 1–33; and Janos Jany, *Judging in the Islamic, Jewish, and Zoroastrian Legal Traditions* (Farnham: 2012).

[190] Macuch, *Das Sasanidische Rechtsbuch*, vol. 2, 14; Macuch, "A Zoroastrian Legal Term in the Dēnkard: Pahikār-Rad," in *La période ancienne*, ed. Philip Huyse, vol. 1, *Iran: Questions et connaissances*. Studia Iranica 25 (Paris: 2002), 77–90.

[191] Macuch, "Jewish Jurisdiction," 150.

[192] The literature is ever-growing. In general, see Peter Brown, *The World of Late Antiquity, From Marcus Aurelius to Muhammad* (London: 1971), 90–99; Simonsohn, *Common*

recognized or authorized a parallel system of adjudication only applicable to particular communities. But Sasanian rule also created space for individuals and groups to resolve disputes legitimately outside of the strict confines of imperial courts. We may speculate that the decisions of an arbitration court could be enforced by imperial courts, but this is nowhere stated explicitly.[193] Local courts did not act with impunity, but rather functioned within certain circumscribed parameters, which explains those rabbinic stories discussed above in which rabbis were pursued by the empire for enacting corporal or capital punishment. These local courts also had to maintain certain standards and adhere to recognizable legal procedures, as indicated by a related story in which a rabbi is brought to the attention of the empire for ruling "without witnesses [most manuscripts continue: and without legal documents]."[194] Other means of conflict resolution were, it seems, ultimately appealable to the empire's courts themselves.

This environment of overlapping mechanisms of legal recourse created the conditions for litigants to pursue what legal scholars call "forum shopping," selecting between the menu of available venues of conflict resolution.[195] Local courts of arbitration, in turn, discouraged their potential litigants from appealing to the imperial court system, and made the case for their superiority as means of resolution on religious, social, or other grounds. Christians established local judges to resolve disputes while discouraging their followers from availing themselves of the courts of "outsiders."[196] Some Christian judges apparently mimicked Iranian laws in their rulings, while others sought to create a stark difference between imperial and Christian forms of resolution. Thus, the Synod of 540 condemns a bishop like Abraham of Bet Lapaṭ for mixing the law of

Justice, 1–62; and Traianos Gagos and Peter van Minnen, *Settling a Dispute: Towards a Legal Anthropology of Late Antique Egypt* (Ann Arbor, MI: 1994), 30–47.

193 Such a situation concerning Jewish law is explicit in Roman legislation. See Linder, *Jews in Roman Imperial Legislation*, 204–211; Alfredo Mordechai Rabello, "Civil Jewish Jurisdiction in the Days of Emperor Justinian (527–565): Codex Justinianus 1.9.8.," *Israel Law Review* 33 (1999): 51–66. For Palestinian rabbis and Roman law, see Martin Goodman, *State and Society in Roman Galilee* (Totowa, NJ: 1983), 155–171; and Lapin, *Rabbis as Romans*, 98–125.

194 b. B. Bat. 58a.

195 Caroline Humfress, "Thinking through Legal Pluralism: 'Forum shopping' in the Later Roman Empire," in *Law and Empire: Ideas, Practices, Actors*, ed. Jeroen Duindam, Jill Harries, Caroline Humfress, and Nimrod Hurvitz (Leiden: 2014), 223–250.

196 E.g., Chabot, *Synodicon Orientale*, 155, 415.

the outsiders (*barrāyē*) with the law of the Church.[197] Theodoret of Cyrrhus describes Jacob of Nisibis' confrontation with a Persian judge, whose unjust verdict he repudiates by cursing a boulder and shattering it into thousands of pieces, leading the judge to revoke his ruling.[198] *The History of Mar Aba* describes Mar Aba's success at luring Christians away from imperial courts, much to the dismay of the magi. It also describes how imperial acquittals might be overturned by Christian judges, setting up direct confrontation between the two legal systems. Christian sources evince local forms of dispute resolution coexisting and competing with formal imperial courts.

The Babylonian Talmud reflects similar dynamics between Jewish and imperial means of resolution. Despite rabbinic literature's tendency to present an idealized image of the place of the rabbis in Jewish society, it provides evidence that Jews too took advantage of the broader Sasanian environment of legal pluralism and forum shopping.[199] Jews had access to non-Jewish courts, which the rabbis often sought to curb, precisely as Church synods and the School of Nisibis threaten those who bring cases to "outsiders." For instance, in one story, rabbis impose a ban on those who resort to the "guard" (פהרגבנא, from Middle Iranian *pāhrag-bān**) of the king to resolve an inter-Jewish dispute over the ownership of a moveable object.[200] Other stories feature Jews reporting other Jews to non-Jewish administrators, although the precise circumstances are unclear.[201]

In one stunning passage, the rabbis distinguish between different kinds of Sasanian courts. It is reported that Palestinian rabbis ruled that a Jew who offers uncoerced testimony in a non-Jewish court against a fellow Jew is to be placed under a ban.[202] An anonymous discussion in the Babylonian Talmud qualifies this principle.

> This holds good if only one witness was concerned but not where there were two. And even to one witness it applies only if he appeared before the court of the

[197] Chabot, *Synodicon Orientale*, 77, 329.

[198] R. M. Price, trans. *History of the Monks of Syria by Theodoret, Bishop of Cyrrhus* (Kalamazoo, MI: 1985), 14–15.

[199] We unfortunately lack the kind of data that we have for Rome in terms of the factors that made various avenues of dispute adjudication more or less appealing, such as relative cost (Simonsohn, *Common Justice*, 29), although in several places in the Talmud Sasanian officials are depicted as bribable (e.g., b. Giṭ. 28b; see also b. Yeb. 63b and b. Ḥag. 5a–b).

[200] b. B. Qam. 117a; cf. b. B. Qam. 113b–114a.

[201] b. B. Qam. 117a–b.

[202] b. B. Qam. 113b–114a.

megista, but not before the court of the *dawār* where they similarly impose an oath upon the evidence of a single witness.[203]

The anonymous discussion first argues that a Jew may in fact testify in a non-Jewish court if a second witness is also involved. It continues to argue that even one Jewish witness may offer uncoerced testimony in the case of a non-Jewish court of the *dawār*, because the court imposes an oath on the witness. However, Jews may not offer testimony in the case of the court of the *megista*, because they do not impose an oath.

As several scholars have argued, *dawār* is most likely to be identified with the Middle Persian *dādwar*, literally a "bearer of law," or judge.[204] As Maria Macuch notes, *MHD* lists "four types of judges with the title dādwar" who were "state officials engaged in the daily work of the courts."[205] The Talmud's anonymous discussion therefore qualified the earlier Palestinian ruling to allow for Jews to serve as voluntary witnesses in these Sasanian courts, reflecting the fact that Jews did make use of them, and that even the rabbis, perhaps begrudgingly, acknowledged that they followed legitimate legal procedures. The court of the *dawār* appears in two other places in the Talmud, and there too reflect the fact that Jews had recourse to them. One source advises that a Jew may excuse himself to a non-Jew by saying "I have an appointment at the court of the *dawār*"; in another, the expectation is that if a Jew wanted to contest the legal action of a non-Jew, they would appeal to the *dawār*.[206]

The *megista*, by contrast, is a different type of non-Jewish court, one with allegedly lower evidentiary standards.[207] Many etymologies have been offered for *megista*, but none are definitive or without problems. Spicehandler suggested that *megista* is simply another form of, or related to the word for magian, such that the rabbis are distinguishing between official imperial courts on the one hand (*dawār*) and arbitration courts

[203] b. B. Qam. 113b–114a. Translation based on MS Escorial.

[204] The various interpretations have been discussed extensively in Ezra Spicehandler, "בי דואר and דמגיסתא דינא: Notes on Gentile Courts in Talmudic Babylonia," *Hebrew Union College Annual* 26 (1955): 333–354. Compare with Shaked, "Notes on the Pahlavi Amulet and Sasanian Courts of Law," *Bulletin of the Asia Institute* (1993): 168–169; and Ciancaglini, *Iranian Loanwords in Syriac*, 221. Simonsohn, *Common Justice*, 46 suggests that *be dawār* was "a direct extension to the Sasanian judicial apparatus," whereas the *be megista*, which "operated in the countryside," was "administered by lay figures," an explanation whose basis is unclear to me.

[205] Macuch, "Jewish Jurisdiction," 154.

[206] b. ʿAbod. Zar. 26a; Giṭ. 58b.

[207] It also appears in b. B. Meṣ. 30b, where it is incredulously juxtaposed with "Torah law (דין תורה)." For a discussion of manuscript variants here, see Spicehandler, "Notes on Gentiles Courts," 344–345.

run by magi on the other (*megista*). Support for Spicehandler's identification of *megista* with magi comes from a talmudic discussion in which a rabbi suggests the temple was destroyed because of judgments that adhered only to biblical law, to which an anonymous comment incredulously retorts "were they to follow the law of *megista*?!" If this source does indeed refer to the courts of the magi, the rabbis are acknowledging and seeking to circumscribe Jewish access to the Sasanian legal marketplace, permitting imperial courts (*dawār*), but disavowing forms of Zoroastrian arbitration (*megista*).[208] The *megista* may have met rabbinic disapproval because of its overtly Zoroastrian legal bases, which is evidenced in a recently published Manichaean text depicting a Zoroastrian judge ruling outside of a fire temple, in which the fire is referred to explicitly to authorize the judge's pronouncements.[209] Although the rabbis here discredit Zoroastrian forms of arbitration on procedural grounds – namely, admitting too few witnesses or not requiring an oath – these may be pretexts to deprecate the overtly Zoroastrian nature of the judgment which provoked rabbinic disapproval.[210]

Given that Jewish litigants had regular access to imperial courts, it is hardly surprising that the Babylonian Talmud reflects familiarity with Sasanian legal terminology and court procedure. The Talmud includes legal discussions concerning Sasanian court documents and the proper use of seals to validate documents.[211] It also discusses the validity of

208 This may be the setting to which Agathias (2.26.5) refers to when he reports that Persians insist that even a "private dispute" must be presided over by the magi. See Joseph Frendo, *Agathias: The Histories* (Berlin: 1975), 61.

209 The Chester Beatty Kephalaia Codex chapter 326 (ed. and trans. Iain Gardner, Jason BeDuhn, and Paul C. Dilley, *The Chapters of the Wisdom of My Lord Mani* [Leiden: 2018], 36–49). Certainly, there were procedural differences between approved forms of conflict resolution; see Macuch, "Jewish Jurisdiction," 155–156.

210 The rabbis were also disdainful of Iranian officials who appear to have been enforcers of court decisions. See b. Shab. 139a; Sanh. 98a; b. Taʿan. 20a; Mokhtarian, *Rabbis, Sorcerers, Kings, and Priests*, 116–120; and Ciancaglini, *Iranian Loanwords in Syriac*, 143. An opaque reference in b. Giṭ. 11a to a document produced in the "assembly of Aramaeans" may also show that Jews approached other local communal courts, which in this case as well, a rabbi rules to be invalid. See Sokoloff, *DJBA*, 575. Compare this assembly of Aramaeans with the report in Amir Harrak, ed., *The Acts of Mār Mārī the Apostle* (Atlanta, GA: 2005), 42ff, and discussion in xxii–xxvi.

211 b. Giṭ. 28b. See Macuch, *Rechtskasuistik*, 727–730; Maria Macuch, "Iranian Legal Terminology in the Babylonian Talmud in the Light of Sassanian Jurisprudence," *Iran-Judaica* IV, ed. Shaul Shaked and Amnon Netzer (Jerusalem: 1999), 91–101; and Maria Macuch, "Allusions to Sasanian Law in the Babylonian Talmud," in *The Talmud in Its Iranian Context*, ed. Carol Bakhos and M. Rahim Shayegan (Tübingen: 2010),

Persian documents composed in non-Jewish courts and used by Jews.[212] Other passages accurately describe differences between Jewish and Sasanian law.[213] Technical Sasanian legal terms are deployed in discussions of Jewish law without any reference to Sasanian law itself, reflecting the internalization of legal concepts to which the rabbis, like other Jews, were regularly exposed.[214]

In one passage, an Exilarch relates several Sasanian laws:[215]

> Rabbah said: These three matters were told to me by ʿUkba b. Nehemiah the Exilarch in the name of Shmuel: the law of the kingdom is law; Persians acquire ownership (*dārišn*) by forty years' occupation; and rich landlords who buy up land and pay the tax on it, the sale is valid.

According to this passage, the Exilarch maintained that the law of the kingdom is binding, a well-known saying to be discussed momentarily, which may serve as a heading to introduce the next two laws.[216] He then explains that possession under Iranian law – using the appropriate

104–105. See also Becker, *Sources*, 81–82n57. For the latter, see b. ʿErub. 62a with Macuch, "Allusions to Sasanian Law," 104; and b. B. Meṣ. 73b with Mokhtarian, *Rabbis, Sorcerers, Kings, and Priests*, 110–111. See also Shai Secunda, "'Lost Property to the King!': The Talmudic Laws of Lost Property in the Shadow of Sasanian Bureaucracy," *Bulletin of the Asia Institute* 28 (2014): 45–55.

212 b. Giṭ. 19b, and cf. b. Giṭ. 11a.

213 b. B. Bat. 173b and B. Meṣ. 71b, with analysis in Secunda, *The Iranian Talmud*, 107–109. See also b. B. Meṣ. 28b and Ber. 60a, discussed in Shai Secunda, "Gaze and Counter-Gaze: Textuality and Contextuality in the Anecdote of R. Assi and the Roman (b. B.M. 28b)," in *The Aggada of the Babylonian Talmud and Its Cultural World*, ed. Geoffrey Herman and Jeffrey Rubenstein (Providence, RI: 2018), 149–171; and b. ʿAbod. Zar. 71a.

214 Macuch, "Iranian Legal Terminology," 91–101 (referring to b. ʿArak. 28a and b. Qid. 60b). Geoffrey Herman has suggested orally that later layers of the Talmud reflect greater awareness of Sasanian legal terminology, although the sample size is quite low, and some references appear to be early (e.g., b. B. Qam. 58b below). But if such a change is meaningful, it may be explained in a host of ways, including greater willingness by the anonymous layer to acknowledge Jewish recourse to imperially sponsored venues and Sasanian realia more generally (see my "Editorial Material in the Babylonian Talmud and Its Sasanian Context," *Association of Jewish Studies Review* 47 [2023], 51–76), or a growing preference among Jews to seek imperial versus local means of recourse. On the latter change in Roman provinces, see Ari Bryen, "Judging Empire: Courts and Culture in Rome's Eastern Provinces," *Law and History Review* 30 (2012): 771–811.

215 b. B. Bat. 55a. See discussion in Herman, *Prince without a Kingdom*, 203–207.

216 Herman, *Prince without a Kingdom*, 204.

Persian technical term, *dārišn* – lasts for forty years,[217] and that wealthy landlords can acquire ownership of a property by paying its overdue property taxes.[218] Here an Exilarch is shown to express particular interest in and familiarity with Sasanian law.

The Exilarch's supposed interest in Sasanian law appears in another passage, which reflects how rabbis might delegitimize other Jewish arbitrators by tarring them for adhering to Sasanian law, just as the Synod of 540 condemned Abraham of Bet Lapaṭ:[219]

A certain person cut down his neighbor's date tree.

He came before the Exilarch, [and the latter] said to him: "I myself saw the place; three date trees stood in a cluster and they were worth one hundred zuz. Pay the other party thirty-three and a third [zuz]."
Said the defendant: "Why do I need the Exilarch who judges in accordance with Persian Law?"
He therefore appeared before R. Naḥman, who said to him [that each tree should be valued at] sixty [*se'ah*, based on rabbinic standards of damage evaluation discussed earlier in the pericope].

The defendant, apparently unhappy with the Exilarch's seemingly commonsensical ruling that cutting down one of three fruit trees reduces the property's productivity, and therefore value, by one third, dismisses the ruling as one based on "Persian law" and brings the case before a rabbi instead.[220] It is striking that the defendant either assumes that the

[217] The precise law in question is unclear, but it does not appear to refer to adverse possession, as it is often understood, but rather the extent of possession, perhaps after which the ownership of land reverts to the state or the previous owner.

[218] This also conforms to what is described as the law of the land in b. B. Bat. 54b. The last law is potentially self-serving, as the Exilarch himself was an acquisitive landowner who might avail himself of this Sasanian law to purchase yet more land. See Chapter 2.

[219] b. B. Qam. 58b, according to MS Vatican 116.

[220] In one of the two other places in which this accusation of ruling in accordance with Persian law appears (b. B. Bat. 173b), the parallel with Sasanian law is clear. See Maria Macuch, "'This is the Law of the Persians': An Allusion to the Sasanian Law of Surety in the Babylonian Talmud," *Iran Namag* 1 (2016): 18–28. In the other location (b. Shebu. 34b), which does not appear in all manuscripts, it is more difficult to determine how the law in question relates to Sasanian law. On the accusation of "Persian law" as derogatory, see Spicehandler, "Notes on Gentile Courts," 354; and Secunda, *Iranian Talmud*, 90–109. Herman, *Prince without a Kingdom*, 208–209 and Secunda, *Iranian Talmud*, 97, based their understanding of the passage on a medieval commentary on the story which has been rightly challenged by Brody, "Irano-Talmudica," 213–214. See Secunda's response in "'This, but Also That': Historical, Methodological, and Theoretical Reflections on Irano-Talmudica," *Jewish Quarterly Review* 106 (2016): 233–241. Interestingly, although here R. Naḥman and the Exilarch are juxtaposed, they are often conflated, on which see Chapter 2.

Exilarch's ruling was in fact based on Iranian law or disparages it by (mis) characterizing it as Iranian law. Here we see how certain Jewish arbitrators may have applied Iranian law in their own conflict resolution, and how the rabbis might rhetorically pit themselves against other arbitrators by portraying the latter's judgments as insufficiently Jewish/rabbinic, or excessively Iranian. The rabbis may well have attracted litigants precisely by laying claim to the mantle of proper Jewish judgment over and against what they marked as "foreign" and "Persian," just as the Exilarch and other Jewish elites may have attracted litigants precisely by offering judgments that were in some form Jewish, while being closely aligned with Sasanian law.

Finally, in the context of the relationship between Jewish and Sasanian law, it is necessary to discuss the famous dictum "the law of the kingdom is the law," found only in the Babylonian Talmud.[221] While it is often presented as articulating a sweeping vision of Jewish acceptance of imperial law, this dictum appears only a handful of times and articulates a narrow legal notion that is already implicit in earlier rabbinic statements.[222] As applied, the dictum does not endorse the replacement of Jewish law by Sasanian law, nor is it equating the two. Instead, the dictum recognizes the validity of the government to expropriate land based on tax law and rules of land tenure. Thus, in one case, a field whose original owners did not pay the tax for a field lose it to those who did pay the tax, because such is the law of the kingdom.[223] When tax collectors act outside of their remit, they are not considered to be following the law of the land and their actions are not deemed valid under Jewish law either.[224] The statement does acknowledge that Sasanian law is halakhically relevant in certain cases, but does not add much to earlier rabbinic material that came to the same conclusion regarding other imperial contexts.[225] For instance, a mishnah states that the contracts of non-Jewish courts are legally valid for Jews, and the Talmud cites "the law of the kingdom is the law" to supply the

[221] b. B. Bat. 54b, 55a; B. Qam. 113a–b; Ned. 27b–28a; Giṭ. 10b; and b. Sanh. 25b according to MS Yad HaRav Herzog I.

[222] The lengthiest discussion is found in Shmuel Shilo, *Dina De-Malkhuta Dina* (Jerusalem: 1974). See also Neusner, *History of the Jews*, 3.43–44; Herman, *Prince without a Kingdom*, 202–207; Yaakov Elman, "Returnable Gifts in Rabbinic and Sasanian Law," in *Irano-Judaica VI*, ed. Shaul Shaked and Amnon Netzer (Jerusalem: 2008), 140–141; and Payne, *State of Mixture*, 104.

[223] b. B. Bat. 54b. [224] b. B. Qam. 113a; b. Ned. 27b–28a.

[225] Contra Gafni, "Political, Social and Economic History," 796, and many others, but in line with Brody, "Irano-Talmudica," 212–213.

mishnah's rationale.[226] The totality of evidence suggests a more dynamic encounter between rabbinic and other courts, in which rabbis permitted access to non-Jewish courts in some cases, erected boundaries in others, and promoted their courts above all.

THE SASANIAN EMPIRE AND ITS COMMUNITIES

The Sasanian Empire oversaw a single overarching administrative and legal system to which all its subjects had recourse. All evidence therefore suggests that Jews, Christians, and other communities were integrated into the state and did not enjoy any formalized semi-autonomy. The Exilarch was not an imperially recognized intermediary on behalf of the Jews and did not head a highly centralized and formal Jewish hierarchy. Instead, he was an elite figure who drew support and power through persuasion and social cachet. The rabbis did not serve as the designated official judges in a Jewish centralized social hierarchy. Instead, like other aspiring Jewish elites, they were in a constant process of competing for prestige, power, and influence.

The Empire nevertheless left spaces for individuals and communities to create alternative means of conflict resolution. Jews, like their Christian and Zoroastrian neighbors, could appeal to Sasanian courts but also to local community-based forms of legal resolution. Some elites, like rabbis and bishops, offered alternative venues for legal settlement, casting rival Sasanian courts as "outsider" or "Persian," and their own courts as governed by communal traditions. Other elites, perhaps including the Exilarch, might draw from Sasanian legal principles in their own judgments. Jews and Christians had access to Sasanian courts, even as the state allowed for communities to resolve conflicts locally through process of arbitration. The existence of multiple avenues of legal recourse, both imperial and communal, forced Jewish and Christian religious experts to compete with imperial courts and persuade followers to choose them instead.

Within this environment, Sasanian communities developed independently from one another. The East Syriac ecclesiastical hierarchy was explicitly modeled on the ecclesiastical hierarchy in the west, even as the loose network of rabbis resembles their Palestinian counterparts. Unlike the Catholicos, the Exilarch did not sit atop a sprawling hierarchy with imperial support. This is not to mention other crucial differences between

226 b. Giṭ. 10b.

the two, such as the fact that the Exilarch was simply the patriarchal head of an aristocratic family, whereas the Catholicos was appointed or elected. These two elites were not commensurate, and their distinctive characters derived from their own contingent histories.

The Sasanian Empire in turn approached Jewish and Christian communities in both similar and dissimilar ways. Sasanian rule offered a single legislative system for all its subjects while tolerating localized forms of dispute resolution. These local forms of social order did not insulate their participants from the Sasanian Empire. Sasanian subjects were invariably embedded in the empire's social and cultural realities. At the same time, given that Christians provoked political anxieties in the context of the Sasanians' protracted conflict with Rome, the Sasanians fostered unique ties with Christian elites through the foundation of an ecclesiastical hierarchy. Even so, the Catholicos was not a formal representative of all Christians at the court, and the Sasanians did not grant Christians semi-autonomy or the right to self-govern. The empire simply elevated elite Christian figures who encouraged their flocks to comply with the Sasanian Empire and functioned as ambassadors and representatives of the court to frontier communities and to the Roman Empire. It seems that Babylonian Jews, who did not provoke similar levels of anxiety, merited neither increased surveillance nor the same scale of benefaction and support.[227]

The integrated picture of Sasanian rule and legal culture sketched above demands a wholesale rethinking of the nature of Jewish society. Indeed, it is in many ways incoherent to speak of Babylonian Jewish society as a single entity at all, outside of the models which assume state sponsorship of a single centralized hierarchy. An alternative approach takes seriously the fact that Babylonian Jews were participants in Sasanian society more broadly, even as some might rhetorically and ideologically seek to stand apart from it. Exilarch and rabbis alike were dynamic figures whose positions depended on the accrual of social prestige and cultural capital as configured within the broader social context in which they were embedded. It is to this more dynamic model of authority in Babylonian Jewish society that we now turn.

[227] For more on the Sasanians' differential treatment of Jews and Christians, see Chapter 3.

2

Competing for Power

Jewish Elites and Sasanian Culture

A lengthy talmudic story tells of a man from the city of Nehardea who entered a butcher's shop in the city of Pumbedita and demanded some meat.[1] When the man was told that he must wait until the attendant of Rav Yehuda b. Ezekiel is served, he rages, "who is Yehuda b. Shewiskel to receive before me!" – omitting Yehuda's title "Rav" and employing a derisive portmanteau of Rav Yehuda's patronymic "Ezekiel," and the word for a type of roasted meat, *shewisqa*.[2] When informed of the slight against him, Rav Yehuda excommunicates the man, while the rabbi's students further advise him that this man regularly insults others by calling them slaves. Rav Yehuda cites a dictum, which he attributes to Shmuel, to the effect that anyone who calls others a slave is himself the descendent of slaves. This man then sues Rav Yehuda for defamation, and they appear before a judge. The man insists that, far from being a slave, he is in fact a descendant of the priestly and royal Hasmonean line. Rav Yehuda counters by conveniently furnishing another statement which he once again attributes to Shmuel: "Whoever says 'I am descended from the house of the Hasmoneans' is a slave."

A strikingly similar talmudic story centers on competition between rabbis.[3] A rabbi named Rav Adda suffers an untimely death, leading several rabbis to debate who bore responsibility for wishing him unwell. Rava suggests that it was he who caused Rav Adda's death, because Rav

[1] b. Qid. 70a–b. See discussion below.

[2] See b. Pesaḥ. 96a, and Sokoloff, *DJBA*, 1118. For a similar play on a name, see b. Qid. 25a.

[3] b. B. Bat. 22a. See the sociological analysis of this story in Wimpfheimer, *Narrating the Law*, 135–137.

Adda used to arrogantly push ahead of Rava's servant at the butcher's shop and say, "I will take before the servant of Rava, because I am superior."

These stories both revolve around the relative social status of rabbis; the first in comparison to a Jew claiming noble lineage, and the second based on rabbinic seniority. The practical stakes – who should be served first by the local butcher – are relatively trivial. But the outcomes – a lawsuit and an untimely death – show how far the involved parties would go to preserve and enforce their social standing and redress slights against them.

This chapter examines the competition for status among Jewish elites according to the integrated model of Sasanian rule proffered in the previous chapter. In the first place, in jettisoning assumptions of a rigid and centralized Jewish social hierarchy, the chapter approaches the Exilarch and the rabbis as players in a dynamic and crowded environment of aspiring elites, all of whom vied for social status and privilege without any guarantee of success, as the two opening stories epitomize.[4] Achieving their aims was largely dependent on their ability to persuade subordinates to recognize them as legitimate authorities who could wield social power.[5] Second, key to these elites' efforts of legitimation was the embrace of habits and symbols that were recognized as distinguishing features of particular elites within both their Sasanian and Jewish contexts. Third, Jewish elites were not simply passive recipients of elite Sasanian cultural symbols and habits or of a monolithic series of Jewish symbols; they were agents selecting and adapting the symbols and habits around them, both in their self-fashioning and in their representation of their competitors.[6] In their competition for recognition, these different elites were engaged in a process of delineating for themselves and others what they considered to be consistent with their definition of Jewish identity, and equally what they framed as antithetical to it.

[4] Here I am informed by Pierre Bourdieu's well-known oeuvre, especially his *Distinction: A Social Critique of the Judgement of Taste* (Cambridge, MA: 1984), and subsequent engagements with these questions.

[5] Cam Grey, *Constructing Communities in the Late Roman Countryside* (Cambridge: 2011), 121.

[6] For methodological reflections, see: Hayim Lapin, "The Law of Moses and the Jews: Rabbis, Ethnic Marking, and Romanization," in *Jews, Christians, and the Roman Empire: The Poetics of Power in Late Antiquity*, ed. Natalie Dohrmann and Annette Yoshiko Reed (Philadelphia, PA: 2014), 79–92.

This chapter therefore casts the relationship of Jews to Sasanian-Iranian culture in a new light. In earlier scholarship, the relative interaction of different Babylonian Jewish elites with Iranian culture was thought to be a byproduct of their positions within the official Jewish hierarchy. Thus, the Exilarch was considered highly acculturated because of his position in court. His habits were deemed typical of "Eastern princes," and an expression of his "feudatory" position in Jewish and Sasanian society.[7] By contrast, the rabbis were, overall, viewed as the defenders of a pristine Jewish tradition that governed the lives of a largely siloed Jewish community, and therefore, with some exceptions, display minimal if any signs of acculturation.[8]

This chapter shows that the acculturation of different Jewish elites was not an epiphenomenon of their proximity to the court. Nor did Jewish elites fall neatly into the binaries that often govern the study of Jews in different historical contexts: acculturated and unacculturated, accommodators and resistors, cosmopolitan and provincial, and – in the case of Sasanian Jews – the elite Exilarch and the ethnocentric rabbis.[9] Indeed, the rabbis too adapted and selected between differing Sasanian and Jewish legitimating symbols, thereby generating tension and conflict, but also perceived harmony between them. Exilarch and rabbis alike are therefore diagnostic for how Sasanian culture and status symbols permeated well outside the royal court itself, and how different actors within particular subject groups straddled their own histories, identities, and traditions with status symbols resonant in the Sasanian Empire.[10] Jews, like all other Sasanian subjects, were not outsiders borrowing from a rigidly bounded Sasanian culture that stood in natural opposition to a similarly rigidly bounded Jewish culture, but were participants who selected from, modified, and

[7] See the influential Heinrich Graetz, *History of the Jews*, vol. 2, trans. Bella Lowy (London: 1891), 508.

[8] See views cited in Introduction, pp. 4–5.

[9] On the supposed "*Kulturkampf*" between the Exilarch and the rabbis – or Persianized and more pristinely Jewish cultures – and between "Accommodating" and "Resisting" rabbis, see Gross, "Rethinking Babylonian Rabbinic Acculturation."

[10] For a reflection on Jews as participants in their cultural environments, see Satlow, "Beyond Influence." For a similar treatment of Jews as exemplifying provincial acculturation and accommodation, see Schwartz, *Imperialism and Jewish Society*; and Lapin, *Rabbis as Romans*.

defined themselves against a repertoire of symbols around them in the process of their own self-realization.[11]

The alternative account offered here begins with the Exilarch. The Exilarch embraced the habits and symbols of the highest Sasanian aristocracy while translating them into recognizable Jewish terms. Like other Sasanian aristocrats, the Exilarch legitimated himself through claims of royal, albeit Jewish, lineage, just as the Hasmonean claimant did in the opening story; like other Sasanian aristocrats, he convened banquets and gatherings, but on Jewish holidays; and like other Sasanian elites, the Exilarch established his own court in which he incorporated and subordinated other Jewish elites. By adopting the bearings of Sasanian Jewish royalty, the Exilarch positioned himself as a high elite who might patronize and rank above lower Jewish elites, who in turn would recognize and reinforce the Exilarch's lofty status. Exilarchs and other Jewish elites stood to benefit from this reciprocal, even transactional, relationship. Those invested in these symbols and relationships were threatened, however, by Jews who delineated the boundaries between Jewish and non-Jewish cultures differently, thereby delegitimating the pretensions of the Exilarch and his ilk.

Rabbis also variously defined themselves and Jewish practice and tradition within and against their broader Sasanian cultural context. They were diverse in the manner in which they adapted and demarcated the dimensions of Jewish and Sasanian culture, and by extension in the relationships they forged with the Exilarch, who often served as proxy for contemplating alternative approaches to Jewish and Sasanian culture.[12] While some rabbis joined the Exilarch's court, others sought to subordinate Sasanian scripts to rabbinic knowledge, setting the latter above the former, and lambasting those Jews, like the Exilarch, but also other rabbis, whom they considered to have elevated certain Sasanian status symbols over Jewish ones. The very notion of a clear distinction between Exilarch and rabbis therefore quickly falls apart, as the two constitute not

[11] I am here informed by studies of cultural hybridity, a nuanced discussion of which can be found in Stephanie M. Langin-Hooper, "Problematizing Typology and Discarding the Colonialist Legacy: Approaches to Hybridity in the Terracotta Figurines of Hellenistic Babylonia," *Archaeological Review from Cambridge* 28 (2013): 95–113, and Mattingly, "Being Roman," 6–7.

[12] This chapter thus challenges a "conflict model" of the relationship between the Exilarch and the rabbis. For previous approaches, see Herman, *Prince without a Kingdom*, 182–188, esp. 186–187; Herman, "In Search of Non-Rabbinic Judaism," 127–131, adopts a conflict model.

separate entities, but overlapping aspiring elites in varying relationships with each other and with the symbols they selectively deployed. Texts about the Exilarch are one prominent site where some rabbis delineated boundaries between Jewish and non-Jewish habits and symbols. But other texts, unrelated to the Exilarch, similarly showcase how rabbis drew from their broader Sasanian context to legitimate themselves, even going so far as analogizing themselves to a rather surprising Sasanian elite figure: the Zoroastrian priest. Whether in their embrace or repudiation of the Exilarch or of certain Sasanian cultural symbols and habits, the rabbis were themselves vying for recognition and prestige against their Sasanian and Jewish backgrounds.

SASANIAN ELITES

The previous chapter demonstrated that the Exilarch did not function as an intermediary on behalf of a centralized Jewish community. This does not mean that the Exilarch was marginal, powerless, or irrelevant. On the contrary, the Exilarch clearly attained a position of considerable prestige and influence among Jews. Judging from rabbinic literature, the Exilarch's position derived not from any formal appointment by the empire, but rather from his ongoing emulation of an elite Sasanian culture that was central to the empire's social makeup and order. The Exilarch's prerogatives and activities are best explicated when situated against the background of the position of elites in Sasanian political and social life.

Elites were essential for the empire's purse and for maintaining social order. These elites appear regularly in sources about Sasanian rule, occupying formal and informal positions of power in times of calm, and providing crucial financial aid, manpower, and support in times of crisis.[13] In some cases, the family name of a noble house became interchangeable with the title of certain imperial positions, indicating the inextricable connection between elite families and imperial administration and governance.[14] The importance of these figures for the authorization and maintenance of the empire is clear from Sasanian inscriptions from the third century, which include lists of nobles and the various roles and

[13] Börm, "König und Gefolgschaft," 32–36.

[14] Börm, "König und Gefolgschaft," 28–29. Procopius, *History of the Wars*, 1.6.12–16, says positions in the Empire only pass through noble families (genealogically; κατὰ γένος), but cf. Theophylact Simocatta, *History*, 1.9.6.

duties they performed. A striking example of the position of nobles is found in Narseh's inscription at Paikuli from the late third century, the only direct record of a royal Sasanian accession.[15] Here, a succession battle broke out between two Sasanian claimants. Each was backed by different elites, and in his narrative of the event, the victor, Narseh, claims that it was the nobles who urged him to take the throne. The Paikuli inscription highlights the importance of noble support to secure the throne, and therefore the need for kings to remain in good standing with them.

Our sources often present these elites as occupying highly stratified positions in society, in what is undoubtedly a schematic simplification. The highest aristocrats were called the *wuzurgān*, the great ones. This upper crust of elites was restricted to specific prominent families. The *wuzurgān* were followed by the *āzādan*, or the free, and other middling landed magnates.[16] Their presence at the side of the king is clear, for instance, from Shapur I's inscription at Hajjiabad, where he boasts of his astonishing feats of marksmanship observed by "the kings (*šahrdārān*) and princes (*wāspuhragān*) and magnates (*wuzurgān*) and nobles (*āzādan*)."[17] The precise duties and roles that attended these different social rungs and the extent to which they constituted clearly demarcated classes is unclear. But Sasanian elites shared certain key features in common. They were wealthy, landholding, and hereditary, and frequently traced their descent back to a noble ancestor.[18] They did not simply benefit freely from their wealth and position but were expected to perform crucial services on imperial and local levels by filling roles in the

[15] See Shenkar, "Coronation of the Early Sasanians," 124–134.

[16] Zeev Rubin, "Nobility, Monarchy and Legitimation under the Later Sasanians," in *The Byzantine and Early Islamic Near East*, vol. 6: *Elites Old and New in the Byzantine and Early Islamic Near East*, ed. John F. Haldon and Lawrence I. Conrad. Studies in Late Antiquity and Early Islam 1 (Princeton: 2004), 235–273; Ahmad Tafazzoli, *Sasanian Society* (New York: 2000), 38–43; and Pourshariati, *Decline and Fall*. See also Payne, "East Syrian Bishops," 5–32.

[17] D. N. MacKenzie, "Shapur's Shooting," *Bulletin for the School of Oriental and African Studies* 41 (1978): 499–511; Michael Back, *Die sassanidischen Staatsinschriften: Studien zur Orthographie und Phonologie des Mittelpersischen der Inschriften zusammen mit einem etymolgischen Index des mittelpersischen Wortgutes und einem Texteorpus der behandelten Inschriften* (Tehran: 1978), 372–378.

[18] Maria Macuch, "Herrschaftskonsolidierung und sasanidische Familienrecht: zum Verhältnis von Kirche und Staat unter den Sasaniden," in *Iran und Turfan: Beiträge Berliner Wissenschaftler, Werner Sundermann zum 60. Geburtstag gewidmet*, ed. Christiane Reck and Peter Zieme (Wiesbaden: 1995), 149–167.

administration, supplying capital and resources, and by ensuring order in the places they resided.[19]

Garnering and maintaining the support of elites was essential for the survival and security of a king and for the prosperity of the empire. The king therefore cultivated relationships with elites across his vast domain, creating a network centered on the court. Gifts were bestowed on elites, such as the magnificent silver vessels found in museum collections across the world, bearing images, for instance, of kings in the hunt.[20] The king created many opportunities to interface with and honor elites, whether in the palace court or on the road.[21]

A crucial element of the formation of a trans-imperial network of elites was a common cosmopolitan culture of behaviors and habits. Distinguished dress, proper behavior, social etiquette, luxury items, and various habits and tastes came to mark elites and facilitate the transregional elite networks. These sets of habits and practices are thematized in works like *Khusro and the Page* (*Xusrō ī Kawādān ud Rēdag*), where a youthful page proves his mettle to the Sasanian king by demonstrating how conversant he is with aristocratic behaviors, practices, and preferences.[22] Participation in elite networks and the adoption of elite habits was a principal way to accrue material, social, and cultural capital, and to gain access to those who controlled them.

While the royal court sought to occupy the center of elite networks, much evidence suggests that elites organized their followers into imperial courts in miniature.[23] One great elite was called, no doubt hyperbolically,

19 See the description of the expected duties of the *dehqān* in: Tafazzoli, *Sasanian Society*, 38–43; and Gyselen, *La géographie administrative de l'empire sassanide*, 28–29.

20 On silver vessels, see Canepa, *Two Eyes of the Earth*, 158–166. For a similar item among the Iranian ruling elite in Georgia, see Stephen H. Rapp, *The Sasanian World through Georgian Eyes: Caucasia and the Iranian Commonwealth in Late Antique Georgian Literature* (Farnham: 2014), 179–181.

21 See esp. Canepa, *Two Eyes of the Earth*; and Börm, "König und Gefolgschaft," 34–35. On the mobility of the Sasanian king, see Jullien, "Parcours à travers l'Histoire d'Īšō'sabran," 179–180.

22 Davoud Monchi-Zadeh, "Xusrōv kavātān ut rētak: Pahlavi Text, Transcription and Translation," in *Momentum Georg Morgenstierne*, vol. 2, ed. Jacques Duchesne-Guillemin and Pierre Lecoq (Leiden: 1982), 70. For a discussion of the precise translation of this word, see Samra Azarnouche, *Husraw ī Kawādān ud Rēdag-ē. Khosrow fils de Kawād et un page: texte pehlevi édité et traduit* (Paris: 2013), 117–118; and Ciancaglini, *Iranian Loanwords in Syriac*, 108.

23 The Armenian royal court and the elites in its orbit share much with Iranian courtly culture, on which see e.g., Nina G. Garsoïan, *The Epic Histories Attributed to P'awstos Buzand (Buzandaran patmut'iwnk')* (Cambridge: 1989), 51–55.

hazarbandag – the man of a thousand followers – but other elites too gathered subelites under their aegis. The result was a system of vertical relationships between the king and other elites, horizontal relationships between some elites, and vertical relationships between elites and subelites in their domain or in close vicinity to them.[24] Elites at various levels of society therefore adopted these habits to distinguish and elevate themselves even on the local level.

Syriac and Armenian sources attest to the presence of imperial elites in their respective communities. Although wealthy lay elites receive less attention in Christian sources composed by ecclesiastical leaders, there is abundant evidence that many such figures achieved positions of prominence and power in the empire. They also served as benefactors to local Christian communities, often passingly mentioned in the acknowledgment of works or honored in the names given to monasteries and other Christian institutions.[25] They could use their considerable capital and power to affect ecclesiastical affairs, throwing their weight behind the elevation of particular Church leaders, which other ecclesiastical figures might perceive as interference. While many of the references to lay elites are oblique, there is sufficient evidence about some especially prominent Christians to allow broader generalizations about how, through their participation in the court and elite networks, they were able to exercise their influence and position to shape the internal affairs of Christians.

Syriac Christian sources sparingly describe elite Sasanian practices and behaviors on their own terms. But paradoxically, we learn about the familiarity Christian authors had with the habits, practices, and privileges of the elite from sources that thematize their renunciation in favor of Christian piety. A particularly striking example of this phenomenon is *The History of Mar Qardagh*, which tells the story of an elite Zoroastrian official who converted to Christianity. Qardagh's family claimed descent from the "stock of the kingdom of the Assyrians (*ʾātorāyē*)," his father descending from Nimrod and his mother from Sennacherib.[26] Qardagh's reputation brings him to the attention of King Shapur, who invites him to

[24] Börm, "König und Gefolgschaft," 30–31.

[25] Jean-Maurice Fiey, "Les laics dans l'histoire de l'Église syrienne orientale," *Proche-Orient chrétien* 14 (1964): 169–183.

[26] Walker, *Legend of Mar Qardagh*, 20. Nimrod also served as royal ancestor in Georgian sources, on which see Rapp, *Sasanian World through Georgian Eyes*, 272–281. For the broader context of "Assyrian" in Classical Syriac, see Aaron Butts, "Assyrian Christians," in *A Companion to Assyria*, ed. Eckart Frahm, Blackwell Companions to the Ancient World (Malden: 2017), 599–612, with this passage discussed on p. 601.

court, where he participates in typical elite Sasanian pastimes like archery and the hunt.[27] The king bestows gifts upon Qardagh and appoints him governor over a large region between north and central Mesopotamia. He relocates to Arbela, where he builds a fortress and palace complex, which includes a fire temple that employed many magi. After converting to Christianity, Qardagh is mocked for abandoning his court position and luxurious lifestyle to live as an ascetic. His family condemns him for turning his back on them and the privileges that attend his association with them, including his ability to oversee and distribute the sizable endowment stored in the fire temple. Undeterred, Qardagh responds to his critics:[28]

> ...while I delighted in finely seasoned tables and exquisite wines in accordance with your polluted will, I was deprived of the pure table of life in Christ ... But today since Christ has made me worthy of the light of His doctrine, behold, I delight in the spiritual table of His holy teaching ...

The decadence of elite Sasanian culture is here the foil by which a Christian culture of renunciation is defined. Christian piety is presented as nourishment served on a spiritual table, more delightful than the finely seasoned tables and exquisite wines of the Sasanian elite. But the author also demonstrates his familiarity with the claims of noble descent, wealth, and habits typical of elites, and how they operated on the local level. The story of Mar Qardagh finds parallels in other stories about ecclesiastical figures from elite wealthy families.[29] For instance, the *Chronicle of Seert* refers to a bishop ʿAqbalaha, whose wealthy father had ties to Shapur II, and even converted to Zoroastrianism. ʿAqbalaha renounced his father's wealth, but not before converting the inhabitants of the city owned by his father to Christianity.[30]

While in the previous two cases the elite Christian figures were originally Zoroastrian who symbolically renounce their elite habits in favor of Christian piety, other sources reflect the way some Christians adopted elite Sasanian practices without reservation. An Armenian text describes the children of the patriarch Yusik, who was descended from a long prominent line of wealthy Church officials. Yusik's two sons apparently felt entitled to luxuriate in the bishop's residence, which was part of the church their great-grandfather had constructed in the city, a sign of their

[27] Walker, *Legend of Mar Qardagh*, 131–140.
[28] Walker, *Legend of Mar Qardagh*, 39.
[29] Ecclesiastical figures serving as bureaucrats or on the frontier is a different matter. See Scott McDonough, "Bishops or Bureaucrats?" 87–92; and Gross, "Being Roman in the Sasanian Empire," 390–397.
[30] Scher, *Chronique de Séert*, 1.222.

intergenerational wealth and status. The sons hosted a lavish banquet, with many boon companions in attendance, all reclining on couches and attended to by "harlots, singing girls, bards, and buffoons."[31] The banquet was akin to those hosted by the king of kings himself at court, described elsewhere in the same source with similar details.[32] In a scene reminiscent of the sons of Aaron in Leviticus 10, the two are struck dead, and their companions dispersed. While the venue and manner in which they banqueted is here targeted for critique, the story shows how elite Christian figures, whose families erected major Christian structures and controlled ecclesiastical offices, were also participants in and reproducers of Sasanian courtly culture, holding banquets modeled on that of the Sasanian court and likewise attended by their supporters.

Elite networks and culture were therefore not limited to the imperial court or high elites, nor were they divorced from their surroundings. Elites were active at various levels of communal life, and the conventions of elitism pervaded outward from the court, where they were adopted and adapted by some local elite figures and were the objects of critiques by others. Elites claimed aristocratic descent, accrued wealth and landholdings, and sought to encourage the support of other elites through the establishment of courts, periodic gatherings, and banquets. This does not mean that local elites adopted all the trappings of Sasanian culture; as Christian sources indicate, such practices might be marked by other Christians as arrogant, even anti-Christian. Local elites, especially Jews and Christians, were in a process of negotiation, adapting aspects of Sasanian elite culture to fit with their understanding of Christian and Jewish traditions, all while contending with Jewish and Christian elites who approached these questions differently.

NOBLE DESCENT

Rabbinic sources represent the Exilarch as a Sasanian-Jewish aristocrat. He undoubtedly adopted the habits and trappings of Sasanian elite culture, which like the author of *The History of Mar Qardagh*, the rabbis of the Talmud understood well and represented accurately.[33] But these norms were clearly integrated with and adapted to his Jewish identity.

[31] Ps.-Pawstos, *Epic Histories* 3.19 (Garsoïan, *Epic Histories*, 93–94).

[32] Ps.-Pawstos, *Epic Histories* 4.54 (Garsoïan, *Epic Histories*, 172–173).

[33] These elements are detailed by Herman, *Prince without a Kingdom*; Geoffrey Herman, "On Table Etiquette and Persian Culture in the Babylonian Talmud" [in Hebrew], *Zion* 77 (2012): 149–188; and Gross, "Rethinking Babylonian Rabbinic Acculturation."

First and foremost, the Exilarch claimed Davidic descent.[34] The Exilarch was not the only Jew in antiquity to trace his descent back to David; the contemporary Patriarch in Palestine appears to have done likewise.[35] But the genealogical claim of the Exilarch met an especially receptive audience in the Sasanian Empire, where great weight was ascribed to noble genealogy. Purported genealogical descent from the house of Sasan remained a precondition for those seeking to rule the empire until the seventh century. Noble descent was transformed into divine descent, as Sasanian kings claimed to be the "seed of the gods."[36] This sacred genealogy was further cemented as Sasanian kings began in the early fifth century to assume titles (e.g., *rāmšāhr*; *Kay*) and names (e.g., Khosrow) related to the Avestan dynasty known as the *Kayānids*. Among the members of this dynasty were benevolent rulers including, according to the Avesta, the patron of Zarathustra himself.[37]

Noble lineage was also of great importance to other imperial elites, as is clear from both literary and sigillographic evidence.[38] Although the

[34] On the Exilarch's purported Davidic descent, see Jacob Liver, *Toldot bet David: mi-hurban mamlekhet Yehudah ve- ʿad le-ahar hurban ha-bayit ha-sheni* (Jerusalem: 1959); Herman, *Prince without a Kingdom*, 54–56; and Franklin, *This Noble House*.

[35] Martin Jacobs, *Die Institution des jüdischen Patriarchen: Eine quellen- und traditionskritische Studie zur Geschichte der Juden in der Spätantike* (Tübingen: 1995), who also discusses whether one of the two claims originated before the other; Albert Baumgarten, "Judah I and his Opponents," *Journal for the Study of Judaism in the Persian, Hellenistic, and Roman Period* 12 (1981): 135–172.

[36] Jamsheed Choksky, "Sacral Kingship in Sasanian Iran," *Bulletin of the Asia Institute* 2 (1988): 35–52. On the etymological debate concerning the word for "seed" (*čihr*), see Antonio Panaino. "L'imperatore sasanide tra umano e divino," in *Divinizzazione, culto del sovrano e apoteosi tra Antichità e Medioevo*, ed. T. Gnoli and F. Muccioli (Bologna: 2014), 331–341.

[37] Touraj Daryaee, "National History or Kayanid History: The Nature of Sasanian Zoroastrian Historiography," *Iranian Studies* 28 (1995): 136–137; Touraj Daryaee, "The Use of Religio-Political Propaganda on the Coinage of Xusro II," *American Journal of Numismatics* 9 (1997): 41–53; Touraj Daryaee, "History Epic, and Numismatics: on the Title of Yazdgerd I (Rāmšāhr)," *American Journal of Numismatics* 14 (2002): 89–95; and Philip Huyse "Die sasanidische Königstitulatur : Eine Gegenüberstellung der Quellen," in *Ērān ud Anērān: Studien zu den Beziehungen zwischen dem Sasanidenreich und der Mittelmeerwelt Oriens et Occidens* 13, ed. J. Wiesehofer and P. Huyse (Stuttgart: 2006), 181–202 (esp. 182–189). Some of these titles captured and consolidated earlier and competing Arsacid claims, on which see Matthew Canepa, "Building a New Vision of the Past in the Sasanian Empire," *Journal of Persianate Studies* 6 (2013): 67–68. The connections are further amplified in the "Iranian epic tradition," on which see E. Yarshater, "Iranian National History," in *The Seleucid, Parthian and Sasanian Periods*, vol. 3, bk. 1, *The Cambridge History of Iran*, ed. E. Yarshater (Cambridge: 1983), 402–411.

[38] Examples of literary sources are Robert Thomson, trans., *Moses Khorenatsi: History of Armenia* (Cambridge: 1978), 214–215; and Procopius, *History of The Wars*, 2. For

notion of a rigid collection of seven noble Parthian families is more historiographic invention than reality, it encapsulates the salience and consistency of hereditary claims, and how they were generally restricted to a select few.[39] Armenian nobles embraced not only Parthian descent, but also descent from notable Armenian ancestors and clans.[40] Syriac Christian hagiographers of the later Sasanian period, like the story of Mar Qadargh discussed above, similarly attributed royal lineage to saints through Assyrian kings like Nimrod and Sennacherib, sometimes fused with Iranian royalty.[41] Given this emphasis on noble genealogy, many important positions across the Sasanian Empire were likely hereditary.[42] Succession and inheritance were major preoccupations of Sasanian law in an effort to ensure the perpetuation of the lines of elite families.[43]

In this context, the Exilarch's claim of Davidic descent represents a parallel Jewish appeal to a royal genealogical past, endowing him with great nobility and authority in terms that resonated both with Sasanians at large and specifically with Jewish audiences, who appear to have been receptive to this claim. In rabbinic literature, the Exilarch was at times caricatured as particularly interested in questions pertaining to royalty, such as whether it is permitted to wear a crown, and his purported

sigillographic evidence, see Rika Gyselen, "The Great Families in the Sasanian Empire: Some Sigillographic Evidence," in *Current Research in Sasanian Archaeology, Art and History*, ed. D. Kennet and P. Luft (Oxford: 2008), 107–113.

39 On the seven families, see Pourshariati, *Decline and Fall*, 48–49; with Gyselen, "Great Families," 107–113. For a possible Georgian imitation of the seven families, see Rapp, *Sasanian World through Georgian Eyes*, 315–316.

40 For Armenian claims, see Nina G. Garsoïan, "Prolegomena to a Study of the Iranian Aspects in Arsacid Armenia," *Handes Amsorea* (1976): 177–234. For a Georgian dynasty claiming genealogical links to both Parthians and Sasanians, see Cyril Toumanoff, *Studies in Christian Caucasian History* (Washington, DC: 1963), 187–192.

41 Walker, *Legend of Mar Qardagh*, 20. Also, see discussion in Richard Payne, "Avoiding Ethnicity: Uses of the Ancient Past in Late Sasanian Northern Mesopotamia," in *Visions of Community in the Post-Roman World: The West, Byzantium and the Islamic World, 300–1100*, ed. Walter Pohle, Clemens Gantner, and Richard Payne (Farnham: 2012), 217–219; and Adam Becker, "The Ancient Near East in the Late Antique Near East: Syriac Christian Appropriation of the Biblical Past," in *Antiquity in Antiquity: Jewish and Christian Pasts in the Greco-Roman World*, ed. Gregg Gardner and Kevin Osterloh (Tübingen: 2008), 394–415. Some sources ascribe Arsacid lineage to Mani. See Iain Gardner and Samuel Lieu, *Manichaean Texts from the Roman Empire* (Cambridge: 2004), 46.

42 Anahit Perikhanian, "Iranian Society and Law," in *The Seleucid, Parthian and Sasanian Periods*, ed. E. Yarsahter, vol. 3, bk. 2, *The Cambridge History of Iran* (Cambridge: 1983), 645; Payne, "Avoiding Ethnicity," 213–214; and Herman, *Prince without a Kingdom*, 37n87.

43 Payne, *State of Mixture*, 144–147.

descent left him vulnerable to critiques that he was not living up to the duties incumbent upon a Davidic claimant.[44] But even these polemical thrusts reflect the underlying acceptance of the Exilarch's core genealogical claim.

The Exilarch may have monopolized genealogical claims to Davidic descent, but the Talmud provides evidence that other aspiring Babylonian Jewish aristocrats laid claim to the other available royal Jewish lineage, that of the Hasmoneans. They believed this claim would likewise bestow upon them prerogatives of the aristocracy, such as the right to be served before others that animated the anecdote with which this chapter opened.[45] A claim of Hasmonean descent may have carried weight in an Iranian context: Parthian kings had enjoyed amicable relations with some of their Hasmonean counterparts. Additionally, one of the final Hasmonean kings was removed to the Parthian court in Babylonia where he was received with great acclaim by Babylonian Jews.[46] Different Jewish elites therefore drew from the past to elevate themselves in a context in which noble genealogy was an important marker of distinction.[47]

SASANIAN COURT IN MINIATURE

The Exilarch's claim to Davidic descent was complemented by his adoption of elite Sasanian habits and customs. These would have been perceived as the appropriate behavior for an aristocrat of his rank. Indeed, the rabbis elsewhere read elite Sasanian practices back into biblical stories about David and other biblical kings, reflecting their parsing of elite

[44] For a critique of the Exilarch for not living up to his Davidic duties, see b. Shab. 54b–56b, with Herman, *Prince without a Kingdom*, 223–231. For the crown, see y. Soṭ. 9.15 (24c); b. Giṭ. 7a; with Herman, *Prince without a Kingdom*, 231–236.

[45] b. Qid. 70a–b; b. B. Bat. 3b–4a, with Kalmin, *Sage in Jewish Society*, 61–67. Incidentally, Josephus claims Hasmonean descent through his mother: Josephus, *Vita*, 1.2.

[46] See, e.g., Josephus, *Antiquities of the Jews*, 15.

[47] My argument about the importance of noble genealogy for aristocratic legitimation should be distinguished from the claim that Sasanian society was highly stratified and rigidly divided into four classes, or that the Talmud reflects the influence of such a caste system, a claim which is highly problematic. For summary and critique, see Yedidah Koren, "'Look through Your Book and Make Me a Perfect Match': Talking about Genealogy in Amoraic Palestine and Babylonia," *Journal for the Study of Judaism in the Persian, Hellenistic and Roman Period* 49 (2018): 417–448; and Gross, "Babylonian Jewish Communities."

Sasanian norms as universal aristocratic behavior.[48] The Exilarch's noble ambitions and his performance of aristocratic status were therefore intertwined and mutually reinforcing.

Rabbinic literature makes clear that the Exilarch overtly behaved as a Sasanian elite would. The Exilarch and the members of his household paraded around in a golden carriage, referred to by an Iranian loanword (גהורקא, Middle Persian *gāhwārag*), an obvious aristocratic status symbol that drew the attention of passersby.[49] Golden carriages were a favored mode of transportation of Sasanian kings.[50] The Sasanian king also sat in a golden throne which symbolized his kingship; lesser officials and dignitaries were made to sit in silver thrones, or in golden thrones positioned at a strategic distance from the king.[51] Female members of the Iranian court, from the Achaemenids to the Sasanians, also traveled in golden carriages, and unsurprisingly rabbinic sources describe the Exilarch's wife doing the same.[52] The golden carriage and throne (*zarrēn gāh*) were so central to elite Sasanian habits that they were still operative in the afterlife, according to the vision described by the Zoroastrian Kerdir in his monumental inscriptions from the second half of the third century, and the later work known as the *Ardā Wīrāz nāmag*.[53] According to these works, elites who properly performed their duties in life rest in the afterlife on golden cushions or sit on golden thrones.

48 See Herman, "One Day David Went Out for the Hunt," 111–136; and b. Meg. 16a, discussed below.

49 See b. Giṭ. 31b, and Sokoloff, *DJBA*, 262.

50 For sources on golden thrones in Sasanian elite culture, see Mokhtarian, "Clusters of Iranian Loanwords in Talmudic Folkore: The Chapter of the Pious (b. Ta'anit 18b–26a) in Its Sasanian Context," in *The Aggada of the Bavli and Its Cultural World*, ed. Jeffrey Rubenstein and Geoffrey Herman (Providence, RI: 2018), 130–135. Beer, *Exilarchate*, 156–157, notes that there are no Palestinian rabbinic equivalences to this mode of transportation.

51 Ahmad Tafazzoli, "The King's Seat in the Fire Temple," in *A Green Leaf: Papers in Honour of Professor Jes P. Asmussen*, ed. W. Sundermann, F. Vahman, and J. Duchesne-Guillemin, Acta Iranica 28 (Leiden: 1988), 101–106.

52 On the Exilarch's wife, see b. Beṣ. 25b and y. Beṣ. 1.6 (60c) (see also b. Shab. 54b where Rav Naḥman notes that his wife Yalta is pampered). On women of royal households in carriages, see Lloyd Llewellyn-Jones, *King and Court in Ancient Persia, 559–331 BCE* (Edinburgh: 2013), 104–105; and Mokhtarian, "Clusters of Iranian Loanwords," 133n37. An Armenian king is reported to have sent his love interest a golden carriage filled with fine raiment. See Robert Thomson, *History of the Armenians by Agathangelos: Translation and Commentary* (Albany, NY: 1976), 172–173.

53 For Kerdir, see MacKenzie, "Kerdir's Inscription," 35–72; for *Ardā Wīrāz-nāmag*, see Fereydun Vahman, *Ardā Wirāz Nāmag: The Iranian "Divina Commedia"* (London: 1986), 200. Cf. b. Ket. 77a (with Sokoloff, *DJBA*, 1207).

The Exilarch and his household also made a point of dressing for the part.[54] In one story, the carriage transporting a member of the Exilarch's household is draped in a leek-green or purple garment, a color with deep aristocratic resonances.[55] The brother of the Exilarch is reported to wear an exceptionally fine type of silk, again referred to with an Iranian loanword (פרנדא, from Middle Persian *parand*), a clear mark of wealth and nobility in the Sasanian Empire. Silk was often used in noble gift exchanges and was a central feature of Sasanian iconography.[56]

The Exilarch's position as elite was also clear from his extensive landholdings.[57] The Babylonian Talmud relates that the Exilarch built a new house, presumably in addition to one(s) he already owned.[58] Elsewhere, the Talmud has an extended discussion predicated on the premise that the Exilarch was constantly looking for properties to add

54 Procopius, *History of the Wars*, 1.17.28, claims that the king regulated who could wear golden jewelry. This is understood literally by Janos Harmatta, "A Turk Officer of the Sasanian king Xusro I," *Acta orientalia Academiae Scientiarum Hungaricae* 55 (2002): 154–155. For a similar claim, see Shaul Shaked, "Esoteric Trends in Zoroastrianism," *Proceedings of the Israel Academy of Sciences and Humanities* 3 (1969): 217–219. al-Jahshiyārī says that only certain groups were authorized, like the king, to ride on "gentle and steady horses" and wear special dress (Tafazzoli, *Sasanian Society*, 27).

55 b. Giṭ. 31b. See Eli Ahdut, "The Talmudic Expression *qaqei hiwware* as an Aid in Understanding the Marking of Social Distinctions among Babylonian Jews" [in Hebrew], in *Irano-Judaica* V, ed. Shaul Shaked and Amnon Netzer (Jerusalem: 2003), 17–18, and discussion below.

56 b. Shab. 20b. A. S. Melikian-Chirvani, "Parand and Parniyān Identified: The Royal Silks of Iran from Sasanian to Islamic Times," *Bulletin of the Asia Institute* 5 (1991): 175–179. Silk was often a royal gift, e.g., Robert Thomson, *The Armenian History Attributed to Sebeos* (Liverpool: 1999), 49–50. On the importance of silk for elite identities in the Sasanian Empire, see Matthew Canepa, "Textiles and Elite Tastes between the Mediterranean, Iran and Asia at the End of Antiquity," in *Global Textile Encounters*, ed. M-L Nosch, Zhao Fang, and L. Varadarajan (Oxford: 2014), 1–14, esp. 2–3; and Richard Payne, "The Silk Road and The Iranian Political Economy in Late Antiquity: Iran, the Silk Road, and the Problem of Aristocratic Empire," in *Bulletin of the School of Oriental and African Studies* 81 (2018): 240. Contrast the Exilarch's *parand* silk with the various references of the more mundane שיראה silk (also deriving from Middle Persian *šērāi*; see Sokoloff, *DJBA*, 1140). Interestingly, in this story other sages refer to the same garment with a different name: מטכסא, from Greek μεταξα.

57 J. Newman, *The Agricultural Life of the Jews in Babylonia: Between the Years 2000 CE and 500 CE* (London: 1932), 37–38. For *dastgird* as the home of the *naxarar*, see Garsoïan, *The Epic Histories*, 520. Compare with, e.g., Thomas of Marga, *The Book of Governors* (E. A. W. Budge, trans., *Thomas of Marga's Book of Governors* [London: 1893], 84); Scher, *Chronique de Séert*, 1.222; and Khalid Yahya Blankinship, *The Challenge to the Empires A.D. 633–635/A.H. 12–13*, vol. 11, *History of al-Ṭabarī* (Albany, NY: 1993), 182.

58 b. Men. 33a.

to his already substantial holdings.[59] Apart from reflecting the Exilarch's great wealth and ability to generate more of it through his possession of land, owning multiple homes and properties would have positioned him and his associates to play a dominant social role in multiple locations.

Indeed, according to a talmudic source discussed in the previous chapter, one of the Exilarch's estates had been a *dastgird*.[60] These elite estates were large landholdings with many servants and employees and were used for both luxury and agricultural production. Given their size and use, *dastgirds* were often located outside of urban centers.[61] For example, the *Life of George* describes a plague in the reign of Khusro II during which the aristocrats all fled Seleucia-Ctesiphon for their *dastgirds*.[62] Sasanian elites likewise retreated to their *dastgirds* to escape the hustle and bustle of urban life.[63] There, they cultivated gardens, hunted, and conducted their affairs away from the congestion and prying eyes of the cities. The *dastgirds* were often adjacent to rivers or canals, facilitating easy irrigation of the fields and grounds, and often contained banquet halls and gardens.[64] Sasanian kings possessed many such estates, spread across their territory, well stocked for hunting and banqueting.[65] For

[59] b. B. Qam. 102b–103a; and see b. B. Bat. 36a, with Beer, *Exilarchate*, 149.

[60] b. ʿErub. 59a.

[61] Bedjan, *Acta martyrum et sanctorum*, 2.317. Elites in the Roman Near East similarly owned homes in the countryside, in which they would vacation or to which they would retreat when displeased with city affairs. See Peter Brown, *Power and Persuasion in Late Antiquity: Towards a Christian Empire* (Madison, WI: 1992), 23–24.

[62] Bedjan, *Histoire de Mar-Jabalaha*, 438–439. For another wealthy individual who survives the ravishes of plague in the city in the comforts of his estate, see Amir Harrak, *The Chronicle of Zuqnin, Parts III and IV* (Toronto: 1999), 97–98.

[63] Kennedy, "From Shahrestan to Medina," 12–14.

[64] For primary sources on *dastgirds*, see Macuch, "Allusions to Sasanian Law," 108; and *Book of a Thousand Judgments* 18 (Perikhanian, 62–63). For examples of *dastgirds*, see Bandian, in northern Khorasan, modern Turkmenistan, which is explicitly identified as a *dastgird* in an inscription (Gignoux, "Les inscriptions en moyen-perse de Bandiān," 251–258). The inscription was part of a large columned hall with stuccoes depicting military, hunting, and banquet scenes. On this site, see Guitty Azarpay, "The Sasanian Complex at Bandian: Palace or Dynastic Shrine," *Bulletin of the Asia Institute* 11 (1997): 193–196; and Samra Azarnouche, "A Zoroastrian Cult Scene on Sasanian Stucco Reliefs at Bandiyān (Daregaz, Khorāsān–e Razavī)," *Sasanian Studies* 1 (2022): 1–28. Other similar structures have been found, such as Massoud Azarnoush, *Sasanian Manor House at Hājīābād, Iran* (Firenze: 1994), and P. R. S. Moorey, *Kish Excavations 1923–1933* (Oxford: 1978).

[65] Matthew Canepa, *Iranian Expanse: Transforming Royal Identity through Architecture, Landscape, and the Built Environment, 550 BCE–642 CE* (Oakland, CA: 2018), 356–374.

both kings and elites, estates served as sites to host and impress guests with the lavish luxuries of elite life.

Considering the Exilarch's landholdings as elite estates offers a solution to a longstanding question about his primary place of residence. A popular view is that the Exilarch lived in the Sasanian capital of Seleucia-Ctesiphon. This argument was based not only on sources that place the Exilarch and his associates in the capital, but mainly on the assumption that as a communal intermediary like the Catholicos, the Exilarch would live in proximity to imperial power.[66] However, the Exilarch and his associates appear in other cities.[67] For instance, the Exilarch at times appears in Nehardea, a city on the Euphrates rather than on the Tigris. A medieval Jewish chronography likewise reports that the annual festival honoring the Exilarch was held in Nehardea. Other medieval sources report that the Exilarchs were buried first in Mata Meḥasia and then in Nehardea, but not in the capital.[68]

Outside of former assumptions concerning the Exilarch, these sources do not need to be reconciled. Like other Sasanian aristocrats, the Exilarch was necessarily mobile; he owned and traveled between *multiple* residences, including urban homes and rural estates.[69] The Exilarch's considerable property holdings allowed him and his associates to appear with some regularity in different locations, interacting with local dignitaries and engaging in local affairs. This is suggested in another talmudic source that reports that an Exilarch died while traveling between cities, and is further supported by the frequent sightings of the Exilarch and his household traveling in their golden carriages, discussed above.[70] The Exilarch

[66] Herman, *Prince without a Kingdom*, 134–161; Elman, "Middle Persian Culture," 191. Oppenheimer, *Babylonia Judaica*, 115–117, attempts to identify the *dastgird* of the Exilarch with references to the king's *dastgird*, but the two are distinct.

[67] For instance, the Exilarch's associates appear in the market of Meḥoza (b. B. Bat. 22a) and Nehardea (b. B. Qam. 59a–b). The rabbis in b. Suk. 26a sleep on the banks of Sura on their way to the house of the Exilarch. A member of his household appears in Nehardea in b. Qid. 70a.

[68] See also Marcus Adler, ed. and trans., *The Itinerary of Benjamin of Tudela* (London: 1907), 53, 69.

[69] The same patterns hold true for Roman elites, on which see essays in Annalisa Marzano and Guy P. R. Métraux eds., *The Roman Villa in the Mediterranean Basin: Late Republic to Late Antiquity* (Cambridge: 2018).

[70] b. Yeb. 115b. The identities of the two cities in this source are enigmatic, but the image of the mobile exilarch is clear. On the cities, see Oppenheimer, *Babylonian Judaica*, 388–389; and Aharon Oppenheimer, "From Qurtava to Aspamia," in *Exile and Diaspora: Studies in the History of the Jewish People Presented to Professor Haim Beinart on the Occasion of his Seventieth Birthday*, ed. A. Mirsky, A. Grossman, and

had multiple abodes, enabling him to remain visible, and facilitating his effort to accumulate both wealth and influence across a wider geographic expanse.

BANQUETS AND GATHERINGS

The Exilarch's landholdings were also sites to gather other elites and served as hubs for communal affairs. There he hosted banquets that comported with the expectation of the Sasanian court. Numerous anecdotes in rabbinic literature center on the Exilarch's banquets and dining habits, described in many cases with appropriate Iranian vocabulary. Thus, the Exilarch hosted meals in a special garden pavilion (אכוורנקא, Middle Persian *xwarnag*, New Persian *xwarangāh*), a term otherwise used in the Babylonian Talmud only to describe the king's palace.[71] This pavilion was located in the Exilarch's garden, also called by its Iranian name, a common setting for a Sasanian feast.[72]

The Exilarch's banquets were staffed by cooks (כוורדיקרא, Middle Persian *xwardīg* + *kār*)[73] and meal attendants (or אכוונגרא, Middle Persian *xwāngar*).[74] This latter term again only appears in the Talmud with reference to the Sasanian king. It also appears prominently in *Sūr*

Y. Kaplan (Jerusalem: 1988), 57–63. See, however, Christa Müller-Kessler, "Interrelations between Mandaic Lead Rolls and Incantation Bowls" in *Mesopotamian Magic: Textual, Historical and Interpretative Perspectives,* ed. Tzvi Abusch and Karel van der Toorn (Leiden: 2000), 201 for an incantation bowl that mentions a בית אספניא. Beer, *Exilarchate*, 23–24, Neusner, *History of the Jews*, 4.184–185, and Goodblatt, *Monarchic Principle*, 279, suggest that it refers to an Exilarch of a *different* Jewish community, an extreme iteration of the institutional approach to the Exilarch. On the medieval reception of this story, see Neil Danzig, "From Oral Talmud to Written Talmud: On the Methods of Transmission of the Babylonian Talmud and Its Study in the Middle Ages," *Bar Ilan Annual* 30–31 (2006): 64.

71 b. ʿErub. 25b–26a; Sokoloff, *DJBA*, 129; b. Taʿan. 14b; and b. Meg. 5b. See the adjacent story in b. ʿErub. 25b for another elite figure's land.

72 בבוסתניה, from *bōstān**. For gardens and wealth, see the interesting story in b. B. Meṣ. 39b–40a. Archaeologists have uncovered what appears to be just such a garden pavilion in the excavations of an elite Sasanian estate at Kish, located south of Babylonia between the Tigris and Euphrates. Moorey, *Kish Excavations*, 138–139. For Jewish Babylonian and other incantation bowls discovered during the Kish excavations of the Sasanian layer, see Moorey, 120–124. Many of the aristocratic residences in Bishapur were surrounded by gardens. See Roman Ghirshman, *Fouilles de Châpour*, vol. 1, *Bîchâpour* (Paris: 1971), 21–36. On other elite Sasanian estates, see Payne, "Avoiding Ethnicity," 217.

73 b. Pesaḥ. 40b; Sokoloff, *DJBA*, 556.

74 b. M. Qaṭ. 11b–12a; Sokoloff, *DJBA*, 129. See broader context of b. M. Qaṭ. 12a for other stories about dispensations made for elites.

saxwan, a Middle Persian text presenting a customary elite banquet toast, in which the toaster gives "Thanks to Ohrmazd, thanks to Holy Immortals, and thanks priests ... thanks meal attendants (*xwāngarān*), entertainers ..."[75] Exilarchal banquets could include over a hundred attendees and an abundance of fine delicacies.[76] Even a dining staple, like bread, was memorable.[77] But the bread was only the beginning; the other items served at the Exilarch's banquets, like the appropriate Iranian words used to describe them, reflect the haute cuisine of the time.[78] For example, one banquet included a serving of oryx (כרבוז; Middle Persian *xarbuz*); this, like other game, was part of the elite Sasanian diet.[79] Elsewhere, the Exilarch is described as serving a type of side dish deriving from the Middle Persian *āmiz*, which appears in *Khusro and the Page* as an archetypical elite spread.[80]

These meals were occasions during which the Exilarch's wealth was displayed before and lavished upon his guests, but also where hierarchical relationships were established and bonds of dependence underscored.[81] The Exilarch here performed his desired position as patron and elite, symbolized by his position as host. It is significant therefore that some rabbis appear to have been regular attendees at the Exilarch's banquets and intimately familiar with his dining habits. The inclusion of these figures at the meal symbolized the Exilarch's desire to bring them under his aegis and to represent his elevated position at the apex of Babylonian Jewish society.[82]

75 b. Ket. 61a and T. Daryaee, "The Middle Persian Text *Sūr ī Saxwan* and the Late Sasanian Court," in *Des Indo-Grecs aux Sassanides: données pour l'histoire et la géographie historique*, vol. 17, *Res Orientales*, ed. Rika Gyselen (Bures-sur-Yvette: 2007), 65–72, esp. 70.

76 b. Ber. 50a and Ber. 42a respectively. 77 b. Ber. 40a.

78 See esp. Herman, "Table Etiquette," 168–170. On Iranian loanwords for food more generally, see Shaul Shaked, "Between Iranian and Aramaic: Iranian Words concerning Food in Jewish Babylonian Aramaic, with Some Notes on the Aramaic Heterograms in Iranian," in *Irano-Judaica* V, ed. Shaul Shaked and Amnon Netzer (Jerusalem: 2003), 120–137.

79 b. Ḥul. 59b; Sokoloff, *DJBA*, 598, with Herman, *Prince without a Kingdom*, 242 n. 14; and Herman, "Table Etiquette," 168.

80 b. Ḥul. 59a, and Monchi-Zadeh, "Xusrōv Kavātān ut Rētak," 70. See Shaked, "Between Iranian and Aramaic," 125; Sokoloff, *DJBA*, 91, D. N. MacKenzie, *A Concise Pahlavi Dictionary* (Oxford: 1971), 8; Sokoloff, *Syriac Lexicon: A Translation from the Latin, Correction, Expansion, and Update of C. Brockelmann's Lexicon Syriacum* (Winona Lake, IN: 2009), 57.

81 Herman, *Prince without a Kingdom*, 239. Rabbis also enjoyed other amenities at the house of the Exilarch, such as baths (b. Shab. 157b, with the Persian word אשונא; see Sokoloff, *DJBA*, 87).

82 A phenomenon that Howard-Johnston, "Two Great Powers," 221, rightly speculated would occur.

The Exilarch appears to have hosted these banquets particularly on the Sabbath and other Jewish holidays.[83] These gatherings were therefore similar to the elaborate feasts hosted by Sasanian kings on Zoroastrian festivals like *Nowrōz*, *Mihragān*, and the *gāhānbār*s (seasonal festivals) for officials and dignitaries, but also for regular subjects.[84] The Exilarch realized this same practice by holding his banquets on occasions of significance in the Jewish calendar. Thus, in the most important medieval rabbinic historiography, the *Epistle* of Sherira Gaon, we hear of an annual gathering (*rigla*) on a particular Sabbath in honor of the Exilarch, which the elites (*rašwata*) and the rabbis were expected to attend.[85] Beyond regularly inviting them to dine with him, the Talmud reports that the Exilarch would attend lectures on the Sabbath at which he expected to encounter other prominent Jewish figures including some rabbis, whose absence the Exilarch noticed with disappointment.[86]

These ties of loyalty and dependence could be quite strong; one source in the Talmud refers to one group as "the rabbis of the house of the Exilarch."[87] What precisely it took to become formal members of the

[83] B. Suk. 26a (compare with b. Suk. 10b).

[84] See Canepa, *Two Eyes of the Earth*, 182–186, and Börm, "König und Gefolgschaft," 38. In the Georgian martyr act of Saint Eustace, the Iranian Zoroastrians in Mtskheta celebrate *Nowrōz* together, and the absence of one of their own was seen as a sign of their severed ties with the community. David Marshall Lang, *Lives and Legends of the Georgian Saints* (New York: 1956), 95; and Rapp, *Sasanian World through Georgian Eyes*, 46–47. The importance of meals on festivals for various elites is also attested for the Parthian period, on which see Albert de Jong, "Religion in Iran: The Parthian and Sasanian Periods (247 BCE–654 CE)," in *From the Hellenistic Age to Late Antiquity*, ed. William Adler, vol. 2, *The Cambridge History of Religions in the Ancient World* (Cambridge: 2012), 33.

[85] Benjamin M. Lewin, *Iggeret Rav Sherira Gaon Mesuderet bi-Shnei Nusḥa'ot: Nusaḥ Sefarad ve-Nusaḥ Ṣarfat 'im Ḥilufei Girsa'ot mi-Khol Qitvei-ha-yad ve-Qitvei ha-"Genizah" sheba-'Olam* (Haifa: 1921), 91–92. See Beer, *Exilarchate*, 129–135. Compare the Exilarch's festival to the biannual gathering at Ctesiphon to honor the Catholicos in Canon 6 of the Synod of 410 (Philip Wood, "Collaborators and Dissidents: Christians in Sasanian Iraq in the Early Fifth Century CE," in *Late Antiquity: Eastern Perspectives*, ed. Teresa Bernheimer and Adam Silverstein [Oxford: 2012], 60).

[86] b. Yom. 78a. The rabbi's presence was not "compulsory," contra Herman, *Prince without a Kingdom*, 193–194. Certainly, there is a literary quality to the story, as seen from the similar structure of b. Shab. 148a. See Eliashiv Fraenkel, "Pirqa Tales in the Babylonian Talmud: Reality and Literature," in *Rabbinic Study Circles: Aspects of Jewish Learning in Its Late Antique Context*, ed. Marc Hirshman and David Satran (Tübingen: 2020), 105–108.

[87] b. Suk. 31a (רבנן דבי ריש גלותא), b. Giṭ. 31b (מאנשי דבי ריש גלותא נינהו), and ms. Munich 95 to 'Erub. 39b–40a. See Goodblatt, *Rabbinic Instruction*, 150; and Herman, *Prince without a Kingdom*, 122 (esp. on why b. Shab. 58a is a later scribal addition and therefore not relevant here).

household is unclear. In one case, Rav Naḥman, a prominent rabbi, married the daughter of the Exilarch and is consistently depicted in rabbinic literature as enjoying particularly close ties with the Exilarch and his household.

The proximity of elites, rabbis, and others to the abode of the Exilarch illuminates a passage discussed in the previous chapter, which says that judges are found at greater concentration at the gate of the Exilarch.[88]

> R. Naḥman said to R. Huna: "Does the law follow our opinion or yours?" He replied: "The law follows your view, since you are closer to the Exilarch's court/gate, where judges are prevalent."

This anecdote features none other than Rav Naḥman, the Exilarch's son-in-law. As noted in the previous chapter, there is little reason to interpret this passage as referring to a full-fledged judicial system situated at the gate or court of the Exilarch. But given the ties the Exilarch fostered with Jewish elites, it is hardly surprising that his son-in-law, Rav Naḥman, as a member of the Exilarch's household, would come into regular contact with Jewish judges, who like some rabbis, may have been frequent guests at the Exilarch's table and home.

TIES WITH THE KING?

Considering the Exilarch's participation in Sasanian elite culture, it is worth reconsidering the question of the potential relationship between the Exilarch and the king. I argued in the previous chapter that there is little evidence that the Exilarch served as an official intermediary on behalf of the Jews. Nevertheless, it is quite possible that the Exilarch's elite Sasanian habits and status afforded him access to an elite network with ties to the Sasanian king himself. Earlier we examined the ample evidence that the Sasanian court fostered connections between local and far-flung elites, including through formal events like festivals in which various elites gathered and reaffirmed their commitment, and subordination, to the Sasanian king.[89] Intriguingly, a medieval text

[88] b. B. Bat. 65a. See discussion in Goodblatt, *Monarchic Principle*, 287; Beer, *Exilarchate*, 77–78.

[89] For the Exilarch gifting money to the "caliph, to the princes and the ministers" at his installation, see Adler, *Itinerary of Benjamin of Tudela*, 41; and on the visual performance of the Exilarchal installation ceremony in the Middle Ages, see Jonathan Decter, "The Hidden Exilarch: Power and Performance in a Medieval Jewish Ceremony," in

pseudonymously attributed to al-Jāḥiẓ, and discussed briefly in Chapter 1, includes the Exilarch in the ritualistic gift exchange that took place at the royal court on the festival of *Nowrōz*:

It happened that when *Nowrōz* fell on a Saturday, the king ordered to give four thousand dirham to the Exilarch.[90]

The source includes the Exilarch as one participant among elites of various rank, including client kings, viziers, scribes, courtiers, generals, nobles, and even wise men and warriors, all of whom brought gifts to the king on this occasion.[91] If this source accurately reflects an event that occurred, regardless of its frequency, it here positions the Exilarch as one elite among many with direct ties to the Sasanian court. But even more so, it shows that the Exilarch's amalgamation of elite Sasanian and Jewish symbols was recognized by the royal court itself, who not only included him among other imperial elites, but symbolically paid him a special distinction when *Nowrōz* fell on the Sabbath.

It is possible that the Exilarch benefited in other ways from his royal connection. The Exilarch's *dastgird*, discussed above and in Chapter 1, may have been bestowed upon him by the Sasanian king. *Dastgirds* were not always granted by the king, but they were one way the king might show favor.[92] This type of royal grant was known to the rabbis, who creatively introduce it into their retelling of the scene from the Book of Esther in which Ahasuerus instructs Haman to reward Mordechai, Haman's rival, for saving the king's life:

"And do even so to Mordecai ... (Esther 6.10)."

Haman said to him [Ahasuerus]: "Who is Mordecai?"
He said to him: "The Jew."
He said: "There are many Mordecais among the Jews."
He replied: "The one who sits at the king's gate."
Said Haman to him: "For him [the reward] of one *dastgird* or one river is sufficient!"
Said Ahasuerus: "Give him that too; let nothing fail of all that you have spoken (Est. 6.10)."[93]

Visualizing Medieval Performance: Perspectives, Histories, Contexts, ed. Elina Gertsman (Aldershot, UK: 2008), 179–191.

90 Text in G. van Vloten, *Le Livre des Beautés*, 362. For further bibliography, see discussion in previous chapter.

91 Tafazzoli, *Sasanian Society*, 42.

92 See Chapter 1, pp. 54–56.

93 b. Meg. 16a.

To avoid bestowing the honor of a full royal procession upon his rival Mordechai, Haman suggests that the king instead more modestly gift Mordechai a single *dastgird*. This is, of course, a fascinating rabbinic retrojection of a well-known Sasanian status symbol – a *dastgird* – onto the earlier Achaemenid period, in which the Book of Esther is set.[94] Perhaps the Exilarch's *dastgird* was also received through royal conferral.[95]

The Exilarch is our best evidence of a kind of Sasanian Jewish elite, one who emulated the Sasanian king and court in miniature and embraced aristocratic habits and behaviors. He claimed noble descent, and he hosted banquets, rode golden chariots, wore fine silk clothes, and embraced other features of elite Sasanian culture. But he expressed Sasanian elite culture in a Jewish idiom, maintaining his elite status vis-à-vis other Jewish elites, and seeking to consolidate them under his aegis. The Exilarch is therefore illustrative of how some Jews navigated Sasanian and Jewish symbols of power and prestige to attain their positions in society.

EXILARCH AND RABBIS

As a network of aspiring elites within Jewish society, the rabbis were faced with the benefits – and potential costs – of associating with the Exilarch, just as the Exilarch stood to benefit from his associations with Jewish experts like the rabbis. Exilarchs and rabbis therefore did not fall into two separate camps; rather, they had overlapping interests which drew some rabbis into the Exilarch's network while alienating others. Instead of static binaries in which the rabbis are either pro- or anti-Exilarch, and the Exilarch either embraced or rejected rabbinic authority and prescriptions, an appreciation of the competitive and dynamic social context painted above renders a far more complicated portrait.

We have ample evidence that the rabbis adopted many individualized approaches to the Exilarch and his embrace of Sasanian elite culture. The spectrum of rabbinic positions vis-à-vis the Exilarch is expressed in a fascinating story:

[94] A different version of Mordechai's potential reward is found in Targum Sheni to the Book of Esther on Est. 6.6; Bernard Grossfeld (ed.), *The Targum Sheni to the Book of Esther: A Critical Edition Based on MS. Sassoon 282 with Critical Apparatus* (New York: Sepher-Hermon, 1994). See discussion in Herman, *Prince without a Kingdom*, 24n17.

[95] The related group of sources, discussed in Chapter 1, that list the Exilarch alongside the king and two other officials, may similarly reflect not his formal position as an intermediary, but his status as an elite who might appear in the royal court. It is worth noting that the Exilarch is not the only Jewish figure to achieve wealth and status and to have participated in the politics of the court. See Whitby and Whitby, *History of Theophylact Simocatta*, 141–142, discussed in Chapter 3.

Rava and Rav Naḥman b. Isaac were sitting when Rav Naḥman b. Jacob passed by, seated in a golden carriage, draped with a leek-green colored garment.

Rava went to him; Rav Naḥman b. Isaac did not go to him, saying [to himself] "perhaps they are member's of the Exilarch's household; Rava is in need of them but I am not in need of them."[96]

Here, a pair of rabbis see an approaching golden carriage which must hold an elite of some kind. Both assume that the figure in the carriage is likely from the house of the Exilarch. Rava moves to greet the member of the Exilarch's household and to pay his respects. By contrast, Rav Naḥman b. Isaac stays seated, reasoning that he is independent of the Exilarch. The figure in the carriage is Rav Naḥman b. Jacob, the son-in-law of the Exilarch, and in the continuation of the story, all three figures converse about earlier rabbinic teachings. Here we see various rabbinic associations with the Exilarch; a rabbi who is considered a member of the Exilarch's household, taking on the same elite trappings as the Exilarch himself, another rabbi who rushes to pay his respects, and a third rabbi who boldly asserts that he is "not in need of them," and remains seated.

Situated within the context of competition for power and influence, the relationship between Exilarch and rabbis becomes highly dynamic.[97] The Exilarch could attract rabbinic supporters while behaving in ways that other rabbis condemned as inconsistent with rabbinic law. Some rabbis could choose to join the Exilarch's ranks for the associated cultural and material benefits, while others distinguished themselves in part by resisting or even criticizing the Exilarch.

The inconsistency of attitudes towards the Exilarch was apparently a source of significant friction among the rabbis. These tensions play out across many rabbinic stories, in which some rabbis are presented as highly permissive of the Exilarch's practices while others actively repudiated them. In two related talmudic accounts, some rabbis ruled in favor of the Exilarch only to be disparaged by their colleagues. In one of these stories, Rav Huna permitted the Exilarch's wife to be carried during a festival on a "chair," presumably a reference to the palanquin discussed earlier.[98] His interlocutor, Rav Ḥisda, notes that this is explicitly forbidden by a tannaitic teaching. Rav Ḥisda therefore declares: "even a student

[96] b. Giṭ. 31b, according to MS Vatican 130. Discussed in Herman, *Prince without a Kingdom*, 216–217.

[97] For diverse Palestinian rabbinic attitudes towards the Patriarch, see Hezser, *Social Structure of the Rabbinic Movement*, 405–449.

[98] y. Beṣ. 1.6 (60c), parallel to y. Shab. 6.1 (7d), which confirms the golden palanquin suggestion, and b. Beṣ. 25b (see Herman, *Prince without a Kingdom*, 236).

would not err in this matter, but Rav Huna has erred!" In another case, Rav Hamnuna permits the Exilarch to dismantle a table on the Sabbath in order to remove it, leading Rav Yehuda to declare: "Whoever permitted him [this] has neither studied nor apprenticed for a sage."[99]

The dispute between those who condoned and condemned the Exilarch's behavior could shift from harsh rhetoric to physical violence. In one story, for example, Rav Naḥman permits the construction of an *'eruv*, or Sabbath boundary marker, around the house of the Exilarch.[100] In response, Rav Sheshet orders his attendant Rav Gadda to pull it down. The Exilarch's household seizes and incarcerates Rav Gadda, who is released, apparently miraculously, by a rabbinic colleague. In another case, Rav Naḥman again rules in favor of the Exilarch on a matter of contract law, and Rav Yehuda responds by tearing up the contract.[101] Physical clashes between rabbis in the Talmud are unusual and reflect the intensity of disagreements about the relationship between rabbis and the Exilarch. The violence ran in both directions; in some stories, members of the Exilarch's household physically abuse and taunt rabbis for their excessive piety.[102]

One story features an extreme accusation of rabbinic complicity in the allegedly exploitative practices of the Exilarch:

A woman came before Rav Naḥman and said to him, "The Exilarch and all of [his] rabbis are sitting in a stolen sukkah."
She complained but Rav Naḥman took no notice of her.
She said to him, "A woman whose father had three hundred and eighteen slaves cries out to you, and you take no notice?"
Rav Naḥman said to them, "She is a noisy woman; but she can claim only the cost of the wood."[103]

[99] y. Shab. 12.1 (13c). Other stories simply report the accommodations made by certain rabbis for the Exilarch, with the Talmud's editors attempting to justify the rabbis' rulings (e.g., b. M. Qaṭ. 12a; Nid. 67b–68a), or simply lodging a disagreement without polemic (b. Suk. 37a; Ḥul. 59b, which in fact says that the rabbi ruling in favor of the Exilarch was not wrong). In one shocking case (b. Pesaḥ. 76b), it appears that a rabbi allows the Exilarch to consume meat cooked simultaneously with pork in the same oven.

[100] b. 'Erub. 11b.

[101] b. B. Meṣ. 66a. Rav Naḥman is said to have ruled differently for the Exilarch and other Jews in b. Ket. 60b.

[102] E.g., b. Giṭ. 67b and b. B. Qam. 59a–b, with Herman, *Prince without a Kingdom*, 219–222. To be sure, the Exilarch's household employed violence against rabbis for more quotidian concerns, such for debt collection (e.g., b. Shab. 121b, with b. Yeb. 120a where the same rabbi seeks to evade the Exilarch's household due to debt).

[103] b. Suk. 31a, according to MS Oxford 366. In b. Shab. 55a, one rabbi questions another for his unwillingness to rebuke the household of the Exilarch. The parallels are discussed

In this story, the Exilarch and his rabbinic coterie are accused by a woman of sitting in a sukkah built of wood that she alleges was stolen from her. Rav Naḥman, a member of the Exilarch's household, responds with indifference and ultimately insults the woman, while granting her nominal recourse. There was apparently some merit to the woman's claim, otherwise Rav Naḥman would have granted her nothing. The rabbis of the Exilarch's household are therefore party to the Exilarch's theft and made matters worse by insulting the old woman. She, in contrast, comments that these rabbis have become so distracted by the wealth of the Exilarch that they have mistreated a woman who has her own noble lineage and wealthy ancestors: She is, after all, a descendent of Abraham, who possessed three hundred and eighteen slaves according to Gen. 14.14.[104] The point of the story is clear: The Exilarch and his rabbinic coterie have privileged their elitism over other Jews. The story paints Rav Naḥman and the other rabbis at the court of the Exilarch as enablers, using the law to insulate the Exilarch from serious liability, rather than redressing the wrongs committed by the Exilarch.[105]

RABBIS AND ELITE SASANIAN CULTURE

The close association of some rabbis with the Exilarch, and the general familiarity of even critical stories in the Talmud with the Exilarch's elite practices, reflect that rabbis too sought to authorize and legitimate themselves through appeals to both Jewish and Sasanian norms. Some adopted similar strategies to the Exilarch. Indeed, in addition to the "rabbis of the house of the Exilarch," other elite rabbinic figures are described as riding through town on golden chariots.[106] In one anecdote, Rav Huna, condemned in a previously discussed story for being overly permissive in allowing the Exilarch's wife to parade around in a

in E. E. Urbach, "Concerning Historical Insight into the Account of Rabbah Bar Naḥmani's Death," *Tarbiz* 34 (1965): 157.

104 Beer, *Exilarchate*, 82.

105 A few later anonymous editorial pericopes appear sympathetic towards the Exilarch; see b. Sanh. 5a–b, with Gross, "Exilarchal Authority," b. Ḥul. 59b, and b. ʿErub. 39b–40a, with Herman, "In Search of Non-Rabbinic Judaism." This is not evidence of a diachronic shift in the way all rabbis viewed the Exilarch, as I am arguing that rabbinic views of the Exilarch were diverse throughout the period (and beyond).

106 b. Ta'an. 20b; B. Meṣ. 73b. See also b. Ket. 77a for a rabbi sitting on thirteen golden "tables/mattresses (תכתקי, from Middle Persian *taxtag*)."

chariot on a festival, is described as similarly riding in a golden chariot and serving as a wealthy benefactor for other Jews.[107] Rava also, who stood up to greet the Exilarch's son-in-law when he arrived in a carriage, is said to have been carried in a chariot of his own (again, from Middle Persian *gāhwārag*). It is not surprising then that Rav Huna and Rava reportedly shared close social ties with the Exilarch and ruled more permissively in his favor, a reflection of their shared interests and shared embrace of symbols of Sasanian elite wealth and position.[108] Certainly, shared interests did not mean total identification between the Exilarch and elite rabbis. Even rabbis like Rav Naḥman, who married the Exilarch's daughter, rode in golden chariots, and occupied the same space as the Exilarch, could still disagree with the Exilarch's opinion.[109]

If some stories depict rabbis with similar elite habits to the Exilarch, others show how some rabbis sought to define elite Sasanian norms as rabbinic, and to subordinate, but not eschew, them. One such discussion begins with the Exilarch expressing his admiration for Iranian dining etiquette:

> The Exilarch said to Rav Sheshet: "Although you are distinguished rabbis, the Persians are better versed than you in meal etiquette. When there are two couches, the senior one takes his place first and then the junior one above him. When there are three couches, the senior occupies the middle one, the next to him [in seniority] takes the place above him, and the third one below him."
> R. Sheshet said to him: "What expertise is this? So, when the two want to speak with one another, the senior must stretch himself in order to do so!"
> He [the Exilarch] replied: "This does not matter to the Persians, because they speak with gesticulation."
> [the Exilarch said:] "They [the Persians] commence the washing of the hands before the meal with the senior one …"
> he [R. Sheshet] replied: "I do not know [about] Persians or Babylonians, but I do know a Tannaitic teaching, in which it is taught: 'What is the order of reclining? When there are two couches, the senior one reclines first, and then the junior takes his place below him. When there are three couches, the senior takes his place first, the second next above him, and then the third one below him…'"[110]

[107] For more on this story, see Gross, "'Whoever is Hungry Come and Eat': On the Origins and Later Development of a Puzzling Passover Passage," *Aramaic Studies* 18 (2020): 171–197.

[108] Contra Beer, *Exilarchate*, 156, who argues that the carriage is a reflection of Rav Huna's connection to the household of the Exilarch.

[109] b. B. Qam. 58b. For the representation of exilarchal cultural proclivities as non- or anti-rabbinic, see b. Shab. 51a, and more below.

[110] b. Ber. 46b, according to ms. Oxford 366 and Paris 671.

The source depicts the Exilarch attempting to present Iranian – and by extension, his own – dining etiquette as superior to that of the rabbis. And yet, while the Exilarch argues for the superiority of Iranian dining etiquette, Rav Sheshet responds that it is largely indistinguishable from that of the rabbis. As Herman argues, the intention of the story is to show that the "Persian" practices celebrated by the Exilarch are no different to the practices promoted in earlier rabbinic teachings.[111] Rav Sheshet's response elegantly punctures the Exilarch's claim of Iranian superiority, while criticizing his unfamiliarity with and lack of appreciation for Jewish traditions. But rather than invalidate Iranian etiquette, Rav Sheshet rabbinizes it, claiming rabbinic teachings dictate the same practices.[112] The Exilarch is faulted for erroneously assuming that there was a superior set of practices to rabbinic teachings, while rabbinic teachings are shown to live up to the highest standards of elite Iranian etiquette. The rabbis are not opposed to Iranian cultural practices as such; they are opposed to the notion that these practices stand above rabbinic practices or reflect poorly on them.

Other rabbinic sources create the sense that exilarchal habits came at the expense of "proper" halakhic observance. The Exilarch himself is at times depicted as having an incomplete understanding of Jewish law, requiring rabbis to enlighten him.[113] His luxurious way of life could clash with how some rabbis understood Jewish law.[114] The Exilarch's servants

[111] Herman, "Table Etiquette," further argues that what the Exilarch characterizes as "Persian" etiquette in fact mirrors Roman etiquette that has been slightly modified to reflect Babylonian Jewish practices, and thus the opposition between Persian and rabbinic practices in the source is contrived. For a critique of some of Herman's suggestions, see Brody, "Irano-Talmudica?" 229–230. For a different focus, see Shaul Shaked, "'No Talking during a Meal': Zoroastrian Themes in the Babylonian Talmud," in *The Talmud in Its Iranian Context*, ed. Carol Bakhos and Rahim Shayegan (Tübingen: 2010), 161–177.

[112] On different uses of the term "Rabbinization," see Raʿanan Boustan, "Rabbinization and the Persistence of Diversity in Jewish Culture in Late Antiquity," in *Diversity and Rabbinization: Jewish Texts and Societies between 400 and 1,000 C.E.*, ed. G. McDowell, R. Naiweld, J. Schlanger, and D. Stökl Ben Ezra (Cambridge: 2021), 427–449.

[113] b. Giṭ. 7a, discussed in Herman, *Prince without a Kingdom*, 234–235. Contrast with Beer, *Exilarchate*, 135–136, who argues that b. Pesaḥ. 115b and b. Beṣ. 29a are both examples of an Exilarch teaching.

[114] y. Meg. 3.2 (74a), and Beer, *Exilarchate*, 157–158 for discussion.

were particularly distrusted in their handling of his meals.[115] They may have been non-Jews, which would have reinforced the impression that the Exilarch was prioritizing elite dinner etiquette, which clashed with halakhic dietary restrictions as defined by some rabbis.[116] These sources that paint the Exilarch or his household as ignorant of rabbinic halakha, or as prioritizing elite behaviors over halakhic conformity, should not be taken as simple statements of fact, but reflect how some rabbis contrasted exilarchal habits with rabbinic excellence, in the service of the latter. They elevate rabbinic knowledge and practice above exilarchal elite habits.

A similar dynamic obtains in a much-studied talmudic story which targets the elite practices of the members of the Exilarch's household.[117] The story is the continuation of the one discussed at the beginning of this chapter, in which a man claims Hasmonean descent and therefore insists he should be served by the butcher prior to Rav Yehuda's servant. When Rav Yehuda asserts that the man in fact descends not from royalty but from slaves, the man sues him for defamation, and brings the case to Rav Naḥman, the Exilarch's son-in-law. Perhaps the story intends to suggest that the Hasmonean claimant appealed specifically to Rav Naḥman because he too was associated with an elite family claiming royal Jewish descent. A rabbinic colleague advises Rav Yehuda that while he is not required to accept the summons, he should nevertheless appear before Rav Naḥman out of respect for the Exilarch.[118]

The story clearly derives from the later period of the Talmud's redaction, as it reuses sayings and motifs that originate elsewhere.[119] It is therefore a constructed work, pitting two opposing characters against each other: Rav Yehuda, who is a rabbinic competitor and critic of the Exilarch, and Rav Naḥman, a rabbinic member of the Exilarch's household. The story offers

115 b. Giṭ. 67b–68a; b. Shab. 48a.

116 See, for instance, b. ʿAbod. Zar. 38b, in which a rabbi is allegedly killed by them, and possibly b. B. Meṣ. 91b. On slaves in Jewish Babylonia, see Laura Lieber, "Daru in the Winehouse: The Intersection of Status and Dance in the Jewish East," *Journal of Religion* 98 (2018): 90–113.

117 For the history of interpretation of this passage, see Gross, "Rethinking Babylonian Jewish Acculturation," 282–285.

118 On Rav Naḥman and the Exilarch, see Chapter 1.

119 Moulie Vidas, "The Bavli's Discussion of Genealogy in *Qiddushin* IV," in *Antiquity in Antiquity: Jewish and Christian Pasts in the Greco-Roman World*, ed. G. Gardner and K. Osterloh (Tübingen: 2008), 306–316; Wimpfheimer, *Narrating the Law*, 147–163; Herman, *Prince without a Kingdom*, 199–200, and n139; and Aaron Amit, "Regards to Yalta: Is There Kol ʾIsha in Bavli Qiddushin 70a–b" [in Hebrew], *Sidra* 30 (2016): 123n8, and compare with b. Ber. 51b.

the clearest articulation of how the Exilarch's rabbinic antagonists sought to portray themselves in opposition to his habits, drawing – and indeed creating – a contrast between elite Sasanian habits and rabbinic, even Jewish, habits. While it criticizes the Exilarch's household, the story reflects the author's deep familiarity with Sasanian elite practices.

The first part of the story focuses on Rav Naḥman's vocabulary:[120]

> A. He (Rav Yehuda) went and found him (Rav Naḥman) making a *ma'aqeh* (railing).[121] Said he (Rav Yehuda) to him (Rav Naḥman): "Does master not accept that which R. Nahilai[122] b. Idi said in Shmuel's name, 'Once a man is appointed a community leader, he may not do labor in the presence of three?'" He (Rav Naḥman) replied: "I am (merely) making a small portion of a *gundrīza*."[123] He (Rav Yehuda) retorted: "Is not *ma'aqeh*, as written in the Torah, or *meḥiṣa*, as used by the rabbis, good enough?"
> B. Said he (Rav Naḥman) to him (Rav Yehuda): "May master sit on a (') *qrpyṭ'*."[124] He (Rav Yehuda) replied: "Do you dislike *safsāl*, as used by the Rabbis, or *'īsṭiba*, as it is commonly called?"
> C. He (Rav Naḥman) said: "Will master partake of *etrongā* (a citron)[125]?" He (Rav Yehuda) replied: "Thus did Shmuel say, 'he who says "etronga', is a third filled with arrogance: he has *'etrog*, as it is called by the Rabbis, or *'etroga*, as it is commonly called [which he should use instead].'"
> D. He (Rav Naḥman) said: "Will you drink *'anbaga*[126] (spiced wine?)?" He (Rav Yehuda) said: "Do you dislike *'īspargos*, as it is called by the Rabbis, or *'anpaka*,[127] as it is commonly called?"

Like many of the stories featuring the Exilarch and his household, this one is also set at a banquet conforming to elite Sasanian habits.[128]

[120] b. Qid. 70a–b. My translation is of MS Munich 95 (M). MS Vatican, Biblioteca Apostolica ebr. 111 (V), selected as the best textual witness by *Ma'agarim: The Historical Dictionary Project of the Academy of the Hebrew Language*, includes several later additions, on which see Amit, "Regards to Yalta," 121–131. The other manuscripts are Bologna, Archivio di Stato Fr. ebr. 210 (B), and Oxford Opp. 248 (367) (O). I note only the significant manuscript variations.

[121] This term also refers to a biblical law, for which see Deut. 22.8. V adds "for his roof."

[122] O and the printed editions have "Huna" here instead.

[123] M גונדר', O גונדריזא, B גונדרייא, V גונדרנא. [124] M קרפיט', O קופיטא, B אקרופיטא, V איקרופיטא.

[125] M אתרונגא, O איתרונגא and אתרונגא, B אתרוגנא, V איתרוגנא and אתרוגנא.

[126] M אנבגא, O אנבג, B אנבגא, V אנבגא. [127] M אנפק, O אנפקא, B אנפ[קא], V אנ(קפ)[פק]א.

[128] On the display of haute cuisine as a marker of class, see Jack Goody, *Cooking, Cuisine, and Class: A Study in Comparative Sociology* (Cambridge: 1982). The Exilarch's elite practices are explicitly criticized elsewhere, such as in b. Giṭ. 31b (also involving Rav Naḥman). For another example of Rav Naḥman and Rav Yehuda jockeying for relative power and prestige, this time explicitly in the Exilarch's court, see b. B. Meṣ. 66a. For criticism of the Exilarch's household set in a banquet scene, see b. Giṭ. 67b–68a. For criticisms of the Exilarch more generally, see Herman, *Prince without a Kingdom*, 210–239.

Rav Naḥman first invites Rav Yehuda to be seated on a bench or couch of some sort. At elite and royal Sasanian banquets, guests regularly sat on special couches.[129] Next, Rav Naḥman offers Rav Yehuda a citron, a luxury food item. In an anecdote elsewhere in the Babylonian Talmud, King Shapur II offers an *ʾetrog* to a Mar Yehuda.[130] The citron was highly regarded in elite cuisine during the Sasanian period;[131] it is listed as one of the principal thirty fruits created.[132] Citrons were included in offerings to the king on the day of *mihragān* and were important to court culture as well, as attested to in the Middle Persian text *Khusro and the Page*.[133] There, one of the best kinds of jam (*ambak*) is made from citron.

Lastly, Rav Naḥman offers Rav Yehuda a cup of unmixed wine (*ʾanbaga*). In the other appearance of this word in the Talmud, this wine is deemed superior to mixed, or diluted, wine.[134] Unmixed wine also appears to have been a preference apparently unique to Iranian aristoc-

[129] Harper, *The Royal Hunter: Art of the Sasanian Empire* (New York: 1978), 75 (no. 25), 146 (no. 70), 148 (no. 73), and sources cited in n115. See, however, the cautionary remarks in Herman, "On Table Etiquette," 162–164.

[130] b. ʿAbod. Zar 76b. See also b. Ket. 61a, where Shapur's wife is said to have eaten an *etrôg*, thereby causing their daughter to be fragrant. See Herman, *Prince without a Kingdom*, 308–309.

[131] It should be noted that the citron is associated with Persia from an early date: Theophrastus (*History of Plants* 4.4.2), as well as Josephus, *Antiquities of the Jews*, 3.244–245 (cf. 13.372), call it the Median or Persian apple. In general, see David Moster, *Etrog: How a Chinese Fruit Became a Jewish Symbol* (Cham, Switzerland: 2018).

[132] Iranian *Bundahišn* 16.26. See B. T. Anklesaria, *Zand-Ākāsīh, Iranian or Greater Bundahišn* (Bombay: 1956), 150–151; and text, translation, and discussion in T. Daryaee, "List of Fruits and Nuts in the Zoroastrian Tradition: An Irano-Hellenic Classification," *Nāme-ye Irān-e Bāstān* 6.1–2 (2006–2007): 1–10. See also J. P. Asmussen, "The List of Fruits in the Bundahišn," in *Henning Memorial Volume*, ed. M. Boyce and I. Gershevitch (London: 1970), 14–19.

[133] For the former, see Shaul Shaked, "From Iran to Islam: On Some Symbols of Royalty," *Jerusalem Studies in Arabic and Islam* 7 (1986), 82–83. For the latter, see Monchi-Zadeh, "Xusrōv Kavātān ut Rētak," 73. See also Azarnouche, *Husraw ī Kawādān*, 52, for French translation, and 125–126 for notes.

[134] b. Ḥul. 94a. See also b. Shab. 109b, which describes this drink as alcohol mixed with sweet clover (see Sokoloff, *DJBA*, 583). The word in these other occurrences is Rav Yehuda's synonymous *anpaka*, on which see below. Diluted and undiluted wine also appears in the context of the Exilarch in b. Giṭ. 67b, but there it pertains to healing practices (and the Aramaic חמרא חייא is used instead).

racy, as Greek and Roman sources reviled unmixed wine.[135] The Exilarch's preference for unmixed wine is consistent with other stories in the Talmud that depict his aristocratic drinking habits.[136]

Though the setting of the story is an elite banquet, the focus is on Rav Naḥman's use of "arrogant" or "haughty" words, and Rav Yehuda's suggestion of alternatives used by rabbis or by Jews colloquially.[137] Some have argued that the difference between the two rabbis' vocabularies is their language of origin, since the words used by Rav Naḥman are Iranian terms while the words preferred by Rav Yehuda are not.[138] Such a solution may appear to work for segment (A), where Rav Naḥman uses the word *gundrīza*, ("fence" or "wall"), derived from an uncertain base word, along with a relatively uncommon Middle Persian diminutive ending, *-īza*.[139] Rav Yehuda prefers a biblical (*ma'aqeh*) or Mishnaic Hebrew (*meḥiṣa*) equivalent.

The ensuing discussion makes clear, however, that both parties in the story use etymologically Iranian words, and sometimes the same words

[135] For Iranian elite culture, see Ps.-Pawstos, *Epic Histories* 5.24 (Garsoïan, *Epic Histories*, 204). For Greek and Roman habits, see Herodotus, *Histories*, 6.84; Plato, *Laws*, 637E (who mentions the Iranian preference for unmixed [ἄκρατος] wine); and Martial, *Epigrams*, 1.11. For a discussion, see Denys Page, *Sappho and Alcaeus: An Introduction to the Study of Ancient Lesbian Poetry* (Oxford: 1955), 307–308.

[136] This is not the only place in the Babylonian Talmud in which the Exilarch's drinking habits earned a remark or are portrayed as lavish. See b. Shab. 62b and 'Abod. Zar. 72b–73a. For the unidentified word קנישק(נ)ין, see Sokoloff, *DJBA*, 1029. See also b. Shab. 140a (on Ukba see Herman, *Prince without a Kingdom*, 309–319).

[137] See also b. 'Abod. Zar 71a and b. Shab. 94a, where Iranians are labeled "arrogant" for certain cultural practices.

[138] Daniel Boyarin, *A Traveling Homeland: The Babylonian Talmud as Diaspora* (Philadelphia, PA: 2015), 83; Yaakov Elman, "Acculturation to Elite Persian Norms and Modes of Thought in the Babylonian Jewish Community of Late Antiquity," in *Neti'ot Ledavid, Jubilee Volume for David Weiss Halivni*, ed. Yaakov Elman, Ephraim Bezalel Halivni, and Zvi Aryeh Steinfeld (Jerusalem: 2004), 48.

[139] For an attempted identification of the base word, see Sokoloff, *DJBA*, 270. It is possible that we have some version of the word *guda* here, which means "wall" in Jewish Babylonian Aramaic, Syriac, and Mandaic. Indeed, in b. B. Bat. 3a, *meḥiṣa* is glossed with *guda*, just as here *meḥiṣa* is synonymous with *gundriza*. For *guda* in Mandaic, see E. S. Drower and R. Macuch, *A Mandaic Dictionary* (Oxford: 1963), 82; for Syriac, Sokoloff, *Syriac Lexicon*, 211; and for Jewish Babylonian Aramaic, see Sokoloff, *DJBA*, 265–266. Elsewhere in the Babylonian Talmud we find the similar word גודריתא, again possessing a Middle Persian diminutive, perhaps with the base word derived from "fence," or גדירא (Hebrew *geder*). See Sokoloff, *DJBA*, 266. See Bedjan, *Acta martyrum et sanctorum* 4.256 for the word *gudna*, which seems to be parallel to "gate." On the diminutive ending, see MacKenzie, *Pahlavi Dictionary*, 46.

with only slightly different pronunciations. Thus, in segment (C), both Rav Naḥman and Rav Yehuda use derivatives of the same Persian word for "citron." The rabbis used *ʾetrog*, which is already found in the Mishnah. Jewish Babylonian Aramaic speakers included the ending of the Aramaic *status emphaticus*, *ʾetroga*, also attested in Syriac. But Rav Naḥman used *ʾetronga*, a word derived from the Middle Persian *wādrang*.[140] This form of the word only appears here in the Babylonian Talmud. Thus, Rav Naḥman uses the contemporary pronunciation for the word, rather than its Hebrew or Aramaic reflex.

In segment (D), about a certain kind of drink, Rav Yehuda prefers the rabbinic usage of a Greek word, *ʾīspargos* (ἀσπάραγος), referred to elsewhere in rabbinic literature as an alcoholic beverage especially suited for healing certain ailments and that is not diluted.[141] Rav Naḥman, however, uses the Persian word *ʾanbaga* which, as mentioned, similarly means unmixed, or undiluted, wine.[142] Strangely, Rav Yehuda instead suggests *ʾanpaka*, the same Persian word used by Rav Naḥman, with only minor differences in pronunciation.[143] However, these differences are telling: Rav Naḥman's *ʾanbaga* reflects the pronunciation of Middle Persian that was common in the Sasanian period, with voiced consonants like b and g. By contrast, Rav Yehuda's *ʾanpaka*, with unvoiced consonants p and k in the same positions, reflects the older pre-Middle Persian usage that would have entered Jewish Babylonian Aramaic before the Sasanian period.[144]

The difference between the words used by the two figures therefore pertains not to the language of origin, but to linguistic register. The words attributed by Rav Yehuda to the rabbis or to Jewish colloquial speech are

[140] Similar words appear in Mandaic as well, although these forms are probably from later periods. See Drower and Macuch, *A Mandaic Dictionary*, 44 and 182.

[141] b. Ber. 51a.

[142] See Zsigmond Telegdi, "Essai sur la phonétique des emprunts iraniens en arameen talmudique," *Journal Asiatique* 226 (1935): 186 and 191; Y. A. Solodukho in Jacob Neusner, *Soviet Views of Talmud Judaism: Five Papers by Yu. A. Solodukho in English Translation* (Leiden: 1973), 91–94; and Sokoloff, *DJBA*, 146.

[143] These words are also associated together in b. B. Bat. 58b, a rather obscure passage. The similarity between the two words appears to have troubled some later transmitters of the text, who removed the second; see She'iltot 43 in Shmuel Mirsky, *She'iltot of Rav Ahai Gaon, Exodus*, vol. 3 (Jerusalem: 1963), 33–35.

[144] See the Middle Persian form *anāb* found in the Pahlavi *Vīdēvdād* 3.23 (twice), 3.24, 3.4 (twice), and 5.52 (twice), with Shaked, "Between Iranian and Aramaic," 128–129.

also found in the Hebrew Bible, the Mishnah, and other rabbinic texts. In addition, the Iranian words preferred by Rav Yehuda entered Jewish Babylonian Aramaic at an earlier stage in the language's history, and therefore had already become familiar words with familiar pronunciations.[145] Rav Naḥman, by contrast, prefers *en vogue* pronunciations of the period – even for words that were in use among Jews, albeit in their older pronunciation. To put it in a contemporary American English context: If some Jews say "croissant" [kɹə'sɑnt], Rav Naḥman, the elite, adopts the French pronunciation ['kʁwa.sɑ̃]; and what some Jews call a "party," Rav Naḥman calls a "*soiree.*" This analogy further indicates that, despite pronouncing the same words differently, or using different words to describe the same object, there is no fundamental difference in the object used by both parties in the story. According to the story, Rav Naḥman is particularly haughty because of his use of language, but the habits themselves are unproblematic.

In the continuation, an ostensibly more significant distinction between the two characters is developed. Rav Yehuda castigates Rav Naḥman for his permissive attitude towards fraternization with women, evidenced by Rav Naḥman's offer to have his daughter come serve them, and his suggestion that Rav Yehuda send greetings to Rav Naḥman's wife. In response, Rav Yehuda cites several dicta from Shmuel, slightly modifying them to fit the circumstances. Thus, when Rav Naḥman suggests that Rav Yehuda send regards to his wife, Rav Yehuda responds, "Thus said Shmuel, 'One must not enquire after a woman's welfare.'" When Rav Naḥman suggests that Rav Yehuda at least send regards through a messenger, Rav Yehuda declares, "Thus said Shmuel, 'One must not enquire after a woman's welfare at all.'" These slight modifications of Shmuel's pronouncements after each of Rav Naḥman's subsequent propositions suggests that they are manufactured for the express purpose of embarrassing Rav Naḥman. Indeed, what Rav Yehuda attributes to Shmuel is unparalleled elsewhere in rabbinic literature. Rather, Rav

[145] In linguistic terms, they are *Lehnwörter*, as opposed to *Fremdwörter*. Note that *Lehnwörter* are not typically perceived as foreign by monolingual speakers of a language. See Aaron Butts, "The Greco-Roman Context of the Syriac Language," in *Les auteurs syriaques et leur langue*, ed. Margherita Farina (Paris: 2018), 141–142. For the historical importance of determining when a loanword entered a particular language, see Aaron Butts, *Language Change in the Wake of Empire: Syriac in Its Greco-Roman Context* (Winona Lake, IN: 2016), 53–60, building upon Ciancaglini, *Iranian Loanwords in Syriac*, 25–28.

Yehuda is here presenting an exaggeratedly conservative approach to women, precisely to draw a greater contrast between him and Rav Naḥman. The point is to emphasize that while Rav Yehuda may participate in the banquet, he is guided first and foremost by rabbinic law. Judging by the ample evidence of the participation of women in elite Sasanian banquets, Rav Naḥman is instead painted as driven by the dictates of aristocratic habits.[146]

This rabbinic story therefore addresses competing claims for social prominence within the Babylonian Jewish community. Rav Yehuda claims privileged standing for himself as a rabbi who represents rabbinic knowledge. He disparages the competing claim of Rav Naḥman, a member of the Exilarch's household, who presents himself as a Jewish Sasanian aristocrat. Indeed, Rav Naḥman's own wife encourages him to dismiss Rav Yehuda before the latter reduces him to nothing more than "a commoner." This is precisely what is at stake in this encounter: who is an elite, and what is deserving of elite status. Rav Yehuda proves that greater weight must be given to rabbinic norms above all else.

Rav Yehuda does not, however, object to Sasanian elite culture per se; after all, he does not rebuff Rav Naḥman's invitation to join him in the banquet. He is not ignorant of these norms; indeed, he understands and partakes of the various foods that Rav Naḥman offers. Rav Yehuda objects instead to what he perceives as the undue prominence given to Sasanian-based cultural pretensions, rather than rabbinic values and norms, using language and practices that distinguish Rav Naḥman from other Jews.[147] The framing narrative emphasizes this point: Recall that the encounter between Rav Yehuda and Rav Naḥman is precipitated by Rav Yehuda's disparagement of an elite who claims Hasmonean descent in order to be served first, a privilege reserved for Rav Yehuda himself. Rav Yehuda is not merely a pious renunciant distancing himself from the luxuries of elite life; he too expects to benefit from his status. As a member of a rabbinic elite, he feels entitled to be served before a Hasmonean claimant, and then to humiliate both the Hasmonean claimant and a member of the household of the Exilarch. Rav Yehuda partakes in Rav Naḥman's banquet, although he criticizes the latter for elevating Sasanian over rabbinic norms. Ultimately, Rav Yehuda represents a different

[146] On the role of women in Sasanian banquets assumed in this story, see Gross, "Rethinking Babylonian Rabbinic Acculturation," 295–298.

[147] Wimpfheimer, *Narrating the Law*, 154–158 (see also pp. 122–146 for a larger discussion of "Torah capital").

hybrid equation, one in which, at least performatively, rabbinic norms are elevated above all else, but where many of the elite habits and expectations remain the same. The difference between alternative pronunciations for a fancy cocktail, which both parties enjoy while sitting on the same banqueting couch is, in the end, rather small.

This rabbinic story is therefore quite different from several non-Jewish texts that treat elite culture and religious piety as diametrically opposed. As we saw above, *The History of Mar Qardagh* valorizes the renunciation of an elite Sasanian lifestyle. Elite Christian figures like the sons of Yusik are denounced for their adoption of the lavish habits of the Sasanian elite.[148] Christian sources condemn those priests seeking higher status who appeal to "the patronage of outside people and worldly believers."[149] A Middle Persian story in the ninth-century *Dēnkard* draws a similar contrast between two ascetic Zoroastrian priests and the opulence of a certain high priest.[150] In this story, two ascetic ("disciplined") and pious Zoroastrian priests live simple lives, working the field for sustenance while reciting the sacred Avesta and Zand, when a Zoroastrian high priest passes by. They explicitly rebuke the high priest for his opulence and merrymaking, which contrast markedly with their modest lifestyles and humble piety. The chief priest attempts to earn – or buy – their affection through patronage. Yet the two priests rebuff his efforts, accepting a tiny fraction of what he had sent them and refusing the rest, returning to their simple lives. In contrast, while some rabbis criticize the Exilarch for what they consider his undue elevation of Sasanian over rabbinic habits, they do not renounce these habits nor elite privileges altogether. More radical renunciations of elite life existed in the Sasanian world, but they are not what we find in the Talmud.

148 See similarly regarding the early seventh century Catholicos Gregory of Prat: Scher, *Chronique de Séert*, 2.202–203; Budge, *Thomas of Marga's Book of Governors*, 86–88; and Bar Hebraeus, *Ecclesiastical Chronicle* (ed. Abeloos and Lamy), 2.108–10.

149 See the Synod of 554, Canon 1, in Chabot, *Synodicon Orientale*, 98–99, 355–356.

150 For text and translation, see Shaked, *Wisdom of the Sasanian Sages* (Denkard VI), *Persian Heritage Series 34* (Boulder, CO: 1979), 176–181. For discussion, see Mansour Shaki, "Fillet of Nobility," *Bulletin of the Asia Institute* 4 (1990): 277–279; Shaked, "Esoteric Trends," 214–219; Shaked, *Dualism in Transformation*, 117–118; Russell, "On Mysticism and Esotericism among the Zoroastrians," *Iranian Studies* 26 (1993): 89; and Gignoux, "Pour une Equisse des Fonctions Religieuses sous les Sassanides," *Jerusalem Studies in Arabic and Islam* 7 (1986): 102–104. More generally on Hērbeds, see: Marie-Louise Chaumont, "Recherches sur le clergé zoroastrien: Le hērbad," *Revue de l'histoire des religions* 158 (1960): 55–80, 161–179.

Rabbis and Exilarchs therefore existed in various kinds of relationship to one another. Some fell under the Exilarch's aegis and legitimated the Exilarch and his habits, while others – and perhaps the very same rabbis who were in his household – sought to elevate rabbinic over exilarchal elitism, without necessarily delegitimizing the Exilarch or his claims of status entirely. This point is encapsulated by the continuation of the medieval account about the Exilarch's annual festival in his honor. According to Sherira Gaon, although the Exilarchs usually held their festivals in Nehardea, they deferred to Rav Ashi (d. 420) – due to his great prominence and prestige – and held their festival instead in his city of Mata Meḥasia, a practice that continued after Rav Ashi died.[151] Regardless of this historicity of this source – indeed any of the sources discussed in this chapter – we see how Exilarchs and rabbis might simultaneously jostle for power and prestige while paying respect to each other, and appeal to different vocabularies of legitimation and power without entirely dismissing that of their competitor.

RABBIS AND SASANIAN COURTLY CULTURE

Rabbis internalized, adapted, and deployed elite Sasanian symbols in the Sasanian Empire in their own self-presentation, even outside of their relationship with the Exilarch.

In a much-studied story in the Talmud, rabbinic academies are depicted as sharing many of the trappings, pomp, and circumstance of the royal Sasanian court.[152] The story contains one of the first descriptions of a rabbinic academy, which represents a major institutional change from the small, localized disciple circles of the so-called Amoraic period (third–fifth centuries CE).[153] Large rabbinic academies first arose near the end of the Sasanian period, after which they persisted far into the

151 Lewin, *Iggeret Rav Sherira Gaon*, 91–92.

152 b. B. Qam. 117a; Sperber, "The Unfortunate Adventures of Rav Kahana," 83–100; Herman, "Story of Rav Kahana," 53–86. More generally on the penetration of Sasanian royal imagery into the Talmud, see Geoffrey Herman, "Insurrection in the Academy: the Babylonian Talmud and the Paikuli Inscription" [in Hebrew], *Zion* 79 (2014): 377–407; Herman, "Ahasuerus, the Former Stable-Master of Belshazzar and the Wicked Alexander of Macedon: Two Parallels between the Babylonian Talmud and Persian Sources," *Association for Jewish Studies Review* 29 (2005): 283–297; and Rubenstein, "King Herod in Ardashir's Court: The Rabbinic Story of Herod (B. Bava Batra 3b–4a) in Light of Persian Sources," *Association for Jewish Studies Review* 38 (2014): 249–274.

153 Goodblatt, *Rabbinic Instruction*.

medieval period.[154] As Daniel Sperber among others has shown, in this story's description of the rabbinic academy, members are hierarchically distinguished by means of two furnishings that were standard features of Iranian court culture. First, the rabbis were seated in a series of seven rows according to rank, and were elevated or demoted depending on their performance in relation to other disciples.[155] Seating by rank was a central organizational feature of Iranian imperial culture for centuries; already ancient Greek authors report that Cyrus the Great's court was set in rows, an aspect of imperial Iranian culture that continued through the Abbasid period.[156] Al-Masʿūdī attributes this seating practice to the first Sasanian king Ardashir, in whose court "the courtiers were arranged according to their rank." As in the rabbinic story, honor and shame in the Sasanian court was expressed by the location or removal of one's seat.[157]

According to the same talmudic story, the leading members of the rabbinic academy also sat on cushions that were stacked according to rank, with the most elevated rabbi sitting on seven cushions. This practice

154 David M. Goodblatt, "New Developments in the Study of the Babylonian *Yeshivot*" [in Hebrew], *Zion* 46 (1981): 14–28; Isaiah Gafni, "Yeshiva and Metivta" [In Hebrew], *Zion* 43 (1978): 12–37; Isaiah Gafni, "Concerning D. Goodblatt's Article" [in Hebrew], *Zion* 46 (1981): 52–56; Rubenstein, *Talmudic Stories*, 206–10; Jeffrey L. Rubenstein, "The Rise of the Babylonian Rabbinic Academy: A Reexamination of the Talmudic Evidence," *Jewish Studies Internet Journal* 1 (2002): 55–68; Brody, "On the Sources", 104–107 (Appendix C); Lightstone, "The Institutionalization of the Rabbinic Academy in Late Sassanid Babylonia and the Redaction of the Babylonian Talmud," *Studies in Religion/ Sciences Religieuses* 22 (1993): 167–186; Sacha Stern, "Rabbinic Academies in Late Antiquity: State of Current Research," in *L'enseignement supérieur dans les mondes antiques et médiévaux. Aspects institutionnels, juridiques et pédagogiques*, ed. Henri Hugonnard-Roche (Paris: 2008), 221–238.

155 This conforms with medieval descriptions of the rabbinic academy. For Arabic, see Menachem Ben-Sasson, "Structure, Purpose, and Content of R. Natan HaBavli's Work" [in Hebrew], in *Culture and Society in Medieval Jewish History: Studies Dedicated to the Memory of Haim Hillel Ben-Sasson*, ed. Menahem Ben-Sasson, Robert Bonfil, and Joseph R. Hacker (Jerusalem: 1989), 194–195. For Hebrew, see Neubauer, *Mediaeval Jewish Chronicles*, 87.

156 Iranian royal court culture has a long history. See, for instance, Llewellyn-Jones, *King and Court*; Rolf Strootman, *Courts and Elites in the Hellenistic Empires: The Near East after the Achaemenids c. 330–30 BCE* (Edinburgh: 2014); and Frantz Grenet, "In Search of Missing Links: Iranian Royal Protocol from the Achaemenids to the Mughals," in *India and Iran in the Longue Durée*, ed. Alka Patel and Touraj Daryaee (Irvine, CA: 2017), 75–90.

157 Shaked, "From Iran to Islam," 31–40. As noted by Herman, "Story of Rav Kahana," 72–73, a similar hierarchically ordered seating arrangement of ecclesiastical figures is mandated in the Synod of 576 CE. See Chabot, *Synodicon Orientale*, 128 (Syr.), 387 (French).

FIGURE 3. Sasanian silver plate, a prestige item here depicting a Sasanian king and queen reclining on cushions in a banquet scene. [Walters Art Gallery, Accession Number 57.709]

is similar to the royal court as depicted, among other places, on Sasanian silver plates, in which the king typically reclines upon seven cushions (see Figure 3).[158] It should not surprise us at this point that the term for "cushion" in the Talmud is an Iranian loanword (from Middle Persian *wistarag*), also used in other texts that describe elite Sasanian culture.

Rabbinic academies were therefore constructed, or at least imagined, in imitation of the royal court. Indeed, in imagining their community, the rabbis adopted other descriptors of royalty, such as describing the heads of academies as "reigning (מלך)" over their students.[159] Even if some rabbis might object to certain competing uses of Sasanian elite culture, they were still shaped by it and used it to express the elevated position in Jewish society to which they aspired.

[158] See Sperber, "Unfortunate Adventures," 91–93; Herman, "The Story of Rav Kahana," 60n7; and Herman, "One Day David Went Out for the Hunt," 130–134.

[159] Rabbis adopted other aspects of Sasanian courtly imagery; see Herman, "Insurrection in the Academy," 377–407. See also Morony, "Religious Communities," 117–118, regarding Christian imitation of Sasanian titles. Manichaean texts present alms offered to the Elect as in some ways equivalent to bestowing gifts on the king. See Iris Colditz, "Manichaean Time-Management: Laymen between Religious and Secular Duties," in *New Light on Manichaeism: Papers from the Sixth International Congress on Manichaeism*, ed. Jason BeDuhn (NHMS 64, Leiden: 2009), 73–99.

THE BENEFITS OF RABBINIC STATUS

If the Exilarch's position as a Sasanian-Jewish aristocrat enabled him to benefit socially and materially, the rabbis could also leverage their self-presentation and claims to elite status to extract material benefits from other Jews. Here too, the rabbis drew on and mimicked other models from Sasanian society that were available to them. This is reflected in one astonishing passage that proposes that rabbis should be exempted from taxes on the grounds that they were somehow analogous to Zoroastrian priests.

This rabbinic statement appears in a larger discussion about rabbinic tax exemptions, which opens with a series of aphorisms that encourages rabbis to refrain from benefiting from their positions.[160] For instance, R. Yoḥanan is quoted as saying: "Whoever puts the crown of the Torah to [profane] use, is uprooted from the world." A similar statement is attributed to the earlier Palestinian rabbi, Eliezer the son of Rabbi Zadok: "Perform deeds for the sake of their Maker and speak of them for their own sake. Do not make them a crown with which to magnify yourself, nor a spade to dig with." Most of these statements are derived from earlier Palestinian discussions.[161]

Yet, immediately following these statements, a series of dicta are attributed to the Babylonian figure Rava describing several ways a rabbi may actively petition to benefit from his position. Rava first appeals to seemingly timeless biblical exegesis, but then turns to the realities of the Sasanian Empire itself.[162]

A. Rava said, "A rabbinic scholar may assert, 'I am a rabbinic scholar; my business should receive first attention; as it is written, 'And David's sons were priests' (2 Sam. 8.18), just as a priest receives [his portion] first, so too does the scholar.'"
And how do we know this of a priest? Because it is written, "You shall sanctify him [the priest], for he offers the bread of your God (Lev. 21.8), and the school of R. Ishmael taught: 'You shall sanctify him' – in all matters pertaining to holiness,

160 b. Ned. 62a–b. There is a parallel to this discussion, with significant differences, in b. B. Bat. 8a. For the rejection of earlier theories of Babylonian rabbinic tax exemption, see Beer, "Were the Babylonian Amoraim Exempt from Taxes"; and Beer, *Babylonian Amoraim*, 227–242.

161 y. Sheb. 4.2 (35b); *Sifre Deuteronomy* ʿeqev 48 (ed. Finkelstein, 114).

162 Rava's advocacy for rabbinic privilege is found elsewhere as well. See Wimpfheimer, *Narrating the Law*, 131–133.

to be the first to commence [the reading of the Torah], the first to pronounce the blessing, and first to receive a good portion."
B. Rava said, "A rabbinic scholar may declare, I will not pay poll tax, for it is written, 'it shall not be lawful to impose *mindāh*, *belo*, or *halāk* upon them [i.e. priests and temple personnel]' (Ezra 7.24)." Rav Judah said, '*mindāh*' is the king's portion; '*belo*' is a poll tax; and '*halāk*' is the crop tax."
C. Rava also said: "A rabbinic scholar may declare, 'I am a servant of fire, and will not pay poll tax.'"
What is the reason? Because it is said to drive away a lion.

Rava first argues that rabbis may use their status to obtain privileges in the market. He analogizes rabbis with priests based on a verse in 2 Sam. 8.18, which says that the sons of David were priests.[163] Of course, there is no other record of David's children serving as priests, so Rava is suggesting that David's children were viewed *as if* they were priests, by enjoying the same benefits as priests. By analogy, the rabbis too should be granted privileges *as if* they were priests.[164] Continuing in this vein, Rava says that a rabbi may exempt himself from the poll tax based on Ezra 7.24, in which the Achaemenids exempted Jewish temple personnel from taxes. Rava therefore justifies both the rabbis' right of first attention in the market and their entitlement to tax exemptions from biblical verses about priestly benefits.

Rava's final statement is therefore odd in two ways: First, it does not introduce a new privilege, but simply provides a new rationale for the previous rabbinic exemption from the poll tax. Second, Rava does not here cite a biblical verse as precedent.[165] Instead, he argues that a rabbi can say that he is an "*avda d-nura*," literally "a servant/worshipper of (the) fire" and thereby exempt himself from the tax.

Rava's final statement has understandably generated many different interpretations. On its face, it rules that a rabbi may claim to be a fire worshipper. This statement is followed by an anonymous interpolation

[163] 1 Chron. 18.17 eliminates this problem.
[164] For rabbis as priests, see Neusner, *History of the Jews in Babylonia*, 2.147–150; and Krista Dalton, "Teaching for the Tithe: Donor Expectations and the Matrona's Tithe," *Association for Jewish Studies Review* 44 (2020): 49–73.
[165] Goodblatt, "Poll Tax," 282, notes these differences, but suggests that the final statement is therefore the only one that can undoubtedly be attributed to Rava, while the first three seem to be later additions. It is unclear to me why one would privilege the final source over the first three.

which appears to have been uncomfortable with Rava's suggestion and therefore offers a justification for it: "What is the reason? Because it is said to drive away a lion." This justification finds a close parallel in another editorial gloss in the Talmud, suggesting that it is a later appendage to Rava's dicta.[166] The gloss here construes Rava to permit the extreme measure of deception only in order to evade "a lion," meaning the tax collector.[167]

Reading Rava's statement outside of the anonymous interpolation raises several questions: What exactly did he mean by "a servant of the fire?" To whom was this claim to be made? How would this claim effectively exempt the rabbinic claimant from paying the poll tax? Some scholars have argued that the term "a servant of the fire" – an expression used to describe Zoroastrians in Greek, Latin, Armenian, and even New Persian – must refer to a run-of-the-mill Zoroastrian.[168] But this would imply that simple Zoroastrians were somehow entitled to a universal poll tax exemption, a notion that is belied by copious evidence.[169] Indeed, it would defy reason to suggest that the empire could somehow afford not to collect this tax from Zoroastrians, who represented a significant percentage of its overall population.

In several publications, Maria Macuch has trenchantly argued that the term "slave of the fire" is in fact a translation of a technical Middle Persian term.[170] Macuch suggests two candidates found in the so-called Sasanian law book, the *Book of a Thousand Judgments*: *Bandag ī ātaxš* (or *ādurān bandag*) and *anšahrīg (ī) ātaxš*. These two terms refer to people either enslaved to or who served as attendants of a fire temple. While semantically these terms both roughly translate to "servant/slave of the fire," they appear to be at odds with Rava's goal throughout his series of statements to claim rabbinic exemption based on their *superior*

[166] b. B. Meṣ.72b. See similarly Goodblatt, "Poll Tax," 283.

[167] For lying to evade certain kinds of tax collection, see m. Ned. 3.4 and b. B. Qam. 113a.

[168] For a summary of this and other scholarly views, see Goodblatt, "The Poll Tax," 282–287. On the term, see Albert de Jong, *Traditions of the Magi: Zoroastrianism in Greek and Latin Literature* (Leiden: 1997), 343n1.

[169] See esp. Rubin, "The Reforms of Khusro Anushirwān," 225–297; and Goodblatt, "Poll Tax," 233–295.

[170] Maria Macuch, "The Talmudic Expression 'Servant of the Fire' in the Light of Pahlavi Legal Sources," *Jerusalem Studies in Arabic and Islam* 26 (2002): 109–129.

position in society.[171] Furthermore, it is unclear whether a non-Zoroastrian could have served in these positions.[172] Even if they could, however, it is not clear what made the rabbis uniquely qualified to make this claim to justify their tax exemption; could any Jew, or for that matter anyone, claim to be enslaved to a fire temple and thereby successfully evade taxes? Was the tax enforcement so lax that one could simply claim an exemption without fear of examination?

Finally, a number of scholars translate the term "servant of the fire" to mean a Zoroastrian *priest* (*hērbad* or *mobed*).[173] At first glance, this interpretation seems more plausible because we do have evidence that priests were exempted from poll taxes under Khusro I's tax reforms, and possibly earlier as well.[174] Rava is therefore suggesting that rabbis demand a comparable tax exemption to Zoroastrian priests, which is consistent with his previous statements that claim priestly privileges for the rabbis by analogy to Jewish priests. This interpretation also fits well with the general thrust of Rava's argument that rabbis should be exempted from paying taxes on account of their elevated communal status.[175] The rabbis were not *claiming* to be Zoroastrian priests but were

[171] To address this issue, Macuch claims that there may be some ambiguity as to whether *bandag ī ātaxš* means a "slave" or a more volitional "worker," but this ambiguity does not seem borne out in the sources. The passages about Mihr Narseh do not seem to be representative, as Macuch suggests, but rather the exception to the rule. See, for example, *MHD* 101.8–11, where *bandag* refers to a full slave, with enslaved children.

[172] In support of this contention, Macuch cites only a report in *Ḥamza Al-Iṣfahānī*, in U. M. Daudpota (trans.), *The Annals of Ḥamza Al-Iṣfahānī* (Bombay: 1932), 40, which is further discussed in Chapter 3. It is problematic to extrapolate broadly from this single episode.

[173] Goodblatt, "Poll Tax," 283–285.

[174] On the reforms, see Rubin, "The Reforms of Khusro Anushirwān," 225–297; Andrea Gariboldi, "The Great 'Restoration' of Husraw I," in *Husraw Ier reconstructions d'un règne: sources et documents*, ed. Christelle Jullien (Paris, 2015), 47–84; and Simcha Gross, "Editorial Material in the Babylonian Talmud and Its Sasanian Context," *Association of Jewish Studies Review* 47 (2023): 56–63.

[175] Goodblatt, "Poll Tax," 283–285 critiques this view on the ground that there is no Middle Persian term that is equivalent to "servant of the fire" (*avda d-nura*) for Zoroastrian priests. He also notes that in Hebrew and Aramaic the term *avda* ("servant") followed by a genitive phrase like *d-nura* ("fire") would typically signify a generic worshipper of fire, not a priest or significant figure. However, many later Arabic sources *do* gloss *hērbad*, or Zoroastrian priest, as "servant of the fire," precisely the group said by al-Ṭabarī to be exempt from Sasanian taxes (C. E. Bosworth, *The Sāsānids, the Byzantines, the Lakhmids, and Yemen*, vol. 5, *The History of al-Ṭabarī*, 259–260, with fn. 625). See Chaumont, "Recherches sur le clerge Zoroastrien," 162–164. Goodblatt may assume that this claim was made to Iranian officials and so must have an Iranian calque, but see my solution below. Moreover, Rava's connection between a "priest" and

instead presenting an *argument* by analogy: If Zoroastrian priests are tax exempt, so too should rabbis be because we perform the same function for Jews.

Moshe Beer suggested that the rabbis made this claim to Zoroastrian tax collectors.[176] However, the notion that this argument might convince them defies belief. Would Zoroastrian tax collectors have known enough about Jewish communal life to differentiate between authentic rabbis and non-rabbis, or between different Jewish ritual experts? Why would they be amenable to exempting Jews of any rank or status from taxes? It is unlikely that tax collectors were in the business of granting discretionary exemptions rather than maximizing revenues.

It is far more likely that Rava's intention was that rabbis could equate themselves to "servants of the fire" to fellow Jews to encourage them to cover their taxes.[177] Indeed, Rava's previous statements justifying rabbinic privileges and exemptions are all addressed to Jews. As other talmudic pericopes show, rabbis sought to have other Jews cover their taxes for them, and in the case of Jewish tax collectors, to exempt them.[178] Rava is therefore here contending that the rabbis could claim to fellow Jews that they constituted the Jewish equivalent to Zoroastrian priests and should be entitled to the same privileges.

fire worshipper is also found in *The Cave of Treasures* 27.12–16 (see Minov, *Memory and Identity*, 163), where the same figure (Ardashir) is described as a "priest" who "served the fire (ܕܡܫܡܫ ܗܘܐ ܠܢܘܪܐ)" where "priest" and "servant of the fire" are treated as synonyms. Ahdut, "The Talmud Expression," 13–26, believes Rava's suggestion is intended to be deceptive, as according to him rabbis were visually indistinguishable from Zoroastrian priests, both wearing specialized dress, specifically white robes. In fact, the passage upon which Ahdut rests his case is best understood as referring to the rabbis as "white," that is, pure, which conforms to the semiotic opposition of black and white clothing found in rabbinic literature, for which see Ishay Rosen-Zvi, *Mishnaic Sotah Ritual: Temple, Gender, and Midrash* (Leiden: 2012), 84–85.

176 Beer, "Were the Babylonian Amoraim Exempt from Taxes," 253.

177 For a similar suggestion, albeit for a later period, see S. D. Goitein, *A Mediterranean Society: The Jewish Communities of the Arab World as Portrayed in the Documents of the Cairo Geniza*, vol. 2 (Berkeley: 1971), 386.

178 For covering others' tax, see b. B. Bat. 55a (with Goodblatt, "Poll Tax," 252–255), b. Sanh. 27a–b; b. ʿAbod. Zar. 4a; B. Bat. 7b–8a (with Michael Satlow, "A Historical Source? B. Baba Batra 7b–8a," *Journal for the Study of Judaism* 28 [1997]: 314–320). For an East Syriac equivalent, see Chabot, *Synodicon Orientale*, 225–226. For Jewish tax collectors, see b. Sanh. 25b–26a; B. Bat. 167a; B. Bat. 8a. For rabbinic exemption from contributing to a communal well, see b. B. Bat. 8a (see partial parallel in b. B. Meṣ. 108a). In b. Soṭ. 10a, the rabbis say a biblical character was punished for imposing a type of tax on the sages.

Rava's analogy therefore conceptualizes Jewish society and the place of the rabbis within it through the lens of the Sasanian social order. For this analogy to hold, Rava must assume a certain structural similarity between Jewish and Iranian society, and an analogy between rabbis and Zoroastrian priests, and that other Jews would find his analogy persuasive.[179] Where the Exilarch drew from the vocabulary of the Sasanian aristocracy, some rabbis analogized themselves to Sasanian religious elites to signal their desired place within Jewish society.[180]

CONCLUSION

Jewish elites, like the Exilarch and the rabbis, competed for social status in an environment redolent with different kinds of Sasanian elite figures and their attending legitimating vocabularies, which they internalized, deployed, and defined themselves against. Different Jews drew from these vocabularies in different configurations and in different ways.

The Exilarch translated Sasanian aristocratic symbols and behaviors into Jewish terms, from his habits, lavish estates, and claims of noble descent, to his cultivation of a royal court in miniature, into whose orbit he drew other Jewish elites. Some rabbis, perhaps because of shared financial and cultural interests or the promise of personal gain, joined the ranks of the Exilarch, helping to legitimate him further. Others,

179 For other examples of analogy between Jewish and Sasanian administrative positions, see b. Ket. 85b–86a with Jonathan Pomeranz, "Concealing the Law: The Limits of Legal Promulgation among the Rabbis of Babylonia," in *Rethinking "Authority" in Late Antiquity: Authorship, Law, and Transmission in Jewish and Christian Tradition*, ed. A. J. Berkovitz and Mark Letteney (London: 2018), 125–126. See also b. Sanh. 98a, with parallel in b. Shab. 139a, where Babylonian Jewish society is in some ways thought to mimic Sasanian society, including how presumably Jewish, but perhaps not rabbinic, judges and Sasanian officers are equivalent (discussion in Secunda, *Iranian Talmud*, 80–82).

180 There are other examples of these analogies used pejoratively. An arrogant rabbi proud of studying with another rabbi could be dismissively referred to as someone elated to have run into a *hargbed*, a high administrative figure (b. Zeb. 96b), on which see Chapter 1. Ignorant reciters of rabbinic study circles (tannaim) are compared to "mumbling magi," deploying a widespread stereotype that painted Zoroastrian recitation as mindless muttering: b. Soṭ. 22a, with Jonas C. Greenfield, "Ratin Megosha," in *Joshua Finkel Festschrift: In Honor of Dr. Joshua Finkel*, ed. Sydney B. Hoenig and Leon D. Stitskin (New York: 1974), 63–69. This should not be confused with Jacob Neusner, "Rabbi and Magus," 169–178; Mokhtarian, *Rabbis, Sorcerers, Kings, and Priests*, 94–123; and Vidas, *Tradition and the Formation of the Talmud*, 115–149, who argue that the rabbis functioned and were organized similarly to the magi.

however, chose to distinguish rabbinic status from the aristocratic habits of the Exilarch, either by subsuming elite Sasanian culture within rabbinic norms, or at times by constructing some, often minor, contrasts between the Exilarch's Sasanian aristocratic habits and an exaggerated version of rabbinic law. Even outside of their interactions with the Exilarch, the rabbis could draw from pervasive symbols of social status by modeling themselves on other Sasanian elites, most astonishingly among them, Zoroastrian priests.

Though we have significant evidence only for the Exilarch and the rabbis, they offer at least a schematic picture of the range of possibilities available to Jewish and other elite aspirants in the dynamic contest for power and status among Sasanian communities. Without formally recognized and guaranteed positions, these various elites competed for power and recognition by drawing from a range of legitimating vocabularies informed by and entrenched in Sasanian and Jewish culture and society.

3

Beyond 'Tolerance'

The Logics of Sasanian Violence against Jews

In an epistle written around the early ninth century, the Babylonian Jewish polemicist Pirqoi ben Baboi chastised Jewish communities around the Mediterranean for adopting certain Palestinian practices that he dubbed "customs of persecution" (*minhagey shmad*).[1] He contended that these customs were not products of the authentic continuous transmission of Jewish tradition extending back to Moses on Mount Sinai, but erroneous corruptions introduced as a result of Roman persecution of Jews. The Babylonian rabbinic tradition, by contrast, was more authentic because Jews had enjoyed consistently peaceable conditions under Persian rule. They were therefore free to practice and preserve traditional Jewish law accurately in an over millennium-long unbroken chain of transmission.

Although Pirqoi ben Baboi wrote in an indisputably polemical vein, the spirit of his remarks continues to animate the historiography of Jews under Sasanian rule. It is therefore almost a truism that Jews were subjected to little violence at the hands of the Sasanians.[2] While allowing

[1] In general, see Robert Brody, *Pirqoy ben Baboy and the History of Internal Polemics in Judaism* [in Hebrew] (Tel Aviv: 2003); and Simcha Gross, "Playing with Persecution: Parallel Jewish and Christian Memories of Late Antiquity in Early Islamic Iraq," *Journal of Near Eastern Studies* 81 (2022): 247–260.

[2] This view has remained largely unchanged for nearly two centuries of the study of Babylonian Jews. In 1865, Joshua Heschel Schorr, "The Circumstances of the Jews in Persia," *HeHalutz* 7 (1865): 75, averred that "the Persians excel in the quality of tolerance (טולירנץ) even to this day." More recent studies include Brody, "Judaism in the Sasanian Empire," 52–62; Gafni, "Babylonian Rabbinic Culture," 236–238; Yaakov Elman and Shai Secunda, "Judaism," in *The Wiley Blackwell Companion to Zoroastrianism*, ed. Michael Stausberg, Yuhan Sohrab-Dinshaw Vevaina, and Anna Tessmann (Hoboken, NJ:

for occasional incidents of violence driven by some zealous Zoroastrian magi, it is largely assumed that Sasanian kings and imperial policy expressed a broad "tolerance" toward Jews and their religious practices.[3] Jewish communities therefore enjoyed relative comfort and security, and thrived in an environment that nurtured and spurred their extraordinary cultural productivity during this period, which is manifest in the Babylonian Talmud. In contrast, Roman persecution had sapped Palestinian Jewry of virtually all of its creative vitality.[4] As one scholar concludes, it was the "centuries of security and tranquillity" that "must have contributed in no small measure to the development of the Babylonian Talmud and of Talmudic Judaism."[5] The peaceable conditions of Sasanian rule created the necessary conditions for the rise and spread of the Babylonian rabbinic movement and the production of the Talmud, forever shaping later Jewish history.[6]

The notion that the Sasanians were particularly tolerant toward Jews was primarily predicated on a dearth of evidence of imperial violence against them, especially in the Babylonian Talmud. The reasoning here is clear enough: if Jews were subject to regular bouts of violence, then surely they would have recorded it in the Talmud and made their displeasure with Sasanian rule known. Indeed, Syriac Christian literature offers an almost mirror image to the Talmud; it is replete with stories about Sasanian violence which valorize martyrs and others who resisted imperial rule. The scholarly tenet that the Sasanians organized religious communities into semi-autonomous corporate bodies supported the idea that the empire also espoused consistently different attitudes to Jews versus Christians, and it consequently used violence against the latter but rarely

2015), 423–436. A few scholars offered polar opposite views; see Salomon Funk, *Die Juden in Babylonien, 200–500*, vol 1. (Berlin: 1902), 67–68.

[3] On the notion that the experience of subject communities fluctuated based on the proclivities of Sasanian kings, see Chapter 6 below.

[4] For a thorough critique of this argument, see Jeremy Cohen, "Roman Imperial Policy towards the Jews from Constantine until the End of the Palestinian Patriarchate (ca. 429)," *Byzantine Studies* 3 (1976): 1–29; and Hayim Lapin, *Rabbis as Romans*, 151–167.

[5] Brody, "Judaism in the Sasanian Empire," 62. See similarly Neusner, "Jews in Iran," 923. For related arguments, see David Kraemer, *Responses to Suffering in Classical Rabbinic Literature* (Oxford: 1994), 209–210; Holger Zellentin, *Rabbinic Parodies of Jewish and Christian Literature* (Tübingen: 2011), 139 and 139n4; Schäfer, *Jesus in the Talmud* (Princeton, NJ: 2007), 115–122; and Secunda, *Talmud's Red Fence*, 68.

[6] Brown, *The World of Late Antiquity*, 165.

against the former. The two communities therefore had wildly divergent experiences under Sasanian rule because of Sasanian "tolerance" towards Jews and "intolerance" towards Christians.[7]

Recent research on Syriac Christians under Sasanian rule has proceeded in a different direction. Greater attention to the tendentiousness and artifice of hagiographical accounts, especially martyr acts, has cautioned scholars against naively reproducing the image of the bloodthirsty, persecutory, and singularly anti-Christian Sasanian Empire that they often project.[8] These works frame imperial violence as unwarranted, irrational, and illegitimate, setting the stage for glorious martyrdom in defense of religion and community. A view that the Sasanians were consistently intolerant of Christians has collapsed under the weight of evidence for Christian elites who served in various prestigious positions within the empire, some even enjoying close ties with the king and his court. Indeed, the Sasanian Empire supported the establishment of a church hierarchy in its domain and under its aegis. The sheer proliferation and spread of Christianity throughout Sasanian lands, both numerically and institutionally, belies narratives of decline or consistent imperial suppression. Any attempt to essentialize a consistent attitude of the Sasanian Empire to Christians is unsustainable.[9]

At the same time, Sasanian violence against Christians cannot be denied.[10] Under various circumstances, Christians were subjected to physical harm and religious interference. The inability to offer explanations that account for both imperial violence and support lies in the prevailing paradigms used to explain Sasanian violence against non-Zoroastrians, especially the binary of tolerance and intolerance, and the

[7] As seen from the dueling titles of the two most influential articles on Sasanian attitudes toward Christians and Jews respectively: Sebastian Brock, "Christians in the Sasanian," 1–19; and Brody, "Judaism in the Sasanian Empire," 52–62.

[8] See Walker, *Legend of Mar Qardagh*; Becker, "Martyrdom, Religious Difference, and 'Fear,'" 300–336; Payne, *State of Mixture*; Wood, *Chronicle of Seert*, 31–65; Lucas van Rompay, "Impetuous Martyrs? The Situation of the Persian Christians in the Last Years of Yazdgard I (419–20)," in *Martyrium in Multidisciplinary Perspective: Memorial Louis Reekmans*, ed. M. Lamberigts and P. van Deun (Leuven: 1995), 363–375; Geoffrey Herman, "The Last Years of Yazdgird I and the Christians," in *Jews, Christians and Zoroastrians: Religious Dynamics in a Sasanian Context*, ed. Geoffrey Herman (Piscataway, NJ: 2014), 67–90; and Butts and Gross, *The History of the "Slave of Christ."*

[9] Pourshariati, *Decline and Fall*, 347–350.

[10] See Gross, "Being Roman in the Sasanian Empire," 390–397.

assumption of a general consistency in imperial attitudes toward particular religious communities.[11] These positions obscure the diverse and even contradictory bases of the Sasanian Empire's actions, attitudes, and policies toward its heterogenous inhabitants.[12]

Instead of reducing Sasanian violence to a reflexive predisposition towards this or that community, it is best understood as a product of a series of political, ideological, and strategic considerations set within particular conditions.[13] The Sasanians could not subdue and pacify their heterogenous subjects solely through the use of force and violence.[14] Violence was typically deployed strategically to target behavior especially objectionable to the state. As Payne explains, "symbolic and physical acts of violence were instruments of organization and regulation in ancient political cultures, and decoding their significance can as often reveal the dynamics of cooperation as of conflict."[15] Imperial violence was not an expression of "prejudice" or "intolerance" toward particular communities, but rather a tool in the empire's arsenal of communication and persuasion, power and control, to be deployed as needed in an ongoing push and pull between the empire and its subjects.

Violence was therefore an imperial instrument applied in response to the behaviors, positionality, and attitudes of its subjects, which similarly determined in what ways and how regularly they triggered Sasanian imperial anxieties. Jews and Christians may, at different points, have come under increased scrutiny and been subjected to greater violence.

[11] See esp. Mary Boyce, "Toleranz und Intoleranz im Zoroastrismus," *Saeculum* 21 (1970): 325–343. In the case of the Sasanian Empire, "tolerance" and "intolerance" are applied not to refer to a broad approach of the Sasanian Empire to its heterogenous populations, but rather to the consistent attitudes the empire and specific kings adopted towards particularly religious communities. Contrast with the use of "tolerance" in the study of the Roman Empire, for instance: Peter Garnsey, "Religious Toleration in Classical Antiquity," *Studies in Church History* 21 (1984): 1–27; and Clifford Ando, "The Edict of Serdica in Religious-Historical Perspective," in *Serdica Edict (311 AD): Concepts and Realizations of the Idea of Religious Toleration*, ed. V. Vatchkova and D. Dmitrov (Sofia: 2014), 51–62.

[12] Payne, *State of Mixture*, 26.

[13] Rogers Brubaker and Frederick Cooper, *Empires in World History: Power and the Politics of Difference* (Princeton, NJ: 2010), 1–22; Myles Lavan, Richard E. Payne, and John Weisweiler, eds., *Cosmopolitanism and Empire: Universal Rulers, Local Elites, and Cultural Integration in the Ancient Near East and Mediterranean* (Oxford: 2016).

[14] Ando, *Imperial Ideology*, 1–5.

[15] Payne, *State of Mixture*, 26.

These groups, regardless of whether and how often they were subjected to violence, were also audiences of Sasanian violence, who developed their own conceptions of what occasioned it and how to elicit or avoid it. A tabulation of the amount of imperial violence against a particular community misses the logics of imperial violence, and the ways in which Jews and Christians did or did not modify or accommodate their behavior in light of it.[16]

We must therefore ask: When and why did the Sasanian Empire employ violence against any of its subjects? What were its strategic calculations in doing so; that is: What kinds of behaviors was it seeking to encourage or discourage? In what ways did Jews fall afoul of these calculations? Did Jews and Christians elicit violence in similar frequencies and for similar reasons? Answering these questions is complicated by the nature of the sources on imperial violence, which, as already mentioned, are often highly ideological, tendentious, and fictionalized. But by comparing and triangulating the available sources on Sasanian imperial violence, patterns emerge that point to certain shared understandings of the causes of Sasanian violence that could then be used as grist for the hagiographer's mill.

This chapter offers a schematic account of the ideological and political factors that precipitated and informed moments of Sasanian imperial violence, within which it situates reports of violence against Jews.[17] Comparisons with Christian evidence, which is far more abundant, clarifies both the catalysts of Sasanian violence and those factors that caused some communities to be subjected to a greater frequency and intensity of violence than others. Sasanian violence, in turn, serves as a window into the ideology of the empire, the types of behaviors it sought to condition and discourage, and how particular communities presented the Sasanians with different degrees and types of challenges. While this chapter will examine the structural realities of Sasanian rule, the way these structural realities were negotiated by Jews and other subject communities will be the subject of the following chapter.

[16] Becker, "Political Theology and Religious Diversity in the Sasanian Empire," in *Jews, Christians, and Zoroastrians: Religious Dynamics in a Sasanian Context*, ed. Geoffrey Herman (Piscataway, NJ: 2014), 7–25.

[17] For an interesting if positivist earlier attempt to schematize the causes of Sasanian violence against Christians, see Sako, *Le rôle de la Hiérarchie Syriaque-Orientale*, 13–14.

THE BOUNDARIES OF IRANIAN IDENTITY

One of the primary catalysts for imperial violence stemmed from threats to the foundational premises of Sasanian imperial ideology, and the categorical and conceptual boundaries between its subjects that the empire sought to impose and reinforce. Sasanian kings consistently presented themselves as Iranian rulers and rulers of Iranians. At the outset of the new dynasty, the first Sasanian king, Ardashir I, adopted the title of "The divine Mazda-worshipping Ardashir, king of kings of the Iranians (*šāhān šāh ērān*, βασιλεὺς βασιλέων Ἀριανῶν), whose image/seed is from the gods," which he displayed on his coins and monumental inscriptions.[18] Ardashir identifies himself as a worshipper of "Mazda," or Ohrmazd, the chief deity of the Iranian pantheon and appears to claim that he is himself divine.[19] The commensurability between king and deities was epitomized in Ardashir I's rock inscription at Naqsh-e Rustam, in which Ohrmazd, who bestows the king with the insignia of office, appears in equivalent size and pose as the king.[20] Both Ardashir and Ohrmazd are mounted on horseback, trampling their respective antagonists; Ardashir tramples the last ruler of the Parthians, Artabanus IV, while Ohrmazd tramples upon the evil deity Ahriman. Ardashir's defeat of Artabanus is here equated to Ohrmazd's besting of Ahriman at the end of days, the ultimate triumph in Iranian cosmology.

Ardashir further entitled himself king of "Iran," a term which evoked genealogical, behavioral, and religious qualities, as well as a shared mythical past.[21] The significance of this term was amplified by Ardashir's successor, Shapur I, who expanded the term to *ērānšāhr* (territory of the Iranians), to refer to his kingdom. As Gherardo Gnoli has influentially argued, in deploying the term *ērānšāhr*, the Sasanians imported its earlier religious and mythical connotations as the homeland

[18] On Ardashir's titulature, see Touraj Daryaee, "Kingship in Early Sasanian Iran," in *The Sasanian Era*, ed. Vesta S. Curtis and Sarah R. A. Stewart, vol. 3, *The Idea of Iran* (London: 2008), 60–70; Huyse, "Die sasanidische Königstitulatur," 182–201 (esp. 182–183).

[19] For these differing views, see Daryaee, "Kingship in Early Sasanian Iran," 67–68.

[20] See Canepa, *Two Eyes of the Earth*, 59–63; Daryaee, "Kingship in Early Sasanian Iran," 66–67.

[21] Shaked, "Religion in the Late Sasanian Period," 10; Payne, "Avoiding Ethnicity," 212–213; Albert de Jong, "Being Iranian in Antiquity (At Home and Abroad)," in *Persianism in Antiquity*, ed. Rolf Strootman and Miguel John Versluys (Stuttgart: 2017), 45–46.

of the ancient Aryans and applied them to the specific political territory ruled by them.[22] This term summoned ancient notions of a sacred central continent of Iranians, around which the others were situated and therefore fundamentally ancillary.[23] Although some aspects of Ardashir's titulature were discontinued by later kings, they introduced additional claims that similarly harkened back to an Iranian mythical past.[24] The categories drawn from sacred and mythical literature continued to inform Sasanian self-definition, notions of alterity, and policy.[25] The Sasanian kings, from first to last, broadcasted their Iranian identities as fundamental to their imperial ideology and legitimacy as rulers, even as the precise contours of these identities were undoubtedly in flux.

Yet, the Sasanians also claimed universal kingship. Following Shapur I's conquests in the Caucuses, Syria, and Asia Minor, he expanded his title to "the king of kings of the Iranians *and non-Iranians*," a title that would endure on Sasanian coins from the third to fifth centuries.[26] In so doing,

[22] Gherardo Gnoli, *Idea of Iran: An Essay on Its Origins* (Leiden: 1989); A. Shapur Shahbazi, "The History of the Idea of Iran," in *The Birth of the Persian Empire*, ed. Vesta S. Curtis and Sarah Stewart (London: 2005), 100–111, argued that the meaning Gnoli attributes to the term can already be found in Avestan texts. My argument is not dependent on the innovation of the Sasanians, but simply their deployment of this term.

[23] Daryaee, "Ethnic and Territorial Boundaries," 123–138; Canepa, *The Iranian Expanse*, 3–14; Antonio Panaino, "Astral Characters of Kingship in the Sasanian and Byzantine Worlds," in *Convegno internazionale: La Persia e Bisanzio (Roma, 14–18 Ottobre 2002)*, ed. Gherardo Gnoli and Antonio Panaino (Rome: 2004), 555–594; and Antonio Panaino, "The King and the Gods in the Sasanian Royal Ideology," in *Sources pour l'histoire et la géographie du monde iranien* ed. Rika Gyselen, Res Orientales 18 (Leuven: 2009), 209–256. On possible backgrounds of Sasanian political ideology, see M. Rahim Shayegan, *Arsacids and Sasanians: Political Ideology in Post-Hellenistic and Late Antique Persia* (Cambridge: 2011).

[24] Touraj Daryaee, "The Construction of the Past in Late Antique Persia," *Historia: Zeitschrift für Alte Geschichte* 55 (2006): 493–503.

[25] Daryaee, "Ethnic and Territorial Boundaries," 124; Richard Payne, "The Reinvention of Iran: The Sasanian Empire and the Huns," in *The Cambridge Companion to the Age of Attila*, ed. Michael Maas (Cambridge: 2014), 282–299; Richard Payne, "Cosmology and the Expansion of the Iranian Empire, 502–628 CE," *Past and Present* 220.1 (2013): 3–33; and Richard Payne, "The Making of Turan: The Fall and Transformation of the Iranian East in Late Antiquity," *Journal of Late Antiquity* 9 (2016): 4–41.

[26] Shapur I's inscription found in Back, *Die sassanidischen Staatsinschriften*, and translation in Frye, *The History of Ancient Iran*, 371–374. This title was also used by other officials, such as Mihr Narseh; see Thomson, *History of Vardan and the Armenian War by Elishē*, 77, 82. On this formula on coins, see Michael Alram, Maryse Blet-Lemarquand, and Prods Oktor Skjærvø, "Shapur, King of Iranians and Non-Iranians," in *Des Indo-Grecs aux Sassanides: Donnees pour l'histoire et la geographie historique* ed. Rika Gyselen (Bures-sur-Yvette: 2007), 11–40.

the Sasanian kings signaled a claim to universal kingship, ruling both Iranians and non-Iranians, while recognizing a fundamental distinction between the two.[27]

There is little evidence to suggest that the Sasanians sought to efface the difference between these categories by compelling non-Iranians to become Iranians, for instance by becoming Zoroastrian.[28] What evidence of compelled conversion we do find is limited primarily to particular moments in the history of Armenia, whose populations had been Zoroastrian and were ruled by members of a branch of the Arsacid dynasty for centuries, even as they maintained close ties with the Romans and converted to Christianity, rendering their status as Iranians or non-Iranians as liminal in the eyes of the Sasanians.[29] Syriac Persian martyr acts often feature attempts by the king or magi to compel the future martyr to worship the sun or fire. However, given the long history of the genre of martyrdom and the type scene in which the martyr is

[27] Shaked, "Religion in the Late Sasanian Period," 103–117; essays in Josef Wiesehöfer and Philip Huyse, eds., *Ērān und Anērān. Studien zu den Beziehungen zwischem dem Sassanidenreich und des Mittelmeerwelt*, Oriens et Occidens 13 (Stuttgart: 2006); Josef Wiesehöfer, "Ērān du Anērān: Sasanian Patterns of Worldview," in *Persianism in Antiquity*, ed. Rolf Strootman and Miguel John Versluys (Stuttgart: 2017), 381–392; and Payne, *State of Mixture*, 27–38. As discussed in Chapter 1, the terms *ēr* and *an-ēr* do not easily map onto modern terminology. Like "Greekness" and "Jewishness" in antiquity, "Iranianness" both encompassed and transcended categories like religion, genealogy, and geography. For Zoroastrianism in the Parthian and Sasanian periods as national, see Albert de Jong, "The First Sin: Zoroastrian Ideas about Time before Zarathustra," in *Genesis and Regeneration: Essays on Conceptions of Origins*, ed. Shaul Shaked (Jerusalem: 2005), 207–208. On Jewishness, see Shaye Cohen, *Beginnings of Jewishness: Boundaries, Varieties, and Uncertainties* (Berkeley: 1999); Steve Mason, "Jews, Judaeans, Judaizing, Judaism: Problems of Categorization in Ancient History," *Journal for the Study of Judaism* 38 (2007): 457–512; Seth Schwartz, "How Many Judaisms were There? A Critique of Neusner and Smith on Definition and Mason and Boyarin on Categorization," *Journal of Ancient Judaism* 2 (2011): 208–238; and Daniel Boyarin, *Judaism: The Genealogy of a Modern Notion* (New Brunswick, NJ: 2018).

[28] For a discussion of Zoroastrian laws related to non-Iranians, conversion, marriage, and study, see Mokhtarian, "Boundaries of an Infidel," 7–8. For changes in conceptualization of conversion from the Avesta to the Middle Ages, see Alberto Cantera, "Legal Implications of conversion in Zoroastrianism," in *Iranian Identity in the Course of History*, ed. Carlo Cereti (Roma: 2010), 53–66.

[29] Nina G. Garsoïan, "The Two Voices of Armenian Mediaeval Historiography: The Iranian Index," *Studia Iranica* 25 (1996): 7–43; Nina G. Garsoïan, "The Iranian Substratum of the 'Agatʿangelos Cycle,'" in *East of Byzantium: Syria and Armenia in the Formative Period*, ed. Nina G. Garsoïan, Thomas F. Mathews, and Robert W. Thomson (Washington, DC: 1982), 151–189; and Nina G. Garsoïan, "Prolegomena to a Study of the Iranian Aspects," 177–234. See, similarly, Rapp, *The Sasanian World through Georgian Eyes*; and de Jong, *Traditions of the Magi*, 442–443.

pressured to convert, it is difficult to gauge the facticity of these accounts.[30] More to the point, the conversion of Christians in these accounts typically arises *after* an initial cause for violence, rather than out of a spontaneous initiative of the empire to convert its masses to Zoroastrianism. Perhaps in certain cases the empire might seek to assimilate certain individuals or populations more actively, but this was the exception, not the norm.

Indeed, in the very inscription in which the expanded title of "the king of kings of the Iranians *and non-Iranians*" is first attested, Shapur I boasts of deporting captive Romans into Iranian territory, without any suggestion that by so doing they became Iranian themselves. Just the opposite: Sasanian kings founded and named cities after their conquests, such as "the better Antioch of Shabur (*weh-antiok-Shabur*)" in Khuzistan, and later "the better Antioch of Khusro (*weh-antiok-xusrō*)" in Babylonia, and employed the deportees to produce characteristically Roman architectural features there, such as baths and a hippodrome.[31] The relocation

[30] A. V. Williams, "Zoroastrians and Christians in Sasanian Iran," *Bulletin of the John Rylands University Library* 78 (1996): 37–53; Van Rompay, "Impetuous Martyrs?" 363–375.

[31] Henning Börm, *Prokop und die Perser: Untersuchungen zu den römisch-sasanidischen Kontakten in der ausgehenden Spätantike* (Stuttgart: 2007), 175–177; Canepa, *Two Eyes of the Earth*, 28. On deportees, see Erich Kettenhofen, "Deportations: (ii) In the Parthian and Sasanian Periods," in *Dārā (b)-Ebn al-Aṯīr*, ed. Ehsan Yarshater, vol. 7, *Encyclopaedia Iranica* (Costa Mesa, CA: 1996), 297–308; Beate Dignas and Engelbert Winter, *Rome and Persia in Late Antiquity: Neighbours and Rivals* (Cambridge: 2007), 254–263; Samuel N. C. Lieu, "Captives, Refugees and Exiles. A Study of Cross-Frontier Civilian Movements and Contacts between Rome and Persia from Valerian to Jovian," in *The Defence of the Roman and Byzantine East: Proceedings of a Colloquium Held at the University of Sheffield in April 1986*, ed. Philip Freeman and David Kennedy (Oxford: 1986), 475–505; Michael G. Morony, "Population Transfers between Sasanian Iran and the Byzantine Empire," in *La Persia e Bisanzio: Atti del Convegno Internazionale, Roma 14–18 ottobre 2002*, ed. Antonio Carile, et al. (Rome: 2004), 161–179; Jullien and Jullien, *Apôtres des confins*, 153–188; Karin Mosig-Walburg, "Deportationen römischer Christen in das Sasanidenreich durch Shapur I. und ihre Folgen – Eine Neubewertung," *Klio* 92 (2010): 117–156; Christelle Jullien, "Les chrétiens déportés dans l'empire sassanide sous Šābūr Ier: À propos d'un récent article," *Studia Iranica* 40 (2011): 285–293; and Warwick Ball, *Rome in the East: The Transformation of an Empire* (London: 2004), 113–122. Jews are said to have been deported in large numbers from Armenia around this time as well, for which see Widengren, "Status of the Jews." The waterworks in Khuzistan are a well-known example of Roman architectural influences; see Canepa, *Two Eyes of the Earth*, 56. For a Syriac Christian text showing awareness of Yazdgird II's city building projects and name, see Bedjan, *Acta martyrum et sanctorum*, 2.518 (Karka d-bet Slokh).

of Romans into Sasanian territory was not intended to erase the identity of the deportees, but to use their distinctive identity to symbolize Sasanian rule over Iranians and non-Iranians alike. According to the Syriac *Martyrdom of Pusai*, Shapur II brought captives from various provinces to Khuzistan and sought to have them intermarry, "so by means of a mixture of them, the captives shall be bound in their families and their love" to their new settlements rather than their previous homes, and therefore would be deterred from flight or revolt. Nevertheless, as becomes apparent in the continuation of the story, these various captives are not Iranian, nor do they become Iranian, but work alongside the "people of [Shapur's] domain." Shapur II even established a palace in Karka d-Ledan, a city built to resettle and house Roman-deported artisans, constructing their quarters alongside his palace.[32] Shapur's inscription is clear that this expanded empire, too, was explicitly attributable to "the help of the gods."[33] Indeed, the Iranian name given to Karka d-Ledan was "the *ērānšāhr* of Shapur (*ērānšāhr-Šāpūr*)." If Karka d-Ledan represented a kind of microcosm of *ērānšāhr*, it reflects the fact that Sasanian kings ruled over distinct subjects without seeking to homogenize them.

This tension between the empire's identity as warden of Iranianness and its universal pretensions shaped its law, as we saw in Chapter 1. Sasanian law applied to both Iranians and non-Iranians, even as it protected and elevated Iranianness in important ways. As Iranian and Mazda-worshipping rulers, the empire sought to define social boundaries and ensure they were not impinged, even while it sought to rule over the many distinct populations in its vast and expanding territory.

TRANSGRESSING BOUNDARIES

The two foci of Sasanian imperial ideology could clash. As a self-professed "Iranian" empire, the Sasanians were responsible for conserving and bolstering Iranians and Iranian cult and cosmology. Any perceived threat to Iranianness therefore provoked political consequences.

[32] Bedjan, *Acta martyrum et sanctorum*, 2.210.

[33] ŠKZ. Translation, Frye, *The History of Ancient Iran*, 372. For more on the inscription, see Philip Huyse, *Die dreisprachige Inschrift šābuhrs I. an der Kaba-i Zardusť (ŠKZ)*, part 3 of Corpus Inscriptionum Iranicarum, 2 vols. (London: 1999); and Michael Back, *Die sassanidischen Staatsinschriften*.

The social boundaries between Iranians and non-Iranians were most blatantly transgressed by the conversion of Zoroastrians to other religions. Christian and Manichaean missionary activity in Sasanian lands was therefore a major cause of imperial concern, as narrativized in many sources. For example, in the *Martyrdom of ʿAqebshma*, the magi challenge Christian missionary activity on the grounds that it threatened Sasanian social order, discouraged procreation, dissuaded some from participating in the military, and violated core tenets of Zoroastrianism:

> The Christians are destroying our teaching. They are teaching people to serve only one God, not to worship the sun, not to honor fire, to defile the waters with despicable ablutions, not to marry women, not to produce sons or daughters, not to enter battle with the kings, not to kill, to slaughter and eat animals without murmuring [the ritual prayers], and to bury and to conceal the dead in the earth. They say that God created serpents and scorpions together with vermin, not Satan. They impair many of the servants of the king and teach them the sorcery that they call books.[34]

In addition to transgressing the boundaries of Iranianness, conversion, especially of elite Zoroastrian officials, could be perceived as a renunciation of political loyalty to the Sasanian king himself, the vaunted protector of Iranianness on earth.[35]

There are numerous cases in which Christians are condemned for missionizing.[36] In some, the king kills the Christian missionaries, while in others, he orders them to forswear future missionary activity. In one striking story, the king even demanded from the missionizing Christian "assurance in his own handwriting that he will not convert to his faith any more Magians in Persia."[37] Christians were not alone: According to many Manichaean accounts, the prophet Mani was condemned to death on account of his missionary activity. In one source, he is accused of leading "humankind astray" for having caused a high-ranking official to leave "our [i.e., Zoroastrian] law" and take up Mani's teachings.[38]

34 *Martyrdom of ʿAqebshma* (Bedjan, *Acta martyrum et sanctorum*, 2.361–362), translated in Payne, *State of Mixture*, 38.

35 See Christelle Jullien, "Conversion to Christianity in the Sasanian Empire: Political and Theological Issues," in *Iranianate and Syriac Christianity in Late Antiquity and the Early Islamic Period*, ed. Chiara Barbati and Vittorio Berti (Vienna: 2021), 12–13; and Gross, "Being Roman in the Sasanian Empire."

36 In general, see Becker, "Martyrdom, Religious Difference, and 'Fear,'" 300–336.

37 Armenian life of ʿAbda in Brock, "Christians in the Sasanian Empire," 11.

38 For these, see Iain Gardner, *The Founder of Manichaeism: Rethinking the Life of Mani* (Cambridge: 2020), 78–79; see also Yuhan Sohrab-Dinshaw Vevaina, "The

The concern with Christian missionary activity also found expression in diplomatic agreements between the Sasanian and Roman Empires. The treaty of 562 between Khusro I and Justinian included a series of provisions related to Christians living under Sasanian rule. For their part, the Sasanians committed to permitting their Christian subjects freedom to "build churches and worship without fear" and guaranteed that they would neither be "compelled to take part in Magian worship" nor "pray to the gods revered by the Medes." In return, Christians committed that they "would not by any means venture to convert the Magians to our [i.e., Christian] beliefs."[39]

If Christian missionaries were targeted for converting Iranians, Iranian converts to Christianity, who had transgressed their commitment to the "Good Tradition" and "Iranianness," received harsh retort from the empire.[40] Several Syriac martyr acts thematize the imperial response to the conversion of a high-ranking Iranian official.[41] Their stories generally follow a similar pattern: The king implores the convert to return to proper conduct, inevitably setting up a confrontation between Christianity, Zoroastrian belief and practices, and even elite Sasanian norms, that results in Christian victory and eventually martyrdom. According to the *Martyrdom of Narsai*, the *mowbed* Ādurbōzē entreated the Sasanian king, saying: "All of your nobles and freemen have abandoned the Magian faith and become Christian. Command me that I might return them to Magianism, which they have abandoned, from Christianity which they have taken up." The destabilizing effects of conversion are underscored in these accounts, as the convert renounces Zoroastrianism, elite Iranian lineage, and a high imperial position, in favor of heavenly reward.

Those Zoroastrians who violated the Empire's social boundaries were therefore compelled to return to proper conduct, or, when recalcitrant,

Hermeneutics of Political Violence in Sasanian Iran: The Death of Mani and the Seizure of Manichaean Property," *Sasanian Studies* 1 (2022): 291–322.

39 Menander, frg. 6.1.398–407; Geoffrey Greatrex and Samuel Lieu, *The Roman Eastern Frontier and the Persian Wars: Part II, AD 363–630* (London: 2002), 134.

40 For the importance of these concepts in the everyday practice of Zoroastrians, see Maria Macuch, "The Pahlavi Model Marriage Contract in the Light of Sasanian Family Law," in *Iranian Languages and Texts from Iran and Turan*, ed. M. Macuch, M. Maggi, and W. Sundermann (Wiesbaden: 2007), 191, although the document dates from the 13th century.

41 See especially Walker, *Legend of Mar Qardagh*; Adam Becker, *Fear of God and the Beginning of Wisdom*; and Payne, *State of Mixture*.

were punished and even executed.[42] In the *Martyrdom of Narsai*, the king is said to order Ādurbōzē: "You are granted authority over them to convert them, without any killing, but only through intimidation, and with some beatings."[43] The Zoroastrian *Letter of Tansar*, often dated to the end of the Sasanian period, instructs that apostates were to be kept prisoner and persuaded to return to the Good Tradition.[44] In a similar vein, a Syriac text known as the *Great Slaughter* describes the martyrdom of a Persian elite named Azad. When the king learns that Azad had disguised himself so as to be among those slaughtered for being Christian, he orders that henceforth:

> "Everyone who is seized on account of Christianity, he should be questioned for the name of his father, and his mother, and his family, and which city or village he is from, and which people he is from . . . and by the pressure of strikes and tortures he should be interrogated repeatedly, and if he does not turn back from his religion (*deḥlta*), then it is upon us to make the gods known, and we give the order as it seems fitting to us."[45]

If some Zoroastrians who converted were spared torture or death, it still resulted in certain legal disadvantages, such as alienation from the inheritance and position afforded by family.[46] Other Iranians, considered aberrant in some ways, were similarly condemned and assailed.[47] Regardless of whether these rules were always enforced, they express the general imperial expectations of proper Iranian comportment and the potential consequences for violators.[48]

Given the possible repercussions, some Christians were reluctant to baptize Iranians, especially those from elite families.[49] Others recognized

42 See Becker, "Martyrdom, Religious Difference, and 'Fear,'" 200–226; Walker, *Legend of Mar Qardagh*; Payne, *State of Mixture*, 27–30; and Mary Boyce, *The Letter of Tansar* (Rome: 1968), 42.

43 Geoffrey Herman, *Persian Martyr Acts under King Yazdgird I* (Piscataway, NJ: 2016), 4–5.

44 P. Bruns, "Beobachtungen zu den Rechtsgrundlagen der Christenverfolgungen im Sasanidenreich," *Römische Quartalschrift für christliche Altertumskunde und für Kirchengeschichte* 103 (2008): 82–112 (esp. 89–92), and passages in the *Letter of Tansar* in Boyce, *Letter of Tansar*, 42; Mēnōg ī Xrad in E. W. West, *The Book of Mainyo-i-khard* (Stuttgart: 1871), 22 and 148.

45 Bedjan, *Acta martyrum et sanctorum*, 2.246.

46 See discussion in Chapter 1, pp. 74–76.

47 The so-called Mazdakites were a particular *cause célèbre*. For a recent review of the literature, see Khodadad Rezakhani, "Mazdakism, Manichaeism and Zoroastrianism: In Search of Orthodoxy and Heterodoxy in Late Antique Iran," *Iranian Studies* 48 (2015): 55–70.

48 For lack of enforcement, see Payne, *State of Mixture*, 52–53.

49 Payne, *State of Mixture*, 54.

the risks to their lives but believed that abstaining from spreading the good word to Iranians was too high a price to pay for peaceable conditions. Thus, for example, the magi ask the king to put the sixth-century Catholicos Mar Aba to death because "he is a repudiator of the *dēn* of Ohrmazd."[50] In response, Mar Aba explains:

> Regarding this faith in God which everyone ought to acknowledge, a person does not have the authority to say, "It is mine alone," as the rest of the empty religions (*deḥlātā*) allow. As this air that we breathe is common to all human beings and as, in turn, the light of the sun, moon, and stars, so by a myriad and more than this Christianity is not mine alone, but rather belongs to all rational beings who have passed on, who are present, and who are going to be, and whose will it is to believe.[51]

Mar Aba rejects the Empire's desired distinction between Iranians and others. Belief in God, he argues, transcends imperially mandated communal divisions.

There is no indication that Jews experienced violence on account of proselytism. While scholars debate whether Jews in antiquity actively sought converts,[52] there is certainly no evidence of regular missionary activity among the Jews of the Sasanian Empire.[53] Indeed, in the case of the rabbis, the Babylonian Talmud adopts a decidedly negative attitude towards converts and imposes more stringent standards for conversion, even discouraging it altogether.[54] To be sure, the Talmud mentions converts who, for instance, are said to be particularly populous in the

[50] Bedjan, *Histoire de Mar-Jabalaha*, 230. For a nearly identical description of another Christian figure, see Joseph Corluy, "Historia Sancti Mar Pethion martyris, syriace et latine: Edidit nunc primum ex cod. Londinensi (Addit. mss. 12174)," *Analecta Bollandiana* 7 (1888): 8 (line 11).

[51] Bedjan, *Histoire de Mar–Jabalaha*, 231; see translation in Becker, "Martyrdom, Religious Difference, and 'Fear,'" 324. On Mar Aba's tribulations, see Macuch, "The Case against Mār Abā," 47–58.

[52] Shaye Cohen, "Was Judaism in Antiquity a Missionary Religion?" in *Jewish Assimilation, Acculturation and Accommodation*, ed. Menahem Mor (Lanham, MD: 1992), 14–23; Martin Goodman, *Mission and Conversion: Proselytizing in the Religious History of the Roman Empire* (Oxford: 1994).

[53] Isaiah Gafni, "Converts and Conversion in Sasanian Babylonia," in *Jews and Judaism in the Rabbinic Era*, ed. Isaiah Gafni (Tübingen: 2019), 257–268 (esp. 204–206), who rightly concludes that we cannot derive Jewish proselytism from Aphrahat's *Demonstrations*. For the earlier conversion of the royal dynasty of Adiabene, see Goodblatt, "The Jews in the Parthian Empire," 269–270; and Lawrence Schiffman, "The Conversion of the Royal House of Adiabene in Josephus and Rabbinic Sources," in *Josephus, Judaism, and Christianity*, ed. Louis Feldman and Gohei Hata (Detroit, MI: 1987), 295.

[54] Moshe Lavee, *The Rabbinic Conversion of Judaism* (Leiden: 2017).

city of Meḥoza, but are disappointingly absent from the city of Mata Meḥasia.[55] The ethnic background of these converts is typically unspecified.[56] By contrast, many clients of the Jewish Babylonian Aramaic incantation bowls had Persian names. Perhaps some of these were Zoroastrians who had become Jewish, but they may equally have been Jews by birth with Persian names or Zoroastrians patronizing Jewish scribes.[57] It is notable that the only extended rabbinic literary account of an explicitly Zoroastrian Iranian convert appears in a Palestinian rather than a Babylonian text, and was composed near or after the Sasanian Empire's decline.[58] This may suggest that Babylonian rabbis themselves did not have occasion to tell stories about Zoroastrian converts. Alternatively, the rabbis thought better than to encourage such conversion for fear of retribution. If Iranians did convert to Judaism, we have no evidence that it occurred frequently, *en masse*, or because of any concerted missionary effort.[59]

The Sasanian Empire was therefore particularly concerned about missionary activity that jeopardized the social fabric predicated on the distinction between Iranians and non-Iranians. Yet, where Christians and Manichaeans appear to have triggered imperial violence with more regular missionary activity, Jews did not. The differing treatment was not the result of the empire's preconceived attitudes to these communities, but of the divergent traditions and decisions of particular communities in relation to distinctions that lay at the heart of Sasanian imperial ideology.

[55] b. Qid. 73a; b. Ber. 17b.

[56] Gafni, "Converts and Conversion," 257–268. For details about the parents of a convert, see b. ʿAbod. Zar. 70a and b. B. Bat. 149a.

[57] Michael Morony, "Magic and Society in Late Antique Iraq," in *Prayer, Magic, and the Stars in the Ancient and Late Antique World*, ed. Scott Noegel, Joel Walker, and Brannon Wheeler (University Park, PA: 2004), 94–95. Morony problematically assumes names automatically align with ethnic (or religious) identity.

[58] Reuven Kiperwasser and Serge Ruzer, "Zoroastrian Proselytes in Rabbinic and Syriac Christian Narratives: Orality-Related Markers of Cultural Identity," *History of Religions* 51 (2011): 197–218; Reuven Kiperwasser and Serge Ruzer, "To Convert a Persian and Teach Him the Holy Scriptures: A Zoroastrian Proselyte in Rabbinic and Syriac Christian Narratives," in *Jews, Christians and Zoroastrians: Religious Dynamics in a Sasanian Context*, ed. Geoffrey Herman (Piscataway, NJ: 2014), 91–127.

[59] For possible medieval evidence of Zoroastrian converts to Judaism, see Moshe Zucker, *Saadya's Commentary on Genesis* (New York: 1984), 135 and 394; which is discussed by Robert Brody, "Zoroastrian Themes in Geonic Responsa," in *Irano-Judaica IV*, ed. Shaul Shaked and Amnon Netzer (Jerusalem: 1999), 179n2; and Lavee, *Rabbinic Conversion of Judaism*, 170.

MEDDLING MAGI

Beyond articulating and defending key ethno-religious distinctions, the principles of Zoroastrian cosmology countenanced certain behaviors and condemned others. Fundamentally, Zoroastrians believed that the world was composed of two types of substance: good and bad, pure and impure, deriving from a similar binary among the gods, and particularly the chief deities – the beneficent Ohrmazd and maleficent Ahriman. A Zoroastrian's chief task was to preserve the purity of the good creation from the encroachment of impurity deriving from the bad creation. Key elements, especially water, fire, and earth, were to be zealously guarded from defilement.

Many sources suggest that Zoroastrian priests played a primary role in enforcing Zoroastrian cosmology, which included interfering in the practices of non-Iranian communities who transgressed it.[60] Our earliest and most infamous set of evidence for the involvement of the magi in the affairs of other religious groups is the four inscriptions in the province of Fārs erected by the Zoroastrian priest Kerdir in the latter half of the third century (see Figure 4). According to his inscriptions, Kerdir served under four successive Sasanian kings. They describe his rise through the ranks: starting from a priest (*herbed*), to a more senior priestly position (*mowbed*), then to magnate (*wuzurg*), and finally, to judge and steward (*āyēnbed*) of the Sasanian ancestral fire cult in Istakhr. His inscriptions are prominently positioned next to those of the kings Ardashir I, Shapur I, and Bahram II, and include reliefs that depict him in profile.[61] In listing his achievements, all purportedly pursued at the behest of the kings he served, Kerdir details at some length the different groups he successfully subdued in the name of the empire and Zoroastrianism:

[60] Kalmin, *Jewish Babylonia*, 130–138; Geoffrey Herman, "Bury My Coffin Deep!" Zoroastrian Exhumation in Jewish and Christian Sources," in *Tiferet leYisrael: Jubilee Volume in Honor of Israel Francus*, ed. Joel Roth, Menahem Schmelzer, and Yaacov Francus (New York: 2010), 31–59.

[61] The four inscriptions are found in Naqš-e Rajab (KNRb), Naqš-e Rustam (KNRm), Sar-e Mašhad (KSM), and on the Kaʿba-ye Zardošt (KKZ). For more, see Prods Oktor Skjaervø, "Kartir," in *Joči-Kāšġari, Saʿd-al-Din*, ed. Ehsan Yarshater, vol. 15, *Encyclopædia Iranica* (London: 2011), 607–628. For the inscriptions, see Back, *Die sassanidischen Staatsinschriften*, 384–489; and Philippe Gignoux, *Les quatre inscriptions du mage Kirdīr, textes et concordances* (Paris: 1991). English translation by D. N. Mackenzie, "Kerdir's inscription," in *The Sasanian Rock Reliefs at Naqsh-i Rustam*, ed. Georgina Herrmann and D. N. MacKenzie (Berlin: 1989), 35–72. See also Frantz Grenet, "Observations sur les titres de Kirdīr," *Studia Iranica* 19 (1990): 87–94.

FIGURE 4. The high priest Kerdir in profile at Naqsh-e Rustam, gazing from the margins at the victory relief of King Shapur I over the submitting emperors Valerian and Philip the Arab. [Photo © Matthew P. Canepa]

And in kingdom after kingdom and place after place throughout the whole empire the services of Ahura Mazda and the gods became preeminent, and great dignity came to the Mazdayasnian religion (*dēn mazdēsn*) and the magi in the empire, and the gods, water, fire, and domestic animals in the empire attained great satisfaction, while Ahriman and the demons were punished and rebuked, and the teachings (*kēš*) of Ahriman and the demons departed from the empire and were abandoned. And Jews (*yahūdī*), Buddhists, Brahmins, Nazarenes, Christians, Baptizers, and Manichaeans in the empire were smitten. Idols were destroyed, and the residences of demons were annihilated, and became the place and seat of the gods.[62]

[62] The inscription at Kaʿba-ye Zardošt, following Gignoux, *Les quatre inscriptions du mage Kirdīr*, 69–70.

Kerdir's inscriptions, composed around half a century from the inception of the Sasanian Empire, reveal a fundamental division between Zoroastrians and non-Zoroastrians. The seven listed groups of non-Zoroastrians are lumped together and dispatched as one. The violence against these communities is meaningfully sandwiched between Kerdir's claim that he punished and rebuked Ahriman, the demons, and their teachings, and destroyed the sites of idol worshippers and demonic residences.

Kerdir's inscription has generated much scholarly debate. Apart from modest difficulties in identifying some of the communities in the list, it is unclear what, if anything, Kerdir actually did to them.[63] He claims to have "smote" (*zadan*) Jews and others, and thus most scholars have interpreted this to mean that he led a physical assault against these communities. Some have accepted this as evidence that Kerdir did in fact commit these acts of violence, while others view the account as yet another instance of inscriptional puffery: empty bragging about imagined victories and achievements that do not reflect real events. They point to the fact that we lack evidence to corroborate widespread violence against other religious communities in the third century.[64] This argument is somewhat disingenuous, however; we simply have *no* relevant Syriac Christian evidence from the third and fourth centuries that would mention these events, and Manichaean sources in fact *do* report Kerdir's presence in the king's court and hold him responsible for Mani's death. Some have tried to identify echoes of Kerdir's violence in the Talmud, although unsuccessfully.[65] Regardless, his prominently placed inscriptions and prestigious career suggest that his actions were most likely

[63] In particular, the terms "Christians" and "Nazorenes" are unclear, on which see Christelle Jullien and Florence Jullien, "Aux frontières de l'iranité: 'Nāsrāyē' et 'Krīstyonē' des inscriptions du mobad Kirdīr: Enquête littéraire et historique," *Numen* 69 (2002): 282–335; Francois de Blois, "Naṣrānī (Ναζωραῖος) and ḥanīf (ἐθνικός): Studies in the Religious Vocabulary of Christianity and of Islam," *Bulletin of the School of Oriental and African Studies* 65 (2002): 5–11; and Françoise Briquel Chatonnet and Simon Brelaud, "Quelques réflexions sur la désignation des chrétiens dans l'inscription du mage Kirdīr et dans l'empire sassanide," *Parole de l'Orient* 43 (2017): 113–136.

[64] de Jong, "Zoroastrian Religious Polemics," 51–52, 62–63; Secunda, *Iranian Talmud*, 118n63.

[65] E. S. Rosenthal, "For the Talmudic Dictionary – Talmudica Iranica" [in Hebrew], in *Irano-Judaica* I, ed. Shaul Shaked (Jerusalem: 1982), 41–42, 58–59, 128–129; Gafni, *Jews of Talmudic Babylonia*, 40n96. See also Amnon Netzer, "Ha-Sasanim ba-Talmud ha-Bavli: Shapur I, Shapur II, and Yazdgird I," *Shevet ve-Am* 7 (1973): 251–262; Moshe Beer, "Notes on the Three Edicts Decreed against Babylonian Jews in the Third Century C.E." [in Hebrew], *Irano-Judaica* I, ed. Shaul Shaked (Jerusalem: 1982), 25–37; and

consistent with Sasanian imperial ideology and policy, and there is little reason to doubt the report's general veracity.

A different understanding of Kerdir's account is offered by Richard Payne who focuses on the verb "smite" used by Kerdir to describe his treatment of the listed communities. Payne argues that "a struck object is neither destroyed nor eliminated. It is, rather, subdued."[66] By way of contrast, Payne argues that Kerdir's treatment of "idols" and "demons" is far more definitive; idols were "destroyed" and residences of demons were "annihilated." These more extreme measures were adopted against groups who were in some ways considered by Kerdir to be deviant Iranians, or so the argument goes.[67] Jews, Christians, and the other communities in the list, by contrast, were "smitten" only in the sense that they were subjected to some sort of religious subordination. This account is necessary for Payne's picture of a coherent and consistent Sasanian Zoroastrian ideology that actively sought to foster a "state of mixture," viewing heterogeneity not as a de facto reality of rule, but as a de jure cosmological ideal for the world's populations. Payne's interpretation aligns Kerdir more closely with the activities of later magi, who – as we will soon see – interfered in Jewish and Christian practices but appear to have targeted them for physical assault only infrequently. But it is difficult to square Payne's understanding with the simple fact that "smite" is unambiguous in meaning. Indeed, instead of contrasting Kerdir's smiting of these communities with his assault on idol worship, in context, both appear to represent equivalent fulfilments of Kerdir's larger boast: "Ahriman and the demons were punished and rebuked, and the teachings (*kēš*) of Ahriman and the demons departed from the empire and were abandoned." The collective smiting and annihilation of these various

Moshe Beer, "The Decrees of Kartir on the Jews of Babylonia" [in Hebrew], *Tarbiẓ* 55 (1986): 525–539. See, however, Kalmin, *Jewish Babylonia*, 127–129.

66 Payne, *State of Mixture*, 24.

67 For the former explanation, see Payne, *State of Mixture*, 32–34. For the latter, see Albert de Jong, "One Nation under God? The Early Sasanians as Guardians and Destroyers of Holy Sites," in *Götterbilder-Gottesbilder-Weltbilder*, ed. R. G. Kratz and H. Spieckermann, vol. 1, *Ägypten, Mesopotamien, Persien, Kleinasien, Syrien, Palästina* (Tübingen: 2006), 223–238; and Albert de Jong, "Regional Variation in Zoroastrianism: The Case of the Parthians," *Bulletin of the Asian Institute* 22 (2008): 19–24. See also James Russell, *Zoroastrianism in Armenia* (Cambridge: 1987), 494; and Perikhanian, *Book of a Thousand Judgments*, 216–217 and 314–315. See Daryaee, *A Middle Persian Text on Late Antique Geography*, 24 and 47, where an idol-temple is established by the mythical anti-Iranian Turanian villain Frāsiyāk. Later in the inscription, Kerdir speaks of removing bad actors from the ranks of the magi.

"others" reflected the victory of Ohrmazd over the forces of evil, delivered with the help of Kerdir.

Even when the historicity of Kerdir's account is accepted, it is quickly dismissed as a brief unhappy moment uncharacteristic of the empire's typical treatment of its Jewish subjects. Kerdir is considered a "religious zealot" and representative of a Zoroastrian priesthood that was the primary antagonist of the empire's other religious communities.[68] It may well be that Kerdir's (imagined?) use of physical violence against these communities would quickly grow out of favor among Sasanian rulers, and perhaps among Zoroastrian priests, as an ideal to be pursued. But it would be a mistake to dismiss Kerdir as a "zealot" or a representative of an extreme form of Zoroastrian priestly "intolerance."

Kerdir may represent a largely abandoned attempt to forcibly eradicate or repress non-Zoroastrian communities. But at its core, Kerdir embraced an understanding of Zoroastrian cosmology that sought to eradicate all obstacles to belief in Ohrmazd and the proper stewardship of his good creations, an ideal that informed the role magi played throughout the Sasanian period. Although Sasanian kings presented themselves as devoted Zoroastrians – patrons of the gods, the cult, and its various requirements – the day-to-day surveillance and custodianship was delegated to the magi. The magi thus served as agents of the empire in enforcing Zoroastrian cosmology among its subjects. During Kerdir's period in power, leading magi may have considered their custodianship to demand smiting non-Iranian communities. But even without physical and bodily harm, magi would continue throughout Sasanian rule to meddle in the affairs of other groups, especially religious groups, when their rituals contravened the dictates of Zoroastrian cosmology. And like Kerdir's inscription, in their role as custodians, the magi did not distinguish between Jews, Christians, and others.

To the magi, then, Zoroastrian cosmology demanded maintenance of the pristine purity and sanctity of Ohrmazd's beneficent creations, especially fire, water, and the earth, which needed to be protected against impurity and the encroachment of Ahriman's evil creations. This concern is also evidenced in Kerdir's inscription where, just prior to listing the religious communities that he smote, Kerdir boasts that on account of his actions "great satisfaction came to the gods, water, fire, and cattle in the

[68] Wiesehöfer, *Ancient Persia*, 212; "ruthless fanatic" in James Russell, "Kartīr and Mānī: A Shamanistic Model of Their Conflict," *Acta Iranica* 30 (1990): 180; see references collected in Payne, *State of Mixture*, 24n3.

empire," suggesting a correlation between the satisfaction of the gods and good creations on the one hand, and the smiting of these communities on the other.[69] Non-Iranian groups, who were not bound by Zoroastrian cosmology or scruples, required regulation and control, and their practices sometimes demanded disruption.

Many sources, for instance, attest to magi interfering in Christian and Jewish burials of the dead. According to Zoroastrian sources, the demon of carrion, Nasuš, the chief force of impurity, rushed newly deceased bodies such that they became primary agents of pollution. Instead of burying the corpse and contaminating the earth with dead matter, Zoroastrians typically exposed them to birds and beasts of prey, often on "towers of silence," whose remains are scattered across the Sasanian expanse. Once the flesh was consumed, the bones were collected and buried in ossuaries (*astōdān*), thereby avoiding any direct contact between dead matter and the elements.[70] While some Zoroastrian sources suggest that non-Zoroastrian corpses did not defile, an abundance of sources depict magi interfering in Jewish and Christian burial customs.[71] Interference in burial of the dead was conspicuous and common enough that Christian sources accurately describe the Zoroastrian basis for it.[72] These encounters are dramatically thematized in Christian martyr acts where the martyr's corpse is left exposed by the magi, and is often

[69] Secunda, *Talmud's Red Fence*, 69n9.

[70] On Zoroastrian funerary practices, see Mary Boyce, *A History of Zoroastrianism* (Leiden: 1975), 325–330; de Jong, *Traditions of the Magi*, 440–444; Michael Shenkar, "Yosef bar El'asa Artaka and the Elusive Jewish Diaspora of Pre-Islamic Iran and Central Asia," *Journal of Jewish Studies* 65 (2014): 71–75; and Azarnouche, "A Zoroastrian Cult Scene," 9–10. Not all Iranians seem to have followed this practice. For archaeological findings of both Iranian burial and exposure of the dead, see St. John Simpson and Theya Molleson, "Old Bones Overturned: New Evidence of Funerary Practices from the Sasanian Empire," in *Regarding the Dead: Human Remains in the British Museum*, ed. Alexandra Fletcher, Daniel Antoine, and J. D. Hill (London: 2014), 77–90.

[71] See Morony, *Iraq after the Muslim Conquest*, 314–316; and Herman, "Bury My Coffin Deep!" 31–59. Elman, "The Other in the Mirror: Iranians and Jews View One Another: Questions of Identity, Conversion and Exogamy in the Fifth-Century Iranian Empire, Part One," *Bulletin of the Asia Institute* 19 (2005): 15–25; Payne, *State of Mixture*, 31–32, downplays the reported events in light of a few theoretical Zoroastrian discussions.

[72] *Martyrdom of Miles* (5th–6th century); Bedjan, *Acta martyrum et sanctorum*, 2.275. See also Oric Basirov, "'Proselytisation' and 'Exposure of the Dead': Two Christian Calumnies Commonly Raised against the Sasanians," in *Faszination Iran: Beiträge zur Religion, Geschichte und Kunst des Alten Iran. Gedenkschrift für Klaus*, ed. Shervin Farridnejad, Anke Joisten-Pruschke, and Rika Gyselen (Wiesbaden: 2015), 1–19.

purloined by fellow Christians under the cover of night.[73] A rabbinic story, discussed in more detail in Chapter 6, depicts a magus purposefully seeking out and exhuming Jewish corpses until the corpse itself miraculously attacks him.[74] The disinterring of Christians is similarly attested.[75] The magi did not act upon their own discretion; they functioned with the license of the Sasanian king. As such, one of the conditions in the terms of peace obtained by Justinian from Khusro I in 562 included "that the Christians [in the Sasanian Empire] would be permitted to bury their dead in graves, as is our custom."[76]

Alongside burial of the dead, the magi appear to have confiscated fire that was not handled properly.[77] This would be essential to ensure the purity of fire, which other communities could not be trusted to uphold. The confiscation of lamps was apparently such a quotidian nuisance that it appears in anecdotes about entirely unrelated legal matters, such as the following:

> Rabbah bar bar Ḥanah was ill. Rav Yehudah and the rabbis entered to ask him a question ... In the meantime, a magus [*ḥabara*] came and took the lamp that was before them ...[78]

The locus classicus for discussions of Zoroastrian interference in Jewish practice is an enigmatic rabbinic source that lists three ways the magi interfered in Babylonian Jewish life. The source follows a discussion in which the biblical verse "with a foolish nation I will anger them" (Deut. 32.21), is understood to refer to the magi, the "foolish nation" who now angers the Jews. The Talmud then anonymously lists three decrees detailing the manner by which Jews were angered by the magi:[79]

73 For some evidence that Christians adopted Zoroastrian-like burial practices, see Payne, *State of Mixture*, 31–32.

74 b. B. Bat. 58a; Herman, "Bury My Coffin Deep," 31–59.

75 *Martyrdom of Peroz*, in Bedjan, *Acta martyrum et sanctorum*, 4.254; Scher, *Chronique de Séert*, 1.219–1.220.

76 Menander Protector, frag. 6.1.398–407, translated in R. C. Blockley, *The History of Menander the Guardsman* (Liverpool: 1985), 74–77.

77 Geoffrey Herman, "Religious Transformation between East and West: Hanukkah in the Babylonian Talmud and Zoroastrianism," in *Religions and Trade: Religious Formation, Transformation and Cross-Cultural Exchange between East and West*, ed. Peter Wick and Volker Rabens (Leiden: 2014), 261–282. For a description of the gathering of fire from "house to house," see the Chester Beatty Kephalaia Codex section 326, in Gardner, BeDuhn, and Dilley, *The Chapters of the Wisdom of My Lord Mani*, 44–45.

78 b. Giṭ. 16b–17a. Compare with b. Shab. 45a, discussed in Chapter 5.

79 In the past, the list was associated with the rabbis who appear just prior, who lived in the mid-third century: Moshe Beer, "Notes on the Three Edicts," 26–37; Beer, "Decrees of

They decreed against three [things] for three [sins]: they decreed against meat because of [negligence in tithing] the priestly gifts; they decreed against the bathhouses because of [negligence in] immersion; they dig up corpses because [the Jews] rejoice on their festivals.[80]

The list adopts a simple schema of sin and punishment, with each decree appearing alongside its corresponding sin. The sins of which Jews are guilty are revealing: Jews do not properly contribute to priestly gifts, a practice that remained in force in Babylonia in the minds of some rabbis despite the destruction of the temple and the absence of clear public service provided by priests;[81] they do not properly follow the laws of bathing, that is purification from menstrual impurity; and most intriguingly of all, Jews apparently celebrate on Zoroastrian festivals. This last sin suggests Jews participated in the conviviality of Zoroastrian meals, which was also a cause of concern for Christians, a topic we will return to in Chapter 5.[82]

Although the source is enigmatic, the three decrees must correspond to practices that were objectionable to the magi. As Geoffrey Herman has suggested, the magi likely prohibited slaughtering meat because it entailed spilling the blood of the animal onto the earth. Zoroastrians instead strangled their sources of meat.[83] In a number of Syriac martyr acts, the Christian is said to be given blood to eat by their Zoroastrian oppressors, which may refer to meat that has not been drained of its blood.[84] A more explicit reference to the differing practices of Jews and Christians, on the one hand, and Zoroastrians, on the other, is found in the Syriac *History of Mar Aba*, in which it is decreed that Christians should avoid eating "magian meat," likely referring to meat that was strangled and not slaughtered.[85]

Kartir," 525–539; Brody, "Judaism in the Sasanian Empire," 58; and Neusner, *History of the Jews*, 2.35–2.36. This resulted in several scholars connecting these edicts to the violence committed against Jews and others according to the boast of the high priest Kerdir, discussed above.

80 b. Yeb. 63b, according to MS Munich 141.

81 On priestly gifts in Babylonia, see Geoffrey Herman, "Priests in Babylonia in the Talmudic Period" [in Hebrew] (MA thesis, Hebrew University of Jerusalem, 1998).

82 Payne, *State of Mixture*, 117–122.

83 Herman, "Priests in Babylonia," 148–153.

84 Brock, "Christians in the Sasanian Empire," 9n37; Herman, "Bury My Coffin Deep!" 47.

85 Bedjan, *Histoire de Mar-Jabalaha*, 238. Also referred to as "meat of muttering" in Bedjan, 229, a common reference to the Zoroastrian ritual "muttering." For more, see Hutter, "Mār Abā and the Impact of Zoroastrianism," 167–173. Payne, *State of Mixture*, 117–122, argues that "magian meat" is in fact a metonym for larger convivial meals crucial to Persian culture, which were attended by Christians. This reading builds much on a few references.

The magi prohibited bathhouses because water was sacred and defiling it was a terrible sin, and a menstruant was considered by Zoroastrians to constitute one of the greatest sources of impurity. According to *Vīdēvdād* 16, for instance, menstruating women are required to stay "fifteen steps from the fire, fifteen steps from the water ... and three steps from the righteous men."[86] Jewish and Syriac sources thematize – and satirize – Zoroastrian notions concerning menstruation. In several Babylonian rabbinic stories, Persians are deterred from laying with Jewish women because the latter claim to be menstruants, even using the proper Persian word (*daštāna*).[87] Other rabbinic texts may also allude to Zoroastrian opposition to Jewish menstrual practices.[88]

The interference of magi in the personal and religious lives of the empire's non-Zoroastrian subjects appears to have been a regular hazard. Here, the traditions and practices of different communities would be a major factor in their relative treatment. Given that both Jews and Christians practiced burial of the dead and did not actively seek to preserve the purity of the beneficent elements according to Zoroastrian cosmology, they were subjected to similar types of violence.

Subsequent chapters will explore how Jews and Christians responded to Zoroastrian interference in religious practices, and whether they sought to mitigate potential conflict by modifying their behavior or whether they obstinately persisted in the face of the inevitability of violence. One possible, albeit scarcely attested, response was to commit acts of violence against the magi. This would undoubtedly have been seen as a frontal assault on the empire and its promotion of the magi as custodians of Zoroastrianism. One of the few non-Jewish reports about Jews living in the Iranian Plateau in the Sasanian period concerns violence committed by Jews against the magi. This report appears in the work of the tenth-century annalist Ḥamza al-Iṣfahānī:[89]

[86] Mahnaz Moazami, *Wrestling with the Demons of the Pahlavi Widēwdād* (Leiden: 2014), esp. 376–379. For more on Zoroastrian views of menstruants, see Shai Secunda, "The Fractious Eye: On the Evil Eye of Menstruants in Zoroastrian Tradition," *Numen* 61 (2014): 83–108; and Secunda, *Talmud's Red Fence*.

[87] b. Taʿan. 22a; ʿAbod. Zar. 18b. See discussion in Chapter 4 below. The Syriac text is found in Bedjan, *Histoire de Mar-Jabalaha*, 449.

[88] Secunda, *Talmud's Red Fence*, 72–73.

[89] English translation in U. M. Daudpota, *The Annals of Ḥamza Al-Iṣfahānī* (Bombay: 1932), 40.

> He [Peroz] ordered half of the Jewish population of Isfahān to be put to death and their children to be sent as slaves to the fire temple of Surush Adhrān in the village of Harwān, as they had flayed the skin from the backs of two Magian priests, joined the two skins and used them for tanning.

According to Ḥamza's report, Jews in Isfahan reacted violently to two magi. It appears that Ḥamza is alleging that the Jews killed the magi, although it is unclear what exactly Ḥamza means by "tanning." As punishment, many Jews were killed, and Jewish children were dedicated as slaves to fire temples.[90] Here, violence against the magi is treated as tantamount to violence against the cult, hence the dedication of children to the fire temple as retributive punishment.[91] Without commenting on the historicity of the report, it plausibly reflects the consequences Jews or other subject communities might suffer for challenging the custodians of Zoroastrian cosmology.

In a similar vein, the Syriac *History of Mar Aba* reports widespread riots and violence against magi in the mid-sixth century.[92] For this, the Catholicos Mar Aba was arrested and threatened with death if he did not put down the revolt, and the king sent a letter to the rebellious Christians warning that, "we will devastate those who persist in rebellion, whether Zoroastrian, Jew, or Christian."[93] Imperial violence in these cases emerged not out of any particular animus for the Christian or Jewish communities, but from the need of the empire to suppress perceived challenges to its authority in the form of violence against the magi, the enforcers of Zoroastrian cosmology.

Sasanian subjects were expected to respect the basic requirements of Zoroastrian cosmology as they pertained to the maintenance of the purity of beneficent creations. Jews and Christians both ran afoul of these considerations on many occasions. The magi appear to have been particularly responsible for surveilling and policing conformity, which could snowball into direct violence between Jews, Christians, and magi.

90 See Macuch, "The Talmudic Expression," 109–129, and discussion in Chapter 2.

91 Discussed in Neusner, *History of the Jews of Babylonia*, 5.60–72. Widengren, "Status of the Jews," 143, suggests that these were trumped-up charges.

92 Particularly in Khuzistan; see Florence Jullien, *Histoire De Mār Abba, catholicos de l'Orient; Martyres de Mār Grigor, général en chef du roi Khusro Ier et, de Mār Yazdpanāh, juge et ouverneur*, 1.35–37 (Syriac), and 2.37–38 (French).

93 Other groups at this time similarly celebrated the death of magi. See Thomson, *History of Vardan and the Armenian War by Elishē*, 129, and Socrates Scholasticus, *Ecclesiastical History*, 7.8.

DISLOYALTY

Like all empires, the Sasanians were apprehensive about the loyalty of their subjects. These concerns were, however, especially acute in Mesopotamia, which was under the constant threat of conflict with Rome. Spies, traitors, and turncoats could share crucial intelligence with the enemy and rally support on a local level for regime change.[94] To mitigate these concerns, the two empires might even collaborate. For example, both empires agreed to limit financial activities of merchants to particular days and sites, "lest the secrets be found out by a foreign kingdom."[95] Yet these agreements did little to prevent the empires from fostering ties with inhabitants living in and around Mesopotamia. Those who were suspected and found guilty of sedition and treachery were treated in the harshest of terms. According to the late Sasanian or early Islamic *Letter of Tansar*, "any who rebelled against a king or fled from the army in the field ... are put to death, to inspire terror and be an example to others ..."[96] Traitors could receive capital punishment and serve as an example to any who might follow in their footsteps.

The general concern with loyalty and disloyalty was aggravated by the increasing Christianization of Rome, which cast doubt on the loyalty of the Sasanians' Christian subjects.[97] Based on the perception that religious and political affiliations in late antiquity were not easily distinguishable, Christians under Sasanian rule were suspected of developing ties with their coreligionists in the west. Christians were therefore perceived as a possible fifth column, presenting "a case of divided loyalties," as Sebastian Brock has influentially put it.[98] Many sources, some roughly contemporary with the events themselves, confirm that around 340, Sasanian violence targeted numerous Christians out of fears of their disloyalty in a period that became known as the Great Persecution. These moments of violence were commemorated in the earliest Persian martyr acts, especially those concerning Simeon bar Ṣabbaʿe, who became the arch-martyr of the East Syriac Church.

[94] See, in general, Gross, "Being Roman in the Sasanian Empire," 390–397.

[95] *Code of Justinian* 4.63.4, translated in Bruce W. Frier, et al., *The Codex of Justinian: A New Annotated Translation with Parallel Latin and Greek Text* (Cambridge: 2016), 1056–1057; Greatrex and Lieu, *The Roman Eastern Frontier*, 33–34; Dignas and Winter, *Rome and Persia in Late Antiquity*, 243ff.

[96] Boyce, *Letter of Tansar*, 42.

[97] Gross, "Being Roman in the Sasanian Empire."

[98] Brock, "Christians in the Sasanian Empire," 1–19.

Thus, in the *Martyrdom of Simeon bar Ṣabba'e*, composed in the late fourth or early fifth century, the bishop Simeon argues that Christians should not pay burdensome taxes. Enraged at Simeon's obstinance, Shapur II declares "For, in your pride and your arrogance, you want to incite your people to rebel against me."[99] The Jews, who are the chief antagonists of Christians in many martyr acts, further provoke the king by noting that the Roman emperor grants more honors to Simeon than to the king himself: "If you, King, were to send your great and learned royal letters, and your glorious offerings and delicious majestic gifts, they would not be well received or much revered in the eyes of Caesar. But if Simeon were to send him a trivial and curt letter, he would arise and bow and receive it with both his hands and diligently fulfill its requests."[100]

Later in the narrative, a high-ranking Persian official named Gushtazad, who had become a Christian but recanted under compulsion, is inspired by Simeon to embrace Christianity once again. When sent to execution, Gushtazad hastily dictates a letter to the Sasanian king in which he clarifies:

> "I have been true and sincere to all your hidden secrets, and I have been sincere to you and your father – as you yourself said. Now grant me this one request that I make of you: let a herald go up and proclaim that Gushtazad, who is being killed, is dying not because he divulged the secrets of the kingdom, nor (because) he was found at fault in anything else, but because he is a Christian and does not deny God."[101]

Gushtazad's claim to have preserved the Sasanian king's "hidden secrets" is clearly intended to address the empire's concern with Christian dual loyalties, which was particularly acute in the case of converts who had once held senior governmental or military positions.[102] Suspicion of Christians in the *Martyrdom* was significantly amplified in the later *History*, where Christian disloyalty remained an ongoing concern.[103] Later sources go even further, such as in the *Martyrdom of Peroz*, where the magi warn the king against active Christian insurrection: "Should a war interpose between the two empires, these

[99] Smith, *Martyrdom and the History*, 22–23.
[100] Smith, *Martyrdom and the History*, 26–27.
[101] Smith, *Martyrdom and the History*, 42–43.
[102] The great poet Narsai is calumniated for having spoken ill of the Sasanian king, which his Persian supporters help him deny. See Becker, *Sources*, 70–71, and Chapter 6 below.
[103] Smith, *Martyrdom and the History*, 76–77.

Christians will turn out as a thorn in your side in any fighting, and through their playing false will bring down your power."[104] Whether the events described in these and related hagiographical sources are historically accurate is beside the point. Their shared depiction of the dynamics of loyalty and disloyalty in the Sasanian Empire capture pervasive imperial anxieties of the time, confirmed by many other sources throughout late antiquity.[105]

According to earlier scholars, Sasanian distrust of Christians calcified into an essential equation of Christians and disloyalty. Violent outbreaks occurred as a reflex of this deep-seated prejudice against Christians. The Sasanians targeted Christians in an ad hoc and sweeping fashion, assuming all to be culpable and untrustworthy. More recently, several scholars have questioned the extent of Sasanian violence and distrust of Christians.[106] They note that hagiographical sources have a propensity to exaggerate the number of martyrs. This tendency is especially apparent in the case of the Great Persecution, where many martyr acts are direct literary spinoffs of the accounts of Simeon bar Ṣabbaʿe's martyrdom.[107] There is indeed little to support the notion of an essential Sasanian distrust of all Christians. Instead, it appears that the Sasanians developed a heightened anxiety about the *possibility* of Christian disloyalty.[108] Violence against Christians was therefore targeted and selective, typically aimed against those in positions of power whose behavior cast their loyalty into doubt.

The absence of any obvious inducement for Sasanian Jews to identify with the Romans, perhaps in addition to presumed Jewish antagonism towards Christian rule, rendered Jews subject to less scrutiny and suspicion than Christians. Yet, when Jewish and Roman interests aligned, they too could elicit imperial anxieties and face violence for perceived disloyalty. This is apparent from a fascinating episode reported in the

104 Bedjan, *Acta martyrum et sanctorum*, 4.258–259; Greatrex and Lieu, *The Roman Eastern Frontier*, 38.

105 Gross, "Being Roman in the Sasanian Empire," 390–397.

106 Mosig-Walburg, "Die Christenverfolgung Shāpūrs II," 171–186; Smith, *Martyrdom and the History*, xvii–l; Smith, *Constantine and the Captive Christians of Persia*; Payne, *State of Mixture*.

107 Adam Becker, "The Invention of the Persian Martyr Acts," in *Syriac Christian Culture: Beginnings to Renaissance*, ed. Aaron Michael Butts and Robin Darling Young (Washington, DC: 2020), 113–148.

108 Gross, "Being Roman in the Sasanian Empire," 390–397.

Martyrdom of Simeon bar Ṣabba'e itself. After the Jews accuse Simeon of being loyal to the Roman king, the text claims that it was the Jews who were ultimately punished for disloyalty, "because they were gathered together in order to go to the rebuilding of Jerusalem at the word of one who led them astray ..."[109] This somewhat cryptic allegation is fleshed out in the *History*, which explains that during Julian's reign, at the instigation of a certain "charlatan," some Babylonian Jews endeavored to travel to Jerusalem to rebuild the temple, but were killed by Shapur II, the very king to whom the Jews had reported Simeon's own alleged perfidy.[110] The agenda of the *Martyrdom* and *History* is apparent: to shift the Jews' accusation of Christian perfidy back upon Jews. But there is no reason to doubt the thrust of the report itself.[111] Jews who sought to return to Roman Jerusalem were simply regarded by the Sasanians as defectors to the Roman Empire, which is consistent with other occasions where the Sasanians sought to curb the defection of their subjects to the west.[112]

109 Smith, *Martyrdom and the History*, 26–29.

110 For the Sasanian Empire seeking to return Christian refugees to their empire, see Socrates Scholasticus, *Ecclesiastical History* 7.18 (Greatrex and Lieu, *The Roman Eastern Frontier*, 38), and Evagrius Scholasticus, *Ecclesiastical History* 5.7 (Michael Whitby, *The Ecclesiastical History of Evagrius Scholasticus* [Liverpool: 2000], 263–264).

111 For the attempted return, see David Levenson, "The Ancient and Medieval Sources for the Emperor Julian's Attempt to Rebuild the Jerusalem Temple," *Journal for the Study of Judaism in the Persian, Hellenistic, and Roman Period* 35 (2004): 409–460 (esp. 426); Smith, *Constantine and the Captive Christians of Persia*, 69–70n15; and Jacob Neusner, "Babylonian Jewry and Shapur II's Persecution of Christianity from 339–379 A.D.," *Hebrew Union College* Annual (1972): 91–92. See the interesting description in Cyril of Scythopolis in R. M. Price, *Lives of the Monks of Palestine: by Cyril of Scythopolis* (Kalamazoo, MI: 1991), 14, on magi guarding the roads during the persecution of Yazdgird I to prevent Christians from fleeing to Rome.

112 For Christians, such a concern is especially clear in the *Martyrdom of Pusai* (Bedjan, *Acta martyrum et sanctorum*, 2.209) and the policy of intermarriage the empire instituted for deportees, discussed above. It is also apparent in Socrates Scholasticus, *Ecclesiastical History* 7.18, who reports that during the violence under Bahram in the first half of the fifth century many Christians fled to the Roman Empire, and the Sasanian king demanded their return. See also the treaty of 562 as described by Menander Protector 6.1.340–347, (Dignas and Winter, *Rome and Persia in Late Antiquity*, 142; Blockley, *History of Menander the Guardsman*, 70–75), which has a provision regarding defectors, distinguishing between those who fled in times of war and those who fled in times of peace, the latter of whom receive no protection. Other sources report allegations against Jews in the Syrian frontier aiding an opposing army, although in these accounts, the Jews are accused of aiding the Persians. See e.g., Frank Trombley and J. W. Watt, *The Chronicle of Pseudo-Joshua the Stylite* (Liverpool: 2000), 60–61.

Treachery was a major preoccupation of the Sasanians, but so was internal dissent. The case of the revolt in Khuzistan that Mar Aba helped quash, discussed above, is one of a number of such examples.[113] Despite the general stability of Sasanian succession, some contests for the throne did arise, none more prominent than that of the short-lived but infamous usurper, Bahrām Chōbīn, who forced Khusro II to flee to the Roman emperor, Maurice, to beg for aid. According to Theophylact Simocatta, Babylonian Jews showered "not … inconsiderable" support on the usurper Bahrām Chōbīn.[114] When Khusro's armies recaptured Mesopotamia, he exacted vengeance, subjecting the Jews to "a variety of deaths." Theophylact attributes Jewish readiness "to slide towards the revolts and conflagrations of the people of Babylonia" to their great wealth, accrued, he claims, from Red Sea trade. Putting the anti-Jewish tenor of Theophylact's report aside, there is little reason to question the veracity of the report itself.[115]

While Jews were blamed for taking a more active role in this revolt, Christians were not entirely exonerated. The Catholicos at the time of the revolt, Isho'yahb of Arzen, chose neither to accompany Khusro as he fled to the Roman Empire nor greet him and his troops as they returned to reclaim Babylonia. The Syriac Christian source justifies the Catholicos' behavior on the grounds that "he feared the wickedness of Bahram, in case he should ruin the Church and stir up a persecution against the Christians."[116] But the source acknowledges that as a result, "Khusro

[113] There are similar stories of Christian involvement in Sasanian rebellions. See, for instance, under Khusro I, Scher, *Chronique de Séert*, 2.70–72, discussed in J. Labourt, *Le Christianisme dans l'empire perse sous la dynastie Sassanide (224–632)* (Paris: 1904), 189–190; and Christensen, *L'Iran sous les Sassanides*, 426; under Khusro II, see sources cited in Sean Anthony, *Crucifixion and Death as Spectacle: Umayyad Crucifixion in Its Late Antique Context* (New Haven, CT: 2014), 16–17.

[114] Theophylact, *History*, 5.7, 4–9, translation in Whitby and Whitby, *History of Theophylact Simocatta*, 141–142. On the revolt, see A. Shapur Shahbazi, "Bahrām VI Čōbīn," in *Ātaš–Bayhaqī, Ẓahīr-al-Dīn*, ed. Ehsan Yarshater, vol. 3, *Encyclopedia Iranica* (London: 1989), 514–522.

[115] On Theophylact's account of the revolt in general, see David Frendo, "Theophylact Simocatta on the Revolt of Bahram Chobin and the Early Career of Khusrau II," *Bulletin of the Asia Institute* 3 (1989): 77–88. On Jewish involvement, see Salo Baron, *A Social and Religious History of the Jews*, 2nd ed. (New York: 1952), 3.58–59; Widengren, "Status of the Jews," 147; Neusner, *History of the Jews*, 5.107–108; and Herman, *Prince without a Kingdom*, 47n145.

[116] Ignazio Guidi, *Chronicum Anonymum de ultimis regibus Persarum, Chronica Minora pars prior*, Corpus Scriptorum Christianorum Orientalium 1–2 (Leuven: 1903), 17; Nasir al-Ka'bi, *A Short Chronicle on the End of the Sasanian Empire and Early Islam* (Piscataway, NJ: 2016), 7–8; Greatrex and Lieu, *Roman Eastern Frontier*, 229.

developed much hatred toward the Catholicos." Not surprisingly, when Khusro II led a campaign against the Roman emperor Phocas a few years later, Isho'yahb's successor was by his side.[117]

Under certain conditions, then, both Jews and Christians could be subject to suspicions of disloyalty and consequently to imperial violence. The differing positionality of Jews and Christians between the Roman and Sasanian Empires was largely responsible for the disparity in the frequency and scope of violence against each. However, an additional factor was the effort each community made to eliminate concerns about their disloyalty, a topic addressed in the next chapter.

Several final reports of imperial violence against Jews are, unfortunately, hopelessly enigmatic. Three early medieval rabbinic chronographies report cases of imperial violence against Jews, but without attributing them to particular causes. *Seder Olam Zuṭa* mentions that around 315 CE, "the Persians declared a persecution against Israel." No further elaboration is provided.[118] Two interrelated medieval rabbinic sources, *Seder Tannaim veAmoraim* and the *Epistle* of Sherira Gaon describe a series of bloody confrontations in the mid-fifth century during which several rabbis and an Exilarch were killed, and Jews were prohibited from observing the Sabbath.[119] Synagogues or houses of study were closed,[120] and one source claims that the Persians "decreed concerning the Jews that they must submit to the laws of the Persians," while the

[117] Guidi, *Chroninca Minora*, 21. See also reports of Christian support, particularly in Khuzistan, of Anoshazadh in 551 CE, which the Catholicos Mar Aba was directed to undercut. See Chronicle of Seert, *PO* 7 (1911), 153, discussed in Chrisensen, *L'Iran sous les Sassanides*, 426; Labourt, *Le Christianisme*, 189–190; Paul Peeters, "Observations sur la vie syriaque de Mar Aba, Catholicos de l'eglise perse," in vol. 2 of *Recherches d'histoire et de philologie orientales* (Brussels: 1951), 157–158.

[118] The persecution is dated to 318 CE ("248 years to the destruction of the Temple") according to MS de Rossi 541, as published by Solomon Schechter, "Seder Olam Suta," *Monatsschrift für Geschichte und Wissenschaft des Judentums* 39 (1895): 27, but 315 CE ("245 years to the destruction of the Temple") according to MS Paris 1279 and MS Oxford Bodleian Heb. E8, in Lazarus, *Die Häupter der Vertriebenen*, 164. For the latter manuscript see also Adolf Neubauer, *Mediaeval Jewish Chronicles* (Oxford: 1895), 2.72. The difference between these two dates is simply due to a common confusion between a ח and ה. See, however, Neusner, *History of the Jews*, 4.101, who inexplicably says *Seder Olam Zuṭa* refers to 313. See Herman, *Prince without a Kingdom*, 366–369, for a discussion of the various manuscripts and editions of *Seder Olam Zuṭa*. See also Widengren, "Status of the Jews," 132–138.

[119] Forbidding Jewish Sabbath observance is a persecutory trope in Jewish literature, e.g., b. Meg. 12b where Vashti is said to have forced Jewish women to violate the Sabbath.

[120] Synagogues in Lewin, *Iggeret Rav Sherira Gaon*, 97; houses of study in Kahan, *Seder Tannaim weAmoraim auf Grund mehrer veröffentlichter und nichtveröffentlichter*

other claims that "Jewish children were given over to the magi."[121] These medieval chronographies similarly describe a general period of Persian interference in rabbinic practice in the sixth century.[122] Following the framing of the medieval chronographies, these events were typically attributed to the Zoroastrian fanaticism of Yazdgird II, Peroz I, and other Sasanian kings.[123]

However, the results of this chapter suggest that, if these accounts do preserve historically accurate information, they do not reflect widespread violence, nor were they caused by untrammeled religious fanaticism.[124] Instead, they likely resulted from one of the grounds for Sasanian violence outlined in this chapter and were probably targeted in scope.[125] Indeed, the forced transfer of Jewish children to the magi described in the medieval rabbinic chronographies is highly reminiscent of Ḥamza Isfahani's report that the Jews of Isfahan were similarly punished for harming two

Texte bearbeitet, übersetzt, mit Einleitung und erklärden Noten versehen (Frankfurt: 1935), 6.

121 On children taken by the magi, see Lewin, *Iggeret Rav Sherira Gaon*, 97; on laws of the Persians, see Kahan, *Seder Tannaim weAmoraim*, 6.

122 Lewin, *Iggeret Rav Sherira Gaon*, 100.

123 Scott McDonough, "A Question of Faith? Persecution and Political Centralization in the Sasanian Empire of Yazdgard II (438–457 CE)," in *Violence in Late Antiquity: Perceptions and Practices*, ed. Hal A. Drake (Aldershot: 2006), 69–81; and Payne, *State of Mixture*, 44–45, attributed it to a period of political and military instability. However, the sparse evidence renders this argument unconvincing.

124 Interestingly, a few late glosses of indeterminate date may indeed allude to these events. In b. Ḥul. 62b, two birds of similar name have opposing validity for sacrifice; one called a *shabur 'andrafta* is permitted, while the other called a *peroz 'andrafta* is forbidden. An anonymous gloss is provided "and your mnemonic is: the wicked Peroz." This appears to be a reference to violence said to take place under the reign of Peroz, as described in the medieval rabbinic chronographies. See Neusner, *History of the Jews*, 5.64. Another late addition in b. Yom. 10a likely refers to the Sasanian destruction of synagogues referenced in Sherira Gaon's *Epistle*. As E. S. Rosenthal, "Talmudica Iranica," 63–64, and Richard Kalmin, "Sasanian Persecution of the Jews: A Reconsideration of the Evidence," in *Irano-Judaica VI*, ed. Shaul Shaked and Amnon Netzer (Jerusalem: 2008), 92–93, both argue, this is likely a later addition postdating the Sasanian period. Contrast with Widengren, "Status of the Jews," 126–128; Moshe Beer, "The Imperial Background and Rav's Activities in Babylonia" [in Hebrew], *Zion* 50 (1984–1985): 155–172; and Gafni, *Jews of Talmudic Babylonia*, 36–43. In a few places, rabbinic sources mention periodic "decrees" against the Jews, but without elaboration; see b. Ta'an. 22a, Beṣ. 4b, and discussion in Chapter 4.

125 There are many reasons to question the historicity of these sources, such as the place persecution plays in their larger narratives, their clear contemporary agendas, and their incorporation of widespread tropes related to persecution. See, for instance, Gross, "When the Jews Greeted Ali," 122–144.

magi, suggesting that we should consider shared root causes.[126] In short, it is possible that lying behind these medieval reports is a reality in which Babylonian Jews ran afoul of the core Sasanian concerns enumerated in this chapter.[127]

CONCLUSION

Sasanian violence adhered to certain patterns and was deployed in furtherance of the empire's ideological and pragmatic aims. Imperial violence was therefore predictable, used to discourage types of behavior that the empire deemed undesirable, and to defend imperial ideology and promote political interests against subjects who might threaten them. A schematic sketch of the principal impetuses of Sasanian violence heuristically divides them into three broad areas: transgressing social boundaries, violating Zoroastrian cosmology, and acts of political disloyalty. Together, they show that Sasanian violence was fundamentally responsive to the behaviors, traditions, and particular positionalities of its subject communities.

Eschewing the categories of tolerance and intolerance offers a different vantage point from which to assess imperial violence against Jews and Christians. Jews were subjected to the same logics of imperial violence as Christians and other Sasanian subjects. However, the distinct practices and positions of Jews and Christians were responsible for the disparate frequency and intensity of the violence they experienced. Christians were more frequently targeted by the empire both because of increased anxiety of their possible ties to an ever-Christianizing Roman Empire and the destabilizing effects of their missionary activities, particularly among Sasanian high elites. Jews were not exempted from violence in these areas, but the apparent absence of proselytism, coupled with their lack of ties with the Roman Empire, elicited fewer occasions for imperial concern and recourse to violence.

126 It is also reminiscent of a report in Elishe (Thomson, *History of Vardan and the Armenian War by Elishē*, 103).

127 A few other medieval sources attribute changes in Jewish ritual to Sasanian persecution. See Jacob Mann, "Changes in the Divine Service of the Synagogue due to Religious Persecutions," *Hebrew Union College Annual* 4 (1927): 282–283. These appear to be an ex post facto explanation rather than have any basis in reality. See Gross, "Playing with Persecution."

Given that imperial violence was a strategy for policing and defending core commitments and concerns of the Sasanian Empire, it was simply one tool in the imperial arsenal for encouraging desirable behaviors among its subjects. As discussed in Chapter 1, the Sasanians not only responded to the possibility of Christian disloyalty with violence, but also fostered closer ties with them, in the form of patronizing a Christian ecclesiastical hierarchy and elevating Christians into positions of power and influence.[128] Jews, by contrast, were not subject to the same frequency of violence, but neither was the empire particularly driven to foster closer ties with Jews collectively through the elevation of Jewish elites. The impetus of increased imperial violence against Christians was also the catalyst for the higher positions they attained in the Empire. Patronage was the carrot to the stick of violence. Ironically, because they posed less of a threat and concern, Jews may have been relegated to a more marginal position than their Christian neighbors.

If Jews were faced with the regular possibility of imperial violence, regardless of its actual frequency, several key questions follow: How did Jews respond to the threat of violence and interference? Did they modify their practices or obdurately challenge the empire? How did Jews conceptualize imperial violence? Lastly, how do we explain the relative dearth of stories about Sasanian violence in the Talmud, especially in contrast with the proliferation of Syriac Christian martyr accounts? As we will see in the next chapter, the structural realities of imperial violence informed rabbinic stories, but it was the concerns and political aims of their authors that determined their shape.

128 I expand on this claim in Gross, "Being Roman in the Sasanian Empire," 390–397.

4

Forgetting Persecution

Memory and Anti-martyrdom in the Babylonian Talmud

Following attacks by Syriac Orthodox Christians around 792, a group of Maronite monks in northern Syria appealed to Timothy I, the Catholicos of the Church of the East, to intervene on their behalf with the Caliph, with whom the Catholicos was believed to have a close relationship. In his response, Timothy encouraged the Maronites to join his own church, noting that its many martyrs established its theological purity:

> For if anyone says that the soil of the east is the soil of holy martyrs, he is never far from the truth. For [during a period of] about four hundred years of Persians [rule], violence and murder did not cease from the Church of the East (*ʿedtā d-madnḥā*). And in all this time and duration of killing and persecution, Satan could never pillage the riches of their confession, nor make any addition or diminution [therefrom].[1]

Timothy also urged the Maronites to read "the books of Martyrdoms, that is, from the acts of the martyrs who suffered martyrdom in the East" and to witness his followers' veneration of the "bones of the holy martyrs."[2] Timothy's remarks invoke the East Syriac Church's

[1] Martin Heimgartner, *Die Briefe 40 und 41 des Ostsyrischen Patriarchen Timotheos I*, 2 vols (CSCO 673–4; Louvain: 2019), 1.107–108. I thank Salam Rassi for sharing his translation with me.

[2] Jeanne-Nicole Saint-Laurent, "Bones in Bags: Relics in Syriac Hagiography," in *Syriac Encounters: Papers from the Sixth North American Syriac Symposium, Duke University, 26–29 June 2011*, ed. Maria E. Doerfler, Emanuel Fiano, and Kyle Smith, Eastern Christian Studies 20 (Leuven: 2015), 439–454; Christelle Jullien and Florence Jullien, "Du ḥnana ou la bénédiction contestée," in *Sur les pas des araméens chrétiens. Mélanges offerts à Alain Desreumaux*, ed. Françoise Briquel-Chatonnet and Muriel Debié (Paris: 2010), 333–348.

longstanding glorification of martyrdom, particularly in defiance of the Sasanian Empire, reflected in its copious martyrological literature and in the many martyr shrines that dotted the East Syriac landscape, which served as sites of annual commemorations and pilgrimage.[3]

Few if any comparable Sasanian-era stories of Jewish martyrdom survive. This absence has fed scholarly narratives about the largely peaceable conditions Jews enjoyed under Sasanian rule. As argued in the previous chapter, notions of Sasanian tolerance toward Jews ignore the ample evidence that the same imperial logics of violence applied to both Jews and Christians, not only in theory but also in practice. But if Jews did suffer imperial violence, it only further calls attention to the odd dearth of Jewish stories of Sasanian persecution.

This absence is only odd, however, if one assumes that the stories groups tell transparently reflect their historical reality, and that the one Sasanian-era Jewish literary source to survive – the Babylonian Talmud – broadly reflects the narratives and experiences of all Sasanian Jews. Yet, over nearly half a century, scholars have continued to show that Jewish and Christian sources about the past are not neutral or straightforward descriptions of historical events: they are narratives constructed in particular moments and which serve a range of social, intellectual, and identitarian functions.[4] They constitute cases of collective or social memory in which communities craft a suitable past, not driven by a concern for accuracy, however that might be measured, but by the function the past serves in the consolidation and ideation of the community in the present.[5] The study of memory is therefore, according to Patrick Geary, "a study of propaganda, of the decisions about what should be remembered and how it should be remembered."[6] These memories are fashioned "through a complex process of transmission, suppression, and re-creation," as individuals and communities "copied, abridged, and

[3] Richard Payne, "The Emergence of Martyrs' Shrines in Late Antique Iran: Conflict, Consensus, and Communal Institutions," in *An Age of Saints? Power, Conflict and Dissent in Early Medieval Christianity*, ed. P. Sarris, M. Dal Santo, and P. Booth (Leiden: 2011), 89–113.

[4] See discussion in Introduction, pp. 13–15.

[5] Elizabeth Castelli, *Martyrdom and Memory: Early Christian Culture Making* (New York: 2004), 10–32, provides a rich historiography of social memory.

[6] Patrick J. Geary, *Phantoms of Remembrance: Memory and Oblivion at the End of the First Millennium* (Princeton, NJ: 1994), 9.

revised archival records, liturgical texts, literary documents."[7] Historical memory is accordingly as much about what to remember as it is about what is worthy of forgetting.[8] As a complicated social process, the formation of communal memory is frequently a subject of disagreement. An interest in historical memory explores precisely "how people together searched for common memories to meet present needs," and how they "agreed, disagreed, or negotiated over its meaning."[9] Communal memory was made by, and for, groups of people, even as they might dispute its precise contours.[10]

The study of social memory is especially productive when applied to the case of narratives of imperial violence and persecution. "Persecution" and a community's response to it are historiographical constructions and do not represent fact as much as the ordering of discrete events – real or imagined – into a specific narrative. As Daniel Boyarin put it well, "Being killed is an event. Martyrdom is a literary form, a genre."[11] That is, accounts of imperial violence do not provide neutral transcripts of historical events, when they correlate with historical events at all. These texts are, first and foremost, literary compositions that conform to rigid conventions and adhere to specific narrative templates.[12] Frequently they were

7 Geary, *Phantoms of Remembrance*, 8. For the use of social memory in the study of the rabbis, see the special issue of *Jewish Studies Quarterly* 30.4 (2023) on "Rethinking Rabbinic History."

8 Geary, *Phantoms of Remembrance*, 28; Eviatar Zerubavel, *Social Mindscapes: An invitation to Cognitive Sociology* (Cambridge, MA: 1997), 84; Michael Schudson, *Watergate in American Memory: How We Remember, Forget, and Reconstruct the Past* (New York: 1992), 5. For the application of this approach to Jews of the medieval period, see Menaḥem Ben-Sasson, "Remembrance and Oblivion of Religious Persecutions: On Sanctifying the Name of God (Qiddush ha-Shem) in Christian and Islamic Countries during the Middle Ages," in *Jews, Christians and Muslims in Medieval and Early Modern Times*, ed. Arnold Franklin, Roxani Eleni Margariti, Marina Rustow, and Uriel Simonsohn (Leiden: 2014), 169–194.

9 David Thelen, "Memory and American History," *Journal of American History* 75 (1989): 1123.

10 Castelli, *Martyrdom and Memory*, 10–11.

11 Boyarin, *Dying for God: Martyrdom and the Making of Christianity and Judaism* (Stanford, CA: 1999), 116.

12 Castelli, *Martyrdom and Memory*; Candida Moss, *The Other Christs: Imitating Jesus in Ancient Christian Ideologies of Martyrdom* (Oxford: 2010); see also the collection edited by Johan Leemans, *More than a Memory: The Discourse of Martyrdom and the Construction of Christian Identity in the History of Christianity* (Leuven: 2005). For periods of persecution, see Brent Shaw, "The Myth of the Neronian Persecution," *Journal of Roman Studies* 105 (2015): 73–100. More generally on the cultural work performed by narratives of violence, see Brent Shaw, *Sacred Violence: African Christians and Sectarian Hatred in the Age of Augustine* (Cambridge: 2011); Thomas Sizgorich,

composed centuries after the events they purport to describe and, in some cases, were provably spun from whole cloth, correlating with no historical event.[13] These accounts have various and complex relationships with historical reality, but as texts they undoubtedly sought to inculcate behaviors, attitudes, and ideas in their audiences in the present.[14]

Sensitivity to the formation and creation of narratives of persecution and violence and the agendas underlying them is now a central scholarly concern. These accounts are, as Daniel Boyarin says, "necessarily evidence for the time and place in which they have come into being as texts and not necessarily for the time and place of which they tell us. That is, they *may* be evidence for earlier times but are certainly evidence that something was being thought or said at the time that the text was promulgated."[15] They are first and foremost "period pieces" before they are evidence for earlier periods.[16] Therefore, questions about the authenticity or veracity of these sources must be subordinated to questions about their contemporary social function.

Memory is not, however, a limited neurological operation in the brains of these writers, and narratives are not simply told for literary edification and entertainment. Memory of a putative past contributes to a community's "formative and normative impulses."[17] Narratives of the past mediate the experience of the community in the present and establish the framework for considering proper responses to it. The study of communal memory is not interested in discourse "for its own sake, as if there was nothing but discourse, but for the sake of its role in social action, present and future."[18] Given the social consequences of memory, and given the differing interests members of a group might have, it should

Violence and Belief in Late Antiquity: Militant Devotion in Christianity and Islam (Philadelphia, PA: 2014); and Butts and Gross, *The History of the "Slave of Christ."*

[13] For one such example, see Simcha Gross, "The Sources of the History of ʿAbdā damšiḥā: The Creation of a Persian Martyr Act," in *Syriac Christian Culture: Beginnings to Renaissance*, ed. Aaron Michael Butts and Robin Darling Young (Washington, DC: 2020), 149–173.

[14] Daniel Boyarin, *Border Lines: The Partition of Judaeo-Christianity* (Philadelphia, PA: 2004), 46; Payne, *State of Mixture*, 18.

[15] Boyarin, *Border Lines*, 46.

[16] See similarly Payne, *State of Mixture*, 18, and Adam Gaiser, *Shurāt Legends, Ibāḍī Identities: Martyrdom, Asceticism, and the Making of an Early Islamic Community* (Columbia, SC: 2016), 8.

[17] Jan Assmann and John Czaplicka, "Collective Memory and Cultural Identity," *New German Critique* 65 (1995): 128. More generally see Assmann, *Moses the Egyptian: The Memory of Egypt in Western Monotheism* (Cambridge, MA: 1998).

[18] Schudson, *Watergate in American Memory*, 4.

be no surprise that multiple narratives could coexist or rival one another: the contest over memory exemplifies the "politics of remembering."[19]

If a community's perception of an empire is shaped, informed, and mediated by memory, communal memory therefore has real material, cultural, and physical consequences.[20] For subject groups, martyrdom and persecution narratives were effective media through which to express views about the empire and prescribe strategies for future encounters with it. Syriac Christian martyr accounts, for instance, had multiple agendas, but a common thread across them is an effort to shape their community's attitude toward the Sasanian Empire, at times formulating areas of accommodation and at other times grounds for resistance.[21] They offered models of the terms for conducive relations between Christians and the empire and articulated the lines that Christians should, sometimes quite literally, die before crossing.[22] These accounts also projected images of the empire and its relationship to Christianity that informed the way Christians approached and interpreted future encounters with it.

While martyrdom accounts reflect one narrative mode of engaging with empire, the relative absence from the Talmud of stories of Sasanian persecution or rabbinic martyrdom cannot serve as evidence of a reality of little imperial violence. This chapter argues that the absence of talmudic stories of imperial violence stems from the decisions of different rabbinic editors and composers about what stories to tell and, as importantly, what stories to forget. These decisions become visible through a dissection of the complicated compositional histories of several rabbinic stories that feature Jewish interactions with the Sasanian Empire. Literary analysis reveals that the rabbis actively subvert, overwrite, erase, and thereby "forget" moments of imperial violence described in earlier rabbinic statements and texts. In other cases, rabbis formulate new stories by means of traceable literary compositional techniques of selection, duplication, and

[19] For a model study of historical memory, see Sarah Bowen Savant, *The New Muslims of Post-Conquest Iran: Tradition, Memory, and Conversion* (Cambridge: 2013).

[20] For the construction of Christian memory to sway political action, see similarly Paul Dilley, "The Invention of Christian Tradition: 'Apocrypha,' Imperial Policy, and Anti-Jewish Propaganda," *Greek, Roman and Byzantine Studies* 50 (2010): 586–615.

[21] See, for instance, Becker, "Martyrdom, Religious Difference, and 'Fear,'" 300–336; Payne, *State of Mixture*; Kyle Smith, "Constantine and Judah the Maccabee"; Smith, *Constantine and the Captive Christians of Persia*; and Wood, *Chronicle of Seert*.

[22] A fascinating example of shifting terms of accommodation can be seen in the differences between the *Martyrdom* and *History of Simeon bar Ṣabba'e*. See Kyle Smith, "Constantine and Judah the Maccabee," and Chapter 1, pp. 46–48.

adaptation that encourage accommodation to an empire they present as unobjectionable.

These processes of forgetting and remembering therefore promoted a particular set of images of the empire and idealized specific strategies for Jewish encounters with it while eschewing others. This chapter will show that the resulting talmudic stories consistently depict a benign empire and idealize the avoidance of outright confrontation with it, in favor of acts of accommodation, or subtle and unostentatious acts of subversion. Earlier rabbinic sayings and sources that allude to episodes of Sasanian imperial persecution were erased or concealed by means of interpolation or even the composition of new stories altogether. The stories the Babylonian rabbis related therefore differ markedly from those told by Christians, not only because the two communities had dissimilar experiences under Sasanian rule but also because some rabbis sought to inculcate a distinct set of perceptions of the Sasanian Empire and strategies for life within it. Indeed, the rabbis were self-reflective about the benefits and costs of their political approach of accommodation and subtle resistance and knowingly contrast it with martyrdom and open resistance, which they pragmatically reject but whose zeal they admire. The rabbis purposefully shaped their audience's relationship with the empire through the stories they told and, as significantly, through those they did not.[23]

The possibility that Babylonian rabbis were invested in offering politically relevant and impactful images for Jewish life in the Sasanian Empire is generally absent in the study of the Talmud to date. Even when scholars study rabbinic representations of the Sasanian Empire and skillfully unpack their compositional histories, they struggle to conceive of rabbinic motives and agendas. They ultimately revert to the conventional conclusion that the rabbis were interested in nothing more than the Torah and its proper interpretation and practice. Thus, in an otherwise pathbreaking article applying the source-critical turn in the study of the Babylonian Talmud to reassess several talmudic references to the Sasanian Empire, some of which are discussed below, Richard Kalmin concludes that "the

[23] For a discussion of Palestinian rabbinic attitudes toward martyrdom, see Daniel Schwartz, "Martyrdom, the Middle Way, and Mediocrity (*Genesis Rabbah* 82:8)," in *Follow the Wise: Studies in Jewish History and Culture in Honor of Lee I. Levine*, ed. Z. Weiss, Oded Irshai, and Jodi Magness (Winona Lake, IN: 2010), 343–353; and Alyssa Gray, "A Contribution to the Study of Martyrdom and Identity in the Palestinian Talmud," *Journal of Jewish Studies* 54 (2003): 242–271.

editors' motive, here as in so many places, is *lehagdil Torah u-leha'dirah* [SG: 'to make the Torah great and exalt it'], to increase the length, complexity, and lavishness of the Talmud's argumentation rather than to make a political, historical, or theological statement." To Kalmin, the redactional interventions are devoid of any larger *Tendenz* beyond mere elaboration for the sake of religious merit. The "primary task" of any editorial intervention, according to Kalmin, was simply "to interpret traditions, to make and resolve objections, and to do so they strive primarily for logical rather than historical cogency."[24] The rabbis are accordingly dismissed for having "little critical control over what they received" and for incorporating "sources into their deliberations primarily for halakhic reasons, or to underscore the moral lessons to be derived from these stories."[25] They were simply uninterested in images of the past for their own sake; their principal pursuit was the resolution of technical textual and legal issues.

The disinclination to conceive of a rabbinic interest in the production of historical memory stems from the older notions of Babylonian Jewish society with which this book began. If Sasanian Jews lived under peaceable conditions, and if they were self-governing and their encounters with the empire minimal to nonexistent, there would be little reason for Jews, and particularly the narrowly focused rabbis, to contemplate how best to represent and navigate Sasanian rule. Outside of those paradigms, the rabbis, like their Syriac Christian counterparts, sought to shape the "normative impulses" of their audience, not only regarding proper religious law and belief, but also political action. They advanced their views through the narratives they told and, equally, through those they chose to forget.

BLAMING THE VICTIM

Our first text offers a striking example of the "forgetting" of Sasanian violence against Jews through later editorial intervention. It opens with a stylistically simple report of the consequences of a Sasanian military campaign that is then recast through subsequent commentary, a formal device that, as we will see, is also deployed in other talmudic accounts of Sasanian violence.

[24] Kalmin, "Sasanian Persecution of the Jews," 101.

[25] Gafni, "Rabbinic Historiography," 297. It should be noted that Gafni here is referring not only to the Babylonian Talmud but also to sages through the early modern period.

[A] Do we rend [clothing] upon [receiving] bad news?

But it was reported to Shmuel, "King Shapur killed 12,000[26] Jews in the city of Caesarea [Mazaca]," yet he [Shmuel] did not rend [his garments]!
They only said one must rend his garment in response to bad tidings when they refer to the majority of the people [of Israel], such as in that case [referred to earlier, when David tore his clothing in response to the tiding of the death of Saul, Jonathan and their troops in 2 Sam. 1.10–11].
[B] But did King Shapur kill Jews? But did not King Shapur say to Shmuel, "may evil befall me if I have killed Jews"?
In that case they brought it upon themselves.
For Rabbi Ami said, "The sound of the bows of Caesarea-Mazaca destroyed the walls of Laodicea."[27]

The historical background to this story is Shapur I's military campaign of 260 CE in which he conquered, among other places, Caesarea-Mazaca in Asia Minor.[28] The campaign is best known for the capture and killing of the Roman Emperor Valerian. The victory is celebrated in Shapur I's monumental inscription at Naqsh-e Rustam, also known as the *Res Gestae Divi Saporis* or "The Things Accomplished by the Divine Shapur."

Based predominantly on the shifting use of Hebrew and Aramaic, Kalmin argued that this passage consists of a core story and several later additions.[29] The core story includes the report of the death of 12,000 Jews in Caesarea-Mazaca, the relaying of this episode to Shmuel, Shmuel explaining why he did not tear his garment upon hearing the tragic news, and Shapur's insistence that he never killed Jews. There are, however, several difficulties with Kalmin's reconstruction. Only seven words of the core story are in Hebrew, and they represent terms commonly found in rabbinic literature.[30] Shapur's statement is entirely in Aramaic and unconnected to the core story. To bring coherence to his reconstructed

26 In other manuscripts, 13,000. This is a common scribal variation. For instance, see the story of Rabbah bar Nahmani below.

27 b. M. Qaṭ. 26a, according to MS Columbia University 294–295.

28 This city may appear elsewhere in rabbinic literature in slightly different forms: Mazaga of Cappadocia (t. Shab. 15.8); Megizah (Magaza) of Cappadocia (y. Yeb. 16.4 [15d], but cf. b. Yeb. 25b). For the historical context of this event, see Neusner, *History of the Jews*, 2.46–48, and references there, especially 46n1; and Isaiah Gafni, "On the Talmudic Chronology in the Iggeret Rav Sherira Gaon," [in Hebrew] *Zion* 52 (1987): 19–22.

29 Kalmin, "Sasanian Persecution of the Jews," 113–121.

30 A near identical statement in b. Yeb. 116b is attributed to Rabbi Hananiah b. Akiva. See also b. Beṣ. 15a.

core story, Kalmin is compelled to insert words into the passage. In the end, Kalmin struggles to explain what motivated the introduction of the secondary additions, concluding that they lack any clear purpose.[31]

Contrary to Kalmin's division between a core text and secondary additions, I would argue that the passage appears to consist of two literarily similar units (A and B above), possibly produced contemporaneously, and both built around an earlier report of Shmuel's response upon hearing of the slaughter of Jews at Caesarea-Mazaca.[32] The literary similarity between the two units can be seen from the nearly identical questions that introduce them (A: "But do we . . .," B: "but did . . ."). Unit A uses Shmuel's conduct to answer a technical halakhic question concerning mourning practice: When does one tear their garment upon hearing tragic news? Unit B addresses a question with political implications: Was Shapur, in fact, responsible for slaughtering Jews? Astonishingly, Shapur issues a denial of any culpability ("may evil befall me if I have killed Jews"), and his denial is accepted at face value. The composer then reappropriates a report from elsewhere in rabbinic literature about a different city attacked by Shapur I in the same military campaign, which makes no mention of Jews.[33] This unrelated report is applied here to now suggest that the slaughtered Jews of Caesarea-Mazaca were somehow responsible for their own deaths.[34] Unit B displays a concerted effort to exonerate Shapur for the Jewish deaths, preferring to place blame on the slaughtered Jews who "brought it upon themselves."[35]

This passage demonstrates the lengths that the rabbis were willing to go to recast reports of Sasanian violence against Jews in ways that reduced or eliminated any culpability by the empire. Although thousands

[31] Kalmin, "Sasanian Persecution of the Jews," 121.

[32] A more detailed textual discussion can be found in Simcha Gross, *Empire and Neighbors: Babylonian Jewish Identity in Its Local and Imperial Context* (PhD diss., Yale University, 2017), 78–89.

[33] y. B. Bat. 2:9; 13b.

[34] On the language of this final statement, see Sokoloff, *DJBA*, 548. Previous discussions can be found in Kalmin, "Sasanian Persecution of the Jews," 117–121; Gafni, "Babylonian Rabbinic Culture," 236; Neusner, *History of the Jews*, 2.45–47. Cf. Widengren, "Status of the Jews," 129 and 129n3; and Netzer, "Ha-Sasanim ba-Talmud ha-Bavli, 256. Baron, *Social and Religious History of the Jews*, 2.177–178, suggests that Shmuel refuses to tear his clothing because of his close relationship with Shapur I. For a similar apologetic explanation for the violence of a Sasanian king, this time offered by Zoroastrians, see Boyce, *Letter of Tansar*, 47.

[35] Kalmin, "Sasanian Persecution of the Jews," 121n108, acknowledges this explanation as a possibility.

of Jews were slaughtered at Caesarea-Mazaca, they are neither celebrated nor romanticized by the rabbis but are instead blamed for their own deaths. The Sasanian king, by contrast, is absolved of any wrongdoing; he denies any blame, and his protestations of innocence are accepted as fact. The Talmud's treatment of a Sasanian attack in which thousands of Jews were killed suggests how far the rabbis were willing to go to whitewash instances of Sasanian violence against Jews.[36]

RABBINIC ANTI-MARTYRDOM

Another story about a Babylonian rabbi named Rabbah bar Naḥmani has traditionally been understood as one of the few talmudic texts to describe an episode of Sasanian persecution against Jews.[37] I will argue that the source is again comprised of two components: a brief, relatively early report of Sasanian violence – this time directed against a leading rabbinic figure rather than masses of Jews – and a later elaborate story that recasts and subverts it. Remarkably, the later story employs literary motifs common in martyrdom stories told by both contemporary Syriac Christians and earlier Palestinian rabbis to generate a set of literary expectations, only to disappoint them and promote the political strategies of accommodation and subtle subversion over outright resistance.

A. Rav Kahana said, "Ḥama, the son of the daughter of Ḥassa, related to me [that] Rabbah bar Naḥmani died on account of persecution."
B. They denounced him (אכלו ביה קורצא) before the government. [the slanderers] said, "There is a man among the Jews who keeps back twelve thousand Jews from the payment of the royal poll tax one month in summer and one in winter." They sent a *frēstaqa* [royal officer][38] for him, but did not find him. He [Rabbah] fled

[36] It is worth noting, in a similar vein, that the Babylonian Talmud does not contain any reference to the deportations of Jews, Christians, and others under Shapur I during the same campaigns in which he conquered Caesarea-Mazaca. This contrasts with Syriac texts, which thematize captivity regularly. See, for instance, *The Martyrdom of Pusai*, *The Captives of Beth Zabdai*, *The Martyrdom of Miles*, and more. For a discussion, see Smith, *Constantine and the Captive Christians of Persia*, 99–180. For the history of these population transfers, see Morony, "Population Transfers," 161–179.

[37] b. B. Meṣ. 86a. I present the text according to MS Vatican 115 because it is complete and relatively clear. The differences in the manuscripts do not affect my arguments.

[38] From Middle Persian *frēstag* [*plystk'*]. See Mackenzie, *A Concise Pahlavi Dictionary*, 34; Ciancaglini, *Iranian Loanwords in Syriac*, 240; and Desmond Durkin-Meisterernst, *Dictionary of Manichaean Middle Persian and Parthian* (Turnhout: Brepols, 2004), 159–161. Cf. Wiessner, *Zur Märtyrerüberlieferung*, 183.

from Pumbedita to Ṣarifa dʿayna, and from Ṣarifa dʿayna to Apadna d'shizha, and from Apadna d'shizha to Agama.
C. The *frēstaqa* chanced upon the same inn in which Rabbah bar Nahmani was [hiding].
They placed a tray before [the *frēstaqa*], gave him two glasses, and then removed the tray from before him; [consequently] his face was turned backwards [i.e., he was incapacitated].[39] They [the inn attendants] said to [Rabbah], "What should we do, he is a royal officer?!" [Rabbah] said, "Bring him the tray again and give him another cup to drink, then remove the tray, so that he may recover." They did so, and he recovered. [The *frēstaqa*] said "I know that the man whom I seek is here." He searched and found him. He said, "I will depart from here; but (even) if they kill that man [i.e., me], I will not disclose [your whereabouts]; but if they torture that man, I will disclose your whereabouts."
D. They brought [Rabbah] before [the *frēstaqa*], and [the *frēstaqa*] led him into an inner chamber and closed the door upon him. [Rabbah] prayed, whereupon the wall fell down, and he fled and went to Agama.
E. There he sat upon the trunk of a palm and was studying. He heard they were disputing in the Heavenly Academy: "If the bright spot preceded the white hair, he is impure; if the white hair preceded the bright spot, he is pure. If [the order is] in doubt, what [is the ruling]?" The Holy One, blessed be He, ruled, "he is pure," while the whole Heavenly Academy maintained "he is impure." "Who shall resolve it? Rabbah bar Naḥmani; for he said, 'I am pre-eminent in the laws of leprosy; I am pre-eminent in tents.'"
A messenger was sent for him, but the Angel of Death could not approach him, because his mouth did not cease studying (Torah). In the meantime, a wind blew and made a noise[40] in the reeds. He thought it was a troop[41] of horsemen. He said, "Let that man [i.e., me] die and not be delivered into the hands of the kingdom (מלכותא)." As he was dying, he exclaimed, "Pure, pure!!" [whereupon] a heavenly voice went out [from Heaven] and said, "Happy are you, Rabbah bar Naḥmani, that your body is pure, and your soul has departed in purity!"
A missive fell from Heaven in Pumbedita of Abaye [upon which was written,] "Rabbah bar Naḥmani has been summoned to the Heavenly Academy."
F. So, Abaye and Raba and all the scholars went forth to attend him [at his burial], but they did not know his whereabouts. They went to Agama and saw birds which were standing and providing shade. They said, "This proves that he is there." They bewailed him for three days and three nights. They wanted to leave, but a missive fell [from Heaven, saying], "He who leaves shall be under a ban." So, they

[39] Pairs (zugot) of food or drink were considered dangerous by the rabbis for fear that they provoked demons; see b. Pesaḥ. 110a–b, which also includes the remedy of an additional third cup of wine found in our story, and includes a late gloss which makes reference to the story of Rabbah bar Naḥmani. For a discussion of this rabbinic pericope and the concern with pairs, see Sara Ronis, *Demons in the Details: Demonic Discourse and Rabbinic Culture in Late Antique Babylonia* (Berkeley, CA: 2022), 130–140.

[40] *'awaš*, Middle Persian *āwāz*, meaning 'to make a sound.' See Sokoloff, *DJBA*, 86–87.

[41] *Gunda*, Middle Persian *gund*. See Sokoloff, *DJBA*, 269–270.

bewailed him for seven days, and [then] a [second] missive fell [from Heaven saying], "Return in peace to your homes."
G. On the day that he died a storm lifted an Arab riding a camel and transported him from one bank of the river Pana to the other. He said, "What is this about?" They answered him, "Rabbah bar Naḥmani has died." He exclaimed before Him, "You are the sovereign of the universe, and Rabbah bar Naḥmani too is yours. Why are you destroying it [the world]?" [Thereupon] the storm subsided.

The literary unit opens (A) with a brief report about a fourth-century rabbi named Rabbah bar Naḥmani who died during a *shmada*.[42] Elsewhere in the Talmud, the word *shmada* refers to a period of religious persecution.[43] The matter-of-fact style of this opening report is typical of basic rabbinic dicta.[44]

Problems arise when this initial report (A) is paired with the story that follows (B–G). The latter does not seem to describe a period of persecution at all, but rather imperial administrators seeking to apprehend Rabbah on account of his seemingly inadvertent instigation of tax evasion by his disciples. Indeed, in the end, Rabbah is not killed by the empire, but by God's hand and by his own request. Contrary to the opening report, the story that follows does not even hint at an episode, let alone a period, of religious persecution.[45]

[42] For a treatment of earlier positivist approaches to this source, see Simcha Gross, "A Persian Anti-Martyr Act: The Death of Rabbah Bar Naḥmani," in *The Aggada of the Bavli and Its Cultural World*, ed. Jeffrey Rubenstein and Geoffrey Herman (Providence, RI: 2018), 219–221. An imaginative reconstruction of the historical events was offered by Moshe Beer, "Concerning the Deposal of Rabbah Bar Naḥmani from the Headship of the Academy: A Chapter in the History of the Relationship between the Sages and the Exilarchs," [in Hebrew] *Tarbiẓ* 33 (1964): 349–357; and strongly criticized by E. E. Urbach, "Concerning Historical Insight into the Account of Rabbah Bar Naḥmani's Death," [in Hebrew] *Tarbiẓ* 34 (1965): 156–161.

[43] For a representative but not exhaustive list, see b. Sanh. 14a; Rosh Hash. 18b; and Beṣ. 4b. For scholarly discussion of the term elsewhere, see Richard L. Kalmin, "Rabbinic Traditions about Roman Persecution of the Jews: A Reconsideration," *Journal of Jewish Studies* 54 (2003): 23 with notes.

[44] The pithy nature of the report and its use of the term *shmada* also resemble in both form and substance medieval rabbinic chronographies that describe periods of Sasanian persecution, e.g., Lewin, *Iggeret Rav Sherira Gaon*, 90–97. See also Isaiah Gafni, "Talmudic Chronology in the Iggeret," 8 and note 29 there for another talmudic pericope that seems to anticipate medieval rabbinic chronographies. Urbach, "Concerning Historical Insight," 156, connects the death of Rabbah to the report in *Seder Olam Zuṭa*, discussed in Chapter 3, pp. 162–163.

[45] Thus, Sokoloff, *DJBA*, 78 and 1155 continues to translate *shmada* as a "religious persecution," even though it does not aptly describe the ensuing story. Indeed, the use of this word was apparently so problematic for Sherira Gaon in the late tenth century that he felt compelled to alter it to שמדא דאורייתא, a persecution against the Torah, and removes

The substantive and stylistic disconnect between the opening report and the story that follows suggests that the latter may have been composed separately from the initial report.[46] Indeed, the latter story incorporates anachronisms – such as references to large rabbinic academies and their semester system (B) – and adapts a significant number of motifs borrowed from elsewhere in the Talmud, which are tell-tale signs of late Babylonian rabbinic compositions.[47] The editorial technique at play here therefore appears similar to that used in the unit concerning the Jews of Caesarea-Mazaca, where an earlier report of Sasanian violence was recast and subverted by the text that immediately followed. In that case, the editorial intervention took the form of a series of questions and answers, while in this case it takes the form of a lengthy and elaborate tale.

BORROWED MOTIFS

Yet if like many late rabbinic compositions, the story of Rabbah is the product of the creative combination and adaptation of literary motifs, themes, and scenes that appear elsewhere in rabbinic literature, it also strongly resembles several foundational Syriac Christian martyr acts. Rabbah's role in his community's evasion of taxes is highly reminiscent of the stories surrounding the principal Syriac Christian martyr, the fourth-century East Syriac leader, Simeon bar Ṣabbaʿe.[48] In the accounts of his martyrdom, Simeon bar Ṣabbaʿe objects to Christians having to pay the poll tax, which results in his prosecution and eventual martyrdom.

the reference to the poll tax entirely (Lewin, *Iggeret Rav Sherira Gaon*, 87). Through this slight emendation, Sherira makes it seem as if the persecution was directed against rabbinic study itself.

46 This explanation differs from that offered by Boyarin, *Socrates and the Fat Rabbis*, 225–227, and Inbar Raveh, *Me'at meharbeh: ma'ase hakhamim–mivnim sifruti'im utefisat olam* (Be'er Sheva: 2008), 88–91, who note the incongruity between the introduction and the rest of the story, but nevertheless treat them as a unity.

47 For academies, see Rubenstein, *Culture of the Babylonian Talmud*, 16–23. For recycled motifs in this story, see Shamma Friedman, "The Orthography of the Names Rabbah and Rava," [in Hebrew] *Sinai* 110 (1992): 156n2; and more extensively, Gross, "Persian Anti-Martyr Act," 239–242. On the semester system, see Gafni, *Jews of Talmudic Babylonia*, 131–144; and Goodblatt, *Rabbinic Instruction in Sasanian Babylonia*, 155–170. The allegation presumes that the period of study was plausibly associated with tax evasion, although given the opacity of the Sasanian tax administration, the details remain unclear; see Goodblatt, "Poll Tax," 273.

48 For a critical edition of the Syriac text with Latin translation, see Michael Kmosko, "S. Simeon bar Ṣabbaʿe," in *Patrología Syriaca* 1.2 (Paris: 1907). For a recent English translation, see Smith, *Martyrdom and History*.

The parallels between this and the story of Rabbah are clear: In each, a Jewish and Christian religious leader – an academy head and a bishop – is accused by the empire of causing their followers to fail to pay taxes.[49] The two figures are also roughly contemporaneous, as their respective accounts place them in the first half of the fourth century.

Some have noticed the connections between these stories, treating them as proof that Jews and Christians were targeted by the Sasanian Empire for similar reasons at roughly the same time.[50] However, as discussed earlier, the story of Rabbah postdates and subverts the original report that his death was the result of persecution. The stories of Simeon's death were likewise composed at least half a century after Simeon's supposed martyrdom and freely reproduce literary topoi from earlier Christian martyrdom literature.[51] Whatever historical episode lies behind Simeon's narratives, the conflict between heroic saint and villainous empire and king at its core is a standard hagiographical template that should be approached with extreme caution. That the parallels between the two stories reflect shared historical circumstances is undermined by the sheer unlikelihood that two leading figures were accused of instigating a similar financial crime among their respective followers at the same historical moment. The historicity of each of these accounts is therefore highly questionable.

If these works do not report history, their uncannily similar premises suggest that they share a literary relationship, with one text's composer aware of and adapting the other. Assuming this is so, then it is the rabbinic story, which postdates the Syriac sources, that would have appropriated material either from some version of the story of Simeon bar Ṣabbaʿe or from one of the many contemporaneous Christian martyrdom stories that derived from it.[52]

In fact, the rabbinic story bears an especially close literary resemblance with one Syriac story that is derivative of Simeon's accounts: the *Martyrdom of Barbaʿshmin*. In this account, Barbaʿshmin, Simeon's nephew, became

49 See Goodblatt, "Poll Tax," 272–276, for a summary of previous scholarship on the question of how exactly Rabbah prevented the Jews from paying taxes. For more on tax collection, see Chapter 1, pp. 45–48 and Chapter 2, pp. 125–130.

50 Neusner, *History of the Jews*, 4.43–44; Goodblatt, "Poll Tax," 249–250; Wiessner, *Zur Märtyrerüberlieferung*, 182–183.

51 On the question of dating, see Gross, "Being Roman in the Sasanian Empire," 369–370. On the anachronism in the *History* related to Simeon's title, see Smith, *Martyrdom and History*, xlv, and references there.

52 On the development of this "corpus," see Becker, "The Invention of the Persian Martyr Acts."

the "head of the Christians" after Simeon's death. Like Simeon, he is martyred for encouraging his followers to subvert the king's authority. The rabbinic story and the *Martyrdom of Barbaʿshmin* share numerous verbal parallels that are even more striking because they include words and phrases otherwise rarely attested in the Babylonian Talmud:[53]

In the sixth year of our persecution, they slandered Barbaʿshmin, the bishop of Seleucia-Ctesiphon, before the king.

They were saying to him, "There is an impudent man here, who stands against our teaching. And he converts many people from our religion (*deḥlta*) and makes them idle from the work of the king, and he disdains the sun and insults fire and water."

The story begins with the slander of Barbaʿshmin, using the same term as the story of Rabbah.[54] While this expression for slander (אכלו ביה קורצא) also appears in three other places in the Babylonian Talmud, it is but one of several similarities between the Syriac and talmudic story.[55] In both, the slanderers explain that "there is a man" whose teachings – whether to talmudic students or Zoroastrians who become Christians – purportedly interfere with the empire's affairs and affect its purse or workforce. Both use the same Aramaic root (*bṭl*) to describe the nature of the wrong-doing.[56] Barbaʿshmin and Rabbah are therefore accused, in an almost identical manner, of the same general offense.[57]

[53] Bedjan, *Acta martyrum et sanctorum* 2.296–297. For a similar general accusation, but which lacks the consistent verbal parallels and thematic similarities shared by the story of Rabbah and that of Barbaʿshmin, see the *Martyrdom of ʿAqebshma* in Bedjan, *Acta martyrum et sanctorum*, 2.261–262.

[54] Slander is also a theme in several Persian martyr acts, such as the martyrdom story of Thecla (Bedjan, *Acta martyrum et sanctorum*, 2.308).

[55] b. Giṭ. 56a; Ber. 58a; and b. B. Bat. 58a. The first text contains an accusation against all Jews, and the other two contain an accusation against a single rabbi for functioning as an independent legislator without proper authority. The expression for slander appears across Aramaic languages deriving from Akkadian, on which see Stephen Kaufman, *The Akkadian Influences on Aramaic* (Chicago: 1974), 63.

[56] Sokoloff, *DJBA*, 197.

[57] While there is no *frēstaqa* in the stories of Simeon or Barbaʿshmin, the *frēstaqa* does appear in other Persian martyr acts as the imperial official who administers the martyr's judgment. See especially Chabot, "Histoire de Jésus-Sabran, 532–533, where a *frēstaqa*, along with a *rad*, plan the execution of Ishoʿsabran. The *frēstaqa* also appears elsewhere in the Talmud. In b. Meg. 7a, a *frēstaqa* is simply an Iranian messenger or official. However, in b. Giṭ. 56b, the *frēstaqa* is oddly a Roman messenger. In b. ʿAbod. Zar. 65a and b. Ket. 62a, fear is associated with the *frēstaqa*, although it should be noted that some manuscripts of the latter lack *frēstaqa*. See Herman, "Talmud in Its Babylonian Context," 84–85, who discusses the appearance of *frēstaqa* in Aramaic incantation bowls and a Manichaean text.

Yet, the composer of the talmudic story did not simply replace the martyred bishop with a rabbinic protagonist. Instead, the rabbinic story evokes verbal and literary motifs typical of this group of Syriac martyr acts, but it consistently veers from their narrative template. The talmudic story appears designed to offer a series of what might be called "structured contrasts" with its Syriac counterparts.

For example, the protagonists in both the Christian and rabbinic stories are accused of preventing their constituents from performing their obligations to the empire. Yet whereas Simeon and Barbaʿshmin acknowledge their role, Rabbah never confirms that he intentionally caused tax evasion; whatever evasion occurred was an inadvertent byproduct of the semester system in which he instructed his many students. This difference between intentional and inadvertent offenses is even clearer in the continuation; Simeon and Barbaʿshmin use their arrest to openly defy the king, declare tax collection unjust, and denigrate his non-Christian beliefs and practices, whereas Rabbah has no interest in defiance; he simply flees (B).[58] If the Christian martyrs represent confrontation, Rabbah represents evasion; if Christians represent "fight," Rabbah represents "flight."

Even as Rabbah is pursued by an imperial official, from whom he initially hides, he nevertheless surrenders himself in order to aid the official when the latter becomes ill, apparently not even wishing any harm on the empire's administrators (C). As a result of Rabbah's assistance, he wins the official's gratitude. Notably, however, the official does not embrace his target's religion as imperial officials sometimes do in other Syriac martyr acts and some rabbinic stories.[59] Instead, the story assumes a pragmatic realism that is almost the opposite of what one finds in Christian martyrdom accounts: The official is willing to help Rabbah, but only up to a point – he is willing to suffer death, but not undergo torture – and imprisons Rabbah while he tries to resolve Rabbah's case with the empire. The message of this scene appears to be that accommodation to imperial officials may offer the possibility – but not certainty – of a better outcome, but this is preferable to defiance that results in certain death.

[58] See Wiessner, *Zur Märtyrerüberlieferung*, 202–204, where he outlines the standard feature of dialogue in Persian martyr acts.

[59] A lengthy version of this type-scene is found in Sebastian Brock and Paul Dilley, *The Martyrs of Mount Berʿain* (Piscataway, NJ: 2014), 54–60. In the Talmud, this type scene is found in stories set in the Roman Empire, such as the death of Rabbi Ḥanina ben Teradion (b. ʿAbod. Zar. 18a), the case of Rabbi Meir in the brothel (b. ʿAbod. Zar. 18a–b), and Onqelos on the mountaintop (b. ʿAbod. Zar. 11a).

Rabbah, like Simeon and Barbaʿshmin, ends up imprisoned, setting the stage for yet another structured contrast (D). The Syriac martyrdom accounts follow a standard narrative template: The martyr is arrested, imprisoned, and brought before the king, who offers him a final chance to recant, which the martyr heroically declines.[60] Rabbah, however, has no interest in such a display of defiance; instead, he prays and is miraculously freed from prison, forestalling any possible encounter with the empire.[61]

In the climax of the story, Rabbah mistakenly believes he hears Sasanian troops approaching (E). Instead of valiantly confronting them, he beseeches Heaven to allow him to "die, rather than be delivered into the hands of the kingdom." This contrasts sharply with the climax of the martyrdoms of Simeon and Barbaʿshmin, who pray for precisely the opposite: an opportunity to be martyred by "the kingdom."[62] The wishes of the protagonists are ultimately fulfilled: Simeon and Barbaʿshmin confront the king and are martyred, whereas Rabbah avoids any confrontation. As a result, Rabbah's death clearly lacks the triumph and spectacle of Simeon and Barbaʿshmin; the latter die surrounded by admirers, while Rabbah's death is a solitary affair.

As we have seen, Simeon, Barbaʿshmin, and even the imperial official all proclaim their willingness to die at the hands of the empire. But Rabbah does not. This does not mean that Rabbah fears death, only that he seeks to avoid death at the hands of the empire. This is emphasized through the incorporation in Rabbah's death scene of the Angel of Death, a motif found in other talmudic stories, but appearing here with a twist. Elsewhere, the Angel of Death comes to take a sage's life but is prevented

60 In some Persian martyr acts, the martyr dies in prison, e.g., Sebastian Brock and Susan Ashbrook Harvey, *Holy Women of the Syrian Orient* (Berkeley: 1998), 78–82. But in most cases, the martyr is brought forth from prison for a final debate.

61 Escape from jail by means of prayer is a widespread folk motif, but for our purposes it is worth noting that it appears in Acts 12 and 16. In *The History of Mar Qardagh* (Walker, *Legend of Mar Qardagh*, 33–34), a Mar Abdišo also prays and is miraculously broken out of prison. Later in the story, after a verbal confrontation between Mar Qardagh and the king's representative, Mar Qardagh also prays and is broken out of prison. But instead of fleeing, Mar Qardagh remains and prays, while "the nobles and pagans" flee to the "rushes of the marsh." This too may be a structured contrast, as in the story of Rabbah's death it is Rabbah who flees to the marshes (*ʾagama*) after being miraculously broken out of jail.

62 Smith, *Martyrdom and History*, 48. For Barbaʿshmin, see Bedjan, *Acta martyrum et sanctorum*, 2.297–298. For other examples, see Brock and Harvey, *Holy Women of the Syrian Orient*, 89 and 95; Walker, *Legend of Mar Qardagh*, 63 (#58), 66 (#63); and *The Martyrdom of 111 Men and 9 Women*, in Bedjan, *Acta martyrum et sanctorum*, 2.292.

from doing so until the sage falters in his Torah study.[63] Yet here, even once Rabbah is distracted by what he believes is the sound of troops, the Angel of Death does not strike until Rabbah prays for death. The Angel of Death motif is thus entirely superfluous to the story, but it appears to emphasize the extent to which Rabbah is in control of his moment of death.[64] It is not Rabbah's time to die; he is choosing death, like a martyr would, but precisely to avoid confrontation with imperial officials.

Rabbah's most prominent students, Abaye and Rava, along with "all the rabbis," receive a missive from Heaven about his death (F). They search for his body and locate it by observing birds "standing and providing shade."[65] This again seems to be a literary motif appropriated from Christian texts; the search for a corpse is almost unattested in rabbinic literature but is common in many Persian martyr acts, where the recently deceased body of a martyr – often left exposed by Zoroastrian officials for whom earthly burial was a religious offense – is sought, found (often at night or under miraculous circumstances), and ceremoniously enshrined.[66] The shading birds appear to be a similarly miraculous motif in the Rabbah account, although the story is otherwise silent as to the disposition of Rabbah's remains. Because he did not die at

63 b. Mak. 10a and b. Shab. 30b. The idea that one cannot die while learning also appears in b. Ket. 104a. On the Angel of Death motif, see Eliezer Diamond, "Wrestling the Angel of Death: Form and Meaning in Rabbinic Tales of Death and Dying," *Journal for the Study of Judaism* 26 (1995), 76–92, esp. 86n49 for the story of Rabbah.

64 As noted by Neusner, *History of the Jews*, 2.44n1.

65 An example of the miraculously marked grave can be found in Butts and Gross, *History of the "Slave of Christ,"* 136–139. Intriguingly, the keen interest in the corpse, the commemoration, and other postmortem miracles expressed in the final sections of the story are also without parallel in the Babylonian Talmud, with one major exception – a text found one folio later that is also indebted to Syriac Christian texts. See Jeffrey L. Rubenstein, "A Rabbinic Translation of Relics," in *Crossing Boundaries in Ancient Judaism and Early Christianity Ambiguities, Complexities and Half-Forgotten Adversaries*, ed. Kimberly Stratton and Andrea Lieber (Leiden: 2016), 314–332.

66 For a partial list of forcible exposure of the martyr's corpse, see Wiessner, *Zur Märtyrerüberlieferung*, 219–221; Hector Ricardo Francisco, "Corpse Exposure in the Acts of the Persian Martyrs and Its Literary Models," *Hugoye* 19 (2016): 193–235; Herman, "Bury My Coffin Deep!" esp. 37–40; and Basirov, "'Proselytisation' and 'Exposure of the Dead,'" 1–19. For miraculous marking of the site of the corpse, see Butts and Gross, *History of the "Slave of Christ,"* 146–153; *The Martyrdom of ʿAqebshma* (Bedjan, *Acta martyrum et sanctorum*, 2.391); *Karka deBet Slokh* (Bedjan, *Acta martyrum et sanctorum*, 2.514; and Bedjan, *Acta martyrum et sanctorum* 2.288). For a discussion of these final sources, see Peter Bruns, "Reliquien und Reliquienverehrung in den syro-persischen Märtyrerakten," *Römische Quartalschrift für christliche Altertumskunde und für Kirchengeschichte* 101 (2006): 194–213 (esp. 203–204).

the hands of the empire, Rabbah's body is not retrieved under the cover of night, nor are there any Sasanian guards to evade in the process of its retrieval.[67]

Abaye, Rava, and all the rabbis mourn Rabbah for three days, a significant period that was clearly intended to convey the impact of Rabbah's death on the rabbinic community at large, but still not the full seven-day mourning period typically observed for one's nuclear family or teacher.[68] However, a heavenly missive orders that the mourning continue until they reach the full seven days.[69] Perhaps the implication is that the rabbis might feel that Rabbah's death was in some ways cowardly or ignominious, but the heavenly missive makes clear that his choice of death over confrontation was praiseworthy.

RABBINIC AWARENESS OF SYRIAC MARTYR ACTS?

The similarities and differences between the rabbinic story and the Syriac martyr acts of Simeon or Barbaʿshmin are significant even if the former is not directly dependent on the latter. Nevertheless, is it indeed possible that the rabbinic composer knew of the Syriac works? While certainty is elusive, it is not a farfetched possibility.[70] Simeon was the most famous of the Syriac Persian martyrs.[71] As discussed in Chapter 1, he was the protagonist of several martyr acts, and throughout Syriac literature his death precipitated the period known as the "Great Persecution" under Shapur II. Simeon's martyrdom served as the archetype for many

[67] Interestingly, the Karaite author Jacob al-Qirqisānī recounts a version of this story which adds that the missive from Heaven was sent to ensure that Rabbah's corpse was, in fact, taken and buried. See Leon Nemoy, "Al-Qirqisānī's Account of the Jewish Sects and Christianity," *HUCA* 7 (1930): 356.

[68] Seven-day mourning is, according to y. M. Qaṭ. 3.5 (82c), based on the seven days that Joseph mourned his father Jacob in Gen. 50.10. Seven-day mourning is attested elsewhere in the Babylonian Talmud, such as in b. Sanh. 108b; M. Qaṭ. 20a; and b. Shab. 152a–b. Cf. the death of Rabbi Judah the Prince in b. Ket. 103b.

[69] On this, see Neusner, *History of the Jews*, 4.101. In the *History of Mar Aba* (Bedjan, *Histoire de Mar-Jabalaha*, 271–272), the martyr's clothing is literally torn off by venerators to be treasured as relics, and his death is followed by a seven-day mourning period.

[70] See Jeffrey L. Rubenstein, "Martyrdom in the Persian Martyr Acts and in the Babylonian Talmud," in *The Aggada of the Bavli and Its Cultural World*, ed. Jeffrey Rubenstein and Geoffrey Herman (Providence, RI: 2018), 175–210.

[71] François Nau, ed., *Martyrologes et ménologes orientaux, I–XIII. Un martyrologie et douze ménologes syriaques édités et traduits*, PO 10.1 (Paris: 1912), 7–26; for a list of the eastern martyrs listed here see Sebastian Brock, *The History of the Holy Mar Maʿin with a Guide to the Persian Martyr Acts* (Piscataway, NJ: 2008), 123–125. For more on the manuscript, see Brock and Van Rompay, *Catalogue of the Syriac Manuscripts*, 389–392.

subsequent stories, such as *Barbaʿshmin*, but also *Pusai*, *Martha*, and *Tarbo*, among others.[72] These are dated based on the "years of persecution" since Simeon's death, and often invoke Simeon as the paradigmatic martyr who they are emulating.[73]

Syriac Persian martyr acts were widely disseminated in late antiquity.[74] Some, including those related to Simeon, were translated into Greek soon after their composition, and thereafter into Armenian, Georgian, and even Sogdian.[75] They were particularly important to Christians living in the Sasanian Empire, as seen from Timothy I's letter cited at the outset of this chapter.[76] Cult sites and martyria dedicated to these saints were established throughout Iraq and Khuzistan, as were special commemorative calendars that marked their death dates.[77] Living in the same cities as their Syriac Christian neighbors, it is quite possible that Babylonian Jews would have grown familiar with Christian martyr stories in some form. The strong resonances between the Rabbah story and these early Syriac martyr acts suggest that the rabbinic composer had some familiarity with them, while the structured contrasts reveal that the purpose in evoking the Syriac martyr acts was, in fact, to juxtapose the rabbinic story with them.

[72] For *Pusai*, Bedjan, *Acta martyrum et sanctorum*, 2:208–232; *Martha*, Bedjan, *Acta martyrum et sanctorum*, 2:233–241; *Tarbo*, Bedjan, *Acta martyrum et sanctorum*, 2:254–260.

[73] On the importance of Simeon to later martyr acts, see Wiessner, *Zur Martyrenüberlieferung*, 34; and Wood, *The Chronicle of Seert*, 61–62n44. Several later texts, such as the *Martyrs of Mount Berʿain*, date themselves earlier in Shapur II's rule, but explicitly refer to details from Simeon's martyrdom, thereby betraying their indebtedness to his story. See e.g., Sebastian Brock, "A Martyr at the Sasanid Court under Vahran II: Candida," *Analecta Bollandiana* 96 (1978), 167–181; and Herman, *Prince without a Kingdom*, 43n117. Simeon also serves as paradigmatic martyr in some Roman accounts in the early and mid-fifth century CE. See Smith, *Constantine and the Captive Christians of Persia*, 53–57.

[74] See in general Becker, "The Invention of the Persian Martyr Acts," and also Wood, *Chronicle of Seert*, 52–65.

[75] For the reception of the stories of the Persian Martyrs in Sozomen's *Ecclesiastical History*, see Paul Devos, "Sozomène et les actes syriaques de S. Syméon bar Sabbaʿe," *Analecta Bollandiana* 84 (1966): 443–456; Wiessner, *Zur Märtyrerüberlieferung*, 148–157; Smith, *Martyrdom and History*, xxxiv–xli; for Sogidan, see Nicholas Sims-Williams, *The Christian Sogdian Manuscript C2* (Berlin: 1985), esp. 137–153.

[76] Persian martyr acts were so popular that some may have been composed outside of the Sasanian Empire, apparently by Christians living on the Roman-Sasanian frontier. Bernard Flusin, *Saint Anastase le Perse et l'histoire de la Palestine au début du VIIe siècle* (Paris: 1992); Brock, *History of the Holy Mar Maʿin*; Herman, "Last Years of Yazdgird I and the Christians," 67–90. Some of these identifications, however, require further evaluation.

[77] Payne, "Emergence of Martyrs' Shrines in Late Antique Iran," 89–113.

STRUCTURED CONTRASTS WITH PALESTINIAN RABBINIC MARTYRS

The Rabbah bar Naḥmani story also invokes and introduces structured contrasts to the well-known rabbinic martyrdom traditions concerning Rabbi Akiva, one of the most prominent and revered early Palestinian rabbis, who was reportedly tortured and executed by the Romans.[78]

In the story of Rabbi Akiva's martyrdom in the Babylonian Talmud, the "wicked government" prohibits Torah study. This does not deter Rabbi Akiva, who flaunts the edict by continuing to teach Torah in public. The Romans imprison and prosecute Rabbi Akiva, who faces the likelihood of death with acceptance and even joy. He explains to his incredulous students that, in dying, he will finally fulfill the biblical charge of Deut. 6.5: "to love your God with all your heart, with all your soul, and with all your might," a verse in the most important prayer, the *Shem'a*. Rabbi Akiva dies when he arrives at the final word of the first verse of the *Shem'a* – "Hear, O Israel: The LORD is our God, the LORD is one."[79] Rabbi Akiva, then, is martyred out of devotion to God while declaring God's unity, invoking the core monotheistic principle.[80] Twice in the narrative, Rabbi Akiva is praised using the expression "Happy are you": once by a Jew who is captured by the Romans for reasons other than Torah study, and then again by a heavenly voice that declares, "Happy are you, Akiva, that you are destined for life in the world to come."[81]

Rabbah's death, with the word "pure" on his lips and the heavenly postmortem praise beginning with "Happy are you" (E), directly evoke the circumstances of Rabbi Akiva's martyrdom, who dies with the word

78 b. Ber. 61b. Paul Mandel, "Was Rabbi Aqiva a Martyr? Palestinian and Babylonian Influences in the Development of a Legend," in *Rabbinic Traditions between Palestine and Babylonia*, ed. Ronit Nikolsky and Tal Ilan (Leiden: 2014), 325–375, has shown that the Babylonian Talmud's version of Akiva's death amplifies its martyrological setting. On the rise of Rabbi Akiva and some of his contemporaries to Jewish martyrs par excellence, see Ra'anan Boustan, *From Martyr to Mystic: Rabbinic Martyrology and the Making of Merkavah Mysticism* (Tübingen: 2005). On the Babylonian Talmud's general tendency to treat Roman imperial violence as a reaction to Torah observance and study, see Kalmin, "Rabbinic Traditions about Roman Persecutions," 21–50.

79 The importance of the proper articulation of the word "one" in the Shema is emphasized by a dictum found in y. Ber. 1.6 (4a) and b. Ber. 13b.

80 Akiva dying with "one" on his Akiva's lips is an addition found only in the Babylonian Talmud's version for the story (absent from y. Ber. 9.5 [14b] = y. Soṭ. 5.7 [20c]).

81 The Vilna printed edition includes an additional praise by a heavenly voice of Akiva for dying with "one" on his lips, similar to what is found in Rabbah's story.

"one" on his lips and is similar praised by a heavenly voice after his death.[82] The association between Rabbi Akiva and Rabbah is amplified by the fact that both Rabbi Akiva and Rabbah are reported to have had twelve thousand students.[83] Yet the parallels between the two stories simply heighten the contrasts between them. Rabbi Akiva is prosecuted and dies for defying a Roman decree and continuing to instruct his students, while Rabbah's circumstances result from his teaching inadvertently causing tax evasion. Rabbi Akiva's students are beside him at his death; Rabbah abandons the academy and never sees his students again. Rabbi Akiva dies in a public spectacle; Rabbah dies alone and in hiding. Rabbi Akiva reaffirms the core monotheistic principle at the moment of his death; Rabbah rules on an obscure halakhic matter.[84] Finally, Rabbi Akiva dies directly at the hand of an "evil kingdom" (מלכות הרשעה), while Rabbah begs God *not* to allow him to die at the hands of the "kingdom" (מלכותא). If Rabbi Akiva is the rabbinic martyr par excellence, in the subtle hands of our story's composer, Rabbah is the anti-martyr. In drawing these connections between the two figures, the composer of Rabbah's story highlights that the two imperial contexts are distinct, and that the defiant approach of Rabbi Akiva is simply unsuitable in Sasanian Babylonia.

Rabbah's story concludes with an enigmatic anecdote that expresses the frustration that follows from the form of political accommodation it proposes: Rabbah's death lacks any clear villain to hold accountable (G). Following Rabbah's death, a storm blows an unnamed Arab riding atop a camel across a river. When the displaced Arab inquires why this occurred to him, he is informed that Rabbah died. The Arab confronts God, saying "You are the sovereign of the universe, and Rabbah bar Naḥmani too is

[82] אשריך appears in other talmudic accounts that similarly feature a heavenly voice inviting the martyrs to heaven (b. ʿAbod. Zar. 10b [Ketiah b. Shalom], and b. ʿAbod. Zar. 17b–18a [R. Ḥanina b. Teradyon]), but only the Akiva parallel mentions the word on the lips of the martyr. Similarly, in t. Ḥul. 2:22–23, = y. ʿAbod. Zar. 2.2 (40d–41a), Ben Dama's death is followed by "happy are you (אשריך), Ben Dama, for you have departed in peace from the world," while in the version of Ben Dama's death in b. ʿAbod. Zar. 27b he is praised for dying "in purity (בטהרה)."

[83] b. Ket. 62b–63a. In the parallel in b. Ned. 50a, R. Akiva has twenty-four thousand, obviously double twelve thousand students, corresponding to two study periods of twelve years each.

[84] Mira Balberg and Moulie Vidas, "Impure Scholasticism: The Study of Purity Laws and Rabbinic Self-Criticism in the Babylonian Talmud," *Prooftexts* 32 (2012): 328–329, strengthen the incongruity between Rabbah's expertise and his "precarious situation."

yours. Why are you destroying it [the world]?"[85] The storm immediately subsides. The Arab essentially reminds God that it is he who ultimately killed Rabbah. God is flailing in search of a villain, lashing out at the world as a whole, but there is no one to blame. Throughout the story, the empire protects its vital revenue interests, without deploying violence needlessly. Their messenger, sent to bring Rabbah in for questioning, is in fact willing to help Rabbah, and although Rabbah fears the arrival of an army, none is dispatched. In the end, the Sasanian Empire does not bear any culpability for Rabbah's death. That the victim of God's momentary misplaced wrath is an Arab highlights who he is not: a Persian.[86]

By repeatedly alluding to the most central martyrdom stories told about contemporary Christians and earlier Palestinian rabbis, the composer of the Rabbah story conveys the message that, unlike the ideological confrontation between Christians and the Sasanian Empire presented by the accounts of Simeon and Barbaʿshmin, or the ideological confrontation between Jews and the Roman Empire presented by the story of Rabbi Akiva, no similar conflict need exist between the Sasanian Empire and Babylonian Jews.[87] Meaningfully, in drawing a contrast with these two groups of exemplars, the composer of the Rabbah story accepts the premise that the position of Babylonian Jews corresponds in certain ways with that of their coreligionists in the west, as well as with their Christian neighbors in the Sasanian Empire. All are similarly situated imperial subjects, who as a result are faced with similar political decisions. Startlingly, this means that the composer saw Jews as broadly inhabiting the same position not just of Palestinian rabbis, but their neighboring Christians. The power of the story lies precisely in its ability to acknowledge congruent circumstances and yet offer an alternative approach, in which defiance of the Sasanian Empire is unsuitable for Babylonian Jews.

[85] Incidentally, the statement attributed to the Arab is reminiscent of what God asks Rabbi Shimon bar Yohai when he leaves the cave and the objects of his gaze burn up, in b. Shab. 33b.

[86] On some uses of the character of the Arab in the Babylonian Talmud, see Sara Ronis, "Imagining the Other: The Magical Arab in Rabbinic Literature," *Prooftexts* 39 (2021): 1–28.

[87] For the suggestion that rabbis elsewhere may have identified with Christian martyrs, see Boyarin, *Dying for God*, 123–125. Gray, "A Contribution to the Study of Martyrdom," 242–272, argues that we find a different kind of negotiation with the idea of martyrdom in several Palestinian rabbinic pericopes, where the editor moves from celebrating public martyrdom to likening intensive Torah observance and study to a kind of martyrdom.

SUBVERTING IMPERIAL EDICTS

A final late Babylonian rabbinic story includes a suggestion of imperial violence while providing a model for subtly subverting – rather than confronting – imperial edicts.[88] Like the story of Rabbah, it redeploys earlier rabbinic motifs as well as a motif from a late antique Persian story.

R. Beroqa Ḥoza'ah was in the market at Be Lapat. Elijah appeared to him.
he asked [Elijah], "is there anyone in this market who has a share in the world to come?" He replied, "No, there is no one."
Meanwhile he caught sight of a man wearing black shoes and who did not have fringes (i.e., *tzitzit*) and he exclaimed, "this man has a share in the world to come."
[R. Beroqa] called after him, but he did not turn around. He ran after him, and the man said: "Go away and come back tomorrow."
The next day he asked him again, "what is your occupation?" And he replied: "I am a jailer (*zendoqa*) and I keep the men and women separate and at night I place my bed between them so that they may not come to sin; when I see a daughter of Israel upon whom the Gentiles cast their eyes, I risk my life and save her.
Once there was amongst us a betrothed girl whom the Gentiles wished to violate. I therefore took dregs of [red] wine and put them in her skirt and I told them that she was a menstruant (*daštāna*)."
[R. Beroqa further] asked the man, "why do you wear black shoes?" He replied, "that the Gentiles amongst whom I constantly move may not know that I am a Jew, so that when a harsh decree is issued [against Jews], they reveal it to me and I inform the rabbis, and they pray [to God] and the decree is annulled."
He further asked him, "why when I called after you did you not turn around?'"
He answered, "they had just issued a decree, and I said I would first go and inform the rabbis of it so that they might pray to God and have it annulled."

In this story, Rav Beroqa from Khuzistan ("Ḥoza'ah") goes to the market of Be Lapat, the capital of the province of Khuzistan, and is told by Elijah that a certain man in the market "has a share in the world to come," meaning that he was righteous. Yet, upon finding the man, Rav Beroqa observes that he does not wear ritual fringes (*tzitzit*), a required religious garment. Puzzled, Rav Beroqa confronts the man to learn why Elijah considered him righteous despite lacking outward signs of Jewish devotion. The man explains that he is a jailer (described with the proper Middle Persian word) who purposefully conceals his identity to protect the purity of imprisoned Jewish men and women from lascivious

[88] b. Ta'an. 22a, according to ms. British Library 400. There are several manuscript variants that do not affect the thrust of the story for our purposes.

non-Jewish guards.[89] He recounts how he once poured wine on a jailed Jewish woman so that she appeared to be a menstruant, thereby dissuading her captors from violating her. This provides an important clue about the identity of the guards; they are undoubtedly Zoroastrians, for whom menstruation was a major source of defilement. The text even uses the Middle Persian word *daštāna* for "menstruant."[90]

This story clearly presupposes that edicts against Jews were regular occurrences requiring ongoing subterfuge on the part of the jailer.[91] The setting of the story similarly points to knowledge of imperial administration; unlike the vast majority of Babylonian rabbinic figures and stories that are situated in Iraq, this story is situated in Be Lapat, the capital of Khuzistan. As Geoffrey Herman and others have shown, the story is undoubtedly set in a famous Sasanian prison in Khuzistan, a central location in many Syriac martyr acts, including those concerning Simeon bar Ṣabbaʿe.[92]

Yet, the shared setting of this rabbinic story and many Syriac martyr acts again reveals a series of different narrative choices. As Yakir Paz has recently illustrated, many Syriac Christian martyr acts set in the Khuzistan prison feature imperial figures who, like the Jewish jailer, also conceal their Christian identities.[93] But, in the Christian martyrdom accounts, the Christian officials ultimately reveal their true identities precisely to trigger a direct confrontation between themselves and the empire. A good example is the story of Gushtazad, which is nested within the accounts of Simeon bar Ṣabbaʿe's martyrdom. Gushtazad is described as the former tutor of the Sasanian king Shapur II and a current imperial

89 On this word, see the extended discussion in Yakir Paz, "Elam Is Dying: The Babylonian Talmud and the Jews of Khuzestan in the Sasanian Period," [in Hebrew] in *Meḥqerei Talmud* IV, ed. Shlomo Naeh and Yoav Rosental (Jerusalem: 2024), 565–572.

90 For a discussion of this motif, see Secunda, *Talmud's Red Fence*, 73–77. For more on Zoroastrian views of menstruants, see Chapter 3, pp. 153–155.

91 The story does not provide enough information to identify the events with any precision, although this has not prevented some scholars from endeavoring to do so. Funk, *Die Juden in Babylonien 200–500*, 2.123, proposes that this desire to mix genders in the prison might have come about during the "revolution" of Mazdak under Kawād I (late fifth century). Alternatively, Neusner, *History of the Jews*, 4.50–51, simply dates the story to the period of Shapur II. For more, see Herman, "One Day David Went Out for the Hunt," 127 and 127n82.

92 Herman, "One Day David Went Out for the Hunt," 111–136; Paz, "Elam Is Dying." On this prison, see Erich Kettenhofen, "Das Staatgefängnis der Sāsāniden," *Die Welt des Orients* 19 (1988): 96–101; and G. Traina and C. A. Ciancaglini, "La Fortresse de l'Oubli," *La Muséon* 115 (2002): 399–422.

93 Paz, "Elam Is Dying."

official. After witnessing Simeon's martyrdom, Gushtazad "stripped off his beautiful clothes, put on black garments of mourning, and returned to sit in his place."[94] When word reaches the king that Gushtazad is not, in fact, a Zoroastrian but a Christian, he too is martyred. By contrast, in the rabbinic story, the Jewish official maintains his disguise precisely to continue protecting Jewish prisoners, undermining the empire from within rather than seeking confrontation. His disguised resistance, rather than open confrontation, earns him "a place in the world to come."

The Jewish official conceals his subversive actions by means of a ruse, tricking the prison guards to believe that the captive Jewish women were menstruants. This ruse is deployed in other Babylonian rabbinic stories, and most strikingly in a late antique story about the escape of the Sasanian king Kawad from the same prison in Be Lapat.[95] Our rabbinic story therefore borrows and reworks available Jewish and non-Jewish literary motifs to valorize subversion and covert resistance over open defiance and confrontation. The use of this ruse, however, again contrasts markedly with scenes in Syriac martyr acts in which the Zoroastrian treatment of menstruation is openly mocked rather than subverted. For instance, in the Syriac *Life of George*, a female convert from Zoroastrianism, while a menstruant, clasps the sacred fire to publicly ridicule Zoroastrianism and demonstrate the finality of her conversion to Christianity.[96] In the case of the Jewish jailer, knowledge of Zoroastrian taboos is deployed not to openly jeer at Zoroastrians, but to surreptitiously save fellow Jews.

If the Jewish jailer undertakes covert action to preserve Jewish life, a Syriac account of a Christian woman named Yazdandukht who gained access to imprisoned Christians again highlights alternative storytelling

[94] Smith, *Martyrdom and History*, 38–39.

[95] Herman, "One Day David Went Out for the Hunt," 129. Herman (pp. 125–127) argues that the first half of the story is a reworking of a story in y. Ta'an. 1.4 (64b), but if there is a parallel, it supplies only a very general framework for the first half of this Babylonian story, and Herman himself notes that "the BT [SG: Babylonian Talmud] has evidently departed some distance from its Palestinian sources" (p. 126).

[96] Bedjan, *Histoire de Mar-Jabalaha*, 449. For more on this, see A. V. Williams, "Zoroastrians and Christians in Sasanian Iran," 51–52; and Gerrit J. Reinink, "Babai the Great's Life of George and the Propagation of Doctrine in the Late Sasanian Empire," in *Portraits of Spiritual Authority: Religious Power in Early Christianity, Byzantium, and the Christian Orient*, ed. Jan Willem Drijvers and John W. Watt (Leiden: 1999), 171–193. In the Chronicle of Seert (Scher, *Chronique de Séert*, 2.75), Mar Aba stumps a magus in debate by asking about a woman carrying a torch in the rain who begins menstruating.

possibilities.[97] In this story, many Christian leaders and elders have been imprisoned by Shapur II in Seleucia-Ctesiphon during the winter months. At this point we learn that:

> There was a great woman there, may her memory be a blessing, whose name was Yazdandukht, whose name means 'daughter of God' . . . who supplied to those martyrs of God from her own possessions, the entire time that they were imprisoned.

Like the Jewish jailer, Yazdandukht is privy to the plans of the state, learning "in secret" that "the following morning the holy martyrs would be killed." However, Yazdandukht's aid is intended to steel the prisoners so that they follow through with their eventual martyrdom. By contrast, the Jewish jailer attempts to save his coreligionists. Ultimately, the story of Yazdandukht glorifies martyrdom, while the Jewish jailer valorizes subterfuge rather than outright confrontation, even when faced with "wicked decrees" of the empire.

Like the story of Rabbah, the tale of the Jewish jailer yet again promotes alternatives to confrontation with the Empire. The story shows that the rabbis were neither ignorant of nor indifferent to imperial cruelty, but they believed it could be more effectively addressed through subversion, rather than direct confrontation. They may well have been aware of alternative Christian strategies, but through stories like that of the Jewish jailer or Rabbah they endorsed a different mode of response for Jews. The subtle subversion glorified in the story of the Jewish jailer is affirmed in other rabbinic stories that, for instance, celebrate Jewish tax or toll collectors who help rabbis and other Jews evade payment but without drawing the attention or ire of the Empire.[98] Like the Jewish jailer, these Jews subvert the imperial administrative system from within.

But the rabbis also apparently realized that in certain instances, the better tactic was to avoid entanglement with the empire altogether. In another talmudic discussion, a rabbi creatively recasts God's curse against Israel in Mal. 2.9 – "I have also made you contemptible and base before all the people" – as a blessing. According to the rabbi, Malachi's prophecy explains why "no river/canal overseers and no officers of the

[97] *Martyrdom of 111 Men and 9 Women*, in Bedjan, *Acta martyrum et sanctorum*, 2.291–295.

[98] B. Sanh. 25b; B. Bat. 167a, b ; B. Bat. 8a; and discussion in Chapter 1.

court shall be appointed to you." These two types of officials were common in the Sasanian Empire, and the use of an Iranian word (גזירפטי) for the latter leaves little doubt that the reference is to the rabbis' Sasanian context.[99] Instead of the plain sense of Malachi's verse as a curse that Israelites would suffer at the hands of other nations, the rabbi treats the contempt as a blessing, sparing Jews from administrative positions that would require them to enforce the will of the empire. Sometimes subtle subversion was needed, but sometimes it was best to avoid any imperial obligations or appointments at all. This, too, could be a blessing.

SELF-AWARENESS

Although the rabbis promoted a strategy of non-confrontation, they recognized that their pragmatism could be seen as a shortcoming in their devoutness. Indeed, one source suggests that while later rabbis embraced non-confrontation, they believed that earlier Babylonian rabbis had embraced, at least rhetorically, the possibility of open confrontation with the empire. This diachronic development is reflected in two almost identical anecdotes appearing in b. Ta'an. 24a–b and b. Ber. 20a.[100] The former version reads as follows:

Rabbah decreed a fast. He prayed for mercy, but rain did not come.

They said to him, "But when Rav Yehuda decreed a fast, rain would come."
He said to them, "What can I do? If the difference between us is due to Torah study, we are superior, as in the years of Rav Yehuda all their studies were limited to the order of *Neziqin*, and we learn all six orders [of the Mishnah]... But when Rav Yehuda would remove one of his shoes, rain would fall. And we cry out all day and no one notices us. If [the difference between me and Rav Yehuda is] due to [inappropriate] deeds, if there is anyone who has seen me do anything [improper], let him say so.
But what can the leaders the great ones of the generation do when their generation is not worthy?"[101]

[99] See b. Ta'an. 20a. On this Iranian official, see also b. Shab. 139a; Sanh. 98a, and Mokhtarian, *Rabbis, Sorcerers, Kings, and Priests*, 116–120.

[100] A parallel to the middle unit in these two stories is also found in b. Sanh. 106b. For the relationship between them, see Jeffrey Rubenstein, "Criteria of Stammaitic Intervention in Aggada," in *Creation and Composition: The Contribution of the Bavli Redactors (Stammaim) to the Aggada* ed. Jeffrey L. Rubenstein (Tübingen: 2005), 434–436.

[101] b. Ta'an. 24a–b, according to MS Yad HaRav Herzog..

In the context of a series of anecdotes about rabbinic wonder workers, Rabbah, a fourth-century Babylonian rabbi, declares a fast day and prays for rain, but his prayers go unheeded. He wonders why his prayers were spurned while the prayers for rain by Rav Yehuda, a third-century rabbi, were promptly answered. Rabbah dismisses the notion that Rav Yehuda or his generation were worthier on account of their greater learning, noting that he and his generation were superior in that regard.[102] Rabbah wonders whether he and his generation are perhaps guilty of some unknown wrongdoing and invites anyone to offer a suggestion – but nobody does. In conclusion, he acknowledges that Rav Yehuda was able to perform greater miracles, and he can only lament that, for some unknown reason, his own generation had been found less worthy.

The parallel account in b. Ber. 20a arrives at a strikingly different conclusion. Here, the discussion is between two different fourth-century Babylonian rabbis. Rav Papa, echoing Rabbah in the earlier version, wonders why miracles were more common in the generation of Rav Yehuda, and he essentially rehashes Rabbah's arguments. But this time, the seemingly unanswerable question receives a response from Abaye:

> [Abaye] replied, "The former generations used to sacrifice their lives for the sanctity of [God's] name; but we do not sacrifice our lives for the sanctity of [God's] name."

According to Abaye, what distinguished Rav Yehuda and his generation was their willingness to sacrifice their lives, unlike the rabbis of Rav Papa and Abaye's own generation. The locution – "to sacrifice one's life for the sanctity of God's name" – could refer to fervent devotion on behalf of Judaism, but it is used more typically to refer to willingly sacrificing one's life, often at the hands of a persecutor, to uphold Judaism.[103] Judging by the continuation of the story, the second meaning holds here. The anonymous editors follow the story with an anecdote intended to highlight the generational gap in willingness "to sacrifice one's life for the sanctity of God's name": Rav Adda bar Ahava, a contemporary of Rav Yehuda, grabbed the forbidden headdress off of a woman in the market that he believed to be Jewish, though she was in fact not Jewish. Fortunately, Rav Adda got off lightly with a large governmental fine to pay but no other punishment. He had, however, risked his life to uphold

[102] For a discussion of the significance of the fields of rabbinic knowledge mentioned here, see Balberg and Vidas, "Impure Scholasticism," 334–337.

[103] For the latter meaning, see b. Pesaḥ. 53b.

Jewish practice. The implication is that Rav Yehuda's generation was similarly willing to jeopardize itself to enforce the law, unlike the later generations of rabbis.

Earlier generations of Babylonian rabbis were, according to Abaye, willing to pursue a strategy of confrontation, jeopardizing their lives in the process, but later generations were not. Here we see how later Babylonian rabbis questioned whether their strategy of accommodation, for all its pragmatism and preservation of life, nevertheless came at a cost to their generation's spiritual stature.

CONCLUSION

Life under Sasanian rule was punctuated by moments of imperial violence and interference. The stories that communities conveyed did not simply recount history; they fashioned and promoted particular attitudes and communal strategies toward the empire. The relative dearth of stories in the Babylonian Talmud about imperial violence directed against the Jewish community neither means that Jews were somehow "tolerated" by the empire nor that their conditions were peaceful. Rather, the talmudic evidence shows that the rabbis consistently minimized images of a persecutory empire, discouraged outright confrontation with its institutions, and instead promoted more surreptitious means of subverting imperial decrees in furtherance of communal self-preservation. They mimic and invoke opposing Palestinian Jewish and Syriac Christian images and narratives to recommend a starkly different and more pragmatic strategy for Jewish life under Sasanian rule. Yet, for all its apparent benefits, the potential ideological cost of this pragmatic strategy continued to haunt its rabbinic proponents.

When comparing contemporary Syriac Christian accounts, with their starkly contrasting reports of Sasanian violence and cruelty, we must again remember that, as with the Babylonian Talmud, we are often dealing with products of communal memory. Certainly, the two are linked; for a variety of reasons, Christians likely encountered a greater frequency of imperial violence than Jews and may therefore have been more willing to view the empire as a hostile entity. However, the two communities also made choices about how to commemorate their imperial circumstances, which informed future encounters with the empire. The valorization of martyrdom by Christians was, no doubt, at least partly responsible for Christians' continued willingness to confront the empire frontally by proselytizing Zoroastrians, evading taxes, and destroying fire temples. This, in turn, produced a predictable imperial response. If Jews encountered fewer instances of imperial violence, it may well have partially resulted from the embrace of accommodationist approaches in stories like those told by the rabbis. The popularity and therefore impact of the rabbis in the Sasanian period itself is difficult to gauge, but the effect their representations had on subsequent Jewish memory is clear. No Babylonian Jewish martyr shrines or books of martyrs would arise in the medieval period; but the notion of a persecution-less Sasanian past would be brandished by medieval Babylonian rabbis to assert their superiority over their Jewish competitors.[104] The stories Babylonian rabbis did and did not tell shaped their audience's behavior in the present, and the perception of the Sasanian period forever after. Forgetting could be as powerful as remembering.

[104] See Gross, "Playing with Persecution."

5

Rabbis and Fire Temples

Navigating a Zoroastrian Empire

The sparse material remains of Jews from the Sasanian Empire include around twenty personal seals, which were used to validate legal, business, and personal documents.[1] These objects typically bore the owner's name and an accompanying image. The identity of the owner is ascertainable from both the names and type of script; Jewish owners likely used square or Hebrew script, Christians used Syriac, and Middle Persian was used by all groups, including Jews and Christians.[2] The images on Jewish and Christian seals are often easily recognizable communal symbols. For example, some Jewish seals depict ritual objects, such as the shofar, palm fronds, and citron (Figure 5).[3] These were common features of Jewish visual culture, present on coins minted by the Judean

[1] On Jewish seals, see Shaul Shaked, "Jewish and Christian Seals of the Sasanian Period," in *Studies in Memory of Gaston Weit*, ed. M. Rosen-Ayalon (Jerusalem: 1977), 17–31; Shaked "Epigraphica Judaeo-Iranica," in *Studies in Judaism and Islam Presented to S. D. Goitein*, ed. Sh. Morag, I. Ben-Ami, and N. A. Stillman (Jerusalem: 1981), 65–82; Shaked, "Jewish Sasanian Sigillography," in *Au carrefour des religions: mélanges offerts à Philippe Gignoux*, ed. Rika Gyselen (Buressur-Yvette: 1995), 239–255; Moshe Beer, "A Reconsideration of Three Ancient Seals from Persia," [in Hebrew] *Tarbiẓ* 52 (1983): 435–445; Daniel Friedenberg, *Sasanian Jewry and Its Culture: A Lexicon of Jewish and Related Seals* (Chicago: 2009); and Geoffrey Herman's critical review in "Sasanian Jewry and Its Culture: A Lexicon of Jewish and Related Seals by Daniel M. Friedenberg, Norman Golb," *Association for Jewish Studies Review* 34 (2010): 121–124. On the uses of seals, see Macuch, "The Use of Seals," 79–87.

[2] For instance, a seal with palm frond, citron, and a Pahlavi inscription: Philippe Gignoux and Rika Gyselen, "Nouveaux cachets sasanides de la Collection Pirouzan," *Studia Iranica* 7 (1978), 39 and pl. 4 (no. 60.02).

[3] Friedenberg, *Sasanian Jewry and Its Culture*, 27–32.

FIGURE 5. Jewish Sasanian seal with Hebrew inscription of the owner Isaac bar Papa and image of a Lulav and Etrog. [National Museum of Denmark, Accession Number 9470, Photo by Lennart Larsen]

rebel Bar Kokhba in the first half of Figure 6. the second century and in late antique synagogue mosaics.[4] Not surprisingly, many Christian seals feature crosses.

Other seals – both Jewish and Christian – contain a more peculiar image: that of a man holding a knife standing alongside an altar, on which rests a child (Figure 6). At the side of the image appears a ram in a thicket. Judith Lerner has shown that these seals depict the Binding of Isaac of Genesis 22, a story which held immense significance for both Jews and Christians.[5] The imagery on these seals is again similar to that found in the famous Dura Europos synagogue of Northern Mesopotamia and other late antique synagogues. What is remarkable about the images on

[4] Levine, *The Ancient Synagogue*, 230–235. See also b. Giṭ. 36a, which discusses the images rabbis used to identify themselves on contracts.

[5] See Judith A. Lerner, *Christian Seals of the Sasanian Period* (Leiden: 1977), 18–22; Judith A. Lerner, "The Sacrifice of Isaac Revisited: Additional Observations on a Theme in Sasanian Glyptic Art," in *Facts and Artefacts: Art in the Islamic World. Festschrift for Jens Kroger on his 65th Birthday*, ed. Annette Hagedorn and Avinoam Shalem (Leiden: 2007), 39–58. See also Judith Lerner, "Considerations on an Aspect of Jewish Culture under the Sasanians: The Matter of Jewish Sigillography," *Journal of the American Oriental Society* 129 (2009): 653–664, with 659n22. For a particularly striking seal of this kind, see Jeffrey Spier, "Late Antique and Early Christian Gems: Some Unpublished Examples," in *Gems of Heaven: Recent Research on Engraved Gemstones in Late Antiquity, c. AD 200–600*, ed. Chris Entwistle and Noël Adams (London: 2012), 202 plate 53.

FIGURE 6. Jewish Sasanian seal made of garnet with Hebrew inscription of owner Shmuel bar Yehuda and image of the Binding of Isaac. [Derek Content Collection]

the seals, however, is that they are also a modified form of a common image on other Sasanians seals that depicts a Zoroastrian priest standing beside a fire altar.[6] Instead of a knife, the priest holds the Zoroastrian ritual barsom twigs, and on the altar is a fire rather than a child. This Zoroastrian imagery was similarly reworked in some Christian seals that replaced elements, like the fire, with one or more crosses.[7] These Jewish

[6] Michael Alram, "Early Sasanian Coinage," in *The Sasanian Era*, ed. Vesta Sarkosh Curtis and Sarah Stewart (London: 2008), 17–30; Michael Alram and Rika Gyselen, *Ardashir I – Shapur I*, vol. 1, *Sylloge Nummorum Sasanidarum: Paris, Berlin, Wien* (Vienna: 2003).

[7] Shaked, "Jewish and Christian Seals," 18, 22–23. See also Marica Cassis, "Kokhe, Cradle of the Church of the East: An Archaeological and Comparative Study," *Journal of the Canadian Society for Syriac Studies* 2 (2002): 62–78, who compares the remains of Sasanian-era churches with imperial Sasanian architecture.

and Christian seals therefore adapt recognizable Zoroastrian imagery to fit within a Biblical frame of reference, simultaneously signaling similarity and alterity. The difference in imagery between this group of Jewish and Christian seals and those that employ common Jewish and Christian motifs is striking.[8]

Alongside these more well-represented Jewish seals are three that adopt other religious imagery. One, a seal belonging to Joseph bar Nathan, depicts a man with arms raised in a cultic performance of some sort, identical to images found on both Zoroastrian and Christian seals.[9] Another, belonging to Aḥa bar Sumaqa, is adorned with a winged symbol Figure 5.with a crescent moon that may have held some religious significance.[10] Most astonishingly, a third includes a Hebrew inscription and depicts a fire altar flanked by priests.[11] Together, this group of seals shows that some Jews went even further, identifying themselves as Jews while using the same religious imagery as other groups, even including an overtly Zoroastrian symbol. Did these Jews simply not have any objections to fire worship? Or had they recast and redefined these images such that they were not, in their mind, contradictory to their Jewish identity?[12]

These different seals are emblematic of how Jews and Christians confronted a world saturated with Zoroastrian symbols. Some apparently eschewed Zoroastrian imagery in favor of plainly Jewish and Christian motifs, perhaps creating a stark divide between the two. Others modified and naturalized Zoroastrian images, reflecting a willingness to engage with an adapted version of the hegemonic culture and its symbols even while differentiating themselves from it. Still others adopted Zoroastrian

[8] Other seals have been identified by some as Daniel in the lion's den, though this is a matter of disagreement. See Lerner, "Considerations on an Aspect of Jewish Culture under the Sasanians."

[9] Shaked, "Jewish and Christian Seals," 25; Friedenberg, *Sasanian Jewry and Its Culture*, 41.

[10] Friedenberg, *Sasanian Jewry and Its Culture*, 52 (compare with p. 51 there); Rika Gyselen, *Catalogue des sceaux, camées et bulles sassanides de la Bibliothèque Nationale et du Musée du Louvre* (Paris: 1994), No. 70.68 (Plate XLV); see also Rika Gyselen, *Sasanian Seals and Sealings in the A. Saeedi Collection* (Louvain: 2007), 120–121.

[11] Shaked, "Jewish Sasanian Sigillography," 240, 243n14 (fig. 3), suggests that the Hebrew name was added to a previously used seal.

[12] Payne, *State of Mixture*, 89–90, provides another example of reappropriation of the symbolism and significance of fire in the Sasanian Empire in a Syriac Persian martyr act.

imagery, apparently experiencing no conflict with their Jewish identities, perhaps not considering them exclusively Zoroastrian symbols at all. Jewish and Christian subjects engaged in acts of definition about themselves and those around them that informed individual and communal postures toward Zoroastrianism and its manifestations, vacillating between resistance, naturalization, appropriation, and even identification.[13]

Outside of former scholarly paradigms of Jewish insularity and isolationism, Jews were incapable of avoiding Zoroastrian cultic practices and imagery altogether because they were simply ubiquitous. Fire altars and temples dotted the urban environment, prominent in both royal compounds and residential communities.[14] Fire temples were essential features of the Mesopotamian landscape, near Jewish population centers.[15] Designated fire temples typically shared certain recognizable architectural features, including four arches and a dome in the middle, under which burned the fire on a central altar, making them immediately

[13] For a similar analysis of Jewish iconographic and inscriptional choices in Palestine, see Schwartz, *Imperialism and Jewish Society*, 129–161.

[14] On fire temples more generally, see Yumiko Yamamoto, "The Zoroastrian Temple Cult of Fire in Archaeology and Literature I," *Orient* 15 (1979): 19–53; Yumiko Yamamoto, "The Zoroastrian Temple Cult of Fire in Archaeology and Literature II," *Orient* 17 (1981): 189–214; Choksy, "Altars, Precincts, and Temples," 1–20; and de Jong, *Traditions of the Magi*, 343–350. For archaeological discoveries, see Ali Mousavi and Touraj Daryaee, "The Sasanian Empire: An Archaeological Survey c. 220–AD 640," in vol. 2, *A Companion to the Archaeology of the Ancient Near East*, ed. Daniel T. Potts (Malden, MA: 2012), 1087–1089; Klaus Schippmann, *Die iranischen Feuerheiligtümer* (Berlin: 1971); Philippe Gignoux, "Le site de Bandiān revisité," *Studia Iranica* 37 (2008): 163–174; Jamsheed K. Choksy, "Reassessing the Material Contexts of Ritual Fires in Ancient Iran," *Iranica Antiqua* 42 (2007): 229–269; and David Stronach, "The Kūh-i Shahrak Fire Altar," *Journal of Near Eastern Studies* 25 (1966): 217–227. For fire temples in Khuzistan and Fars, see Kennedy, "From Shahristan to Medina," 15–17. Russell, *Zoroastrianism in Armenia*, 481–503, discusses the fire cult in Armenia throughout this period.

[15] On fire temples in Iraq, see Theodore Nöldeke, *Geschichte der Perser und Araber zur Zeit der Sasaniden aus der arabischen Chronik des Tabari* (Leiden: 1879), 353. In the *History of Mar Qardagh* (see Walker, *Legend of Mar Qardagh*, 22–23 and 274), Qardagh, while still a Zoroastrian *marzbān*, is said to have visited a fire temple in Arbela and to have built a fire temple (*bet nurwātā*) at the base of the "tell" nearby. Morony, *Iraq after the Muslim Conquest*, 283, lists a few other literary attestations of fire temples in Iraq. For the requisition of a Christian church for the sake of a fire temple in Amida, see Muriel Debié, "Guerres et religions en Mésopotamie du Nord dans l'antiquité tardive: un mimro inédit de Jacques de Saroug sur l'église Saint-Étienne que les Perses ont transformée en temple du feu à Amid (Diyarbakır) en 503 è.c.," *Syriac Orthodox Patriarchal Journal* 56 (2018): 29–80 (esp. 45–46).

recognizable.[16] Zoroastrian festivals, closely linked to the calendrical cycle, were highly visible and could include fire worship.[17] The visibility of fire worship and Zoroastrianism more generally in these various contexts and media was due in large part to its central symbolic importance to Sasanian imperial political theology. The reverse of Sasanian coins depicted fire altars flanked by officiating priests (Figure 7).[18] Royal reliefs depicted the Sasanian king and benevolent deity Ohrmazd in parallel, both bringing order to the world by trampling on their respective enemies (Figure 8). Jews, Christians, and other non-Zoroastrians navigated a cultural environment pervaded by Zoroastrian practices and images.[19]

Like the owners of the seals surveyed above, the Babylonian rabbis similarly negotiated Zoroastrian practices, institutions and symbols. Their stories and legal discussions illuminate the kinds of complicated and even contradictory conceptual and definitional operations performed by at least some Jews that were seeking to accommodate Jewish practice to a Sasanian context. The Babylonian rabbis proscribe Jewish interaction

[16] On the architecture of fire temples, see: Dietrich Huff, "Čahārṭāq: (i) In Pre-Islamic Iran," in *Bāyjū-Carpets*, ed. Ehsan Yarshater, vol. 4, *Encyclæpedia Iranica* (London: 1990), 634–648; Huff, "Beobachtungen zum Chahartaq und zur Topographie von Girre," *Iranica Antique* 30 (1995): 71–92; Soroor Ghanimati, "Kuh-e Khwaja and the Religious Architecture of Sasanian Iran," in *Oxford Handbook of Ancient Iran*, ed. D. Potts (Oxford: 2013), 892–900. For an in-depth study of one site, see Yousef Moradi and Edward Keall, "The Sasanian Fire Temple of Gach Dawar in Western Iran: New Evidence," *Journal of the British Institute of Persian Studies* 58 (2020): 27–40.

[17] Jenny Rose, "Festivals and the Calendar," in *The Wiley-Blackwell Companion to Zoroastrianism*, ed. Michael Stausberg and Yuhan Sohrab-Dinshaw Vevaine (Chichester: 2015), 384.

[18] Michael Alram, "The Beginning of Sasanian Coinage," *Bulletin of the Asia Institute* 13 (1999): 67–76. On earlier coinage, see Daniel T. Potts, "Foundation Houses, Fire Altars and the Frataraka: Interpreting the Iconography of some Post-Achaemenid Persian Coins," *Iranica Antiqua* 42 (2007): 271–300.

[19] The early Iranian Manichaeans represent an interesting counterpoint, as they sought to portray their teachings as a realization of Iranian traditions. See Paul Dilley, "Also schrieb Zarathustra? Mani as Interpreter of the 'Law of Zarades,'" in *Mani at the Court of the Persian Kings: Studies on the Chester Beatty Kephalaia Codex*, ed. Iain Gardner, Jason BeDuhn, and Paul Dilley (Leiden: 2015), 101–135; Jason BeDuhn, "Iranian Epic in the Chester Beatty Kephalaia," in *Mani at the Court of the Persian Kings: Studies on the Chester Beatty* Kephalaia *Codex*, ed. Iain Gardner, Jason BeDuhn, and Paul Dilley (Leiden: 2015), 136–158; and Yuhan Sohrab–Dinshaw Vevaina, "The Hermeneutics of Political Violence in Sasanian Iran: The Death of Mani and the Seizure of Manichaean Property," *Sasanian Studies* 1 (2022): 291–322. In the case of fire worship, see Gardner, BeDuhn, and Dilley, *The Chapters of the Wisdom of My Lord Mani*, 36–49, where Mani debates the Zoroastrian judge Adourpat about the meaning of fire worship and its various components.

FIGURE 7. Drachm of King Bahram IV (r. 388-99 CE); on obverse image of king with his particular headgear, on reverse typical image of fire altar flanked by priestly attendants. [Metropolitan Museum of Art, Accession Number 99.35.2965]

FIGURE 8. Investiture relief at Naqsh-e Rustam symmetrically presenting the first Sasanian king, Ardashir I, on the left, accepting the diadem of sovereignty from the deity, Ohrmazd, on the right. [Photo © Matthew P. Canepa]

with Zoroastrian institutions and practices, applying rabbinic legal precedents from Palestine that had been developed in a Roman context. Yet some rabbis also made dispensations for certain kinds of Jewish interaction with Zoroastrian cultic practice and institutions that required them to stretch, if not outright transgress, earlier rabbinic law. Their permissive approach differed dramatically not only from their rabbinic predecessors, but also from some of their contemporary Syriac Christian neighbors, reflecting alternative approaches subjects adopted to defining themselves and their traditions, Zoroastrianism and imperial symbols, and the boundaries between them.

JEWS AND IDOLATRY

To appreciate the Babylonian rabbis' engagement with Zoroastrianism, we must position them against the background of the extreme opposition to all forms of idolatry established in the Pentateuch. Pentateuchal laws address an idealized (and imagined) setting in which the Israelites live in a society over which they exercise absolute power and therefore can regulate and control proper and improper cultic worship. The Israelites were expected, as one of the Ten Commandments declares, to "not make any graven image . . . not bow to them, nor serve them" (Ex. 20.4-6), but also to eradicate whatever idolatry they encountered (Deut. 12.2-3). But with the demise of Jewish autonomy in Palestine in the first century of the Common Era, and with an ever-growing Jewish diaspora, Jews were confronted by a world permeated with images, festivals, and cultic practices that they could neither ignore nor abolish, even as many Jews remained uncompromisingly opposed to idolatry. To avoid needless conflict with the Jewish population, the Romans generally granted Jews special dispensation and excused them from offering sacrifices to the imperial cult.[20] The Jewish refusal to participate in such sacrifices was understood to embody the unique character of the Jewish *ethnos*.[21] Even when their opposition to idolatry was accommodated, Jews, and soon

[20] On the imperial cult, see Glen Bowersock, "The Imperial Cult: Perceptions and Persistence," in *Jewish and Christian Self-Definition*, vol. 3, *Self-Definition in the Graeco-Roman World*, ed. Ben Meyer and E. P. Sanders (London: 1982), 171–182; and more generally S. R. F. Price, *Rituals and Power: The Roman Imperial Cult in Asia Minor* (Cambridge: 1983).

[21] Some, however, marked Jewish non-participation as a sign of "misanthropy" and anti-social Jewish behavior. See Peter Schäfer, *Judeophobia: Attitudes toward the Jews in the Ancient World* (Cambridge, MA: 1997), 170–177, and more generally, Katell Berthelot,

Christians, still could not escape the images and cultic objects that permeated their largely pagan environment. The third-century North African Christian author Tertullian describes a world in which "the streets, the market, the baths, the taverns, even our houses are none of them altogether clear of idols. The whole world is filled with Satan and his angels."[22]

Over time, Jewish communities fashioned a *modus vivendi* according to which they could thrive alongside the cultic practices of their neighbors. In an influential article, Seth Schwartz showed how the Palestinian rabbis laid the legal and conceptual groundwork for Jewish coexistence with their non-Jewish neighbors in the idolatry-saturated cities of Roman Palestine.[23] The rabbis' approach was best encapsulated in a mishnaic story in which Rabban Gamaliel is challenged by a non-Jew, identified as the son of a philosopher, for having visited a bathhouse that was adorned with an image of Aphrodite, in apparent violation of biblical prescriptions against tolerating idolatry.[24] Rabban Gamaliel justifies his actions by explaining that "One does not say, 'Let us make a bathhouse to adorn Aphrodite,' rather Aphrodite was made as an adornment for the bathhouse." He therefore draws a fundamental distinction between *functional* iconography that was legally deemed idolatrous and prohibited, and *ornamental* iconography that was not, a distinction not found in the Pentateuch's sweeping injunctions against idolatry. Indeed, Rabban Gamliel's distinction would likely not have been accepted by earlier, less compromising Palestinian rabbinic authorities.[25] As Moshe Halbertal explains, "the distinction between the cultic and the aesthetic" created "a neutral space between pagans and Jews," which allowed "for a

Philanthrôpia judaica: Le débat autour de la "misanthropie" des lois juives dans l'antiquité (Leiden: 2003).

[22] Tertullian, *De Spectaculis* 8.9.

[23] Seth Schwartz, "Gamaliel in Aphrodite's Bath: Palestinian Judaism and Urban Culture in the Third and Fourth Centuries," in *The Talmud Yerushalmi and Graeco-Roman Culture*, vol. 1, ed. Peter Schäfer (Tübingen: 1998), 203–217. In this chapter, the terms "pagan." "paganism," and "idolatry" reflect rabbinic categories and thought, while "religious" refers to matters of deities, cult, and worship. I recognize that these terms are problematic and do not fully capture the self-understanding of either the rabbis or the groups about which the rabbis speak.

[24] m. ʿAbod. Zar. 3.4. For a critical edition of the text, see David Rosenthal, "*Mishnah Avodah Zara:* A Critical Edition (with Introduction)," [in Hebrew] (PhD diss., Hebrew University of Jerusalem, 1980), 2.40–43.

[25] See, for instance, Mekhilta deRabbi Ishmael, Baḥodesh 6 (Hayim Saul Horovitz, and Israel A. Rabin, eds. *Mekhilta deRabbi Ishmael* [Jerusalem: 1998], 224–225).

broader interaction in that space."[26] The rabbis understood that certain accommodations had to be made in light of the ubiquity of iconic images in the Roman Empire.[27] Their response was therefore "modified rigorism, with its uncompromising rejection of anything remotely connected to pagan cult, but acceptance of most non-cultic manifestations of Greco-Roman pagan culture, permitting them to live and function in the cities."[28]

At the same time, the rabbis applied the strictest of standards to functional idolatry and categorized it as one of three cardinal sins for which a Jew, even under duress, must choose death rather than transgress.[29] Deriving any benefit from idolatry was also prohibited by the rabbis, who

[26] Moshe Halbertal, "Co-existing with the Enemy: Jews and Pagans in the Mishnah," in *Tolerance and Intolerance in Early Judaism and Christianity*, ed. Graham N. Stanton and Guy G. Stroumsa (Cambridge: 1998), 159–172, esp. 167.

[27] See, for instance, Yaron Eliav, "Viewing the Sculptural Environment: Shaping the Second Commandment," in *The Talmud Yerushalmi and Graeco-Roman Culture*, vol. 3, ed. Peter Schafer (Tübingen: 2002), 411–433, although see the caveats in Zeev Weiss, "Sculptures and Sculptural Images in the Urban Galilean Context," in *The Sculptural Environment of the Roman Near-East: Reflection on Culture, Ideology, and Power*, ed. Y. Z. Eliav, Elise A. Friedland, and Sharon Herbert (Leuven: 2008), 559–574.

[28] Schwartz, "Gamaliel in Aphrodite's Bath," 217. Compare this with the Council of Elvira (canons 59–60), which forbids Christians sacrificing to idols, but also condemns Christians who destroy idols and are killed by idolaters as a result.

[29] This conclusion is consistent with E. E. Urbach, "The Rabbinical Laws of Idolatry in the Second and Third Centuries in the Light of Archaeological and Historical Facts," *Israel Exploration Journal* 9 (1959): 229–245, who argued that the rabbis replaced the biblical command to physically *destroy* idolatrous objects with a prohibition against *benefiting* from objects whose cultic significance had not been "neutralized" (*biṭul*). The rabbis may not have been as unanimous as Urbach suggested: see Ishay Rosen-Zvi, "The Polemic on the Requirements to Destroy Avodah Zarah in Tannaitic Literature," [in Hebrew] *Reishit* 1 (2009): 91–115. Cf. Noam Zohar, "The Relationship of Non-Jews and Their Statues in Mishnah Avodah Zarah," [in Hebrew] *Reshit* 1 (2009): 145–164. Urbach's own explanation for rabbinic leniency – namely, a response to changing economic conditions in the Roman Near East and a decline of paganism in the third century – has been roundly rejected. See Sacha Stern, "Figurative Art and Halakha in the Mishnaic-Talmudic Period," [in Hebrew] *Zion* 61 (1996): 397–399; and Sacha Stern, "Pagan Images in Late Antique Palestinian Synagogues," in *Ethnicity and Culture in Late Antiquity*, ed. Stephen Mitchell and Geoffrey Greatrex (London: 2000), 243. Rabbinic notions of idolatry may even reflect the circumambient notions and practices of idolatry of the time: Yaron Eliav, "On Idolatry in the Roman Bathhouse – Two Comments," [in Hebrew] *Cathedra* 110 (2003): 173–180; Yair Furstenberg, "Idolatry Annulment and Roman Rule," [in Hebrew] *Reshit* 1 (2009): 118–144. For other studies of the story in m. 'Abod. Zar. 3.4, see Azzan Yadin, "Rabban Gamaliel, Aphrodite's Bath, and the Question of Pagan Monotheism," *Jewish Quarterly Review* 96 (2006): 149–179; and R. Rafe Neis, *The Sense of Sight in Rabbinic Culture: Jewish Ways of Seeing in Late Antiquity* (Cambridge: 2013), 170–201.

imposed safeguards to avoid even inadvertently supporting idolatrous practices. They similarly enacted a variety of constraints on business interactions with idolaters, especially around the time of their festivals, to avoid giving idolators any cause for increased celebration on these occasions.[30]

BABYLONIAN RABBIS AND IDOLATRY

Like their Palestinian counterparts, the Babylonian rabbis regularly encountered idolatry.[31] Mesopotamia had a long and rich tradition of Assyrian, Babylonian, and Greco-Roman cultic practices, and these persisted long after the emergence of the Babylonian rabbis at the beginning of the third century CE.[32] Assyrian and Babylonian cults and their related shrines persisted through the Sasanian period.[33] Greco-Roman cults, which had a long history in the region, would also have been reintroduced to the region by the captives of war deported by Shapur I and II.[34] While native populations slowly assimilated with other local religious groups, including Jews and Christians, many other cults endured for quite some time.[35]

The Babylonian Talmud itself mentions several temples dedicated to well-known deities in which "worship takes place all year round." These include "the temple of Bel in Babylon, the temple of Nebo in Kursi, Tar'ata which is in Mabbug, Zerifa which is in Askelon, and Nishtra which is in Arabia."[36] The continuation of this passage lists the festivals observed by Babylonians. These active temples and festivals are distinct

[30] This is the primary focus of the first chapters of m. 'Abod. Zar. 1.

[31] Josephus (*Against Apion* 1.192) cites Hecataeus of Abdera (fl. late 4th–early third century BCE) to the effect that Jews in Alexander's army refused to aid in the reconstruction of the temple of Bel in Babylon. For discussion, see Menahem Stern, *Greek and Latin Authors on Jews and Judaism*, vol. 1 (Jerusalem: 1974), 42–43. For a related discussion, see Geoffrey Herman, "Idolatry, God(s), and Demons among the Jews of Sasanian Babylonia," in *Expressions of Sceptical Topoi in (Late) Antique Judaism* ed. Geoffrey Herman and Reuven Kiperwasser (Berlin: 2021), 85–99.

[32] Hunter, "Aramaic Speaking Communities of Sasanid Mesopotamia," 319–335; de Jong, "Zoroastrian Religious Polemics," 49.

[33] See the useful survey and references in Walker, *Legend of Mar Qardagh*, 251–254. See also Markham Geller, "The Last Wedge," *Zeitschrift für Assyriologie* 87 (1997): 49–95. This is not to suggest that all of these sites were preserved, but despite the abandonment of some, others seem to have remained active for some time. S. Downey, *Mesopotamian Religious Architecture: Alexander through the Parthians* (Princeton, NJ: 1988), 174–178.

[34] See, for instance, Morony, "Population Transfers," 161–179.

[35] Jaakko Hämeen-Anttila, *The Last Pagans of Iraq: Ibn Wahshiyya and His Nabatean Agriculture* (Leiden: 2006); Lerner, "Considerations on an Aspect of Jewish Culture," 657n17.

[36] b. 'Abod. Zar. 11b, MS Paris, Bibliotheque Nationale, 1337.

from others described elsewhere in the Talmud as defunct, such as the "temple of Nimrod."[37] Part of the Talmud's list of temples is also found in a Mandaic magical lead roll from the late Sasanian period, which reads "Bel is turned from Babylon, Nabu (Nebo) is turned from Borsippa, Nishra is turned from Kashkar."[38] Other ancient historians report the existence of temples of Bel, Artemis or Aphrodite, Nanaia, and other gods in western Iran before the Common Era, and Aramaic dedicatory inscriptions up to the early third century CE mention the temples of Bel and Nabu (Nebo).[39] Still other cults, such as that of Ishtar, may have continued to flourish into the fourth century and even later.[40] Syriac Christian sources speak of missionaries arriving in Mesopotamia during this period to convert idolaters; for example, in *The Acts of Mar Mari*, the city of Kashkar is reported to worship Nishar, among the deities mentioned in the Babylonian Talmud and the Mandaic lead roll. In other martyr acts, Christians are reportedly pressured to worship several idols.[41] All this suggests that the rabbis were regularly exposed to what they would have deemed idolatry.

This historical record has nevertheless been challenged by Richard Kalmin, who claims that Babylonian rabbis "encountered idols only when they went out of their way to find them," a marked difference from the Palestinian rabbinic experience.[42] Of Babylonian rabbinic engagement with questions of idolatry, he therefore concludes that the "continued

[37] b. ʿAbod. Zar. 53b, based on m. ʿAbod. Zar. 4.6. Relatedly, see b. Ber. 57b.

[38] See Yakir Paz, "'Meishan Is Dead': On the Historical Contexts of the Bavli's Representations of the Jews in Southern Babylonia," in *Babylonian Aggada in Its Historical Context*, ed. Geoffrey Herman and Jeffrey Rubenstein (Providence, RI: 2018), 13. Other Mandaic texts suggest the survival of certain Mesopotamian deities as well. See Christa Müller-Kessler and Karlheinz Kessler, "Spätbabylonische Gottheiten in spätantiken mandäischen Texten," *Zeitschrift für Assyriologie* 89 (1999): 65–87.

[39] See references in Mary Boyce and Frantz Grenet, *History of Zoroastrianism III. Zoroastrianism under Macedonian and Roman Rule* (Leiden: 1991), 35–48. For Nanaia, see Bedjan, *Acta martyrum et sanctorum* 2.516; Basile Aggoula, *Inscriptions et graffites araméens d'Assour* (Napoli: 1985), 16–17.

[40] Stephanie Dalley, "Occasions and Opportunities: Persian, Greek, and Parthian Overlords," in *Legacy of Mesopotamia*, ed. Stephanie Dalley (Oxford: 2005), 38, on Ishtar of Arbela. But see Joel Thomas Walker, "The Legacy of Mesopotamia in Late Antique Iraq: The Christian Martyr Shrine at Melqi (Neo-Assyrian Milqia)," *ARAM Periodical* 18–19 (2006–2007): 493. For more on "paganism" in Iraq in Late Antiquity, see Morony, *Iraq after the Muslim Conquest*, 384–400.

[41] See references in Paz, "Meishan Is Dead," 58–59. Similarly, the prophet Mani's father is said to have been an idolater. See Michel Tardieu, *Manichaeism* (Chicago, IL: 2008), 3 and 68.

[42] Kalmin, *Jewish Babylonia*, 103.

vitality [of idolatry] was more in the minds of the rabbis than grounded in the realities of life in Sasanian Persia."[43]

Kalmin bases his argument on an internal reading of rabbinic literature, yet the very sources he cites in support of his claims reveal precisely the opposite: a world in which idolatry was prevalent. For example, Kalmin cites a story where Rav Menasheh travels to Be Torta and there encounters an idol that is identified as "Mercury."[44] Kalmin argues that this passage demonstrates how *rare* idolatry was in Babylonia, for it was only when Rav Menasheh visited Be Torta that he encountered an idol. However, Be Torta was apparently adjacent to Rav Menasheh's main dwelling in Pumbedita, so Rav Menasheh likely visited or passed through it regularly. In fact, the only other source in the Babylonian Talmud that mentions Rav Menasheh situates him in Be Torta.[45] That the statue is named after Mercury should not surprise us, given that other Greco-Roman deities, such as Hercules, had devotees in Iraq and Iran.[46] Indeed, another rabbinic story describes two Babylonian *amoraim* (Rav Hamnuna and Rav Ashi) encountering a statue of Hermes.[47] In yet another story, Rava bar Rav Yizḥak tells Rav Yehuda that there is a temple with an idol in the area that is regularly prayed to for rain.[48] Kalmin dismisses this source simply because the idol is unnamed, which he claims casts doubt on its historicity. But it is unclear how the absence of a name negates the implication that idols and their worship persisted in the region.

[43] Kalmin, *Jewish Babylonia*, 109. [44] b. Sanh. 64a.

[45] b. ʿAbod. Zar. 25b–26a. See Oppenheimer, *Babylonia Judaica*, 359 and 367n84. Moreover, Be Torta also seems to be associated with Ishtar in a Babylonian Jewish incantation bowl and appears with a list of other locations, once again suggesting that it is not an exception to the rule, as Kalmin presents it. See Dan Levene and Gideon Bohak, "A Babylonian Jewish Aramaic Incantation Bowl with a List of Deities and Toponyms," *Jewish Studies Quarterly* 19 (2012): 8.

[46] For Hercules, see Paul Bernard, "Vicissitudes au gré de l'histoire d'une statue en bronze d'Heracles entre Seleucie du Tigre et la Mesene," *Journal des savants* 1 (1990): 3–68. This is not the only Hercules discovered. See Richard N. Frye, *The Heritage of Persia* (London: 1962), 156 (with plates 68–71, 87). For Nergal as Hercules, see Lucinda Dirven, "'My Lord with His Dogs': Continuity and Change in the Cult of Nergal in Parthian Mesopotamia," in *Edessa in hellenistisch-römischer Zeit. Religion, Kultur und Politik zwischen Ost und Wes*, ed. Lutz Greisiger, Claudia Rammelt, and Jürgen Tubach (Beirut: 2009), 47–69; and Dirven, "Religious Frontiers in the Syrian-Mesopotamian Desert," in *Frontiers in the Roman World: Proceedings of the Ninth Workshop of International Network Impact of Empire*, ed. Ted Kaizer and Olivier Hekster (Leiden: 2011), 165. See also Tacitus, *Annals*, 12.13. For references to Mercury in rabbinic literature, see for instance m. Sanh. 7.6; ʿAbod. Zar. 4.1; and t. ʿAbod. Zar. 6.13 (Zuckermandel). See also y. ʿAbod. Zar. 4.1 (43c) and 9.1 (12d), for slightly different but related uses of the word.

[47] b. Ber. 57b. [48] b. ʿAbod. Zar. 55a.

The reality of the Babylonian rabbis was most likely broadly similar to that of their Palestinian predecessors: Both encountered what they defined as idolatry regularly, and their responses to idolatry were typically consistent.[49] Even Kalmin accepts that the Babylonian rabbis *imagined* a world filled with idolatry and adopted the same stipulations that governed attitudes toward idolatry in Palestinian sources, especially Rabban Gamaliel's distinction between functional and ornamental idols – a view attributed in the Talmud to Babylonian rabbis as well.[50] Yet unexpectedly, the Babylonian rabbis charted a more inconsistent course in negotiating the realities of Zoroastrianism in the Sasanian Empire.

ZOROASTRIANISM

In theory, Zoroastrianism was, in many ways, distinct from Assyrian, Babylonian, and Greco-Roman religions. The Sasanian-era Zoroastrian cult centered on fire and fire temples, not graven images.[51] Given the prominence of fire in Zoroastrian worship, images and idols were, at the very least, not the primary vehicle of worship among Zoroastrians.[52]

[49] Although there were differences between Babylonia and Palestine regarding the laws of idolatry. See Hayes, *Between the Babylonian and Palestinian Talmuds*, esp. 127–153 on non-Jewish midwives and 154–170 on idolatrous festivals.

[50] b. ʿAbod. Zar. 40b–41a.

[51] M. Azarnoush, "Fire Temple and Anahita Temple: A Discussion on Some Iranian Places of Worship," *Mesopotamia* 22 (1987): 391–401; Choksy, "Reassessing the Material Contexts of Ritual Fires;" Choksy, "Altars, Precincts, and Temples in Medieval and Modern Zoroastrian Praxis," *Iran* 43 (2006): 1–20; Mary Boyce, "On the Sacred Fires of the Zoroastrians," *Bulletin of the School of Oriental and African Studies* 31 (1968): 52–68; Mary Boyce, "On the Zoroastrian Cult Temple Cult Fire," *Journal of the American Oriental Society* 95 (1975): 454–465. See Kalmin, *Jewish Babylonia*, 103–120, with discussion below.

[52] It is quite possible that, for much of the Sasanian period, iconic imagery was still used by some Zoroastrians in cultic settings. See Choksy, "Reassessing the Material Contexts of Ritual Fires," 251, and in general see Shenkar, *Intangible Spirits and Graven Images: The Iconography of Deities in the Pre-Islamic Iranian World* (Leiden: 2014). An Armenian Christian text at the end of the Sasanian period mentions statues of the Iranian deities Ohrmazd and Anahita. See S. der Nersessian, "Une apologie des images du septieme siècle," *Byzantion* 17 (1944–1945): 58–88. See also *The History of Karka d-Bet Slokh* (Bedjan, *Acta martyrum et sanctorum*, 2.510), for the historical memory that Seleucus built both a fire temple and a temple with idols, side by side. Statues may therefore still have been part of some Zoroastrian worship in Babylonia during the Sasanian period. Admittedly far removed from Babylonia, Iranian pantheons with images are found in Bactria and Sogdiana. See Frantz Grenet, "Iranian Gods in Hindu Garb: the Zoroastrian Pantheon of the Bactrians and Sogdians, Second–Eighth Centuries," *Bulletin of the Asia Institute* 20 (2006): 87–99.

Indeed, it has been argued, most forcefully by Mary Boyce, that the Sasanian-era cult was not only aniconic, but also iconoclastic, deliberately pursuing and destroying idols and idol-worshipping temples. Instead, the center of the cult was the fire. But Boyce's arguments have come under serious scrutiny in recent years, in part because of surviving Sasanian-era imagery that depicts human-like deities.[53] Among the most impressive are massive royal rock inscriptions with anthropomorphic depictions of the chief Zoroastrian deity, Ohrmazd.[54] In Ardashir I's inscription at Naqsh-e Rustam, Ohrmazd is also identified in a trilingual description as a figure on horseback standing opposite Ardashir I.[55] Similar iconic art is visible on arches and columns of palaces and other monumental rock inscriptions, such as at Ṭaq-e Bostan, Naqsh-e Rajab, and Bishapur. Iconic imagery has also been found on more mundane objects, such as on seals, coins, cups, silver plates, and more.[56] If Aphrodite was on Roman

[53] Boyce's claim regarding iconoclasm has been challenged by Frantz Grenet, "Mary Boyce's Legacy for the Archaeologists," *Bulletin of the Asia Institute* 22 (2012): 29–47; Gherardo Gnoli, *Zoroaster's Time and Homeland* (Naples: 1980), 222; and esp. Shenkar, "Rethinking Sasanian Iconoclasm," *Journal of the American Oriental Society* 135 (2015): 477–478. Shenkar might be going too far in his claim (p. 491) that "no real iconoclastic movement ever existed in Sasanian Zoroastrianism." See also van Bladel, *From Sasanian Mandaeans*, 109–110.

[54] See, for instance, Georgina Herrmann, "The Rock Reliefs of Sasanian Iran," in *Mesopotamia and Iran in the Parthian and Sasanian Periods: Rejection and Revival c. 238 BC–AD 652*, ed. J. Curtis (London: 2000), 35–46.

[55] Canepa, "Technologies of Memory," 576. The site also includes Hebrew graffiti, but these are from a much later date; see Bruno Overlaet, "Hidden in Plain Sight: The Hebrew Inscription on Ardashir I's Rock Relief at Naqsh-I Rustam," *Iranica Antiqua* 46 (2011): 331–340; and Theodore Kwasman, "Hebrew Graffiti on Ardashir I's Relief at Naqsh-i Rustam," *Iranica Antiqua* 47 (2012): 399–403.

[56] For coins and seals, see Rika Gyselen, "Note de glyptique sassanide: Quelques éléments d'iconographie religieuse," in *Contribution à l'histoire de l'Iran: mélanges offerts à Jean Perrot*, ed. François Vallat (Paris: 1990), 253–267. For a general overview, with specific references to imagery of deities on Sasanian coins, see Robert Göbl, "Sasanian Coins," in *The Seleucid, Parthian and Sasanian Periods*, vol. 3, bk. 1, *The Cambridge History of Iran*, ed. Ehsan Yarshater (Cambridge: 1983), 322–339, esp. 327–328. For a representative but by no means comprehensive list, see Prudence O. Harper, *Silver Vessels of the Sasanian Period: I Royal Imagery* (New York: 1981), 32–34; Jamsheed K. Choksy, "A Sasanian Monarch, his Queen, Crown Prince, and Deities: The Coinage of Wahram II," *American Journal of Numismastics* 2.1 (1989): 117–135; and Georgina Herrmann with Rosalind Howell, *Naqsh-i Rustam 5 and 8: Sasanian Reliefs attributed to Hormuzd II and Narseh* (Berlin: 1977). For Anāhīta on a seal, see Jacques Duchesne-Guillemin, "Art et religion sous les Sassanides," *Atti del Convegno Internazionale sul Tema: La Persia nel Medioevo* (Rome: 1971), 378 and plate III, fig. 3. For a useful survey of a single goddess on various objects, see Jenny Rose, "Three Queens, Two Wives, and a Goddess: Roles and Images of Women in Sasanian Iran," in *Women in the Medieval Islamic World: Power, Patronage, and Piety*, ed. Gavin R. G. Hambly (New York: 1998), 29–54. For a

bathhouses, Ohrmazd was on palace architecture and elite silverware. Still, the most common symbols of the Zoroastrian cult were fire, the fire altar, and the fire temple.

The rabbis appear not to have distinguished between Roman festivals that focused on idols and other iconic imagery and Persian festivals that did not; both were idolatrous. Both the Palestinian and Babylonian Talmuds include Persian festivals in their lists of idolatrous festivals. Jews were therefore instructed to avoid certain economic transactions and social interactions with Zoroastrians in proximity to festivals.[57] Some of the names of these Persian festivals are garbled and difficult to identify definitively, but others can be firmly established, such as Nōwrōz, on which fire worship was performed at a temple.[58]

Despite the prohibitions they imposed around Zoroastrian festivals, the rabbis elsewhere reluctantly admit that some Jews nevertheless participated in them. As discussed in Chapter 3, one talmudic passage alleged that Jews suffered religious interference in the Sasanian Empire as divine retribution for, among other things, those who "rejoice on their festivals (*yom ʾeidam*)."[59] This presumably refers to Jews who participated in Zoroastrian festivals in some form. Here we have some indication that not all Jews honored the boundaries articulated by the rabbis. Indeed, a few stories in the Babylonian Talmud depict rabbis distributing gifts to non-Jews on festival days, who may have been Zoroastrians. In one case,

helpful list of deities on Sasanian coins, see Shenkar, "Rethinking Sasanian Iconoclasm," 489n124.

57 b. ʿAbod. Zar. 11b. For more on these festivals, see de Jong, *Traditions of the Magi*, 367–383 and references there. See also the earlier study of Mary Boyce, "Iranian Festivals," in *The Seleucid, Parthian and Sasanian Periods*, vol. 3, bk. 2, *The Cambridge History of Iran*, ed. E. Yarshater (Cambridge: 1983), 792–815.

58 See David Oppenheim, "Die Namen der persischen und babylonischen Feste im Talmud," *Monatsschrift für Geschichte und Wissenschaft des Judentums* 7 (1854): 347–352; Alexander Kohut, "Les fêtes persanes et babyloniennes dans les Talmuds de Babylon et de Jerusalem," *Revue des Études Juives* 24 (1892): 256–271; Alexander Kohut, "The Talmudic Records of Persian and Babylonian Festivals Critically Illustrated," *The American Journal of Semitic Languages and Literatures* 14 (1898): 183–194; S. H. Taqizadeh, "The Iranian Festivals Adopted by the Christians and Condemned by the Jews," *Bulletin of the School of Oriental Studies* 10 (1940–1941): 632–639; Neusner, "How Much Iranian in Jewish Babylonia?" 185–186; Baruch Micah Bokser, "Talmudic Names of the Iranian Festivals," *Journal of the American Oriental Society* 95 (1975): 261–262; Gafni, "Babylonian Rabbinic Culture," 242–243; and the helpful survey in Mokhtarian, *Rabbis, Sorcerers, Kings, and Priests*, 65–66. These identifications are based partly on the parallel in y. ʿAbod. Zar. 1.3 (39c), such as *nōwrōz*.

59 b. Yeb. 63b.

Rava offers a gift (*qurbana*) to a Bar Sheshak, whose identity is not entirely clear, on his festival day (*yom'eido*), which he implausibly justifies by saying, "I know he does not worship idolatry."[60] In fact, as described in Chapter 2, gift giving itself was a central component of certain Zoroastrian festivals.[61] Some Jews, and even rabbis, may therefore have participated in the general ceremony of gift giving and conceptualized Zoroastrian festivals in a way that diminished or recast their religious connotations, viewing them instead as an opportunity for conviviality. Syriac Christian texts similarly attest to the participation of Christians in Zoroastrian feasts and festivals, and the attempt by ecclesiastical figures to check this trend.[62] While the rabbis were rather laconic about the thought worlds of Jews who "rejoiced on their festivals," we might heuristically think of them as akin to those Jews who adopted Zoroastrian imagery on their seals; both did not see Jewish identity as incompatible with at least some aspects of Zoroastrianism. Indeed, they may not have categorized them as Zoroastrian at all, drawing boundaries and definitions differently from the rabbis.

A similar tension between the attraction of aspects of Zoroastrianism for some Jews and the restrictions imposed on them by rabbinic regulation is found in a Talmudic discussion concerning Zoroastrianism:

[A] Rav Zutra b. Tuviya said that Rav said, ... "he who learns something (*davar*) from a magus is worthy of death ..."
[B] [Concerning] Magianism (*['a]mgushta*), [63] Rav and Shmuel [disagree]: One said [that it is classified as] sorcery (*ḥarshe*), the other said [that it is] blasphemy (*giddufe*).
[C] It may be concluded that it is Rav who maintains that it is blasphemy. For Rav Zutra b. Tuviya said that Rav said, "he who learns something from a magus is worthy of death." Now should you think that it is sorcery, surely it is written "you shall not learn to do [the abhorrent practices of those nations] (Deut. 18.9)," [which implies that] you may learn in order to understand and instruct. This proves it.[64]

60 b. 'Abod. Zar. 65a. Geoffrey Herman, "Talmud in Its Babylonian Context," 79–96 seeks to situate this story in a Manichaean context, but see Secunda, "Babylonian Judaism and Zoroastrianism."

61 Chapter 2, pp. 106–107. 62 Payne, *State of Mixture*, 117–122.

63 In MS Vatican 108 the word is slightly modified and can be vocalized to mean "the magi" in the plural. Cf. Secunda, *Iranian Talmud*, 186–187n35.

64 b. Shab. 75a. Text according to MS Oxford Opp. Add., fol. 23. Translation following Secunda, *Iranian Talmud*, 71.

The discussion opens with a statement in the name of Rav, one of the earliest Babylonian rabbis, declaring that one who studies with a magus – that is, a Zoroastrian priest – is deserving of death. This statement is immediately followed by a debate between Rav and Shmuel that focuses not on study with a Zoroastrian teacher, but on how to classify the transgression of "magianism," using an abstract form of the word otherwise unattested in the Babylonian Talmud. One rabbi categorizes it as blasphemy and the other as sorcery.

Shai Secunda suggests that this debate about the nature of "magianism" (B) should be removed from its current location and read separately from the opening statement of Rav (A) and the anonymous concluding paragraph (C).[65] Reading Section B in isolation, he notes that one rabbinic opinion considers Zoroastrianism to be a form of blasphemy; for example, "a sacrilegious speech act," and the same might be said for the rabbi who considers magianism to constitute a kind of sorcery. He therefore concludes that the rabbis are not debating the nature of "Zoroastrianism" as a whole, but rather something ritually recited, namely Zoroastrian "sacred texts," particularly the Avesta.[66] In Section B, Rav and Shmuel are therefore more narrowly debating "the legal status of this Zoroastrian ritual in rabbinic jurisprudence."[67]

While the textual unit is undoubtedly the product of editing, there is no reason to isolate the debate in Section B from Rav's initial pronouncement in Section A.[68] If anything, *both* Sections B and C can be considered later editorial attempts to make sense of Rav's severe ruling in Section A. In context, the two rabbis in Section B are debating the transgression related to studying "magianism" itself and not a particular – and unidentified – Zoroastrian ritual; after all, "magianism" is also the abstract noun for

65 See discussion in Secunda, *Iranian Talmud*, 43–44 and 70–75.

66 Secunda, *Iranian Talmud*, 44, 71. In this, Secunda generally follows the early medieval explanation of this passage, found in Benjamin M. Lewin, *Oṣar ha-Geonim: Teshuvot geone Bavel u-ferusheihem ʿal pi seder ha-Talmud*, 13 vols. (Haifa: 1928–1943), 2.34, which argues that the passage refers to the Zoroastrian practice to mumble during a meal, given a prohibition against outright speech. Secunda makes this connection in his "Studying with a Magus/Like Giving a Tongue to a Wolf," *Bulletin of the Asia Institute* 19 (2005): 152. On this practice, see Shaul Shaked, "No Talking during a Meal!" 208–234; and Geoffrey Herman, "On Table Etiquette," 175–182.

67 Secunda, *Iranian Talmud*, 72.

68 On this editorial template, see Noah Bickart, *Tistayem: An Investigation into the Scholastic Culture of the Bavli* (PhD diss., Jewish Theological Seminary of America, 2015).

Zoroastrianism in Syriac sources.[69] If "magianism" in this passage refers to Zoroastrianism, the textual progression is quite logical: After declaring study with a magus to be worthy of death (A), the next section (B) seeks to understand under what classification of transgression the mere study of magianism could merit capital punishment, according to Rav. It compares the study of magianism with two other sins related to study – blasphemy and sorcery – and concludes in the final section (C) that Rav must view magianism as a type of blasphemy to believe its study warranted the death penalty.[70]

The different proposed classification of the study of magianism as either blasphemy or sorcery are highly significant under rabbinic jurisprudence. Elsewhere in the Talmud, blasphemy is explicitly understood by some rabbis to be a form of idolatry. By extension, if Zoroastrianism is a form of blasphemy, then it is also idolatry. As idolatry, the study of Zoroastrianism is prohibited under the express provision of Deut. 18.9.[71] Thus, by linking Zoroastrianism to blasphemy, and thereby to idolatry, the *study* of Zoroastrianism, not just its *practice*, is strictly prohibited. Shmuel, by contrast, treats Zoroastrianism as sorcery, not blasphemy; as a *practice*, sorcery is prohibited, but its study is not prohibited.[72] In treating Zoroastrianism as sorcery, Shmuel (or the composer of this passage) may have been invoking an ancient association between the two; indeed, in Greek, as eventually in English, the word for "magic" derives from the word for Zoroastrian priests, "magus," an association that was pervasive throughout the ancient world.[73]

Putting aside this debate's jurisprudential nuances, the fact that it is recorded at all suggests that the rabbis were indeed concerned with Jews engaging in some form of study of Zoroastrianism.[74] A similar concern is expressed in Zoroastrian and Syriac Christian sources, albeit for different reasons. The *Hērbedestān*, a work dedicated to the study and transmission of Zoroastrian knowledge, discusses the conditions under which one may teach Zoroastrianism to "a student who sacrifices to the demons," which is glossed in the Sasanian-era Middle Persian commentary as

69 See Butts and Gross, *History of the "Slave of Christ,"* 39–40n120, 89; and A. V. Williams, "Zoroastrians and Christians in Sasanian Iran," 51.

70 For the prohibition against studying magic to perform it, see b. Sanh. 68a; and discussion in Gideon Bohak, *Ancient Jewish Magic: A History* (New York: 2012), 359–386.

71 y. Sanh. 7.9 (25b); b. Ker. 7b.

72 Bohak, *Ancient Jewish Magic*, 359–386.

73 In general, see de Jong, *Traditions of the Magi*; and Fritz Graf, *Magic in the Ancient World*, trans. Franklin Philip (Cambridge: 1997), 20–29.

74 Compare with Secunda, "Studying with a Magus," 151–152.

"non-Iranians (*anērān*)."[75] The text states with some ambivalence that a teacher in financial straits may instruct a non-Iranian, but with the warning that this is akin to giving "a tongue to the wolf" and providing ammunition for enemies of Zoroastrianism.[76] The choice of "wolf" is significant because in Zoroastrian cosmology, the wolf is one of the evil class of creatures (*xrafstar*) created by Ahriman.[77] This source is the mirror image of the discussion in the Babylonian Talmud; while acknowledging the possibility of non-Iranian study of Zoroastrian tradition, it attempts to curtail its practice, this time from the perspective of Zoroastrians, and therefore from the vantage point of the teacher rather than the student.

That non-Iranians at times sought to study Zoroastrianism – and the reasons they might do so – is clear from other sources as well. For instance, the ninth-century collection of saint biographies produced by Ishoʿdnaḥ of Basra tells the tale of the Sasanian-era George of Merv, who was born to wealthy Christians. His parents sent their son to be trained "in the doctrines of the Persians, like the elites of the world."[78] Similarly, the elites in the Lakhmid Arab capital of al-Ḥīra, who were themselves Christians, sent their children to board with Iranian elites, who would train them in Iranian language and traditions.[79] Jews may also have learned Zoroastrian traditions to prepare to participate in Sasanian elite life.

The debate between Rav and Shmuel therefore does not challenge the rabbinic classification of Zoroastrian practices like festivals as constituting idolatry; indeed, it enhances and extends certain prohibitions to the *study* of Zoroastrianism. And yet, the same rabbinic texts that erect

[75] *Hērbedestān* 19.1. For text, see Kotwal and Kreyenbroek, *Herbedestan and Nerangestan*, 1.78–81; Helmut Humbach and Josef Elfenbein. *Erbedestan: An Avest-Pahlavi Text* (Munich: 1990), 118–123; and Prods Oktor Skjærvø, "'OL' News: ODs and Ends," in *Exegisti Monumenta: Festschrift in Honour of Nicholas Sims-Williams*, ed. W. Sundermann, Almut Hintze, and François de Blois (Wiesbaden: 2009), 484–491. For discussion, see esp. Secunda, "Studying with a Magus," 155; and Payne, *State of Mixture*, 70. For the date of the Middle Persian commentary, see Alberto Cantera, *Studien zur Pahlavi-Übersetzung der Avesta* (Wiesbaden: 2004), 164–239.

[76] A similar law that incorporates a prohibition on teaching a heretic or an "evil person" is found in Dēnkard 4, on which see Shaked, *Wisdom of the Sasanian Sages*, 156.

[77] Mahnaz Moazami, "Evil Animals in the Zoroastrian Religion," *History of Religions* 44 (2005): 300–317.

[78] French translation in J. B. Chabot, *Le livre de la chasteté composé par Jésusdenah, Évêque de Baçrah, publié et traduit* (Rome: 1896), 245.

[79] Isabel Toral-Niehoff, "Late Antique Iran and the Arabs: The Case of al-Hira," *Journal of Persianate Studies* 6 (2013): 120–122.

barriers between Jews and the study of Zoroastrianism also suggest that at least some Jews might have been compelled to pursue such knowledge. Indeed, the rabbis themselves occasionally exhibit detailed knowledge of Zoroastrianism. In one fascinating textual parallel already noted in the mid-nineteenth century, the Talmud reproduces a typology of different fires that appears to derive from Zoroastrian sources.[80] Knowledge of Zoroastrianism is on display in a rabbinic anecdote in which a rabbi debates, and unsurprisingly bests, a magus.[81] Other suggestions of the influence of Zoroastrian ideas on the rabbis have been furnished, some more plausibly than others.[82] Outside of rabbinic literature and alongside the Jewish seals discussed above, the Iranian theophoric names of clients on Jewish Babylonian Aramaic bowls, in some cases undoubtedly belonging to Jews, further suggest at least some basic familiarity with Zoroastrian cosmology and traditions.[83] The incantations on the bowls attest some knowledge of Zoroastrian traditions.[84] The prohibitions against study with Zoroastrians, in addition to the various prohibitions related to business and personal interactions around Zoroastrian festivals, seek to dissuade Jews from participating in Zoroastrian festivals and studying Zoroastrian traditions, precisely because it seems some Jews were doing so.

80 b. Yom. 21b. See James Darmesteter, "Les six feux dans le Talmud et dans le Bundehesh," *Revue des Études Juives* 1 (1880): 186–196; Geoffrey Herman, "Fire Typologies in Zoroastrianism and in the Babylonian Talmud: A Methodological Consideration," in *Iran, Israel, and the Jews: Symbiosis and Conflict from the Achaemenids to the Islamic Republic*, ed. Aaron Koller and Daniel Tsadik (Eugene, OR: 2019), 108–120. For more on Zoroastrian discussions of fire, see Dan Shapira, "Pahlavi Fire, Bundahishn 18," *ARAM* 26 (2014): 129–151.

81 b. Sanh. 39a. For discussion, see Secunda, *Iranian Talmud*, 128–133. On religious debates in the Sasanian Empire, see Richard Payne, "Les polémiques syro-orientales contre le Zoroastrisme et leur contexte politique," in *Les controverses religieuses en syriaque*, ed. Flavia Ruani (Paris: 2017), 1–22. On Syriac texts that polemicize against Zoroastrian learning, see Walker, *Legend of Mar Qardagh*, and Kiperwasser and Ruzer, "To Convert a Persian and Teach Him the Holy Scriptures," 91–127.

82 See review in Secunda, "Babylonian Judaism and Zoroastrianism." Herman, "Religious Transformation between East and West," 261–282, argues that the relative emphasis on the ritual lighting of fire on Hannukah is greater in the Babylonian Talmud and is a product of Zoroastrian influence, but the festival was associated with fire long before this.

83 Intriguingly, Mandaic texts suggest an intimate connection between Jews and Zoroastrians. See Shapira, "Manichaeans (Marmanaiia), Zoroastrians (Iazuqaiia), Jews, Christians, and Other Heretics," 243–280.

84 Shaul Shaked, "Bagdana, King of the Demons, and Other Iranian Terms in Babylonian Aramaic Magic," *Acta Iranica* 25 (1985): 511–525; Shaked, "Jesus in the Magic Bowls," 309–319.

SELLING WOOD TO THE FIRE TEMPLE

Despite rabbinic restrictions on Zoroastrian festivals and study, several rabbinic texts display a strikingly permissive stance toward the Zoroastrian cult itself.

Rav Ashi owned a forest, which he sold to a fire temple.

Said Ravina to Rav Ashi, "But there is [the biblical injunction]. 'You shall not put a stumbling-block before the blind (Lev. 19.14)!'"
He replied, "Most wood is used for heating."[85]

Rav Ashi reportedly sells his forest to a fire temple (*be nura*). His interlocuter Ravina is apparently aware that the sale of wood to a fire temple appears to indirectly enable idolatry. He therefore challenges Rav Ashi, saying that his sale of wood caused Zoroastrians to "stumble" and sin, that is, by worshipping idolatry. For his part, Rav Ashi contends that wood is most commonly used for heating and so is not a "stumbling block" per se; this legal presumption, he claims, allows him to ignore the fact that in this particular case, the wood will almost certainly be used for cultic purposes.

Rav Ashi's presumption that wood is primarily used for heating is drawn from another Babylonian rabbinic discussion, but one entirely unrelated to fire worship or idolatry.[86] There, a highly technical legal debate concludes that wood is not classified as "food" because it is not harvested for immediate consumption in most cases, but rather stored for heating at a later date. Yet, in the context of fire temples, such a presumption appears comical; the wood is, of course, used to stoke the idolatrous

[85] b. Ned. 62b. See also the story of Ifra Hormiz in b. B. Bat. 10b–11a.

[86] The principle is found in both b. B. Qam. 101b–102a and Beṣ. 33a. Yaakov Elman, "Shopping in Ctesiphon: A Lesson in Sasanian Commercial Practice," in *The Archaeology and Material Culture of the Babylonian Talmud*, ed. Markham J. Geller (Leiden: 2015), 242, refers only to b. B. Qam. 101b–102a, which may have led him to believe that the principle means heating in general, whereas in b. Beṣ. 33a it clearly means burning. Tellingly, Rav Ashi's formulation differs slightly from the other appearances of this principle, as the latter says undesignated wood (*stam 'ezim*), whereas he says most wood (*rov 'eiṣim*). Accordingly, Rav Ashi acknowledges that some wood *will* be used for idolatrous purposes, itself a problem, given that the laws of nullification do not apply in the case of idolatry. See m. 'Abod. Zar. 5.8–9. Neusner, *History of the Jews*, 5.24 says that "it is difficult to suppose Rav Ashi was ignorant of the real use to which his wood probably would be put. He provided not a reason but an excuse for his action ..." Neusner also connects this source to b. 'Abod. Zar. 16a cited below, and from this concludes that "the two stories together suggest he was not averse to cooperating with the Iranian government and church."

fire, as Ravina protests.[87] Why, then, did Rav Ashi adopt such a permissive stance regarding commercial exchange with fire temples?

GIFTS TO THE FIRE TEMPLE

A second source appears in the context of a weighty talmudic discussion that establishes the principle that under coercion and threat of death, a Jew should violate virtually all commandments save the three cardinal sins of forbidden relations, idolatry, and murder. This principle is then qualified: If coerced in public, before onlookers, one must die before transgressing *any* commandment, regardless of its relative severity.[88] This principle is considered so foundational that the anonymous editors of the passage declare it to be "obvious." Up to this point, the discussion in the Babylonian Talmud closely parallels a similar one in the Palestinian Talmud.[89] However, the Babylonian Talmud proceeds to challenge this "obvious" principle in the following way:

> But was [the transgression of] Esther public?
>
> Abaye said, "Esther was [like] the soil of the earth."
> Rava said, "[When the persecutors demand the sin for] their personal benefit, it is different [that is, a Jew may transgress the divine commandment rather than die]. For if you do not say this, how do we give these *qawāqī* and *dīmōnīqī* to the fire [temple]? But [conclude from this that] their personal pleasure is different; so too here [in Esther's case], their pleasure is different."

The story of Queen Esther is adduced to contradict the principle that when in public, one must die rather than transgress even a minor

[87] The basic procedure of the fire cult was widely known. See, for instance, the second-century Greek geography, Pausanias; see W. H. S. Jones and H. A. Ormerof, ed. and trans., *Pausanias: Description of Greece*, vol. 2, Loeb Classical Library 188 (Cambridge: 1918), 5.27.5–6. Intriguingly, Rav Ashi's forest appears in another context (b. M. Qaṭ. 12b), in which he once again engages in questionable behavior. There, he wishes to cut a part of his tree on a Jewish festival, ruling permissively against the injunctions of earlier rabbis. Yet, he persists in his behavior despite opposition. The anecdote concludes that "The hatchet then slipped, threatening to cut off his leg. He then abandoned his task and came again [on another, nonfestival, day]." Rav Ashi retracts his permissive position regarding a Jewish festival, but not when it involves commerce with a fire temple itself. On Rav Ashi's forest, see Aharon Oppenheimer, "Relations between Jews and Gentiles in the Localities of Talmudic Babylonia," *Proceedings of the World Congress of Jewish Studies* (1985): 33. Other rabbis owned forests as well (b. B. Meṣ. 107b).

[88] b. Sanh. 74b. [89] y. Sheb. 4.2 (35a) = y. Sanh. 3.6 (21b).

commandment. The text does not explicitly identify Esther's transgression, but the unstated implication is that it was her cohabitation with the non-Jewish Persian King Ahasuerus, not one of the three cardinal sins, but one performed publicly.[90] If even noncardinal sins must not be committed in public, then how could Esther do so without resisting, even dying?

Abaye justifies Esther's conduct by arguing that she was "merely soil" (קרקע עולם, *qarqaʿ ʿolam*), by which he seems to mean that she was entirely passive and therefore did not effectively transgress any law.[91] The sex act was something done *to* Esther, not *by* her. Thus, Abaye accepts the presumptive legal premise, that one must die rather than commit even a minor sin publicly, but maintains that it is inapplicable to Esther's case, because there simply was no transgression at all.

Rava offers a different explanation for Esther's actions, one that significantly limits the scope of the presumptive legal premise: a Jew must not die, even if coerced to sin publicly, if the coercer is seeking to personally benefit from the transgression. Death is only required when the coercer is seeking to denigrate Jews through the public flaunting of Jewish law. In the case of Esther, King Ahasuerus was not seeking to denigrate Jews nor Jewish practice; indeed, according to the book of Esther, he did not even know that Esther was Jewish until after they had wed. Rather, the king desired Esther for his personal pleasure, and therefore Esther could commit a sin even in public.

Rava defends his position in a rather surprising way. Instead of offering a biblical or rabbinic precedent, he refers to a contemporary practice whose permissibility he takes for granted: giving *qawāqī* and *dīmōnīqī* to fire temples.[92] These terms refer to two kinds of utensils used

90 Christiane Tzuberi "Rescue from Transgression through Death; Rescue from Death through Transgression," in *Rabbinic Traditions between Palestine and Babylonia*, ed. Ronit Nikolsky and Tal Ilan (Leiden: 2014), 137 and 137n13, notes how difficult it is to identify the "sin" in this passage. See also Aryeh Cohen, "Towards an Erotics of Martyrdom," *The Journal of Jewish Thought and Philosophy* 7 (1997): 236–237. The earliest Babylonian rabbinic work to comment on this passage (*She'iltot* 44, ed. Mirsky, 3.47) identifies the sin as intercourse. For Josephus' earlier attempt to deal with Esther's marriage to Ahasuerus, see Louis Feldman, *Studies in Josephus' Rewritten Bible* (Leiden: 1998), 497–512.

91 C. F. Cohen, "Towards an Erotics of Martyrdom," 238–242.

92 The rhetorical presumption that this behavior is permitted and that a justification is needed is rare in rabbinic literature. For more on this rhetorical posture, see Beth Berkowitz, "Reconsidering the Book and the Sword: A Rhetoric of Passivity in Rabbinic Hermeneutics," in *Violence, Scripture, and Textual Practices in Early Judaism and Christianity*, ed. Raʿanan Boustan, Alex Jassen and Calvin Roetzel (Leiden: 2010),

for fire worship.[93] The word *qawāqī* comes from the Greek καυκίον, καῦκος, a cup or vessel, also attested in Syriac and Mandaic.[94] The *dīmōnīqī* derives from Middle Persian *damēnag*, referring to a fan or bellows used to stoke the flames.[95] That is, Rava is describing the donation by Jews of implements of fire worship to fire temples.[96]

Rava's position is clearly adopted post facto, seeking to justify the preexisting practice of the donation of these implements to fire temples, a practice he acknowledges appears to constitute a public transgression and therefore to demand death. His justification for this radical practice is that these contributions, although coerced at some level, were not part of a concerted effort to publicly denigrate Jewish law. Rather, they were intended solely to provide an economic benefit to the fire temples and to Zoroastrians. In effect, Rava argues that just as Esther could engage in a prohibited sex act under certain circumstances, so too could Jews in his period facilitate fire temples. He therefore limits the scope of the laws of Jewish martyrdom in order to justify the preexisting practice of donating implements to fire temples.

The reception history of this passage reflects the unease with which it was greeted by later scribes, transmitters, and commentators. The earliest witnesses to the Talmud, such as the Geonic-era *She'iltot* and *Halakhot Gedolot*, make explicit that the recipients of the implements are in fact none other than "the fire" or the "house/temple of fire."[97] The *She'iltot* also explicitly acknowledges that these implements are used for idolatry, while *Halakhot Gedolot* goes so far as to say that Rava's opinion allows

145–173; and Christine Hayes' use of the "rhetoric of concealment" in her *What's Divine about Divine Law? Early Perspectives* (Princeton: 2015).

93 Rosenthal, "Talmudica Iranica," 41, 74–75n29–30, which includes discussion of manuscript variants and medieval commentators. See also Brody, "Zoroastrian Themes," 179–186.

94 Indeed, a Mandaic text mentions a vessel (*qāwaqa*) for the fire in a ritual context. See E. S. Drower, *The Canonical Prayerbook of the Mandaeans* (Leiden: 1959), 29. On a Mandaic passage describing Zoroastrian ritual in some depth, see Shapira, "Manichaeans (Marmanaiia), Zoroastrians (Iazuqaiia), Jews, Christians, and Other Heretics," 248–253. The word also appears in y. ʿAbod. Zar. 3.3 (42d).

95 Brody, "Judaism in the Sasanian Empire," 57, and again in Brody, "Zoroastrian Themes," 184, suggests that the term refers to a type of clay pan used to hold fire, relying on Mary Boyce's fieldwork in the heavily Zoroastrian village of Sharifabad-e Yazd, in Iran, in her *A Persian Stronghold of Zoroastrianism* (Oxford: 1977), 85. However, it is problematic to rely on modern rituals to explain ancient ones.

96 Rosenthal, "Talmudica Iranica," 81n99.

97 *She'iltot* 44 (ed. Mirsky, 3:47–48); *Halakhot Gedolot* 54, Hilkhot Avodah Zarah (ed. Hildesheimer, 575). See also MS Munich 95.

for Jews to even commit idolatry under duress if it is for the personal benefit of the idolator! Rava's opinion appears, however, to have scandalized later scribes and interpreters. Several manuscripts amend the recipients of the ritual accoutrements to the generic pronoun "them," so as not to explicitly name fire temples. This amended version was adopted in the standard printed edition of the Talmud still in use today.[98] Later interpreters likewise sought to downplay the scope and implications of Rava's ruling.[99] To them, Rava's permissive approach was incongruous with the rest of this critical legal discussion establishing the core principles of Jewish martyrdom.[100]

Indeed, an anonymous discussion immediately following Rava's opinion further seeks to justify it as nothing more than rabbinic law as usual. It attributes to Rava a distinction between the case of a gentile who orders a Jew to violate the Sabbath by cutting grass to feed the gentile's cattle – which is permitted because the act is intended to benefit the gentile economically – and the case of a gentile who orders grass to be cut and then thrown into the sea – which is prohibited because the gentile derives no economic benefit from the violation. In the second case, it is presumed that the coercer intends to publicly denigrate Jewish law. Yet while the consideration of personal benefit in the case of the Sabbath appears reasonable given that non-Jews do not recognize its importance, it is far more dubious to introduce it in the case of idolatry, which may always be said to serve the personal benefit of idolators. There is in fact a long chain of rabbinic and earlier Jewish precedents permitting the violation of the Sabbath in order to preserve one's life.[101] This permissive stance,

[98] MS Yad HaRav Herzog; MS Karlsruhe Reuchlin 2; and the printed editions of Venice, Vilna, and Berko.

[99] Rosenthal, "Talmudica Iranica," 75n31.

[100] Some medieval commentators argued that according to Rava, even the other two foundational sins – murder and forbidden relations – do not require martyrdom if performed for the benefit of the coercer. Later interpreters, however, distance themselves from this position. For a list of several early commentaries on the passage, see Rosenthal, "Talmudica Iranica," 75n31.

[101] The permission to transgress the Sabbath rather than die is found in the second temple period through to tannaitic literature. See Moshe David Herr, "On the Problem of the Laws of War on the Sabbath in the Second Temple Period and the Mishnaic and Talmudic Period," [in Hebrew] *Tarbiẓ* 30 (1961): 242–256, 341–356; and Menahem Kister, "Plucking Grain on the Sabbath and the Christian-Jewish Polemic," *Meḥqere Yerushalayim beMaḥshevet Yisrael* 3 (1983/1984): 349–366. Interestingly, in some versions of the story of the famous Hasmonean-era mother and her seven sons, the youngest son chooses death over even the appearance of idolatry, on which see Shaye Cohen, "The Name of the Ruse: The Toss of a Ring to Save Life and Honor," in *'Follow*

however, is unprecedented in the case of even the facilitation of idolatry. Indeed, the example of the Sabbath cited by the anonymous editor has a parallel in the Palestinian Talmud, but no parallel exists for Rava's permissive stance regarding idolatry.[102] Whether or not the case of violating the Sabbath and facilitating idolatry are equivalent, Rava's own position stems not from earlier precedent but from the need to justify a contemporary practice. We must understand the circumstances of this preexisting practice, and why Rava attempts to accommodate, rather than proscribe, the contribution of implements to fire temples.

The precise circumstances under which Jews contributed implements to fire temples remains uncertain. The implication of the context of the talmudic discussion is that these gifts were made under coercion, but only for the personal benefit of Zoroastrians. This interpretation has been echoed by scholars who argue that the coercion of donations to fire temples was "motivated by extreme reverence for fire, rather than by any desire to involve Jews in Zoroastrian ritual to persecute them, or even to inconvenience them."[103] In other words, the coerced contributions provided a "personal benefit" in that they helped the temple worshipers satisfy their extreme reverence for fire, with little heed to what such contributions would have meant to Jews.

These interpretations, however, may too readily accept Rava's presentation of the circumstances. Ample evidence suggests that there would have almost certainly have been religious symbolism in the coercion of non-Zoroastrians to contribute to the Zoroastrian cult. The Sasanian king Peroz (r. 459–484) reportedly forced Christians to provide wood for fire temples, a requirement that was later abolished under a peace treaty with the emperor Leo.[104] According to the Armenian historian

the Wise': Studies in Jewish History and Culture in Honor of Lee Levine, ed. Zeev Weiss, Oded Irshai, Jodi Magness, and Seth Schwartz (Winona Lake, IN: 2010), 25–36.

102 y. Sheb. 4.2 (35a–b) and Sanh. 3.6, 21b. For a full discussion see Gray, "Contribution to the Study of Martyrdom," 242–272.

103 Brody, "Judaism in the Sasanian Empire," 58. See also Jacob Levy, *Neuhebräisches und chaldäisches wörterbuch über die Talmudim und Midraschim* (Leipzig: 1889), 4.273, followed by Neusner, *History of the Jews*, 4.51.

104 E. Gismondi, ed., *Maris, Amri, et Salibae: De Patriarchis Nestorianorum Commentaria II: Maris textus arabicus et versio Latina* (Rome: 1899), 41 lines 13ff; with Stephen Gerö, *Barsauma of Nisibis and Persian Christianity in the Fifth Century* (Louvain: 1981), 19n30. Intriguingly, a Geonic responsum glosses *qawāqī* as wood tax extracted for fire temples; see Avraham Harkavy, *Zikhron Kamah Geonim: uve-Yiḥud Rav Sherira ve-Rav Hai beno veha-Rav R. Yiṣḥaq Alfasi* (Berlin: 1887), 144 (no. 297; see also no. 298 for a Geonic identification of *dīmōnīqī*).

Moses Khorenats'i, Ardashir I (r. 224–241) invaded Armenia and ordered that the conquered Armenians maintain the "fire of Ormizd."[105] Similar compulsion around the fire cult in Armenia is also reported for the later period of Yazdgird II (r. 438–457).[106] As discussed in Chapter 3, a medieval Persian historian reports that during the Sasanian period, the Jews of Isfahan killed two magi, for which their children were forcibly conscripted as slaves to the local fire temple.[107] These episodes are more than simple attempts to benefit and enrich the cult; they purposefully compel non-Zoroastrians to acknowledge Zoroastrian dominance. They are consistent with other Zoroastrian texts from the period, such as Kerdir's inscription also discussed in Chapter 3. If this is the true background, Rava downplays and neutralizes the symbolism of coerced Jewish contribution to fire worship in order to permit it.

It is worth exploring an alternative setting for these contributions to fire temples. Though the legal context in which Rava invokes and justifies contributions to fire temples concerns coercion, the practice itself may have been entirely voluntary on the part of Jews. Jewish contributions to non-Jewish institutions in Mesopotamia would not be unique to this circumstance. According to the sixth-century Syriac Christian author John of Ephesus, Jews in Amida (modern Diyarbakir) maintained close ties with their Christian neighbors; Christians conducted regular financial exchanges with local Jews who in turn "used to pay many contributions to the members of the church."[108] This rendered the members of the church "their supporters," inciting the recluse Sergius and his followers, visitors who disapproved of the close social ties between Jews and Christians they observe, to destroy the local synagogue. Perhaps behind Rava's description lies a local practice whereby some Jews willingly

105 Thomson, *Moses Khorenats'i*, 221. Moses' *floruit* is disputed. See Thomson, *Moses Khorenats'i*, 1–6.

106 See Russell, *Zoroastrianism in Armenia*, 491–494. The coerced donation of vessels might be contextualized with reports in the Talmud about the coerced confiscation of fire by magi, discussed in Chapter 3 (e.g., b. Giṭ. 16b–17a and Shab. 45a). See Brody, "Zoroastrian Themes," 182–183. For an interesting report about adopting fire worship to curry favor with the magi, see Dirk Kruisheer, "Theodore bar Koni's *Ketābā d-'Eskolyon* as a Source for the Study of Early Mandaeism," *Jaarbericht Ex Oriente Lux* 33 (1993–1994): 164.

107 Daudpota, *Annals of Ḥamza Al-Iṣfahānī*, 40. See discussion in Chapter 3.

108 John of Ephesus, *Lives of the Eastern Saints* (ed. and trans. E. W. Brooks), 90–91. On this episode, see Fergus Millar, "A Rural Jewish Community in Late Roman Mesopotamia, and the Question of a "Split" Jewish Diaspora," *Journal for the Study of Judaism* 42 (2011): 356–361.

contributed implements to fire temples out of a sense of amity, a practice which Rava legitimizes by claiming it is coerced.

Regardless of the precise motivation for this practice, what is clear is that Rava's stance in the Talmud is a legal strategy specifically tailored to accommodate Jewish contributions to fire temples and represents a significant extension of – if not a wholesale departure from – longstanding rabbinic law. The fact that this discussion centers around Esther is no coincidence; after all, she cohabited with the Persian king Ahasuerus. She is therefore an apt paradigm for considering a kind of Jewish accommodation to Persian rule in the rabbis' own time, one which tolerated certain practices that, at first blush, appeared inconsistent with rabbinic ideals.[109]

Together, these two Talmudic sources show that despite the rabbinic classification of Zoroastrian festivals and even study as idolatry, some rabbis stretched existing legal presumptions to accommodate different kinds of transactions with fire temples, in part by denuding them of their cultic associations. Why did these Babylonian rabbis adopt such unprecedented and permissive dispensations for Jewish interactions with fire temples, and what are we to make of their seemingly flimsy legal justifications?

SYRIAC CHRISTIANS AND FIRE TEMPLES

The permissive stance of these rabbis is even more remarkable when contrasted with the uncompromisingly *adversarial* approach toward the fire cult featured in several near-contemporary Syriac Christian martyr acts. Where the Babylonian rabbis justified forms of accommodation, these Christian texts valorize those who demolished fire temples and were martyred as a result.[110]

In the *Martyrdom of Narsai the Ascetic*, a sick Zoroastrian is healed and converted to Christianity, and donates land for the construction of a

[109] For other examples of the book of Esther serving as a template for Jews contemplating life under the Sasanians, see b. Ket. 61a–b, with Alyssa Gray, "Redaction and Meaning in *b. A. Z. 10a–11a*," in *Creation and Composition: The Contribution of the Bavli Redactors (Stammaim) to the Aggada*, ed. Jeffrey Rubenstein (Tübingen: 2005), 67; and de Jong, "Zoroastrian Religious Polemics," 57.

[110] I do not here take a stance on the question of the historicity of these accounts or on the purported periods of violence that ensued. See van Rompay, "Impetuous Martyrs," 363–375; Herman, "The Last Years of Yazdgird I and the Christians," 67–90; and Gross, "Being Roman in the Sasanian Empire."

church.[111] Alarmed by the growing phenomenon of conversions of Zoroastrians to Christianity, the Zoroastrian authorities compel the donor to renounce his conversion and rescind his donation of the land to the church, building a fire temple in its stead. A Christian named Narsai, unaware of the donor's change of heart, comes to the building expecting to find a church. When he instead discovers a fire temple occupying the site, he proceeds to remove all its cultic accoutrements:

> "He extinguished it [the fire on the altar] and took out the bricks of the brazier and the magian vessels and he disposed of them outside. And he assembled and fixed the church, and he dwelled within it."[112]

Among the activities attributed to him, Narsai removes "the magian vessels."[113] To Narsai, cultic vessels like these had to be removed from a church. Compare his stance with Rava's, who justifies *donating* vessels to a fire temple. When ordered to restore the fire temple or face death, Narsai proudly opts for martyrdom. Rava might argue that restoring a fire temple is merely of practical benefit to the Zoroastrians, and a Jew is therefore *prohibited* from opting for martyrdom in this case. The contrast could not be more striking.

In the *Martyrdom of 'Abda*, Christian antagonism toward fire temples reaches a higher pitch.[114] Here, the future martyr Hosea unprovokedly destroys a fire temple. When interrogated by the king himself, Hosea admits to the charge, saying: "I did destroy the building and extinguished

[111] For the Syriac of the *Martyrdom of Narsai*, see Bedjan, *Acta martyrum et sanctorum*, 4.170–180. Whether this story and the one that follows are historical is not crucial to my argument. Herman, "Last Years of Yazdgird I and the Christians," 88–89, argues that these stories were written in the Roman Near East and do not reflect real historical events. By contrast, Payne, *State of Mixture*, 48, treats them as historical. Herman, "Last Years of Yazdgird I and the Christians," 88–89, also argues that the account of Narsai is a "little short of a closely argued apology and cautionary tale for something that should never have happened, but that occurred through a misunderstanding." However, I do not see any basis for this evaluation (see similarly Payne, 48).

[112] Bedjan, *Acta martyrum et sanctorum*, 4.173.3.

[113] ܡܐܢܝ̈ܗܘܢ ܕܡܓܘܫܐ; Bedjan, *Acta martyrum et sanctorum*, 4.173.3. r

[114] For 'Abda, the incomplete Syriac text appears in Bedjan, 4.250–253. For a discussion of 'Abda with French translation of the Syriac, see F. Jullien, "La passion syriaque de Mār 'Abdā: quelques relations entre chrétiens et mazdéens" in *Rabban l'Olmyn: Florilège offert à Philippe Gignoux pour son 80e anniversaire*, ed. Rika Gyselen, C. Jullien, and F. Jullien (Leuven: 2011), 195–205. For an English translation and discussion of both texts, see Herman, *Persian Martyr Acts under Yazdgird I*. Both 'Abda and Narsai are discussed by van Rompay, "Impetuous Martyrs?" 363–375 (who discusses surviving versions in other languages); and Herman, "The Last Years of Yazdgird I and the Christians," 67–90.

the fire, because it is not a house of God, and fire is not the daughter of God . . . It is generated from dry wood." Rav Ashi might have argued that this dry wood was mostly used for heating, not worship.

Lastly, in *The History of Mar Qardagh*, the eponymous protagonist transforms from Zoroastrian elite and Sasanian general to zealous Christian martyr. Before his conversion, Mar Qardagh's patrimony includes fire temples, but after his conversion, he promises to "tear down the fire temples and build martyr shrines," to "overturn the fire altars" and to "establish holy altars in their places." He therefore "ordered the demolition of the fire temples that had been built by his parents, and he made them into holy temples for the Highest One, and he tore down the fire altars in which the fire was carried in procession by the impious magi and set up shining altars to Christ."[115] Mar Qardagh's conversion from Persian general to Christian warrior is mirrored in his transformation of fire temples to churches and monasteries.[116] To him, church and fire temples were incompatible – not so for Rava and Rav Ashi.

Regardless of the historicity of these stories, they exemplify and promote attitudes toward fire temples that differ markedly from those found in these talmudic stories. It is unlikely that either these few talmudic discussions or hagiographical Christian texts are representative of the practices and ideologies of all Jews or Christians. But the juxtaposition of these two collections highlights the particular approach some rabbis embraced and those they eschewed.

FIRE TEMPLES IN SASANIAN SOCIETY

Why, then, did some Babylonian rabbis adopt so permissive a stance with respect to Zoroastrian fire temples, and why did some Syriac Christians promote a different course? To answer this question, we must understand the place of fire temples within Sasanian society. While fire temples were, of course, sites of cultic significance, they also served as centers of political, cultural, administrative, and financial import. Indeed, even enumerating the discrete functions of fire temples occludes the extent to which

[115] Walker, *Legend of Mar Qardagh*, 53.

[116] See also *Acts of Mar Mari* (Harrak, *The Acts of Mār Māri the Apostle*, sections 23–24), which similarly thematizes Christianity versus the worshipped fire, but in that case, Mar Mari agrees to go through the fire to prove that it is not a deity, extinguishing it in the process.

they were undifferentiated and indistinguishable in imperial rhetoric and in the eyes of many Iranians.[117]

Fire worship permeated imperial self-representation, where Sasanian kings consistently modeled themselves as patrons of fire temples and the fire cult. The king and his household, as well as other Sasanian elites, would endow fire temples to assert their patronage of the cult.[118] The Sasanians established rituals and performed public donations to advertise their investment in fire temples and identify kings with the fire cult.[119] Sasanian kings broadcast their support for the fire cult in a variety of media, from coins to monumental reliefs (Figures 7 and 8).[120] King Shapur I boasted about the mutual relationship between king and cult in a well-known monumental inscription at Naqsh-e Rustam:

> "Thus, for this reason, that the gods have made us their ward, and with the aid of the gods we have searched out and taken so many lands, so that in every land we have founded many Bahram fires and have conferred benefices upon many magi, and we have magnified the cult of the gods."[121]

According to the inscription, the spread of Shapur's empire advances a parallel spread of fire temples, a claim also found in the high priest Kerdir's inscriptions discussed in Chapter 3.[122] Elsewhere in Shapur's inscription, he reports that he established a fire for himself and for "the souls" of four other family members, each of whom he endowed with property.[123] The Sasanians elevated three central imperially sponsored

[117] I am here informed by Brent Nongbri, "Dislodging 'Embedded' Religions: A Brief Note on a Scholarly Trope," *Numen* 55 (2008): 440–460.

[118] Maria Macuch, "Die sasanidische Stiftung 'für die Seele'—Vorbild für islamischen waqf?" in *Iranian and Indo-European Studies: Memorial Volume of Otakar Kilma*, ed. Petr Vavroušek (Prague: 1994), 163–180; Maria Macuch, "Herrschaft skonsolidierung und sasanidische Familienrecht, 149–167; and Maria Macuch, "Pious Foundations in Byzantine and Sasanian Law," in *La Persia e Bisanzio: Convegno internazionale, Roma 14–18 ottobre 2002*, ed. Gherardo Gnoli (Rome: 2004), 181–196. For temples in cities, see Anahita Mittertrainer, *Sinnbilder politischer Autorität? Frühsasanidische Städtebilder im südwesten Irans* (PhD diss., Ludwig-Maximilians-Universität Münchenvorgelegt, 2020), 282–289.

[119] de Jong, "Sub Specie Maiestatis," 345–365; and more generally, Canepa, *Two Eyes of the Earth*, 13–18.

[120] Choksy, "Reassessing the Material Contexts of Ritual Fires," 259–260.

[121] Translation from Frye, *The History of Ancient Iran*, 372; original in Back, *Die Sassanidischen Staatsinschriften*, 328–330; see also Georgina Herrmann, *The Sasanian Rock Reliefs at Naqsh-i Rustam: Naqsh-i Rustam 6, The Triumph of Shapur I* (Berlin: 1989).

[122] Gignoux, *Les quatre inscriptions du mage Kirdīr*.

[123] Macuch, "Pious Foundations," 191–192.

fire temples and drew associations between them and sites mentioned in the Avesta, further bolstering the ties between the dynasty and Iranian history.[124] Some fire temples appear to have had designated thrones to honor the king when he was present.[125] Later Sasanian kings were coronated in fire temples, corresponding to Roman coronations within churches.[126] There is some evidence that the Sasanians carried a sacred fire on their military campaigns, representing and materializing the connection between the fate of the empire and the care of the gods.[127]

Other Sasanian elites similarly founded and patronized fire temples.[128] The Syriac *History of Mar Qardagh* presupposes this context when it reports that prior to his conversion to Christianity, the elite Zoroastrian Mar Qardagh sponsored a fire temple at great personal expense.[129] A fascinating inscription on a fire altar (*adurgāh*) dated to 241–242 CE, discovered in the region of Fars, reveals this intersection of the gods, the

[124] Canepa, "Building a New Vision," 64–69; Matthew P. Canepa, "Technologies of Memory in Early Sasanian Iran: Achaemenid Sites and Sasanian Identity," *American Journal of Archaeology* 114 (2010): 563–596; Canepa, *Iranian Expanse*, 283–290.

[125] Tafazzoli, "The King's Seat in the Fire Temple," 101–106; Shokouh Khosravi, Sajjad Alibaigi, and Mehdi Rahbar, "The Functions of Gypsum Bases in Sasanid Fire Temples: A Different Proposal," *Iranica Antiqua* 53 (2018): 267–298.

[126] Shenkar, "The Coronation of the Early Sasanians," 133–134. For the notion that a fire was lit to commemorate the coronation of a king, see A. Sh. Shahbazi, "Coronation," in *Coffeehouse-Dārā*, vol. 6, *Encyclopaedia Iranica*, ed. E. Yarshater (London: 1993), 277–279; and Fabrizio Sinisi, Alison Betts, and Ghairatdin Khozhaniyazov, "Royal Fires in the Ancient Iranian World: The Evidence from Akchakhan-kala, Chorasmia," *Parthica* 20 (2018): 9–30.

[127] E. W. Brooks, *Iohannis Ephesini Historiae Ecclesiasticae Pars Tertia*, 2 vols, CSCO 105–106, Scriptores Syri 54–55 (Leuven: 1935–1936), 299 [Syr.], 226 [Latin]; Andrew Palmer, trans., *The Qartmin Trilogy*, Microfiche Supplement to *Monk and Mason on the Tigris Frontier: The Early history of Ṭur ʿAbdin* (Cambridge, 1990), IV; and Muriel Debié, "St. Stephen in Amida in a New Mimro of Jacob of Serugh: Christianity vs. Zoroastrianism in a Clash of Religious Shrines," in *Syriac Hagiography: Texts and Beyond*, ed. Sergey Minov and Flavia Ruani (Leiden: 2021), 344.

[128] For an example of the importance of building projects to project elite status and as signs of commitment to the gods, see the inscription in R. N. Frye and P. O. Skjaervo, "The Middle Persian Inscription from Meshkinshahr," *Bulletin of the Asia Institute* 10 (1996): 53–61. For the implications of these buildings, see D. Huff, "Architecture: (iii) Sasanian," *in Ānāmaka-Aṯār-Al-Wozarāʾ*, vol. 2, *Encyclopædia Iranica*, ed. E. Yarshater (London: 1987), 329–334. See also the descriptions of foundation of several fire temples by Mihr Narseh in Bosworth, *Sāsānids, the Byzantines, the Lakhmids, and Yemen*, 104–105; and Perikhanian, *Book of a Thousand Judgments*, 312–313, 318–319, with Macuch, "Pious Foundations," 189–190. For a fascinating story of a noble Christian who is condemned for arrogantly emulating Persian benefaction, building a monastery and assigning it a Persian name, see E. A. W. Budge, *Thomas of Marga's Book of Governors*, 2.43 (136–137, 282–283).

[129] Walker, *Legend of Mar Qardagh*, 22–23.

empire, kingship, and fire worship. A Sasanian official named Abnūn pledges to donate a fire altar if Shapur I is victorious in his campaign against the Romans. When Shapur ultimately succeeds, Abnūn donates the fire altar, which he dubs "Long live Shapur and Abnūn!"[130] Fire temples thus became sites for public displays of power, benefaction, and loyalty to both the gods and the king.[131]

Fire temples also functioned as centers of financial wealth and opportunity. As Maria Macuch notes, they possessed "enormous endowments" and "income-producing property."[132] They employed workers and owned slaves that helped maintain them.[133] Elites were incentivized to establish and patronize temples because what was invested in the temple remained under their control and authority, to be allocated as they wished. Assets invested in the temple became the means for providing secure incomes for descendants, extended families, friends, and the community.[134] Indeed, when Mar Qardagh converts to Christianity, his father warns that he has lost "the authority to distribute to the Nazarenes the possessions and riches of the fire temple."[135] These institutions therefore accumulated massive amounts of capital, provided employment for many, and required large quantities of materials and goods. This is the context for the financial incentive behind Rav Ashi's sale of his forest to a fire temple. Indeed, other sources report the sale of forests to fire temples, an undoubtedly lucrative proposition for the seller.[136]

Zoroastrian magi played a crucial role in administering a massive empire, and their authority extended, in part, from their superintending the fire.[137] Fire temples therefore also held larger administrative

[130] Mackenzie, "The Fire Altar of Happy Frayosh," *Bulletin of the Asia Institute* 7 (1993): 105–109.

[131] See, for instance, Canepa, *Two Eyes of the World*, 148–149.

[132] Macuch, "Pious Foundations," 191.

[133] See Macuch, "Talmudic Expression," 109–129.

[134] Macuch, "Pious Foundations," 191. As such, at least on some occasions, their holdings could be requisitioned by the king during times of financial disarray to alleviate the tax burden and economic troubles of his inhabitants. See Tafazzoli, "The King's Seat in the Fire Temple," 101–102.

[135] Walker, *Legend of Mar Qardagh*, 46. On the careful selection of inheritors to serve as trustees of a family-controlled fire temple, see Perikhanian, *Book of a Thousand Judgments*, 312–313.

[136] See Bosworth, *Sāsānids, the Byzantines, the Lakhmids, and Yemen*, 105.

[137] For the notion that city fire temples served as administrative headquarters for magi, see Negin Miri, *Sasanian Pārs: Historical Geography and Administrative Organization* (Costa Mesa, CA: 2012), 114, based in part on the mention in MHD (78.11–14) of an archive in a fire temple in Ardashir-Xwarrah.

significance. These "champions of the fire," as they were described in Kerdir's inscription, were also often state officials, a fact well attested in the surviving literary and material evidence.[138] Some magi reportedly served as judges at fire temples themselves.[139] The official function of these institutions provides possible context for Rava's reference to *coerced* donations to the fire temples.[140]

Fire temples were therefore much more than cultic sites alone. They were centers of financial, cultural, and political capital, around which coalesced imperial interests. Yet the nexus of significations surrounding them became, for the rabbis, an opportunity to distinguish and select between them. Some rabbis permitted limited interaction with fire temples through staggeringly bold acts of compartmentalization, treating them predominantly as sites of commerce and trade, and even of conviviality, while largely ignoring their cultic associations. They accomplished this through the creative application of rabbinic law and precedent, with the goal of enabling Jews to engage in financial and personal transactions with a prominent Sasanian institution. Through their conceptual alchemy, donations of cultic accoutrements became economic transactions for "personal benefit," and the sale of wood to these temples was used "only for heating," with no cultic significance.

Some Syriac Christian stories refused to sideline the cultic character of fire temples. They were not oblivious to the assorted functions fire temples played in Sasanian society. In fact, they explicitly target these functions to draw a starker contrast between Christianity and Zoroastrianism and to emphasize their uncompromising stance toward competing cultic systems. The political implications of this act of resistance were not lost to the composer of *The Martyrdom of ʿAbda*. The king confronts the future martyr who had destroyed a fire temple and asks: "Why did one of you uproot that base of the fire and dare to stretch forth his hand over a thing by which our sovereignty stands?" The author understood that attacking a fire temple would be perceived as tantamount to a direct assault against Sasanian sovereignty. Yet to the Christian composer, the cultic significance of the fire temple ultimately outweighs its other significations. The story of Mar Qardagh similarly highlights and disparages the significance of fire temples as centers of finance and elite status. Qardagh's

138 See discussion in Chapter 3.

139 The Chester Beatty Kephalaia Codex chapter 326 (ed. and trans. Gardner, BeDuhn, and Dilley, *The Chapters of the Wisdom of My Lord Mani*, 36–49).

140 For more on this, see Herman, "Bury My Coffin Deep!" 31–59.

story is a subversion of Sasanian mores, using his Persian noble status and privileges to aid his new coreligionists, saying that "the treasures and riches that my parents dedicated and gave to the fire temples, I will distribute them to the churches and monasteries."[141] Qardagh was fully cognizant of the various hierarchies of power and prestige in which fire temples were pivotal, sublimating them in favor of Christianity.

These Jewish and Christian sources therefore offer sharply divergent responses to fire temples which, in turn, may index and may have generated different attitudes toward Zoroastrianism and Sasanian rule at large among their audiences. Their responses tell us much about the multifaceted nature of a Sasanian institution like the fire temple and the way different subjects positioned themselves in relation to it.

A RABBINIC ZOROASTRIAN SACRIFICE?

If rabbis could neutralize the cultic associations of some aspects of the fire cult, one story suggests that some rabbis could even imagine the mutual validity of both Jewish and Zoroastrian sacrificial practice.

The story features Ifra Hormiz, the supposed mother of the fourth century Sasanian King Shapur II, who appears in several undoubtedly fictional talmudic anecdotes, typically as a supporter of the Jews and of the rabbis.[142] There is little historical evidence to support the existence of Ifra Hormiz and, needless to say, her fondness for her Jewish subjects. The different talmudic anecdotes featuring Ifra Hormiz recycle similar formulaic templates and are therefore the products of literary construction.[143] The distinct plotline and details introduced by the composer of each particular story reflect choices of narration, and the use of the figure of Ifra Hormiz conveys larger ideas that were of interest to them.

This particular story featuring Ifra Hormiz appears in the context of a discussion about sacrifices in a post-temple world. The discussion raises the following question: While Jews are prohibited from offering sacrifices

141 Walker, *Legend of Mar Qardagh*, 50–51. See also Shirin, who puts out the family fire after converting; Paul Devos, "La jeune martyre perse sainte Širin († 559)," *Analecta Bollandiana* 112 (1994): 22 (§11).

142 b. Ta'an. 24b; B. Bat. 8a–b, 10b–11a; Zeb. 116a; Nid. 20b. On these, see Neusner, *History of the Jews*, 4.35–39; and Neusner, "Babylonian Jewry," 93–95.

143 Michal Bar-Asher Siegal, "Ifra Hormiz and the Use of Mini-Corpora in the Study of the Babylonian Talmud," *Jewish Quarterly Review* 113 (2023): 615–638. For instance, Ifra Hormiz and Rava appear together in the ensuing anecdote, and in another story in b. B. Bat. 10b–11a.

outside of the now destroyed Temple, can Jews nevertheless aid non-Jews in sacrificing, presumably to the Jewish God? A Palestinian rabbi observes that, while it is permitted for gentiles to sacrifice outside of the Temple, Jews cannot "assist them or act as their agents." The Babylonian Rava, however, opines that "we may instruct them" in proper sacrificial practice, even in the present. Yet, if at first glance Rava appears to narrowly permit Jews to instruct non-Jews in Jewish sacrificial practice, a story follows that depicts Rava not only actively arranging a sacrifice for the queen mother Ifra Hormiz, but a rather unusual sacrifice at that:

Ifra Hormiz, mother of King Shabur, sent a three-year-old calf[144] to Rava, with the request, "offer it up for me in the honor of Heaven."

Said Rava to R. Safra and Rav Aḥa b. Huna: "Go, fetch two of-age young men,[145] identify a spot where the sea has thrown up alluvial mud, take new [unused] pieces of wood, transfer a fire from a new vessel,[146] and offer it up in the honor of Heaven."[147]

Remarkably, the sacrifice Rava arranges does not conform to rabbinic sacrificial regulations. Indeed, it includes several features unattested in any Jewish sacrificial practice, such as the participation of two young men, unused wood, a transferred fire, and a location with a deposit of alluvial mud. A discussion appended to the story attempts to make sense of Rava's instructions based on rabbinic sacrificial law, but to little avail.[148]

The sacrifice's features do, however, broadly accord with what evidence survives of Zoroastrian sacrificial practice.[149] Rava's instruction to

144 On this term, see Shamma Friedman, "Now You See It, Now You Don't: Can Source-Criticism Perform Magic on Talmudic Passages about Sorcery?" in *Rabbinic Traditions between Palestine and Babylonia*, ed. Ronit Nikolsky and Tal Ilan (Leiden: 2014), 65–66. The printed edition replaces this term with "sacrifice."

145 On the word translated as "of-age" or "of the same age," see Sokoloff, *DJBA*, 280, who follows Rashi.

146 The standard dictionary of the field notes that the word for vessel is of uncertain etymology and meaning (Sokoloff, *DJBA*, 640), and the manuscripts fluctuate to some degree.

147 b. Zeb. 116b.

148 In all of the manuscripts, this ensuing discussion is attributed to Abaye, but it nevertheless carries the discursive features typical of a later editorial addition.

149 See especially de Jong, *Traditions of the Magi*, 357–362; Albert de Jong, "Animal Sacrifice in Ancient Zoroastrianism: A Ritual and Its Interpretations," in *Sacrifice in Religious Experience*, ed. Albert Baumgarten (Leiden: 2002), 127–148; and Alberto Cantera, "The Offering to Satisfy the *ratu* (*miiazda ratufrī*): The Dual System of the Animal Sacrifice in Zoroastrian Rituals," in *The Reward of the Righteous: Festschrift in*

find an area with a deposit of alluvial mud parallels what we find in the *Nērangestān*, a Zoroastrian ritual manual for priests, which stipulates that when offering an animal sacrifice, one must dig a pit around it.[150] A similar Zoroastrian practice is described by the first-century geographer Strabo, who says that Zoroastrians dig a trench before sacrificing the victim near water.[151] This pit or trench was intended to contain the blood and prevent it from spilling into the water or spreading on the earth, thereby polluting it.[152] The use of new, or unused, wood suggests an interest in maintaining the fire's purity, a major concern of Zoroastrian literature.[153] The two young officiating men call to mind the two men flanking the fire altar on the reverse of all Sasanian coins (Figure 7).[154] The instruction to take a new vessel and transfer fire from elsewhere accords with the Zoroastrian practice of seeding new fires from old fires.[155] While much about the passage remains obscure, a problem compounded by a

Honour of Almut Hintze, ed. Alberto Cantera, Maria Macuch, and Nicholas Sims-Williams (Wiesbaden: 2022), 39–96, for comprehensive discussion and earlier references. For some continuities between Achaemenid and Sasanian sacrificial ritual, see Antonio Panaino, "Sheep, Wheat, and Wine: An Achaemenian Antecedent of the Sasanian Sacrifices *pad ruwān*," *Bulletin of the Asia Institute* 19 (2005): 111–118. For a later Pahlavi document that appears to mention animal sacrifice, see Dieter Weber, "Villages and Estates in the Documents from the Pahlavi Archive: The Geographical Background," *Bulletin of the Asia Institute* 24 (2010): 37–65 (esp. 51–52).

150 Firoze M. Kotwal and Philip G. Kreyenbroek, *The Hērbedestān and Nērangestān III: Nērangestān. Fragard* 2, Studia Iranica Cahier 16 (Paris: 2003), 206–207.

151 Strabo, *Geography* 15.3.14.

152 de Jong, "Animal Sacrifice in Ancient Zoroastrianism," 137.

153 See especially *Vīdēvdād* 5.1–5.4, which takes it for granted that pure wood is necessary. *Dēnkard* 8.37.32 discusses maintaining the purity of wood used for fire. Further regulations concerning wood for the fire are discussed in Cantera, "The Offering to Satisfy the *ratu*," 67–68, 76–77.

154 See, for instance, Christopher Brunner, *Stamp Seals in the Metropolitan Museum of Art* (New York: 1978), 65 (#52). In general, see the description of the Yasna ritual in *Dādestān ī dēnīg* 48, which includes purified wood introduced to the fire by a priest and his assistant.

155 Jacques Duchesne-Guillemin, *Religion of Ancient Iran* (Bombay: 1973), 62–63; Jivanji Jamshedji Modi, *The Ceremonies and Customs of the Parsees* (Bombay: 1937), 200–226; Boyce, "On the Sacred Fires of the Zoroastrians," 52–68; and the polemic against it in the *Martyrdom of Narsai* (Herman, *Persian Martyr Acts under King Yazdgird I*, 14). An interesting etiology of this practice is found in Ammianus Marcellinus, *History* (*Res Gestae*), 23.6, who also mentions in passing Zoroastrian animal sacrifice. This practice also appears to be referred to in a Manichaean text (Gardner, BeDuhn, and Dilley, *The Chapters of the Wisdom of My Lord Mani*, 44–45). For some historical incidents of fire transfer, see Kennedy, "From Shahristan to Medina," 15–17. See *MHD* 110.4 (Perikhanian, *Book of a Thousand Judgments*, 244–245) for the need to remove the fire to fix the fire foundation.

dearth of evidence on Zoroastrian animal sacrifice, the similarities are sufficient to recognize that Rava facilitated Ifra Hormiz's sacrifice in a manner that was consistent with Zoroastrian cultic practice.

To be sure, Ifra Hormiz's sacrifice is not directed to Zoroastrian deities, but to the Jewish God. She is therefore described as wishing to offer a sacrifice "for the sake of Heaven," a generic term employed throughout rabbinic literature to refer to proper gentile worship.[156] Similarly, she sacrifices a "three-year-old calf," using the term employed by the Aramaic Targumim to describe Abraham's sacrifice in Gen. 15.9. This suggests that Ifra Hormiz's desire to sacrifice to Heaven is in some ways akin to Abraham's pre-Sinaitic sacrifices.[157] Neither may conform to post-Sinaitic stipulations, but both are surely meritorious acts of worship.

The story's composer therefore engages in a form of comparison, equating Jewish and Zoroastrian sacrificial practice as similarly valid vehicles of worship, provided they are directed toward the proper source. The political implications of this comparison can be read in two, perhaps compatible ways. The story could embody a form of mimicry and critique that exposes the hollowness and artificiality of Zoroastrian worship and the imperial actors for whom it was a central authorizing symbol, by demonstrating that they could, with some ease, be rechanneled to serve the deity of minor imperial subjects. But the story may also express how non-Iranian subjects, even those as immersed in a particular tradition as the rabbis, could come to perceive imperial Zoroastrianism as nonsectarian, leaving open the possibility that at any given moment, imperial worship and its various entailments could also possibly serve to worship the Jewish god.

The distinctive thrust of this story within rabbinic literature is observable by comparing it with two intertextually related stories.[158] In one, which appears in the Palestinian Talmud, the Roman emperor Antoninus

156 See e.g., b. Sanh. 39b; 'Abod. Zar. 8a; and interestingly, the Jewish temple of Onias in Egypt in b. Men. 109b.

157 Other contexts in the Talmud suggest that a three-year-old calf was considered a particularly sumptuous meat. See Friedman, "Now You See It, Now You Don't," 65–66; and e.g., b. Ḥul.133a; Shab. 136a. The use of the sumptuous three-year-old calf conforms to Zoroastrian stipulations about the preferred use of valuable animals. Cantera, "The Offering to Satisfy the *ratu*," 41. Similarly, it conforms with rules regulating the use of immature animals, on which see p. 42.

158 y. Meg. 1.2 (72b). See discussion in Shaye Cohen, "Conversion of Antoninus," in vol. 1, *The Talmud Yerushalmi and Graeco-Roman Culture*, ed. Peter Schäfer (Tübingen: 1998), 142–145.

asks Rabbi Yehuda the Patriarch if he can build an altar and offer incense on it. Rabbi Yehuda answers that he can build the altar, if he afterwards hides the now-sanctified stones, and that he may offer incense, provided he excludes one of the original spices from the mix. However, an earlier teaching (*baraita*) is cited which rules that Jews cannot presently build an altar or sacrifice, but gentiles are not similarly constrained. Why then did Rabbi Yehuda instruct Antoninus to leave out a spice? The answer given is that since a rabbi was assisting Antoninus in preparing the spices, he had to leave out a spice so that he, as a Jew, would not violate the commandment. Whereas a Palestinian rabbi helps a non-Jewish emperor offer a modified rabbinically-appropriate sacrifice, Rava assists a non-Jewish emperor with sacrificing in a manner consistent with non-Jewish sacrificial norms.

The second story appears in the Babylonian Talmud.[159] There, the Roman emperor sends a "three-year-old calf" to be sacrificed at the Temple, which in the story was still standing. But a dark scheme is afoot: The sacrifice has been sent at the suggestion of a Jew who, unbeknownst to the emperor, has a personal score to settle with the rabbis. Seeking to incite the emperor, the schemer tells the emperor that the rabbis will refuse his sacrifice. The schemer secretly wounds the calf, thereby invalidating it for temple sacrifice. The rabbis, recognizing the potential for insult if they refuse to sacrifice the emperor's animal, debate whether or not to sacrifice it despite its blemish. Unfortunately, excessive scrupulosity prevails; the animal is not sacrificed, and this leads to the eventual destruction of the Temple by the Roman emperor. In many ways, the story of Ifra Hormiz offers a direct contrast to the story of the Roman emperor. Ifra Hormiz herself is not trying to trip up or test the rabbis, but simply wishes to offer a sacrifice. Rava readily offers her "three-year-old calf" and tailors the sacrificial procedures to address the queen mother's sensibilities. While the circumstances are undoubtedly distinct – a sacrifice sent to the Jerusalem Temple versus a sacrifice to be offered outside of the Temple's strictures – the intertextual connections between the two stories highlight the extent to which Babylonian rabbis adapted literary templates to depict Sasanian rulers and their (reoriented) sacrificial practices in a positive light.

[159] b. Giṭ. 56a. This story and the larger literary context in which it appears are discussed by Rubenstein, *Talmudic Stories*, 139–175.

MODIFYING PRACTICE

Rabbinic accommodation to Zoroastrian veneration of the fire is further visible in modifications they introduced to rabbinic laws. The following dialogue appears in the context of a discussion about the prohibition to relocate lamps on the Sabbath:

> Rav was asked, "is it permitted to move the Hanukkah candelabrum before the Zoroastrian priests (*ḥabare*) on the Sabbath?"
> He answered them, "it is well, for a time of danger is different."[160]

As discussed in Chapter 3, as part of their resolve to safeguard beneficent creations, especially fire, the magi apparently confiscated lamps used by rabbis. The Hanukkah candelabrum would have posed a particular problem because of the additional stipulation that the candelabrum should be placed in a publicly visible location.[161] Given the presence of the magi, Rav is asked if, despite the prohibition against relocating a lamp on the Sabbath, it is permissible to relocate the Hanukkah candelabrum. He answers that it is permissible because it qualifies as a "time of danger."[162]

Rav therefore rules that it is better to violate a relatively minor commandment than incite the magi, though it remains unclear what might happen if the magi were indeed to see the candelabrum. In another rabbinic story, the magi simply confiscate a lamp without any further repercussions.[163] Does Rav fear that the candelabrum will incense the magi and lead them to further suppress Jewish practice or commit acts of violence against Jews? Or is he attempting to eliminate anything that might irritate the magi, regardless of the consequences to Jews? No matter what the risk, Rav endeavors to reduce possible points of tension between Jews and magi, rather than encourage confrontation or

[160] b. Shab. 45a. There have been unconvincing attempts to reconstruct a different original text that makes no mention either of Hanukkah or even the Zoroastrian priests; see discussion in Moshe Benovitz, "Times of Danger in Israel and Babylonia," *Tarbiẓ* 74 (2004), 6n6.

[161] As discussed in b. Shab. 21b–22a.

[162] On this term here and elsewhere, see Benovitz, "Times of Danger in Israel and Babylonia," 5–20. According to a Tannaitic teaching cited in b. Shab. 21b, the laws requiring the public display of Hanukkah lights are suspended in "times of danger," allowing one to light them in a private space from the outset, but not to relocate them once they are lit.

[163] b. Giṭ. 16b–17a, discussed in Chapter 3.

insist that Jewish practice must remain unchanged under pressure, consistent with the strategies proffered in other rabbinic stories discussed in Chapter 4.

CONCLUSION

Jews adopted various approaches to negotiating the ubiquity and symbolic force of Zoroastrianism under Sasanian rule. Some imitated and adapted Zoroastrian symbols in their personal seals, while others eschewed them completely. At least some Jews were apparently attracted to Zoroastrian festivals and teachings, even as the rabbis prohibited them. The rabbis simultaneously set boundaries around Zoroastrianism and its practice and study, even as they neutralized fire temples and permitted certain forms of Jewish exchange with them, often by modifying or departing from earlier rabbinic precedents. The permissive approach of the rabbis was, I have suggested, responsive to the nexus of religious, cultural, social, and political capital invested in fire temples, even as it is consistent with the rabbinic rejection of modes of resistance explored in the previous chapter. The rabbinic evidence can be contrasted with several Syriac texts that adopt an overwhelmingly antagonistic posture toward fire temples, despite recognizing their multifaceted significations. While Zoroastrianism is a particularly clear case of imperial hegemonic symbols and power, the complex and often internally contradictory negotiations adopted by Jews and Christians in this case undoubtedly extended to various aspects of life under Sasanian rule.

6

Kings and Religion in the Talmud and in the Imagination of Sasanian Communities

In a landmark essay, Stephen Greenblatt discussed a telling comment attributed to Elizabeth I in 1601.[1] The queen learned that the steward of the Earl of Essex commissioned Shakespeare's own theatre company, the Lord Chamberlain's Men, to perform *Richard II*. Given the earl's well-known seditious intentions, the queen responded, "I am Richard II. Know ye not that?" As Francis Bacon explained in his treatise indicting the Earl of Essex for treason, the earl's steward supported the production "to satisfy his eyes with the sight of that Tragedy, which he thought soon his Lord should bring from the Stage to the State."[2] Greenblatt argues that the earl's steward, and apparently the queen herself, recognized that the story had "the power to wrest legitimation from the established ruler and confer it on another." In short, "the queen understood the performance as a threat," and the steward understood its galvanizing potential. The earl commenced his ultimately unsuccessful rebellion against the queen the day after the performance.

According to *The Cause of the Foundation of the Schools*, a text intended to initiate new disciples into the East Syriac School of Nisibis, the famous late fifth-century Syriac Christian poet and school master Narsai was accused of slandering the Sasanian king Kawad.[3] His enemies

[1] Stephen Greenblatt, "Introduction," in *The Power of Forms in the English Renaissance*, ed. Stephen Greenblatt (Norman, OK: 1982), 3–6.

[2] Jonathan Bate, *Soul of the Age: The Life, Mind and World of William Shakespeare* (London: 2008), 253.

[3] On the School of Nisibis, see Becker, *Fear of God and the Beginning of Wisdom*; on this work, see Becker, *Sources*, 86–93. On the theological profile of Narsai in the *Cause of the Foundation of the Schools*, see Karl Pinggéra, "Das Bild Narsais des Großen bei

claimed that a *mēmrā* he composed, entitled "Friend of human beings, who has turned human beings to knowledge of himself, turn my mind toward the teaching of the word of life," constituted a critique of the Sasanian king, and brought it to the attention of the royal court.[4] To dispel this accusation, Narsai composed a new *mēmrā* with the title "Summit of the (four) quarters (of the world), turn to the order of authority," which appears to encourage his followers to obey the king, presumably mimicking the Sasanian's own claims of universal kingship.[5] Narsai translated the *mēmrā* into Middle Persian with the help of Persian-speaking Christians from Khuzistan, many of whom may have been deported by the Sasanians as captives of war from Nisibis, and had it delivered to the king himself. Christians and the king understood how the power of poetry might affect the loyalty of Sasanian subjects.

Though separated by over a thousand years, these two anecdotes reflect the perception among contemporary actors that representations of, or even allusions to, ruling powers could shape the behaviors and attitudes of their audiences toward them. These representations therefore were not formed in a vacuum; rulers sought to foster certain attitudes toward themselves by producing specific images and encouraging communities to internalize and reproduce them, while discouraging the production of those images that cast the king or empire in a negative light. Individuals and communities would variously adopt, mimic, alter, reject, and parody those same images and claims, as Narsai's two homilies did. Representations of empire by subjects were invariably produced at the nexus of imperial self-presentation and communal attitudes.

Barḥadbšabbā ʿArḇāyā. Zum theologischen Profil der 'Geschichte der heiligen Väter'," in *Inkulturation des Christentums im Sasanidenreich*, ed. Arafa Mustafa, Jürgen Tubach, and Sophia Vashalomidze (Wiesbaden: 2007), 245–259. For Narsai, see Aaron M. Butts, "Narsai's Life and Work," in *Narsai: Rethinking His Work and His World*, ed. Aaron M. Butts, Kristian S. Heal, and Robert A. Kitchen (Tübingen: 2020), 1–8.

4 François Nau, ed., *La seconde partie de l'Histoire de Barhadbešabba 'Arbaïa et controverse de Théodore de Mopsueste avec les Macédoniens*, Patrologia Orientalis 9.5 [45] (Paris: 1913), 612–613; Becker, *Sources*, 70–71. This *mēmrā* is not extant; see *Mēmrā 83 in Aaron M. Butts, Kristian S. Heal, and Sebastian P. Brock, *Clavis to the Metrical Homilies of Narsai*, Corpus Scriptorum Christianorum Orientalium 690 (Leuven: 2020). On the translation of Christian letters for the Sasanian king, see also the Synod of 410 where the letter of the western fathers is translated from Greek to Persian.

5 This *mēmrā* is also not extant. See *Mēmrā 84 in Butts, Heal, and Brock, *Clavis to the Metrical Homilies of Narsai*. On Sasanian claims to universal kingship, see Canepa, *Two Eyes of the Earth*; Payne, "Iranian Cosmopolitanism," 209–230; and Touraj Daryaee, "Kingship in Early Sasanian Iran," 60–70.

The Talmud's explicit references to the Sasanian Empire, its constituent figures, and its various manifestations, are therefore rich sites for considering rabbinic attitudes toward their imperial environment. Consistently, the Talmud offers a dichotomous portrait of Sasanian rule and its impact on Jews. On the one hand, Sasanian kings are typically portrayed as benevolent: they converse with rabbis, demonstrate a genuine interest in and admiration for rabbinic teachings, and honor Jews and Jewish interests.[6] At no point do they coerce Jewish compliance with Zoroastrian tenets or direct religiously inspired violence against them. In some cases, they even appear eager to accommodate Jewish practices and beliefs. On the other hand, a variety of talmudic stories portray Zoroastrian magi interfering in Jewish practices and beliefs. Most scholars of Sasanian Jews have embraced and reproduced this dichotomous portrait of Sasanian society as historical fact.[7] In their telling, Sasanian kings were generally accepting – and even fond – of Jews, and any violence directed against the Jews was a result of the pernicious influence and religious zealotry of the magi.

A similar dichotomy between benevolent kings and malicious magi appear in stories told by other groups in the Sasanian Empire, and this has shaped the scholarly accounts of their histories in much the same way.[8] Sasanian history as a whole is therefore framed as a perennial tug-of-war between Sasanian kings and the Zoroastrian magi.[9] In the words of one scholar, "The whole history of the Sasanians can be envisaged in terms of the relation between the temporal and spiritual powers, which

[6] See Brody, "Judaism in the Sasanian Empire," 56; and Gafni, "Political, Social, and Economic History," 796, 799.

[7] Brody, "Judaism in the Sasanian Empire," 58; Yaakov Elman, "Marriage and Marital Property in Rabbinic and Sasanian Law," in *Rabbinic Law in Its Roman and Near Eastern Context*, ed. Catherine Hezser (Tübingen: 2003), 260; Gafni, "Babylonian Rabbinic Culture," 237; Mokhtarian, *Rabbis, Sorcerers, Kings, and Priests*, 105; and János Jany, "Criminal Justice in Sasanian Persia," *Iranica Antiqua* 42 (2007): 375–377.

[8] Brock, "Christians in the Sassanian Empire," 6; Touraj Daryaee, "The Idea of Eranshahr: Jewish, Christian and Manichaean Views in Late Antiquity," in *Iranian Identity in the Course of History: Proceedings of the Conference Held in Rome, 21–24 September 2005*, ed. Carlo G. Cereti (Rome: 2010), 95. Contrast with Becker, "Martyrdom, Religious Difference, and 'Fear,'" 325–326.

[9] See, for instance, Williams, "Zoroastrians and Christians in Sasanian Iran," 37–53; Macuch, "Zoroastrian Principles and the Structure of Kinship," 231–232; and references in Payne, *State of Mixture*, 28n8. Critiqued by Becker, "Political Theology and Religious Diversity," 7–25.

now support, now oppose one another."[10] The kings are thus broadly seen as political pragmatists and the magi as religious zealots.[11] As the power and influence of the one rose, that of the other fell, leaving the latter to bide their time until they could once again regain the upper hand. The fate of non-Iranians was heavily dependent on which of the two was ascendant; fluctuating between kings and magi, periods of tolerance and intolerance, concord and persecution, in a perpetual but unpredictable historical cycle.[12]

According to this narrative, Sasanian kings viewed the empire's heterogenous communities differently from the magi. The kings were, fundamentally, driven by considerations of political expediency, not an ideological alignment with any one religion.[13] The empire's relentless signaling of its patronage of Zoroastrianism across different forms of media, whether on coins, monumental reliefs, or the public sponsorship of fire temples, were simply examples of disingenuous imperial propaganda, or so the argument goes. Sasanian kings did not harbor an unwavering commitment to Iranian identity or Zoroastrianism; instead, they strategically – even cynically – deployed and exploited religion to gain supporters and appease various entrenched sources of power, including Iranian nobility and subjects, and especially the Zoroastrian magi. The kings' support for Zoroastrianism and the magi was grounded in a calculation of their relative prominence and utility at any particular moment. In short, Sasanian kings were largely "secular," while the magi were "religious." The Zoroastrian "church" imposed "religion" on the "state" whenever the "church" somehow accumulated sufficient power and influence, goading the king to privilege Zoroastrians and to interfere – or license the magi to interfere – in the lives of non-Zoroastrians.

This dichotomous view of Sasanian society suffers from both theoretical and historical problems. As Adam Becker has noted, it employs

[10] J. Duchesne-Guillemin, "Zoroastrian Religion," in *The Seleucid, Parthian, and Sasanian Periods*, vol. 3, bk. 2, *The Cambridge History of Iran*, ed. E. Yarshater (Cambridge: 1983), 874–906 (esp. 874).

[11] Lee Paterson, "Minority Religions in the Sasanian Empire: Suppression, Integration and Relations with Rome," in *Sasanian Persia: Between Rome and the Steppes of Eurasia*, ed. Eberhard W. Sauer (Edinburgh, 2017), 181–198.

[12] Schippmann, *Grundzüge*, 92–102; Herman, *Prince without a Kingdom*, 40–49.

[13] See, for instance, Philip G. Kreyenbroek, "How Pious Was Shapur I? Religion, Church and Propaganda under the Early Sasanians," in *The Idea of Iran*, vol. 3, *The Sasanian Era*, ed. Vesta Sarkhosh Curtis and Sarah Stewart (New York: 2008), 7–16; and especially the works reviewed and critiqued in Becker, "Political Theology and Religious Diversity," 7–25.

modern categories and distinctions – such as politics and religion – that were "not simply intermingled, but imbricated and impossible to separate."[14] The dichotomous view posits that Sasanian kings were somehow uniquely able to live outside of their historical moment, in this case remaining determinately "secular," a term with little applicability to the ancient world. On historical grounds, this dualistic model proposes a neat, cyclical account of Sasanian rule revolving around two institutions endlessly competing for power and influence, without one ever managing to permanently overcome the other. Cyclical storylines may reduce the vicissitudes of a long-enduring empire into an appealing core animating tension, but they rarely pass muster as productive renderings of the past.

It cannot be denied that textual sources produced during this period by Jews, Christians, and Manichaeans often depict a stark binary between kings and magi. They also frequently portray Sasanian history as unfolding along a repetitious cycle of individual kings who were either religious "persecutors" – often because of their close ties to the magi – or benign, even invested in other religious communities and their institutions.[15] Other sources, however, including Sasanian reliefs and coins, Zoroastrian texts, and some Christian evidence, offer a conflicting picture, in which Sasanian kings were fervent Zoroastrians, sharing a commonality of purpose with the magi. This picture, too, had been accepted by some scholars as reflecting the true convictions of Sasanian kings, even as others dismissed it as propaganda by the kings or self-deception by the magi.[16] This puts scholars in the unenviable position of choosing one set of representations as ideologically neutral and historically accurate, and the other as the work of dupes or a product of wishful thinking.

This chapter revisits the incongruous and competing representations of the Sasanian kings found in the works of various communities and the empire's own self-projections. By situating these representations in their respective literary, communal, and cultural contexts, we find that non-Zoroastrian sources that create a dichotomy between king and magi do not necessarily reveal "how things really were" in the Sasanian Empire,

[14] Becker, "Political Theology and Religious Diversity," 12. See also Nongbri, "Dislodging 'Embedded' Religion". On the applicability of the term "religion" to late antique Zoroastrianism, see Kianoosh Rezania, "'Religion' in Late Antique Zoroastrianism and Manichaeism: Developing a Term in Counterpoint," *Entangled Religions* 11 (2020): 1–32.

[15] Likewise, Payne, *State of Mixture*, 25–26.

[16] Shaked, *Dualism in Transformation*, 2. See similarly Pourshariati, *Decline and Fall*, 325–326.

any more than Zoroastrian sources do. At the same time, these various portrayals presumably had to contain some element of verisimilitude for audiences to find them persuasive. This chapter therefore endeavors to explain how Sasanian political culture, ideology, and self-projections may have generated competing perceptions among its Zoroastrian and non-Zoroastrian subjects. In the case of the rabbis, the chapter offers an alternative to binary approaches that approach rabbinic stories as either roughly reliable reflections of historical reality or the product of rabbinic culture, showing that the two possibilities cannot be so easily disentangled.[17]

RELIGIOUSLY NEUTRAL KINGS

The Babylonian Talmud regularly portrays Sasanian kings as religiously neutral.[18] In several stories, Sasanian kings, including Shapur I, Shapur II, and Yazdgird I, engage rabbis in discussions of Jewish law, biblical interpretation, or theology.[19] The king is rarely, if ever, presented as

[17] For the former, see Moshe David Herr, "The Historical Significance of the Dialogues between Jewish Sages and Roman Dignitaries," in *Studies in Aggadah and Folk-Literature*, ed. Joseph Heinemann and Dov Noy (Jerusalem: 1971), 123–150. For the latter, see Christine Hayes, "Displaced Self-Perceptions: The Deployment of Minim and Romans in B. Sanhedrin 90b–91a," in *Religious and Ethnic Communities in Later Roman Palestine*, ed. Hayim Lapin (Bethesda, MD: 1998), 249–289; and Jenny Labendz, *Socratic Torah: Non-Jews in Rabbinic Intellectual Culture* (Oxford: 2013).

[18] For previous studies on representations of the Sasanian king in rabbinic literature and the cultural work they perform, see Kalmin, *Sage in Jewish Society*, 52–53; Jason Sion Mokhtarian, "Empire and Authority in Sasanian Babylonia: The Rabbis and King Shapur in Dialogue," *Jewish Studies Quarterly* 19 (2012): 148–180; Mokhtarian, *Rabbis, Sorcerers, Kings, and Priests*, 74–93, esp. 90–93; Secunda, *The Iranian Talmud*, 100–106; and Geoffrey Herman, "'In Honor of the House of Caesar': Attitudes to the Kingdom in the Aggada of the Babylonian Talmud and other Sasanian Sources," in *The Aggada of Bavli and Its Cultural World*, ed. Geoffrey Herman and Jeffrey Rubenstein (2018), 103–124. On rabbinic reflections on Achaemenid's kings, see Jason Sion Mokhtarian, "Rabbinic Depictions of the Achaemenid King Cyrus the Great: The Babylonian Esther Midrash (b. Meg. 10b–17a) in Its Iranian Context," in *The Talmud in Its Iranian Context*, ed. Carol Bakhos and M. Rahim Shayegan (Tübingen: 2010), 112–139. For the representation of "the other" in tractate ʿAvodah Zarah, see Mira Beth Wasserman, *Jews, Gentiles, and Other Animals: The Talmud after the Humanities* (Philadelphia: 2017).

[19] The following are the explicit references to Sasanian kings in the Babylonian Talmud: b. Ber. 56a; Shab. 113a; Pesaḥ. 54a; Suk. 53a; Taʿan. 24b; M. Qaṭ. 26a; Ḥag. 5b; Ket. 61b; Ned. 49b; B. Qam. 96b; B. Meṣ. 70b, 85a, 119a; B. Bat. 8a, 10b; Sanh. 46b, 98a; ʿAbod. Zar. 76b; Zeb. 19a, 116b; and Nid. 20b. For a full list, see Gerd A. Wewers, "Israel zwischen den Mächten: Die rabbinischen Traditionen über König Schabhor," *Kairos* 22 (1980): 77–100; Mokhtarian, "Empire and Authority," 5; Herman, "Ahasuerus, the

possessing any strong religious or theological views of his own.[20] If anything, these stories present the Sasanian kings as open and amenable to rabbinic instruction and practice, where they often serve the literary function of the nonthreatening outsider who is able to evaluate rabbinic ideas and express rabbinic anxieties.[21]

In one story, Shapur II questions a fourth-century rabbi about the scriptural basis for Jewish practices concerning burial of the dead:

King Shapur asked Rav Ḥama, "From where in the Torah do you derive the law of burial [of the dead]?" He did not offer any reply.
Rav Aḥa b. Jacob exclaimed, "The world has been given over into the hands of fools! He should have quoted, 'For you shall bury!' (Deut. 21.23)."
[That is not proof, since] it might merely have meant to make a coffin [for the deceased, even above the ground].
But it is also written, "Bury, you shall bury him (Deut. 21.23) [and the redundancy indicates burial in the ground]."
He [King Shapur] would not have understood it thus.
Then let him prove it from the fact that the righteous were buried (e.g., Gen. 49.31)!
[He might object] That was merely a general custom.
[He should prove it then] from the fact that the Holy One, blessed be He, buried Moses (Deut. 34.6)!
But [he might retort] that was so as not to deviate from the general custom ...[22]

King Shapur's question to Rav Ḥama reflects an interest in understanding Jewish burial practices, presumably as opposed to the Zoroastrian practice of exposure of the dead, or excarnation. There is nothing menacing in the king's questions, nor any suggestion that he wishes to impose Zoroastrian law on Jews. On the contrary, the rabbis engage in side discussions of what explanations should or should not be presented to the king, suggesting that he is viewed as a discerning and analytical thinker, albeit not necessarily willing to follow all of the rabbis' hermeneutical assumptions. Shapur's perceived neutrality and discernment, in addition to the fact that he ruled over a large Zoroastrian population for whom burial of the dead was a severe transgression, makes him a

Former Stable Master," 291n39. Strangely, Kalmin, "Sasanian Persecution of the Jews," 121, says that "the Talmud contains numerous unambiguous criticisms of Persians and Persian kings ..." but cites no supporting evidence.

20 The king shows interest in or even approval of rabbinic halakhic rulings, especially in b. B. Meṣ. 119a; Sanh. 46b; and ʿAbod. Zar. 76b.

21 On the attribution of rabbinic anxieties to various "others," see Hayes, "Displaced Self-Perceptions," 249–289.

22 b. Sanh. 46b, according to MS Jerusalem, Yad Harav Herzog 1.

particularly useful figure through which to address rabbinic anxieties about the absence of a clear biblical prooftext for Jewish burial practices. The king questions the persuasiveness of the scriptural prooftext but without challenging the legitimacy of the practice as such. This is a discussion, not an inquisition.

In another dialogue, King Shapur exposes rabbinic anxieties about messianism.[23] In the process, he is portrayed as a somewhat naïve supporter of Jewish messianic hopes. Several rabbis note the existence of contradictory biblical verses about the nature of the messiah's arrival. One verse (Dan. 7.13) suggests that the messiah will arrive astride heavenly clouds, while another (Zech. 9.9) suggests that he will arrive astride a simple ass. The rabbis conclude that there is no contradiction between the two verses: "if they [Israel] are meritorious, [he will come] with the clouds of heaven; if not, [he will come] lowly and riding upon an ass."[24] This debate recognizes that an ass did not quite offer the fabulous spectacle that one might anticipate for the triumphal arrival of the messiah. The concern for an appropriately triumphal arrival of the messiah is at the heart of the short, seemingly good-natured exchange between Shmuel and Shapur, replete with Middle Persian loanwords, that appears at the end of the talmudic discussion:[25]

> King Shapur said to Shmuel, "You maintain that the Messiah will come upon an ass: Let me instead send him my horse (*bārag*)."
> He [Shmuel] replied, "Do you have a donkey of a thousand colors (*xar hazār gōnag*)?"

The story represents King Shapur possessing familiarity with Jewish messianic expectations, a subject which could be construed as threatening to him. Indeed, one of the reports of Sasanian imperial violence against Jews stemmed from a "charlatan" who encouraged Babylonian Jews to go to Jerusalem and rebuild the Temple during the reign of the emperor Julian.[26] Yet in this talmudic story, the king is portrayed as untroubled. He instead inquires about the messiah's undignified mount, again serving as a mouthpiece for a rabbinic anxiety. The king prods Shmuel with a double-edged

[23] b. Sanh. 98a, according to MS Jerusalem, Yad Harav Herzog 1.
[24] The second verse was the basis for the scene of Jesus' arrival in Jerusalem in Matt. 21.1–11, the fulfillment of Jewish messianic expectations of the time.
[25] As is frequently the case, some of the Persian loanwords are corrupted in a few of the manuscript witnesses, and in the better manuscripts some of the Persian words appear with Aramaic glosses. See Sokoloff, *DJBA*, 183.
[26] See Chapter 3.

proposal, offering to send a horse to bear Shmuel's messiah, at once reminiscent of the honor the Achaemenid king, Ahasuerus, bestows on Mordecai in Esther 6, but also implying that the Jews were unable to provide an appropriate mount for the messiah. Shmuel offers a double-edged riposte: that the donkey serving as the messiah's mount will be no ordinary ass, but one adorned with a thousand colors. It will be miraculous, as befitting the messiah, and much more impressive than any horse offered by the king.

Overall, the gentle ribbing between the king and Shmuel suggests they share a degree of intimacy and comfort. With the use of Middle Persian loanwords, the text simultaneously accentuates both the otherness of the Sasanian king and the ease with which king and rabbi conversed with each other directly, rather than through an interpreter or intermediary. The king shows that he understands Jewish messianic hopes and is unthreatened by them. At the same time, Shmuel defends and even expands the messianic myth in response to Shapur's queries, crafting an image of the messiah mounted on a spectacular multicolored ass that would satisfy the king, despite having no precedent in earlier Jewish sources. The king again is a neutral interlocuter, approaching the rabbis as an interested outsider.

The neutrality of the Sasanian king is especially on display in a third story, which follows a legal discussion that establishes that one may purify a knife by plunging it into the ground ten times:[27]

> ... Mar Yehuda and Bati bar Tovi were sitting in front of King Shapur and a citron was brought before him [the king].
> [King Shapur] cut [a slice] and ate it. He cut [another slice] and gave it to Bati bar Tovi. He then stuck the knife into the ground ten times, cut [a slice], and gave it to Mar Yehuda.
>
> Bati bar Tovi said, "And is this man [i.e., me, Bati bar Tovi] not a Jew as well?"
> [King Shapur] said to him, "Regarding this master [Mar Yehuda], I am certain [of his adherence to the Torah, or alternatively his Jewish identity], whereas regarding this master [Bati bar Tovi], I am uncertain."
> Others say, "Thus did [King Shapur] say to [Bati bar Tovi]: 'Remember what you did last night!'"

Here, two Jews, a rabbi (Mar Yehuda) and a non-rabbi (Bati bar Tovi), sit before the king, who serves them a citron, which we saw in Chapter 2 was considered a Persian delicacy.[28] The king is therefore treating the two Jews as distinguished guests. He also takes care to purify the knife before serving a slice of the citron to Mar Yehuda, demonstrating his familiarity

[27] b. ʿAbod. Zar. 76b, according to MS JTS Rab. 15.   [28] Chapter 2, pp. 116–117.

with this rabbinic stringency, but he does not do the same for Bati.[29] The king explains that the Jewish identity of Mar Yehuda is clear, while Bati's is not. An alternative version of the story attributed to "others" suggests that the king knew of Bati's conduct, which he considered to be inconsistent with Jewish observance.[30] The story shows that the Sasanian king respected rather than challenged the scrupulous observance of religious boundaries and traditions, such that he can serve as judge for behaviors characteristic of proper – that is, rabbinic – Jews.[31]

In each of these stories, the Sasanian king shows no interest in promoting or enforcing Zoroastrian law or opinions. Instead, kings are portrayed as students of rabbinic law, Jewish eschatology, and halakhic practice. This image holds true for other Sasanian royalty as well. Five rabbinic stories feature Ifra Hormiz, Shapur II's mother, who maintains extraordinarily close ties with the rabbis.[32] She sends them money for charity,[33] and most shockingly, consults rabbis about her menstrual status.[34] Together, these stories reflect a consistent rabbinic depiction of Sasanian royalty as supportive of Jewish, and particularly rabbinic, teachings and practice. The Talmud contains no hint of royal interference in Jewish practice, or even an effort to promote or contrast alternative religious practices.[35]

There is internal rabbinic precedent for these favorable portraits of the Sasanian king. Palestinian rabbinic literature offers similar depictions of the relationship between some rabbis and Roman emperors.[36] Several of

29 For a highly positivistic attempt to identify Bati, see Otakar Klíma, "*Baat the Manichee*," *Archív orientální* 26 (1958): 342–346.

30 Mokhtarian, "Empire and Authority," 177–179.

31 On the placement of this story at the conclusion of tractate ʻAvodah Zarah, see Secunda, *Iranian Talmud*, 103; and Wasserman, *Jews, Gentiles, and Other Animals*, 227–233.

32 See references in Chapter 5, p. 232.

33 b. B. Bat. 8a–b, 10b–11a.

34 b. Nid. 20b. Shai Secunda, "Talmudic Text and Iranian Context: On the Development of Two Talmudic Narratives," *Association for Jewish Studies Review* 33 (2009): 48–58, interprets the story as related to Zoroastrianism. The Zoroastrian queen-mother, according to Secunda, was testing Jewish leaders. However, this blood sample is never explicitly identified as her blood; Secunda, *Talmud's Red Fence*, 84–103.

35 Of course, the king could be depicted as defending imperial prerogatives and institutions; for instance, related to law and taxes. See Chapter 1, pp. 46–48, and Chapter 4, pp. 175–184.

36 For an early study of these sources, see Herr, "Historical Significance of the Dialogues," 123–150. The parallel between Palestinian and Babylonian stories of encounters with royalty somewhat challenges the extent to which these Babylonian stories are primarily intended, as Mokhtarian, *Rabbis, Sorcerers, Kings, and Priests*, 92–93, contends, to "highlight Babylonian rabbinic claims to power," and to what extent they echo Iranian discourse in the mere fact of drawing on the king's "reputation as a ruler," as the same move is found in Palestinian rabbinic literature, but also in later Islamic-era Syriac literature, on which see Michael Morony, "History and Identity in the Syrian Churches," in *Redefining Christian*

these stories pertain to Rabbi Yehuda the Patriarch and the Roman emperor Antoninus Pius, such as one examined at the end of Chapter 5. In the Palestinian Talmud, the emperor informs the rabbi that he wishes to offer a sacrifice, and he donates a lampstand to a synagogue. There is even a discussion whether Antoninus converted to Judaism.[37] There are also dialogues between Rabban Gamaliel and an unnamed emperor about cosmology and scriptural interpretation. In two cases in the Babylonian Talmud, identical stories about an encounter between a Palestinian rabbi and Roman emperor, and a Babylonian rabbi and Sasanian king, appear one after the other.[38] It is hard to avoid the conclusion that these Palestinian stories served as models for Babylonian rabbinic dialogues between rabbis and Sasanian kings.[39]

That being said, the encounters with Roman emperors are typically portrayed as more tendentious and provocative, with the emperor seeking to win some type of debate with his rabbinic interlocutor.[40] The Babylonian Talmud consistently portrays the Sasanian king as religiously neutral by highlighting his openness to conversations about topics that were anathema to Zoroastrians. The Talmud offers no countervailing stories that suggest that Sasanian kings engaged in any type of religiously inspired violence or interference in communal affairs.[41] The same is not true of Roman emperors in Palestinian rabbinic literature, who are often depicted as the source of violence against Jews.

INTERFERING MAGI

The Babylonian Talmud's depiction of religiously neutral Sasanian kings stands in marked contrast to its depiction of magi, who are consistently

Identity: Cultural Interaction in the Middle East since the Rise of Islam, ed. J. J. van Ginkel, H. L. Murre-Van Den Berg, and T. M. Van Lint (Leuven: 2005), 28.

37 Cohen, "Conversion of Antoninus," 141–171.

38 b. Ber. 56a; 'Abod. Zar. 10b–11a.

39 Gray, "Redaction and Meaning in b. A. Z. 10a–11a," 64–68, contends that although in the Babylonian Talmud "Persian rulers are portrayed on the whole in a neutral to good manner, and largely without hostility," the rabbis still did not depict themselves as overly friendly with Sasanian rulers. However, this assessment is the result of Gray's choice to measure stories about rabbis interacting with Sasanian rulers by the standard of the friendship between rabbis and royalty on display in the stories of Rabbi and Antoninus.

40 Interestingly, several tendentious debates between Palestinian rabbis and Roman emperors are included together in b. Sanh. 39a, and they are followed by a story of dialogue between a rabbi and a magus, rather than the Sasanian king.

41 The empire could be depicted as financially oppressive/extractive. See the story of Rabbah bar Naḥmani in b. B. Meṣ. 86a, discussed in Chapter 4, and the story featuring Rava in b. Ḥag. 5a–b.

portrayed as zealots who regularly seek to interfere in Jewish religious practices.[42] Instances of this interference are discussed in Chapter 3. Here, I will highlight a specific series of cases in which the Talmud attributes Sasanian violence and religious interference to magi, while at the same time exonerating the king from any direct responsibility or guilt by association.

In one anecdote, discussed in previous chapters, a magus interrupts a rabbinic discussion by confiscating a lamp. This anecdote becomes an occasion for rabbis to muse about the Sasanian Empire itself:

> Rabbah bar bar Ḥanah was ill. Rav Yehuda and the rabbis entered to ask him a question ... In the meantime, a certain magus [*ḥabara*] came and took the lamp that was before them. Said [Rabbah bar bar Ḥanah], "Merciful One, either [conceal us] in your shade or in the shade of the son of Esau [Rome]."
>
> Is this to say that [Rabbah bar bar Ḥanah believed that] the Romans are better than the Persians? But behold, R. Ḥiyya taught, "What is written, 'God understands her [i.e., Wisdom/Torah's] way; He knows her place (Job 28.23)'? God knows that Israel cannot stand the decree of the Romans, so he exiled them to Babylonia!"
>
> [Why then did Rabbah bar bar Ḥanah say he preferred the Romans to the Babylonians?] It is not difficult. This [R. Ḥiyya's statement] was said before the magi [*ḥabare*] came to Babylonia, and this [Rabbah bar bar Ḥanah's statement] was said after the magi came to Babylonia.[43]

As a result of the interference of a magus, Rabbah bar bar Ḥanah exclaims, likely in exasperation and hyperbolically, that Roman rule is preferable to Persian rule.[44] If there is something intolerable about the Sasanian Empire, it is the activities of the magi. The anonymous editors, who notoriously lack sensitivity for humor or the sarcastic tone of earlier rabbinic statements, take umbrage at the implication that the Romans might be preferable to the Persians, and cite a statement by Rabbi Hiyya to the effect that Roman rule is *more* persecutory than Persian rule, such that it is impossible to even contemplate that Rome would be preferable to Persia. The anonymous interpolation explains that "[R. Ḥiyya's statement] was said before the magi [*ḥabare*] came to Babylonia, and this [Rabbah bar bar Ḥanah's statement] was after the magi came to Babylonia." The conclusion is that it is only during the ascendency of the magi that life under Persian rule could be compared unfavorably to Roman rule.

[42] This is also noted in passing by Herman, "In Honor of the House of Caesar," 115.

[43] b. Giṭ. 16b–17a, according to MS Munich 95.

[44] Kalmin, "Sasanian Persecution of the Jews," 102.

Unlike the open dialogues between Sasanian kings and rabbis, rabbinic stories depict the magi as incorrigible enforcers of Sasanian cosmology. Where a Sasanian king could engage in a discussion about Jewish burial of the dead, the magi are described as exhuming Jewish corpses to force them to decompose in the open, in a manner consistent with Zoroastrian practice. In one story, the rabbis imagine that the exhuming magus receives his just comeuppance:

There was a certain magus who used to dig up burial caves. When he came to the burial cave of Rav Tobi bar Mattenah, he [R. Tobi, the corpse] took hold of his [the magus'] beard. Avuha[45] came and said to him [R. Tobi, the corpse], "Please, leave [the magus]."

A year later he again came, and he [the corpse] took hold of his beard, and Avuha again came, but he [the corpse] did not leave him until [Avuha] brought scissors and cut off [the magus'] beard.[46]

The interfering magus is here stymied by the very object of impurity he seeks to remove, the corpse.[47] The story is a parody of Zoroastrian ideas about impurity; what Zoroastrians consider "dead matter" is in fact alive enough to teach the magus a lesson.

If the dialogue about burial of the dead with Shapur differs markedly from this encounter with the magus, the one direct dialogue between a rabbi and a magus further reinforces their clashing representations in the Talmud.[48] The interaction begins with the assertion by the magus that "From your waist upwards is of Hormiz [i.e., Ohrmazd], from your waist downwards is of Ahriman," a theological pronouncement that already departs from the religiously neutral image of the Sasanian king. As Shai Secunda has shown, the view attributed to the magus in this story is consistent with certain Zoroastrian cosmologies that mapped dualism onto human anatomy. The rabbi denigrates this cosmology, using

45 Other manuscripts read "Abaye."

46 b. B. Bat. 58a. Text according to MS Hamburg 165. On magi exhuming the dead, see Herman, "Bury My Coffin Deep!" and Chapter 3 above.

47 Incidentally, later sources suggest that magi were prohibited from shaving, which may add an extra level of parody to this text. See Mario Vitalone, *The Persian Rivayat 'Ithoter': Zoroastrian Rituals in the Eighteenth Century* (Napoli, 1996), 180 (Rivayat 32). However, Kerdir is beardless in his self-portrait at Naqsh-e Rustam (see Figure 4), although the reasons for this have been the subject of much speculation. On Kerdir and beardlessness in a Sasanian context, see Judith Lerner and P. O. Skjaervo, "The Seal of a Eunuch in the Sasanian Court," *Journal of Inner Asian Art and Archaeology* 1 (2006), 113–118.

48 b. Sanh. 39a. For discussion, see Ahdut, "Jewish-Zoroastrian Polemics," 13–26; and Secunda, *Iranian Talmud*, 64–66, 128–131.

scatological humor: "[If so,] how does Ahriman let Hormiz pass urine through his land?" This polemical tack is similar to that deployed by the fifth-century Armenian author Yeznik of Kolb in his diatribe against Zoroastrianism, who similarly mocks Zoroastrian dualism for the fact that "the waters, which we drink continually, and we turn their sweetness into stench in our bowels" then pass through the body and "dishonor those creatures which are held as gods."[49] The scornful tenor of this debate could not differ more radically from the portrayals of conversations between kings and rabbis.

The Babylonian Talmud therefore offers a consistently contrasting portrait of kings and magi. The king is portrayed as religiously neutral while the magi are persecutors who are essentially the catalysts for all religious interference. The magi aggressively seek to restrict practices that are inconsistent with Zoroastrian law, whereas Sasanian kings are more interested in understanding the practices of their Jewish subjects, even when they conflict with Zoroastrian law. The activity of the magi is presented as if it were independent of the king himself, and it is their interference in the lives of Jews that casts a pall over the experience of Jews in the Empire.

KINGS IN SASANIAN COMMUNAL IMAGINATION

A similar dichotomous portrait of neutral kings and zealous magi characterizes Manichean sources, most notably in the encounter between the prophet Mani and Shapur I.[50] According to several versions of Mani's life, the apostle Mani was welcomed by Shapur, who granted him permission to preach across the empire.[51] Accepting the historicity of this story, scholars have seen Shapur's reception of Mani as inconsistent with the king's claim to be a devotee of Ohrmazd and with his documented support, for instance, for the priest Kerdir. Shapur's simultaneous support for both Mani and Kerdir was touted as the best evidence for the cynical use of religion by Sasanian kings, proving that he was not "a person who

[49] Monica Blanchard and Robin Darling Young, *A Treatise on God Written in Armenian by Eznik of Kołb (floruit c. 430–c. 450)* (Leuven: 1998), 40.

[50] The wavering commitment of the king is read into a range of materials. See, for instance, Dietrich Huff, "Formation and Ideology of the Sasanian State in the Context of Archaeological Evidence," in *The Sasanian Era*, vol. 3, *The Idea of Iran*, ed. Vesta S. Curtis and Sarah R. A. Stewart (London: 2008), 39–40.

[51] A general discussion of the sources can be found in Gardner, *Founder of Manichaeism*. See also Gardner and Lieu, *Manichaean Texts from the Roman Empire*, 73–76 (*Kephalaia* 14.3–16.2).

[was] filled with religious zeal," and challenging the idea that "his kingdom has behind it a religious drive."[52] He was therefore "not wedded to one particular religious tradition," but was a consumer in a marketplace of religious alternatives, seeking the best tool with which to solidify his rule.[53] Manichaean sources further buoyed this paradigm, as Mani's fortunes at the Sasanian court rapidly declined as a result of a magian conspiracy against him.[54] Particular blame is placed on a Zoroastrian priest named Kardel, who of course is to be identified with Kerdir himself.[55] The story of Mani therefore epitomized the speed with which a king might switch his support from one religious group to another, as political calculations shifted.[56]

In recent years, several scholars have challenged the credibility of the relevant Manichaean sources about Mani's reception in the Sasanian court. They claim that "records of Mani's audience with Shapur are heavily mythologised," which is equally true of his encounters with the next Sasanian king, Vahrām I.[57] Part of this turn in scholarly thinking stems from the realization that the Manichaean accounts conform to narrative patterns found in Iranian, Christian, and other traditions.[58] For example, Albert de Jong has highlighted similarities between the story of Mani's appearance before King Shapur and that of Zarathushtra's audience with King Vishtaspa recorded in the Avesta.[59] Mani's

[52] Shaked, "Religion in the late Sasanian Period," 103–104.

[53] Kreyenbroek, "How Pious Was Shapur I?" 11.

[54] See Gardner and Lieu, *Manichaean Texts from the Roman Empire*, 81–82. For critical evaluation of this account's historicity, see de Jong, "Cologne Mani Codex," 138–139.

[55] Gardner and Lieu, *Manichaean Texts from the Roman Empire*, 84; Iain Gardner, "The Final Ten Chapters," in *Mani at the Court of the Persian Kings: Studies on the Chester Beatty* Kephalaia *Codex*, ed. Iain Gardner, Jason BeDuhn, and Paul Dilley (Leiden: 2015), 81–88. See also W. B. Henning, "Mani's Last Journey," *Bulletin of the School of Oriental and African Studies* 10 (1942): 949–950.

[56] Some scholars suggest that Shapur was drawn to the universalism offered by Mani's preaching, which incorporated the prophets of other Sasanian communities, such as Buddha, Jesus, and Zarathustra, into his own prophetology, and its related protean ability to speak in the language, imagery, and terminology of the various communities it reached. See Manfred Hutter, "Manichaeism in the Early Sasanian Empire," *Numen* 40.1 (1993): 2–15, esp. 7; and Manfred Hutter, "Manichaeism in Iran," in *The Wiley Blackwell Companion to Zoroastrianism*, ed. Michael Stausberg, Yuhan Sohrab-Dinshaw Vevaina, and Anna Tessmann (Hoboken: 2015), 477–489, esp. references on 477–478. See also Gardner and Lieu, *Manichaean Texts from the Roman Empire*, 6.

[57] Gardner, *Founder of Manichaeism*, 58.

[58] Peter Brown, "The Diffusion of Manichaeism in the Roman Empire," *Journal of Roman Studies* 59 (1969): 93–94.

[59] de Jong, "Cologne Mani Codex," esp. 138–139. More technically, the argument that Mani and Shapur enjoyed a sustained relationship throughout their respective careers appears to be a confusion in the sources. See Gardner, *Founder of Manichaeism*, 38–58 and passim.

appearance before the Sasanian king also conforms to a popular literary trope of the period in which a wise man or saint meets and converts a king, such as in the *Acts of Thomas* and in various early Christian martyr accounts.[60] Indeed, Mani reportedly converted other kings in his missionary journeys, including in India, just like the apostle Thomas.[61] Instead of offering an unvarnished historical transcript, the story of Mani's encounter with Sasanian kings expresses, above all, Manichaean aspirations to spread their tradition across territories and social ranks. The stories convey the idea that anyone, even the Sasanian king himself, was potentially amenable to Mani's teaching. It was the magi, and only the magi, who impeded the king and the progress of Mani's mission.

The malevolent role of the magi is emphasized in other Manichaean works, such as in the Manichaean Psalm Book where they are responsible for Mani's death:

> The lover of fighting, the peaceless one (i.e., Vahrām II) roared in flaming anger, he commanded them to fetter the righteous one that he [the king] might please the Magians, the teachers of Persia, the servants of fire.[62]

As Iain Gardner notes, this source displays "an interesting tendency to take the blame from the king and focus it on the priests."[63] It explicitly attributes the persecution of Mani to the king's need to mollify the magi, rather than to any core conviction of his own.

The notion that Shapur seriously contemplated adopting Mani's preaching as a unifying ideology of the state, as many have suggested, is based on a positivist reading of Manichaean sources and should be dismissed.[64] The story instead reflects a common narrative pattern about encounters between missionaries and kings, where the king is amenable to non-Zoroastrian teaching, and it is the zealous magi who guard against foreign influence in the court and Iranian lands more broadly. The divide

60 They also mirror the death of Jesus. See Gardner, *Founder of Manichaeism*, 60–80 and passim.

61 On Thomas, see Nathanel Andrade, *The Journey of Christianity to India in Late Antiquity: Networks and the Movement of Culture* (Cambridge: 2018), 27–66; Jeanne-Nicole Mellon Saint-Laurent, *Missionary Stories and the Formation of the Syriac Churches* (Oakland, CA: 2015), 17–35.

62 Lieu, *Manichaeism in Mesopotamia*, 10; and Gardner and Lieu, *Manichaean Texts from the Roman Empire*, 97–101. Other striking passages in the Manichaean Psalms similarly blame the magi. See Lieu, *Manichaeism in Mesopotamia*, 12.

63 Iain Gardner, "Mani's Last Days," in *Mani at the Court of the Persian Kings: Studies on the Chester Beatty* Kephalaia *Codex*, ed. Iain Gardner, Jason BeDuhn, and Paul Dilley (Leiden: 2015), 200.

64 See similarly Vevaina, "Hermeneutics of Political Violence," 294.

between king and magi in these Manichaean sources is consistent with their representation in the Babylonian Talmud. Yet where the rabbis offered two sets of stories – of rabbis dialoguing with kings and of magi committing acts of violence against them – Mani's biography incorporates the two into the life of one figure.

GREEK AND CHRISTIAN SOURCES

Viewed as a narrative pattern, the division between king and magi in the Babylonian Talmud and Manichaean sources strongly resembles many other sources about encounters between Sasanian kings and charismatic non-Zoroastrian figures, on the one hand, and the interfering presence of the magi, on the other. For instance, the dichotomous picture of the nonaligned Sasanian king and religiously zealous magi is found in a work by the fourth-century Greek sophist, Eunapius. In his *Lives of the Philosophers*, he describes an encounter between the philosopher Eustathius and King Shapur.[65] Eustathius accepts an invitation to dine with the Sasanian king because the latter appeared to "have a natural bent for virtue." Eustathius charmed the king with his eloquence, winning "such influence over him that the king of Persia came within an ace of renouncing his upright tiara, laying aside his purple and bejeweled attire, and putting on instead the philosopher's cloak of Eustathius." However, Eustathius was hindered by "certain magi who happened to be at the court, and kept asserting that the man was nothing but a mere conjuror ..."[66]

A similar story is told about the bishop Marutha of Maypherqaṭ (fl. early fifth century). His *Vita* survives in Greek, Armenian, and later Arabic works, all of which likely derive from an original Syriac source.[67] In these works, the institutionalization of the East Syrian ecclesiastical hierarchy is attributed to Marutha's successful embassy to the Sasanian king Yazdgird I. At court, Marutha is repeatedly undermined by the magi who fear that he might "persuade the king to embrace Christianity." In their final ploy to sway the king, the magi conceal a man underneath the fire altar who mimics the voice of God. The same ploy is attributed in other sources to the priests of Baal in their battle against Elijah on Mount

65 Wilmer Cave Wright, ed. and trans., *Philostratus and Eunapius*, Loeb Classical Library 134 (Cambridge: 1952), 396–399.

66 See the similar accounts in Scher, *Chronique de Séert*, 1.142–143; and Procopius, *History of the Wars*, 1.3, where the magi advise the king how to deceptively make a treaty and then break it.

67 See Marcus, "Armenian Life of Marutha of Maipherkat," 47–71.

Carmel described in 1 Kings 18, a scene depicted on the frescoes of the third-century synagogue of Dura Europos.[68] Marutha, channeling Elijah, exposes the ruse of the wicked magi, here the embodiments of the priests of Baal.[69] Yazdgird, in turn, grants Marutha the right "to erect churches wherever he wished," and the king reportedly almost became Christian himself, but his death "prevented his making an open profession of Christianity." According to this account, Yazdgird is amenable to Christian overtures were it not for the interfering magi, and Marutha's power in this case is displayed precisely in his ability to break the narrative pattern and best the magi. Other Christian stories from the late sixth and seventh century similarly imagine that when the magi did not interfere, several Sasanian kings became Christian, including Ardashir I, Khusro I, and Khusro II.[70]

Multiple other sources portray the king as receptive to the teachings of other communities. One story appearing in the ninth-century Christian-Arabic *Chronicle of Seert* even offers a striking parallel to the conversation between Shapur and the rabbi regarding Jewish burial practices. In this version, the Sasanian king Jamasp (r. 496–498) asks the Catholicos Babai the following question:

> "Dead bodies rot and turn to dust. Why do you honor the bones of the dead? Why do you venerate them and not put them in coffins, like the Magi?"
>
> [Babai] responded to him: "We know that the bodies of men are in a state of absolute inertia and rot and turn to dust. But we believe that they will be resurrected in a more beautiful and dazzling state than before..."
> [Jamasp] approved of his response. Babai came away from him in joy.[71]

King Jamasp's questions target Christian burial practices, even referencing the cult of relics in which bones of saints and martyrs are venerated, a

[68] See Uzi Leibner, "An Illustrated Midrash of Mekilta de R. Ishmael, Vayeḥi Beshalaḥ, 1 – Rabbis and the Jewish Community Revisited," *Talmuda de-Eretz Israel: Archaeology and the Rabbis in Late Antique Palestine*, ed. Steven Fine and Aaron Koller (2014), 92–94.

[69] Socrates Scholasticus (*Ecclesiastical History* 7.8). For a discussion of Marutha, see Elizabeth Key Fowden, *Barbarian Plain: Saint Sergius between Rome and Iran* (Berkeley, CA: 1999), 52–57.

[70] See Alexander Markus Schilling, *Die Anbetung der Magier und die Taufe der Sāsāniden: Zur Geistesgeschichte des iranischen Christentums in der Spätantike* (Leuven: 2008); 91–96 (Ardashir I), 185–189 (Khusro I), and 247–261 (Khusro II); Christelle Jullien, "Christianiser le pouvoir: Images de rois sassanides dans la tradition syro-orientale," *Orientalia christiana periodica* 75 (2009): 285–293; and Payne, *State of Mixture*, 164–165.

[71] Scher, *Chronique de Séert*, 2.37–38, with Bruns, "Reliquien und Reliquienverehrung," 194–195.

practice that Zoroastrians would consider a gross act of defilement and a serious transgression. As in the rabbinic story, there is no threat, tension, or suggestion of compulsion in this exchange. The king himself is presented as a curious observer of the practices of his subjects, willing to consider and compare Christian practices with those of the Zoroastrians, without explicitly or impliedly endorsing one or the other. Unlike the rabbinic story, in which the rabbi fails to proffer a biblical prooftext, the Catholicos successfully responds to the king.

The literary trope of neutral kings and scheming magi is also found in the work of Miaphysite Christians living in the Roman Near East. In the account of the sixth-century John of Ephesus, King Khusro II was never "an enemy of the Christians, and though incited by the Magians against them, he was not often prevailed upon to consent to their being persecuted."[72] Khusro serves in John's account as a neutral arbiter in a debate between the East Syriac Catholicos and a miaphysite, and decides that reason favors the latter. Other accounts similarly present Sasanian kings as neutral arbiters in disputations between Christian sects.[73]

This picture of intellectual and ideologically neutral kings was widespread, even in the Roman world, to the point that it shaped the decisions of real actors there as well. According to the sixth-century Roman historian Agathias, when the philosophical school in Athens was forcibly closed in the mid-sixth century, its teachers fled to the Sasanian court of Khusro I (r. 531–579) because they believed that "Persia was the land of Plato's philosopher king."[74] Agathias describes at some length the pervasiveness of this belief. Yet, he further details how the philosophers were deeply disappointed by their conversation with the king; the king boasted "that he was a student of philosophy," but in fact "his knowledge of the subject was

72 Payne Smith, *The Third Part of the Ecclesiastical History of John Bishop of Ephesus*, 417–420. For discussion of the larger context of this debate, and the question of its general historicity, see Walker, *Legend of Mar Qardagh*, 178–180.

73 Payne, "Les polémiques syro-orientales," 239–260.

74 Agathias, *Histories* 2.30.3–2.31.1, with Joseph Frendo, *Agathias: The Histories* (Berlin: 1975), 65. For Agathias' views on the Sasanians, see Averil Cameron, "Agathias on the Sassanians," *Dumbarton Oaks* 23/24 (1969–1970): 67–183. On Byzantine views toward the Sasanians more generally, see the bibliography in Smith, *Constantine and the Captive Christians of Persia*, 74–75; Jan W. Drijvers, "A Roman Image of the 'Barbarian' Sasanians," in *Romans, Barbarians, and the Transformation of the Roman World.: Cultural Interaction and the Creation of Identity in Late Antiquity*, ed. Ralph Mathisen and Danuta Shanzer (Farnham: 2011), 67–76; and Jan W. Drijvers, "Ammianus Marcellinus' Image of Sasanian Society," in *Ērān und Anērān, Studien zu den Beziehungen zwischen dem Sasanidenreich und der Mittelmeerwelt*, ed. Philip Huyse, and Josef Wiesehöfer (Stuttgart: 2006), 45–69.

utterly superficial." Similar stories about the Sasanian "philosopher king" created expectations that could be upset when faced with the reality of the king himself. For instance, an epistle sent by Gregory the Great to Domitian of Melitene reveals that the latter, presumably while accompanying Khusro II in his effort to regain his throne in 590–591 CE, had sought unsuccessfully to convert the Sasanian king.[75] Discourse and reality were two very different things.

The Talmud's stories about the Sasanian kings and the rabbis are therefore of a piece with the texts of other Sasanian communities. While employing tropes, motifs, and storylines familiar from their own traditions, Jewish, Syriac, Manichaean, and even late-antique Roman sources all adopt a similar narrative template in depicting the Sasanian king as religiously neutral and receptive to the teachings and charismatic figures of his various subjects. It is the magi, in most cases, who impede the king from following through on his "natural bent for virtue," and it is they who are responsible when these communities face violence and religious interference.

KINGS VERSUS MAGI

Syriac martyr acts offer a similar binary between kings and magi as that found in the Babylonian Talmud, even when it pertains to violence. Yet whereas the Talmud does not discuss kings and magi together, in the Syriac accounts, the magi instigate the king to persecute the Christians, while the king opposes them or has no choice but to submit to their will.[76] A striking example of the deployment of this trope is found in the *Martyrdom of Peroz of Be Lapat*, which purports to describe events that transpired in 422 CE:[77]

> [King Vahram] owed a favor to the impure magi and the pagan nobles who were at the gate of the king, because they gave him the crown from among all his brothers. On account of this, he made his will the same as theirs. And he obeyed the command of the slandering Mihrshabur, head of the magi. He exhumed the dead

[75] Gregory the Great (*Correspondences*, III.67).

[76] In addition to the texts discussed below, see *Martyrdom of the Captives of Beth Zabdai* (Syriac in Bedjan, *Acta martyrum et sanctorum*, 2.316–324; English translation in Smith, *Constantine and the Captive Christians*, 184–190). More generally, see I. Gillman and H.-J. Klimkeit, *Christians in Asia before 1500* (Surrey: 1999), 109–127; and Jullien and Jullien, *Apôtres des confins*.

[77] *Martyrdom of Peroz of Be Lapat* (Bedjan, *Acta martyrum et sanctorum*, 4.253–254). This account was known to Socrates Scholasticus, who in his *Ecclesiastical History* (7.18) follows the *Martyrdom of Peroz* quite closely.

that were buried during the years of his fathers and exposed them to the sun. When this law was in place for five years, and this evil that he caused did not suffice, then he commanded that even [with regard to] their tranquility and worship, there should be pressure and persecution on the people of God, and there should be a harsh persecution on all of those who believed in the "fear" of the Christians.

In this account, the king harbors no ill will toward Christians. However, he cannot withstand the pressure of the magi because of the debt he believes he owes them for their help attaining the throne.

According to other accounts, such as the *Acts of Grigor*, the king provided Christians with letters of passage that protected them from the interference and violence of magi.[78] Similarly, in the *History of Mar Aba*, a distinction is drawn between the head of the magi, who consistently seeks to have the king deploy force against the Christians, and the king himself, who only rarely complies. According to Philip Wood, "the hagiographer is underlining the distinction between the shah's absolute authority, which Aba respects, and the religious law of the Zoroastrian clergy," which he disdains.[79]

We find similar attempts by the king to restrain the magi in the *Martyrdom of Narsai*.[80] They beseech the king for the right to punish the rise of converts to Christianity. The king responds: "you are granted authority over them to convert them, without any killing, but only through intimidation and with some beatings."[81] Once again, the magi advocate deploying force and violence, while the king seeks to curtail them. In these accounts, the king is released from any accountability for anti-religious violence, and culpability is laid squarely at the feet of the magi.[82]

78 Bedjan, *Histoire de Mar-Jabalaha*, 347–348.

79 Wood, *Chronicle of Seert*, 113; Wood, "The Christian Reception of the Xwadāy-Nāmag: Hormizd IV, Khusrau II and Their Successors," *Journal of the Royal Asiatic Society* 26 (2016): 416–417. See also McDonough, *Power by Negotiation*, 250–251, on many Syriac martyr acts downplaying the involvement of the king.

80 Herman, "In Honor of the House of the Caesar," 108. See the discussion of this text in Chapter 3, pp. 143–145, and Chapter 5, pp. 225–226.

81 Herman, *Persian Martyr Acts under King Yazdgird I*, 4.

82 Wiessner, *Zur Martyrerüberlieferung*, 169–175; Philippe Gignoux "Die religiöse Administration in sasanidischer Zeit: Ein Überblick," in *Kunst, Kultur, und Geschichte der Achämenidenzeit und ihr Fortleben*, ed. Heidemarie Koch and David N. Mackenzie (Berlon: 1983), 256. Some Persian martyr acts do not involve the king at all and thematize the cruelty of the magi, a notion cleverly deployed in cases where a magus converts due to the sanguinity with which Christians face torture and martyrdom at the hands of other magi. See *Martyrdom of Abbot Barshebya, Ten Fellow Brothers, and One Magus* (Bedjan, *Acta martyrum et sanctorum*, 2.281–284; Smith, *Constantine and the Captive Christians*, 191–196).

PERSECUTORY KINGS

The dichotomy between king and magi was, however, contested. Many Syriac Christian sources do not hesitate to attribute anti-religious violence to the king himself, portraying him as the leading agent in the persecution of Christians.[83] Indeed, in the earliest Syriac martyr act, the *Martyrdom of Simeon bar Ṣabba'e*, it is the king who is largely responsible for the violence deployed against Christians, as part of an effort to turn them to Zoroastrianism. Similarly, in another likely fifth-century text, the *Martyrdom of Pusai*, the king is the chief provocateur. The story is set in Khuzistan, where many Roman captives had been forcibly resettled. The protagonist Pusai is an artisan who rises to a position of prominence in the guild administered by the king. Yet, when it is revealed that Pusai is not a Zoroastrian but a Christian, the king goes to great lengths to convert him. It is the king, not a magus, who declares:

> I was unaware that this man is a Christian, for were I aware of this, I would not have entrusted him with our work even one day, O Gods, nor would I have deemed him worthy of this great honor. However, I assumed that he was a Persian, and espoused our "fear," O Gods.[84]

In other accounts, even when persecution begins with the magi, it is ultimately the king who unleashes violence against Christians. In the *Martyrdom of Barba'shmin*, after the king learns that Christians are missionizing and scorning sun worship, he arrests church leaders and declares, "I will root out your teaching from the earth, and I will remove your "fear" from the world." There are no pretensions about a religiously neutral king; the Christians, therefore, mock the king and his gods and openly flout his command, leading the enraged king to declare: "From this day onwards, I write to the troops I have in all lands, that anyone who has this name [Christianity] upon him, they should wipe out his memory from the earth by sword and blade."[85] Numerous other examples could be furnished of Sasanian kings directly participating in violence against Christians.[86]

[83] Williams, "Zoroastrians and Christians in Sasanian Iran," 37–53.

[84] Bedjan *Acta martyrum et sanctorum*, 2.213.

[85] Bedjan, *Acta martyrum et sanctorum*, 2.301.

[86] E.g., *Martyrdom of 111 Men and 9 Women* (Bedjan, *Acta martyrum et sanctorum*, 2.291–295). While some have sought to downplay the extent of the king's involvement in the *Martyrdom of Simeon bar Ṣabba'e* and the *History of Simeon bar Ṣabba'e*, this often requires special pleading. See Payne, *State of Mixture*, 38–44.

Whether or not these accounts reflect actual moments of religiously inspired and royally directed violence, they are the products of Christian composers who chose to portray the Sasanian kings as religiously motivated, at times even fanatical. These stories are no more or less reliable than earlier Christian works that blamed violence entirely on the magi while exonerating the kings. Instead, different literary representations of the Sasanian kings likely reflect their authors' competing attitudes toward the empire, and how, through their literary production, they sought to engender these attitudes in their audiences.

ZOROASTRIAN REPRESENTATIONS OF KING AND RELIGION

If some non-Iranians emphasized the dichotomy between king and magi, state and religion, several Zoroastrian texts emphasized the *interdependence* of the two.[87] A series of late and post-Sasanian texts affirm the notion that the kings and the Zoroastrian priesthood march in lockstep.[88] As the *Letter of Tansar* says, "Religion (*dēn*) and kingship (*malik*) were born of one womb, joined together and never to be sundered."[89] The ninth-century encyclopedic compilation of earlier traditions, the *Dēnkard*, which Shaked explains represents "how the religious history of Iran was interpreted in priestly circles,"[90] states that "kingship (*xwadāyīh*) and religion (*dēn*), religion and kingship, are countrymen."[91] The *Testament of Ardašīr*, a work of the *Mirror of Princes* genre, says "Know that kingship and religion are twin brothers, no one of which can be maintained without the other. For religion is the foundation of kingship, and kingship is the guardian of religion."[92] In these texts, king and religion are aligned and inseparable.

This image of alliance between king and magi did not emerge only in the post-Sasanian era, as some scholars have argued. Instead, Iranian

87 The possibility of pious Zoroastrians using religion against the empire is an acute concern of the *Testament of Ardashir*. See Shaked, "Esoteric Trends," 214–219.

88 Robert C. Zaehner, *Dawn and Twilight of Zoroastrianism* (London: 1961), 296–299; Shaked, "Notes on Some Themes in Transmission," 31–40; Gnoli, *Idea of Iran*, 164–166. For sources, see Marijan Molé, *Culte, mythe et cosmologie dans l'Iran ancien. Le problème zoroastrien et la tradition mazdéenne* (Paris: 1963), 37–58.

89 Persian text in M. Minuvi, *Nāma-ye Tansar* [The Letter of Tansar] (Tehran: 1932), 52–53; Boyce, "Letter of Tansar," 33–34. On post-Islamic details in the letter, see Shenkar, "Coronation of the Early Sasanians," 122.

90 Shaked, *Dualism in Transformation*, 101.

91 *Dēnkard* 3.58.2. See Shaked, *Dualism in Transformation*, 39.

92 Surviving in Arabic in Ibn Miskawayh's *Tajārib al-umam*. Hutter, "Manichaeism in Iran," 479; and Shaked, "Esoteric Trends," 214.

sources composed during the Sasanian period paint a similarly harmonious picture, with the king serving as an agent and enforcer of Zoroastrian tradition[93] For example, Kerdir's inscriptions portray king and magus as marching in lockstep, with Sasanian kings serving as patrons of the cult, echoing similar formulations in early Sasanian royal inscriptions. Kerdir attributes his success in constructing fire temples and promoting the magi's interests to the "command of the King of Kings." Kerdir equates the spread of the Sasanian Empire with the expansion of the fire cult to the new territories: "And in kingdom after kingdom and place after place throughout the whole empire, the services of Ahura Mazda and the gods became preeminent." If nothing else, Kerdir's inscription reveals much about the way Iranians could perceive the religious commitment of the Sasanian kings.

Other Iranian sources consider gods and kings as corresponding entities. *Sūr Saxwan*, a late Sasanian elite banquet toast, blesses the gods, beginning with Ohrmazd, "who among the spiritual and material world is the greatest," and the imperial hierarchy, beginning with the king, who is "foremost of men," ending with the prayer to "give sovereignty to *ērānšāhr*, and splendor amidst it."[94] The inscription on an administrative figure's seal similarly boasts of having been tested by the gods and by "Iranian sovereignty *(ērīh-xwadāyīhā)*," while another administrative figure could donate a fire altar in the king's honor.[95] An early fifth-century Syriac martyr act reflects widespread Iranian belief when it has a magus describe Zoroastrianism as "the fear of the King of Kings, whose nature is from the gods."[96]

The notion that king and religion went hand in hand was shared by many Iranians throughout the Sasanian period. As some scholars have sensed, such statements of concord between king and religion paint an idealized image that was no more a reflection of reality than the dichotomous portrait offered by non-Iranian subjects like the Babylonian rabbis and Syriac Christians.[97]

93 Minov, "Dynamics of Christian Acculturation," 181–186, argues that the Syriac *Cave of Treasures* is aware of the notion of the unity of kingship and priesthood.

94 Daryaee, "The Middle Persian Text Sūr ī Saxwan," 68–69.

95 Philippe Gignoux, "D'Abnū à Māhān: Étude de deux inscriptions sassanides," *Studia Iranica* 20 (1991): 9–22, esp. 21.

96 Bedjan, *Acta martyrum et sanctorum*, 2.160.21–161.01.

97 See Gignoux, "Church-State Relations," 72–80; Shaked, "Religion in the Late Sasanian Period," 104–105; and Shaked, *Dualism in Transformation*, 115–116.

JANUS-FACED EMPIRE

What then explains these different portrayals of the relationship between king and magi? Rather than determine which portrait most closely represents the "true" Sasanian king, the pervasiveness and consistency of both suggest that they respond to different images the Sasanian Empire projected of itself to its heterogenous communities.

To borrow a term employed by Ludwig Koenen to describe the presentations of Ptolemaic kings to their dual Greek and Egyptian audiences, we should think of the Sasanian kings as "Janus-faced," proffering distinct – even contradictory – images of themselves depending on their audience.[98] This was not exclusive to Ptolemaic kings; Roman rulers similarly projected various images to which their heterogenous communities might be more receptive. As Noel Lenski has shown, during Constantine's lifetime, different images of the emperor were in circulation among different communities, and "each conceptualized along locally conditioned parameters that reflect in part images projected by the emperor himself and in part the expectations and desires" of the communities presenting him.[99] The Sasanians were similarly keenly aware of their various audiences. The images they projected allowed their various inhabitants the opportunity to conceptualize Sasanian rule from the vantage point of their own traditions, expectations, and desires.

As discussed in Chapter 3, Sasanian kings divided their subjects into Iranians and non-Iranians. In ordering their subjects this way, they recognized the need to persuade two broad groups to acquiesce to their rule. To their Iranian subjects, the message was clear: The kings and the gods existed in a symbiotic relationship, in which the gods appointed and sustained the kings, who, in turn, supported the gods. In their coinage, monumental reliefs, inscriptions, and imperially sponsored writings, Sasanian kings consistently vaunt their anointment by the Zoroastrian deities as the fulfillment of their duties as devout patrons of their cult.[100]

[98] Ludwig Koenen, "The Ptolemaic King as a Religious Figure," in *Images and Ideologies: Self-definition in the Hellenistic World*, ed. Anthony W. Bulloch, Eric S. Gruen, A. A. Long, and Andrew Steward, Hellenistic Culture and Society 12 (Berkeley, CA: 1993), 25–115.

[99] Noel Lenski, *Constantine and the Cities: Imperial Authority and Civic Politics* (Philadelphia, PA: 2016), 210. Compare with Ando, *Imperial Ideology*, and Dohrmann, "Law and Imperial Idioms," 63–78.

[100] Choksy, "Sacral Kingship in Sasanian Iran," 35–52; de Jong, "Sub Specie Maiestatis," 345–349; Shaked, *Dualism in Transformation*, 99–131.

These inscriptions were often accompanied by investiture reliefs in which the gods are depicted bestowing rulership upon Sasanian kings.[101] On the reverse of their coins, each Sasanian king portrayed a fire altar flanked by priests, a portable reminder of the relationship between empire and the cult, discussed in Chapter 5.[102] Empire and religion were not perceived as separate spheres, such that in a work of Sasanian *belles-lettres*, an aspiring elite courtier boasts of his excellence in both courtly culture and priestly knowledge:

> I memorized the *Yašt*, the *Hādōxt*, the *Bagān Yasn*, and the *Vīdēvdād* like a *herbed* and passage by passage heard the *Zand* ... And my skill in riding and archery is such that the other (i.e., opponent) must be taken for fortunate who can escape through my racecourse.[103]

Similarly, dynastic histories and stories which lauded the combined courtly, martial, and spiritual prowess of Sasanian kings were propagated by the court, likely in the second half of the Sasanian period.[104] As discussed in Chapter 1, Sasanian laws enshrined certain protections for Iranians and Iranianness. The Sasanians modeled themselves as Iranians, patrons of the Iranian cult, and preservers of Iranianness.[105]

Given the Sasanians' commitment to upholding Iranian distinctiveness, Iranian subjects were relied upon to conduct the affairs of the state. The magi in particular were well-integrated into Sasanian administration.[106]

[101] Matthew Canepa, "Topographies of Power: Theorizing the Visual, Spatial and Ritual Contexts of Rock Reliefs in Ancient Iran," in *Of Rocks and Water: Towards and Archaeology of Place*, ed. Ö. Harmanşah, Joukowsky Institute Publication 5 (Oxford: 2014), 55–92.

[102] Alram, "Beginning of Sasanian Coinage," 67–76. On earlier coinage, see Potts, "Foundation Houses, Fire Altars and the *Frataraka*," 271–300.

[103] Monchi-Zadeh, "Xusrōv Kavātān ut Rētak," 47–92, esp. 51–64.

[104] On the *Xwadāy-nāmag*, see Jaakko Hämeen-Anttila, *Khwadāynāmag: the Middle Persian Book of Kings* (Leiden: 2018). On the *Kārnāmag ī Ardaxšēr ī Pāpakān* ("Book of the Deeds of Ardashir, Son of Papak"), see Grenet, *La geste d'Ardashir fils de Pâbag*.

[105] De Jong, "One Nation under God?" 223–238.

[106] Daryaee, *Sasanian Persia*, 126–133; Shaul Shaked, "Administrative Functions of Priests in the Sasanian Period," in *Proceedings of the First European Conference of Iranian Studies: Part I, Old and Middle Iranian Studies*, ed. Gherardo Gnoli and Antonio Panaino (Rome: 1990), 261–273; Albert de Jong, "The Contribution of the Magi," vol. 1, *Birth of the Persian Empire*, ed. Vesta Sarkhosh Curtis and Sarah Stewart (New York: 2005), 92–93; Wiesehöfer, *Ancient Persia*, 183–191; Philippe Gignoux, "Titres et fonctions religieuses sasanides d'après les sources syriaques hagiographiques," *Acta Antiqua Academiae Scientiarum Hungaricae* 28 (1983): 191–203; Philippe Gignoux, "Pour une esquisse des fonctions religieuses," 93–108; Philippe Gignoux, "Une catégorie de mages à la fin de l'époque sasanide: les mogvēh," *Jerusalem Studies in Arabic and Islam* 9 (1987): 19–23; and Philippe Gignoux, "Die religiöse Administration in

They filled the posts of judges, arbiters, and more, and they appear in Syriac martyrdom accounts and rabbinic stories as possessing the authority to arrest, question, torture, and even execute.[107] While much remains opaque about Sasanian administration, aristocracy, elite families, and various other elite figures, the totality of the evidence, especially sigillographic, demonstrates that most Sasanian officials were of Iranian extraction.[108]

A commitment to Iranianness did not, however, preclude the Sasanian king from engaging with other communities. On the contrary, by conceiving of Iranians as a distinct population, Sasanian kings were free to acknowledge and support the particularities of non-Iranian communities, as part of their claim to universal kingship. The kings could sponsor the establishment of a church hierarchy in their lands, gift lavish furnishings to churches in the capital city of Ctesiphon, and even send relics of the true cross to the Catholicos.[109] Given their strategic importance, Christian martyr cults located in key frontier cities along the border with the Roman Empire were patronized by the Sasanian kings.[110] Kings could serve as arbiters of disputes between and among non-Iranian communities.[111] A Sasanian general could seek a ceasefire from the Romans so that "the Nazarenes and Jews who are in the army that is with me" could celebrate Easter and Passover.[112] Rabbinic stories, discussed above, can describe imperial support of individual rabbis and rabbinic law, while Christian synods portray the contemporary Sasanian king as a benevolent patron guided by the hand of God.[113] Christians and Jews did not see Sasanian support of Iranianness as compromising the empire's ability to favor other communities.

sasanidischer Zeit," 253–266. For material evidence, see Rika Gyselen, *La géographie administrative de l'empire sassanide*, 27–40; Gignoux, *Sasanian Seals and Sealings*, 34–67 and 130–295. Jean de Menasce, *Feux et fondations pieuses dans le droit sassanide* (Paris: 1964), 51–55, discusses the evidence for the officials in fire temples.

107 See discussion in Chapter 1. Even allowing for exaggeration, Agathias' account (*Histories*, 2.26.5) is illustrative of the place of magi in Sasanian society.

108 See Chapter 2.

109 For the former, see *Martyrdom of Peroz* (Bedjan, *Acta martyrum et sanctorum*, 4.256); for the latter, see *The History of Mar Sabrisho* (Bedjan, *Histoire de Mar-Jabalaha*, 302–303).

110 Fowden, *Barbarian Plain*; Marcus, "Armenian Life of Marutha of Maipherkat," esp. 69–70.

111 See e.g., Becker, *Sources*, 155.

112 Pseudo-Zachariah Rhetor, *Chronicle*, in Brooks, *Historia ecclesiastica Zachariae*, 95; translation in Hamilton and Brooks, *Syriac Chronicle*, 225–226. The passage is discussed in Neusner, *History of the Jews*, 5.106. See also Widengren, "Status of the Jews," 145–146.

113 See Chabot, *Synodicon Orientale*, 121 (Canon 14).

In addition, Sasanian kings promoted their claim to universal kingship through displays of benevolence, competence, and strength. They built and maintained infrastructure like bridges and canals, especially in Mesopotamia, to promote agricultural productivity and the circulation of goods and trade while projecting themselves as benefactors of local communities.[114] Jewish and Christian sources describe royal processions and periodic gatherings at the royal court, offering denizens a sense of access to and intimacy with the king.

Alongside these demonstrations of soft power, Mesopotamia was a borderland in which the Sasanian kings displayed hard power as well. Jewish and Christian sources mention the procession and billeting of troops, often unwelcome presences, but which effectively conveyed both the strength and vigilance of the king.[115] The constant movement of forces to and from Mesopotamia made the proximity of the king apparent, and military victories were powerful symbols of the imperial protection the king afforded these communities.[116] Sasanian kings projected the strength and stability of their rule by shaping the urban landscape; founding cities in Mesopotamia with names praising the king and commemorating their victories.[117] Iranians and non-Iranians therefore lived in cities named after the victories of Sasanian kings, such as "the victory of Shapur (Pērōz Shābuhr)," signifying Shapur's defeat of the emperor Gordian in 244 CE and subsequent ratification of a highly favorable treaty.[118]

The embrace by non-Iranians of imperial protection is visible in the following talmudic discussion:

Said Rav Adda b. Ahavah, "One should not sell them bars of iron."

Why? Because they may hammer weapons out of them ...
Why then do we sell it now?
Said Rav Ashi, "[We sell it] to the Persians because they protect us."[119]

[114] That bridge building was an important kind of benefaction is seen, for instance, from Mihr Narseh's bridge inscription in Gur. See Walter B. Henning, "The Inscription of Firuzabad," *Asia Major* 4 (1954): 98–102. Public building was one of the most prominent ways a king displayed his beneficence and rule, reflected, for instance, in the *Kārnāmag ī Ardaxšēr ī Pābagān* (Grenet, *La geste d'Ardashir fils de Pâbag*, 94–95; 106–107).

[115] E.g., b. Ḥul. 46a. [116] Rubin, "Sasanid Monarchy," 641.

[117] Zeev Rubin, "The Sasanid Monarchy," in *Late Antiquity: Empire and Successors, AD 425–600*, vol. 14, *The Cambridge Ancient History* ed. Averil Cameron, Bryan Ward-Perkins, and Michael Whitby (Cambridge: 2000), 639.

[118] Described in Naqsh-e Rustam, the so-called *Res Gestae Divi Saporis*, 3–4.

[119] b. ʿAbod. Zar. 16a according to MS Paris, Bibliotheque Nationale, 1337.

Here, an established rabbinic prohibition against selling weapons-grade iron to gentiles is openly flaunted by accepted communal practice, requiring an ex post facto justification. Rav Ashi explains that the practice is limited "to the Persians because they protect us."[120] The rhetorical pattern of the introduction of a change to the law as a result of an already existent practice recalls Rava's opinion, discussed in Chapter 5, regarding the donation of vessels to fire temples. In the case of donations to the fire temple, the prohibitions were waived, and the donations were permitted on the grounds that they provided an economic benefit to the fire temples and were not intended to denigrate Judaism. Here, the prohibition is waived because Persians allegedly enhance the security of the Jewish community. The categorical assertion that the Persians protect the Jews mimics Sasanian imperial claims to afford security and protection to its subjects.[121]

By viewing their subjects as a conglomeration of Iranians and non-Iranians, rather than as a unitary whole, the Sasanians also recognized the differing cultural, linguistic, and religious expressions of these communities.[122] Instead of seeking to unify and homogenize their subjects based on a common cultural identity, the Sasanians promoted a general sense of unity around the model of a universal king, one who served all of his subjects and was owed allegiance by them. We therefore find little evidence of Aramaic-speaking communities in Mesopotamia during the Sasanian period explicitly classifying themselves as Iranians; instead, they preserved their own, distinct communal identities.[123] Despite this, their

120 On this text, see Hayes, *Between the Babylonian and Palestinian Talmuds*, 171–179; and Gafni, "Political, Social, and Economic History," 799.

121 The existence of Jewish soldiers in the Sasanian military is suggested in several sources. See the report in Pseudo-Zachariah Rhetor: Syriac in E. W. Brooks, ed., *Historia ecclesiastica Zachariae rhetori vulgo adscripta* (Paris: 1919–1924), 95; English in Robert Phenix and Cornelia Horn, trans. *The Chronicle of Pseudo-Zachariah Rhetor: Church and War in Late Antiquity* (Liverpool: 2001), 322–323; and discussion in Neusner, *History of the Jews*, 5.106; b. Ta'an. 21b; Yeb. 121b. For a survey of earlier views, see Itzchak Geiger, *The Yeshiva of Pumbedita from Its Foundation until Abbaye's Days* [in Hebrew] (PhD diss., Hebrew University of Jerusalem, 2006), 233–234.

122 Attempts to attribute to the Sasanians an affirmative Zoroastrian cosmology and theology that actively sought to incorporate non-Iranians into not only its political, but also its eschatological ends, is unnecessary to explain the inclusion of non-Iranians in the Sasanian Empire and its hierarchies. Contra Payne, *State of Mixture*, 30–38, and suggested in de Jong, "First Sin," 192–209.

123 Daryaee, "Ethnic and Territorial Boundaries," 123–137, suggests that Jews, Christians, and others saw themselves as Iranians. This, however, is based on a likely ninth-century Christian funerary inscription. See de Blois, "The Middle Persian Inscription from

non-Iranian identities did not preclude community members from attaining positions in the imperial bureaucracy, some even rising to the status of elite courtiers.[124] Sasanian kings deftly navigated their overlapping commitments, allowing both Iranian and non-Iranian populations to see themselves as proper subjects of Sasanian rule.

In this context, the magi functioned as enforcers of Iranian and Zoroastrian cosmology on behalf of the king, as discussed in Chapter 3. Protection of this cosmology, which viewed certain practices of the empire's non-Iranian communities as adversely impacting the sacredness of Iranian space, necessarily created conflict between Iranians and non-Iranians – something that the kings could not have ignored. The suggestion, found in some of the non-Iranian sources discussed earlier, that the magi somehow functioned independently of the king, is therefore difficult to accept because it is belied by Kerdir's inscriptions, treaties between Sasanian and Roman rulers, and more.[125] It was the king who ultimately permitted the magi to enforce the tenets of Iranian cosmology, and it was he who had the ability to restrain them when necessary. This is not to suggest that king and magi always acted in unison, just as emperors and bishops often found themselves in conflict.[126] Yet, as Adam Becker argues, "there was conflict between the priestly class and the Shahanshah or between the priestly class and the nobles, but these were frictions within a fundamentally political *and* religious system of social networks that made up the Sasanian state and elite society." Their interests, ideas, and actions were not always entirely aligned; but king and magi collaborated in their shared desire to maintain Iranian identity and Zoroastrian principles, even when they defined these differently.

The very existence of the magi, however, helped created distance between their activities and the will of the king. As the visible protectors of Iranian cosmology, the magi could be used to exonerate the king from

Constantinople: Sassanian or Post-Sassanian?" *Studia Iranica* 19 (1990): 209–218. It appears instead, as Daryaee, 134, himself suggests, that the term lost its political and religious valence after the fall of the Sasanians. Gnoli, *The Idea of Iran*, 151–156, notes that Manichaeans similarly do not adopt "ērān" as an endonym.

124 For Christians achieving high status positions in the empire, see Introduction, p. 28. The *Martyrdom of Pusai* (Bedjan, *Acta martyrum et sanctorum*, 2.213), discussed and quoted earlier, reflects this imperial preference for Iranian over Christian officials.

125 Menander Protector, fragment 6.1.398–407 (Blockley, *The History of Menander the Guardsman*, 74–77).

126 Gignoux, "Church-State Relations," 72–80. On the Byzantine Empire, see esp. Harold Drake, "Intolerance, Religious Violence, and Political Legitimacy in Late Antiquity," *Journal of the American Academy of Religions* 79 (2011): 193–235.

their acts of violence against inhabitants. Non-Iranians were able to imagine that the magi behaved without the king's permission or impressed their will upon him. The king therefore remained above the fray. This was not a strategy of duplicity or disingenuousness on the part of the Sasanian kings, but rather a reflection of the uneasy balancing act that they often had to maintain between competing constituencies.

The dueling images of the Sasanian king proffered by its different subjects appears most starkly in two sources, both composed in Arabic in the ninth-tenth century, which describe the same encounter between the Sasanian king Ohrmazd and the magi, albeit with significantly different conclusions. The famous Iranian historian al-Ṭabarī reports the encounter as follows:

> The Hērbadhs (Zoroastrian priests) presented Ohrmazd with a petition that embodied their desire to persecute the Christians. The king endorsed the document with the words: "Just as our royal throne cannot stand on its two front legs without the two back ones, our kingdom cannot stand or endure firmly if we cause the Christians and adherents of other faiths, who differ in belief from ourselves, to become hostile to us. So renounce this desire to persecute the Christians and become assiduous in good works, so that the Christians and the adherents of other faiths may see this, praise you for it, and feel themselves drawn toward your religion."[127]

The Sasanian King Ohrmazd IV (r. 579–590) admonishes the magi not to persecute Christians or other groups because they are an essential part of the Empire, here analogized to legs of the throne. The king, however, adds a further inducement to the magi that by not persecuting these groups and remaining committed to the performance of their duties as Zoroastrians, Christians and others may be *more* inclined to accept Zoroastrianism.

A different version of this episode appears in the Christian Arabic *Chronicle of Seert*. It is nearly identical to that reported by al-Ṭabarī, but with one crucial difference.[128] Instead of the king's final inducement to the magi that Christians may convert, the king cautions the magi that:

> ... as a throne with four legs cannot be stable on the two in front if it does not also rest on the two behind, so also the religion of the Magi will not be stable if there is no other religion to counterbalance it.

[127] Bosworth, *The Sāsānids, the Byzantines, the Lakhmid*, 298.

[128] Scher, *Chronique de Séert*, 2.103–104. See partial translation and discussion in Shaked, *Dualism in Transformation*, 114–115.

According to the Christian source, what matters most to the king is that his subjects – Iranian or non-Iranian – embody the two traits he ascribes in particular to his Christian subjects: faithfulness and obedience.[129] Whereas the source in al-Ṭabarī represents a king whose pragmatism toward non-Zoroastrians is in fact a guileful ploy intended to benefit the magi, in the Christian source the king's pragmatism is due to his appreciation of loyal subjects, no matter their religious background. The king, in fact, wanted balance between the magi and other groups, not the triumph of one over the other. The very same episode – whether real or imagined – could be refracted through the different images the king projected, on the one hand, and the ingrained and selective perceptions of different subjects, on the other.

CONCLUSION

We can now better respond to the questions posed at the outset of the chapter: How could neighboring communities have produced such different portrayals of king and empire? And which of them should we accept as historical fact? The latter is simply the wrong question. These differing and competing communal perceptions all resulted from a political culture carefully cultivated by Sasanian kings to appeal to two distinct audiences. Zoroastrians could view the king as their loyal patron, one who maintained the fire cult and Iranian cosmology. To them, the king was first and foremost an Iranian, and this perspective is reflected in the Zoroastrian sources discussed above. Non-Zoroastrian communities could view the king as religiously and philosophically neutral, informed by the king's benefaction of their communities, on the one hand, and the absence of overt imperial efforts to challenge their communal practices, on the other. To them, the king was religiously neutral, whereas the magi were religious zealots. The dichotomous portrayals of king and magi in non-Iranian sources therefore reflect the perspective of the non-Iranian communities who saw, were made to see, and wished to see, Sasanian royalty as a group with which they could cooperate.

By portraying a religiously unaffiliated king who prevented or at least limited religiously based violence, the Talmud, Manichaean sources, and Christian sources internalized a discrete set of images the empire projected to its subjects. This allowed them and their followers to see the state as a

[129] E.g., Payne, *State of Mixture*, 167.

place in which their communities could flourish. As Payne provocatively put it with regard to several Christian sources, by locating "imperial Zoroastrianism in the religious authorities rather than in the rulers" of the Sasanian Empire, East Syriac leaders became "more docile servants of the empire than the bishops of the Christian Roman Empire."[130] The Babylonian Talmud's portrayal of an unfailingly neutral king, never even appearing with magi in the same story, offers a similar idyll of an empire with which rabbis and Jews could negotiate, one in which religious interference was an aberration rather than a fundamental feature, an empire against which, as we saw in Chapter 4, direct and hostile conflict was the wrong political tack. The representations of kings and magi in the Talmud, like those in Manichaean, Syriac, and indeed Zoroastrian sources, were forged at the intersection of imperial ideology and communal desires.

This chapter demonstrates the benefits of an historical approach that studies rabbinic representation alongside those of neighboring communities, and that situates them within the context of Sasanian rule. On their own, each community's representations might be treated as an accurate historical description or as a reflection of an isolated community's perception of its surroundings. Taken together, however, these works furnish a far more multifaceted portrait of an ongoing and animated conversation between empire and subjects that defined their ever-evolving relationship.

[130] Payne, *State of Mixture*, 13–14.

Conclusion

The Sasanian Empire from the Perspective of the Jews

While presiding over a legal dispute, Rav Naḥman's student persistently pestered him with questions. Exasperated, Rav Naḥman reprimanded the student:

> Did I not say to you that when I am sitting in judgment you should not say anything to me, for Huna our colleague said with reference to me that I and King Shapur are brothers in respect of judgement (*dina*) . . . ?[1]

The comparison Rav Naḥman draws between himself and King Shapur has traditionally been understood as a reference not to the Sasanian king himself, but to the third-century Babylonian rabbi Shmuel. This is based on another talmudic pericope discussed in the introduction of this book, where a rabbi boasts that he will say something "that not even King Shapur said," which an anonymous gloss there suggests refers not to King Shapur, but to a nickname of the rabbi Shmuel.[2] As I argued there, there is no reason to accept the late anonymous explanation, and there is certainly no compelling reason to apply it here to the story of Rav Naḥman where no such interpolation appears.[3] Taking the above story

[1] b. B. Qam. 96b.

[2] b. Pesaḥ. 54a = B. Bat. 115b. See discussion in Secunda, *Iranian Talmud*, 104–106. This reading is also based, in part, on a late editorial gloss in b. Bek. 49b that says that in matters of civil law, or *dine*, the law follows Shmuel rather than Rav. However, the context of the story in b. B. Qam. 96b is not civil law (*dine*) in general, but a court case (*dina*), and Rav Naḥman takes umbrage at the fact that a student is questioning him *during* a court case.

[3] In MS Escorial, Rav Naḥman elaborates that his analogy is to King Shapur himself, adding the explanation "just as King Shapur can expropriate money without judgment, so too can I expropriate money without judgment." MS Vatican 116 contains a marginal gloss that

on its own terms, Rav Naḥman is not comparing his expertise in judgement to Shmuel, but to King Shapur himself.

Minimally, Rav Naḥman's analogy to King Shapur is intended to convey that Rav Naḥman, like the Sasanian king, outranks his student. But the comparison is more than a generic boast. Rav Naḥman invokes Shapur in the context of judgement, in which he claims they are equal. This reflects the perception of the Sasanian king as a benchmark for just judgment, a perception the king undoubtedly fostered and that the rabbis apparently internalized.[4] Indeed, stories told by other subject communities reflect the notion that the Sasanian king was perceived as an authoritative and dependable judge, even in matters of internecine conflict.[5] Yet the analogy's target may be even narrower. Rav Naḥman compares himself to the king to demand his disciple's silence. This may invoke the expectation of silence in the court of the Sasanian king until one was invited to speak.[6] The analogy to King Shapur then not only distinguished the rabbi as a supremely worthy judge, but it may additionally import the cultural codes and expectations of the Sasanian court to the rabbinic court.

Stories like this typify the ongoing conversation between the Sasanian Empire and its Jewish subjects that lies at the heart of this book. Rabbis not only express familiarity with the royal court, but adopted, adapted, and naturalized imperial projections about it, changing their own self-perception and social expectations in the process. The story reveals rabbinic pretensions to elite status, fashioning themselves after prominent Sasanian figures, including the king himself. A rabbi could embrace images projected by the empire of the king as legal paragon, paradoxically to authorize his own legal arbitration in a world in which Jews had recourse to the very Sasanian courts nominally administered by the king himself. Rabbis sought to wrest some power and influence for themselves even as they legitimated the empire and presented it as worthy of accommodation. Even seemingly parochial encounters between a rabbinic master and his irritating disciple were deeply enmeshed in the Sasanian world.

identifies King Shapur with Shmuel, following Rashi and other medieval commentaries ad loc.

4 See similarly Dohrmann, "Law and Imperial Idioms," about early Palestinian rabbis and Rome.

5 Becker, *Sources*, 155.

6 Canepa, *Two Eyes of the Earth*, 144–146. For silence at Persian meals, see Herman, "Table Etiquette and Persian Culture," 176–178.

This book has contended that Jews were necessarily and unavoidably entrenched in, vigorously navigated, and were dramatically shaped by Sasanian rule. Recognition of this fact has radical implications for how we understand Sasanian Jewish social and cultural history, as well as Sasanian imperial ideologies and strategies for governing its diverse populations. This conclusion recapitulates the major claims of the book, with an eye toward future directions and broader implications for the study of Jews, other Sasanian subjects, and the Sasanian Empire.

BABYLONIAN JEWISH SOCIETY AND CULTURE

The first two chapters of this book challenged the three pillars of semi-autonomy, central hierarchy, and insularity which have underpinned nearly every scholarly account of Babylonian Jewish history to date. Together, they supported an image of a highly stable, static, and siloed Jewish community throughout late antiquity and even beyond it. This community was supposedly headed by the Exilarch, who served as the intermediary and representative of the Jews with the Sasanian Empire, and it was governed by Jewish officials, especially the rabbis. The Jews exemplified the neatly bounded communities fostered by the Sasanians, who correspondingly organized their Christian and even Zoroastrian subjects.

A thorough study in Chapter 1 of the responsibilities attributed to the Exilarch in rabbinic literature and the Talmud's portrayal of rabbinic judgment, in conjunction with Christian and Sasanian evidence, revealed no signs of a consistent Sasanian policy to organize its subjects into self-governing and siloed religious communities. Subjects were, first and foremost, governed directly by imperial administration and had recourse to imperial courts, an arrangement reflected in Sasanian legal sources. This is visible in Talmudic and Christian anecdotes about encounters with Sasanian courts and administrators, as well as rabbinic and Christian familiarity with the technicalities of Sasanian law. Many texts into which have been read the notions of semi-autonomy and delegated legal authority are in fact evidence of Jewish participation in imperial systems and imperial indignation at attempted arrogations of its authority by its subjects.

Elites like the Exilarch, rabbis, bishops, and priests sought to occupy the informal spaces left open for local forms of conflict resolution and communal influence attainable not through imperial *diktat*, but through persuasion. In the case of legal adjudication, the rabbis, like Christian ecclesiastical leaders, sought to coax followers to submit themselves to their arbitration, even as they acknowledged, begrudgingly permitted, and circumscribed recourse to some forms of official imperial judgment. One way that rabbis and Christians sought to sway their followers was to present their judgment as authentically Jewish or Christian, while delegitimating their opponents for what they labeled excessive reliance or mimicry of Persian law, and by extension undermining Persian law as a legitimate venue for Jewish or Christian judgment. Their opponents, however, may well have adopted principles and the particulars of Sasanian law to ground their own rulings and make them legible (and perhaps admissible) in an imperial legal context.

Without a central hierarchy with guaranteed imperially sponsored positions that served to distinguish a functionary elite class, aspiring Jewish elites competed for status and prominence. As with modes of judgment, these figures variously and selectively mimicked and translated recognizable elite Sasanian symbols and habits into Jewish terms, and tactically denigrated their opponents' cultural choices. Against older ideas of a siloed Jewish community sheltered from so-called foreign Iranian influence, excepting the Exilarch, whose place at court demanded certain cultural concessions, all Jews were thoroughly embedded within their Iranian cultural and social context, which they positioned themselves within and against. They articulated their desired position within Jewish society through recognizable Sasanian modes of authority.

Chapter 2 focused on the aspiring Jewish elites best attested in the Talmud: the Exilarch and the rabbis. The Exilarch's cultural choices were reflective not of his formal position at court, but were instead a product of his imitation of high Sasanian aristocrats, whose legitimating claims and behaviors he expressed in Jewish terms. The Exilarch's public displays of wealth, assertion of noble descent, multiple abodes, and lavish banquets are consistent with our evidence for other high Sasanian elites, but he traced his noble descent to King David rather than an Iranian ancestor, and he hosted banquets on Jewish festivals instead of Zoroastrian ones. Like other high elites, the Exilarch sought to draw various lower elites into his orbit, establishing a royal court in miniature, but now populated by Jews. Included among these were rabbis, some of whom earned the moniker "rabbis of the house of the Exilarch," and who appear to have welcomed the patronage and validation of the Exilarch. Other rabbis, however, contested aspects of the Exilarch's self-presentation, and claimed to be equally or more deserving of status and influence owing to their expertise in Jewish tradition, which they elevated above all other claims to authority and power. Even these rabbis, however, did not reject Sasanian elite culture as such, adopting and adapting it for their own ends. The rabbinic academy was modeled, at least in rabbinic imagination, after the Sasanian royal court, and the leading rabbi was considered its king. Other rabbis claimed that they deserved public support from fellow Jews because they served a function similar to another Sasanian elite, the Zoroastrian priest. As subjects integrated into Sasanian administration, law, and society, Jews of various stripes invariably negotiated Sasanian and Jewish cultures in their jockeying for recognition.

A central feature in previous accounts of Babylonian Jewish history was the supposedly peaceable conditions Jews enjoyed under Sasanian rule, in direct contrast to the experience of Christians. Their relatively positive treatment was attributed to the personal proclivities of Sasanian kings who overall "tolerated" Jews and Jewish practice, but often displayed intolerance toward Christians. Even as models that assume a broad Sasanian intolerance for Christians are in a process of revision, Sasanian "tolerance" of Jews and Judaism informs scholarly notions of a flourishing Jewish community left to its own devices. Chapter 3 argued that Jews did not merit special tolerance from the empire, nor were Christians targeted on account of imperial intolerance. Sasanian violence was not typically applied at the capricious whims of the Sasanian king, nor did it indiscriminately target all members of a particular religious community. Instead, Sasanian violence was a strategically deployed imperial instrument, the proverbial stick used alongside the carrot of patronage and support to enforce the principles and social boundaries that lay at the heart of Sasanian political theology.

Key to Sasanian political theology was the assertion that its kings were simultaneously Iranian and universal rulers, constituting a corresponding division between two sets of subjects, Iranians and non-Iranians. The Sasanians bore different responsibilities to these two communities; it had to safeguard and promote Iranian identities and Zoroastrianism, even as it sought to extend order over all of its subjects. Imperial violence was often used when subjects were perceived to threaten Iranian identity or Zoroastrianism, or when they challenged Sasanian rule over its vast territories, a major concern in Mesopotamia, which lay at the border of the Roman-Sasanian frontier. Sasanian violence was therefore fundamentally responsive to the behaviors, choices, and positions of its subjects; the differing scope and regularity of imperial violence experienced by Jews and Christians illuminates much about how and why they triggered imperial concerns.

By collecting reports of violence against Jews and Christians, Chapter 3 argued that Jews were subjected to fewer incidents of violence because it seems like they did not missionize Zoroastrians to the same degree as Christians did, nor did they trigger the same geopolitical anxieties. The fraught position of Christians in the context of the enduring Roman-Sasanian conflict led to more regular bouts of imperial violence against them, but also to more overt and sweeping acts of patronage, such as the foundation of the East Syriac ecclesiastical hierarchy at the behest of the Sasanian king. As a result of their relative insignificance in the context of the Roman-Sasanian conflict, Jews elicited fewer anxieties than their Christian neighbors, but carried less importance, accounting for both the likely fewer instances of imperial violence against them and the lack of evidence of significant imperial sponsorship of Jews. The position and behavior of Jews often placed them outside of the immediate purview of imperial concern, but hardly spared them entirely from episodes of imperial violence.

If Jews were indeed subjected to Sasanian violence, and especially to the same logics of Sasanian violence as their neighbors, the absence of stories of imperial persecution from the Babylonian Talmud requires explanation, especially when compared with the prodigious body of Syriac Christian works dedicated to stories of martyrdom and direct confrontation with the Empire. Chapters 4 through 6 argued that such a question misguidedly approaches the Talmud as a passive repository of information about Jews and the Sasanian Empire. Rabbinic representations of the empire were intended to convey and shape Jewish attitudes toward it. In the case of stories of violence, Chapter 4 argued that attention to their compositional history reveals that the rabbis selectively crafted representations that encouraged an accommodationist stance toward the Sasanian Empire and avoidance of direct confrontation with it, and accomplished this in part by altering, and perhaps expunging, those stories that could convey a different message. The empire in these stories is never anti-Jewish, and imperial violence never targets Jews in particular. When necessary, the empire was to be subverted and circumvented, but not openly challenged. The stories that survive in the Talmud consistently reflect how some Jews communicated what they deemed the optimal political strategies to endure within the imperial system in which they were integrated.

Stories of Sasanian violence – and their absence – were only one of the ways Jews reflected on strategies to thrive in the Sasanian Empire. Outside of assumptions of an insular and siloed community, Jews simply could not avoid the prominence and prevalence of Zoroastrian practices, institutions, and symbols. Chapter 5 explored the varied and conflicting ways Sasanian Jews approached Zoroastrianism. Surviving Jewish personal seals as well as rabbinic sources suggest that some Jews were comfortable adopting Zoroastrian symbols or participating in Zoroastrian festivals, while other Jews eschewed or condemned them. This tension lives within the pages of the Talmud. Rabbis classified Zoroastrianism as idolatry, thereby applying a body of laws intended to separate Jews from even the remotest possible facilitation of idolatrous practice. Yet in several remarkable stories, rabbis devised highly creative – bordering on dubious – legal justifications for financial exchange with fire temples as well as the donation of implements of worship to them. Such accommodation to Zoroastrianism is legible in light of the central political, social, cultural, and economic functions and valences of fire temples in particular, and Zoroastrianism in general, within the Sasanian Empire. The same valences of fire temples and Zoroastrianism were known to Syriac Christians, who often told stories not of accommodation, but open resistance to them. As in the case of representations of imperial violence studied in Chapter 4, the fact that Jews and Christians differ here may suggest that certain political views were more prevalent amongst the members of one group than the other, perhaps the result of the popularity of the metanarrative framework of martyrdom among Christians and its relative absence among Jews.[7] We must be open to the possibility that the stories communities told about the Empire shaped their interactions with it.

Chapter 6 explored talmudic representations of Sasanian kings and magi. The former are regularly depicted as largely religiously neutral, and the latter as custodians of Zoroastrianism whose enforcement often entailed interfering directly in Jewish life and practice. Syriac and Manichaean texts offer similar binary representations of kings and magi. Scholars have understood this dualistic image as a reflection of a reality in which Sasanian kings were broadly tolerant toward Jews, and the magi principally responsible for interference in Jewish practice and life. In turn, scholars have imagined a perennial conflict at the heart of the Sasanian Empire between the religiously zealous magi and the secular king, who at times was powerful enough to disregard the magi, but at other times had no choice but to capitulate to their radical demands. Yet in treating these representations of kings and magi as transparent reflections of reality,

[7] Kyle Smith, *Cult of the Dead: A Brief History of Christianity* (Berkeley, CA: 2022).

scholars ignore or dismiss the ample testimony from imperial and Zoroastrian sources that portray a harmonious relationship between king and magi, royalty and religion. The chapter argued that the contradictory representations offered by non-Iranian and Iranian subjects reflect the different images the empire projected to its diverse populations. To Iranian subjects, the king was a champion of the gods and the cult; to non-Iranian subjects, the king represented the empire's order, prosperity, and security. We need not choose one imperial projection over the other, but Sasanian subjects did, embracing imperial projections that best fit their histories and needs.

Given the lasting impact of notions of imperial feudalism and tolerance, on the one hand, and of Jewish semi-autonomy, centralization, and insularity, on the other, on all aspects of Sasanian Jewish history, the revisionist account offered in this book stands to transform the social and cultural histories not only of the Jews, but especially of the rabbis and their only literary legacy, the Talmud.[8]

REVERSING THE GAZE

This book's focus on Jews has required addressing aspects of the Sasanian Empire and its other subjects in a piecemeal and episodic fashion as they were prompted by the Jewish evidence. We will here reverse the gaze and address how Jewish sources, in conjunction with the evidence of other subject groups, affect our understanding of the Sasanian Empire.

Though Jewish society has served as a lynchpin in earlier histories of the Sasanian Empire, the Jewish evidence belies any Sasanian propensity to organize its subjects into corporate religious communities (Chapter 1). Rather, individuals and groups were directly subjected to the state apparatus. At the same time, the Sasanians recognized and distinguished between two broad sets of subjects: Iranians and non-Iranians (Chapters 1, 3, and 6). This division reflects the deep and often conflicting ideological commitments and aspirations of the empire: to rule Iran and Iranians and be universal rulers over all who resided in their territory. The balancing act between these two commitments serves to define much of

[8] I explore some of the implications and future directions in Gross, "Prolegomena to a Study of Babylonian Rabbinization in Late Antiquity"; Gross, "Babylonian Jewish Communities"; and Gross, "The Impact of Sasanian Imperialism on the Culture and Literature of the Babylonian Rabbis," in *What is the Talmud: The State of the Question*, ed. Christine Hayes and Jay Harris (Forthcoming).

the empire's rhetoric, administrative policy, and encounters with particular groups. The history of scholarship has sought to reduce these two aspirations into one, portraying the empire as driven either by religious zealotry or political pragmatism (or claiming that certain individual kings vacillated between the two), and more recently by seeking to harmonize a single Sasanian political-theological commitment to foster a "state of mixture" that seamlessly integrated Iranian and non-Iranians into a single polity.[9] Instead of questioning the genuineness of the convictions of the empire and its rulers, or projecting a modern notion of cultural pluralism onto the Sasanians, this book explored how the empire sought to realize and achieve equilibrium between these two ideological foci.

Among the empire's strategies was legislation that enshrined protections for Iranians and Iranianness, while at the same time creating a system of law that applied to all its subjects (Chapter 1). Another strategy was the deliberate and selective deployment of violence in order to protect Iranian interests from the encroachments and desecrations of non-Iranians, even as the empire supported and patronized non-Iranian communities in sundry ways (Chapter 3). The empire projected distinct images of itself to its dual audiences, allowing both Iranians and non-Iranians to emphasize the imperial interests that best suited them (Chapter 6).[10] These dual projections and their effects are visible when the literatures of subject communities are examined collectively, militating against persistent models that reduce Sasanian rule into a perennial and irresolvable tension between kings and magi, pragmatism and religion.

Even if the Sasanians broadly divided their subjects into two, which accounts for the general logics of imperial behavior and the shared experience of non-Iranian subjects, the empire could also forge distinct relationships with particular religious elites depending on the prospects and threats they presented to Sasanian imperial ambitions (Chapters 1 and 3). One of the recurring conclusions of this book is that the Sasanians ultimately had very different relationships with Christians than with Jews. The former constituted a regular and central concern to the Sasanians because their religious identities positioned them squarely at the intersection of the empire's ongoing conflict with an increasingly Christianized Rome, and their practices habitually threatened the division between Iranians and non-Iranians.[11] Christians therefore attracted special

[9] Payne, *State of Mixture*.
[10] See by comparison Ando, *Imperial Ideology*, 5; and Lenski, *Constantine and the Cities*.
[11] Gross, "Being Roman."

scrutiny and were subject to intense surveillance and violence, but also to otherwise unparalleled imperial patronage. The patronage of an East Syriac ecclesiastical hierarchy is not a reflection of a general Sasanian policy toward the organization of its non-Iranian religious communities, but was tailored to the particularities of Christians, intended to parallel the Church hierarchy established under the auspices of the Roman Empire. Even this church hierarchy, however, did not amount to a Christian state within a state, nor did it approximate any semblance of semi-autonomy (Chapter 1). Instead, the existence of a church bureaucracy allowed the Sasanians to foster strong ties with Christian elites, who in turn would promote the interests of the state to their communities, even to the point of policing their own Christian flock on behalf of the state.[12] Jews, whose position in the late antique Near East did not elicit similar imperial anxiety nor promise similar benefits, never drew imperial attention to the same degree. This spared them from the frequency and scale of violence employed against Christians, but also never incentivized the Sasanians to invest in Jewish communities to the same extent. The relationship between the empire and its subjects was determined by structural forces of imperial political culture, by the contingency of historical circumstance, and by the agency of the subjects themselves.

Lastly, this book has pushed back against a tendency to treat the Sasanian Empire as the curious oriental despotic stepsibling of the Roman Empire, equivalent perhaps in military capability and economic power, but profoundly distinct in its political organization. The pervasiveness of the analogy between supposed Sasanian feudalism and a caricature of the Ottoman millet system, despite the thousand years separating them, signals an essentialism that flattens various eastern empires into a convenient antipode of the more sophisticated Roman and other "western" empires. But the Sasanians employed neither a caricature of feudalism nor a political theology that celebrated multiculturalism. Allowing for meaningful differences, this book portrayed a Sasanian Empire driven by similar policies, strategies of rule, and stimuli as the contemporary Roman and other empires in the ancient world vis-à-vis their heterogenous subjects. Like the Christian Roman Empire, they struggled between commitments to a given subset of their population and to their diverse subjects as a whole. They integrated populations into their legal system while allowing for arbitration and local conflict resolution;

[12] For a bold example of this, see Gross, "Being Roman in the Sasanian Empire," 386–387.

they used violence as an instrument of rule, and they were deliberate in the projections they offered their different communities. These commonalities should hardly be surprising. Scholars continue to show the extent to which the Romans and Sasanians were responsive to the others' modes of self-presentation, which mutually shaped their titles, inscriptions, images, coins, urban planning, architecture, and so much more.[13] Further comparative work must explore similarities and differences between the Sasanians and other imperial contexts without exoticizing or belittling the former.

One of the key shortcomings of the Sasanian Jewish record is that it does not readily speak to diachronic change over the course of late antiquity. This, however, may also be a strength, as it shifts focus away from a historiographic tendency to narrate Sasanian rule as a constant vacillation between the personalities and attitudes of individual kings to the broader logics and animating principles that lay at the heart of Sasanian rule in its encounters with different subject groups. An emphasis on broader patterns does not discount the possibility of various contingent forces affecting the short-term policies of the empire and its treatment of its subjects, or other factors that produced change over time, but it contends that the abstractions offered in this book possess important explanatory power.

SASANIAN SUBJECTS

An approach that treats Jews as one subject group among many also allows for broader generalizations about their shared context and their negotiation with it. As this book has emphasized repeatedly, a process of triangulation between different subject groups must not elide or collapse the differing experiences they had or the distinct choices they made in their encounters with Sasanian rule.

In the first place, a collective study of subject communities reflected that they were integrated into the same administrative apparatus and positioned themselves within and against it in similar ways (Chapter 1). Sasanian rule, habits, and symbols similarly pervaded the lives of subjects in a range of socio-economic positionalities, including those who lived predominately outside of the purview of the court (Chapter 2). Against an emphasis on high elites and their life at court as the central nodes of a

[13] See esp. Canepa, *Two Eyes of the Earth*.

group's acculturation, predicated on older models of semi-autonomous and siloed communities, future research will continue to uncover the ways individuals, groups, and texts from varying social locations embraced, adapted, and contested the ambient culture, imperial projections, and other aspects of life under Sasanian rule. Based primarily on the Jewish evidence, the book therefore offered a schematic portrayal of how groups positioned themselves, their histories, traditions, and institutions within, alongside, and against imperial administration and elite Sasanian culture.

In aggregate, certain attitudes and images were more prevalent in Jewish versus Christian sources. The surviving Christian evidence evinces a greater willingness to describe imperial violence against Christians and valorize active Christian resistance and martyrdom in response (Chapters 3–5). These differences are primarily literary but may also reflect the relative prevalence of these attitudes and strategies among the two groups. Why might the members of particular communities have embraced different attitudes? Was it due to the prominence of a robust tradition of martyrdom among Christians and its absence among Jews? Did the greater violence that Christians experienced because of their position generate greater willingness for resistance, in turn occasioning further violence, in a repetitive cycle?

Yet the relative prevalence of certain images or attitudes among Sasanian Jews and Christians that this method of triangulation exposed should not suggest that the two groups are easily divided according to the monolithic attitudes toward the Sasanian Empire they espoused. Groups, and even the same individuals, espoused different and often contradictory views and made assorted choices. The rabbis could both permit recourse to certain Sasanian courts and jostle for recognition against them. They could view Zoroastrian fire temples as idolatrous and permit financial exchange with them. They could embrace Sasanian habits and frames of reference while critiquing others for doing so, drawing the lines between tradition and empire in different places. This is to say nothing of the disagreements and contests between and among Jews over these questions (Chapters 2 and 5). Given the variety of approaches on display in the limited surviving body of Jewish evidence alone, it is never justifiable to reduce a given group to a single set of views.

The Jewish evidence examined in this book is not necessarily the most copious, the most diverse, or the most comprehensive to survive from a group of Sasanian subjects. But whatever its shortcomings, this evidence encapsulates the unique experience, attitudes, and strategies of one subject group, which in turn are diagnostic of the possibilities available to other subjects and the constraints they faced living under Sasanian rule. The parochial nature of much of the Jewish evidence is precisely what makes it so valuable as a litmus test for the impact of Sasanian rule on many aspects of its various subjects' lives well outside of the direct purview of the royal court. The Talmud's technical legal and hermeneutical debates and edifying stories show just how deeply Babylonian Jews were entrenched in and shaped by the Sasanian Empire. This must be the starting point from which to discuss the integrated history of Jews, Christians, and other subjects under Sasanian rule.

Bibliography

Adams, Robert McC. *Land behind Baghdad: A History of Settlement on the Diyala Plains*. Chicago, IL: 1965.

Heartland of Cities: Surveys of Ancient Settlement and Land Use on the Central Floodplain of the Euphrates. Chicago, IL: 1981.

Adler, Marcus, ed. and trans. *The Itinerary of Benjamin of Tudela*. London: 1907.

Aggoula, Basile. *Inscriptions et graffites araméens d'Assour*. Napoli: 1985.

Ahdut, Eli. "Jewish-Zoroastrian Polemics in the Babylonian Talmud." In *Irano-Judaica* IV, edited by Shaul Shaked and Amnon Netzer, 17–40. Jerusalem: 1999.

"The Talmudic Expression *qaqei hiwware* as an Aid in Understanding the Marking of Social Distinctions among Babylonian Jews" [in Hebrew]. In *Irano-Judaica* V, edited by Shaul Shaked and Amnon Netzer, 13–26. Jerusalem: 2003.

al-Ka'bi, Nasir. *A Short Chronicle on the End of the Sasanian Empire and Early Islam*. Piscataway, NJ: 2016.

Alram, Michael. "The Beginning of Sasanian Coinage." *Bulletin of the Asia Institute* 13 (1999): 67–76.

"Early Sasanian Coinage." In *The Idea of Iran*, vol. 3: *The Sasanian Era*, edited by Vesta Sarkhosh Curtis and Sarah Stewart, 17–30. London: 2008.

Alram, Michael, and Rika Gyselen. *Ardashir I – Shapur I. Vol. 1 of Sylloge Nummorum Sasanidarum: Paris – Berlin – Wien*. Vienna: 2003.

Alram, Michael, Maryse Blet-Lemarquand, and Prods Oktor Skjærvø. "Shapur, King of Iranians and Non-Iranians." In *Des Indo-Grecs aux Sassanides: données pour l'histoire et la géographie historique*, edited by Rika Gyselen, 11–40. Vol. 17 of *Res Orientales*. Bures-sur-Yvette: 2007.

Alstola, Tero. *Judeans in Babylonia: A Study of Deportees in the Sixth and Fifth Centuries BCE*. Leiden: 2020.

Altheim, Franz, and Ruth Stiehl. *Ein asiatischer Staat, Feudalismus unter den Sasaniden und ihren Nachbarn*. Wiesbaden: 1954.

Amit, Aaron. “Regards to Yalta: Is There Kol ʾIsha in Bavli Qiddushin 70a–b?” [in Hebrew]. *Sidra* 30 (2016): 121–131.

Ando, Clifford. *Imperial Ideology and Provincial Loyalty in the Roman Empire*. Berkeley, CA: 2000.

“The Edict of Serdica in Religious-Historical Perspective.” In *Serdica Edict (311 AD): Concepts and Realizations of the Idea of Religious Toleration*, edited by Dimitr Dmitrov and Veselina Vachkova, 51–62. Sofia: 2014.

Andrade, Nathanael. *The Journey of Christianity to India in Late Antiquity: Networks and the Movement of Culture*. Cambridge: 2018.

Anisfeld, Rachel A. Sustain Me with Raisin-Cakes: Pesikta DeRav Kahana and the Popularization of Rabbinic Judaism. Leiden: 2009.

Anklesaria, B. T. *Zand-Ākāsīh, Iranian or Greater Bundahišn*. Bombay: 1956.

Anthony, Sean. *Crucifixion and Death as Spectacle: Umayyad Crucifixion in Its Late Antique Context*. New Haven, CT: 2014.

Asatrian, Mushegh. “Iranian Elements in Arabic: The State of Research.” *Iran & the Caucasus* 10 (2006): 87–106.

Asmussen, P. “The List of Fruits in the Bundahišn.” In *Henning Memorial Volume*, edited by Mary Boyce and Ilya Gershevitch, 14–19. London: 1970.

Azarnouche, Samra. *Husraw ī Kawādān ud Rēdag-ē. Khosrow fils de Kawād et un page: texte pehlevi édité et traduit*. Paris: 2013.

“A Zoroastrian Cult Scene on Sasanian Stucco Reliefs at Bandiyān (Daregaz, Khorāsān-e Razavī).” *Sasanian Studies* 1 (2022): 1–28.

Azarnoush, Massoud. “Fire Temple and Anahita Temple: A Discussion on Some Iranian Places of Worship.” *Mesopotamia* 22 (1987): 391–401.

The Sasanian Manor House at Hājīābād, Iran. Firenze: 1994.

Azarpay, Guitty. “The Sasanian Complex at Bandian: Palace or Dynastic Shrine.” *Bulletin of the Asia Institute* 11 (1997): 193–196.

Bachmann-Medick, Doris. *Cultural Turns: New Orientations in the Study of Culture*. Berlin: 2016.

Back, Michael. *Die sassanidischen Staatsinschriften: Studien zur Orthographie und Phonologie des Mittelpersischen der Inschriften zusammen mit einem etymolgischen Index des mittelpersischen Wortgutes und einem Texteorpus der behandelten Inschriften*. Tehran: 1978.

Baker, Cynthia. *Jew*. New Brunswick, NJ: 2017.

Balberg, Mira, and Moulie Vidas. “Impure Scholasticism: The Study of Purity Laws and Rabbinic Self-Criticism in the Babylonian Talmud.” *Prooftexts* 32 (2012): 312–356.

Ball, Warwick. *Rome in the East: The Transformation of an Empire*. London: 2004.

Banaji, Jairus. “On the Identity of Shahrālānyōzān in the Greek and Middle Persian Papyri from Egypt.” In *Documents and the History of the Early Islamic World*, edited by Alexander Schubert and Petra Sijpesteijn, 27–42. Leiden: 2014.

Bar-Asher Siegal, Michal. *Early Christian Monastic Literature and the Babylonian Talmud*. Cambridge: 2016.

“Ifra Hormiz and the Use of Mini-corpora in the Study of the Babylonian Talmud.” *Jewish Quarterly Review* 113 (2023): 615–638.

Baron, Salo. *A Social and Religious History of the Jews*, 2nd edition. 18 vols. New York: 1952.
Basirov, Oric. "'Proselytisation' and 'Exposure of the Dead': Two Christian Calumnies Commonly Raised against the Sasanians." In *Faszination Iran: Beiträge zur Religion, Geschichte und Kunst des Alten Iran. Gedenkschrift für Klaus*, edited by Shervin Farridnejad, Anke Joisten-Pruschke, and Rika Gyselen, 1–19. Wiesbaden: 2015.
Bate, Jonathan. *Soul of the Age: The Life, Mind and World of William Shakespeare*. London: 2008.
Baumgarten, Albert. "Judah I and His Opponents." *Journal for the Study of Judaism in the Persian, Hellenistic, and Roman Period* 12 (1981): 135–172.
Becker, Adam. "Anti-Judaism and Care of the Poor in Aphrahat's Demonstration 20." *Journal of Early Christian Studies* 10 (2002): 305–327.
Fear of God and the Beginning of Wisdom: The School of Nisibis and Christian Scholastic Culture in Late Antique Mesopotamia. Philadelphia, PA: 2006.
"The Ancient Near East in the Late Antique Near East: Syriac Christian Appropriation of the Biblical Past." In *Antiquity in Antiquity: Jewish and Christian Pasts in the Greco-Roman World*, edited by Gregg Gardner and Kevin Osterloh, 394–415. Tübingen: 2008.
Sources for the History of the School of Nisibis. Liverpool: 2008.
"Martyrdom, Religious Difference, and 'Fear' as a Category of Piety in the Sasanian Empire: The Case of the Martyrdom of Gregory and the Martyrdom of Yazdpaneh." *Journal of Late Antiquity* 2 (2009): 300–336.
"The Comparative Study of 'Scholasticism' in Late Antique Mesopotamia: Rabbis and East Syrians." *Association for Jewish Studies Review* 34 (2010): 91–113.
"Positing a 'Cultural Relationship' between Plato and the Babylonian Talmud: Daniel Boyarin's *Socrates and the Fat Rabbis* (2009)." *Jewish Quarterly Review* 101 (2011): 255–269.
"Polishing the Mirror: Some Thoughts on Syriac Sources and Early Judaism." In *Envisioning Judaism: Studies in Honor Peter Schäfer on the Occasion of His Seventieth Birthday*, edited by Ra'anan Boustan, Klaus Herrmann, Reimund Leicht, Annette Yoshiko Reed, and Giuseppe Veltri, 897–916. Vol. 2. Tübingen: 2013.
"Political Theology and Religious Diversity in the Sasanian Empire." In *Jews, Christians, and Zoroastrians: Religious Dynamics in a Sasanian Context*, edited by Geoffrey Herman, 7–25. Piscataway, NJ: 2014.
"L'antijudaïsme syriaque: entre polémique et critique interne." In *Les controverses religieuses en syriaque*, edited by Flavia Ruani, 181–208. Paris: 2016.
"The Invention of the Persian Martyr Acts." In *Syriac Christian Culture: Beginnings to Renaissance*, edited by Aaron Michael Butts and Robin Darling Young, 113–148. Washington, DC: 2020.
Bedjan, Paul, ed. *Acta martyrum et sanctorum*. 4 vols. Leipzig and Paris: 1890–1897.
Histoire de Mar-Jabalaha, de trois autres patriarches, d'un prêtre et de deux laïques, nestoriens. Paris: 1895.
BeDuhn, Jason. "Iranian Epic in the Chester Beatty Kephalaia." In *Mani at the Court of the Persian Kings: Studies on the Chester Beatty Kephalaia Codex*,

edited by Iain Gardner, Jason BeDuhn, and Paul Dilley, 136–158. Leiden: 2015.

Beer, Moshe. "Concerning the Deposal of Rabbah Bar Naḥmani from the Headship of the Academy: A Chapter in the History of the Relationship between the Sages and the Exilarchs" [in Hebrew]. *Tarbiẓ* 33 (1964): 349–357.

"Were the Babylonian Amoraim Exempt from Taxes and Customs?" [in Hebrew]. *Tarbiẓ* 33 (1964): 247–258.

"Exilarchs of the Talmudic Epoch Mentioned in R. Sherira's Responsum." *Proceedings of the American Academy for Jewish Research* 35 (1967): 43–74.

The Exilarchate in Babylonia in the Mishnaic and Talmudic Period [in Hebrew]. Tel Aviv: 1970.

The Babylonian Amoraim: Aspects of Economic Life [in Hebrew]. Ramat Gan: 1982.

"Notes on the Three Edicts against the Jews in Babylonia in the Third Century C.E. [in Hebrew]." In *Irano-Judaica* I, edited by Shaul Shaked, 25–37. Jerusalem: 1982.

"A Reconsideration of Three Ancient Seals from Persia" [in Hebrew]. *Tarbiẓ* 52 (1983): 435–445.

"The Imperial Background and Rav's Activities in Babylonia" [in Hebrew]. *Zion* 50 (1984–1985): 155–172.

"The Decrees of Kartir on the Jews of Babylonia" [in Hebrew]. *Tarbiẓ* 55 (1986): 525–539.

Belinitzky, Bar, and Yakir Paz, "Bound and Banned: Aphrahaṭ and Excommunication in the Sasanian Empire." In *Jews and Syriac Christians: Intersections across the First Millennium*, edited by Aaron M. Butts and Simcha Gross, 67–88. Tübingen: 2020.

Benovitz, Moshe. "Times of Danger in Israel and Babylonia." *Tarbiẓ* 74 (2004): 5–20.

Ben-Sasson, Menaḥem. "Structure, Purpose, and Content of R. Natan HaBavli's Work." In *Culture and Society in Medieval Jewish History: Studies Dedicated to the Memory of Haim Hillel Ben-Sasson*, edited by Menahem Ben-Sasson, Robert Bonfil, and Joseph R. Hacker, 137–196. Jerusalem: 1989.

"Remembrance and Oblivion of Religious Persecutions: On Sanctifying the Name of God (Qiddush ha-Shem) in Christian and Islamic Countries during the Middle Ages." In *Jews, Christians and Muslims in Medieval and Early Modern Times*, edited by Arnold Franklin, Roxani Eleni Margariti, Marina Rustow, and Uriel Simonsohn, 169–194. Leiden: 2014.

Berkowitz, Beth. "Reconsidering the Book and the Sword: A Rhetoric of Passivity in Rabbinic Hermeneutics." In *Violence, Scripture, and Textual Practices in Early Judaism and Christianity*, edited by Raʿanan Boustan, Alex Jassen and Calvin Roetzel, 145–173. Leiden: 2010.

Bernard, Paul. "Vicissitudes au gré de l'histoire d'une statue en bronze d'Héraclès entre Séleucie du Tigre et la Mésène." *Journal des savants* 1 (1990): 3–68.

Bernheimer, Teresa, and Adam Silverstein, eds. *Late Antiquity: Eastern Perspectives*. Warminster: 2012.

Berthelot, Katell. *Philanthrôpia judaica: Le débat autour de la "misanthropie" des lois juives dans l'antiquité*. Leiden: 2003.

Jews and their Roman Rivals: Pagan Rome's Challenge to Israel. Princeton, NJ: 2021.

Bhabha, Homi. *The Location of Culture*. London: 1994.

Bickart, Noah. *Tistayem: An Investigation into the Scholastic Culture of the Bavli*. PhD diss. Jewish Theological Seminary of America, 2015.

Blanchard, Monica, and Robin Darling Young, *A Treatise on God Written in Armenian by Eznik of Kołb (floruit c.430–c.450)*. Leuven: 1998.

Blankinship, Khalid Yahya. *The Challenge to the Empires A.D. 633–635/A.H. 12–13. Vol. 11 of History of al-Ṭabarī*. Albany, NY: 1993.

Blockley, R. C. *The History of Menander the Guardsman*. Liverpool: 1985.

Blois, François de. "The Middle Persian Inscription from Constantinople: Sassanian or Post-Sassanian?" *Studia Iranica* 19 (1990): 209–218.

"*Naṣrānī* (Ναζωραῖος) and *ḥanīf* (ἐθνικός): Studies in the Religious Vocabulary of Christianity and of Islam." *Bulletin of the School of Oriental and African Studies* 65 (2002): 1–30.

Bohak, Gideon. *Ancient Jewish Magic: A History*. New York: 2012.

Bokser, Baruch Micah. "Talmudic Names of the Iranian Festivals." *Journal of the American Oriental Society* 95 (1975): 261–262.

Börm, Henning. *Prokop und die Perser: Untersuchungen zu den römisch-sasanidischen Kontakten in der ausgehenden Spätantike*. Stuttgart: 2007.

"König und Gefolgschaft im Sasanidenreich: Zum Verhältnis zwischen Monarch und imperialer Elite im spätantiken Persien." In *Die Interaktion von Herrschern und Eliten in imperialen Ordnungen des Mittelalters*, edited by Wolfram Drews, 23–42. Berlin: 2018.

Bosworth, C. E. *The Sāsānids, the Byzantines, the Lakhmids, and Yemen. Vol. 5 of The History of al-Ṭabarī*. Albany, NY: 1999.

Bourdieu, Pierre. *Distinction: A Social Critique of the Judgement of Taste*. Cambridge, MA: 1984.

Boustan, Raʿanan S. *From Martyr to Mystic: Rabbinic Martyrology & the Making of Merkavah Mysticism*. Tübingen: 2005.

"The Spoils of Jerusalem at Rome and Constantinople: Jewish Counter-Geography in a Christianizing Empire." In *Antiquity after Antiquity: Jewish and Christian Pasts in the Greco-Roman World*, edited by G. Gardner and K. I. Osterloh, 327–372. Tübingen: 2008.

"Rabbinization and the Persistence of Diversity in Jewish Culture in Late Antiquity." In *Diversity and Rabbinization: Jewish Texts and Societies between 400 and 1,000 CE*, edited by Gavin McDowell, Ron Naiweld, Judith Schlanger, and Daniel Stökl Ben Ezra, 427–449. Cambridge: 2021.

Boustan, Raʿanan, Oren Kosansky, and Marina Rustow. "Anthropology, History, and the Remaking of Jewish Studies." In *Jewish Studies at the Crossroads of Anthropology and History: Authority, Diaspora, Tradition*, edited by Raʿanan S. Boustan, Oren Kosansky, and Marina Rustow, 1–28. Philadelphia, PA: 2011.

Bowersock, Glen. "The Imperial Cult: Perceptions and Persistence." In *Jewish and Christian Self-Definition*, edited by Ben Meyer and Ed Parish Sanders,

171–182. Vol. 3 of *Self-Definition in the Graeco-Roman World*. London: 1982.

Boyarin, Daniel. *Dying for God: Martyrdom and the Making of Christianity and Judaism*. Stanford, CA: 1999.

Border Lines: The Partition of Judaeo-Christianity. Philadelphia, PA: 2004.

Socrates and the Fat Rabbis. Chicago, IL: 2009.

A Traveling Homeland: The Babylonian Talmud as Diaspora. Philadelphia, PA: 2015.

Judaism: The Genealogy of a Modern Notion. New Brunswick, NJ: 2018.

Boyce, Mary. *The Letter of Tansar*. Rome: 1968.

"On the Sacred Fires of the Zoroastrians." *Bulletin of the School of Oriental and African Studies* 31 (1968): 52–68.

"Toleranz und Intoleranz im Zoroastrismus." *Saeculum* 21 (1970): 325–343.

A History of Zoroastrianism. Leiden: 1975.

"On the Zoroastrian Temple Cult of Fire." *Journal of the American Oriental Society* 95 (1975): 454–465.

A Persian Stronghold of Zoroastrianism. Oxford: 1977.

"Iranian Festivals." In *The Cambridge History of Iran*, vol. 3, bk. 1: *The Seleucid, Parthian and Sasanian Periods*, edited by Ehsan Yarshater, 792–815. Cambridge: 1983.

"On the Orthodoxy of Sasanian Zoroastrianism." *Bulletin of the School of Oriental and African Studies, University of London* 59 (1996): 11–28.

Boyce, Mary, and Frantz Grenet. *History of Zoroastrianism III. Zoroastrianism under Macedonian and Roman Rule*. Leiden: 1991.

Braude, Benjamin. "Foundation Myths of the Millet System." In *The Central Lands*, edited by Benjamin Braude and Bernard Lewis, 69–88. Vol. 1 of *The Christians and Jews in the Ottoman Empire*. New York: 1982.

The History of the Holy Mar Ma'in with a Guide to the Persian Martyr Acts. Piscataway, NJ: 2008.

Brock, Sebastian P. "Review of G. Wiessner's *Zur Märtyrerüberlieferung*." *Journal of Theological Studies* 19 (1968): 300–309.

"A Martyr at the Sasanid Court under Vahran II: Candida." *Analecta Bollandiana* 96 (1978): 167–181.

"Christians in the Sassanian Empire: A Case of Divided Loyalties." In *Religious and National Identity: Papers Read at the Nineteenth Summer Meeting and the Twentieth Winter Meeting of the Ecclesiastical History Society*, edited by Stuart Mews, 1–19. Oxford: 1982.

Brock, Sebastian P., and Lucas van Rompay. *Catalogue of the Syriac Manuscripts and Fragments in the Library of Deir al-Surian, Wadi al-Natrun (Egypt)*. Leuven: 2014.

Brock, Sebastian P., and Paul Dilley. *The Martyrs of Mount Ber'ain*. Piscataway, NJ: 2014.

Brock, Sebastian P., and Susan Ashbrook Harvey. *Holy Women of the Syriac Orient*. Berkeley, CA: 1987.

Brodd, Jeffrey, and Jonathan L. Reed, eds. *Rome and Religion: A Cross-Disciplinary Dialogue on the Imperial Cult*. Atlanta, GA: 2011.

Brody, Robert. "Judaism in the Sasanian Empire: A Case Study in Religious Coexistence." In *Irano-Judaica* II, edited by Shaul Shaked and Amnon Netzer, 52–62. Jerusalem: 1990.

The Geonim of Babylonia and the Shaping of Medieval Jewish Culture. New Haven, CT: 1998.

"Zoroastrian Themes in Geonic Responsa." In *Irano-Judaica* IV, edited by Shaul Shaked and Amnon Netzer, 179–186. Jerusalem: 1999.

"On the Sources for the Chronology of the Talmudic Period" [in Hebrew]. *Tarbiẓ* 70 (2000–2001): 75–107.

Pirqoy ben Baboy and the History of Internal Polemics in Judaism. Tel Aviv: 2003.

"Epistle of Sherira Gaon." In *Rabbinic Texts and the History of Late-Roman Palestine*, edited by Martin Goodman and Philip Alexander, 253–264. Oxford: 2010.

Sa'adyah Gaon. Oxford: 2013.

"Irano-Talmudica: The New Parallelomania?" *Jewish Quarterly Review* 106 (2016): 209–232.

Brooks Ernest Walter, ed. *Historia ecclesiastica Zachariae Rhetori vulgo adscripta*. Paris: 1919–1924.

ed. and trans. *John of Ephesus. Lives of the Eastern Saints, Patrologia Orientalis* 17.1, 18.4, 19.2. Paris: Firmin-Didot, 1923–1925.

ed. and trans. *John of Ephesus, Ecclesiastical History*, as *Iohannis Ephesini Historiae Ecclesiasticae Pars Tertia*, 2 vols., Corpus Scriptorum Christianorum Orientalium 105–106, Scriptores Syri 54–55 Leuven: 1935–1936.

Brown, Elizabeth. "The Tyranny of a Construct: Feudalism and Historians of Medieval Europe." *The American Historical Review* 79 (1974): 1063–1088.

Brown, Peter. "The Diffusion of Manichaeism in the Roman Empire." *Journal of Roman Studies* 59 (1969): 92–103.

The World of Late Antiquity, From Marcus Aurelius to Muhammad. London: 1971.

Power and Persuasion in Late Antiquity: Towards a Christian Empire. Madison, WI: 1992.

Brubaker, Rogers, and Frederick Cooper. *Empires in World History: Power and the Politics of Difference*. Princeton, NJ: 2010.

Brunner, Christopher. *Stamp Seals in the Metropolitan Museum of Art*. New York: 1978.

"Geographical and Administrative Divisions: Settlement and Economy." In *The Cambridge History of Iran*, vol. 3, bk. 1: *The Seleucid, Parthian and Sasanian Periods*, edited by Ehsan Yarsahter, 747–777. Cambridge: 1983.

Bruns, Peter. "Reliquien und Reliquienverehrung in den syro-persischen Märtyrerakten." *Römische Quartalschrift für christliche Altertumskunde und für Kirchengeschichte* 101 (2006): 194–213.

"Beobachtungen zu den Rechtsgrundlagen der Christenverfolgungen im Sasanidenreich." *Römische Quartalschrift für christliche Altertumskunde und für Kirchengeschichte* 103 (2008): 82–112.

Bryen, Ari. "Judging Empire: Courts and Culture in Rome's Eastern Provinces." *Law and History Review* 30 (2012): 771–811.

Budge, E. A. W., trans. *Thomas of Marga's Book of Governors*. London: 1893.

Butts, Aaron. *Language Change in the Wake of Empire: Syriac in Its Greco-Roman Context*. Winona Lake, IN: 2016.

"Assyrian Christians." In *A Companion to Assyria*, edited by Eckart Frahm, 599–612. Blackwell Companions to the Ancient World. Malden: 2017.

"The Greco-Roman Context of the Syriac Language." In *Les auteurs syriaques et leur langue*, edited by Margherita Farina, 137–166. Paris: 2018.

"Narsai's Life and Work." In *Narsai: Rethinking his Work and his World*, edited by Aaron Butts, Kristian S. Heal, and Robert A. Kitchen, 1–8. Tübingen: 2020.

Butts, Aaron, and Simcha Gross. *The History of the "Slave of Christ": From Jewish Child to Christian Martyr*. Piscataway, NJ: 2016.

"Introduction." In *Jews and Syriac Christians: Intersections across the First Millennium*, edited by Aaron Michael Butts and Simcha Gross, 1–26. Tübingen: 2020.

Butts, Aaron M., Kristian S. Heal, and Sebastian P. Brock. *Clavis to the Metrical Homilies of Narsai*, Corpus Scriptorum Christianorum Orientalium 690. Leuven: 2020.

Cameron, Averil. "Agathias on the Sassanians." *Dumbarton Oaks* 23/24 (1969–1970): 67–183.

"The Jews in Seventh-Century Palestine." *Scripta Classica Israelica* 13 (1994): 75–93.

Camplani, Alberto. "L'Esposizione XIV di Afraate: una retorica antiautoritaria nel contesto dell'evoluzione istituzionale della Chiesa siriaca." In *Storia e pensiero religioso nel Vicino Oriente. L'età bagratide – Maimonide – Afraate*, edited by C. Baffioni, R. Bianchi Finazzi, A. Passoni Dell'Acqua, and E. Vergani, 191–235. Milan: 2014.

Canepa, Matthew P. *The Two Eyes of the Earth: Art and Ritual Kingship between Rome and Sasanian Iran*. Berkeley, CA: 2009.

"Technologies of Memory in Early Sasanian Iran: Achaemenid Sites and Sasanian Identity." *American Journal of Archaeology* 114 (2010): 563–596.

"Building a New Vision of the Past in the Sasanian Empire." *Journal of Persianate Studies* 6 (2013): 64–90.

"Sasanian Rock Reliefs." In *The Oxford Handbook of Ancient Iran*, edited by Daniel T. Potts, 856–877. Oxford: 2013.

"Textiles and Elite Tastes between the Mediterranean, Iran and Asia at the End of Antiquity." In *Global Textile Encounters*, edited by Marie-Louise Nosch, Feng Zhao, Lotika Varadarajan, 1–14. Oxford: 2014.

"Topographies of Power: Theorizing the Visual, Spatial and Ritual Contexts of Rock Reliefs in Ancient Iran." In *Of Rocks and Water: Towards and Archaeology of Place*, edited by Ömür Harmanşah, 55–92. Oxford: 2014.

The Iranian Expanse: Transforming Royal Identity through Architecture, Landscape, and the Built Environment, 550 BCE–642 CE. Oakland, CA: 2018.

Cantera, Alberto. *Studien zur Pahlavi-Übersetzung der Avesta*. Wiesbaden: 2004.

"Legal Implications of Conversion in Zoroastrianism." In *Iranian Identity in the Course of History*, edited by Carlo Cereti, 53–66. Rome: 2010.

"The Offering to Satisfy the *ratu* (*miiazda ratufrī*): The Dual System of the Animal Sacrifice in Zoroastrian Rituals." In *The Reward of the Righteous: Festschrift in Honour of Almut Hintze*, edited by Alberto Cantera, Maria Macuch, and Nicholas Sims-Williams, 39–96. Wiesbaden: 2022.

Cassis, Marica. "Kokhe, Cradle of the Church of the East: An Archaeological and Comparative Study." *Journal of the Canadian Society for Syriac Studies* 2 (2002): 62–78.

Castelli, Elizabeth. *Martyrdom and Memory: Early Christian Culture Making*. New York: 2004.

Chabot, J. B. "Histoire de Jésus-Sabran, écrite par Jésus-Yab d'Adiabène." *Archives des missions scientifiques et littéraires* 7 (1897): 485–584.

Le livre de la chasteté composé par Jésusdenah, Évêque de Baçrah, publié et traduit. Rome: 1896.

Synodicon orientale, ou recueil de synodes nestoriens. Paris: 1902.

Chatonnet, Françoise Briquel, and Simon Brelaud. "Quelques réflexions sur la désignation des chrétiens dans l'inscription du mage Kirdīr et dans l'empire sassanide." *Parole de l'Orient* 43 (2017): 113–136.

Chaumont, Marie-Louise. "Recherches sur le clergé zoroastrien: Le hērbad." *Revue de l'histoire des religions* 158 (1960): 55–80, 161–179.

Choksy, Jamsheed K. "Sacral Kingship in Sasanian Iran." *Bulletin of the Asia Institute* 2 (1988): 35–52.

"A Sasanian Monarch, His Queen, Crown Prince, and Deities: The Coinage of Wahram II." *American Journal of Numismastics* 2.1 (1989): 117–135.

"Altars, Precincts, and Temples in Medieval and Modern Zoroastrian Praxis." *Iran* 43 (2006): 1–20.

"Reassessing the Material Contexts of Ritual Fires in Ancient Iran." *Iranica Antiqua* 42 (2007): 229–269.

Christensen, Arthur. "Sassanid Persia." In *The Imperial Crisis and Recovery, A.D. 193–324*, edited by Stanley Arthur Cook et al., 109–137. Vol. 12 of *The Cambridge Ancient History*. Cambridge: 1939.

L'Iran sous les Sassanides. Copenhagen: 1944.

Ciancaglini, Claudia, *Iranian Loanwords in Syriac*. Wiesbaden: 2008.

Clark, Elizabeth. *History, Theory, Text: Historians and the Linguistic Turn*. Cambridge, MA: 2004.

Cohen, Aryeh. "Towards an Erotics of Martyrdom." *The Journal of Jewish Thought and Philosophy* 7 (1997): 227–256.

Cohen, Avinoam. "More on the Question of the Amora Mar Zutra as Exilarch: A Study of Geonic Chronicles," *Sidra* 26 (2011): 19–60.

Cohen, Barak. "Local Academies in Talmudic Babylonia" [in Hebrew]. *Zion* 70 (2005): 447–471.

"The Distinction between Sage and Exilarch in Sassanian Babylonia: The Case of (Rav) Huna bar Natan." *Jewish History* 36 (2022): 1–24.

Cohen, Jeremy. "Roman Imperial Policy towards the Jews from Constantine until the End of the Palestinian Patriarchate (ca. 429)." *Byzantine Studies* 3 (1976): 1–29.

Cohen, Mark. *Jewish Self-Government in Medieval Egypt: The Origins of the Office of the Head of the Jews, ca. 1065–1126*. Princeton, NJ: 1981.

Cohen, Shaye J. D. "The Place of the Rabbi in Jewish Society of the Second Century." In *Galilee in Late Antiquity*, edited by Lee Levine, 157–173. New York: 1992.

"Was Judaism in Antiquity a Missionary Religion?" In *Jewish Assimilation, Acculturation and Accommodation*, edited by Menahem Mor, 14–23. Lanham, MD: 1992.

"Conversion of Antoninus." In *The Talmud Yerushalmi and Graeco-Roman Culture*, edited by Peter Schäfer, 141–171. Vol. 1. Tübingen: 1998.

Beginnings of Jewishness: Boundaries, Varieties, and Uncertainties. Berkeley, CA: 1999.

"The Rabbi in Second-Century Jewish Society." In *The Roman Period*, edited by William Horbury, W. D. Davies, and John Sturdy, 922–990. Vol. 3 of *The Cambridge History of Judaism*. Cambridge: 1999.

"The Name of the Ruse: The Toss of a Ring to Save Life and Honor." In *"Follow the Wise": Studies in Jewish History and Culture in Honor of Lee Levine*, edited by Zeev Weiss, Oded Irshai, and Jodi Magness, 25–36. Winona Lake, IN: 2010.

Colditz, Iris. "Manichaean Time-Management: Laymen between Religious and Secular Duties." In *New Light on Manichaeism. Papers from the Sixth International Congress on Manichaeism*, edited by Jason BeDuhn, 73–99. Leiden: 2009.

Contini, Riccardo. "Hypothèses sur l'araméen manichéen." *Annali di Ca' Foscari: Rivista della Facoltà di lingue e letterature straniere dell'Università Ca' Foscari di Venezia* 34 (1995): 65–107.

Corluy, Joseph. "Historia Sancti Mar Pethion martyris, syriace et latine: Edidit nunc primum ex cod. Londinensi (Addit. mss. 12174)." *Analecta Bollandiana* 7 (1888): 5–45.

Crone, Patricia and Michael Cook. *Hagarism: The Making of the Islamic World*. New York: 1977.

Dalley, Stephanie. "Occasions and Opportunities: Persian, Greek, and Parthian Overlords." In *Legacy of Mesopotamia*, edited by Stephanie Dalley, 35–56. Oxford: 2005.

Dalton, Krista. "Teaching for the Tithe: Donor Expectations and the Matrona's Tithe." *Association for Jewish Studies Review* 44 (2020): 49–73.

Danzig, Neil. "From Oral Talmud to Written Talmud: On the Methods of Transmission of the Babylonian Talmud and Its Study in the Middle Ages." *Bar-Ilan Annual* 30–31 (2006): 49–112.

Darmesteter, James. "Les six feux dans le Talmud et dans le Bundehesh." *Revue des études Juives* 1 (1880): 186–196.

Daryaee, Touraj. "National History or Keyanid History? The Nature of Sasanian Zoroastrian Historiography." *Iranian Studies* 28 (1995): 121–145.

"The Use of Religio-Political Propaganda on the Coinage of Xusro II." *American Journal of Numismatics* 9 (1997): 41–53.
"The Changing 'Image of the World': Geography and Imperial Propaganda in Ancient Persia." *Electrum* 6 (2002): 99–109.
"History, Epic, and Numismatics: On the Title of Yazdgerd I (*Rāmšahr*)." *American Journal of Numismatics* 14 (2002): 89–95.
Šahrestānīhā ī Ērānšahr: A Middle Persian Text on Late Antique Geography, Epic and History. Costa Mesa, CA: 2002.
"Ethnic and Territorial Boundaries in Late Antique and Early Medieval Persia (Third to Tenth Century)." In *Borders, Barriers, and Ethnogenesis, Frontiers in Late Antiquity and Middle Ages*, edited by Florin Curta, 123–137. Turnhout: 2005.
"The Construction of the Past in Late Antique Persia." *Historia: Zeitschrift für Alte Geschichte* 55 (2006): 493–503.
"List of Fruits and Nuts in the Zoroastrian Tradition: An Irano-Hellenic Classification." *Nāme-ye Irān-e Bāstān* 6.1–2 (2006–2007): 1–10.
"The Middle Persian Text Sūr ī Saxwan and the Late Sasanian Court." In *Des Indo-Grecs aux Sassanides: données pour l'histoire et la géographie historique*, edited by Rika Gyselen, 65–72. Vol. 17 of *Res Orientales*. Bures-sur-Yvette: 2007.
"Kingship in Early Sasanian Iran." In *The Idea of Iran*, vol. 3: *The Sasanian Era*, edited by Vesta Sarkhosh Curtis and Sarah Stewart, 60–70. London: 2008.
Sasanian Persia: The Rise and Fall of an Empire. London: 2009.
"The Idea of Eranshahr: Jewish, Christian and Manichaean Views in Late Antiquity." In *Iranian Identity in the Course of History: Proceedings of the Conference Held in Rome, 21–24 September 2005*, edited by Carlo Cereti, 91–108. Rome: 2010.
"To Learn and to Remember from Others: Persians Visiting the Dura-Europos Synagogue." *Scripta Judaica Cracoviensia* 8 (2010): 29–37.
"The Limits of Sasanian History: Between Iranian, Islamic, and Late Antique Studies." *Iranian Studies* 49 (2016): 193–203.
"Palmyra and the Sasanians." In *Palmyra and the East*, edited by Kenneth Lapatin and Rubina Raja, 39–44. Turnhout: 2022.
Daudpota, Umar bin Muhammad. trans. *The Annals of Ḥamza al-Iṣfahānī*. Bombay: 1932.
Debié, Muriel. "L'Empire perse et ses marges." In *Histoire générale du christianisme, v. I. Des origines au XVe siècle*, edited by Jean-Robert Armogathe, Pascal Montaubin, and Michel-Yves Perrin, 611–646. Paris: 2010.
"Guerres et religions en Mésopotamie du Nord dans l'antiquité tardive: un mimro inédit de Jacques de Saroug sur l'église Saint-Étienne que les Perses ont transformée en temple du feu à Amid (Diyarbakır) en 503 è.c." *Syriac Orthodox Patriarchal Journal* 56 (2018): 29–80.
"St. Stephen in Amida in a New Mimro of Jacob of Serugh: Christianity vs. Zoroastrianism in a Clash of Religious Shrines." In *Syriac Hagiography: Texts and Beyond*, edited by Sergey Minov and Flavia Ruani, 340–364. Leiden: 2021.

Decter, Jonathan. "The Hidden Exilarch: Power and Performance in a Medieval Jewish Ceremony." In *Visualizing Medieval Performance: Perspectives, Histories, Contexts*, edited by Elina Gertsman, 179–191. Aldershot, UK: 2008.

De Jong, Albert. *Traditions of the Magi: Zoroastrianism in Greek and Latin Literature*. Leiden: 1997.

"Animal Sacrifice in Ancient Zoroastrianism: A Ritual and Its Interpretations." In *Sacrifice in Religious Experience*, edited by Albert Baumgarten, 127–148. Leiden: 2002.

"Zoroastrian Self-Definition in Contact with Other Faiths." In *Irano-Judaica V*, edited by Shaul Shaked and Amnon Netzer, 16–26. Jerusalem: 2003.

"Sub Specie Maiestatis: Reflections on Sasanian Court Rituals." In *Zoroastrian Ritual in Context*, edited by Michael Stausberg, 345–365. Leiden: 2004.

"Zoroastrian Religious Polemics and Their Contexts: Interconfessional Relations in the Sasanian Empire." In *Religious Polemics in Context: Papers Presented to the Second International Conference of the Leiden Institute for the Study of Religions (LISOR) Held at Leiden, 27–28 April 2000*, edited by Arie van der Kooij and Theo L. Hettema, 48–63. Studies in Theology and Religion 11. Assen: 2004.

"The Contribution of the Magi." In *The Idea of Iran*, vol. 1: *Birth of the Persian Empire*, edited by Vesta Sarkhosh Curtis and Sarah Stewart, 85–99. London: 2005.

"The First Sin: Zoroastrian Ideas about Time before Zarathustra." In *Genesis and Regeneration: Essays on Conceptions of Origins*, edited by Shaul Shaked, 192–209. Jerusalem: 2005.

"One Nation under God? The Early Sasanians as Guardians and Destroyers of Holy Sites." In *Götterbilder-Gottesbilder-Weltbilder*, edited by Reinhard G. Kratz and Hermann Spieckermann, 223–238. Vol. 1 of *Ägypten, Mesopotamien, Persien, Kleinasien, Syrien, Palästina*. Tübingen: 2006.

"Regional Variation in Zoroastrianism: The Case of the Parthians." *Bulletin of the Asia Institute* 22 (2008): 17–27.

"Religion in Iran: The Parthian and Sasanian Periods (247 BCE–654 CE)." In *From the Hellenistic Age to Late Antiquity*, edited by William Adler, 23–53. Vol. 2 of *The Cambridge History of Religions in the Ancient World*. Cambridge: 2012.

"The Cologne Mani Codex and the Life of Zarathustra." In *Jews, Christians and Zoroastrians: Religious Dynamics in a Sasanian Context*, edited by Geoffrey Herman, 129–147. Piscataway, NJ: 2014.

"Being Iranian in Antiquity (at Home and Abroad)." In *Persianism in Antiquity*, edited by Rolf Strootman and Miguel John Versluys, 35–47. Stuttgart: 2017.

Devos, Paul. "Sozomène et les actes syriaques de S. Syméon bar Sabbaʿe," *Analecta Bollandiana* 84 (1966): 443–456.

"La jeune martyre perse sainte Širin († 559)." *Analecta Bollandiana* 112 (1994): 5–31.

Diamond, Eliezer. "Wrestling the Angel of Death: Form and Meaning in Rabbinic Tales of Death and Dying." *Journal for the Study of Judaism* 26 (1995): 76–92.

Dignas, Beate, and Engelbert Winter. *Rome and Persia in Late Antiquity: Neighbours and Rivals*. Cambridge: 2007.

Dilley, Paul. "The Invention of Christian Tradition: 'Apocrypha,' Imperial Policy, and Anti-Jewish Propaganda." *Greek, Roman and Byzantine Studies* 50 (2010): 586–615.

"Also schrieb Zarathustra? Mani as Interpreter of the 'Law of Zarades.'" In *Mani at the Court of the Persian Kings: Studies on the Chester Beatty Kephalaia Codex*, edited by Iain Gardner, Jason BeDuhn, and Paul Dilley, 101–135. Leiden: 2015.

Dirven, Lucinda. "Religious Competition and the Decoration of Sanctuaries: The Case of Dura-Europos." *Eastern Christian Art* 1 (2004): 1–19.

"'My Lord with His Dogs': Continuity and Change in the Cult of Nergal in Parthian Mesopotamia." In *Edessa in hellenistisch-römischer Zeit. Religion, Kultur und Politik zwischen Ost und West*, edited by Lutz Greisiger, Claudia Rammelt, and Jürgen Tubach, 47–69. Beirut: 2009.

"Religious Frontiers in the Syrian-Mesopotamian Desert." In *Frontiers in the Roman World: Proceedings of the Ninth Workshop of International Network Impact of Empire*, edited by Ted Kaizer and Olivier Hekster, 157–173. Leiden: 2011.

Dohrmann, Natalie. "Law and Imperial Idioms: Rabbinic Legalism in a Roman World." In *Jews, Christians, and the Roman Empire: The Poetics of Power in Late Antiquity*, edited by Natalie Dohrmann and Annette Yoshiko Reed, 63–78. Philadelphia, PA: 2014.

Downey, Susan. *Mesopotamian Religious Architecture: Alexander through the Parthians*. Princeton, NJ: 1988.

Drower, Ethel Stefana. *The Canonical Prayerbook of the Mandaeans*. Leiden: 1959.

Drower, Ethel Stefana, and Macuch, Rudolf. *A Mandaic Dictionary*. Oxford: 1963.

Duchesne-Guillemin, Jacques. "Art et religion sous les Sassanides." In *Atti del Convegno Internazionale sul Tema: La Persia nel Medioevo*, 377–388. Rome: 1971.

Religion of Ancient Iran. Bombay: 1973.

"Zoroastrian Religion." In *The Cambridge History of Iran*, vol. 3, bk. 1: *The Seleucid, Parthian and Sasanian Periods*, edited by Ehsan Yarshater, 866–908. Cambridge: 1983.

Drake, Harold. "Intolerance, Religious Violence, and Political Legitimacy in Late Antiquity." *Journal of the American Academy of Religions* 79 (2011): 193–235.

Drijvers, Jan Willem "Ammianus Marcellinus' Image of Sasanian Society." In *Ērān und Anērān, Studien zu den Beziehungen zwischen dem Sasanidenreich und der Mittelmeerwell*, edited by Josef Wiesehöfer and Philip Huyse, 45–69. Stuttgart: 2006.

"A Roman Image of the 'Barbarian' Sasanians." In *Romans, Barbarians, and the Transformation of the Roman World: Cultural Interaction and the Creation of Identity in Late Antiquity*, edited by Ralph Mathisen and Danuta Shanzer, 67–76. Farnham: 2011.

Ehrlich, R. "The Celebrations and Gifts of the Persian New Year (Now Ruz) According to the Arabic Sources." In *Dr. Modi Memorial Volume: Papers on Indo–Iranian and Other Subjects Written by Several Scholars in Honour of Shams-ul-Ulama Dr. Jivanji Jamshedji Modi*, edited by The Dr. Modi Memorial Volume Editorial Board, 95–101. Bombay: 1930.

Eliav, Yaron. "Viewing the Sculptural Environment: Shaping the Second Commandment." In *The Talmud Yerushalmi and Graeco-Roman Culture*, edited by Peter Schäfer, 411–433. Vol. 3. Tübingen: 2002.

"On Idolatry in the Roman Bathhouse – Two Comments" [in Hebrew]. *Cathedra* 110 (2003): 173–180.

Elman, Yaakov. "Orality and the Redaction of the Babylonian Talmud." *Oral Tradition* 14 (1999): 52–99.

"Marriage and Marital Property in Rabbinic and Sasanian Law." In *Rabbinic Law in Its Roman and Near Eastern Context*, edited by Catherine Hezser, 227–276. Tübingen: 2003.

"Acculturation to Elite Persian Norms and Modes of Thought in the Babylonian Jewish Community of Late Antiquity." In *Neti'ot Ledavid, Jubilee Volume for David Weiss Halivni*, edited by Yaakov Elman, Ephraim Bezalel Halivni, and Zvi Aryeh Steinfeld, 31–56. Jerusalem: 2004.

"The Other in the Mirror: Iranians and Jews View One Another: Questions of Identity, Conversion and Exogamy in the Fifth-Century Iranian Empire, Part One." *Bulletin of the Asia Institute* 19 (2005): 15–25.

"Middle Persian Culture and Babylonian Sages: Accommodation and Resistance in the Shaping of Rabbinic Legal Tradition." In *The Cambridge Companion to the Talmud and Rabbinic Literature*, edited by Charlotte Elisheva Fonrobert and Martin S. Jaffe, 165–197. Cambridge: 2007.

"Returnable Gifts in Rabbinic and Sasanian Law." In *Irano-Judaica VI*, edited by Shaul Shaked and Amnon Netzer, 150–195. Jerusalem: 2008.

"The Other in the Mirror: Questions of Identity, Conversion, and Exogamy in the Fifth-Century Iranian Empire, Part Two." *Bulletin of the Asia Institute* 20 (2010): 25–46.

"Shopping in Ctesiphon: A Lesson in Sasanian Commercial Practice." In *The Archaeology and Material Culture of the Babylonian Talmud*, edited by Markham J. Geller, 225–244. Leiden: 2015.

Elman, Yaakov, and Oktor Skjaervo. "Concepts of Pollution in Late Sasanian Iran: Does Pollution Need Stairs, and Does It Fill Space?" *Aram* 26 (2013): 21–45.

Elman, Yaakov, and Shai Secunda. "Judaism." In *The Wiley Blackwell Companion to Zoroastrianism*, edited by Michael Stausberg and Yuhan Sohrab-Dinshaw Vevaina, 423–436. Hoboken, NJ: 2015.

Erhart, Victoria. "The Development of Syriac Christian Canon Law in the Sasanian Empire." In *Law, Society, and Authority in Late Antiquity*, edited by Ralph W. Mathisen, 115–129. Oxford: 2001.

Feldman, Louis. *Studies in Josephus' Rewritten Bible*. Leiden: 1998.

Fiey, Jean-Maurice. "Les laics dans l'histoire de l'Église syrienne orientale." *Proche–Orient chrétien* 14 (1964): 169–183.

Fine, Steven. "Jewish Identity at the Limus: The Earliest Reception of the Dura Europos Synagogue Paintings." In *Cultural Identity in the Ancient Mediterranean*, edited by Erich Gruen, 303–320. Getty Research Institute Issues & Debates. Los Angeles: 2011.

Finkelstein, Louis, ed. *Sifre Deuteronomy*. New York, 1939.

Flusin, Bernard. *Saint Anastase le Perse et l'histoire de la Palestine au début du VIIe siècle*. Paris: 1992.

Fowden, Elizabeth Key. *The Barbarian Plain: Saint Sergius between Rome and Iran*. Berkeley, CA: 1999.

Fowler, Richard, and Olivier Hekster. "Imagining Kings: From Persia to Rome." In *Imaginary Kings: Royal Images in the Ancient Near East, Greece and Rome*, edited by Richard Fowler and Olivier Hekster, 9–38. Stuttgart: 2005.

Fraade, Steven. *From Tradition to Commentary: Torah and Its Interpretation in the Midrash Sifre to Deuteronomy*. Albany, NY: 1991.

Fraenkel, Eliashiv. "Pirqa Tales in the Babylonian Talmud: Reality and Literature." In *Rabbinic Study Circles: Aspects of Jewish Learning in Its Late Antique Context*, edited by Marc Hirshman and David Satran, 86–114. Tübingen: 2020.

Fraenkel, Jonah. "The Story of Rabbi Sheila" [in Hebrew]. *Tarbiẓ* 40 (1970): 33–40.

Francisco, Hector Ricardo. "Corpse Exposure in the Acts of the Persian Martyrs and Its Literary Models." *Hugoye* 19 (2016): 193–235.

Franklin, Arnold. *This Noble House: Jewish Descendants of King David in the Middle Ages*. Philadelphia, PA: 2013.

Frendo, Joseph. *Agathias: The Histories*. Berlin: 1975.

"Theophylact Simocatta on the Revolt of Bahram Chobin and the Early Career of Khusrau II." *Bulletin of the Asia Institute* 3 (1989): 77–88.

Friedenberg, Daniel. *Sasanian Jewry and Its Culture, A Lexicon of Jewish and Related Seals*. Chicago, IL: 2009.

Friedman, Shamma. "Literary Development and Historicity in the Aggadic Narrative of the Babylonian Talmud: A Study Based upon BM 83b–86a." In *Community and Culture: Essays in Jewish Studies in Honor of the 90th Anniversary of Gratz College, 1895–1985*, edited by Nahum W. Waldman, 67–80. Philadelphia, PA: 1987.

"The Orthography of the Names Rabbah and Rava" [in Hebrew]. *Sinai* 110 (1992): 140–164.

"Historical Narrative in the Babylonian Talmud [in Hebrew]." In *Saul Lieberman Memorial Volume*, edited by Shamma Friedman, 119–164. New York: 1993.

"'Wonder not at a gloss in which the Name of an Amora is Mentioned': The Amoraic Statements and the Anonymous Material in the Sugyot of the Bavli Revisited" [in Hebrew]. In *Melekhet Mahshevet: Studies in the Redaction and Development of Talmudic Literature*, edited by Aaron Amit and Aharon Shemesh, 73–116. Ramat Gan: 2011.

"Now You See It, Now You Don't: Can Source-Criticism Perform Magic on Talmudic Passages about Sorcery?" In *Rabbinic Traditions between Palestine and Babylonia*, edited by Ronit Nikolsky and Tal Ilan, 32–83. Leiden: 2014.

Frier, Bruce W., ed. *The Codex of Justinian: A New Annotated Translation with Parallel Latin and Greek Text*. Cambridge: 2016.

Frye, R. N. *The Heritage of Persia*. London: 1962.

Golden Age of Persia: The Arabs in the East. New York: 1975.

"The Political History of Iran under the Sasanians." In *The Cambridge History of Iran*, vol. 3, bk. 1: *The Seleucid, Parthian and Sasanian Periods*, edited by Ehsan Yarshater, 116–181. Cambridge: 1983.

The History of Ancient Iran. Munich: 1984.

"Feudalism in Sasanian and Early Islamic Iran." *Jerusalem Studies in Arabic and Islam* 9 (1987): 13–18.

Frye, Richard N., and Prods Oktor Skjaervo. "The Middle Persian Inscription from Meshkinshahr." *Bulletin of the Asia Institute* 10 (1996): 53–61.

Funk, Salomon. *Die Juden in Babylonien, 200–500*. 2 vols. Berlin: 1902.

Furstenberg, Yair. "Idolatry Annulment and Roman Rule" [in Hebrew]. *Reshit* 1 (2009): 118–144.

Gafni, Isaiah. "Yeshiva and Metivta" [in Hebrew]. *Zion* 43 (1978): 12–37.

"Concerning D. Goodblatt's Article" [in Hebrew]. *Zion* 46 (1981): 52–56.

"Court Cases in the Babylonian Talmud: Literary Forms and Historical Implications." *Proceedings of the American Academy of Jewish Research* 49 (1982): 23–40.

"On the Talmudic Chronology in the Iggeret Rav Sherira Gaon" [in Hebrew]. *Zion* 52 (1987): 19–22.

The Jews of Talmudic Babylonia: A Social and Cultural History [in Hebrew]. Jerusalem: 1990.

Land, Center and Diaspora: Jewish Constructions in Late Antiquity. Sheffield: 1997.

"Babylonian Rabbinic Culture." In *Cultures of the Jews: A New History*, edited by David Biale, 223–265. New York: 2002.

"The Political, Social, and Economic History of Babylonian Jewry, 224–638 CE." In *The Cambridge History of Judaism: The Late Roman–Rabbinic Period*, edited by Steven Katz, 792–820. Cambridge: 2006.

"How Babylonia Became 'Zion': Shifting Identities in Late Antiquity." In *Jewish Identities in Late Antiquity: Studies in Memory of Menahem Stern*, edited by Lee I. Levine and Daniel R. Schwartz, 333–348. Tübingen: 2009.

"Rethinking Talmudic History: The Challenge of Literary and Redaction Criticism." *Jewish History* 25 (2011): 355–375.

"Converts and Conversion in Sasanian Babylonia." In *Jews and Judaism in the Rabbinic Era*, edited by Isaiah Gafni, 257–268. Tübingen: 2019.

Gagos, Traianos, and Peter van Minnen. *Settling a Dispute: Towards a Legal Anthropology of Late Antique Egypt*. Ann Arbor, MI: 1994.

Gaiser, Adam. *Shurāt Legends, Ibāḍī Identities: Martyrdom, Asceticism, and the Making of an Early Islamic Community*. Columbia, SC: 2016.

Gardner, Iain. "The Final Ten Chapters." In *Mani at the Court of the Persian Kings: Studies on the Chester Beatty Kephalaia Codex*, edited by Iain Gardner, Jason BeDuhn, and Paul Dilley, 75–97. Leiden: 2015.

"Mani's Last Days." In *Mani at the Court of the Persian Kings: Studies on the Chester Beatty Kephalaia Codex*, edited by Iain Gardner, Jason BeDuhn, and Paul Dilley, 159–208. Leiden: 2015.

The Founder of Manichaeism: Rethinking the Life of Mani. Cambridge: 2020.

Gardner, Iain, and Samuel Lieu. *Manichaean Texts from the Roman Empire*. Cambridge: 2004.

Gardner, Iain, Jason BeDuhn, and Paul Dilley. *The Chapters of the Wisdom of My Lord Mani*. Leiden: 2018.

Gariboldi, Andrea. "The Great 'Restoration' of Husraw I." In *Husraw Ier reconstructions d'un règne: sources et documents*, edited by Christelle Jullien, 47–84. Paris: 2015.

Garnsey, Peter. "Religious Toleration in Classical Antiquity." *Studies in Church History* 21 (1984): 1–27.

Garsoïan, Nina G. "Armenia in the Fourth Century: An Attempt to Redefine the Concepts 'Armenia' and 'Loyalty.'" *Revue des Etudes Arméniennes* 8 (1971): 341–352.

"Le rôle de l'hiérarchie chrétienne dans les rapports diplomatiques entre Byzance et les Sassanide." *REArm* 10 (1973–1974): 119–138.

"Prolegomena to a Study of the Iranian Aspects in Arsacid Armenia." *Handes Amsorea* 90 (1976): 177–234.

"The Iranian Substratum of the 'Agatʿangełos Cycle.'" In *East of Byzantium: Syria and Armenia in the Formative Period*, edited by Nina G. Garsoïan, Thomas F. Mathews, and Robert W. Thomson, 151–189. Washington, DC: 1982.

The Epic Histories Attributed to Pʿawstos Buzand (Buzandaran patmutʿiwnkʾ). Cambridge: 1989.

"The Two Voices of Armenian Mediaeval Historiography: The Iranian Index." *Studia Iranica* 25 (1996): 7–43.

"The Arshakuni Dynasty." In *The Dynastic Periods: From Antiquity to the Fourteenth Century*, edited by Richard G. Hovannisian, 75–81. Vol. 1 of *The Armenian People from Ancient to Modern Times*. New York: 1997.

Geary, Patrick J. *Phantoms of Remembrance: Memory and Oblivion at the End of the First Millennium*. Princeton, NJ: 1994.

Geiger, Itzchak. "The Yeshiva of Pumbedita from Its Foundation until Abbaye's Days" [in Hebrew]. PhD diss. Hebrew University of Jerusalem, 2006.

Geller, Markham. "The Last Wedge." *Zeitschrift für Assyiologie* 87 (1997): 43–95.

Gerö, Stephen. *Barsauma of Nisibis and Persian Christianity in the Fifth Century*. Louvain: 1981.

"The See of Peter in Babylon: Western Influences on the Ecclesiology of Early Persian Christianity." In *East of Byzantium: Syria and Armenia in the Formative Period*, edited by Nina G. Garsoïan, Thomas F. Mathews, and Robert W. Thomson, 45–51. Dumbarton Oaks, Washington, DC: 1982.

Ghanimati, Soroor. "Kuh-e Khwaja and the Religious Architecture of Sasanian Iran." In *The Oxford Handbook of Ancient Iran*, edited by Daniel T. Potts, 892–900. Oxford: 2013.

Ghirshman, Roman. *Fouilles de Châpour*. Vol. 1 of *Bîchâpour*. Paris: 1971.

Gignoux, Philippe. "Problèmes de distinction et de priorité des sources." In *Prolegomena to the Sources on the History of Pre-Islamic Central Asia*, edited by Janos Harmatta, 137–141. Budapest: 1979.

"Die religiöse Administration in sasanidischer Zeit: Ein Überblick." In *Kunst, Kultur, und Geschichte der Achämenidenzeit und ihr Fortleben*, edited by Heidemarie Koch and David N. Mackenzie, 253–266. Berlin: 1983.

"Titres et fonctions religieuses sasanides d'après les sources syriaques hagiographiques," *Acta Antiqua Academiae Scientiarum Hungaricae* 28 (1983): 191–203.

"Church-State Relations in the Sasanian Period." In *Monarchies and Socio–Religious Traditions in the Ancient Near East*, edited by Prince Takahito Mikasa, 72–80. Wiesbaden: 1984.

"Les quatre régions administratives de l'Iran sasanide et la symboliques des nombres trois et quatre." *Annali dell' Istituto Orientali di Napoli* 44 (1984): 555–572.

"L'organisation administrative sasanide: le cas du marzbān." *Jerusalem Studies in Arabic and Islam* 4 (1984): 1–29.

"Pour une nouvelle histoire de l'Iran sasanide." In *Middle Iranian Studies: Proceedings of the International Symposium Organized by the Katholieke Universiteit Leuven from the 17th to the 20th of May 1982*, edited by Wojciech Skalmowski and Alois Van Tongerloo, 253–262. Leuven: 1984.

"Pour une Esquisse des Fonctions Religieuses sous les Sasanides." *Jerusalem Studies in Arabic and Islam* 7 (1986): 93–108.

"Une catégorie de mages à la fin de l'époque sasanide: les *mogvēh*." *Jerusalem Studies in Arabic and Islam* 9 (1987): 19–23.

"D'Abnū à Māhān: Étude de deux inscriptions sassanides." *Studia Iranica* 20 (1991): 9–22.

Les quatre inscriptions du mage Kirdīr, textes et concordances. Paris: 1991.

"Dastgerd." In *Dārā(b)–Ebn al-Aṯīr*, edited by Ehsan Yarshater, 105–106. Vol. 7 of *Encyclopaedia Iranica*. Costa Mesa, CA: 1996.

"Les inscriptions en moyen-perse de Bandiān." *Studia Iranica* 27 (1998): 251–258.

Man and Cosmos in Ancient Iran. Rome: 2001.

"La site de Bandiān revisite." *Studia Iranica* 37 (2008): 163–174.

"Une archive post–sassanide du Tabaristān (I)." In *Objets et documents inscrits en pārsīg*, edited by Rika Gyselen, 29–96. Res Orientales 21. Bures-sur-Yvette: 2012.

Gignoux, Philippe, and Rika Gyselen. "Nouveaux cachets sasanides de la Collection Pirouzan." *Studia Iranica* 7 (1978): 23–48, pls. I–VII.

Gil, Moshe. "The Babylonian Encounter and the Exilarchic House in the Light of Cairo Geniza Documents and Parallel Arab Sources." In *Judaeo-Arabic Studies: Proceedings of the Founding Conference of the Society for Judaeo-Arabic Studies*, edited by Norman Golb, 135–173. Amsterdam: 1997.

Jews in Islamic Countries in the Middle Ages, trans. David Strassler. Leiden: 2004.

Gillman, I., and Hans-Joachim Klimkeit. *Christians in Asia before 1500*. Surrey: 1999.

Gismondi, E., ed. *Maris, Amri, et Salibae: De Patriarchis Nestorianorum Commentaria II: Maris textus arabicus et versio Latina*. Rome: 1899.

Gnoli, Gherardo. *Zoroaster's Time and Homeland*. Naples: 1980.

The Idea of Iran: An Essay on Its Origin. Leiden: 1989.

Go, J. *Postcolonial Thought and Social Theory*. Oxford: 2016.

Göbl, Robert. "Sasanian Coins." In *The Cambridge History of Iran*, vol. 3, bk. 1: *The Seleucid, Parthian and Sasanian Periods*, edited by Ehsan Yarshater, 322–339. Cambridge: 1983.

Goitein, S. D. *A Mediterranean Society: The Jewish Communities of the Arab World as Portrayed in the Documents of the Cairo Geniza*. 6 vols. Berkeley, CA: 1967–1993.

Goldziher, Ignaz. "Renseignements de source musulmane sur la dignité de resch-galuta." *Revue des études Juives* 8 (1884): 121–125.

Goodblatt, David M. *Rabbinic Instruction in Sasanian Babylonia*. Leiden: 1975.

"The Poll Tax in Sasanian Babylonia: The Talmudic Evidence." *Journal of the Economic and Social History of the Orient* 22 (1979): 233–295.

"The Babylonian Talmud." In *The Study of Ancient Judaism: The Palestinian and Babylonian Talmuds*, edited by Jacob Neusner, 120–199. New York: 1981.

"New Developments in the Study of the Babylonian *Yeshivot*" [in Hebrew]. *Zion* 46 (1981): 14–38.

"Josephus on Parthian Babylonia (Antiquities XVIII, 310–379)." *Journal of the American Oriental Society* 107 (1987): 605–622.

The Monarchic Principle: Studies in Jewish Self-Government in Antiquity. Tübingen: 1994.

"A Generation of Talmudic Studies." In *The Talmud in Its Iranian Context*, edited by Carol Bakhos and M. Rahim Shayegan, 1–20. Tübingen: 2010.

"The Jews in the Parthian Empire: What We Don't Know." In *Judaea–Palaestina, Babylon and Rome*, ed. Yuval Shaḥar and Benjamin Isaac, 263–278. Leiden: 2012.

Goodenough, Erwin R. *Jewish Symbols in the Greco-Roman Period*. Princeton, NJ: 1988.

Goodman, Martin. *State and Society in Roman Galilee*. Totowa, NJ: 1983.

Mission and Conversion: Proselytizing in the Religious History of the Roman Empire. Oxford: 1994.

Goody, Jack. *Cooking, Cuisine, and Class: A Study in Comparative Sociology*. Cambridge: 1982.

Graetz, Heinrich. *History of the Jews*. Vol. 2. Translated by Bella Löwy. London: 1891.

Graf, Fritz. *Magic in the Ancient World*. Translated by Franklin Philip. Cambridge: 1997.

Gray, Alyssa. "A Contribution to the Study of Martyrdom and Identity in the Palestinian Talmud." *Journal of Jewish Studies* 54 (2003): 242–272.

"Redaction and Meaning in *b. A. Z. 10a–11a*." In *Creation and Composition: The Contribution of the Bavli Redactors (Stammaim) to the Aggada*, edited by Jeffrey Rubenstein, 26–72. Tübingen: 2005.

Greatrex, Geoffrey, and Samuel Lieu. *The Roman Eastern Frontier and the Persian Wars: Part II, AD 363–630*. London: 2002.

Green, William Scott. "What's in a Name? The Problematic of Rabbinic Biography." In *Approaches to Ancient Judaism: Theory and Practice*, edited by William Scott Green, 77–96. Missoula, MT: 1978.

Greenblatt, Stephen. "Introduction." In *The Power of Forms in the English Renaissance*, edited by Stephen Greenblatt, 3–6. Norman, OK: 1982.

Greenfield, Jonas C. "Ratin Magosha." In *Joshua Finkel Festschrift: In Honor of Dr. Joshua Finkel*, edited by Sydney B. Hoenig and Leon D. Stitskin, 63–69. New York: 1974.

Grenet, Frantz. "Observations sur les titres de Kirdīr." *Studia Iranica* 19 (1990): 87–94.

La geste d'Ardashir fils de Pâbag. Kārnāmag ī Ardaxšēr ī Pābagān. Paris: 2003.

"Iranian Gods in Hindu Garb: The Zoroastrian Pantheon of the Bactrians and Sogdians, Second–Eighth Centuries." *Bullet of the Asia Institute* 20 (2006): 87–99.

"Mary Boyce's Legacy for the Archaeologists." *Bulletin of the Asia Institute* 22 (2012): 29–47.

"In Search of Missing Links: Iranian Royal Protocol from the Achaemenids to the Mughals." In *India and Iran in the Longue Durée*, edited by Alka Patel and Touraj Daryaee, 75–90. Irvine, CA: 2017.

Grey, Cam. *Constructing Communities in the Late Roman Countryside*. Cambridge: 2011.

Gross, Simcha. "Irano-Talmudica and Beyond: Next Steps in the Contextualization of the Babylonian Talmud." *Jewish Quarterly Review* 106 (2016): 248–255.

"Empire and Neighbors: Babylonian Jewish Identity in Its Local and Imperial Context." PhD diss. Yale University, 2017.

"When the Jews Greeted Ali: Sherira Gaon's Epistle in Light of Arabic and Syrac Historiography." *Jewish Studies Quarterly* 24 (2017): 122–144.

"A Persian Anti-Martyr Act: The Death of Rabbah Bar Naḥmani." In *The Aggada of the Bavli and Its Cultural World*, edited by Jeffrey Rubenstein and Geoffrey Herman, 211–242. Providence, RI: 2018.

"Rethinking Babylonian Rabbinic Acculturation in the Sasanian Empire." *Journal of Ancient Judaism* 9 (2019): 280–310.

"The Sources of the History of ʿAbdā damšiḥā: The Creation of a Persian Martyr Act." In *Syriac Christian Culture: Beginnings to Renaissance*, edited by Aaron Michael Butts and Robin Darling Young, 149–173. Washington, DC: 2020.

"Whoever Is Hungry, Come and Eat": On the Origins and Later Development of a Puzzling Passover Passage." *Aramaic Studies* 18 (2020): 171–197.

"Being Roman in the Sasanian Empire: Revisiting the Great Persecution under Shapur II." *Studies in Late Antiquity* 5 (2021): 390–397.

"The Curious Case of the Jewish Sasanian Queen Šīšīnduxt: Exilarchal Propaganda and Zoroastrians in Tenth- to Eleventh-Century Baghdad." *Journal of the American Oriental Society* 141 (2021): 365–380.

"Playing with Persecution: Parallel Jewish and Christian Memories of Late Antiquity in Early Islamic Iraq." *Journal of Near Eastern Studies* 81 (2022): 247–260.

"Reassessing Exilarchal Authority between Sasanian and Early Islamic Rule." *Journal of Jewish Studies* 73 (2022): 263–287.

"Where Did Rav and Shmuel Preside? Lingering Institutional Assumptions in the Study of the Late Antique Babylonian Rabbis." *Jewish History* 36 (2022): 1–28.

"Editorial Material in the Babylonian Talmud and Its Sasanian Context." *Association of Jewish Studies Review* 47 (2023): 51–76.

"Hopeful Rebels and Anxious Romans: Jewish Interconnectivity in the Great Revolt and Beyond." *Historia: Zeitschrift für Alte Geschichte* 72 (2023): 1–135.

"Babylonian Jewish Communities." In *The Routledge Companion to Jews in Late Antiquity*, edited by Catherine Hezser, 414–434. Abington, Oxon: 2024.

"The Impact of Sasanian Imperialism on the Culture and Literature of the Babylonian Rabbis." In *What Is the Talmud: The State of the Question* ed. Christine Hayes and Jay Harris, Cambridge, MA: Forthcoming.

"Prolegomena to a Study of Babylonian Rabbinization in Late Antiquity." In vol. 2 of *Rabbinization & Diversity*, edited by Ra'anan Boustan, Geoffrey Herman, Eve Krakowski, and D. Stökl Ben Ezra, Forthcoming.

Gross, Simcha, and Avigail Manekin-Bamberger. "Babylonian Jewish Society: The Evidence of the Incantation Bowls." *Jewish Quarterly Review* 112 (2022): 1–30.

Gross, Simcha and Yakir Paz. *The Great Persecution: Martyrs at the Court of Shapur II*. Piscataway, NJ, Forthcoming.

Grossfeld, Bernard. *The Targum Sheni to the Book of Esther: A Critical Edition Based on MS Sassoon 282 with Critical Apparatus*. New York: 1994.

Grossman, Abraham. *Rashut ha-Golah bi-Tequfat ha-Geʾonim*. Jerusalem: 1984.

Guidi, Ignazio. *Chronicum Anonymum de ultimis regibus Persarum, Chronica Minora pars prior*. Corpus Scriptorum Christianorum Orientalium 1–2. Leuven: 1903.

Gyselen, Rika. *La géographie administrative de l'empire sassanide: Les témoignages sigillographiques*. Paris: 1989.

"Note de glyptique sassanide: Quelques éléments d'iconographie religieuse." In *Contribution à l'histoire de l'Iran: mélanges offerts à Jean Perrot*, edited by François Vallat, 253–269. Paris: 1990.

Catalogue des sceaux, camées et bulles sassanides de la Bibliothèque Nationale et du Musée du Louvre du Louvre. Paris: 1994.

"Les témoignages sigillographiques sur la présence chrétienne dans l'Empire Sassanide." In *Chrétiens en terre d'Iran: Implantation et Acculturation*, edited by Rika Gyselen, 17–78. Paris: 2006.

Sasanian Seals and Sealings in the A. Saeedi Collection. Louvain: 2007.

"The Great Families in the Sasanian Empire: Some Sigillographic Evidence." In *Current Research in Sasanian Archaeology, Art and History*, edited by Derek Kennet and Paul Luft, 107–113. Oxford: 2008.

"Primary Sources and Historiography on the Sasanian Empire." *Studia Iranica* 38 (2009): 163–190.

Halbertal, Moshe. "Co-existing with the Enemy: Jews and Pagans in the Mishnah." In *Tolerance and Intolerance in Early Judaism and Christianity*, edited by Graham N. Stanton and Guy G. Stroumsa, 159–172. Cambridge: 1998.

Halivni, David Weiss. *The Formation of the Babylonian Talmud*, trans. Jeffrey Rubenstein. New York: 2013.

Hämeen–Anttila, Jaakko. *The Last Pagans of Iraq: Ibn Wahshiyya and His Nabatean Agriculture*. Leiden: 2006.

Khwadāynāmag: the Middle Persian Book of Kings. Leiden: 2018.

Hamilton, F. J., and E. W. Brooks, eds., *The Syriac Chronicle Known as That of Zachariah of Mitylene*. London: 1899.

Han, Jae. "Mani's Metivta: Manichaean Pedagogy in Its Late Antique Mesopotamian Context." *Theological Review* 114 (2021): 346–370.

Harkavy, Avraham. *Zikhron Kamah Geonim: uve-Yiḥud Rav Sherira ve-Rav Hai beno veh—Rav R. Yiṣḥaq Alfasi*. Berlin: 1887.

Harmatta, Janos. "A Turk Officer of the Sasanian King Xusro I." *Acta Orientalia Academiae Scientiarum Hungaricae* 55 (2002): 153–159.

Harper, P. O., *The Royal Hunter: Art of the Sasanian Empire*. New York: 1978.

Silver Vessels of the Sasanian Period: I Royal Imagery. New York: 1981.

Harrak, Amir. *The Chronicle of Zuqnin, Parts III and IV*. Toronto: 1999.

The Acts of Mār Māri the Apostle. Atlanta, GA: 2005.

The Law Code of Simeon, Bishop of Rev-Ardashir. Piscataway, NJ: 2020.

The Law Code of Išōʿyahb I, Patriarch of the Church of the East. Piscataway, NJ: 2022.

Harviainen, Tapani. "Pagan Incantations in Aramaic Magic Bowls." in *Studia Aramaica: New Sources and New Approaches*, edited by Markham Geller, Jonas C. Greenfield, and Michael P. Weitzman, 53–60. Oxford: 1995.

Hayes, Christine. *Between the Babylonian and Palestinian Talmuds: Accounting for Halakhic Difference in Selected Sugyot from Tractate Avodah Zarah*. New York: 1997.

Displaced Self-Perceptions: The Deployment of Minim and Romans in B. Sanhedrin 90b–91a." In *Religious and Ethnic Communities in Later Roman Palestine*, edited by Hayim Lapin, 249–289. Bethesda, MD: 1998.

Gentile Impurities and Jewish Identities: Intermarriage and Conversion from the Bible to the Talmud. Oxford: 2002.

What's Divine about Divine Law? Early Perspectives. Princeton, NJ: 2015.

Heimgartner, Martin. *Die Briefe 40 und 41 des Ostsyrischen Patriarchen Timotheos I*. 2 vols. Louvain: 2019.

Henning, Walter Bruno. "Mani's Last Journey." *Bulletin of the School of Oriential and African Studies* 10 (1942): 941–953.

"The Inscription of Firuzabad." *Asia Major* 4 (1954): 98–102.

Herman, Geoffrey. "Priests in Babylonia in the Talmudic Period" [in Hebrew]. MA diss. Hebrew University of Jerusalem, 1998.

"Ahasuerus, the Former Stable-Master of Belshazzar, and the Wicked Alexander of Macedon: Two Parallels between the Babylonian Talmud and Persian Sources." *Association for Jewish Studies Review* 29 (2005): 283–297.

"Iranian Epic Motifs in Josephus' Antiquities (XVIII, 314–370)." *Journal of Jewish Studies* 57 (2006): 245–268.

"The Story of Rav Kahana (BT Baba Qamma 117a–b) in Light of Armeno-Persian Sources." *Irano-Judaica* VI, edited by Shaul Shaked and Amnon Netzer, 53–86. Jerusalem: 2008.

"'Bury My Coffin Deep!' Zoroastrian Exhumation in Jewish and Christian Sources." *Tiferet leYisrael; Jubilee Volume in Honor of Israel Francus*, edited by Joel Roth, Menahem Schmelzer, Yaacov Francus, 31–59. New York: 2010.

"Persia in Light of the Babylonian Talmud: Echoes of Contemporary Society and Politics: *hargbed* and *bidaxš*." In *The Talmud in Its Iranian Context*, edited by Carol Bakhos and Rahim Shayegan, 61–84. Tubingen: 2010.

"Sasanian Jewry and Its Culture: A Lexicon of Jewish and Related Seals by Daniel M. Friedenberg, Norman Golb," *Association for Jewish Studies Review* 34 (2010): 121–124.

"The Jews of Parthian Babylonia." In *The Parthian Empire and Its Religions*, edited by Peter Wick and Markus Zehnder, 141–150. Gutenberg: 2012.

"One Day David Went Out for the Hunt of the Falconers: Persian Themes in the Babylonian Talmud." In *Shoshanat Yaakov: Jewish and Iranian Studies in Honor of Yaakov Elman*, edited by Shai Secunda and Steven Fine, 111–136. Leiden: 2012.

A Prince without a Kingdom: The Exilarch in the Sasanian Era. Tübingen: 2012.

"On Table Etiquette and Persian Culture in the Babylonian Talmud" [in Hebrew]. *Zion* 77 (2012): 149–188.

"Insurrection in the Academy: The Babylonian Talmud and the Paikuli Inscription" [in Hebrew]. *Zion* 79 (2014): 377–407.

"The Last Years of Yazdgird I and the Christians." In *Jews, Christians, and Zoroastrians: Religious Dynamics in a Sasanian Context*, edited by Geoffrey Herman, 67–90. Judaism in Context. Piscataway, NJ: 2014.

"'Like a Slave before His Master': A Persian Gesture of Deference in Sasanian Jewish and Christian Sources." *Aram* 26 (2014): 101–108.

"Midgets and Mules, Elephants, and Exilarchs: On the Metamorphosis of a Polemical Amoraic Story." In *Rabbinic Traditions between Palestine and Babylonia*, edited by Tal Ilan and Ronit Nikolsky, 117–132. Leiden: 2014.

"Religious Transformation between East and West: Hanukkah in the Babylonian Talmud and Zoroastrianism." In *Religions and Trade: Religious Formation, Transformation and Cross-Cultural Exchange between East and West*, edited by Peter Wick and Volker Rabens, 261–282. Leiden: 2014.

"The Mysterious Mar Zutra." *Segula* 27 (2015): 40–47.

Persian Martyr Acts under Yazdgird I. Piscataway, NJ: 2016.

"The Talmud in Its Babylonian Context: Rava and Bar-Sheshakh; Mani and Mihrshah." In *Between Babylonia and the Land of Israel: Studies in Honor of Isaiah M. Gafni*, edited by Geoffrey Herman, Meir ben Shahar, and Aharon Oppenheimer, 79–96. Jerusalem: 2017.

"Back to Bustanay: The History of a Legend." In *Irano-Judaica* VII, edited by Geoffrey Herman and Julia Rubanovich, 311–339. Jerusalem: 2018.

"'In Honor of the House of Caesar': Attitudes to the Kingdom in the Aggada of the Babylonian Talmud and Other Sasanian Sources." In *The Aggada of Bavli and Its Cultural World*, edited by Geoffrey Herman and Jeffrey Rubenstein, 103–124. Providence: 2018.

"Fire Typologies in Zoroastrianism and in the Babylonian Talmud: A Methodological Consideration." In *Iran, Israel, and the Jews: Symbiosis and Conflict from the Achaemenids to the Islamic Republic*, edited by Aaron Koller and Daniel Tsadik, 108–120. Yeshiva University Center for Israel Studies, 2019.

"Jewish Identity in Babylonia in the Period of the Incantation Bowls." In *A Question of Identity: Social, Political, and Historical Aspects of Identity Dynamics in Jewish and Other Contexts*, edited by Dikla Rivlin Katz, Noah Hacham, Geoffrey Herman, and Lilach Sagiv, 131–152. Berlin: 2019.

"Exilarch and Catholicos: A Paradigm for the Commonalities of the Jewish and Christian Experience under the Sasanians." In *Jews and Syriac Christians: Intersections across the first Millennium*, edited by Aaron Michael Butts and Simcha Gross, 145–153. Tubingen: 2020.

"In Search of Non-Rabbinic Judaism in Sasanian Babylonia." In *Diversity and Rabbinization: Jewish Texts and Societies between 400 and 1,000 CE*, edited by Gavin McDowell, Ron Naiweld, Judith Schlanger, and Daniel Stökl Ben Ezra, 121–138. Cambridge: 2021.

"Idolatry, God(s), and Demons among the Jews of Sasanian Babylonia," in *Expressions of Sceptical Topoi in (Late) Antique Judaism* ed. Geoffrey Herman and Reuven Kiperwasser, 85–99. Berlin: 2021.

Herrmann, Georgina. *The Sasanian Rock Reliefs at Naqsh-I Rustam: Naqsh-i Rustam 6, The Triumph of Shapur I*. Berlin: 1989.

"The Rock Reliefs of Sasanian Iran." In *Mesopotamia and Iran in the Parthian and Sasanian Periods: Rejection and Revival c. 238 BC–AD 652*, edited by John Curtis, 35–45. London: 2000.

Herrmann, Georgina with Rosalind Howell. *Naqsh-i Rustam 5 and 8: Sasanian Reliefs attributed to Hormuzd II and Narseh*. Berlin: 1977.

Herr, Moshe David. "On the Problem of the Laws of War on the Sabbath in the Second Temple Period and the Mishnaic and Talmudic Period" [in Hebrew]. *Tarbiẓ* 30 (1961): 242–256, 341–356.

"The Historical Significance of the Dialogues between Jewish Sages and Roman Dignitaries." In *Studies in Aggadah and Folk-Literature*, edited by Joseph Heinemann and Dov Noy, 123–150. Jerusalem: 1971.

Hezser, Catherine. *Social Structure of the Rabbinic Movement in Roman Palestine*. Tübingen: 1997.

Hidary, Richard. *Dispute for the Sake of Heaven: Legal Pluralism in the Talmud*. Providence, RI: 2010.

Hildesheimer, Azriel. *Halakhot Gedolot*. Berlin: 1888.
Hirshman, Marc. *The Stabilization of Rabbinic Culture, 100 C.E.–350 C.E.: Texts on Education and their Late Antique Context*. Oxford: 2009.
Horovitz, Hayim Saul, and Israel A. Rabin, eds. *Mekhilta deRabbi Ishmael*. Jerusalem: 1998.
Horowitz, Elliot. "'The Vengeance of the Jews Was Stronger than Their Avarice': Modern Historians and the Persian Conquest of Jerusalem in 614." *Jewish Social Studies* 4 (1998): 1–39.
Howard-Johnston, James. "The Two Great Powers in Late Antiquity: A Comparison." In *The Byzantine and Early Islamic Near East, v. III: States, Resources, and Armies*, edited by Averil Cameron, 157–226. Princeton, NJ: 1995.
"State and Society in Late Antique Iran." In *The Idea of Iran*, vol. 3: *The Sasanian Era*, edited by Vesta Sarkhosh Curtis and Sarah Stewart, 118–129. London: 2008.
Huff, Dietrich. "Architecture: (iii) Sasanian." In *Ānāmaka–Aṯār–Al-Wozarā'*, edited by Ehsan Yarshater, 329–334. Vol. 2 of *Encyclopædia Iranica*. London: 1987.
"Čahārṭāq: (i) In Pre-Islamic Iran." In *Bāyjū–Carpets*, edited by Ehsan Yarshater, 634–648. Vol. 4 of *Encyclæpedia Iranica*. London: 1990.
"Beobachtungen zum Chahartaq und zur Topographie von Girre." *Iranica Antique* 30 (1995): 71–92.
"Formation and Ideology of the Sasanian State in the Context of Archaeological Evidence." In *The Idea of Iran, vol. 3: The Sasanian Era*, edited by Vesta S. Curtis and Sarah R. A. Stewart, 31–59. London: 2008
Humbach, Helmut, and Josef Elfenbein. *Erbedestan: An Avesta-Pahlavi Text*. Munich: 1990.
Humfress, Caroline. *Orthodoxy and the Courts in Late Antiquity*. Oxford: 2007.
"Thinking through Legal Pluralism: 'Forum Shopping' in the Later Roman Empire." In *Law and Empire: Ideas, Practices, Actors*, edited by Jeroen Duindam, Jill Diana Harries, Caroline Humfress, and Hurvitz Nimrod, 223–250. Leiden: 2014.
Hunter, Erica. "Aramaic Speaking Communities of Sasanid Mesopotamia." *ARAM Periodical* 7 (1995): 319–335.
Hutter, Manfred. "Manichaeism in the Early Sasanian Empire." *Numen* 40.1 (1993): 2–15.
"Mār Abā and the Impact of Zoroastrianism on Christianity in the 6th Century." In *Religious Themes and Texts of Pre-Islamic Iran and Central Asia*, edited by Carlo Cereti, Mauro Maggi, and Elio Provasi, 167–173. Wiesbaden: 2003.
"Manichaeism in Iran." In *The Wiley Blackwell Companion to Zoroastrianism*, edited by Michael Stausberg, Yuhan Sohrab-Dinshaw Vevaina and Anna Tessmann, 477–489. Hoboken, NJ: 2015.
Huyse, Philip. *Die dreisprachige Inschrift šābuhrs I. an der Kaba-I Zardušt (šKZ)*. In *Corpus Inscriptionum Iranicarum*, pt. 3. 2 vols. London: 1999.
"Die sasanidische Königstitulatur: Eine Gegenüberstellung der Quellen." In *Ērān und Anērān, Studien zu den Beziehungen zwischen dem*

Sasanidenreich und der Mittelmeerwelt, *Oriens et Occidens 13*, edited by Josef Wiesehöfer and Philip Huyse, 182–201. Stuttgart: 2006.

Jaafari-Dehaghi, Mahmoud, ed. and trans. *Dādestān ī Dēnīg: Part I, Transcription, Translation and Commentary*. Paris: 1998.

Jacobs, Louis. "The Economic Conditions of the Jews in Babylon in Talmudic Times Compared with Palestine." *Journal of Semitic Studies* 2 (1957): 349–359.

Jacobs, Martin. *Die Institution des jüdischen Patriarchen: Eine quellen- und traditionskritische Studie zur Geschichte der Juden in der Spätantike*. Tübingen: 1995.

Jamali, Nima. "A Study of the Interactions among Zoroastrian, Jewish and Roman Legal Systems during the 7th and 8th Centuries CE Based on a Critical Edition of Īšōʿ-boḵt's Corpus Juris with Commentary and an English Translation." PhD diss. University of Toronto, 2021.

Jany, János. "Criminal Justice in Sasanian Persia." *Iranica Antiqua* 42 (2007): 347–386.

"Sasanian Law," *e-Sasanika* 9 (2011): 1–33.

Judging in the Islamic, Jewish, and Zoroastrian Legal Traditions. Surrey: 2012.

Jones, W. H. S. and H. A. Ormerod, ed. and trans. *Pausanias: Description of Greece*. Vol. 2, *Loeb Classical Library 188*. Cambridge: 1918.

Jullien, Christelle. "Christianiser le pouvoir: Images de rois sassanides dans la tradition syro–orientale." *Orientalia christiana periodica* 75 (2009): 119–131.

"Les chrétiens déportés dans l'empire sassanide sous Šābūr Ier. À propos d'un récent article." *Studia Iranica* 40 (2011): 285–293.

"Conversion to Christianity in the Sasanian Empire: Political and Theological Issues." In *Iranianate and Syriac Chrisitanity in Late Antiquity and the Early Islamic Period*, edited by Chiara Barbati and Vittorio Berti, 11–32. Vienna: 2021.

Jullien, C., and F. Jullien. *Apôtres des confins: processus missionnaires chrétiens dans l'Empire Iranien*. Bures-sur-Yvette: 2002.

"Aux frontières de l'iranité: 'nāṣrāyē' et "krīstyonē" des inscriptions du mobad Kirdīr: enquête littéraire et historique." *Numen* 49 (2002): 282–335.

"Du ḥnana ou lan contestée." In *Sur les pas des Araméens chrétiens. Mélanges offerts à Alain Desreumaux*, edited by Françoise Briquel-Chatonnet and Muriel Debié, 333–348. Cahiers d'études syriaques 1. Paris: 2010.

Jullien, Florence. "Parcours à travers l'Histoire d'Īšōʿsabran, martyr sous Khosrau II." In *Contributions à l'histoire et la géographie historique de l'Empire sassanide*, edited by Rika Gyselen, 171–183. Bures-sur-Yvette: 2004.

"La passion syriaque de Mār ʿAbdā: quelques relations entre chrétiens et mazdéens." In *Rabban l'Olmyn: florilège offert à Philippe Gignoux pour son 80e anniversaire*, edited by Rika Gyselen, C. Jullien, and F. Jullien, 195–205. Leuven: 2011.

Histoire de Mār Abba, catholicos de l'Orient. Martyres de Mār Grigor, général en chef du roi Khusro Ier et, de Mār Yazd–panāh, juge et gouverneur. 2 vols. Louvain: 2015.

Juusola, H. "Who Wrote the Syriac Incantation Bowls." *Studia Orientalia* 85 (1999): 75–92.

"Manichaean Incantations Bowls in Syriac." *Jerusalem Studies in Arabic and Islam* 24 (2000): 58–92.

Kahan, Kalman. *Seder Tannaim weAmoraim auf Grund mehrer veröffentlichter und nichtveröffentlichter Texte bearbeitet, übersetzt, mit Einleitung und erklärden Noten versehen*. Frankfurt: 1935.

Kalmin, Richard L. *The Sage in Jewish Society of Late Antiquity*. New York: 1999.

"Rabbinic Traditions about Roman Persecutions of the Jews: A Reconsideration." *Journal of Jewish Studies* 54 (2003): 21–50.

"The Formation and Character of the Babylonian Talmud." In *Cambridge History of Judaism IV: The Late-Roman Period*, edited by S. T. Katz, 840–876. Cambridge: 2006.

Jewish Babylonia between Persia and Roman Palestine. Oxford: 2006.

"Sasanian Persecution of the Jews: A Reconsideration of the Evidence." In *Irano-Judaica* VI, edited by Shaul Shaked and Amnon Netzer, 87–125. Jerusalem: 2008.

Migrating Tales: The Talmud's Narratives and Their Historical Context. Oakland, CA: 2014.

Kaufhold, Hubert. "Sources of Canon Law in the Eastern Churches." In *The History of Byzantine and Eastern Canon Law to 1500*, edited by Wilfried Hartmann and Kenneth Pennington, 215–342. Washington, DC: 2012.

Kaufman, Stephen. *The Akkadian Influences on Aramaic*. Chicago, IL: 1974.

Kennedy, Hugh. "From Shahristan to Medina." *Studia Islamica* 102 (2006): 5–34.

Kettenhofen, Erich. "Das Staatgefängnis der Sāsāniden." *Die Welt des Orients* 19 (1988): 96–101.

"Deportations: (ii) In the Parthian and Sasanian Periods." In *Dārā (b)–Ebn al-Aṯīr*, edited by Ehsan Yarshater, 297–308. Vol. 7 of *Encyclopaedia Iranica*. Costa Mesa, CA: 1996.

Khosravi, Shokouh, Sajjad Alibaigi, and Mehdi Rahbar. "The Functions of Gypsum Bases in Sasanid Fire Temples: A Different Proposal." *Iranica Antiqua* 53 (2018): 267–298.

Kiperwasser, Reuven, and Serge Ruzer. "Zoroastrian Proselytes in Rabbinic and Syriac Christian Narratives: Orality-Related Markers of Cultural Identity." *History of Religions* 51 (2011): 197–218.

"To Convert a Persian and Teach Him the Holy Scriptures: A Zoroastrian Proselyte in Rabbinic and Syriac Christian Narratives." in *Jews, Christians and Zoroastrians: Religious Dynamics in a Sasanian Context*, edited by Geoffrey Herman, 91–127. Piscataway, NJ: 2014.

Kister, Menahem. "Plucking Grain on the Sabbath and the Christian–Jewish Polemic." *Meḥqere Yerushalayim b'Maḥshevet Yisrael* 3 (1983/1984): 349–366.

Klíma, Otakar. "*Baat the Manichee*." *Archív orientální* 26 (1958): 342–346.

Kmosko, Michael. "S. Simeon bar Ṣabba'e." In *Patrología Syriaca* 1.2. Paris: 1907.

Koenen, Ludwig. "The Ptolemaic King as a Religious Figure." In *Images and Ideologies: Self-definition in the Hellenistic World*, edited by Anthony W.

Bulloch, Erich S. Gruen, A. A. Long, and Andrew Steward, 25–115. Berkeley, CA: 1993.

Kohut, Alexander. "The Talmudic Records of Persian and Babylonian Festivals Critically Illustrated." *The American Journal of Semitic Languages and Literatures* 14 (1898): 183–194.

"Les fêtes persanes et babyloniennes dans les Talmuds de Babylon et de Jerusalem." *Revue des Études Juives* 24 (1892): 256–271.

Koltun-Fromm, Naomi. *Hermeneutics of Holiness: Ancient Jewish and Christian Notions of Sexuality and Religious Community*. Oxford: 2010.

Koren, Yedidah. "'Look through Your Book and Make Me a Perfect Match': Talking about Genealogy in Amoraic Palestine and Babylonia." *Journal for the Study of Judaism in the Persian, Hellenistic and Roman Period* 49 (2018): 417–448.

Kosmin, Paul. *Land of the Elephant Kings: Space, Territory, and Ideology in the Seleucid Empire*. Cambridge, MA: 2014.

Kotwal, Firoze M., and Kreyenbroek, Philip G. *The Hērbedestān and Nērangestān*. Paris, 1992.

The Hērbedestān and Nērangestān III: Nērangestān. Fragard 2. Paris: 2003.

Kraemer, David. *Responses to Suffering in Classical Rabbinic Literature*. Oxford: 1995.

Kreyenbroek, Philip G. "How Pious Was Shapur I? Religion, Church and Propaganda under the Early Sasanians." In *The Idea of Iran*, vol. 3: *The Sasanian Era*, edited by Vesta Sarkhosh Curtis and Sarah Stewart, 7–16. New York: 2008.

Kruisheer, Dirk. "Theodor bar Koni's *Ketābā d-'Eskolyon* as a Source for the Study of Early Mandaeism." *Jaarbericht Ex Oriente Lux* 33 (1993–1994): 151–169.

Kwasman, Theodore. "Hebrew Graffiti on Ardashir I's Relief at Naqsh-I Rustam." *Iranica Antiqua* 47 (2012): 399–403.

Labendz, Jenny. *Socratic Torah: Non-Jews in Rabbinic Intellectual Culture*. Oxford: 2013.

Labourt, Jérôme. *Le Christianisme dans l'empire perse sous la dynastie Sassanide (224–632)*. Paris: 1904.

Lacerenza, G. "Jewish Magicians and Christian Clients in Late Antiquity." In *What Athens Has to Do with Jerusalem: Essays on Classical, Jewish, and Early Christian Art and Archaeology in Honor of Gideon Foerster*, edited by Leonard Rutgers, 393–419. Leuven: 2002.

Lang, David Marshall. *Lives and Legends of the Georgian Saints*. New York: 1956.

Langin-Hooper, Stephanie M. "Problematizing Typology and Discarding the Colonialist Legacy: Approaches to Hybridity in the Terracotta Figurines of Hellenistic Babylonia." *Archaeological Review from Cambridge* 28 (2013): 95–113.

Lapin, Hayim. *Rabbis as Romans: The Rabbinic Movement in Palestine, 100–400 CE*. Oxford: 2012.

"The Law of Moses and the Jews: Rabbis, Ethnic Marking, and Romanization," in *Jews, Christians, and the Roman Empire: The Poetics of*

Power in Late Antiquity, edited by Natalie Dohrmann and Annette Yoshiko Reed, 79–92. Philadelphia, PA: 2014.

Lavan, Myles, Richard Payne, and John Weisweiler, eds. *Cosmopolitanism and Empire: University Rulers, Local Elites, and Cultural Integration in the Ancient Near East and Mediterranean*. Oxford: 2016.

Lavee, Moshe. *The Rabbinic Conversion of Judaism*. Leiden: 2017.

Lazarus, Felix. *Die Häupter der Vertriebenen: Beiträge zu einer Geschichte der Exilsführsten in Babylonien unter den Arsakiden und Sassaniden*. Frankfurt: 1890.

Lee, Kyong-Jin. *The Authority and Authorization of Torah in the Persian Period*. Leuven: 2011.

Leemans, Johan, ed. *More than a Memory: The Discourse of Martyrdom and the Construction of Christian Identity in the History of Christianity*. Leuven: 2005.

Lehto, Adam. *The Demonstrations of Aphrahat, the Persian Sage*. Piscataway, NJ: 2010.

Leibner, Uzi. "An Illustrated Midrash of Mekilta de R. Ishmael, Vayeḥi Beshalaḥ, 1 – Rabbis and the Jewish Community Revisited." In *Talmuda de-Eretz Israel: Archaeology and the Rabbis in Late Antique Palestine*, edited by Steven Fine and Aaron Koller, 83–96. 2014.

Lenski, Noel. *Constantine and the Cities: Imperial Authority and Civic Politics*. Philadelphia, PA: 2016.

Lerner, Judith. *Christian Seals of the Sasanian Period*. Leiden: 1977.

"The Sacrifice of Isaac Revisited: Additional Observations on a Theme in Sasanian Glyptic Art." In *Facts and Artefacts: Art in the Islamic World. Festschrift for Jens Kröger on His 65th Birthday*, edited by Annette Hagedorn and Avinoam Shalem, 39–58. Leiden: 2007.

"Considerations on an Aspect of Jewish Culture under the Sasanians: The Matter of Jewish Sigillography." *Journal of the American Oriental Society* 129 (2009): 653–664.

Lerner, Judith, and P. O. Skjaervo. "The Seal of a Eunuch in the Sasanian Court." *Journal of Inner Asian Art and Archaeology* 1 (2006): 113–118.

Levene, Dan. "'... and by the name of Jesus ...,' An Unpublished Magic Bowl in Jewish Aramaic." *Jewish Studies Quarterly* 6 (1999): 283–308.

A Corpus of Magic Bowls: Incantation Texts in Jewish Aramaic from Late Antiquity. London: 2003.

Levene, Dan, and Gideon Bohak. "A Babylonian Jewish Aramaic Incantation Bowl with a List of Deities and Toponyms." *Jewish Studies Quarterly* 19 (2012): 56–72.

Levene, Dan, and Siam Bhayro. "'Bring to the Gates ... upon a good smell and upon good fragrances': An Aramaic Incantation Bowl for Success in Business." *Archiv für Orientforschung* 51 (2005/2006): 242–246.

Levine, Lee. *The Rabbinic Class of Roman Palestine in Late Antiquity*. New York: 1990.

The Ancient Synagogue: The First Thousand Years. New Haven, CT: 2005.

Visual Judaism in Late Antiquity: Historical Contexts of Jewish Art. New Haven, CT: 2013.

Levine, Lee, and Daniel Schwartz, eds. *Jewish Identities in Antiquity: Studies in Memory of Menachem Stern*. Tübingen: 2009.

Levenson, David. "The Ancient and Medieval Sources for the Emperor Julian's Attempt to Rebuild the Jerusalem Temple." *Journal for the Study of Judaism in the Persian, Hellenistic, and Roman Period* 35 (2004): 409–460.

Levy, Jacob. *Neuhebräisches und chaldäisches wörterbuch über die Talmudim und Midraschim*. 4 vols. Leipzig: 1876–1889.

Lewin, Benjamin M. *Iggeret Rav Sherira Gaon Mesuderet bi-Shnei Nusḥa'ot: Nusaḥ Sefarad ve-Nusaḥ Ṣarfat 'im ḥilufei Girsa'ot mi-Khol Qitvei-ha-yad ve-Qitvei ha-"Genizah" sheba-'Olam*. Haifa: 1921.

Oṣar ha-Geonim: Teshuvot Geonei Bavel u-Feirushehem 'al pi Seder ha–Talmud. 13 vols. Haifa: 1928–1943.

Libson, Gideon. "Determining Factors in Ḥerem and Nidui (Ban and Excommunication) during the Tannaitic and Amoraic Periods" [in Hebrew]. *Annual of the Institute for Research in Jewish Law* 2 (1975): 292–342.

Lieber, Laura. "Daru in the Winehouse: The Intersection of Status and Dance in the Jewish East." *Journal of Religion* 98 (2018): 90–113.

Lieu, Judith. *Image and Reality: The Jews in the World of the Christians in the Second Century*. Edinburgh: 1996.

"Accusations of Jewish Persecution in Early Christian Sources, with Particular Reference to Justin Martyr and the *Martyrdom of Polycarp*." In *Tolerance and Intolerance in Early Judaism and Christianity*, edited by G. Stanton and G. Stroumsa, 239–295. Cambridge: 1998.

Lieu, Samuel N. C. "Captives, Refugees, and Exiles: A Study of Cross-Frontier Civilian Movements and Contacts between Rome and Persia from Valerian to Jovian." In *The Defence of the Roman and Byzantine East: Proceedings of a Colloquium Held at the University of Sheffield in April 1986*, edited by Philip Freeman and David Kennedy, 475–505. Oxford: 1986.

Manichaeism in Mesopotamia and the Roman East. Leiden: 1994.

Lightstone, Jack. "The Institutionalization of the Rabbinic Academy in Late Sassanid Babylonia and the Redaction of the Babylonian Talmud." *Studies in Religion/ Sciences Religieuses* 22 (1993): 167–186.

Linder, Amnon. *Jews in Roman Imperial Legislation*. Detroit, MI: 1987.

Liver, Jacob. *Toldot bet David: mi-hurban mamlekhet Yehudah ve- 'ad le-ahar hurban ha–bayit ha-sheni*. Jerusalem: 1959.

Llewellyn-Jones, Lloyd. *King and Court in Ancient Persia, 559–331 BCE*. Edinburgh: 2013.

Loomba, Ania. *Colonialism/Postcolonialism*. London: 1998.

Ma, John. *Antiochus III and the Cities of Western Asia Minor*. Oxford: 2000.

MacKenzie, D. N. *A Concise Pahlavi Dictionary*. London: 1971.

"Kerdir's inscription." In *The Sasanian Rock Reliefs at Naqsh-i Rustam*, edited by Georgina Herrmann and D. N. MacKenzie, 35–72. Berlin: 1989.

"The Fire Altar of Happy Frayosh." *Bulletin of the Asia Institute* 7 (1993): 105–109.

Macuch, Maria. *Das Sasanidische Rechtsbuch "Mātakdān i Hazār Dātistān*. 2 vols. Wiesbaden: 1981.

"Ein mittelpersischer terminus technicus im syrischen Rechtsbuch des Īšōʿbōḫt und im sasanidischen Rechtsbuch." In *Studia Semitica necnon Iranica Rudolpho Macuch septuagenario ab amicis et discipulis dedicata*, edited by Maria Macuch, Christa Müller, and Bert Fragner, 149–160. Wiesbaden: 1989.

Rechtskasuistik Und Gerichtspraxis Zu Beginn Des Siebenten Jahrhunderts in Iran: Die Rechtssammlung Des Farroḫmard i Wahrāmān. Wiesbaden: 1993.

"Die sasanidische Stiftung 'für die Seele'—Vorbild für islamischen waqf?" In *Iranian and Indo-European Studies: Memorial Volume of Otakar Kilma*, edited by Petr Vavroušek, 163–180. Prague: 1994.

"Herrschaftskonsolidierung und sasanidische Familienrecht: Zum Verhältnis von Kirche und Staat unter den Sasaniden." In *Iran und Turfan: Beiträge Berliner Wissenschaftler, Werner Sundermann zum 60. Geburtstag gewidmet*, edited by Christiane Reck and Peter Zieme, 149–167. Wiesbaden: 1995.

"The Use of Seals in Sasanian Jurisprudence." In *Sceaux d'Orient et leur emploi*, edited by Rika Gyselen, 79–87. Bures-sur-Yvette: 1997.

"Iranian Legal Terminology in the Babylonian Talmud in the Light of Sassanian Jurisprudence." In *Irano-Judaica* IV, edited by Shaul Shaked and Amnon Netzer, 91–101. Jerusalem: 1999.

"The Talmudic Expression 'Servant of the Fire' in Light of Pahlavi Legal Sources." *Jerusalem Studies in Arabic and Islam* 26 (2002): 109–129.

"A Zoroastrian Legal Term in the Dēnkard: Pahikār-Rad." In *Iran: Questions et connaissances. Vol. 1, La période ancienne*, edited by Philip Huyse, 77–90. Studia Iranica, Cahier 25. Paris: 2002.

"Zoroastrian Principles and the Structure of Kinship in Sasanian Iran." In *Religious Themes and Texts of Pre-Islamic Iran and Central Asia*, edited by Carlo Cereti, Mauro Maggi, and Elio Provasi, 231–246. Wiesbaden: 2003.

"Pious Foundations in Byzantine and Sasanian Law." In *La Persia e Bisanzio: Convegno internazionale, Roma 14–18 ottobre 2002*, edited by Antonio Carile, Lellia Cracco Ruggini, Gherardo Gnoli, et al., 181–196. Rome: 2004.

"The Hērbedestān as a Legal Source: A Section on the Inheritance of a Convert to Zoroastrianism." *Bulletin of the Asia Institute* 19 (2005): 91–102.

"The Pahlavi Model Marriage Contract in the Light of Sasanian Family Law." In *Iranian Languages and Texts from Iran and Turan*, edited by Maria Macuch, Mauro Maggi, and Werner Sundermann, 183–204. Wiesbaden: 2007.

"Pahlavi Literature." In *The Literature of Pre-Islamic Iran*, edited by Ronald E. Emmerick and Maria Macuch, 116–196. New York: 2009.

"Allusions to Sasanian Law in the Babylonian Talmud." In *The Talmud in Its Iranian Context*, edited by Carol Bakhos and M. Rahim Shayegan, 100–111. Tübingen: 2010.

"Legal Constructions of Identity in the Sasanian Period." In *Iranian Identity in the Course of History*, edited by Carlo Cereti, 193–212. Rome: 2010.

"The Case against Mār Abā, the Catholicos, in the Light of Sasanian Law." *ARAM Periodical* 26 (2014): 47–58.

"Jewish Jurisdiction within the Framework of the Sasanian Legal System." In *Encounters by the Rivers of Babylon: Scholarly Conversations between*

Jews, Iranians and Babylonians in Antiquity, edited by Uri Gabbay and Shai Secunda, 147–160. Tübingen: 2014.

"'This Is the Law of the Persians': An Allusion to the Sasanian Law of Surety in the Babylonian Talmud." *Iran Namag* 1 (2016): 18–28.

Mandel, Paul. "Was Rabbi Aqiva a Martyr? Palestinian and Babylonian Influences in the Development of a Legend." In *Rabbinic Traditions between Palestine and Babylonia*, edited by Ronit Nikolsky and Tal Ilan, 325–375. Leiden: 2014.

Manekin-Bamberger, Avigail. "Who Were the Jewish 'Magicians' behind the Aramaic Incantation Bowls?" *Journal of Jewish Studies* 71 (2020): 235–254.

Mann, Jacob. "Changes in the Divine Service of the Synagogue due to Religious Persecutions." *Hebrew Union College Annual* 4 (1927): 241–310.

Marcus, Ralph. "The Armenian Life of Marutha of Maipherkat." *The Harvard Theological Review* 25 (1932): 47–71.

Markwart, Josef. *A Catalogue of The Provincial Capitals of Ērānshahr, Pahlavi Text, Version and Commentary*, edited by Giuseppe Messina. Rome: 1931.

Marzano, Annalisa, and Guy P. R. Métraux, eds. *The Roman Villa in the Mediterranean Basin: Late Republic to Late Antiquity*. Cambridge: 2018.

Mason, Steve. "Jews, Judaeans, Judaizing, Judaism: Problems of Categorization in Ancient History." *Journal for the Study of Judaism* 38 (2007): 457–512.

Mattingly, David. "Being Roman: Expressing Identity in a Provincial Setting." *Journal of Roman Archaeology* 17 (2004): 5–25.

May, Natalie N. "Gates and Their Functions in Mesopotamia and Ancient Israel." In *The Fabric of Cities: Aspects of Urbanism, Urban Topography and Society in Mesopotamia, Greece and Rome*, edited by Natalie N. May and Ulrike Steinert, 77–123. Leiden: 2014.

McDonough, Scott John. "Power by Negotiation: Institutional Reform in the Fifth Century Sasanian Empire." PhD diss. University of California, Los Angeles, 2005.

"A Question of Faith? Persecution and Political Centralization in the Sasanian Empire of Yazdgard II (438–457 CE)." In *Violence in Late Antiquity: Perceptions and Practices*, edited by Hal A. Drake, 69–81. Aldershot: 2006.

"Bishops or Bureaucrats?: Christian Clergy and the State in the Middle Sasanian Period." In *Current Research in Sasanian Archaeology, Art and History*, edited by Derek Kennet and Paul Luft, 87–92. Oxford: 2008.

"A Second Constantine?: The Sasanian King Yazdgard in Christian History and Historiography." *Journal of Late Antiquity* 1 (2008): 127–140.

Melikian-Chirvani, A. S. "Parand and Parniyān Identified: The Royal Silks of Iran from Sasanian to Islamic Times." *Bulletin of the Asia Institute* 5 (1991): 175–179.

Menasce, Jean de. "Inscriptions pehlevies en écriture cursive." *Journal Asiatique* 244 (1956): 423–31.

Feux et fondations pieuses dans le droit sassanide. Paris: 1964.

Millar, Fergus. "A Rural Jewish Community in Late Roman Mesopotamia, and the Question of a 'Split' Jewish Diaspora," *Journal for the Study of Judaism* 42 (2011): 351–374.

Miller, Stuart. *Sages and Commoners in Late Antique 'Ereẓ Israel: A Philological Inquiry into Local Traditions in Talmud Yerushalmi*. Tübingen: 2006.
Minorsky, Vladimir. *Studies in Caucasian History*. London: 1953.
Minov, Sergey. "Dynamics of Christian Acculturation in the Sasanian Empire: Some Iranian Motifs in the *Cave of Treasures*." In *Jews, Christians and Zoroastrians: Religious Dynamics in a Sasanian Context*, edited by Geoffrey Herman, 159–212. Piscataway, NJ: 2014.
Memory and Identity in the Syriac Cave of Treasures: Rewriting the Bible in Sasanian Iran. Leiden: 2020.
"Christians, Jews, and Magic in the Sasanian Realm: Between Confrontation and Cooperation." *Entangled Religions* 13.3 (2022), 1–28.
Minuvi, M. *Nāme–ye Tansar* [The Letter of Tansar]. Tehran, 1932.
Miri, Negen. *Sasanian Pārs: Historical Geography and Administrative Organization*. Costa Mesa: 2012.
Mirsky, Shmuel. *She'iltot of Rav Ahai Gaon*. Vol. 3, *Exodus*. Jerusalem: 1963.
Mittertrainer, Anahita. *Sinnbilder politischer Autorität? Frühsasanidische Städtebilder im südwesten Irans*. PhD diss. Ludwig-Maximilians-Universität Münchenvorgelegt, 2020.
Moazami, Mahnaz. "Evil Animals in the Zoroastrian Religion." *History of Religions* 44 (2005): 300–317.
Wrestling with the Demons of the Pahlavi Widēwdād. Leiden: 2014.
Modi, Jivanji Jamshedji. *Aiyādgār-I-Zarirān, Shatrōihā-I-Airān and Afdiya va Sahigiya-I-Sistān. Translated with Notes*. Bombay: 1899.
The Ceremonies and Customs of the Parsees. Bombay: 1937.
Mokhtarian, Jason Sion. "Rabbinic Depictions of the Achaemenid King Cyrus the Great: *The Babylonian Esther Midrash* (bMeg. 10b–17a) in Its Iranian Context." In *The Talmud in Its Iranian Context*, edited by Carol Bakhos and M. Rahim Shayegan, 112–139. Tübingen: 2010.
"Empire and Authority in Sasanian Babylonia: The Rabbis and King Shapur in Dialogue." *Jewish Studies Quarterly* 19 (2012): 148–180.
"The Boundaries of an Infidel in Zoroastrianism: A Middle Persian Term of Otherness for Jews, Christians, and Muslims." *Iranian Studies* 48 (2015): 99–115.
Rabbis, Sorcerers, Kings, and Priests: The Culture of the Talmud in Ancient Iran. Oakland, CA: 2015.
"Excommunication in Jewish Babylonia: Comparing Bavli Mo'ed Qatan 14b–17b and the Aramaic Bowl Spells in a Sasanian Context." *Harvard Theological Review* 108 (2015): 552–578.
"Clusters of Iranian Loanwords in Talmudic Folkore: The Chapter of the Pious (b. Ta'anit 18b–26a) in Its Sasanian Context." In *The Aggada of the Bavli and Its Cultural World*, edited by Jeffrey Rubenstein and Geoffrey Herman, 125–148. Providence, RI: 2018.
"Zoroastrian Polemics against Jews in the *Doubt-Dispelling Exposition*." *Mizan* 3 (2018): 53–81.
Molé, Marijan. *Culte, mythe et cosmologie dans l'Iran ancient. Le problème zoroastrien et la tradition mazdéenne*. Paris: 1963.

Monchi-Zadeh, Davoud. "Xusrōv Kavātān ut Rētak: Pahlavi Text, Transcription and Translation." In vol. 2 of *Monumentum Georg Morgenstierne*, edited by Jacques Duchesne-Guillemin and Pierre Lecoq, 47–92. Leiden: 1982.

Montgomery, James. *Aramaic Incantation Texts from Nippur*. Philadelphia, PA: 1913.

Moorey, P. R. S. *Kish excavations, 1923–1933*. Oxford: 1978.

Moradi, Yousef, and Keall, Edward. "The Sasanian Fire Temple of Gach Dawar in Western Iran: New Evidence." *Journal of the British Institute of Persian Studies* 58 (2020): 27–40.

Morony, Michael. "Religious Communities in Late Sasanian and Early Muslim Iraq." *Journal of the Economic and Social History of the Orient* 17 (1974): 113–135.

"The Effects of the Muslim Conquest on the Persian Population of Iraq." *Iran* 14 (1976): 41–59.

"Magic and Society in Late Sasanian Iraq." In *Prayer, Magic and the Stars in the Ancient and Late Antique World*, edited by Scott Noegel, Joel Walker, and Brannon Wheeler, 83–107. University Park, PA: 2003.

"Population Transfers between Sasanian Iran and the Byzantine Empire." In *La Persia e Bisanzio: Convegno internazionale, Roma 14–18 ottobre 2002*, edited by Gherardo Gnoli. 161–179. Rome: 2004.

"History and Identity in the Syrian Churches." In *Redefining Christian Identity: Cultural Interaction in the Middle East since the Rise of Islam*, edited by Jan Jacob van Ginkel, Heleen L. Murre-van den Berg, and Theo Maarten Van Lint, 1–33. Leuven: 2005.

Iraq after the Muslim Conquest, 2nd ed. Piscataway, NJ: 2005.

"Religion and the Aramaic Incantation Bowls." *Religion Compass* 1 (2007): 414–429.

Mosig-Walburg, Karin. "Die Christenverfolgung Shāpūrs II. vor dem Hintergrund des persisch-römischen Krieges." In *Inkulturation des Christentums im Sasanidenreich*, edited by Arafa Mustafa, Jürgen Tubach, and Sophia Vashalomidze, 171–186. Wiesbaden: 2007.

"Deportationen römischer Christen in das Sasanidenreich durch Shapur I. und ihre Folgen—Eine Neubewertung." *Klio* 92 (2010): 117–156.

Moss, Candida. *The Other Christs: Imitating Jesus in Ancient Christian Ideologies of Martyrdom*. Oxford: 2010.

Moster, David. *Etrog: How a Chinese Fruit Became a Jewish Symbol*. Cham, Switzerland: 2018.

Mousavi, Ali, and Touraj Daryaee. "The Sasanian Empire: An Archaeological Survey, c. 220–AD 640." In vol. 2 of *A Companion to the Archaeology of the Ancient Near East*, edited by Daniel T. Potts, 1076–2094. Malden, MA: 2012.

Müller-Kessler, Christa. "Interrelations between Mandaic Lead Rolls and Incantation Bowls." In *Mesopotamian Magic: Textual, Historical and Interpretative Perspectives*, edited by Tzvi Abusch and Karel van der Toorn, 197–209. Leiden: 2000.

Müller-Kessler, Christa, and Karlheinz Kessler. "Spätbabylonische Gottheiten in spätantiken mandäischen Texten." *Zeitschrift für Assyriologie* 89 (1999): 65–87.

Nau, François, ed. *Martyrologes et ménologes orientaux, I–XIII. Un martyrologie et douze ménologes syriaques édités et traduits*. Patrologia Orientalis 10.1. Paris: 1912.

ed. *La seconde partie de l'Histoire de Barhadbešabba 'Arbaïa et controverse de Théodore de Mopsueste avec les Macédoniens*. Patrologia Orientalis 9.5. Paris: 1913.

Naveh, Joseph, and Shaked, Shaul. *Amulets and Magic Bowls*. Jerusalem: 1985.

Magic Spells and Formulae. Jerusalem: 1993.

Neis, R. Rafe. *The Sense of Sight in Rabbinic Culture: Jewish Ways of Seeing in Late Antiquity*. Cambridge: 2013.

Nemoy, Leon. "Al-Qirqisānī's Account of the Jewish Sects and Christianity." *HUCA* 7 (1930): 317–398.

Nersessian, S. der. "Une apologie des images du septieme siècle." *Byzantion* 17 (1944–1945): 58–88.

Netzer, Amnon. "Ha-Sasanim ba-Talmud ha-Bavli: Shapur I, Shapur II, and Yazdgird I." *Shevet ve-Am* 7 (1973): 251–262.

Neubauer, Adolf. *Mediaeval Jewish Chronicles and Chronological Notes*. 2 vols. Oxford: 1887.

Neusner, Jacob. *A History of the Jews in Babylonia*. 5 vols. Leiden: 1966–1969.

"Rabbi and Magus in Third-Century Sasanian Babylonia." *History of Religions* 6 (1966): 169–178.

Development of a Legend: Studies on the Traditions concerning Yohanan ben Zakkai. Leiden: 1970.

"Rabbis and Community in Third Century Babylonia." In *Religions in Antiquity Essays in Memory of Erwin Ramsdell Goodenough*, edited by Jacob Neusner, 438–459. Leiden: 1970.

"Babylonian Jewry and Shapur II's Persecution of Christianity from 337 to 379 A.D." *Hebrew Union College Annual* 43 (1972): 77–102.

Eliezer ben Hyrcanus. The Tradition and the Man. Leiden: 1973.

"How Much Iranian in Jewish Babylonia?" *Journal of the American Oriental Society* 95 (1975): 184–190.

"Jews in Iran: Jewish Settlement in the Western Satrapies of Iran." In *The Cambridge History of Iran*, vol. 3, bk. 1: *The Seleucid, Parthian and Sasanian Periods*, edited by Ehsan Yarsahter, 909–923. Cambridge: 1983.

Israel's Politics in Sasanian Iran: Jewish Self-Government in Talmudic Times. Lanham, MD: 1986.

School, Court, Public Administration: Judaism and Its Institutions in Talmudic Babylonia. Atlanta, GA: 1987.

Newman, Hillel I. "Closing the Circle: Yonah Fraenkel, the Talmudic Story, and Rabbinic History." In *How Should Rabbinic Literature be Read in the Modern World?*, edited by Matthew Kraus, 105–113. Piscataway, NJ, 2006.

Newman, J. *The Agricultural Life of the Jews in Babylonia: Between the Years 200 CE and 500 CE*. London: 1932.

Nirenberg, David. *Anti-Judaism: The Western Tradition*. New York: 2013.

Nöldeke, Theodore. *Geschichte der Perser und Araber zur Zeit des Sasaniden aus der arabischen Chronik des Tabari*. Leiden: 1879.

Nongbri, Brent. "Dislodging 'Embedded' Religion: A Brief Note on a Scholarly Trope." *Numen* 55 (2008): 440–460.

Oppenheim, David. "Die Namen der persischen und babylonischen Feste im Talmud." *Monatsschrift für Geschichte und Wissenschaft des Judentums* 7 (1854): 347–352.

Oppenheimer, Aharon. *Babylonia Judaica in the Talmudic Period*. Wiesbaden: 1983.

"Relations between Jews and Gentiles in the Localities of Talmudic Babylonia." *Proceedings of the World Congress of Jewish Studies* (1985): 33–38.

"From Qurtava to Aspamia." In *Exile and Diaspora: Studies in the History of the Jewish People Presented to Professor Haim Beinart on the Occasion of His Seventieth Birthday*, edited by Aharon Mirsky, Avraham Grossman, and Yosef Kaplan, 57–63. Jerusalem: 1988.

Overlaet, Bruno. "Hidden in Plain Sight – The Hebrew Inscription on Ardashir I's Rock Relief at Naqsh-I Rustam." *Iranica Antiqua* 46 (2011): 331–340.

Page, Denys. *Sappho and Alcaeus: An Introduction to the Study of Ancient Lesbian Poetry*. Oxford: 1955.

Palmer, Andrew, trans. "Monk and Mason on the Tigris Frontier: The Early history of Ṭur ʿAbdin." The Qartmin Trilogy. Cambridge: 1990. Microfiche supplement.

Panaino, Antonio. "Astral Characters of Kingship in the Sasanian and Byzantine Worlds." In *Convegno internazionale: La Persia e Bisanzio (Roma, 14–18 Ottobre 2002)*, edited by Gherardo Gnoli and Antonio Panaino, 555–594. Rome: 2004.

"Sheep, Wheat, and Wine: An Achaemenian Antecedent of the Sasanian Sacrifices *pad ruwān*." *Bulletin of the Asia Institute* 19 (2005): 111–118.

"The King and the Gods in the Sasanian Royal Ideology." In *Sources pour l'histoire et la géographie du monde iranien*, Res Orientales XVIII, edited by R. Gyselen. (Leuven: 2009): 209–256.

"L'imperatore sasanide tra umano e divino." In *Divinizzazione, culto del sovrano e apoteosi tra Antichità e Medioevo*, edited by Tommaso Gnoli and Federicomaria Muccioli, 331–341. Bologna: 2014.

"Between Semantics and Pragmatics: Origins and Developments in the Meaning of *dastgerd*. A New Approach to the Problem." *Sasanian Studies* 1 (2022): 215–242.

Papaconstantinou, Arietta. "Confrontation, Interaction, and the Formation of the Early Islamic Oikoumene." *Revue des études byzantines* 63 (2005): 166–181.

Parisot, J. *Aphraatis Sapientis Persae Demonstrationes*. Patrologia Syriaca 1.1–2. Paris: 1894–1907.

Paterson, Lee. "Minority Religions in the Sasanian Empire: Suppression, Integration and Relations with Rome." In *Sasanian Persia: Between Rome and the Steppes of Eurasia*, edited by Eberhard W. Sauer, 181–198. Edinburgh, 2017.

Payne, Richard. "The Emergence of Martyrs' Shrines in Late Antique Iran: Conflict, Consensus, and Communal Institutions." In *An Age of Saints? Power, Conflict and Dissent in Early Medieval Christianity*, edited by Peter Sarris, Matthew Dal Santo, and Phil Booth, 89–113. Leiden: 2011.

"Avoiding Ethnicity: Uses of the Ancient Past in Late Sasanian Northern Mesopotamia." In *Visions of Community in the Post–Roman World: The West, Byzantium and the Islamic World, 300–1100*, edited by Walter Pohl, Clemens Gantner, and Richard E Payne, 205–221. Farnham: 2012.

"Cosmology and the Expansion of the Iranian Empire, 502–628 CE." *Past and Present* 220.1 (2013): 3–33.

"Review of *Commutatio et Contention*." *Journal of Late Antiquity* 6 (2013): 187–190.

"The Archaeology of Sasanian Politics." *Journal of Ancient History* 2 (2014): 80–92.

"The Reinvention of Iran: The Sasanian Empire and the Huns." In *The Cambridge Companion to the Age of Attila*, edited by Michael Maas, 282–299. Cambridge: 2014.

"East Syrian Bishops, Elite Households, and Iranian Law after the Muslim Conquest." *Iranian Studies* 48 (2015): 5–32.

State of Mixture: Christians, Zoroastrians, and Iranian Political Culture in Late Antiquity. Oakland, CA: 2015.

"Iranian Cosmopolitanism: World Religions at the Sasanian Court." In *Cosmopolitanism and Empire: University Rulers, Local Elites, and Cultural Integration in the Ancient Near East and Mediterranean*, edited by Myles Lavan, Richard Payne, and John Weisweiler, 209–230. Oxford: 2016.

"The Making of Turan: The Fall and Transformation of the Iranian East in Late Antiquity." *Journal of Late Antiquity* 9 (2016): 4–41.

"Les polémiques syro-orientales contre le Zoroastrisme et leur contexte politique." In *Les controverses religieuses en syriaque*, edited by Flavia Ruani, 1–22. Paris: 2017.

"Territorializing Iran in Late Antiquity: Autocracy, Aristocracy, and the Infrastructure of Empire." In *Ancient States and Infrastructural Power*, edited by Clifford Ando and Seth Richardson, 179–217. Philadelphia, PA: 2017.

"The Silk Road and the Iranian Political Economy in Late Antiquity: Iran, the Silk Road, and the Problem of Aristocratic Empire." *Bulletin of the School of Oriental and African Studies* 81 (2018): 227–250.

Paz, Yakir. "'Meishan Is Dead': On the Historical Contexts of the Bavli's Representations of the Jews in Southern Babylonia." In *Babylonian Aggada in Its Historical Context*, edited by Geoffrey Herman and Jeffrey Rubenstein, 47–102. Providence, RI: 2018.

"Elam Is Dying: The Babylonian Talmud and The Jews of Khuzestan in the Sasanian Period" [in Hebrew]. In *Meḥqerei Talmud IV*, edited by Shlomo Naeh and Yoav Rosenthal, 519–606. Jerusalem: 2024.

Pearce, Laurie E., and Cornelia Wunsch. *Documents of Judean Exiles and West Semites in Babylonia in the Collection of David Sofer*. Ithaca, NY: 2014.

Peeters, Paul. "Observations sur la vie syriaque de Mar Aba, Catholicos de l'eglise perse." In *Recherches d'histoire et de philologie orientales*, 117–163. Vol. 2. Brussels: 1951.

Pellat, Charles. *Le Livre de la Couronne*. Paris: 1954.

Perikhanian, Anahit. "Iranian Society and Law." In *The Cambridge History of Iran*, vol. 3, bk. 1: *The Seleucid, Parthian and Sasanian Periods*, edited by E. Yarsahter, 627–680. Cambridge: 1983.

Mādayān ī Hazār ī Dādestān: The Book of a Thousand Judgments, a Sasanian Law-Book. Costa Mesa, CA: 1997.

Phenix, Robert R., and Horn, Cornelia B., trans. *The Chronicle of Pseudo-Zachariah Rhetor: Church and War in Late Antiquity*. Liverpool: 2001.

Pigulevskaja, Nina Viktorovna. *Les villes de l'État iranien aux époques parthe et sassanide: contribution à l'histoire sociale de la basse Antiquité*. Paris: 1963.

Pinggéra, Karl. "Das Bild Narsais des Großen bei Barḥadbšabbā ʿArḇāyā. Zum theologischen Profil der 'Geschichte der heiligen Väter.'" In *Inkulturation des Christentums im Sasanidenreich*, edited by Arafa Mustafa, Jürgen Tubach, and Sophia Vashalomidze, 245–259. Wiesbaden: 2007.

Pomeranz, Jonathan. *Ordinary Jews in the Babylonian Talmud: Rabbinic Representations and Historical Interpretation*. PhD diss. Yale University, 2016.

"Concealing the Law: The Limits of Legal Promulgation among the Rabbis of Babylonia." In *Rethinking "Authority" in Late Antiquity: Authorship, Law, and Transmission in Jewish and Christian Tradition*, edited by A. J. Berkovitz and Mark Letteney, 123–135. London: 2018.

Potts, Daniel. "Foundation Houses, Fire Altars and the Frataraka: Interpreting the Iconography of some Post-Achaemenid Persian Coins." *Iranica Antiqua* 42 (2007): 271–300.

Pourshariati, Parvaneh. *Decline and Fall of the Sasanian Empire: The Sasanian-Parthian Confederacy and the Arab Conquest of Iran*. London: 2008.

"Further Engaging the Paradigm of Late Antiquity." *Journal of Persianate Studies* 6 (2013): 1–14.

"New Vistas on the History of Iranian Jewry in Late Antiquity, Part I: Patterns of Jewish Settlement in Iran." In *The Jews of Iran*, edited by Houman Sarshar, 1–32. London: 2014.

Price, R. M., trans. *History of the Monks of Syria by Theodoret, Bishop of Cyrrhus*. Kalamazoo, MI: 1985.

Lives of the Monks of Palestine: by Cyril of Scythopolis. Kalamazoo, MI: 1991.

Price, S. R. F. *Rituals and Power: The Roman Imperial Cult in Asia Minor*. Cambridge: 1984.

Rabello, Alfredo Mordechai. "Civil Jewish Jurisdiction in the Days of Emperor Justinian (527–565): Codex Justinianus 1.9.8." *Israel Law Review* 33 (1999): 51–66.

Rapp, Stephen H. *The Sasanian World through Georgian Eyes: Caucasia and the Iranian Commonwealth in Late Antique Georgian Literature*. Farnham: 2014.

Raveh, Inbar. *Me'at meharbeh: ma'ase hakhamim—mivnim sifruti'im utefisat olam*. Be'er Sheva: 2008.

Reinink, Gerrit J. "Babai the Great's Life of George and the Propagation of Doctrine in the Late Sasanian Empire." In *Portraits of Spiritual Authority: Religious Power in Early Christianity, Byzantium, and the Christian Orient*, edited by Jan Willem Drijvers and John W. Watt, 171–193. Leiden: 1999.

Reynolds, Susan. *Fiefs and Vassals: The Medieval Evidence Reinterpreted*. Oxford: 1994.

Rezakhani, Khodadad. "Mazdakism, Manichaeism and Zoroastrianism: In Search of Orthodoxy and Heterodoxy in Late Antique Iran." *Iranian Studies* 48 (2015): 55–70.

Rezania, Kianoosh. "'Religion' in Late Antique Zoroastrianism and Manichaeism: Developing a Term in Counterpoint." *Entangled Religions* 11 (2020): 1–32.

Rives, J. B. "The Decree of Decius and the Religion of Empire." *Journal of Roman Studies* 89 (1999): 135–154.

Ronis, Sara. *Demons in the Details: Demonic Discourse and Rabbinic Culture in Late Antique Babylonia*. Berkeley, CA: 2022.

Rose, Jenny. "Three Queens, Two Wives, and a Goddess: Roles and Images of Women in Sasanian Iran." In *Women in the Medieval Islamic World: Power, Patronage, and Piety*, edited by Gavin R. G. Hambly, 29–54. New York: 1998.

"Festivals and the Calendar." In *The Wiley-Blackwell Companion to Zoroastrianism*, edited by Michael Stausberg and Yuhan Sohrab-Dinshaw Vevaina, 379–392. Chichester, England: 2015.

Rosenthal, David. "*Mishnah Avodah Zara: A Critical Edition (with Introduction)*" [in Hebrew]. 2 vols. PhD diss. Hebrew University of Jerusalem, 1980.

Rosenthal, E. S. "For the Talmudic Dictionary – Talmudica Iranica" [in Hebrew]. *Irano-Judaica* I, edited by Shaul Shaked, 38–134. Jerusalem: 1982.

Rosen-Zvi, Ishay. "The Polemic on the Requirements to Destroy Avodah Zarah in Tannaitic Literature" [in Hebrew]. *Reishit* 1 (2009): 91–115.

The Mishnaic Sotah Ritual: Temple, Gender, and Midrash. Leiden: 2012.

"Is the Mishnah a Roman Composition?" In *The Faces of Torah. Studies in the Texts and Contexts of Ancient Judaism in Honor of Steven Fraade*, edited by Christian Hayes, Tzvi Novick and Michal Bar-Asher Segal, 487–508. Journal of Ancient Judaism Supplements 22. Göttingen: 2017.

Rubin, Zeev. "The Reforms of Khusro Anushirwān." In *States, Resources and Armies*, edited by Averil Cameron, 225–297. Vol. 3 of *The Byzantine and Early Islamic Near East*. Princeton, NJ: 1995.

"The Sasanid Monarchy." In *Late Antiquity: Empire and Successors, AD 425–600*, edited by Averil Cameron, John Bryan Ward-Perkins, and Michael Whitby, 638–661. Vol. 14 of *The Cambridge Ancient History*, 2nd edition. Cambridge: 2000.

"Nobility, Monarchy and Legitimation under the Later Sasanians." In *The Byzantine and Early Islamic Near East, vol. 6: Elites Old and New in the Byzantine and Early Islamic Near East*, edited by John F. Haldon and Lawrence I. Conrad, 235–273. Princeton, NJ: 2004.

"Persia and the Sasanian Monarchy (224–651)." In *The Cambridge History of the Byzantine Empire c. 500–1492*, edited by Jonathan Shepard, 130–155. Cambridge: 2008.

Rubenstein, Jeffrey L. *Talmudic Stories: Narrative Art, Composition, and Culture*. Baltimore, MD: 1999.

"The Rise of the Babylonian Rabbinic Academy: A Reexamination of the Talmudic Evidence." *Jewish Studies Internet Journal* 1 (2002): 55–68.

The Culture of the Babylonian Talmud. Baltimore, MD: 2003.

"Criteria of Stammaitic Intervention in Aggada." In *Creation and Composition: The Contribution of the Bavli Redactors (Stammaim) to the Aggada*, edited by Jeffrey L. Rubenstein, 417–440. Tübingen: 2005.

"King Herod in Ardashir's Court: The Rabbinic Story of Herod (B. Bava Batra 3b–4a) in Light of Persian Sources." *Association for Jewish Studies Review* 38 (2014): 249–274.

"A Rabbinic Translation of Relics." In *Crossing Boundaries in Ancient Judaism and Early Christianity: Ambiguities, Complexities and Half-Forgotten Adversaries*, edited by Kimberly Stratton and Andrea Lieber, 314–332. Leiden: 2016.

"Martyrdom in the Persian Martyr Acts and in the Babylonian Talmud." In *The Aggada of the Bavli and Its Cultural World*, edited by Jeffrey Rubenstein and Geoffrey Herman, 175–210. Providence, RI: 2018.

Rubenstein, Jeffrey, and Herman, Geoffrey. "Introduction." In *The Aggada of the Bavli and Its Cultural World*, edited by Jeffrey Rubenstein and Geoffrey Herman, xi–xxxv. Providence, RI: 2018.

Russell, James. *Zoroastrianism in Armenia*. Cambridge: 1987.

"Kartīr and Mānī: A Shamanistic Model of Their Conflict." *Acta Iranica* 30 (1990): 180–193.

"On Mysticism and Esotericism among the Zoroastrians." *Iranian Studies* 26 (1993): 73–94.

Rustow, Marina. *Heresy and the Politics of Community: The Jews of the Fatimid Caliphate*. Ithaca, NY: 2008.

"Jews and the Islamic World: Transitions from Rabbinic to Medieval Contexts." In *The Bloomsbury Companion to Jewish Studies*, edited by Dean Phillip Bell, 90–120. London: 2013.

Sachau, Eduard. *Syrische Rechtsbücher*. Vols. 1–3. Berlin: 1907–1914.

Saint-Laurent, Jeanne-Nicole. "Bones in Bags: Relics in Syriac Hagiography." In *Syriac Encounters: Papers from the Sixth North American Syriac Symposium, Duke University, 26–29 June 2011*, edited by Maria E. Doerfler, Emanuel Fiano and Kyle Smith, 439–454. Eastern Christian Studies 20. Leuven: 2015.

Missionary Stories and the Formation of the Syriac Churches. California: 2015.

Sako, Louis. *Le rôle de la hiérarchie syriaque orientale dans les rapports diplomatiques entre la Perse et Byzance aux Ve–VIIe siècles*. Paris: 1986.

Sanger, Patrick. "The Administration of Sasanian Egypt: New Masters and Byzantine Community." *Greek, Roman, and Byzantine Studies* 51 (2011): 653–665.

Satlow, Michael. "A Historical Source? B. Baba Batra 7b–8a." *Journal for the Study of Judaism* 28 (1997): 314–320.

"Beyond Influence: Toward a New Historiographic Paradigm." In *Jewish Literatures and Cultures: Context and Intertext*, edited by Yaron Eliav and Anita Norwich, 37–53. Providence, RI: 2008.

Sauer, Eberhard W., Hamid Omrani Rekavandi, Tony James Wilkinson, and Jebrael Nokandeh. *Persia's Imperial Power in Late Antiquity. The Great Wall of Gorgan and Frontier Landscapes of Sasanian Iran*. Oxford: 2013.

Savant, Sarah Bowen. *The New Muslims of Post-Conquest Iran: Tradition, Memory, and Conversion*. Cambridge: 2013.

Schäfer, Peter. *Judeophobia: Attitudes toward the Jews in the Ancient World*. Cambridge: 1997.

Jesus in the Talmud. Princeton, NJ: 2007.

Schechter, Solomon. "Seder Olam Suta." *Monatsschrift für Geschichte und Wissenschaft des Judentums* 39 (1895): 23–28.

Scher, Addai, ed. *Histoire nestorienne inédite (Chronique de Séert)*. 2 vols. Paris: 1907–1919.

Schiffman, Lawrence. "The Conversion of the Royal House of Adiabene in Josephus and Rabbinic Sources." In *Josephus, Judaism, and Christianity*, edited by Louis Feldman and Gohei Hata, 293–312. Detroit, MI: 1987.

Schilling, Alexander Markus. *Die Anbetung der Magier und die Taufe der Sāsāniden: Zur Geistesgeschichte des iranischen Christentums in der Spätantike*. Louvain: 2008.

Schindel, Nikolaus. "The 3rd Century 'Marw Shah' Bronze Coins Reconsidered." In *Commutatio et Contentio. Studies in the Late Roman, Sasanian and Early Islamic Middle East*, edited by Henning Börm and Josef Wiesehöfer, 23–36. Düsseldorf: 2010.

Schippmann, Klaus. *Die iranischen Feuerheiligtümer*. Berlin: 1971.

Grundzüge der Geschichte des sasanidischen Reiches. Darmstadt: 1990.

Schorr, Joshua Heschel. "The Circumstances of the Jews in Persia." *HeHalutz* 7 (1865): 74–79.

Schremer, Adiel. "Stammaitic Historiography." In *Creation and Composition: The Contribution of the Bavli Redactors (Stammaim) to the Aggada*, edited by Jeffrey L. Rubenstein, 219–235. Tübingen: 2005.

Schudson, Michael. *Watergate in American Memory: How We Remember, Forget, and Reconstruct the Past*. New York: 1992.

Schwartz, Daniel. "Martyrdom, the Middle Way, and Mediocrity (*Genesis Rabbah* 82:8)." In *Follow the Wise: Studies in Jewish History and Culture in Honor of Lee I. Levine*, edited by Zeev Weiss, Oded Irshai, and Jodi Magness, 343–353. Winona Lake, IN: 2010.

Schwartz, Seth. "Language, Power and Identity in Ancient Palestine." *Past and Present* 148 (1995): 3–47.

"D. Goodblatt, *The Monarchic Principle*." *Journal of Jewish Studies* 47 (1996): 167–169.

"Gamaliel in Aphrodite's Bath: Palestinian Judaism and Urban Culture in the Third and Fourth Centuries." In *The Talmud Yerushalmi and Graeco-Roman Culture*, edited by Peter Schäfer, 203–217. Vol. 1. Tübingen: 1998.

Imperialism and Jewish Society: 200 BCE to 640 CE. Princeton, NJ: 2001.

"Rabbinization in the Sixth Century." In *The Talmud Yerushalmi and Greco-Roman Culture*, edited by Peter Schäfer, 55–69. Vol. 3. Tübingen: 2002.

"Big Men or Chiefs: Against an Institutional History of the Palestinian Patriarchate." In *Jewish Religious Leadership: Image and Reality*, edited by Jack Wertheimer, 155–173. Vol. 1. New York: 2004.

"The Political Geography of Rabbinic Texts." In *The Cambridge Companion to the Talmud and Rabbinic Literature*, edited by Charlotte Fonrobert and Martin Jaffee, 75–96. Cambridge: 2007.

"How Many Judaisms Were There? A Critique of Neusner and Smith on Definition and Mason and Boyarin on Categorization." *Journal of Ancient Judaism* 2 (2011): 208–238.

"Was There a 'Common Judaism' after the Destruction?" In *Envisioning Judaism: Studies in Honor of Peter Schäfer on the Occasion of His Seventieth Birthday*, edited by Ra'anan S. Boustan, Klaus Herrmann, Reimund Leicht, Annette Y. Reed and Giuseppe Veltri, with the collaboration of Alex Ramos, 3–22. Tübingen: 2013.

Scott, James C. *Domination and the Arts of Resistance: Hidden Transcripts*. New Haven, CT: 1990.

Secunda, Shai. "Studying with a Magus/Like Giving a Tongue to a Wolf." *Bulletin of the Asia Institute* 19 (2005): 151–157.

"Talmudic Text and Iranian Context: On the Development of Two Talmudic Narratives." *Association for Jewish Studies Review* 33 (2009): 45–69.

The Iranian Talmud: Reading the Bavli in Its Sasanian Context. Philadelphia, PA: 2013.

"The Fractious Eye: On the Evil Eye of Menstruants in Zoroastrian Tradition." *Numen* 61 (2014): 83–108.

"'Lost Property to the King!': The Talmudic Laws of Lost Property in the Shadow of Sasanian Bureaucracy." *Bulletin of the Asia Institute* 28 (2014): 45–55.

"'This, but Also That': Historical, Methodological, and Theoretical Reflections on Irano-Talmudica." *Jewish Quarterly Review* 106 (2016): 233–241.

"Gaze and Counter-Gaze: Textuality and Contextuality in the Anecdote of R. Assi and the Roman (b. B.M. 28b)." In *The Aggada of the Babylonian Talmud and Its Cultural World*, edited by Geoffrey Herman and Jeffrey Rubenstein, 149–171. Providence: 2018.

The Talmud's Red Fence: Menstrual Impurity and Religious Difference in Babylonian Judaism and Its Sasanian Context. Oxford: 2020.

"Babylonian Judaism and Zoroastrianism." In *The Routledge Companion to Jews in Late Antiquity*, edited by Catherine Hezser, 435–446. Abington, Oxon: 2024.

Segal, Eliezer. *Case Citation in the Babylonian Talmud: The Evidence of Tractate Neziqin*. Atlanta, GA: 1990.

Selb, Walter, and Hubert Kaufhold. *Das syrisch-römische Rechtsbuch*. 3 vols. Vienna: 2002.

Shafir, Nir. "Vernacular Legalism in the Ottoman Empire: Confession, Law, and Popular Politics in the Debate over the "Religion of Abraham (millet-i Ibrāhīm)." *Islamic Law and Society* 28 (2020): 32–75.

Shahbazi, A. Shapur. "Bahrām VI Čōbīn." in *Ātaš–Bayhaqī, Ẓahīr-al-Dīn*, edited by Ehsan Yarshater, 519–522. Vol. 3 of *Encyclopædia Iranica*. London: 1989.

"Coronation." In *Coffeehouse–Dārā*, edited by Ehsan Yarshater, 277–279. Vol. 6 of *Encyclopaedia Iranica*. London: 1993.
"The History of the Idea of Iran." In *The Idea of Iran*, vol. 1: *The Birth of the Persian Empire*, edited by Vesta Sarkhosh Curtis and Sarah Stewart, 100–111. London: 2005.
Shaked, Shaul. "Esoteric Trends in Zoroastrianism." *Proceedings of the Israel Academy of Sciences and Humanities* 3 (1969): 175–221.
"Some Legal and Administrative Terms of the Sasanian Period." In *Monumentum H. S. Nyberg*, 213–225. Vol. 2. Leiden: 1975.
"Jewish and Christian Seals of the Sasanian Period." In *Studies in Memory of G. Wiet*, edited by Myriam Rosen Ayalon, 17–31. Jerusalem: 1977.
The Wisdom of the Sasanian Sages (Denkard VI). Boulder, CO: 1979.
"Epigraphica Judaeo-Iranica." In *Studies in Judaism and Islam Presented to S. D. Goitein*, edited by Shelomo Morag, Issachar Ben-Ami, and Norman A. Stillman, 65–82. Jerusalem: 1981.
"From Iran to Islam: Notes on Some Themes in Transmission." *Jerusalem Studies in Arabic and Islam* 4 (1984): 31–40.
"Bagdana, King of the Demons, and Other Iranian Terms in Babylonian Aramaic Magic." *Acta Iranica* 25 (1985): 511–525.
"From Iran to Islam: On Some Symbols of Royalty." *Jerusalem Studies in Arabic and Islam* 7 (1986): 75–91.
"Administrative Functions of Priests in the Sasanian Period." In *Proceedings of the First European Conference of Iranian Studies: Part I, Old and Middle Iranian Studies*, edited by Gherardo Gnoli and Antonio Panaino, 261–273. Rome: 1990.
"Zoroastrian Polemics against Jews in the Sasanian and Early Islamic Period." *Irano-Judaica II*, edited by Shaul Shaked and Amnon Netzer, 85–104. Jerusalem: 1990.
"Notes on the Pahlavi Amulet and Sasanian Courts of Law." *Bulletin of the Asia Institute* 7 (1993): 165–172.
Dualism in Transformation: Varieties of Religion in Sasanian Iran. London: 1994.
"Jewish Sasanian Sigillography." In *Au carrefour des Religions: mélanges offerts à Philippe Gignoux*, edited by Rika Gyselen, 239–256. Bures-sur-Yvette: 1995.
"Popular Religion in Sasanian Babylonia." *Jerusalem Studies in Arabic and Islam* 21 (1997): 101–117.
"Jesus in the Magic Bowls. Apropos Dan Levene's '... and by the name of Jesus ...,'" *Jewish Studies Quarterly* 6 (1999): 309–319.
"Jews, Christians and Pagans in the Aramaic Incantation Bowls of the Sasanian Period." In *Religions and Cultures: First International Conference of Mediterraneum*, edited by A. Destro and M. Pesce, 61–89. Binghamton, NY: 2001.
"Between Iranian and Aramaic: Iranian Words Concerning Food in Jewish Babylonian Aramaic, with Some Notes on the Aramaic Heterograms in Iranian." *Irano-Judaica V*, edited by Shaul Shaked and Amnon Netzer, 120–137. Jerusalem: 2003.

"Religion in the Late Sasanian Period: Eran, Aneran, and Other Religious Designations." In *The Idea of Iran*, vol. 3: *The Sasanian Era*, edited by Vesta Sarkhosh Curtis and Sarah Stewart, 103–117. London: 2008.

"'No Talking during a Meal!': Zoroastrian Themes in the Babylonian Talmud." In *The Talmud in Its Iranian Context*, edited by Carol Bakhos and M. Rahim Shayegan, 208–34. Tübingen: 2010.

Shaked, Shaul, J. N. Ford, and Siam Bhayro. *Aramaic Bowl Spells: Jewish Babylonian Aramaic Bowls. Vol. 1 of Magical and Religious Literature of Late Antiquity*. Leiden: 2013.

Shaki, Mansour. "The Cosmogonical and Cosmological Teachings of Mazdak." *Acta Iranica* 24 (1985): 527–543.

"Fillet of Nobility," *Bulletin of the Asia Institute* 4 (1990): 277–279.

Shapira, Dan D. Y. "Manichaeans (Marmanaiia), Zoroastrians (Iazuqaiia), Jews, Christians and Other Heretics: A Study in the Redaction of Mandaic Texts." *Le Muséon* 117 (2004): 243–280.

"Pahlavi Fire, Bundahishn 18." *ARAM Periodical* 26 (2014): 129–151.

Shaw, Brent. *Sacred Violence: African Christians and Sectarian Hatred in the Age of Augustine*. Cambridge: 2011.

"The Myth of the Neronian Persecution." *Journal of Roman Studies* 105 (2015): 73–100.

Shayegan, M. Rahim. *Arsacids and Sasanians: Political Ideology in Post-Hellenistic and Late Antique Persia*. Cambridge: 2011.

Shenkar, Michael. *Intangible Spirits and Graven Images: The Iconography of Deities in the Pre-Islamic Iranian World*. Leiden: 2014.

"Yosef bar El'asa Artaka and the Elusive Jewish Diaspora of Pre-Islamic Iran and Central Asia." *Journal of Jewish Studies* 65 (2014): 58–76.

"Rethinking Sasanian Iconoclasm." *Journal of the American Oriental Society* 135 (2015): 471–498.

"The Coronation of the Early Sasanians, Ctesiphon, and the Great Diadem of Paikuli." *Journal of Persianate Studies* 11 (2018): 113–139.

Shepardson, Christine. *Anti-Judaism and Christian Orthodoxy: Ephrem's Hymns in Fourth-Century Syria*. Washington, DC: 2008.

Sherwin-White, Susan, and Amelie Kehrt. *From Samarkhand to Sardis: A New Approach to the Seleucid Empire*. London: 1993.

Shilo, Shmuel. *Dina De-Malkhuta Dina*. Jerusalem: 1974.

Simonsohn, Uriel. "Seeking Justice among the 'Outsiders': Christian Recourse to Non-Ecclesiastical Judicial Systems under Early Islam." *Church History and Religious Culture* 89 (2009): 191–216.

A Common Justice: The Legal Allegiances of Christians and Jews under Early Islam. Philadelphia, PA: 2011.

Simpson, St. John. "Merv, an Archaeological Case-Study from the Northeastern Frontier of the Sasanian Empire." *Journal of Ancient History* 2 (2014): 1–28.

"The Land behind Ctesiphon: The Archaeology of Babylonia during the Period of the Babylonian Talmud." In *The Archaeology and Material Culture of the Babylonian Talmud*, edited by Markham Geller, 6–38. Leiden: 2015.

Simpson, St. John, and Theya Molleson. "Old Bones Overturned: New Evidence of Funerary Practices from the Sasanian Empire." In *Regarding the Dead:*

Human Remains in the British Museum, edited by Alexandra Fletcher, Daniel Antoine, and J. D. Hill, 77–90. London: 2014.
Sims-Williams, Nicholas. *The Christian Sogdian Manuscript C2*. Berlin: 1985.
Sinisi, Fabrizio, Alison Betts, and Ghairatdin Khozhaniyazov. "Royal Fires in the Ancient Iranian World: The Evidence from Akchakhan-kala, Chorasmia." *Parthica* 20 (2018): 9–30.
Sivertsev, Alexei. *Judaism and Imperial Ideology in Late Antiquity*. Cambridge: 2011.
Sizgorich, Thomas. *Violence and Belief in Late Antiquity: Militant Devotion in Christianity and Islam*. Philadelphia, PA: 2014.
Skjærvø, Prods Oktor. "OL' News: ODs and Ends." In *Exegisti Monumenta: Festschrift in Honour of Nicholas Sims-Williams*, edited by Werner Sundermann, Almut Hintze, and François de Blois, 484–491. Wiesbaden: 2009.
"Kartīr." In *Joči-Kāšġari, Sa'd-al-Din*, edited by Ehsan Yarshater, 607–628. Volume 15 of *Encyclopædia Iranica*. London: 2011.
"The Zoroastrian Oral Tradition as Reflected in the Texts." In *The Transmission of the Avesta*, edited by Alberto Cantera, 3–48. Wiesbaden: 2012.
Skolmowski, Wojciech. "On Middle Iranian *dstkrt(y)*." In *Medioiranica: Proceedings of the International Colloquium Organized by the Katholieke Universiteit Leuven*, edited by Wojciech Skalmowski and Alois Van Tongerloo, 157–162. Leuven: 1993.
Smith, Kyle. "Constantine and Judah the Maccabee: History and Memory in the Acts of the Persian Martyrs." *Journal of the Canadian Society for Syriac Studies* 12 (2012): 16–33.
The Martyrdom and the History of Blessed Simon Bar Ṣabba'e. Piscataway, NJ: 2014.
Constantine and the Captive Christians of Persia: Martyrdom and Religious Identity in Late Antiquity. Oakland, CA: 2016.
Cult of the Dead: A Brief History of Christianity. Berkeley, CA: 2022.
Smith, R. Payne. *The Third Part of the Ecclesiastical History of John Bishop of Ephesus*. Oxford: 1860.
Sokoloff, Michael. *A Dictionary of Jewish Babylonian Aramaic of the Talmudic and Geonic Periods*. Baltimore, MD: 2002.
Syriac Lexicon: A Translation from the Latin, Correction, Expansion, and Update of C. Brockelmann's Lexicon Syriacum. Winona Lake, IN: 2009.
Solodukho Y. A., and Neusner, Jacob. *Soviet Views of Talmud Judaism: Five Papers by Yu. A. Solodukho in English Translation*. Leiden: 1973.
Sperber, Daniel. "On the Office of the Agoranomos in Roman Palestine." *Zeitschrift der Deutschen Morgenländischen Gesellschaft* 127 (1977): 227–243.
"The Unfortunate Adventures of Rav Kahana: A Passage of Saboraic Polemic from Sasanian Persia." *Irano-Judaica I*, edited by Shaul Shaked, 83–100. Jerusalem: 1982.
Spicehandler, Ezra. "*Be Dawar and Dine DeMegista*: Notes on Gentile Courts in Talmudic Babylonia." *Hebrew Union College Annual* 26 (1955): 333–354.

Spier, Jeffrey. "Late Antique and Early Christian Gems: Some Unpublished Examples." In *Gems of Heaven: Recent Research on Engraved Gemstones in Late Antiquity, c. AD 200-600*, edited by Chris Entwistle and Noël Adams, 193–207. London: 2012.

Spivak, Gayatri. "Can the Subaltern Speak?" In *Marxism and the Interpretation of Culture*, edited by Cary Nelson and Lawrence Grossberg, 271–313. Urbana, IL: 1988.

Stampfer, Y. Zvi. "Jews in Baghdad during the Abbasid Period." In *Baghdād: From Its Beginnings to the 14th Century*, edited by Jens Scheiner and Isabel Toral, 731–764. Leiden: 2022.

Stern, Menahem. *Greek and Latin Authors on Jews and Judaism*. Vol. 1. Jerusalem: 1974.

Stern, Sacha. "Figurative Art and Halakha in the Mishnaic-Talmudic Period" [in Hebrew]. *Zion* 61 (1996): 397–399.

"Pagan Images in Late Antique Palestinian Synagogues." In *Ethnicity and Culture in Late Antiquity*, edited by Stephen Mitchell and Geoffrey Greatrex, 241–252. London: 2000.

"Rabbi and the Origins of the Patriarchate." *Journal of Jewish Studies* 54 (2003): 193–215.

"Rabbinic Academies in Late Antiquity: State of Current Research." In *L'enseignement supérieur dans les mondes antiques et médiévaux. Aspects institutionnels, juridiques et pédagogiques*, edited by Henri Hugonnard-Roche, 221–238. Paris: 2008.

Stronach, David. "The Kūh-i Shahrak Fire Altar." *Journal of Near Eastern Studies* 25 (1966): 217–227.

Strootman, Rolf. *Courts and Elites in the Hellenistic Empires: The Near East after the Achaemenids c. 330–30 BCE*. Edinburgh: 2014.

Tafazzoli, Ahmad. "The King's Seat in the Fire Temple." In *A Green Leaf: Papers in Honour of Professor Jes P. Asmussen*, edited by Jes Peter Asmussen et al., 101–106. Acta Iranica 28. Leiden: 1988.

Sasanian Society: Warriors, Scribes, Dehqans. New York: 2000.

Tannous, Jack. *The Making of the Medieval Middle East: Religion, Society, and Simple Believers*. Princeton, NJ: 2018.

Taqizadeh, S.H. "The Iranian Festivals Adopted by the Christians and Condemned by the Jews." *Bulletin of the School of Oriental Studies* 10 (1940–1941): 632–639.

Tardieu, Michel. *Manichaeism*. Chicago, IL: 2008.

Taylor, Miriam. *Anti-Judaism and Early Christian Identity: A Critique of the Scholarly Consensus*. Leiden: 1995.

Telegdi, Zsigmond. "Essai sur la phonétique des emprunts iraniens en araméen talmudique." *Journal Asiatique* 226 (1935): 177–256.

Thelen, David. "Memory and American History." *The Journal of American History* 75 (1989): 1117–1129.

Thomson, Robert, trans. *History of the Armenians by Agathangelos: Translation and Commentary*. Albany, NY: 1976.

trans. *Moses Khorenatsi: History of the Armenians*. Cambridge: 1978.

trans. *History of Vardan and the Armenian War by Elishē*. Cambridge: 1982.

trans. *The Armenian History attributed to Sebeos*. Liverpool: 1999.
Thrope, Samuel. "Contradictions and Vile Utterances: The Zoroastrian Critique of Judaism in the Škand Gumānīg Wizār." PhD diss. University of California, Berkeley, 2012.
Tillier, Mathieu. *L'invention du cadi: La justice des musulmans, des juifs et des chrétiens aux premiers siècles de l'Islam*. Paris, 2017.
Topchyan, Aram. "Jews in Ancient Armenia (1st Century BC – 5th Century AD)." *Le Muséon* 120 (2007): 435–476.
Toral–Niehoff, Isabel. "Late Antique Iran and the Arabs: The Case of Al-Hira." *Journal of Persianate Studies* 6 (2013): 115–126.
Toumanoff, Cyril. *Studies in Christian Caucasian History*. Washington, DC: 1963.
Traina, G., and C. A. Ciancaglini. "La Fortresse de l'Oubli." *La Muséon* 115 (2002): 399–422.
Trombley, Frank, and J. W. Watt. *The Chronicle of Pseudo-Joshua the Stylite*. Liverpool: 2000.
Tropper, Amram. *Rewriting Ancient Jewish History: The History of the Jews in Roman Times and the New Historical Method*. 2016.
Tykocinski, Chaim. "Bustanai rosh ha-gola" [in Hebrew]. *Devir* 1 (1923): 145–179.
Tzuberi, Christiane. "Rescue from Transgression through Death; Rescue from Death through Transgression." In *Rabbinic Traditions between Palestine and Babylonia*, edited by Ronit Nikolsky and Tal Ilan, 133–146. Leiden: 2014.
Urbach, E. E. "The Rabbinical Laws of Idolatry in the Second and Third Centuries in the Light of Archaeological and Historical Facts." *Israel Exploration Journal* 9 (1959): 229–245.
"Concerning Historical Insight into the Account of Rabbah Bar Naḥmani's Death" [in Hebrew]. *Tarbiẓ* 34 (1965): 156–161.
Vahman, Fereydun. *Ardā Wirāz Nāmag: The Iranian "Divina Commedia."* London: 1986.
van Bladel, Kevin. *From Sasanian Mandaeans to Ṣābians of the Marshes*. Leiden: 2017.
van Rompay, Lucas. "Impetuous Martyrs? The Situation of the Persian Christians in the Last Years of Yazdgard I (419–420)." In *Martyrium in Multidisciplinary Perspective: Memorial Louis Reekmans*, edited by Mathijs Lamberigts and Peter van Deun, 363–375. Leuven: 1995.
Verkinderen, Peter. *Waterways of Iraq and Iran in the Early Islamic Period: Changing Rivers and Landscapes of the Mesopotamian Plain*. London/New York: 2015.
Vevaina, Yuhan Sohrab-Dinshaw. "'Enumerating the Dēn': Textual Taxonomies, Cosmological Deixis, and Numerological Speculations in Zoroastrianism." *History of Religions* 50 (2010): 111–143.
"The Hermeneutics of Political Violence in Sasanian Iran: The Death of Mani and the Seizure of Manichaean Property." *Sasanian Studies* 1 (2022): 291–322.
Vidas, Moulie. "The Bavli's Discussion of Genealogy in *Qiddushin* IV." In *Antiquity in Antiquity: Jewish and Christian Pasts in the Greco-Roman World*, edited by Gregg Gardner and Kevin Osterloh, 285–326. Tübingen: 2008.

Tradition and the Formation of the Talmud. Princeton, NJ: 2014.
Vitalone, Mario. *The Persian Rivayat "Ithoter": Zoroastrian Rituals in the Eighteenth Century*. Napoli: 1996.
Vloten, G. van. *Le Livre des beautés et des antithèses, attribuè á Abou Othman Amr ibn Bahr Al-Djahiz de Basra*. Leiden: 1898.
Vööbus, Arthur. *Syriac and Arabic Documents Regarding Legislation Relative to Syrian Asceticism*. Stockholm: 1960.
The Statutes of the School of Nisibis. Stockholm: 1961.
The Syro-Roman Lawbook: The Syriac Text of the Recently Discovered Manuscripts Accompanied by a Facsimile Edition and Furnished with an Introduction and Translation. Stockholm: 1982.
Wagner, K. A. "Resistance, Rebellion, and the Subaltern." In *The Oxford World History of Empire, vol. 1: The Imperial Experience*, ed. Peter F. Bang, C. A. Bayly, and Walter Scheidel, 416–436. Vol. 1 of *The Oxford World History of Empire*. New York: 2021.
Walker, Joel Thomas. "The Limits of Late Antiquity: Philosophy between Rome and Iran." *Ancient World* 33 (2002): 45–69.
The Legend of Mar Qardagh: Narrative and Christian Heroism in Late Antique Iraq. Berkeley, CA: 2006.
"The Legacy of Mesopotamia in Late Antique Iraq: The Christian Martyr Shrine at Melqi (Neo-Assyrian Milqia)." *ARAM Periodical* 18–19 (2006–2007): 483–508.
"From Nisibis to Xi'an: The Church of the East in Late Antique Eurasia." In *The Oxford Handbook of Late Antiquity*, edited by Scott. F. Johnson, 994–1052. Oxford: 2012.
Walters, James. "Reconsidering the Compositional Unity of Aphrahat's Demonstrations." In *Syriac Christian Culture: Beginnings to Renaissance*, edited by Aaron Michael Butts and Robin Darling Young, 50–64. Washington, DC: 2020.
Wansbrough, John. *Quranic Studies: Sources and Methods of Scriptural Interpretation* Oxford: 1977.
The Sectarian Milieu: Content and Composition of Islamic Salvation History. Oxford: 1978.
Wasserman, Mira Beth. *Jews, Gentiles, and Other Animals: The Talmud after the Humanities*. Philadelphia, PA: 2017.
Weber, Dieter. "Eine spätsassanidische Rechtsurkunde aus Ägypten." *Tyche* 17 (2002): 185–192.
"Villages and Estates in the Documents from the Pahlavi Archive: The Geographical Background." *Bulletin of the Asia Institute* 24 (2010): 37–65.
Weiss, Isaac, ed. *Sifra de-bei rav*. 1st edition. Vienna: 1862.
Weiss, Zeev. "Sculptures and Sculptural Images in the Urban Galilean Context." In *The Sculptural Environment of the Roman Near-East: Reflection on Culture, Ideology, and Power*, edited by Y. Z. Eliav, Elise A. Friedland, and Sharon Herbert, 559–574. Leuven: 2008.
Weitz, Lev. *Between Christ and Caliph: Law, Marriage, and Christian Community in Early Islam*. Philadelphia, PA: 2018.
West, E. W. *The Book of Mainyo-i-khard*. Stuttgart: 1871.

Sacred Books of the East: Pahlavi Texts, Part IV. Oxford: 1892.

Wewers, Gerd A. "Israel zwischen den Mächten: Die rabbinischen Traditionen über König Schabhor." *Kairos* 22 (1980): 77–100.

Whitby, Michael. *The Ecclesiastical History of Evagrius Scholasticus*. Liverpool: 2000.

Whitby, Michael, and Mary Whitby. *The History of Theophylact Simocatta*. New York: 1986.

Widengren, Geo. "Recherches sur le feodalisme iranien." *Orientalia Suecana* 5 (1956): 79–182.

"The Status of the Jews in the Sassanian Empire." *Iranica Antiqua* 1 (1961): 117–162.

Der Feudalismus im alten Iran: Männerbund, Gefolgswesen, Feudalismus in der iranischen Gesellschaft im Hinblick auf die indogermanischen Verhältnisse. Köln: 1969.

Wiesehöfer, Josef. *Ancient Persia: From 550 BC to 650 AD*. London: 1996.

"Ērān ud Anērān: Sasanian Patterns of Worldview," in *Persianism in Antiquity*, edited by Rolf Strootman and Miguel John Versluys, 381–392. Stuttgart: 2017.

Wiesehöfer, Josef, and Philip Huyse, eds. *Ērān und Anērān. Studien zu den Beziehungen zwischem dem Sassanidenreich und des Mittelmeerwelt*. Oriens et Occidens 13. Stuttgart: 2006.

Wiessner, Gernot. *Untersuchungen zur syrischen Literaturegeschichte I: Zur Märtyrerüberlieferung aus der Christenverfolgung Schapurs II*. Göttingen: 1967.

Williams, A. V. "Zoroastrians and Christians in Sasanian Iran." *Bulletin of the John Rylands University Library of Manchester* 78 (1996): 37–53.

Wimpfheimer, Barry S. *Narrating the Law: A Poetics of Talmudic Legal Stories*. Philadelphia, PA: 2011.

Wood, Philip. "Collaborators and Dissidents: Christians in Sasanian Iraq in the Early Fifth Century CE." In *Late Antiquity: Eastern Perspectives*, edited by Teresa Bernheimer and Adam Silverstein, 57–70. Oxford: 2012.

Chronicle of Seert: Christian Historical Imagination in Late Antique Iraq. Oxford: 2013.

"The Christian Reception of the Xwadāy-Nāmag: Hormizd IV, Khusrau II and Their Successors." *Journal of the Royal Asiatic Society* 26 (2016): 407–422.

The Imam of the Christians: The World of Dionsyius of Tel-Mahre, c. 750–850. Princeton, NJ: 2021.

Woolf, Greg. *Tales of the Barbarians: Ethnography and Empire in the Roman West. Blackwell Bristol Lectures on Greece, Rome and the Classical Tradition*. Chichester, MA: 2011.

Wright, Wilmer Cave, ed. and trans. *Philostratus and Eunapius*. Loeb Classical Library 134. Cambridge: 1952.

Yadin, Azzan. "Rabban Gamaliel, Aphrodite's Bath, and the Question of Pagan Monotheism." *Jewish Quarterly Review* 96 (2006): 149–179.

Yamamoto, Yumiko. "The Zoroastrian Temple Cult of Fire in Archaeology and Literature I." *Orient* 15 (1979): 19–53.

"The Zoroastrian Temple Cult of Fire in Archaeology and Literature II," *Orient* 17 (1981): 189–214.

Yarshater, Ehsan. "Iranian National History." In *The Cambridge History of Iran*, vol. 3, bk. 1: *The Seleucid, Parthian and Sasanian Periods*, edited by Ehsan Yarshater, 359–478. Cambridge: 1983.

Zaehner, Robert C. *Dawn and Twilight of Zoroastrianism*. London: 1961.

Zakeri, Mohsen. *Sāsānid Soldiers in early Muslim Society*. Wiesbaden: 1995.

Zellentin, Holger. *Rabbinic Parodies of Jewish and Christian Literature*. Tübingen: 2011.

Zerubavel, Eviatar. *Social Mindscapes: An invitation to Cognitive Sociology*. Cambridge, MA: 1997.

Zohar, Noam. "The Relationship of Non–Jews and their Statues in Mishnah Avodah Zarah" [in Hebrew]. *Reshit* 1 (2009): 145–164.

Zucker, Moshe. *Saadya's Commentary on Genesis*. New York: 1984.

General Index

acculturation
  Exilarch, 88–89
  rabbis, 88
Achaemenid kings
  Ahasuerus, 10, 107, 220, 225, 247
  Cyrus the Great, 123
Acts of Thomas, 254
Agathias, 257–258
Ahasuerus, King, 10, 107, 220, 225, 247
Ahriman, deity, 137, 147, 149–150, 251
  creations, 151, 216
al-Jāḥiẓ, 41–42, 107
al-Masʿūdī, 123
al-Ṭabari, historian, 269
āmiz, 104
anšahrīg (ī) ātaxš, 127
Antoninus Pius, Emperor, 236, 248–249
Aphrahat, 50
Ardashir I, King, 123, 137–138, 147, 211, 224, 256
  devotee of Ohrmazd, 137
Armenian, 127
Artabanus IV, King, 137
Aryans, 138

Babylonia
  festivals, 207
  Jews, 61
  Parthian court, 98
  priestly gifts, 154
  rabbinic authority, 3
  rabbinic courts, 59
  rabbis, 60, 62
  temples, 207
  urban Jewish life, 19
Babylonian Jewish society
  centralization, 3, 50
  insularity, 3
  integrationist model, 38–39
  semi-autonomy, 3
  three pillars model, 274
Babylonian Talmud
  depiction of Sasanian kings, 249
  as historical source, 284
Bacon, Francis, 239
Bahram II, King, 147
bandag ī ātaxš (ādurān bandag), 127
Bati bar Tovi, 247–248
Bē Torta, 209
Becker, Adam, 242–243
Beer, Moshe, 129
Bei Lapat, 189–190
  prison, 191
Belinitzky, Bar, 65
Book of a Thousand Judgments (MHD)
  circumscription of non-Iranians, 74–76
Boyce, Mary, 211
Bustanai, exilarch, 40–41, 45

Caesarea-Mazaca, 173
Christensen, Arthur, 37
Christians
  imperial violence against, 283
  martyrdom, 283
  resistance to imperial rule, 283
  triangulation with Jews, 27, 282–283

Chronicle of Seert, 94, 256–257, 269–270
citron, 247
Cohen, Shaye, 59
Ctesiphon. *See* Seleucia-Ctesiphon
Cyrus the Great, king, 123

dādwar, 79
daštāna, 190
dastgird, 54
David, King, 3, 12, 33, 96, 98
  as ancestor of Exilarchs, 275
  sons of, 126
de Jong, Albert, 253
disciple circles, 122
Domitian of Melitene, 258
Dura Europos, 19
Dura Europos synagogue
  frescoes, 60, 256
  graffiti, 10
  imagery, 198

Earl of Essex, 239
Elijah, 189
Elizabeth I, Queen, 239
Elman, Yaakov, 15
ʿEruvin, tractate, 53
Eunapius, 255
Eustathius, philosopher, 255
Exilarch
  acculturation, 88
  Davidic descent, 275
  imitation of elites, 275–276
  three pillars model, 274
  Sasasian habits and symbols, 89

Fars, 6, 229
Fārs, 147
festivals
  Nowrōz, 41–42, 105–107
fire temples, 201
  financial exchange with, 283
  in rabbinic thought, 283

Gafni, Isaiah, 4, 61
gāhwārag, 99, 112
Gnoli, Gherardo, 137
Goodblatt, David, 61–62
Goodenough, E. R., 60–61
Greek, 127
Greenblatt, Stephen, 239
Gregory the Great, 258
Gushtazad, Persian official, 158, 190–191

Halbertal, Moshe, 205
hargbed, 43
Hebrew Bible, 119
Hērbedestān, 215
Hercules, deity, 209
Herman, Geoffrey, 12, 190
History of Simeon bar Ṣabbaʿe
  relationship to *Martyrdom*, 46–48
Huna, exilarch, 39–40

Ifra Hormiz, mother of Shapur II, 64, 232–233, 236
  and rabbinic practice, 163
  sacrifices, 234–235
incantation bowls
  Aramaic, 16, 25
  Jewish Babylonian Aramaic, 16–17, 19, 146, 217
  Mandaic, 16
  Syriac, 16–17
Iranian deities. *See* Zoroastrian deities

Jerusalem, 160, 246
Jerusalem Temple, 160, 236, 246
Jewish Babylonian Aramaic, 16, 118
  incantation bowls, 16–17, 19, 146, 217
Julian, emperor, 246

Kashkar, 208
Kalmin, Richard, 61, 171–174, 208–210
kārframān, 57
Kawad, King, 191, 239
Kerdir, Zoroastrian priest, 252
Khusro I, King, 128, 143, 153, 256
Khusro II, King, 40, 101, 161–162, 256
Khuzistan, 33, 140–141, 161, 185, 189–190, 240, 260
Koenen, Ludwig, 263

Lapin, Hayim, 65
Latin, 127
Lenski, Noel, 263
Leo, Emperor, 223
Lerner, Judith, 198
Life of George, 101, 191

Macuch, Maria, 73, 79, 127–128, 230
magi
  and Ohrmazd IV, 269–270
  relationship to Sasanian kings, 279
  religious interference, 249–252
  Talmudic representations, 278
Mandaic, 16, 221
  incantation bowls, 16
Mani
  relationship to Shapur I, 252–255
Manichaeans, 243
  Mesopotamia, 7, 32
  missionary activity, 146
Manichaeism
  Mani, 252–255
Mar Aba
  repudiator of Ohmrad, 145
Mar Yehuda, 247–248
martyrdom, 283
Martyrdom of Simeon bar Ṣabbaʿe
  relationship to *History*, 46–48
Marutha of Maypherqaṭ, 66–67, 255–256
Mata Mehasia, 122
Maurice, Emperor, 161
Mazda. *See* Ohrmazd
Mehasia, 146
Mehoza, 49, 146
Mesopotamia, 6–8, 161, 198, 201, 207–208, 224, 266–267, 276
Middle Persian, 118, 197
Middle Persian words, 2, 63, 247
  āmiz, 104
  anšahrīg (ī) ātaxš, 127
  bandag ī ātaxš (ādurān bandag), 127
  dādwar, 79
  daštāna, 190
  dastgird, 54
  diminuitive ending (*-īza*), 117
  gāhwārag, 99, 112
  hargbed, 43
  influence of pronunciation, 118
  kārframān, 57
  parand, 100
  pursišn-nāmag, 58
  rēš-galūdag, 35
  wādrang, 118
  wāzārbed, 49
  wistarag, 124
  xarbuz, 104
  xwāngar, 103
  xwāngarān, 104
  xwardīg + kār, 103
  xwarnag, 103
Mishnah, 56, 118–119
Mordecai, 10, 108, 247

Naqsh-e Rustam, 173
  inscription, 211
Narsai, 239–240
Nehardea, 49, 86, 122
Neusner, Jacob, 3–4, 60–61
New Persian, 127
Nippur, 17
Nisibis, 240
Nitzwoi, 56
Nowrōz, festival, 41–42
  feasts, 105
  gift exchange, 106–107
  on Sabbath, 107

Ohrmazd IV, King
  and magi, 269–270
Ohrmazd, deity, 137, 147, 151, 211–212, 251–252, 262
  creations, 151
  and Sasanian kings, 202

Palestine
  rabbinic courts, 59
  rabbis, 60
Palestinian Talmud
  depiction of Roman emperors, 248–249
parand, 100
Parthian kings
  Artabanus IV, 137
Parthians, 7, 137
Payne, Richard, 11, 69–70
Paz, Yakir, 65, 190
Phocas, Emperor, 162
Pirqoi ben Baboi, 132
priestly gifts, 154
Pseudo-al-Jāḥiẓ, 41–42, 107
Pumbedita, 86, 209
  rabbinic academy, 40
pursišn-nāmag, 58

Qayrawan, 40

Rabbah, 189, 192
Rabbah bar Nahmani, 175–178
Rabban Gamaliel, 210, 249

Rabbi Ḥanina, 42–43
Rabbi Yehuda, patriarch, 248–249
rabbinic academy
  imitation of royal court, 122–124, 276
  organization, 123–124
  Pumbedita, 40
rabbinic courts, 59
rabbis
  acculturation, 88
  authority, 3
  Babylonia, 60, 62
  communal influence, 274–275
  conflict resolution, 274–275
  courts, 59
  disciple circles, 122
  dialogues with Sasanian kings, 249
  elite status, 273
  and fire temples, 283
  Palestine, 60
  rabbinic academy, 40, 122–124, 276
  and royal court, 273
  and Sasanian courts, 283
  and Sasanian habits, 283
  Shmuel, 272–273
  social status, 87
  three pillars model, 274
Rav, 213–217, 237–238
Rav Adda bar Ahava, 49–50
Rav Ashi, 39–40, 122, 209, 218–219, 227, 230, 267
Rav Beroqa, 189–190
Rav Dimi, 49–51
Rav Gadda, 110
Rav Hama, 245–246
Rav Hamnuna, 110, 209
Rav Hisda, 109
Rav Huna, 51–52, 106, 109, 111–112
Rav Joseph, 50
Rav Menasheh, 209
Rav Nahman, 51–53, 56, 105–106, 110–112, 114–121
  analogy to Shapur I, 272–273
Rav Nahman b. Isaac, 108–109
Rav Nahman b. Jacob, 108–109
Rav Sheshet, 110, 112–113
Rav Shmuel, 214
Rav Yehuda, 53–56, 86–87, 110, 114–121, 209
Rava, 49–50, 87, 108–109, 111–112, 125–130, 227, 235–236, 267
Rava bar Rav Yizḥak, 209
Ravina, 50, 218–219
religious interference
  magi, 249–252
rēš-galūdag, 35
Roman emperors, 158
  Antoninus Pius, 235, 248–249
  Julian, 246
  Leo, 223
  Maurice, 161
  in Palestinian Talmud, 248–249
  Phocas, 162
  religious neutrality, 248–249
  Valerian, 173
Rubenstein, Jeffrey, 62

Sasanian kings
  Ardashir I, 123, 137–138, 147, 211, 224, 256
  Bahram II, 147
  dialogues with rabbis, 249
  and Jewish purity norms, 247–248
  as judge, 273
  Kawad, 191, 239
  Khusro I, 128, 143, 153, 256
  Khusro II, 40, 101, 161, 256
  and messianism, 246–247
  and Ohrmazd, 202
  Ohrmazd IV, 269–270
  relationship to magis, 279
  religious neutrality, 249
  Shapur I, 137–138, 147, 173, 244, 252–255, 272–273
  Shapur II, 46, 94, 116, 141, 158, 160, 184, 190, 192, 232, 244–248
  Talmudic representations, 278
  Vahrām I, 253
  Yazdgird I, 244, 255–256
  Yazdgird III, 40
  and Zoroastrianism, 243
Sasanian rule
  court codes, 273
  political theology, 276–277
  representation, 239–240
  violence, 276–277, 283
Sasanian subjects
  acculturation, 282
  differing attitudes, 283
  heterogeneity, 283
  imperial violence against, 283
  integration, 282

resistance to imperial rule, 283
triangulation, 27, 282–283
School of Nisibis, 239
seals, 9
Jewish, 24
Secunda, Shai, 15, 214, 251
Seder Tannaim veAmoraim, 162
Seleucia-Ctesiphon, 7, 19, 67, 71, 101–102, 192, 265
bishop of, 50
Shaked, Shaul, 15, 199, 261
Shapur I, King, 137–138, 147, 173
devotee of Ohrmazd, 252
nickname of Shmuel, 272–273
relationship to Mani, 252–255
religious neutrality, 244
support for Kerdir, 252
Shapur II, King, 94, 116, 141, 158, 160, 190, 192, 232
Great Persecution, 46, 184
and Jewish purity norms, 247–248
and messianism, 246–247
religious neutrality, 244–248
Sherira Gaon, 39–40, 105, 122, 162
Shmuel, 86, 216, 246–247
and Shapur I, 272–273
Simeon bar Ṣabbaʿe
martyrdom of, 190–191
Simeon bar Ṣabbaʿe, bishop, 45, 66, 158, 190
martyrdom, 159
Simeon bar Ṣabbaʿe, bishop, 160
Simeon of Rev-Ardashir, 72
Šīšīnduxt, wife of Yazdgird I, 33–35, 40–41, 45
Smith, Kyle, 47
Sozomen
story of Simeon in *History*, 46–48
Sperber, Daniel, 123
Spicehandler, Ezra, 79–80
Susa, 33–34
Šuštar, 33
Syria, 2, 6, 138, 166
Syriac, 16, 118, 197, 221
incantation bowls, 16–17

Temple. *See* Jerusalem Temple
three pillars model, 274
Exilarch, 274
Jews, 274
triangulation, 32, 282–283

Vahrām I, King, 253
Valerian, Emperor, 173

wādrang, 118
Wahrām Gōr, son of Šīšīnduxt, 35
Walker, Joel, 11
wāzārbed, 49
Wiessner, Gernot, 46–47
Wimpfheimer, Barry, 49
wistarag, 124

xarbuz, 104
xwāngar, 103
xwāngarān, 104
xwardīg + kār, 103
xwarnag, 103

Yazdandukht, 191–192
Yazdgird I, King, 255–256
religious neutrality, 244
Yazdgird III, King, 40

Zoroastrianism, 210
Ahriman, 137, 147, 149–151, 216, 251
festivals, 41–42, 105–107
fire temples, 283
Nowrōz, 41–42, 105–107
Ohrmazd, 137, 147, 151, 202, 211–212, 251–252, 262
and Sasanian kings, 243

Source Index

Hebrew Bible
  Genesis
    14.14, 110–111
    22, 198
    49.31, 245
  Exodus
    19.6, 39
    20.4–6, 204
  Leviticus
    19.14, 218
    21.8, 125
  Deuteronomy
    6.5, 186
    12.2–3, 204
    18.9, 213, 215
    21.23, 245
    22.8, 115
    32.21, 153
    34.6, 245
  2 Samuel
    8.18, 125–126
    1.10–11, 173
  1 Kings
    18, 256
  Isaiah
    49.23, 39
  Zechariah
    9.9, 246
  Malachi
    2.9, 192
  Job
    28.23, 250
  Esther
    6, 247
    6.10, 107
  Daniel
    7.13, 246
  Ezra
    7.24, 126
  1 Chronicles
    18.17, 126
Second Temple Jewish Literature
  Josephus
    Against Apion
      1.192, 207
    Antiquities of the Jews
      3.244–245, 116
      11.133, 2
      15, 98
      18.110–79, 38
      13.372, 116
    Vita
      1.2, 98
New Testament
  Matthew
    21.1–11, 246
Targum
  Targum Sheni to Esther
    6.6, 108
Mishnah
  ʿErubin
    5.6, 53–54
  Nedarim
    3.4, 127

Mishnah (cont.)
Sanhedrin
7.6, 209
'Abodah Zarah
1, 207
3.4, 127, 205–206
4.1, 209
4.6, 208
5.8–9, 218
Mekhilta deRabbi Ishmael
Baḥodesh 6, 205
Sifra
Qedoshim 8, 48
Sifre Deuteronomy
'eqev 48, 125
Ki Teṣei 394, 48
Tosefta
Shabbat
15.8, 173
'Abodah Zarah
6.13, 209
Ḥullin
124a, 187
Palestinian Talmud
Berakhot
1.6 (4a), 186
2.4 (5a), 44
9.5 (14b), 186
Bikkurim
3.3 (65d), 52
Shabbat
12.1 (13c), 110
6.1 (7d), 109
Beṣah
1.6 (60c), 99, 109
Ta'anit
1.4 (64b), 191
Megillah
1.2 (72b), 235
3.2 (74a), 64, 113
Mo'ed Qaṭan
3.5 (82c), 184
Yebamot
16.4 (15d), 173
Soṭah
5.5 (20b), 45
5.7 (20c), 186
9.15 (24c), 98
Baba Batra
5.5 (15a–b), 48
Sanhedrin
3.6 (21b), 219, 223
7.9 (25b), 215
Shebu'ot
1.2 (32d), 42–44
4.2 (35a-b), 125, 221, 223
'Abodah Zarah
1.3 (39c), 212
2.2 (40d–41a), 187
3.3 (42d), 221
4.1 (43c), 209
9.1 (12d), 209
Babylonian Talmud
Berakhot
13b, 186
17b, 146
20a, 45, 80, 184, 193–195
40a, 104
42a, 104
46b, 57, 112–113, 244–245
50a, 104, 187
51a, 112, 118
56a, 180, 236, 244, 249
57b, 208–209
58a, 53, 63, 181
60a, 81
61b, 186
Shabbat
20b, 100
21b, 237
30b, 79, 183
33b, 188
45a, 153, 224, 237
48a, 114
51a, 112
54b, 99
54b–56b, 98
55a, 110
58a, 105
59b, 63
62b, 117, 163, 218
75a, 213
93a, 55
94a, 116
109b, 116
110a, 62
113a, 244
126b, 52
136a, 235
139a, 80, 130, 193
140a, 117
148a, 105
152a–b, 184

157b, 104
21b–22a, 50, 237
'Erubin
11b, 110, 207, 212
25b, 45, 65, 83, 99, 103, 109, 173, 192, 209
25b–26a, 103, 129
59a, 40, 54–57, 101, 104
62a, 58, 81
Pesaḥim
40b, 103
53b, 194, 208
54a, 1, 244, 272
76b, 110
96a, 86
110a–b, 176
115b, 1, 102, 113, 272
Yoma
10a, 129, 163
19a, 62
21a, 217
78a, 105
Sukkah
10b, 52, 84, 105, 187, 244
26a, 79, 102, 105, 172–175, 244
31a, 45, 105, 110–111
37a, 110
53a, 244
Beṣah
4b, 163, 177
15a, 173
25b, 99, 109
29a, 113
33a, 100, 218
Rosh HaShanah
18b, 177
Ta'anit
14b, 103
20a, 45, 80, 193
21b, 237, 267
22a, 155, 163, 189
24a–b, 193–194
24b, 63, 232, 244
Megillah
5b, 62, 103
7a, 181
12b, 162, 219
16a, 55, 99, 107, 218, 266
Mo'ed Qaṭan
11b–12a, 103
12a, 103, 110
12b, 219
17a–b, 62
20a, 184
26a, 173–175, 244
28a, 40, 81
Ḥagigah
5a–b, 78, 249
5b, 62, 103, 244
Yebamot
25b, 173
63b, 78, 153–154, 212
115b, 102
116b, 173, 233, 244
121b, 267
Ketubbot
60b, 81, 110
61a, 104, 116
61a–b, 39–40, 225
61b, 186, 244
62a, 58, 81, 180
62b–63a, 187
77a, 99, 111
85b–8a, 130
94b, 53
103b, 184
104a, 183
105a–b, 63
Nedarim
27b–28a, 83
49b, 40, 244, 272
50a, 187
62a–b, 125
62b, 218
66b, 52
Soṭah
6b, 55
10a, 129
22a, 130
49b, 40
Giṭṭin
7a, 98, 113, 180
10b, 83–84
11a, 80–81, 181
14a–b, 40
16b–17a, 153, 224, 237, 250
16b–17a, 153
19b, 81
28b, 55, 58, 78, 80
31b, 99–100, 105, 108–109, 115
40a, 55, 104
56a, 180, 236
56b, 180

Babylonian Talmud (cont.)
58b, 79
59a, 40
67b, 50, 110, 116
67b–68a, 110, 114–115
Qiddushin
25a, 86
39b, 64, 209
60b, 81
70a, 52, 62, 102, 146
70a–b, 86, 98, 100, 115–116
73a, 146
Baba Qamma
58b, 53, 79, 81–82, 112, 118
59a–b, 102, 110
83a, 40
96b, 244, 272
98a, 49
101b–102a, 218
102b–103a, 101
113a, 83, 127, 244
113a–b, 83
113b–114a, 78–79
117a, 64, 78, 122
117a–b, 78
Baba Meṣiʿa
28b, 81
30b, 79
39b–40a, 103
47a, 55
65a, 50
66a, 53, 110, 115
70b, 244
71b, 81
72b, 127
73b, 81, 111
85a, 244
86a, 175–178, 249
91b, 114
107b, 219
108a, 129
119a, 244
Baba Batra
3a, 117
3b–4a, 98
7b–8a, 129
8a, 45, 125, 129, 192, 235, 244
8a–b, 232, 248
10b, 244
10b–11a, 218, 232, 248–249
22a, 48, 86, 102, 130, 155, 163, 189, 214
21b–22a, 50
36a, 101
46b, 57
54b, 82–83, 99
55a, 81, 83, 110, 129, 209
58a, 52–53, 63, 77, 105, 153, 180, 251
58b, 118
65a, 50–52, 106, 180, 213
89a, 48–49
115b, 1, 272
149a, 146
167a, 45, 65, 129, 192
167b, 192
173b, 81–82
Sanhedrin
5a, 53, 64
7b, 52, 215
14a, 177
25b, 45, 83, 192
25b–26a, 129
27a–b, 53, 129
39a, 217, 249, 251
39b, 235
43a, 40
46b, 244, 245–246
64a, 209
68a, 215
74b, 219
98a, 49, 80, 130, 193, 244, 246
99b, 62
106ba, 193
108b, 184
Shebuʿot
6b, 42–44, 55
34b, 82
ʿAbodah Zarah
4a, 129
8a, 235
10b, 187
10b–11a, 249
11a, 181
11b, 207, 212
16a, 218, 266
17b–18a, 187
18a, 181
18a–b, 181
18b, 155, 177
25b-26a, 209
27b, 187

38b, 114
40b–41a, 210
53b, 208
55a, 209
65a, 180, 213
70a, 146
71a, 81, 117
72b–73a, 117
76b, 110, 244, 247
Zebaḥim
19a, 39–40, 62, 244
96b, 44, 130
116a, 232
116b, 233, 244
Menaḥot
33a, 100
109b, 116, 235
Ḥullin
46a, 266
59a, 104
59b, 63, 104, 110
62b, 163
94a, 116
124a, 52
133a, 235
Bekorot
31a, 45
49b, 272
'Arakin
28a, 81
Kerithot
7b, 215
Niddah
20b, 100, 232, 244, 248
25b, 65
67b–68a, 110
Geonim
Halakhot Gedolot, 221–222
54, 221
Oṣar ha-Geonim, 214
Seder Tannaim veAmoraim, 40, 162
She'iltot of Rav Ahai, 221–222
43, 118
44, 220–221
Sherira Gaon, *Epistle*, 39–40, 105, 122, 162–163, 177
Other Responsa, 223
Greco-Roman Literature, 72
Ammianus Marcellinus
Roman History (Res Gestae)
23.6, 234
Code of Justinian
4.63.4, 157
Eunapius
Lives of the Philosophers, 255
Herodotus
Histories
6.84, 117
Martial
Epigrams
1.11, 117
Menander Protector
fragments
6.1.304–397, 268
6.1.340–347, 160
6.1.398–407, 143
6.1.405–407, 153
Pausanias
5.27.5–6, 219
Plato
Laws
637E, 117
Strabo
Geography, 234
Syro-Roman Lawbook, 72
Tacitus
Annals
12.13, 209
Theophrastus
History of Plants
4.4.2, 116
Early Christian Literature, 11, 13, 26, 28, 44, 46–48, 66, 68–71, 78, 80, 93–94, 97, 101, 117, 121, 134, 140–145, 152–156, 158–161, 169–170, 175, 178–185, 191–192, 201, 208, 210, 215, 217, 225–227, 229–232, 234, 254–255, 258–260, 262, 265, 268
Acts of Grigor, 259
Acts of Mar Mari, 80, 208, 227
Acts of Thomas, 254
Agathangelos
History of the Armenians, 99
Agathias
Histories
2.26.5, 80, 265
2.30.3–31.1, 257–258
Aphrahat
Demonstrations
14, 50, 71–72

Early Christian Literature (cont.)
14.3, 71
14.7, 71
14.44, 72
Bar Hebraeus
Ecclesiastical Chronicle, 121
Barḥadbshabba ʿArbaya
Cause of the Foundation of the Schools, 239–240
Cave of Treasures
27.12–16, 129
Chronicle of Khuzistan, 44, 68, 161
Chronicle of Seert
1.90, 47
1.142–143, 255
1.219–220, 153
1.222, 94, 100
2.202–203, 121
2.37–38, 256–257
2.75, 191
2.103–104, 269
2.270–272, 161
Chronicle of Zuqnin, 101
Cyril Scythopolis
Life of Euthymius, 160
Elishe
History of Vardan and the Armenian War, 47, 138, 164
Evagrius Scholasticus
Ecclesiastical History
5.7, 160
Great Slaughter, 144
Gregory the Great
Correspondences 3.67, 258
History of Ishoʿsabran, 44, 180
History of Karka d-beth Slokh, 140, 183, 210
History of Mar Aba, 70, 78, 145, 154, 156, 259
History of Mar Pethion, 44, 145
History of Mar Qardagh, 11, 93–95, 97, 121, 182, 201, 227, 229–232
History of Mar Sabrishoʿ, 71, 265
History of Simeon bar Ṣabbaʿe, 45–48, 158–159, 170, 178–179, 190–191, 260
History of the "Slave of Christ," 183, 215
Ishoʿbokht
Maktbānutā d-ʿal Dinē, 72
Ishoʿdnaḥ of Basra
Book of Chastity, 216
John of Ephesus
Ecclesiastical History
6.20, 67, 257
Lives of the Eastern Saints, 224
Life of George, 101, 191
Life of Marutha of Maypherqaṭ, 66–67, 255–256, 265
Martyrdom of 111 Men and 9 Women, 182, 260
Martyrdom of ʿAbda, 142, 226–227, 231
Martyrdom of ʿAqebshma, 142, 180, 183
Martyrdom of Barbaʿshmin, 179–182, 260
Martyrdom of Miles, 152, 175
Martyrdom of Narsai, 143–144, 225–226, 234, 259
Martyrdom of Peroz, 153, 158–159, 258, 265
Martyrdom of Pethion, 44–45, 145
Martyrdom of Pusai, 141, 160, 175, 185, 260, 268
Martyrdom of Simeon bar Ṣabbaʿe, 45–48, 158–160, 170, 178–179, 190–191, 260
Martyrdom of Tarbo, 185
Martyrdom of the Captives of Beth Zabdai, 175, 258
Martyrdom of Thecla, 180
Martyrs of Mount Berʿain, 181, 185
Moses Khorenatsʿi
History of Armenia, 96, 224
Procopius
History of the Wars
1.6.12–16, 90
1.17.28, 100
1.3, 255
2, 96
Pseudo-Joshua the Stylite
Chronicle, 160
Pseudo-Pawstos
Epic Histories
3.19, 95
4.54, 95
5.24, 117
Pseudo-Zachariah Rhetor
Chronicle, 160, 265, 267
Sebeos
Armenian History, 100
Simeon of Rev-Ardashir
On the Law of Inheritance, 72

Socrates Scholasticus
Ecclesiastical History
7.8, 156, 256
7.18, 160, 258
Sozomen
Ecclesiastical History, 46
Synodicon Orientale
Synod of 410, 43, 47, 67, 105, 240
Synod of 484, 69, 71
Synod of 497, 68
Synod of 544, 78
Synod of 554, 121
Synod of 576, 67, 123, 265
Synod of 585, 77
Synod of 676, 19, 72, 129
Tertullian
De spectaculis
8.9, 205
Theodoret of Cyrrhus
History of the Monks of Syria, 78
Theophylact Simocatta
History
1.9.6, 90
5.7.4–9, 45, 108, 161
Thomas of Marga
Book of Governors, 100, 121, 229
Timothy I, Catholicos
Letters 40–41, 166–167
Yeznik of Kolb
Treatise on God, 252
Manichean Literature, 252–254
Homilies
42.9–50.17, 253
Kephalaia
(Berlin) 14.3–16.2, 252
(Chester Beatty) 326, 80, 153, 202, 231, 234
Manichean Psalm-Book, 254
Šābuhragān, 253
Persian and Zoroastrian Literature, 33–35, 40, 57, 73–76, 79, 92, 99, 104, 116, 144, 157, 173–174, 215, 234, 261–262, 264, 266
Ardā Wīrāz-nāmag, 99
Book of a Thousand Judgments (MHD), 55, 73–76, 127
1.10–13, 74
1.13–15, 74
101.8–11, 127
110.4, 234
18, 55, 101
38, 55
39, 55
48.7–10, 57
60.16–17, 75
78.11–14, 230
94.3–6, 150
A35.16–A36.6, 229–230
A36, 55
A37.1–15, 150
A39.1–17, 229
Bundahišn
16.26, 116
Dādestān ī Dēnīg
40.1–2, 74
48, 234
Dēnkard
3.58.2, 261
3.140.1–6, 74
6, 121, 216
8.16.6, 76
8.20.29, 75
8.37.32, 234
Ḥamza Al-Iṣfahānī
Annals, 128, 155–156, 224
Hērbedestān, 215–216
11.6–7, 74
12.1–5, 74
12.3–5, 75
12.4–5, 75
19.1, 216
Kārnāmag ī Ardaxšēr ī Pābagān, 57, 266
Letter of Tansar, 144, 157, 174, 261
Mēnōg ī Xrad, 144
Nērangestān, 74–75, 216, 234
Provincial Capitals of Ērānšahr, 33–35, 40, 55
Res Gestae Divi Saporis, 173, 266
Sūr saxwan, 103–104, 262
Testament of Ardašīr, 261
Vīdēvdād
3.4, 118
3.24, 118
5.1–5.4, 234
5.52, 118
16, 155
Xusrō ī Kawādān ud Rēdag (Khusro and the Page), 92, 104, 116, 264
Islamic Literature, 41, 100, 128

Islamic Literature (cont.)
al-Shahrastānī
Kitābu ʾl-milal wa ʾl-niḥal (Book of Sects and Creeds), 44
History of al-Ṭabarī, 100, 128
Ibn Miskawayh
Tajārib al-umam (Experiences of Nations), 261
Kitāb al-Tāj (Book of the Crown), 41–42
Ps. al-Jāḥiẓ
al-Maḥāsin wal-aḍdād (Good Qualities and [their] Opposites), 41–42, 107

For EU product safety concerns, contact us at Calle de José Abascal, 56–1°, 28003 Madrid, Spain or eugpsr@cambridge.org.

www.ingramcontent.com/pod-product-compliance
Lightning Source LLC
LaVergne TN
LVHW041619060526
838200LV00040B/1344
9781009280501